GNU Image Manipulation Program

User Manual

September 29, 2016

GNU Image Manipulation Program

Copyright © 2002, 2003, 2004, 2005, 2006, 2007, 2008, 2009, 2010, 2011, 2012, 2013, 2014, 2015, 2016 The GIMP Documentation Team

Contents

I   Getting Started   1

1   Introduction   3
- 1.1   Welcome to GIMP 3
  - 1.1.1   Authors 3
  - 1.1.2   The GIMP Help system 3
  - 1.1.3   Features and Capabilities 3
- 1.2   What's New in GIMP 2.8? 4

2   Fire up the GIMP   11
- 2.1   Running GIMP 11
  - 2.1.1   Known Platforms 11
  - 2.1.2   Language 11
  - 2.1.3   Command Line Arguments 12
- 2.2   Starting GIMP the first time 13
  - 2.2.1   Finally 13

3   First Steps with Wilber   15
- 3.1   Basic Concepts 15
- 3.2   Main Windows 17
  - 3.2.1   The Toolbox 20
  - 3.2.2   Image Window 22
  - 3.2.3   Dialogs and Docking 25
- 3.3   Undoing 31
  - 3.3.1   Things That Cannot be Undone 31
- 3.4   Common Tasks 32
  - 3.4.1   Intention 32
  - 3.4.2   Change the Size of an Image for the screen 32
  - 3.4.3   Change the Size of an Image for print 34
  - 3.4.4   Compressing Images 35
  - 3.4.5   Crop An Image 38
  - 3.4.6   Find Info About Your Image 39
  - 3.4.7   Change the Mode 40
  - 3.4.8   Flip An Image 42
  - 3.4.9   Rotate An Image 44
  - 3.4.10 Separating an Object From Its Background 45
- 3.5   How to Draw Straight Lines 47
  - 3.5.1   Intention 47
  - 3.5.2   Examples 50

4   Getting Unstuck   53
- 4.1   Getting Unstuck 53
  - 4.1.1   Stuck! 53
  - 4.1.2   Common Causes of GIMP Non-Responsiveness 53

II   How do I Become a GIMP Wizard?   57

5   Getting Images into GIMP   59
- 5.1   Image Types 59
- 5.2   Creating new Files 61
- 5.3   Opening Files 61
  - 5.3.1   Open File 61

	5.3.2	Open Location	62
	5.3.3	Open Recent	63
	5.3.4	Using External Programs	63
	5.3.5	File Manager	63
	5.3.6	Drag and Drop	63
	5.3.7	Copy and Paste	64
	5.3.8	Image Browser	64

6 Getting Images out of GIMP — 65
- 6.1 Files — 65
  - 6.1.1 Save / Export Images — 65
  - 6.1.2 File Formats — 65
- 6.2 Preparing your Images for the Web — 72
  - 6.2.1 Images with an Optimal Size/Quality Ratio — 72
  - 6.2.2 Reducing the File Size Even More — 73
  - 6.2.3 Saving Images with Transparency — 74

7 Painting with GIMP — 77
- 7.1 The Selection — 77
  - 7.1.1 Feathering — 78
  - 7.1.2 Making a Selection Partially Transparent — 79
- 7.2 Creating and Using Selections — 79
  - 7.2.1 Moving a Selection — 79
  - 7.2.2 Adding or subtracting selections — 81
- 7.3 The QuickMask — 81
  - 7.3.1 Overview — 82
  - 7.3.2 Properties — 82
- 7.4 Using QuickMask Mode — 83
- 7.5 Paths — 83
  - 7.5.1 Path Creation — 83
  - 7.5.2 Path Properties — 84
  - 7.5.3 Paths and Selections — 85
  - 7.5.4 Transforming Paths — 85
  - 7.5.5 Stroking a Path — 85
  - 7.5.6 Paths and Text — 86
  - 7.5.7 Paths and SVG files — 86
- 7.6 Brushes — 87
- 7.7 Adding New Brushes — 89
- 7.8 The GIH Dialog Box — 90
- 7.9 Varying brush size — 94
  - 7.9.1 How to vary the height of a brush — 94
  - 7.9.2 Creating a brush quickly — 95
- 7.10 Gradients — 96
- 7.11 Patterns — 98
- 7.12 Palettes — 101
  - 7.12.1 Colormap — 102
- 7.13 Presets — 103
- 7.14 Drawing Simple Objects — 103
  - 7.14.1 Drawing a Straight Line — 103
  - 7.14.2 Creating a Basic Shape — 105

8 Combining Images — 107
- 8.1 Introduction to Layers — 107
  - 8.1.1 Layer Properties — 107
- 8.2 Layer Modes — 111
- 8.3 Creating New Layers — 126
- 8.4 Layer Groups — 126

9 Text Management   129
   9.1   Text Management 129
     9.1.1   Text Area 129
     9.1.2   Managing Text Layer 130
     9.1.3   Text Toolbox 131
     9.1.4   Text Context Menu 132
   9.2   Text 134
     9.2.1   Embellishing Text 134
     9.2.2   Adding Fonts 134
     9.2.3   Font Problems 136

10 Enhancing Photographs   137
   10.1   Working with Digital Camera Photos 137
     10.1.1   Introduction 137
     10.1.2   Improving Composition 137
     10.1.3   Improving Colors 138
     10.1.4   Adjusting Sharpness 140
     10.1.5   Removing Unwanted Objects from an Image 141
     10.1.6   Saving Your Results 142

11 Color Management with GIMP   145
   11.1   Color Management in GIMP 145
     11.1.1   Problems of a non Color Managed Workflow 145
     11.1.2   Introduction to a Color Managed Workflow 146

12 Enrich my GIMP   149
   12.1   Preferences Dialog 149
     12.1.1   Introduction 149
     12.1.2   Environment 150
     12.1.3   Interface 151
     12.1.4   Theme 152
     12.1.5   Help System 153
     12.1.6   Tool Options 154
     12.1.7   Toolbox 155
     12.1.8   Default Image Preferences 156
     12.1.9   Default Image Grid 157
     12.1.10   Image Windows 158
     12.1.11   Image Window Appearance 159
     12.1.12   Image Window Title and Statusbar 160
     12.1.13   Display 161
     12.1.14   Color Management 162
     12.1.15   Input Devices 165
     12.1.16   Input Controllers 166
     12.1.17   Window Management 168
     12.1.18   Folders 169
     12.1.19   Data Folders 170
   12.2   Grids and Guides 171
     12.2.1   The Image Grid 171
     12.2.2   Guides 172
   12.3   Rendering a Grid 173
   12.4   How to Set Your Tile Cache 173
   12.5   Creating Shortcuts to Menu Functions 174
   12.6   Customize Splash-Screen 176

13 Scripting   **177**

13.1 Plugins 177
    13.1.1 Introduction 177
    13.1.2 Using Plugins 178
    13.1.3 Installing New Plugins 178
    13.1.4 Writing Plugins 179

13.2 Using Script-Fu Scripts 180
    13.2.1 Script-Fu? 180
    13.2.2 Installing Script-Fus 180
    13.2.3 Do's and Don'ts 180
    13.2.4 Different Kinds Of Script-Fus 180
    13.2.5 Standalone Scripts 182
    13.2.6 Image-Dependent Scripts 183

13.3 A Script-Fu Tutorial 183
    13.3.1 Getting Acquainted With Scheme 183
    13.3.2 Variables And Functions 185
    13.3.3 Lists, Lists And More Lists 187
    13.3.4 Your First Script-Fu Script 190
    13.3.5 Giving Our Script Some Guts 196
    13.3.6 Extending The Text Box Script 198
    13.3.7 Your script and its working 200

III   Function Reference   **203**

14 Tools   **205**

14.1 The Toolbox 205
    14.1.1 Introduction 205
    14.1.2 Tool Icons 206
    14.1.3 Color and Indicator Area 206
    14.1.4 Tool Options 208

14.2 Selection Tools 209
    14.2.1 Common Features 209
    14.2.2 Rectangle Selection 211
    14.2.3 Ellipse Selection 215
    14.2.4 Free Selection (Lasso) 218
    14.2.5 Fuzzy selection (Magic wand) 220
    14.2.6 Select By Color 222
    14.2.7 Intelligent Scissors 224
    14.2.8 Foreground Select 226

14.3 Paint Tools 230
    14.3.1 Common Features 230
    14.3.2 Dynamics 235
    14.3.3 Brush Tools (Pencil, Paintbrush, Airbrush) 243
    14.3.4 Bucket Fill 243
    14.3.5 Blend 246
    14.3.6 Pencil 249
    14.3.7 Paintbrush 251
    14.3.8 Eraser 252
    14.3.9 Airbrush 254
    14.3.10 Ink 256
    14.3.11 Clone 257
    14.3.12 Heal 261
    14.3.13 Perspective Clone 263
    14.3.14 Blur/Sharpen 265
    14.3.15 Smudge 267
    14.3.16 Dodge/Burn 268

14.4 Transform Tools 270
    14.4.1 Common Features 270

14.4.2 Align 273
14.4.3 Move 276
14.4.4 Crop 278
14.4.5 Rotate 281
14.4.6 Scale 283
14.4.7 Shear 285
14.4.8 Perspective 287
14.4.9 Flip 289
14.4.10 The Cage Tool 290
14.5 Color Tools 292
14.5.1 Overview 292
14.5.2 Color Balance 293
14.5.3 Hue-Saturation 295
14.5.4 Colorize 297
14.5.5 Brightness-Contrast 298
14.5.6 Threshold 299
14.5.7 Levels 303
14.5.8 Curves 308
14.5.9 Posterize 312
14.5.10 Desaturate 313
14.6 Other 314
14.6.1 Overview 314
14.6.2 Paths 315
14.6.3 Color Picker 318
14.6.4 Zoom 320
14.6.5 Measure 321
14.6.6 Text 322
14.6.7 GEGL Operation 325

15 Dialogs 329
15.1 Dialog Introduction 329
15.2 Image Structure Related Dialogs 329
15.2.1 Layers Dialog 329
15.2.2 Channels Dialog 334
15.2.3 Paths Dialog 340
15.2.4 Colormap Dialog 344
15.2.5 Histogram dialog 346
15.2.6 Navigation Dialog 349
15.2.7 Undo History Dialog 350
15.3 Image-content Related Dialogs 352
15.3.1 FG/BG Color Dialog 352
15.3.2 Brushes Dialog 355
15.3.3 Patterns Dialog 359
15.3.4 Gradients Dialog 362
15.3.5 Palettes Dialog 369
15.3.6 Tagging 376
15.3.7 Fonts Dialog 377
15.4 Image Management Related Dialogs 379
15.4.1 Buffers Dialog 379
15.4.2 Images Dialog 381
15.4.3 Document History Dialog 382
15.4.4 Templates Dialog 383
15.5 Misc. Dialogs 386
15.5.1 Tool Presets Dialog 386
15.5.2 Tool Preset Editor 388
15.5.3 Device Status Dialog 388
15.5.4 Error Console 389
15.5.5 Save File 390
15.5.6 Export File 391

15.5.7 Sample Points Dialog 393
15.5.8 Pointer Dialog 395

16 Menus **397**
16.1 Introduction to Menus 397
16.1.1 The Image Menu Bar 397
16.1.2 Context Menus 397
16.1.3 Tear-off menus 397
16.1.4 Tab menus 398
16.2 The "File" Menu 399
16.2.1 Overview 399
16.2.2 New... 399
16.2.3 Create 402
16.2.4 Open.... 404
16.2.5 Open as Layers... 406
16.2.6 Open Location... 406
16.2.7 Open Recent 407
16.2.8 Save 407
16.2.9 Save as.... 407
16.2.10 Save a Copy.... 409
16.2.11 Revert 409
16.2.12 Export... 410
16.2.13 Export As... 410
16.2.14 Create Template... 410
16.2.15 Print 411
16.2.16 Close 411
16.2.17 Close all 412
16.2.18 Quit 412
16.3 The "Edit" Menu 413
16.3.1 "Edit" Menu Entries 413
16.3.2 Undo 413
16.3.3 Redo 414
16.3.4 Fade 414
16.3.5 Undo History 414
16.3.6 Cut 415
16.3.7 Copy 415
16.3.8 Copy Visible 415
16.3.9 Paste 416
16.3.10 Paste Into 416
16.3.11 Paste as 416
16.3.12 Buffer 418
16.3.13 Clear 418
16.3.14 Fill with FG Color 419
16.3.15 Fill with BG Color 419
16.3.16 Fill with Pattern 420
16.3.17 Stroke Selection 420
16.3.18 Stroke Path 421
16.3.19 The "Preferences" Command 423
16.3.20 Keyboard Shortcuts 423
16.3.21 Modules 423
16.3.22 Units 424
16.4 The "Select" Menu 425
16.4.1 Introduction to the "Select" Menu 425
16.4.2 Select All 426
16.4.3 None 426
16.4.4 Invert 426
16.4.5 Float 427
16.4.6 By Color 428
16.4.7 From Path 428

16.4.8 Selection Editor 428
16.4.9 Feather 431
16.4.10 Sharpen 432
16.4.11 Shrink 432
16.4.12 Grow 433
16.4.13 Border 434
16.4.14 Distort 435
16.4.15 Rounded Rectangle 436
16.4.16 Toggle QuickMask 437
16.4.17 Save to Channel 437
16.4.18 To Path 437
16.5 The "View" Menu 438
16.5.1 Introduction to the "View" Menu 438
16.5.2 New View 438
16.5.3 Dot for Dot 439
16.5.4 Zoom 439
16.5.5 Shrink Wrap 441
16.5.6 Full Screen 441
16.5.7 Navigation Window 442
16.5.8 Display Filters 442
16.5.9 Show Selection 447
16.5.10 Show Layer Boundary 447
16.5.11 Show Guides 448
16.5.12 Show Grid 448
16.5.13 Show Sample Points 448
16.5.14 Snap to Guides 448
16.5.15 Snap to Grid 448
16.5.16 Snap to Canvas 449
16.5.17 Snap to Active Path 449
16.5.18 Padding Color 449
16.5.19 Show Menubar 450
16.5.20 Show Rulers 450
16.5.21 Show Scrollbars 450
16.5.22 Show Statusbar 450
16.6 The "Image" Menu 451
16.6.1 Overview 451
16.6.2 Duplicate 451
16.6.3 Mode 452
16.6.4 RGB mode 452
16.6.5 Grayscale mode 452
16.6.6 Indexed mode 452
16.6.7 Transform 454
16.6.8 Flip Horizontally; Flip Vertically 455
16.6.9 Rotation 455
16.6.10 Guillotine 455
16.6.11 Canvas Size 455
16.6.12 Fit Canvas to Layers 459
16.6.13 Fit Canvas to Selection 459
16.6.14 Print Size 459
16.6.15 Scale Image 460
16.6.16 Crop to Selection 461
16.6.17 Autocrop Image 462
16.6.18 Zealous Crop 462
16.6.19 Merge Visible Layers 463
16.6.20 Flatten Image 464
16.6.21 Align Visible Layers... 465
16.6.22 Guides 468
16.6.23 New Guide 468
16.6.24 New Guide (by Percent) 469

16.6.25 New Guides from Selection 470
16.6.26 Remove all guides 470
16.6.27 Configure Grid. 470
16.6.28 Image Properties 471
16.7 The "Layer" Menu 474
16.7.1 Introduction to the "Layer" Menu 474
16.7.2 New Layer 475
16.7.3 New Layer Group 475
16.7.4 New From Visible 476
16.7.5 Duplicate layer 476
16.7.6 Anchor layer 476
16.7.7 Merge Down 477
16.7.8 Delete Layer 477
16.7.9 The Text Commands of the Layer Menu 477
16.7.10 Discard Text Information 478
16.7.11 "Stack" Submenu 478
16.7.12 Select Previous Layer 479
16.7.13 Select Next Layer 479
16.7.14 Select Top Layer 480
16.7.15 Select Bottom Layer 480
16.7.16 Raise Layer 481
16.7.17 Lower Layer 481
16.7.18 Layer to Top 481
16.7.19 Layer to Bottom 481
16.7.20 The "Reverse Layer Order" command 481
16.7.21 The "Mask" Submenu 482
16.7.22 Add Layer Mask 482
16.7.23 Apply Layer Mask 483
16.7.24 Delete Layer Mask 484
16.7.25 Show Layer Mask 484
16.7.26 Edit Layer Mask 484
16.7.27 Disable Layer Mask 484
16.7.28 Mask to Selection 485
16.7.29 Add Layer Mask to Selection 485
16.7.30 Subtract Layer Mask from Selection 486
16.7.31 Intersect Layer Mask with Selection 486
16.7.32 The "Transparency" Submenu of the "Layer" menu 487
16.7.33 Add Alpha Channel 487
16.7.34 Remove Alpha Channel 488
16.7.35 Color to Alpha 488
16.7.36 Semi-flatten 488
16.7.37 Threshold Alpha 488
16.7.38 Alpha to Selection 489
16.7.39 Add Alpha channel to Selection 490
16.7.40 Subtract from Selection 491
16.7.41 Intersect Alpha channel with Selection 491
16.7.42 The "Transform" Submenu 492
16.7.43 Flip Horizontally 492
16.7.44 Flip Vertically 493
16.7.45 Rotate 90° clockwise 493
16.7.46 Rotate 90° counter-clockwise 494
16.7.47 Rotate 180° 494
16.7.48 Arbitrary Rotation 495
16.7.49 Offset 495
16.7.50 Layer Boundary Size 497
16.7.51 Layer to Image Size 499
16.7.52 Scale Layer 499
16.7.53 Crop to Selection 500
16.7.54 Autocrop Layer 500

16.8 The "Colors" Menu 501
    16.8.1 Introduction to the "Colors" Menu 501
    16.8.2 Colors Tools 502
    16.8.3 Invert 502
    16.8.4 Value Invert 503
    16.8.5 Use GEGL 503
    16.8.6 The "Auto" Submenu 504
    16.8.7 Equalize 506
    16.8.8 White Balance 506
    16.8.9 Color Enhance 507
    16.8.10 Normalize 508
    16.8.11 Stretch Contrast 508
    16.8.12 Stretch HSV 509
    16.8.13 The "Components" Submenu 509
    16.8.14 Channel Mixer 510
    16.8.15 Compose 513
    16.8.16 Decompose 515
    16.8.17 Recompose 517
    16.8.18 The "Map" Submenu 517
    16.8.19 Rearrange Colormap 519
    16.8.20 Set Colormap 520
    16.8.21 Alien Map 521
    16.8.22 Color Exchange 522
    16.8.23 Gradient Map 524
    16.8.24 Palette Map 524
    16.8.25 Rotate Colors 525
    16.8.26 Sample Colorize 528
    16.8.27 The "Info" Submenu 530
    16.8.28 Histogram 531
    16.8.29 Border Average 531
    16.8.30 Colorcube Analysis 532
    16.8.31 Smooth Palette 533
    16.8.32 The Color Filters 533
    16.8.33 Colorify... 534
    16.8.34 Color to Alpha... 535
    16.8.35 Filter Pack... 536
    16.8.36 Hot... 538
    16.8.37 Maximum RGB... 539
    16.8.38 Retinex 540
16.9 The "Tools" Menu 542
    16.9.1 Introduction to the "Tools" Menu 542
16.10 The "Filters" Menu 542
    16.10.1 Introduction to the "Filters" Menu 542
    16.10.2 Repeat Last 543
    16.10.3 Re-show Last 543
    16.10.4 Reset All Filters 544
    16.10.5 The "Python-Fu" Submenu 544
    16.10.6 The "Script-Fu" Submenu 546
16.11 "Windows" Menu 548
16.12 The "Help" Menu 549
    16.12.1 Introduction to the "Help" Menu 549
    16.12.2 Help 550
    16.12.3 Context Help 550
    16.12.4 Tip of the Day 550
    16.12.5 About 551
    16.12.6 Plug-In Browser 552
    16.12.7 The Procedure Browser 553
    16.12.8 GIMP online 554

17 Filters 555

  17.1 Introduction 555

     17.1.1 Preview 555

  17.2 Blur Filters 556

     17.2.1 Introduction 556

     17.2.2 Blur 558

     17.2.3 Gaussian Blur 558

     17.2.4 Selective Gaussian Blur 560

     17.2.5 Motion Blur 561

     17.2.6 Pixelise 563

     17.2.7 Tileable Blur 564

  17.3 Enhance Filters 566

     17.3.1 Introduction 566

     17.3.2 Antialias 566

     17.3.3 Deinterlace 567

     17.3.4 Despeckle 568

     17.3.5 Destripe 569

     17.3.6 NL Filter 570

     17.3.7 Red Eye Removal 572

     17.3.8 Sharpen 573

     17.3.9 Unsharp Mask 574

  17.4 Distort Filters 577

     17.4.1 Introduction 577

     17.4.2 Blinds 577

     17.4.3 Curve Bend 578

     17.4.4 Emboss 580

     17.4.5 Engrave 581

     17.4.6 Erase Every Other Row 583

     17.4.7 IWarp 584

     17.4.8 Lens Distortion 586

     17.4.9 Mosaic 588

     17.4.10 Newsprint 590

     17.4.11 Page Curl 592

     17.4.12 Polar Coords 593

     17.4.13 Ripple 595

     17.4.14 Shift 597

     17.4.15 Value Propagate 598

     17.4.16 Video 601

     17.4.17 Waves 602

     17.4.18 Whirl and Pinch 604

     17.4.19 Wind 605

     17.4.20 Apply Lens 608

  17.5 Light and Shadow Filters 609

     17.5.1 Introduction 609

     17.5.2 Gradient Flare 609

     17.5.3 Lens Flare 614

     17.5.4 Lighting Effects 616

     17.5.5 Sparkle 620

     17.5.6 Supernova 622

     17.5.7 Drop Shadow 624

     17.5.8 Perspective 625

     17.5.9 Xach-Effect 628

     17.5.10 Glass Tile 629

  17.6 Noise Filters 630

     17.6.1 Introduction 630

     17.6.2 HSV Noise 631

     17.6.3 Hurl 632

     17.6.4 Pick 634

     17.6.5 RGB Noise 635

17.6.6 Slur 637
17.6.7 Spread 638
17.7 Edge-Detect Filters 639
17.7.1 Introduction 639
17.7.2 Difference of Gaussians 640
17.7.3 Edge 642
17.7.4 Laplace 644
17.7.5 Neon 644
17.7.6 Sobel 645
17.8 Generic Filters 646
17.8.1 Introduction 646
17.8.2 Convolution Matrix 646
17.8.3 Dilate 651
17.8.4 Erode 652
17.9 Combine Filters 652
17.9.1 Introduction 652
17.9.2 Depth Merge 652
17.9.3 Filmstrip 655
17.10 Artistic Filters 657
17.10.1 Introduction 657
17.10.2 Apply Canvas 657
17.10.3 Cartoon 659
17.10.4 Clothify 660
17.10.5 Cubism 661
17.10.6 GIMPressionist 663
17.10.7 Oilify 672
17.10.8 Photocopy 674
17.10.9 Predator 676
17.10.10 Softglow 678
17.10.11 Van Gogh (LIC) 679
17.10.12 Weave 682
17.11 Decor Filters 683
17.11.1 Introduction 683
17.11.2 Add Bevel 684
17.11.3 Add Border 685
17.11.4 Coffee Stain 686
17.11.5 Fuzzy Border 687
17.11.6 Old Photo 689
17.11.7 Round Corners 691
17.11.8 Slide 693
17.11.9 Stencil Carve 694
17.11.10 Stencil Chrome 696
17.12 Map Filters 699
17.12.1 Introduction 699
17.12.2 Bump Map 699
17.12.3 Displace 701
17.12.4 Fractal Trace 705
17.12.5 Illusion 706
17.12.6 Make Seamless 708
17.12.7 Map Object 708
17.12.8 Paper Tile 712
17.12.9 Small Tiles 714
17.12.10 Tile 715
17.12.11 Warp 716
17.13 Rendering Filters 719
17.13.1 Introduction 719
17.13.2 Difference Clouds 719
17.13.3 Fog 720
17.13.4 Plasma 721

17.13.5 Solid Noise 722
17.13.6 Flame 723
17.13.7 IFS Fractal 726
17.13.8 Checkerboard 731
17.13.9 CML Explorer 732
17.13.10 Diffraction Patterns 737
17.13.11 Grid 738
17.13.12 Jigsaw 740
17.13.13 Maze 742
17.13.14 Qbist 743
17.13.15 Sinus 744
17.13.16 Circuit 746
17.13.17 Fractal Explorer 747
17.13.18 Gfig 752
17.13.19 Lava 754
17.13.20 Line Nova 755
17.13.21 Sphere Designer 757
17.13.22 Spyrogimp 759
17.14 Web Filters 761
17.14.1 Introduction 761
17.14.2 ImageMap 761
17.14.3 Semi-Flatten 766
17.14.4 Slice 767
17.15 Animation Filters 770
17.15.1 Introduction 770
17.15.2 Blend 770
17.15.3 Burn-In 771
17.15.4 Rippling 773
17.15.5 Spinning Globe 774
17.15.6 Waves 775
17.15.7 Optimize 776
17.15.8 Playback 777
17.16 Alpha to Logo Filters 777
17.16.1 Introduction 777
17.16.2 3D Outline 778
17.16.3 Alien Glow 781
17.16.4 Alien Neon 782
17.16.5 Basic I & II 783
17.16.6 Blended 784
17.16.7 Bovination 785
17.16.8 Chalk 786
17.16.9 Chip Away 788
17.16.10 Chrome 790
17.16.11 Comic Book 791
17.16.12 Cool Metal 792
17.16.13 Frosty 793
17.16.14 Glossy 794
17.16.15 Glowing Hot 796
17.16.16 Gradient Bevel 798
17.16.17 Neon 799
17.16.18 Particle Trace 800
17.16.19 Textured 802

18 Keys and Mouse Reference 805
  18.1 Help 805
  18.2 Tools 805
  18.3 File 806
  18.4 Dialogs 807
  18.5 View 808
  18.6 Edit 809
  18.7 Layer 809
  18.8 Select 810
  18.9 Filters 810
  18.10 Zoom tool 810

IV   Glossary 811

V   Bibliography 829
  18.11 Books 831
  18.12 Online resources 831

VI   GIMP History 835
  .1 The Very Beginning 837
  .2 The Early Days of GIMP 837
  .3 The One to Change the World 838
  .4 Version 2.0 838
  .5 What's New in GIMP 2.2? 841
  .6 What's New in GIMP 2.4? 842
  .7 What's New in GIMP 2.6? 844

VII   Reporting Bugs and Requesting Enhancements 849
  .8 Making sure it's a Bug 851
    .8.1 Find a Specific Bug 852
    .8.2 The Advanced Bug Search Form 852
  .9 Reporting the Bug 853
  .10 What Happens to a Bug Report after you Submit it 855

VIII   GNU Free Documentation License 857
  .11 PREAMBLE 859
  .12 APPLICABILITY AND DEFINITIONS 859
  .13 VERBATIM COPYING 860
  .14 COPYING IN QUANTITY 860
  .15 MODIFICATIONS 861
  .16 COMBINING DOCUMENTS 862
  .17 COLLECTIONS OF DOCUMENTS 862
  .18 AGGREGATION WITH INDEPENDENT WORKS 862
  .19 TRANSLATION 862
  .20 TERMINATION 863
  .21 FUTURE REVISIONS OF THIS LICENSE 863
  .22 ADDENDUM: How to use this License for your documents 863

IX   Eeek! There is Missing Help 865

    Index 869

List of Examples

16.1 Crop marks 516
17.1 Simple "Slice" filter example output 767
17.2 With separate image folder 768
17.3 Space between table elements 768
17.4 JavaScript code snippet 769
17.5 Skipped animation for table caps (simplified HTML code) 769

Preface

GIMP User Manual Authors and Contributors

Content Writers Alex Muñoz (Spanish) , Alexandre Franke (French) , Alexandre Prokoudine (Russian) , Angelo Córdoba Inunza (Spanish) , Christian Kirbach (German) , Daniel Francis (Spanish) , Daniel Mustieles (Spanish) , Daniel Winzen (German) , Delin Chang (Chinese) , Dimitris Spingos (Greek) , Djavan Fagundes (Brasilian) , Enrico Nicoletto (Brasilian) , Felipe Ribeiro (Brasilian) , Guiu Rocafort (Spanish) , Jiro Matsuzawa (Japanese) , Joe Hansen (Danish) , João S. O. Bueno (Brasilian) , Julien Hardelin (French, English) , Kenneth Nielsen (Danish) , Kolbjørn Stuestøl (Norwegian) , Marco Ciampa (Italian) , María Majadas (Spanish) , Milagros Infante Montero (Spanish) , Milo Casagrande (Italian) , Piotr Drąg (Polish) , Rafael Ferreira (Brasilian) , Róman Joost (German, English) , Seong-ho Cho (Korean) , SimaMoto,RyōTa (　　) (Japanese) , Sven Claussner (German, English) , Timo Jyrinki (Finnish) , Ulf-D. Ehlert (German) , Vitaly Lomov (Russian) , Willer Gomes Junior (Brasilian) , Yuri Myasoedov (Russian)

Proof Reading Stéphane Poumaer (French) , Axel Wernicke (German, English) , Alessandro Falappa (Italian) , Manuel Quiñones (Spanish) , Ignacio AntI (Spanish) , Choi Ji-Hui(　) (Korean) , Nickolay V. Shmyrev (Russian) , Albin Bernharsson (Swedish) , Daniel Nylander (Swedish) , Patrycja Stawiarska (Polish) , Andrew Pitonyak (English) , Jakub Friedl (Czech, English) , Hans De Jonge (Dutch) , Raymon Van Wanrooij (Dutch) , Semka Kuloviæ-Debals (Croatian) , Sally C. Barry (English) , Daniel Egger (English) , Sven Neumann (English, German) , Domingo Stephan (German) , Thomas Lotze (German) , Thomas Güttler (German) , Zhong Yaotang (Chinese) , Calum Mackay (English) , Thomas S Lendo (German) , Mel Boyce (syngin) (English) , Oliver Ellis (Red Haze) (English) , Markus Reinhardt (German) , Alexander Weiher (German) , Michael Hölzen (German) , Raymond Ostertag (French) , Cédric Gémy (French) , Sébastien Barre (French) , Niklas Mattison (Swedish) , Daryl Lee (English) , William Skaggs (English) , Cai Qian (　) (Chinese) , Yang Hong (　) (Chinese) , Xceals (Chinese) , Eric Lamarque (Chinese) , Robert van Drunen (Dutch) , Marco Marega (Italian) , Mike Vargas (Italian) , Andrea Zito (Italian) , Karine Delvare (French) , David 'Ilicz' Klementa (Czech) , Jan Smith (English) , Adolf Gerold (German) , Roxana Chernogolova (Russian) , Grigory Bakunov (Russian) , Oleg Fritz (Russian) , Mick Curtis (English) , Vitaly Lomov (Russian) , Pierre PERRIER (French) , Oliver Heesakke (Dutch) , Susanne Schmidt (English, German) , Ben (German) , Daniel Hornung (English) , Sven Claussner (English, German)

Graphics, Stylesheets Jakub Steiner , Øyvind Kolås

Build System, Technical Contributions Kenneth Nielsen , Róman Joost , Axel Wernicke , Nickolay V. Shmyrev , Daniel Egger , Sven Neumann , Michael Natterer (mitch) , Henrik Brix Andersen (brix) , Thomas Schraitle , Chris Hübsch , Anne Schneider , Peter Volkov , Daniel Richard

Part I

Getting Started

Chapter 1

Introduction

1.1 Welcome to GIMP

GIMP is a multi-platform photo manipulation tool. GIMP is an acronym for GNU Image Manipulation Program. The GIMP is suitable for a variety of image manipulation tasks, including photo retouching, image composition, and image construction.

GIMP has many capabilities. It can be used as a simple paint program, an expert quality photo retouching program, an online batch processing system, a mass production image renderer, an image format converter, etc.

GIMP is expandable and extensible. It is designed to be augmented with plug-ins and extensions to do just about anything. The advanced scripting interface allows everything from the simplest task to the most complex image manipulation procedures to be easily scripted.

One of The GIMP's strengths is its free availability from many sources for many operating systems. Most GNU/Linux distributions include The GIMP as a standard application. The GIMP is also available for other operating systems such as Microsoft Windows or Apple's Mac OS X (Darwin). The GIMP is a Free Software application covered by the General Public License [GPL]. The GPL provides users with the freedom to access and alter the source code that makes up computer programs.

1.1.1 Authors

The first version of the GIMP was written by Peter Mattis and Spencer Kimball. Many other developers have contributed more recently, and thousands have provided support and testing. GIMP releases are currently being orchestrated by Sven Neumann and Mitch Natterer and the other members of the GIMP-Team.

1.1.2 The GIMP Help system

The GIMP Documentation Team and other users have provided you with the information necessary to understand how to use GIMP. The User Manual is an important part of this help. The current version is on the web site of the Documentation Team [GIMP-DOCS] in HTML format. The HTML version is also available as context sensitive help (if you installed it) while using GIMP by pressing the **F1** key. Help on specific menu items can be accessed by pressing the **F1** key while the mouse pointer is focused on the menu item. Read on to begin your GIMP journey.

1.1.3 Features and Capabilities

The following list is a short overview of some of the features and capabilities which GIMP offers you:

- A full suite of painting tools including brushes, a pencil, an airbrush, cloning, etc.

- Tile-based memory management, so image size is limited only by available disk space

- Sub-pixel sampling for all paint tools for high-quality anti-aliasing

- Full Alpha channel support for working with transparency

- Layers and channels

- A procedural database for calling internal GIMP functions from external programs, such as Script-Fu

- Advanced scripting capabilities

- Multiple undo/redo (limited only by disk space)

- Transformation tools including rotate, scale, shear and flip

- Support for a wide range of file formats, including GIF, JPEG, PNG, XPM, TIFF, TGA, MPEG, PS, PDF, PCX, BMP and many others

- Selection tools, including rectangle, ellipse, free, fuzzy, bezier and intelligent scissors

- Plug-ins that allow for the easy addition of new file formats and new effect filters.

1.2   What's New in GIMP 2.8?

GIMP 2.8 is another important release from a development point of view, even more that it was for 2.6. It features a big change to the user interface addressing one of the most often received complaints: the lack of a single window mode. Moreover the integration effort of GEGL library had taken a big step forward, reaching more than 90% of the GIMP core, a new powerful transformation tool, layer groups, new common options, new brushes, improved text tool, and more.

User Interface

New single window mode With this new feature it will be possible to work with all the GIMP dialogs inside one big window, usually with the image(s) centered inside. No more floating panels or toolbox but the dialogs could be arranged inside this single window. This mode could be enabled or disabled all the time, even while working, and the option will be remembered through the sessions.

Figure 1.1 The new look of the single window mode

New file save workflow Now Save and Save as work only with xcf formats. If you want to export an image in another format, say jpg or png, you have to explicitly Export it. This enhances the workflow and lets you simply overwrite the original file or export to various other formats.

Figure 1.2 The new image workflow

New image bar A new useful image bar comes with the single window mode, which lets you switch easily between open images through the means of a tab bar with image thumbnails.

Figure 1.3 The new image bar

New arrangement options GIMP will make users working with two screens (one for dialogs, the other for images) happy: now it is possible to arrange the dialogs one over the other, in tabs and in columns too.

Figure 1.4 Multi column docks

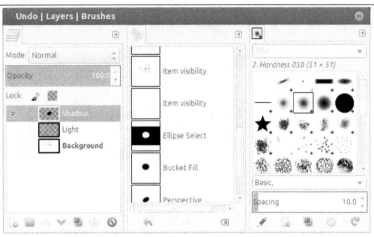

New resources tags GIMP Brushes, Gradients, Pattern and Palettes can be filtered and searched via tags. Tags are text labels that the user can assign to resources. With Tags the user can easily find the resources by means of an input text box. Tags can be manually assigned by the user with the same input box used for searching tags, or they can be automatically tagged using the directory name of the imported items.

Figure 1.5 Resource tags

Simple math in size entries Enhancements have also been made to the size entry widget, which is used for inputting most of the x, y, width, height parameters. For example, in the scale dialog it is now possible to write "50%" in the Width field to scale the image to 50% of the width. Expressions such as "30in + 40px" and "4 * 5.4in" work, too.

Figure 1.6 Math size entries

Minor changes

- The new "Lock Pixels" option in the layers dialog can avoid undesired painting on a layer when working with several layers.

Figure 1.7 The new Lock Pixels option

- Now you can move between images in single and multi window mode using the shortcuts Ctrl-PageUp/PageDown or Alt-Number.

- Add support for F2 to rename items in lists.

- You can now Alt-Click on layers in the Layers dialog to create a selection from it. Add, subtract and intersect modifiers **Click**, **Shift** and Ctrl-Shift keys work too. This makes it easy to compose contents of a layer based on the contents of other layers, without detours.

- Since the keyboard shortcuts Ctrl-E and Ctrl-Shift-E have been redirected to image export mechanisms, new keyboard shortcuts have been setup for "Shrink Wrap" and "Fit Image in Window", namely Ctrl-J and Ctrl-Shift-J respectively.

- Added Windows → Hide docks menu item that does what "Tab" does and also displays its state, which is now persistent across sessions, too.

- The layer modes have been rearranged into more logical and useful groups based on the effect they have on layers. Layer modes that make the layer lighter are in one group, layer modes that make the layer darker in another group, and so forth.

- In multi-window mode, you can now close the Toolbox without quitting GIMP.

- Allow binding arbitrary actions to extra mouse buttons.

- Now it is possible to change the application language directly from the preference menu.

Tools, Filters and Plug-ins

A new tool: Cage Transform With this new tool is now possible to create custom bending of a selection just moving control points. This is the result of one of our Google Summer of Code 2010 students.

Figure 1.8 Cage Transform

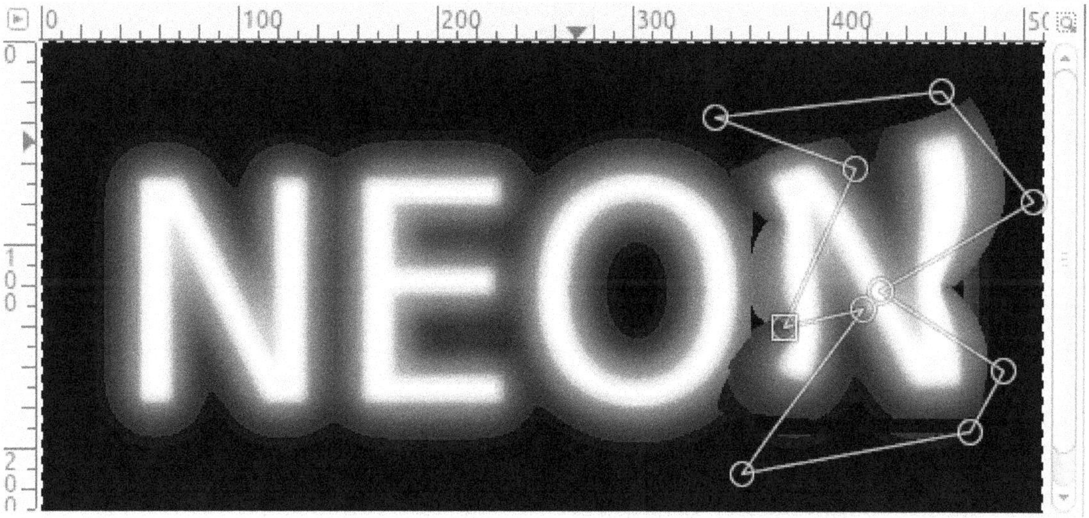

Improved Text Tool The text tool has been enhanced to support on canvas text writing and make possible changing the attributes of a single char.

Figure 1.9 Improved text tool

New layer groups It is now possible to group set of layers and treat them like an entity. It is possible to switch a group on or off and to move the group in the layers dialog. It is easy to add / remove existing layers to a group or to create / delete a layer inside the group and it is even possible to create embedded groups of groups. It is possible to apply a layer mode to a group as you do with a single layer. All this greatly improves the workflow with complex multilayer images making them easier to manage.

Figure 1.10 New layer groups

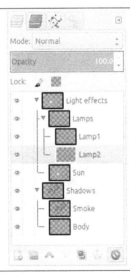

Rotating brushes Brushes can now be rotated at will, acting on the brush option "Angle".

Figure 1.11 Rotating brushes

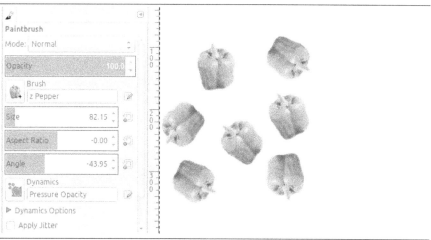

Minor changes

- The default Quick Mask color is now configurable.
- The RTL mode (right to left writing) has been improved in the Text tool.
- You can specify the written language in the Text Tool. This helps choosing an appropriate font, or appropriate glyphs for the selected language.
- Added optional diagonal guides to the crop tool.
- Added "Rule of fifths" crop guide overlay.
- A Cairo based PDF exporter has been implemented. Although being somewhat simplistic, the exporter saves text, embedding fonts into the final PDF file, and attempts to convert bitmaps to vector objects.
- Brush dynamics improved.
- Added plug-in for loading JPEG2000 images.
- Added plug-ins for X11 Mouse Cursor import and export support.
- Added fundamental OpenRaster (.ora) import and export support.
- Added RGB565 support to the csource plug-in.
- Added a new "Create" command that allows loading a Web page directly into GIMP using Webkit.

Under the Hood

GEGL The porting of the GIMP core towards the new high bit-depth and non-destructive editing GEGL [GEGL] library has taken big steps and now more than 90% of the task is already finished.

In addition to porting color operations to GEGL, an experimental GEGL Operation tool has been added, found in the Tools menu. It enables applying GEGL operations to an image and it gives on-canvas previews of the results. The screenshot below shows this for a Gaussian Blur.

Figure 1.12 GEGL operation

Cairo porting Started with GIMP version 2.6, all tools rendering on canvas is now completely ported to [CAIRO]. It provides smooth antialiased graphics and improves GIMP look. Some plug-ins have been upgraded to Cairo as well. Additionally all tools now use an on-canvas progress indicator instead of the one in the statusbar.

Figure 1.13 Progress indicator

Miscellaneous

License change The GIMP license has been changed to (L)GPLv3+.

New script API

- A lot of GIMP APIs have been rebuilt to simplify developing new scripts.
- To further enhances scripting abilities, API changes to support layer groups have been made.

Backwards Compatibility To allow migrating from the old tools presets system to the new one, there is a Python script, which you can download from the GIMP wiki site. However, the old tools presets are not 100% convertible to the new tool presets. For instance, brush scale from 2.6 can't be converted to brush size in 2.8.

Known Problems Working with graphics tablets could be problematic due to the GTK+2 library in use. If in this case either use the older version 2.6 or wait for the up coming version 3.0 for the full GTK+3 support.

Chapter 2

Fire up the GIMP

2.1 Running GIMP

Most often, you start GIMP either by clicking on an icon (if your system is set up to provide you with one), or by typing **gimp** on a command line. If you have multiple versions of GIMP installed, you may need to type **gimp-2.8** to get the latest version. You can, if you want, give a list of image files on the command line after the program name, and they will automatically be opened by GIMP as it starts. It is also possible, though, to open files from within GIMP once it is running.

Most operating systems support file associations, which associates a class of files (as determined by their filename extension, such as .jpg) with a corresponding application (such as GIMP). When image files are properly "associated" to GIMP, you can double click on an image to open it in GIMP.

2.1.1 Known Platforms

The GIMP is the most widely supported image manipulation available today. The platforms on which GIMP is known to work include:

GNU/Linux, Apple Mac OS X, Microsoft Windows, OpenBSD, NetBSD, FreeBSD, Solaris, SunOS, AIX, HP-UX, Tru64, Digital UNIX, OSF/1, IRIX, OS/2, and BeOS.

The GIMP is easily ported to other operating systems because of its source code availability. For further information visit the GIMP developers homepage. [GIMP-DEV].

2.1.2 Language

GIMP automatically detects and uses the system language. In the unlikely event that language detection fails, or if you just want to use a different language, since GIMP-2.8, you can do so through: Edit → Preferences → Interface.

You can also use:

Under Linux *In LINUX*: in console mode, type **LANGUAGE=en gimp** or **LANG=en gimp** replacing en by fr, de, ... according to the language you want. Background: Using **LANGUAGE=en** sets an environment variable for the executed program **gimp**.

Under Windows XP Control Panel → System → Advanced → Environment button in "System Variables" area: Add button: Enter LANG for Name and fr or de... for Value. Watch out! You have to click on three successive OK to validate your choice.

If you change languages often, you can create a batch file to change the language. Open NotePad. Type the following commands (for french for instance):

```
set lang=fr
start gimp-2.8.exe
```

Save this file as GIMP-FR.BAT (or another name, but always with a .BAT extension). Create a shortcut and drag it to your desktop.

Another possibility: Start → Programs → GTK Runtime Environment Then Select language and select the language you want in the drop-down list.

Under Apple Mac OS X From System Preferences, click on the International icon. In the Language tab, the desired language should be the first in the list.

Another GIMP instance Use **−n** to run multiple instances of GIMP. For example, use **gimp-2.8** to start GIMP in the default system language, and **LANGUAGE=en gimp-2.8 −n** to start another instance of GIMP in English; this is very useful for translators.

2.1.3 Command Line Arguments

Although arguments are not required when starting GIMP, the most common arguments are shown below. On a Unix system, you can use **man gimp** for a complete list.

Command line arguments must be in the command line that you use to start GIMP as **gimp-2.8 [OPTION...] [FILE | URI...]**.

-?, --help Display a list of all commandline options.

--help-all Show all help options.

--help-gtk Show GTK+ Options.

-v, --version Print the GIMP version and exit.

--license Show license information and exit.

--verbose Show detailed start-up messages.

-n, --new-instance Start a new GIMP instance.

-a, --as-new Open images as new.

-i, --no-interface Run without a user interface.

-d, --no-data Do not load patterns, gradients, palettes, or brushes. Often useful in non-interactive situations where start-up time is to be minimized.

-f, --no-fonts Do not load any fonts. This is useful to load GIMP faster for scripts that do not use fonts, or to find problems related to malformed fonts that hang GIMP.

-s, --no-splash Do not show the splash screen while starting.

--no-shm Do not use shared memory between GIMP and plugins.

--no-cpu-accel Do not use special CPU acceleration functions. Useful for finding or disabling buggy accelerated hardware or functions.

--session=_name_ Use a different `sessionrc` for this GIMP session. The given session name is appended to the default `sessionrc` filename.

--gimprc=_filename_ Use an alternative `gimprc` instead of the default one. The `gimprc` file contains a record of your preferences. Useful in cases where plugins paths or machine specs may be different.

--system-gimprc=_filename_ Use an alternate system gimprc file.

-b, --batch=_commands_ Execute the set of commands non-interactively. The set of commands is typically in the form of a script that can be executed by one of the GIMP scripting extensions. When the command is **−**, commands are read from standard input.

--batch-interpreter=_proc_ Specify the procedure to use to process batch commands. The default procedure is Script-Fu.

--console-messages Do not popup dialog boxes on errors or warnings. Print the messages on the console instead.

--pdb-compat-mode=_mode_ PDB compatibility mode (off | on | warn).

--stack-trace-mode=_mode_ Debug in case of a crash (never | query | always).

--debug-handlers Enable non-fatal debugging signal handlers. Useful for GIMP debugging.

--g-fatal-warnings Make all warnings fatal. Useful for debug.

--dump-gimprc Output a gimprc file with default settings. Useful if you messed up the gimprc file.

--display=*display* Use the designated X display (does not apply to all platforms).

2.2 Starting GIMP the first time

When first run, GIMP performs a series of steps to configure options and directories. The configuration process creates a subdirectory in your home directory called `.gimp-2.8`. All of the configuration information is stored in this directory. If you remove or rename the directory, GIMP will repeat the initial configuration process, creating a new `.gimp-2.8` directory. Use this capability to explore different configuration options without destroying your existing installation, or to recover if your configuration files are damaged.

2.2.1 Finally . . .

Just a couple of suggestions before you start, though: First, GIMP provides tips you can read at any time using the menu command Help → Tip of the Day. The tips provide information that is considered useful, but not easy to learn by experimenting; so they are worth reading. Please read the tips when you have the time. Second, if at some point you are trying to do something, and GIMP seems to have suddenly stopped functioning, the section Getting Unstuck may help you out. Happy Gimping!

Chapter 3

First Steps with Wilber

3.1 Basic Concepts

Figure 3.1 Wilber, the GIMP mascot

The Wilber_Construction_Kit (in src/images/) allows you to give the mascot a different appearance. It is the work of Tuomas Kuosmanen (tigertATgimp.org).

This section provides a brief introduction to the basic concepts and terminology used in GIMP. The concepts presented here are explained in much greater depth elsewhere. With a few exceptions, we have avoided cluttering this section with a lot of links and cross-references: everything mentioned here is so high-level that you can easily locate it in the index.

Images Images are the basic entities used by GIMP. Roughly speaking, an "image" corresponds to a single file, such as a TIFF or JPEG file. You can also think of an image as corresponding to a single display window (although in truth it is possible to have multiple windows all displaying the same image). It is not possible to have a single window display more than one image, though, or for an image to have no window displaying it.

A GIMP image may be quite a complicated thing. Instead of thinking of it as a sheet of paper with a picture on it, think of it as more like a stack of sheets, called "layers". In addition to a stack of layers, a GIMP image may contain a selection mask, a set of channels, and a set of paths. In fact, GIMP provides a mechanism for attaching arbitrary pieces of data, called "parasites", to an image.

In GIMP, it is possible to have many images open at the same time. Although large images may use many megabytes of memory, GIMP uses a sophisticated tile-based memory management system that allows GIMP to handle very large images gracefully. There are limits, however, and having more memory available may improve system performance.

Layers If a simple image can be compared to a single sheet of paper, an image with layers is likened to a sheaf of transparent papers stacked one on top of the other. You can draw on each paper, but still see the content of the other sheets through the transparent areas. You can also move one sheet in relation to the others. Sophisticated GIMP users often deal with images containing many layers, even dozens of them. Layers need not be opaque, and they need not cover the entire extent of an

15

image, so when you look at an image's display, you may see more than just the top layer: you may see elements of many layers.

Resolution Digital images comprise of a grid of square elements of varying colors, called pixels. Each image has a pixel size, such as 900 pixels wide by 600 pixels high. But pixels don't have a set size in physical space. To set up an image for printing, we use a value called resolution, defined as the ratio between an image's size in pixels and its physical size (usually in inches) when it is printed on paper. Most file formats (but not all) can save this value, which is expressed as ppi — pixels per inch. When printing a file, the resolution value determines the size the image will have on paper, and as a result, the physical size of the pixels. The same 900x600 pixel image may be printed as a small 3x2" card with barely noticeable pixels — or as a large poster with large, chunky pixels. Images imported from cameras and mobile devices tend to have a resolution value attached to the file. The value is usually 72 or 96ppi. It is important to realize that this value is arbitrary and was chosen for historic reasons. You can always change the resolution value inside GIMP — this has no effect on the actual image pixels. Furthermore, for uses such as displaying images on line, on mobile devices, television or video games — in short, any use that is not print — the resolution value is meaningless and is ignored, and instead the image is usually displayed so that each image pixel conforms to one screen pixel.

Channels A Channel is a single component of a pixel's color. For a colored pixel in GIMP, these components are usually Red, Green, Blue and sometimes transparency (Alpha). For a Grayscale image, they are Gray and Alpha and for an Indexed color image, they are Indexed and Alpha.

The entire rectangular array of any one of the color components for all of the pixels in an image is also referred to as a Channel. You can see these color channels with the Channels dialog.

When the image is displayed, GIMP puts these components together to form the pixel colors for the screen, printer, or other output device. Some output devices may use different channels from Red, Green and Blue. If they do, GIMP's channels are converted into the appropriate ones for the device when the image is displayed.

Channels can be useful when you are working on an image which needs adjustment in one particular color. For example, if you want to remove "red eye" from a photograph, you might work on the Red channel.

You can look at channels as masks which allow or restrict the output of the color that the channel represents. By using Filters on the channel information, you can create many varied and subtle effects on an image. A simple example of using a Filter on the color channels is the Channel Mixer filter.

In addition to these channels, GIMP also allows you to create other channels (or more correctly, Channel Masks), which are displayed in the lower part of the Channels dialog. You can create a New Channel or save a selection to a channel (mask). See the glossary entry on Masks for more information about Channel Masks.

Selections Often when modify an image, you only want a part of the image to be affected. The "selection" mechanism makes this possible. Each image has its own selection, which you normally see as a moving dashed line separating the selected parts from the unselected parts (the so-called "marching ants"). Actually this is a bit misleading: selection in GIMP is graded, not all-or-nothing, and really the selection is represented by a full-fledged grayscale channel. The dashed line that you normally see is simply a contour line at the 50%-selected level. At any time, though, you can visualize the selection channel in all its glorious detail by toggling the QuickMask button.

A large component of learning how to use GIMP effectively is acquiring the art of making good selections—selections that contain exactly what you need and nothing more. Because selection-handling is so centrally important, GIMP provides many tools for doing it: an assortment of selection-making tools, a menu of selection operations, and the ability to switch to Quick Mask mode, in which you can treat the selection channel as though it were a color channel, thereby "painting the selection".

Undoing When you make mistakes, you can undo them. Nearly everything you can do to an image is undoable. In fact, you can usually undo a substantial number of the most recent things you did, if you decide that they were misguided. GIMP makes this possible by keeping a history of your actions. This history consumes memory, though, so undoability is not infinite. Some actions use very little undo memory, so that you can do dozens of them before the earliest ones are deleted from this history; other types of actions require massive amounts of undo memory. You can configure the amount of memory GIMP allows for the undo history of each image, but in any situation, you should always be able to undo at least your 2-3 most recent actions. (The most important action that is not undoable is closing an image. For this reason, GIMP asks you to confirm that you really want to close the image if you have made any changes to it.)

Plug-ins Many, probably most, of the things that you do to an image in GIMP are done by the GIMP application itself. However, GIMP also makes extensive use of "plug-ins", which are external programs that interact very closely with GIMP, and are capable of manipulating images and other GIMP objects in very sophisticated ways. Many important plug-ins are bundled with GIMP, but there are also many available by other means. In fact, writing plug-ins (and scripts) is the easiest way for people not on the GIMP development team to add new capabilities to GIMP.

All of the commands in the Filters menu, and a substantial number of commands in other menus, are actually implemented as plug-ins.

Scripts In addition to plug-ins, which are programs written in the C language, GIMP can also make use of scripts. The largest number of existing scripts are written in a language called Script-Fu, which is unique to GIMP (for those who care, it is a dialect of the Lisp-like language called Scheme). It is also possible to write GIMP scripts in Python or Perl. These languages are more flexible and powerful than Script-Fu; their disadvantage is that they depend on software that does not automatically come packaged with GIMP, so they are not guaranteed to work correctly in every GIMP installation.

3.2 Main Windows

The GIMP user interface is now available in two modes:

- multi-window mode,

- single window mode.

When you open GIMP for the first time, it opens in multi-window mode by default. You can enable single-window mode through Windows → >Single-Window Mode) in the image menu bar. After quitting GIMP with this option enabled, GIMP will start in single-window mode next time.

Multi-Window Mode

Figure 3.2 A screenshot illustrating the multi-window mode.

The screenshot above shows the most basic arrangement of GIMP windows that can be used effectively.

You can notice two panels, left and right, and an image window in middle. A second image is partially masked. The left panel collects Toolbox and Tool Options dialog together. The right panel collects layers, channels, paths, undo history dialogs together in a multi-tab dock, brushes, patterns and gradients dialogs together in another dock below. You can move these panels on screen. You can also mask them using the **Tab** key.

1. *The Main Toolbox:* Contains a set of icon buttons used to select tools. By default, it also contains the foreground and background colors. You can add brush, pattern, gradient and active image icons. Use Edit → Preferences → Toolbox to enable, or disable the extra items.

2. *Tool options:* Docked below the main Toolbox is a Tool Options dialog, showing options for the currently selected tool (in this case, the Move tool).

3. *Image windows:* Each image open in GIMP is displayed in a separate window. Many images can be open at the same time, limited by only the system resources. Before you can do anything useful in GIMP, you need to have at least one image window open. The image window holds the Menu of the main commands of GIMP (File, Edit, Select...), which you can also get by right-clicking on the window.

   An image can be bigger than the image window. In that case, GIMP displays the image in a reduced zoom level which allows to see the full image in the image window. If you turn to the 100% zoom level, scroll bars appear, allowing you to pan across the image.

4. The *Layers, Channels, Paths, Undo History* dock — note that the dialogs in the dock are tabs. The Layers tab is open : it shows the layer structure of the currently active image, and allows it to be manipulated in a variety of ways. It is possible to do a few very basic things without using the Layers dialog, but even moderately sophisticated GIMP users find it indispensable to have the Layers dialog available at all times.

5. *Brushes/Patterns/Gradients:* The docked dialog below the layer dialog shows the dialogs (tabs) for managing brushes, patterns and gradients.

Dialog and dock managing is described in Section 3.2.3.

Single Window Mode

Figure 3.3 A screenshot illustrating the single-window mode.

You find the same elements, with differences in their management:

- Left and right panels are fixed; you can't move them. But you can decrease or increase their width by dragging the moving pointer that appears when the mouse pointer overflies the right border of the left pane. If you want to keep the left pane narrow, please use the slider at the bottom of the tool options to pan across the options display.

  If you reduce the width of a multi-tab dock, there may be not enough place for all tabs;then arrow-heads appear allowing you to scroll through tabs.

  As in multi-window mode, you can mask these panels using the **Tab** key.

- The image window occupies all space between both panels.

  When several images are open, a new bar appears above the image window, with a tab for every image. You can navigate between images by clicking on tabs or either using Ctrl-Page Up or Page Down or Alt-Number. "Number" is tab number; you must use the number keys of the upper line of your keyboard, not that of keypad (Alt-shift necessary for some national keyboards).

This is a minimal setup. There are over a dozen other types of dialogs used by GIMP for various purposes, but users typically open them when they need them and close them when they are done. Knowledgeable users generally keep the Toolbox (with Tool Options) and Layers dialog open at all times. The Toolbox is essential to many GIMP operations. The Tool Options section is actually a separate dialog, shown docked to the Main Toolbox in the screenshot. Knowledgeable users almost always have it set up this way: it is very difficult to use tools effectively without being able to see how their options are set. The Layers dialog comes into play when you work with an image with multiple layers: after you advance beyond the most basic stages of GIMP expertise, this means *almost always*. And of course it helps to display the images you're editing on the screen; if you close the image window before saving your work, GIMP will ask you whether you want to close the file.

Note

 If your GIMP layout is lost, your arrangement is easy to recover using Windows → Recently Closed Docks ; the Windows menu command is only available while an image is open. To add, close, or detach a tab from a dock, click ◈ in the upper right corner of a dialog. This opens the Tab menu. Select Add Tab, Close Tab , or Detach Tab.

The following sections walk you through the components of each of the windows shown in the screenshot, explaining what they are and how they work. Once you have read them, plus the section describing the basic structure of GIMP images, you should have learned enough to use GIMP for a wide variety of basic image manipulations. You can then look through the rest of the manual at your leisure (or just experiment) to learn the almost limitless number of more subtle and specialized things that are possible. Have fun!

3.2.1   The Toolbox

Figure 3.4 Screenshot of the Toolbox

The Toolbox is the heart of GIMP. Here is a quick tour of what you will find there.

> **Tip**
>
> In the Toolbox, as in most parts of GIMP, moving the mouse over something and letting it rest for a moment, usually displays a "tooltip" that describes the thing. Short cut keys are also frequently shown in the tooltip. In many cases, you can hover the mouse over an item and press the **F1** key to get help about the thing that is underneath the mouse.

By default, only the Foreground-background icon is visible. You can add Brush-Pattern-Gradient icons and Active Image icon through Edit → Preferences → Toolbox: Tools configuration.

1. *Tool icons:* These icons are buttons which activate tools for a wide variety of purposes: selecting parts of images, painting an image, transforming an image, etc. Section 14.1 gives an overview of how to work with tools, and each tool is described systematically in the Tools chapter.

2. *Foreground/Background colors:* The color areas here show you GIMP's current foreground and background colors, which come into play in many operations. Clicking on either one of them brings up a color selector dialog that allows you to change to a different color. Clicking on the double-headed arrow swaps the two colors, and clicking on the small symbol in the lower left corner resets them to black and white.

3. *Brush/Pattern/Gradient:* The symbols here show you GIMP's current selections for: the Paintbrush, used by all tools that allow you to paint on the image ("painting" includes operations like erasing and smudging, by the way); for the Pattern, which is used in filling selected areas of an image; and for the Gradient, which comes into play whenever an operation requires a smoothly varying range of colors. Clicking on any of these symbols brings up a dialog window that allows you to change it.

4. *Active Image:* In GIMP, you can work with many images at once, but at any given moment, only one image is the "active image". Here you find a small iconic representation of the active image. Click the icon to display a dialog with a list of the currently open images, click an image in the dialog to make it active. Usually, you click an image window in multi-window mode, or an image tab in single-window mode, to make it the active image.

   You can "Drop to an XDS file manager to save the image". XDS is an acronym for "X Direct Save Protocol": an additional feature for the X Window System graphical user interface for Unix-like operating systems.

> **Note**
>
> At every start, GIMP selects a tool (the brush), a color, a brush and a pattern by default, always the same. If you want GIMP to select the last tool, color, brush and pattern you used when quitting your previous session, check the Save input device settings on exit in Preferences/Input Devices.

> **Tip**
>
> The Toolbox window displays "Wilber's eyes" along the top of the dialog. You can get rid of the "Wilber's eyes" by adding the following line to your `gimprc` file: `(to olbox-wilber no)`. It only affects the toolbox. The eyes in the Image window are only visible when you do not have an open image.

> **Tip**
>
> Drag and drop an image from a file browser into the Toolbox window to open the image in its own Image window or tab.

3.2.2 Image Window

GIMP user interface is now available in two modes: multi-window mode (default), and single-window mode (optional, through Windows → >Single-Window Mode. But, if you quit GIMP with this option enabled, GIMP will open in single mode next time).

In single-window mode, no new window is added: images and dialogs are added in tabs. Please see Single Window Mode.

When you start GIMP without any image open, the image window seems to be absent in single-window mode, while, in multi-window mode, an image window exists, even if no image is open.

We will begin with a brief description of the components that are present by default in an ordinary image window. Some of the components can be removed by using commands in the View menu.

Figure 3.5 The Image Window in Multi-Window Mode

Figure 3.6 The Image Area in Single-Window Mode

Note

 Despite *Single*-window Mode, we will use "image window" for "image area".

---

1. *Title Bar:* The Title Bar in an image window without an image displays "GNU Image Manipulating Program". An image window with an image displays the image name and its specifications in the title bar according to the settings in Preference Dialog. The Title Bar is provided by the operating system, not by GIMP, so its appearance is likely to vary with the operating system, window manager, and/or theme — in Linux systems, this title bar has a button to display the image window on all your desktops. You also have this button in toolbox window and layer window.

   If you have opened a non-xcf image, it is "(imported)" as a .xcf file and its original name appears in the status bar at the bottom of the image window.

   When an image is modified, an asterisk appears in front of title.

2. *Image Menu:* Directly below the Title Bar appears the Menu bar (unless it has been suppressed). The Image Menu provides access to nearly every operation you can perform on an image. You can also right-click on an image to display a pop-up image menu, [1], or by left-clicking on the little "arrow-head" symbol in the upper left corner, called *Menu Button*, described just below. Many menu commands are also associated with keyboard *shortcuts* as shown in the menu. You can define your own custom shortcuts for menu actions, if you enable Use Dynamic Keyboard Shortcuts in the Preferences dialog.

---

[1] Users with an Apple Macintosh and a one button mouse can use Ctrl-Mouse Button instead.

3. *Menu Button:* Click the Menu Button to display the Image Menu in a column,(essential in full screen mode). If you like to use keyboard shortcuts, use Shift-F10 to open the menu.

4. *Ruler:* In the default layout, rulers are shown above and to the left of the image. Use the rulers to determine coordinates within the image. The default unit for rulers is pixels; use the settings described below to use a unit other than pixels.

   One of the most important uses of rulers is to create *guides*. Click and drag a ruler into the image to create a guide. A guide is a line that helps you accurately position things—or verify that another line is truly horizontal or vertical. Click and drag a guide to move it. Drag a guide out of the image to delete it; you can always drag another guide into the image. You can even use multiple guides at the same time.

   In ruler area, the mouse pointer position is marked with two small arrow-heads pointing vertically and horizontally.

5. *QuickMask Toggle:* The small button in the lower left corner of the image toggles the Quick Mask on and off. When the Quick Mask is on, the button is outlined in red. See QuickMask for more details on this highly useful tool.

6. *Pointer Coordinates:* When the pointer (mouse cursor, if you are using a mouse) is within the image boundaries, the rectangular area in the lower left corner of the window displays the current pointer coordinates. The units are the same as for the rulers.

7. *Units Menu:* Use the Units Menu to change the units used for rulers and several other purposes. The default unit is pixels, but you can quickly change to inches, cm, or several other possibilities using this menu. Note that the setting of "Dot for dot" in the View menu affects how the display is scaled: see Dot for Dot for more information.

8. *Zoom Button:* There are a number of ways to zoom the image in or out, but the Zoom Button is perhaps the simplest. You can directly enter a zoom level in the text box for precise control.

9. *Status Area:* The Status Area is at the bottom of the image window. By default, the Status Area displays the original name of the image.xcf file, and the amount of system memory used by the image. Please use Edit → Preferences → Image Windows → Title & Status to customize the information displayed in the Status Area. During time-consuming operations, the status area temporarily shows the running operation and how complete the operation is.

Note

 Note that the memory used by the image is very different from the image file size. For instance, a 70Kb .PNG image may occupy 246Kb in RAM when displayed. There are two primary reasons the difference in memory usage. First, a .PNG file is compressed format, and the image is reconstituted in RAM in uncompressed form. Second, GIMP uses extra memory, and copies of the image, for use by the Undo command.

---

10. *Cancel Button:* During complex time-consuming operations, usually a plug-in, a Cancel button temporarily appears in the lower right corner of the window. Use the Cancel button to stop the operation.

Note

 A few plug-ins respond badly to being canceled, sometimes leaving corrupted pieces of images behind.

---

11. *Navigation Control:* This is a small cross-shaped button at the lower right corner of the image display. Click and hold (do not release the mouse button) on the navigation control to display the Navigation Preview. The Navigation Preview has a miniature view of the image with the displayed area outlined. Use the Navigation Preview to quickly pan to a different part of the image—move the mouse while keeping the button pressed. The Navigation Window is often the most convenient way to quickly navigate around a large image with only a small portion displayed. (See Navigation Dialog for other ways to access the Navigation Window). (If your mouse has a middle-button, click-drag with it to pan across the image).

12. *Inactive Padding Area:* When the image dimensions are smaller than the image window, this padding area separates the active image display and the inactive padding area, so you're able to distinguish between them. You cannot apply any Filters or Operations in general to the inactive area.

13. *Image Display:* The most important part of the image window is, of course, the image display or canvas. It occupies the central area of the window, surrounded by a yellow dotted line showing the image boundary, against a neutral gray background. You can change the zoom level of the image display in a variety of ways, including the Zoom setting described below.

14. *Image Window Resize Toggle:* Without enabling this feature, if you change the size of the image window by click-and-dragging border limits, the image size and zoom does not change. If you make the window larger, for example, then you will see more of the image. If this button is pressed, however, the image resizes when the window resizes so that (mostly) the same portion of the image is displayed before and after the window is resized.

> **Tip**
>
> Drag and drop an image into the Toolbox window from a file browser to open the image in its own Image window or tab.
>
> Dragging an image file into the Layer dialog adds it to the image as a new layer.

Image size and image window size can be different. You can make image fit window, and vice versa, using two keyboard shortcuts:

- Ctrl-J: this command keeps the zoom level; it adapts window size to image size. The Shrink Wrap command does the same.

- Ctrl-Shift-J: this command modifies the zoom level to adapt the image display to the window.

3.2.3 Dialogs and Docking

3.2.3.1 Organizing Dialogs

GIMP has great flexibility for arranging dialog on your screen. A "dialog" is a moving window which contains options for a tool or is dedicated to a special task. A "dock" is a container which can hold a collection of persistent dialogs, such as the Tool Options dialog, Brushes dialog, Palette dialog, etc. Docks cannot, however, hold non-persistent dialogs such as the Preferences dialog or an Image window.

GIMP has three default docks:

- the Tool Options dock under the Toolbox in the left panel,

- the Layers, Channels, Paths and Undo dock in the upper part of the right panel,

- the Brushes, Patterns and Gradients dock in the lower part of the right panel.

In these docks, each dialog is in its own tab.

In multi-window mode, the Toolbox is a *utility window* and not a dock. In single-window mode, it belongs to the single window.

Use Windows → Dockable Dialogs to view a list of dockable dialogs. Select a dockable dialog from the list to view the dialog. If the dialog is available in a dock, then it is made visible. If the dialog is not in a dock, the behavior is different in multi and single window modes:

- In multi-window mode, a new window, containing the dialog, appears on the screen.

- In single-window mode, the dialog is automatically docked to the Layers-Undo dock as a tab.

You can click-and-drag a tab and drop it in the wanted place:

- either in the tab bar of a dock, to integrate it in the dialog group,

- or on a docking bar that appears as a blue line when the mouse pointer goes over a dock border, to anchor the dialog to the dock.

In multi-window mode, you can also click on the dialog title and drag it to the wanted place.

Figure 3.7 Integrating a new dialog in a dialog group

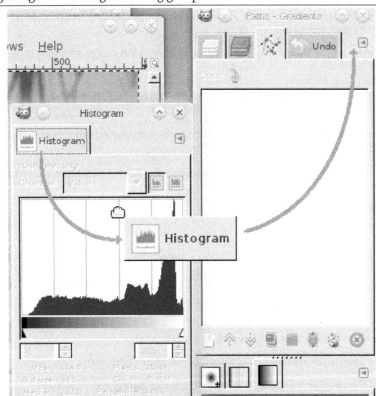

Here, in multi-window mode, the Histogram dialog was dragged to the tab bar of the Layers-Undo dock.

More simple: the **Add tab** command in the Tab menu Section 3.2.3.2.

Figure 3.8 Anchoring a dialog to a dock border

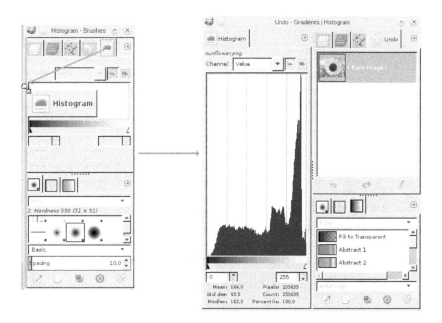

The Histogram dialog dragged to the left vertical docking bar of the right panel and the result: the dialog anchored to the left border of the right panel. This dialog now belongs to the right panel.
So, you can arrange dialogs in a multi-column display, interesting if you work with two screens, one for dialogs, the other for images.

 Tip

Press the **Tab** key in an Image window to toggle the visibility of the docks. This is useful if the docks hide a portion of the image Window. You can quickly hide all the docks, do your work, then display all the docs again. Pressing the **Tab** key inside a dock to navigate through the dock.

3.2.3.2   Tab Menu

Figure 3.9 A dialog in a dock, with the Tab menu button highlighted.

In each dialog, you can access a special menu of tab-related operations by pressing the Tab Menu button, as highlighted in the figure above. Exactly which commands are shown in the menu depends on the active dialog, but they always include operations for creating new tabs, closing or detaching tabs.

Figure 3.10 The Tab menu of the Layers dialog.

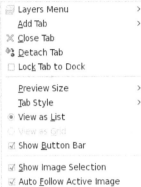

The Tab menu gives you access to the following commands:

Context Menu At the top of each Tab menu, an entry opens the dialog's context menu, which contains operations specific to that particular type of dialog. For example, the context menu for the Layers tab is Layers Menu, which contains a set of operations for manipulating layers.

Add Tab Add Tab opens into a submenu allowing you to add a large variety of dockable dialogs as new tabs.

Figure 3.11 "Add tab" sub-menu

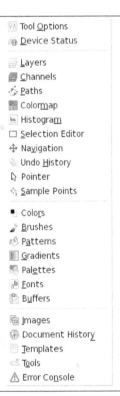

Close Tab Close the dialog. Closing the last dialog in a dock causes the dock itself to close.

Detach Tab Detach the dialog from the dock, creating a new dock with the detached dialog as its only member. It has the same effect as dragging the tab out of the dock and releasing it at a location where it cannot be docked.

It's a way to create a paradoxical new window in single-window mode!

If the tab is locked, this menu item is insensitive and grayed out.

Lock Tab to Dock Prevent the dialog from being moved or detached. When activated, Detach Tab is insensitive and grayed out.

Preview Size

Figure 3.12 Preview Size submenu of a Tab menu.

Many, but not all, dialogs have Tab menus containing a Preview Size option, which opens into a submenu giving a list of sizes for the items in the dialog (see the figure above). For example, the Brushes dialog shows pictures of all available brushes: the Preview Size determines how large the pictures are. The default is Medium.

Tab Style

Figure 3.13 Tab Style submenu of a Tab menu.

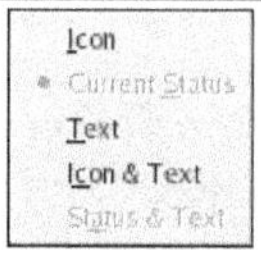

Available only when multiple dialogs are in the same dock, Tab Style opens a submenu allowing you to choose the appearance of the tabs at the top (see the figure above). There are five choices, not all are available for every dialog:

Icon Use an icon to represent the dialog type.

Current Status Is only available for dialogs that allows you to select something, such as a brush, pattern, gradient, etc. Current Status shows a representation of the currently selected item in the tab top.

Text Use text to display the dialog type.

Icon and Text Using both an icon and text results in wider tabs.

Status and Text Show the currently selected item and text with the dialog type.

View as List; View as Grid These entries are shown in dialogs that allow you to select an item from a set: brushes, patterns, fonts, etc. You can choose to view the items as a vertical list, with the name of each beside it, or as a grid, with representations of the items but no names. Each has its advantages: viewing as a list gives you more information, but viewing as a grid allows you to see more possibilities at once. The default for this varies across dialogs: for brushes and patterns, the default is a grid; for most other things, the default is a list.

When the tree-view is View as List, you can use tags. Please see Section 15.3.6.

You can also use a list search field:

Figure 3.14 The list search field.

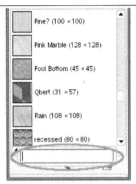

Use Ctrl-F to open the list search field. An item must be selected for this command to be effective.

The list search field automatically closes after five seconds if you do nothing.

> **Note**
>
> The search field shortcut is also available for the tree-view you get in the "Brush", "Font" or "Pattern" option of several tools.

Show Button Bar Some dialogs display a button bar on the bottom of the dialog; for example, the Patterns, Brushes, Gradients, and Images dialogs. This is a toggle. If it is checked, then the Button Bar is displayed.

Figure 3.15 Button Bar on the Brushes dialog.

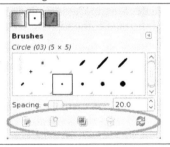

Show Image Selection This option is available in multi-window mode only. This is a toggle. If it is checked, then an Image Menu is shown at the top of the dock:

Figure 3.16 A dock with an Image Menu highlighted.

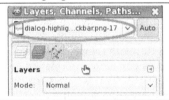

It is not available for dialogs docked below the Toolbox. This option is interesting only if you have several open images on your screen.

Auto Follow Active Image This option is available in multi-window mode only. This option is also interesting only if you have several images open on your screen. Then, the information displayed in a dock is always that of the selected image in the Image Selection drop-down list. If the Auto Follow Active Image is disabled, the image can be selected only in the Image Selection. If enabled, you can also select it by activating the image directly (clicking on its title bar).

3.3 Undoing

Almost anything you do to an image in GIMP can be undone. You can undo the most recent action by choosing Edit → Undo from the image menu, but this is done so frequently that you really should memorize the keyboard shortcut, Ctrl-Z.

Undoing can itself be undone. After having undone an action, you can *redo* it by choosing Edit → Redo from the image menu, or use the keyboard shortcut, Ctrl-Y. It is often helpful to judge the effect of an action by repeatedly undoing and redoing it. This is usually very quick, and does not consume any extra resources or alter the undo history, so there is never any harm in it.

Caution

If you undo one or more actions and then operate on the image in any way except by using Undo or Redo, it will no longer be possible to redo those actions: they are lost forever. The solution to this, if it creates a problem for you, is to duplicate the image and then test on the copy. (Do *Not* test the original, because the undo/redo history is not copied when you duplicate an image.)

If you often find yourself undoing and redoing many steps at a time, it may be more convenient to work with the Undo History dialog, a dockable dialog that shows you a small sketch of each point in the Undo History, allowing you to go back or forward to that point by clicking.

Undo is performed on an image-specific basis: the "Undo History" is one of the components of an image. GIMP allocates a certain amount of memory to each image for this purpose. You can customize your Preferences to increase or decrease the amount, using the Environment page of the Preferences dialog. There are two important variables: the *minimal number of undo levels*, which GIMP will maintain regardless of how much memory they consume, and the *maximum undo memory*, beyond which GIMP will begin to delete the oldest items from the Undo History.

Note

Even though the Undo History is a component of an image, it is not saved when you save the image using GIMP's native XCF format, which preserves every other image property. When the image is reopened, it will have an empty Undo History.

GIMP's implementation of Undo is rather sophisticated. Many operations require very little Undo memory (e.g., changing visibility of a layer), so you can perform long sequences of them before they drop out of the Undo History. Some operations, such as changing layer visibility, are *compressed*, so that doing them several times in a row produces only a single point in the Undo History. However, there are other operations that may consume a lot of undo memory. Most filters are implemented by plug-ins, so the GIMP core has no efficient way of knowing what changed. As such, there is no way to implement Undo except by memorizing the entire contents of the affected layer before and after the operation. You might only be able to perform a few such operations before they drop out of the Undo History.

3.3.1 Things That Cannot be Undone

Most actions that alter an image can be undone. Actions that do not alter the image generally cannot be undone. Examples include saving the image to a file, duplicating the image, copying part of the image to the clipboard, etc. It also includes most actions that affect the image display without altering the underlying image data. The most important example is zooming. There are, however, exceptions: toggling QuickMask on or off can be undone, even though it does not alter the image data.

There are a few important actions that do alter an image but cannot be undone:

Closing the image The Undo History is a component of the image, so when the image is closed and all of its resources are freed, the Undo History is gone. Because of this, unless the image has not been modified since the last time it was saved, GIMP always asks you to confirm that you really want to close the image. (You can disable this in the Environment page of the Preferences dialog; if you do, you are assuming responsibility for thinking about what you are doing.)

Reverting the image "Reverting" means reloading the image from the file. GIMP actually implements this by closing the image and creating a new image, so the Undo History is lost as a consequence. Because of this, if the image is unclean, GIMP asks you to confirm that you really want to revert the image.

"Pieces" of actions Some tools require you to perform a complex series of manipulations before they take effect, but only allow you to undo the whole thing rather than the individual elements. For example, the Intelligent Scissors require you to create a closed path by clicking at multiple points in the image, and then clicking inside the path to create a selection. You cannot undo the individual clicks: undoing after you are finished takes you all the way back to the starting point. For another example, when you are working with the Text tool, you cannot undo individual letters, font changes, etc.: undoing after you are finished removes the newly created text layer.

Filters, and other actions performed by plugins or scripts, can be undone just like actions implemented by the GIMP core, but this requires them to make correct use of GIMP's Undo functions. If the code is not correct, a plugin can potentially corrupt the Undo History, so that not only the plugin but also previous actions can no longer properly be undone. The plugins and scripts distributed with GIMP are all believed to be set up correctly, but obviously no guarantees can be given for plugins you obtain from other sources. Also, even if the code is correct, canceling a plugin while it is running may corrupt the Undo History, so it is best to avoid this unless you have accidentally done something whose consequences are going to be very harmful.

3.4 Common Tasks

This tutorial is based on text Copyright © 2004 Carol Spears. The original tutorial can be found online: [TUT02].

3.4.1 Intention

GIMP is a powerful image editing program with many options and tools. However, it is also well suited for smaller tasks. The following tutorials are meant for those who want to achieve these common tasks without having to learn all the intricacies of GIMP and computer graphics in general.

Hopefully, these tutorials will not only help you with your current task, but also get you ready to learn more complex tools and methods later, when you have the time and inspiration.

All you need to know to start this tutorial, is how to find and open your image. (File → Open from the Image window).

3.4.2 Change the Size of an Image for the screen

You have a huge image, possibly from a digital camera, and you want to resize it so that it displays nicely on a web page, online board or email message.

Figure 3.17 Example Image for Scaling

The first thing that you might notice after opening the image, is that GIMP opens the image at a logical size for viewing. If your image is very large, like the sample image, GIMP sets the zoom so that it displays nicely on the screen. The zoom level is shown in the status area at the bottom of the Image window. This does not change the actual image.

The other thing to look at in the title-bar is the mode. If the mode shows as RGB in the title bar, you are fine. If the mode says Indexed or Grayscale, read the Section 3.4.7.

Figure 3.18 GIMP Used for Image Scaling

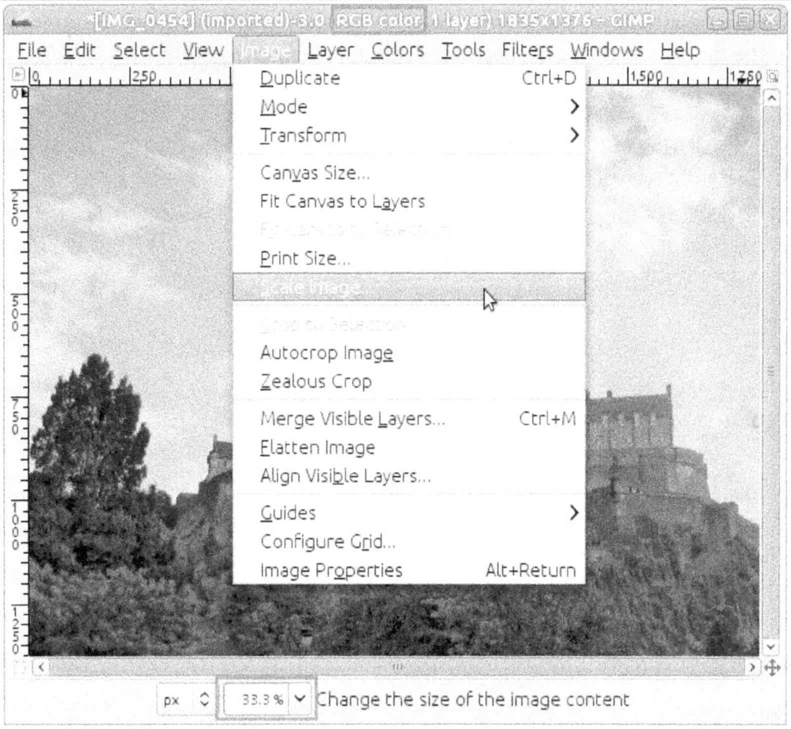

Use Image → Scale Image to open the "Scale Image" dialog. You can right click on the image to open the menu, or use the menu along the top of the Image window. Notice that the "Scale Image" menu item contains three dots, which is a hint that a dialog will be opened.

Figure 3.19 Dialog for Image Scaling in Pixels

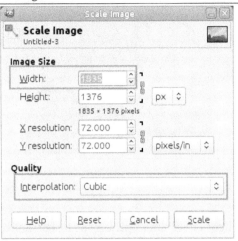

The unit of size for the purpose of displaying an image on a screen is the pixel. You can see the dialog has two sections: one for width and height and another for resolution. Resolution applies to printing only and has no effect on the image's size when it is displayed on a monitor or a mobile device. The reason is that different devices have different pixels sizes and so, an image that displays on one device (such as a smartphone) with a certain physical size, might display on other devices (such as an LCD projector) in another size altogether. For the purpose of displaying an image on a screen, you can ignore the resolution parameter. For the same reason, do not use any size unit other than the pixel in the height / width fields.

If you know the desired width, enter it in the dialog at the top where it says Width. This is shown in the figure above. If you don't have such a number in mind, choose an appropriate width for the desired use. Common screen sizes range between 320 pixels for simpler phones, 1024 pixels for a netbook, 1440 for a wide-screen PC display and 1920 pixels for an HD screen. for the purpose of displaying an image on-line, a width of 600 to 800 pixels offers a good compromise.

When you change one of the image's dimensions, GIMP changes the other dimension proportionally. To change the other dimension, see Section 3.4.5. Bear in mind that when you change the two dimensions arbitrarily, the image might become stretched or squashed.

3.4.3   Change the Size of an Image for print

As discussed before, pixels don't have a set size in the real world. When you set out to print an image on paper, GIMP needs to know how big each pixels is. We use a parameter called resolution to set the ratio between pixels and real-world units such as inches.

By default, most images open with the resolution set to 72. This number was chosen for historical reasons as it was the resolution of screens in the past, and means that when printed, every pixel is 1/72 of an inch wide. When printing images are taken with modern digital cameras, this produces very large but chunky images with visible pixels. What we want to do is tell GIMP to print it with the size we have in mind, but not alter the pixel data so as not to lose quality.

To change the print size use Image → Print Size to open the "Print Size" dialog. Select a size unit you are comfortable with, such as "inches". Set one dimension, and let GIMP change the other one proportionally. Now examine the change in resolution. If the resolution is 300 pixels per Inch or over, the printed image's quality will be very high and pixels will not be noticeable. With a resolution of between 200 and 150 ppi, pixels will be somewhat noticeable, but the image will be fine as long as its not inspected too closely. Values lower than 100 are visibly coarse and should only be used for material that is seen from a distance, such as signs or large posters.

Figure 3.20 Dialog for Setting Print Size

3.4.4   Compressing Images

Figure 3.21 Example Image for JPEG Saving

If you have images that take up a large space on disk, you can reduce that space even without changing the image dimensions. The best image compression is achieved by using the JPG format, but even if the image is already in this format, you can usually still make it take up less space, as the JPG format has an adaptive compression scheme that allows saving in varying levels of compression. The trade-off is that the less space an image takes, the more detail from the original image you lose. You should also be aware that repeated saving in the JPG format causes more and more image degradation.

Since GIMP-2.8, images are loaded and saved as .XCF files. Your JPG image has been loaded as XCF. GIMP offers you to Overwrite image-name.jpg or File → Export As to open the "Export Image" dialog.

Figure 3.22 "Export Image" Dialog

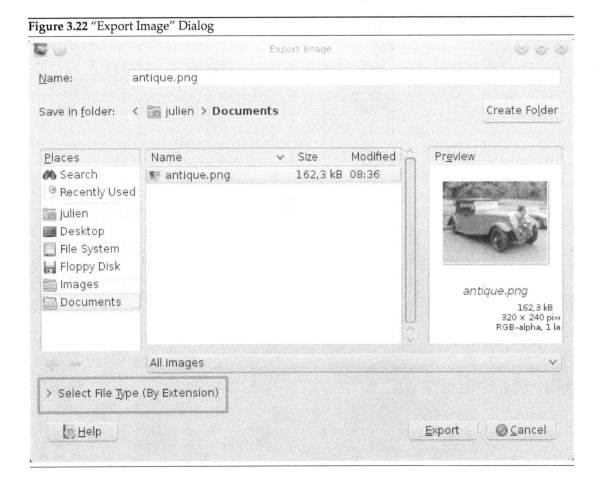

The dialog opens with the file name already typed in the Name box, with the default.png extension. Delete the existing extension and type JPG instead, and GIMP will determine the file type from the file extension. Use the file extension list, red circled in the figure above, to see the types supported by GIMP. The supported extensions change depending on your installed libraries. If GIMP complains, or if "JPEG" is grayed out in the Extensions menu, cancel out of everything and step through the Section 3.4.7. Once you have done this, click Save. This opens the "Export Image as JPEG" dialog that contains the quality control.

The "Export Image as JPEG" dialog uses default values that reduce size in memory while retaining good visual quality; this is the safest and quickest thing to do.

Figure 3.23 "Export Image as JPEG" dialog with default quality

Reduce the image Quality to make the image even smaller. Reduced quality degrades the image, so be certain to check "Show preview in image window" to visually gauge the degradation. A Quality setting of 10 produces a very poor quality image that uses very little disk space. The figure below shows

a more reasonable image. A quality of 75 produces a reasonable image using much less disk space, which will, in turn, load much faster on a web page. Although the image is somewhat degraded, it is acceptable for the intended purpose.

Figure 3.24 "Export Image as JPEG" dialog with quality 75

Finally, here is a comparison of the same picture with varying degrees of compression:

Figure 3.25 Example for High JPEG Compression

(a) *Quality: 10; Size: 3.4 KiloBytes*   (b) *Quality: 40; Size: 9.3 KiloBytes*

Figure 3.26 Example for Moderate JPEG Compression

(a) *Quality: 70; Size: 15.2 KiloBytes*   (b) *Quality: 100; Size: 72.6 KiloBytes*

3.4.5   Crop An Image

Figure 3.27 Example Image for Cropping

(a) *Source image*   (b) *Image after cropping*

There are many reasons to crop an image; for example, fitting an image to fill a frame, removing a portion of the background to emphasize the subject, etc. There are two methods to activate the crop tool. Click the ✎ button in the Toolbox, or use Tools → Transform Tools → Crop in the image window. This changes the cursor and allow you to click and drag a rectangular shape. The button in the toolbox is the easiest way to get to any of the tools.

Figure 3.28 Select a Region to Crop

    Click on one corner of the desired crop area and drag your mouse to create the crop rectangle. You don't have to be accurate as you can change the exact shape of the rectangle later.

Figure 3.29 Dialog for Cropping

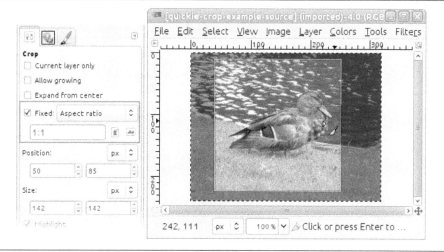

After completing the click and drag motion, a rectangle with special regions is shown on the canvas. As the cursor is moved over the different areas of the selected crop area, the cursor changes. You can then drag the rectangle's corners or edges to change the dimensions of the selected area. As shown in the figure above, as the crop area is resized, the dimensions and ratio are shown in the status bar. Double-click inside the rectangle or press **Enter** to complete cropping. See Section 14.4.4 for more information on cropping in GIMP.

If you would like to crop the image in a specific aspect ratio, such as a square, make sure the tool options are visible (Windows → Dockable Dialogs → Tool Options). In the Tool Options dockable, check the mark next to Fixed and make sure the drop-down box next to it is set to Aspect Ratio. You can now type the desired aspect ratio on the text box below, such as "1:1".

You also have controls to change the aspect from landscape to portrait. After you set the aspect ratio, drag one of the corners of the crop rectangle to update it. The rectangle changes to the chosen ratio, and when you drag it should maintain that ratio.

3.4.6   Find Info About Your Image

Figure 3.30 Finding Info

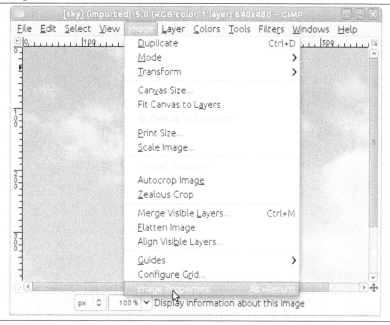

When you need to find out information about your image, Use Image → Image Properties to open the "Image Properties" dialog, which contains information about the image size, resolution, mode and much more.

Figure 3.31 "Image Properties" Dialog

3.4.7 Change the Mode

As with anything else, images come in different kinds and serve different purposes. Sometimes, a small size is important (for web sites) and at other times, retaining a high color depth (e.g., a family portrait) is what you want. GIMP can handle all of this, and more, primarily by converting between three fundamental modes, as seen in this menu. In order to switch your image to one of these modes, you open it and follow that menu and click the mode you want.

Figure 3.32 Dialog for changing the mode

RGB- This is the default mode, used for high-quality images, and able to display millions of colors. This is also the mode for most of your image work including scaling, cropping, and even flipping. In RGB mode, each pixel consists of three different components: R->Red, G->Green, B->Blue. Each of these in turn can have an intensity value of 0-255. What you see at every pixel is an additive combination of these three components.

Indexed- This is the mode usually used when file size is of concern, or when you are working with images with few colors. It involves using a fixed number of colors (256 or less) for the entire image to represent colors. By default, when you change an image to a palleted image, GIMP generates an "optimum palette" to best represent your image.

Figure 3.33 Dialog "Convert Image to Indexed Colors"

As you might expect, since the information needed to represent the color at each pixel is less, the file size is smaller. However, sometimes, there are options in the various menus that are grayed-out for no apparent reason. This usually means that the filter or option cannot be applied when your image is in its current mode. Changing the mode to RGB, as outlined above, should solve this issue. If RGB mode doesn't work either, perhaps the option you're trying requires your layer to have the ability to be transparent. This can be done just as easily via Layer → Transparency → Add Alpha Channel.

Figure 3.34 Add Alpha Channel

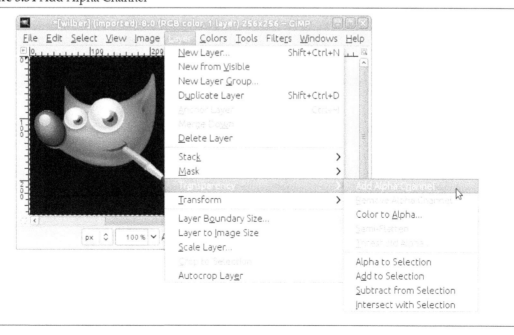

Grayscale- Grayscale images have only shades of gray. This mode has some specific uses and takes less space on the hard drive in some formats, but is not recommended for general use as reading it is not supported by many applications.

There is no need to convert an image to a specific mode before saving it in your favorite format, as GIMP is smart enough to properly export the image.

3.4.8   Flip An Image

Use this option when you need the person in the photo looking in the other direction, or you need the

top of the image to be the bottom. Use Tools → Transform Tools → Flip , or use the 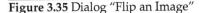 button on the toolbox. After selecting the flip tool from the toolbox, click inside the canvas. Controls in the Tool Options dockable let you switch between Horizontal and Vertical modes.

Figure 3.35 Dialog "Flip an Image"

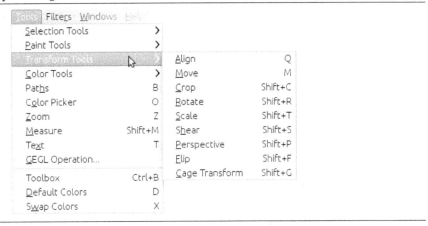

After selecting the flip tool from the toolbox, click inside the canvas. The tool flips the image horizontally. Use the options dialog to switch between horizontal and vertical. If it is not already displayed in the dock under the toolbox, double click the toolbox button. You can also use the **Ctrl** key to switch between horizontal and vertical.

In the images below, all possible flips are demonstrated:

Figure 3.36 Example Image to Flip

Source image

Horizontal flipped image

Vertical flipped image

Horizontal and vertical flipped image

3.4.9 Rotate An Image

Figure 3.37 Menu for "Rotate An Image"

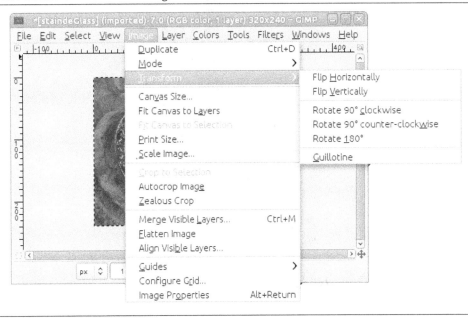

Images that are taken with digital cameras sometimes need to be rotated. To do this, use Image →
Transform → Rotate 90° clockwise (or counter-clockwise). The images below demonstrate a 90 degrees
CCW rotation.

Figure 3.38 Example for "Rotate An Image"

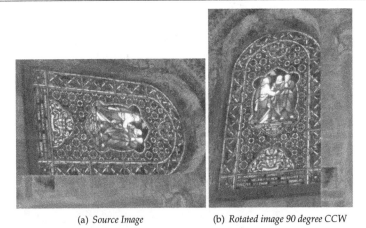

(a) *Source Image*   (b) *Rotated image 90 degree CCW*

3.4.10   Separating an Object From Its Background

Figure 3.39 Object with Background

Sometimes you need to separate the subject of an image from its background. You may want to have the subject on a flat color, or keep the background transparent so you can use it on an existing background, or any other thing you have in mind. To do this, you must first use GIMP's selection tools to draw a selection around your subject. This is not an easy task, and selecting the correct tool is crucial. You have several tools to accomplish this.

The "Free Select Tool" allows you to draw a border using either freehand or straight lines. Use this when the subject has a relatively simple shape. Read more about this tool here: Section 14.2.4

Figure 3.40 Free Select Tool

The "Intelligent Scissors Select Tool" lets you select a freehand border and uses edge-recognition algorithms to better fit the border around the object. Use this when the subject is complex but distinct enough against its current background. Read more about this tool here: Section 14.2.7

Figure 3.41 Intelligent Scissors Select Tool

The "Foreground Select Tool" lets you mark areas as "Foreground" or "Background" and refines the selection automatically. Read more about this tool here: Section 14.2.8

Figure 3.42 Foreground Select Tool

Once you have selected your subject successfully, use Select → Invert. Now, instead of the subject, the background is selected. What you do now depends on what you intended to do with the background.

- To fill the background with a single color:

  Click the foreground color swatch (the top left of the two overlapping colored rectangles) in the toolbox and select the desired color. Next, use Section 14.3.4 to replace the background with your chosen color.

Figure 3.43 Result of Adding a Plain Color Background

- To make a transparent background:

  Use Layer → Transparence → Add Alpha Channel to add an alpha channel. Next, use Edit Clear or hit the **Del** key on the keyboard to remove the background. Please note that only a small subset of file formats support transparent areas. Your best bet is to save your image as PNG.

Figure 3.44 Result of Adding a Transparent Background

- To make a black-and-white background while keeping the subject in color:

  Use Colors → Desaturate. In the dialog that opens, cycle between the modes and select the best-looking one, then click OK.

Figure 3.45 Result of Desaturating the Background

3.5 How to Draw Straight Lines

This tutorial is based on Text and images Copyright © 2002 Seth Burgess. The original tutorial can be found in the Internet [TUT01].

3.5.1 Intention

Figure 3.46 Example of straight lines

This tutorial shows you how to draw straight lines with GIMP. Forcing a line to be straight is a convenient way to deal with the imprecision of a mouse or tablet, and to take advantage of the power of a computer to make things look neat and orderly. This tutorial doesn't use Straight Lines for complex tasks; its intended to show how you can use it to create quick and easy straight lines.

1. Preparations

Figure 3.47 Introducing the **Shift**-key

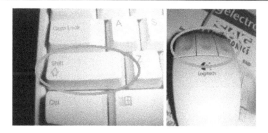

The invention called the typewriter introduced the **Shift** Key. You generally have 2 of them on your keyboard. They look something like the figure above. The keys are located on the left and right sides of your keyboard. The mouse was invented by Douglas C. Engelbart in 1970. These come in different varieties, but always have at least one button.

2. Creating a Blank Drawable

Figure 3.48 New image

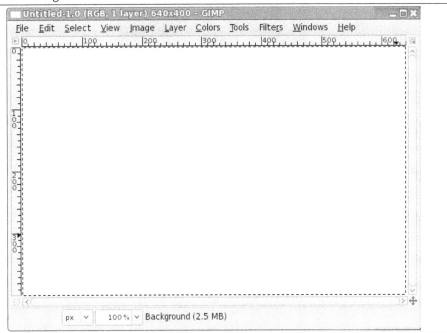

First, create a new image. Any size will do. Use File → New to create a new image.

3. Choose a Tool

Figure 3.49 Paint tools in the toolbox

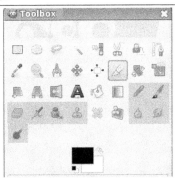

Any of the red-highlighted tools on the above toolbox can do lines.

4. Create a Starting Point

Figure 3.50 Starting point

Click on the paintbrush in the toolbox. Click in the image where you want a line to start or end. A single dot will appear on the screen. The size of this dot represents the current brush size, which you can change in the Brush Dialog (see Section 15.3.2).Now, lets start drawing a line. Hold down the **Shift** key, and keep it down.

5. Drawing the Line

Figure 3.51 Drawing the line

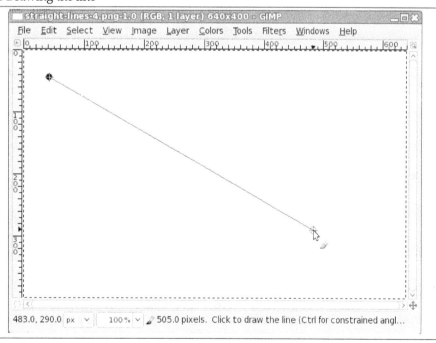

After you have a starting point and while pressing the **Shift** key, you will see a straight line that follows the cursor. Press the first button on the mouse (the leftmost one usually) and let it go. During that whole "click" of the mouse button, you need to keep the **Shift** key held down.

6. Final

Figure 3.52 Final Image

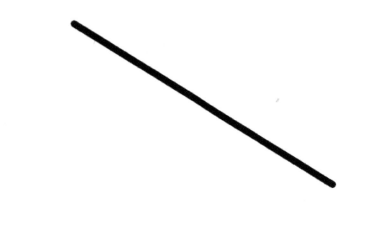

This is a powerful feature. You can draw straight lines with any of the draw tools. You can even draw more lines at the end of this one. Our last step is to let go of the **Shift** key. And there you have it. Some more examples are shown below. Happy GIMPing!

3.5.2 Examples

Figure 3.53 Examples I

(a) *Check Use color from gradient.*

(b) *Select the Clone tool and set the source to "Maple Leaves" pattern.*

Figure 3.54 Examples II

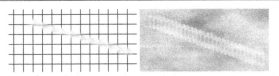

(a) *Use Filters → Render → Pattern → Grid to create a grid. Use the Smudge Tool to draw a cool line with a slightly larger brush.*

(b) *Use Filters → Render → Clouds → Plasma to create the plasma cloud. Use the Erase Tool with a square brush to draw a line.*

Figure 3.55 Example III

Use the rectangle select tool to select a rectangle, and then fill the selection with a light blue color. Select the dodge/burn tool. Set the type to Dodge and paint along the top and left side using an appropriately sized brush. Set the type to Burn and paint along the right and bottom.

Chapter 4

Getting Unstuck

4.1 Getting Unstuck

4.1.1 Stuck!

All right, okay: you're stuck. You're trying to use one of the tools on an image, and nothing is happening, and nothing you try makes any difference. Your fists are starting to clench, and your face is starting to feel warm. Are you going to have to kill the program, and lose all your work? This sucks!

Well, hold on a second. This happens pretty frequently, even to people who've used GIMP for a long time, but generally the cause is not so hard to figure out (and fix) if you know where to look. Lets be calm, and go through a checklist that will probably get you GIMPing happily again.

4.1.2 Common Causes of GIMP Non-Responsiveness

4.1.2.1 There is a floating selection

Figure 4.1 Layers dialog showing a floating selection.

How to tell: If there is a floating selection, many actions are impossible until the floating section is anchored. To check, look at the Layers dialog (making sure it's set to the image you're working on) and see whether the top layer is called "Floating Selection".

How to solve: Either anchor the floating selection, or convert it into an ordinary (non-floating) layer. If you need help on how to do this, see Floating Selections.

4.1.2.2   The selection is hidden

Figure 4.2 Unstuck show selection menu

In the View menu, make sure that "Show Selection" is checked.

How to tell: If this is the problem, merely reading this will already have made you realize it, probably, but to explain in any case: sometimes the flickering line that outlines the selection is annoying because it makes it hard to see important details of the image, so GIMP gives you the option of hiding the selection, by unchecking Show Selection in the View menu. It is easy to forget that you have done this, though.

   How to fix: If this hasn't rung any bells, it isn't the problem, and if it has, you probably know how to fix it, because it doesn't happen unless you explicitly tell it to; but anyway: just go to the View menu for the image and, if Show Selection is unchecked, click on it..

4.1.2.3   You are acting outside of the selection

Figure 4.3 Unstuck select all

Click "All" in the Select menu to make sure that everything is selected.

How to fix: If doing this has destroyed a selection that you wanted to keep, hit Ctrl-Z (undo) a couple of times to restore it, and then we'll figure out what the problem is. There are a couple of possibilities. If you couldn't see any selection, there may have been a very tiny one, or even one that contained no pixels. If this was the case, it surely is not a selection that you wanted to keep, so why have you gotten this far in the first place? If you can see a selection but thought you were inside it, it might be inverted from what you think. The easiest way to tell is to hit the Quick Mask button: the selected area will be clear and the unselected area will be masked. If this was the problem, then you can solve it by toggling Quick Mask off and choosing Invert in the Select menu.

4.1.2.4   The active drawable is not visible

Figure 4.4 Unstuck layer invisibility

Layers dialog with visibility off for the active layer.

How to tell: The Layers dialog gives you ability to toggle the visibility of each layer on or off. Look at the Layers dialog, and see if the layer you are trying to act on is active (i.e., darkened) and has an eye symbol to the left of it. If not, this is your problem.

  How to fix: If your intended target layer is not active, click on it in the Layers dialog to activate it. (If none of the layers are active, the active drawable might be a channel -- you can look at the Channels tab in the Layers dialog to see. This does not change the solution, though.) If the eye symbol does not appear, click in the Layers dialog at the left edge to toggle it: this should make the layer visible. See the Help section for the Layers Dialog if you need more help.

4.1.2.5   The active drawable is transparent

Figure 4.5 Unstuck layer transparency

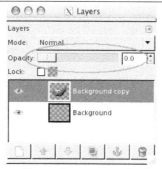

Layers dialog with opacity set to zero for the active layer.

How to tell: When the opacity is set 0 on the layer, you cannot see anything which you draw on it. Look the Opacity slider, and see which side the slider placed at. If it is at the leftmost side, that is your problem.

  How to fix: Move the slider.

4.1.2.6   You are trying to act outside the layer

How to tell: In GIMP, layers don't need to have the same dimensions as the image: they can be larger or smaller. If you try to paint outside the borders of a layer, nothing happens. To see if this is happening, look for a black-and-yellow dashed rectangle that does not enclose the area you're trying to draw at.

How to fix: You need to enlarge the layer. There are two commands at the bottom of the Layer menu that will let you do this: Layer to Image Size, which sets the layer bounds to match the image borders; and Layer Boundary Size, which brings up a dialog that allows you to set the layer dimensions to whatever you please.

4.1.2.7   The image is in indexed color mode.

How to tell: GIMP can handle three different color modes: RGB(A), Indexed and Grayscale. The indexed colormode uses a colormap, where all used colors on the image are indexed. The color picker in GIMP however, let you choose RGB colors. That means, if you try to paint with a different color than it is indexed in the colormap, you end up in very undetermined results (e.g. it paints with the wrong color or you can't paint).

How to fix: Always use the RGB Color mode to paint on images. You can verify and select another color mode from the Mode menuitem in the Image menu.

4.1.2.8   Eraser and brushes no longer work

You have selected the clipboard brush and the clipboard is empty.

Figure 4.6 Empty Clipboard Brush

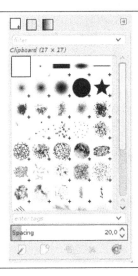

Part II

How do I Become a GIMP Wizard?

Chapter 5

Getting Images into GIMP

This chapter is about getting images into GIMP. It explains how to create new images, how to load images from files, how to scan them and how to make screenshots.

But first we want to introduce you to the general structure of images in GIMP.

5.1 Image Types

It is tempting to think of an *image* as something that corresponds with a single display window, or to a single file such as a JPEG file. In reality, however, a GIMP image is a a complicated structure, containing a stack of layers plus several other types of objects: a selection mask, a set of channels, a set of paths, an "undo" history, etc. In this section we take a detailed look at the components of a GIMP image, and the things that you can do with them.

The most basic property of an image is its *mode*. There are three possible modes: RGB, grayscale, and indexed. RGB stands for Red-Green-Blue, and indicates that each point in the image is represented by a "red" level, a "green" level, and a "blue" level; representing a full-color image. Each color channel has 256 possible intensity levels. More details in Color Models

In a grayscale image, each point is represented by a brightness value, ranging from 0 (black) to 255 (white), with intermediate values representing different levels of gray.

Figure 5.1 Components of the RGB and CMY Color Model

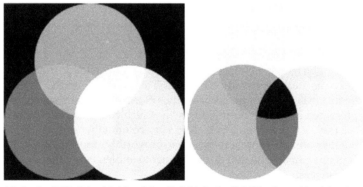

(a) *In the RGB Color Model, mixing Red, Green and Blue gives White, which is what happens on your screen.*

(b) *In the CMY(K) color model, mixing Cyan, Magenta and Yellow gives Black, which is what happens when you print on a white paper. The printer will actually use the black cartridge for economical reasons and better color rendering.*

Conceptually, the difference between a grayscale image and an RGB image is the number of "color channels": a grayscale image has one; an RGB image has three. An RGB image can be thought of as three superimposed grayscale images, one colored red, one green, and one blue.

Actually, both RGB and grayscale images have one additional color channel called the *alpha* channel, which represents opacity. When the alpha value at a given location in a given layer is zero, the layer is completely transparent (you can see through it), and the color at that location is determined by what lies underneath. When alpha is maximal (255), the layer is opaque (you cannot see through it), and the color is determined by the color of the layer. Intermediate alpha values correspond to varying degrees of transparency / opacity: the color at the location is a proportional mixture of color from the layer and color from underneath.

Figure 5.2 Example of an image in RGB and Grayscale mode

(a) *An image in RGB mode, with the channels corresponding to Red, Green and Blue.* (b) *An image in Grayscale mode, with the channel corresponding to Luminosity.*

In GIMP, every color channel, including the alpha channel, has a range of possible values from 0 to 255; in computing terminology, a depth of 8 bits. Some digital cameras can produce image files with a depth of 16 bits per color channel. GIMP cannot load such a file without losing resolution. In most cases the effects are too subtle to be detected by the human eye, but in some cases, mainly where there are large areas with slowly varying color gradients, the difference may be perceptible.

Figure 5.3 Example of an image with alpha channel

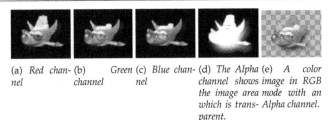

(a) *Red chan-nel* (b) *Green channel* (c) *Blue chan-nel* (d) *The Alpha channel shows the image area which is trans-parent.* (e) *A color image in RGB mode with an Alpha channel.*

The third type, *indexed* images, is a bit more complicated to understand. In an indexed image, only a limited set of discrete colors are used, usually 256 or less. These colors form the "colormap" of the image, and each point in the image is assigned a color from the colormap. Indexed images have the advantage that they can be represented inside a computer in a way which consumes relatively little memory, and back in the dark ages (say, ten years ago), they were very commonly used. As time goes on, they are used less and less, but they are still important enough to be worth supporting in GIMP. (Also, there are a few important kinds of image manipulation that are easier to implement with indexed images than with continuous-color RGB images.)

Some very commonly used types of files (including GIF and PNG) produce indexed images when they are opened in GIMP. Many of GIMP's tools don't work very well on indexed images–and many filters don't work at all–because of the limited number of colors available. Because of this, it is usually best to convert an image to RGB mode before working on it. If necessary, you can convert it back to indexed mode when you are ready to save it

GIMP makes it easy to convert from one image type to another, using the Mode command in the Image menu. Some types of conversions, of course (RGB to grayscale or indexed, for example) lose information that cannot be regained by converting back in the other direction.

Note

If you are trying to use a filter on an image, and it appears grayed out in the menu, usually the cause is that the image (or, more specifically, the layer) you are working on is the wrong type. Many filters can't be used on indexed images. Some can be used only on RGB images, or only on grayscale images. Some also require the presence or absence of an alpha channel. Usually the fix is to convert the image to a different type, most commonly RGB.

5.2   Creating new Files

Use File → New to open the Create a new image dialog. Modify the initial width and height of the file or use the standard values, then create a new image file. More information about the Create a new image dialog can be found in Section 16.2.2.

5.3   Opening Files

There are several ways of opening an existing image in GIMP:

5.3.1   Open File

The most obvious way to open an existing image is the menu. Use File → Open to open the Open Image dialog,allowing you to navigate to the file and click on its name. This method works well if you know the name and location of the file you want to open. Although the Open Image dialog does have a preview pane, it is not convenient (easy) to find an image based on a thumbnail.

Note

While opening a file, GIMP must determine the file type. Unfortunately, the file extension, such as .jpg, is not reliable: file extensions vary from system to system; any file can be renamed to have any extension; and there are many reasons why a file name might lack an extension. GIMP first tries to recognize a file by examining its contents: most of the commonly used file formats have "magic headers" that permit them to be recognized. Only if the magic yields no result does GIMP resort to using the extension.

Figure 5.4 The "Open Image" dialog

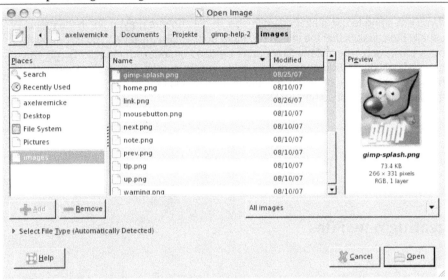

GIMP 2.2 introduced a new Open Image dialog that provides several features to help you navigate quickly to a file. Perhaps the most important is the ability to create "bookmarks", or Places, for folders that you use often. Your list of bookmarks appears on the left side of the dialog. The ones at the top, such as "Desktop", are provided automatically. Use the the Add button to add the current directory to the list. Use the Remove button to remove the selected bookmark. Double-click on a bookmark to navigate directly to that directory.

The center of the dialog contains a listing of the contents of the selected directory. Subdirectories are shown at the top of the list, files below them. By default, all files in the directory are listed, but you can restrict the listing to image files of a specific type using the File Type selection menu that appears beneath the directory listing.

When you select an image file entry in the listing, a preview appears on the right side of the dialog, along with some basic information about the image. Note that previews are cached when they are generated, and there are some things you can do that may cause a preview to be incorrect. If you suspect that this may be happening, you can force a new preview to be generated by holding down the **Ctrl** key and clicking in the Preview area.

By default, a Location text box is present in the File Open dialog. It may be absent: the Ctrl-L key combination toggles this text box. Alternatively, you can click on the icon of the paper and pencil in the upper left corner to toggle the text box.

> **Note**
>
> If you select a file name from the list, and click the "Open" button in the lower right corner or the dialog, it is almost always true that GIMP will automatically determine the file type for you. On rare occasions, mainly if the file type is unusual and the name lacks a meaningful extension, GIMP may fail to correctly identify the file type. Use Select File Type at the bottom of the dialog to manually specify the file type if this is required. More commonly, though, if GIMP fails to open an image file, it is either corrupt or not a supported format.

5.3.2 Open Location

If instead of a file name, you have a URI (i.e., a web address) for the image, you can open it using the menu, by choosing File → Open Location... from an image menu. This brings up a small dialog that allows you to enter (or paste) the URI.

Figure 5.5 The "Open Location" dialog

The "Open Location" dialog.

5.3.3 Open Recent

The easiest way to open an image that was recently open in GIMP, may be using File → Open Recent. This displays a scrollable list of the mostly recently opened images with icons beside them. Select and open the desired image.

5.3.4 Using External Programs

GIMP uses plugins for reading and writing all file formats except XCF. These plugins may use external libraries or programs. For example, GIMP does not directly support PostScript. Instead, for reading (or writing) PostScript files (file extension .ps or .eps), GIMP requires a powerful free software program called Ghostscript.

5.3.4.1 Installing Ghostscript

Linux distributions almost always come with Ghostscript already installed (not necessarily the most recent version). For other operating systems, you may have to install it yourself. Here are instructions for installing it on Windows:

- Go to the Ghostscript project page on Sourceforge [GHOSTSCRIPT].

- Look for the package gnu-gs or ghostscript (for non-commercial use only) and go to the download section.

- Download one of the prepared Windows distributions, such as gs650w32.exe or gs700w32.exe.

- Start the executable and follow the instructions for the installation procedure.

- Set the GS_PROG environment variable to the full file name of the gswin32c binary (e.g. C:\\gs\\gsX.YY\\bin\\gswin32c.exe).

Now you should be able to read PostScript files with GIMP. Please note that you must not move the Ghostscript directories once the installation is complete. The installation creates registry entries which allow Ghostscript to find its libraries. (These instructions courtesy of http://www.kirchgessner.net.)

5.3.5 File Manager

If you have associated an image file type with GIMP, either when you installed GIMP or later, then you can navigate to the file using a file manager (such as Nautilus or Konqueror in Linux, or Windows Explorer in Windows), and once you have found it, double-click on the file. If properly configured, the image will open in GIMP.

5.3.6 Drag and Drop

Drag and drop a file onto the GIMP Toolbox to open the file. Drag an image into an open GIMP image to add dropped file as a new layer, or set of layers, to the already open image.

Many applications support dragging and dropping an image into GIMP; for example, drag an image from Firefox and drop it onto GIMP's toolbox.

5.3.7 Copy and Paste

Use File → Create → From Clipboard to create a new image from the clipboard; alternatively, you can use Edit → Paste as → New Image. Many applications support copying an image to the clipboard that can then be pasted into GIMP. Many operating systems support copying screens to the clipboard. **Print Screen** typically copies the screen to the clipboard, and Alt-Print Screen copies only the active window. Print screen is not universally supported, and just because your operating system can copy an image to the clipboard, does not mean that GIMP can use the image from the clipboard. Your best bet is to try it and see if it works.

5.3.8 Image Browser

Linux supports an image-management application named gThumb. Besides being an excellent image browser, you can right click an image, choose Open with, then select GIMP from the list of options. You can also drag an image from gThumb onto the GIMP toolbox. See the gThumb home page [GTHUMB] for more information. Other similar applications are : GQview [GQVIEW], and XnView [XNVIEW].

Chapter 6

Getting Images out of GIMP

6.1 Files

GIMP is capable of reading and writing a large variety of graphics file formats. With the exception of GIMP's native XCF file type, file handling is done by Plugins. Thus, it is relatively easy to extend GIMP to support new file types when the need arises.

6.1.1 Save / Export Images

> **Note**
>
> In former GIMP releases, when you loaded an image in some format, let us say JPG or PNG, the image kept its format and was saved in the same format by **Save**. With GIMP-2.8, images are loaded, imported, in the XCF format as a new project. For example, a "sunflower.png" image will be loaded as "*[sunflower] (imported)-1.0 (indexed color, 1 layer)". The leading asterisk indicates that this file has been changed. This image will be saved as "sunflower.xcf" by **Save**. To save this image in a format other than XCF, you must use **Export**.

When you are finished working with an image, you will want to save the results. (In fact, it is often a good idea to save at intermediate stages too: GIMP is a pretty robust program, but we have heard rumors, possibly apocryphal, that it may have been known on rare and mysterious occasions to crash.) Most of the file formats that GIMP can open, can also be used for saving. There is one file format that is special, though: XCF is GIMP's native format, and is useful because it stores *everything* about an image (well, almost everything; it does not store "undo" information). Thus, the XCF format is especially suitable for saving intermediate results, and for saving images to be re-opened later in GIMP. XCF files are not readable by most other programs that display images, so once you have finished, you will probably also want to export the image in a more widely used format, such as JPEG, PNG, TIFF, etc.

6.1.2 File Formats

There are several commands for *saving* images. A list, and information on how to use them, can be found in the section covering the File Menu.

GIMP allows you to *export* the images you create in a wide variety of formats. It is important to realize that the only format capable of saving *all* of the information in an image, including layers, transparency, etc., is GIMP's native XCF format. Every other format preserves some image properties and loses others. It is up to you to understand the capabilities of the format you choose.

Exporting an image does not modify the image itself, so you do not lose anything by exporting. See Export file.

Note

When you close an image (possibly by quitting GIMP), you are warned if the image is "dirty"; that is, if it has been changed without subsequently being saved (an asterisk is in front of the image name).

Figure 6.1 Closing warning

Saving an image in any file format will cause the image to be considered "not dirty", even if the file format does not represent all of the information from the image.

6.1.2.1 Export Image as GIF

Figure 6.2 The GIF Export dialog

Warning

The GIF file format does not support some basic image properties such as *print resolution*. If you care for these properties, use a different file format like PNG.

GIF Options

Interlace Checking interlace allows an image on a web page to be progressively displayed as it is downloaded. Progressive image display is useful with slow connection speeds, because you can stop an image that is of no interest; interlace is of less use today with our faster connection speeds.

GIF comment GIF comments support only 7-bit ASCII characters. If you use a character outside the 7-bit ASCII set, GIMP will export the image without a comment, and then inform you that the comment was not saved.

Animated GIF Options

Loop forever When this option is checked, the animation will play repeatedly until you stop it.

Delay between frames where unspecified You can set the delay, in milliseconds, between frames if it has not been set before. In this case, you can modify every delay in the Layer Dialog.

Frame disposal where unspecified If this has not been set before, you can set how frames will be superimposed. You can select among three options :

- I don't care: you can use this option if all your layers are opaque. Layers will overwrite what is beneath.
- Cumulative Layers (combine): previous frames will not be deleted when a new one is displayed.
- One frame per layer (replace): previous frames will be deleted before displaying a new frame.

Use delay entered above for all frames Self-explanatory.

Use disposal entered above for all frames Self-explanatory.

6.1.2.2   Export Image as JPEG

JPEG files usually have an extension .jpg, .JPG, or .jpeg. It is a very widely used format, because it compresses images very efficiently, while minimizing the loss of image quality. No other format comes close to achieving the same level of compression. It does not, however, support transparency or multiple layers.

Figure 6.3 The JPEG Export dialog

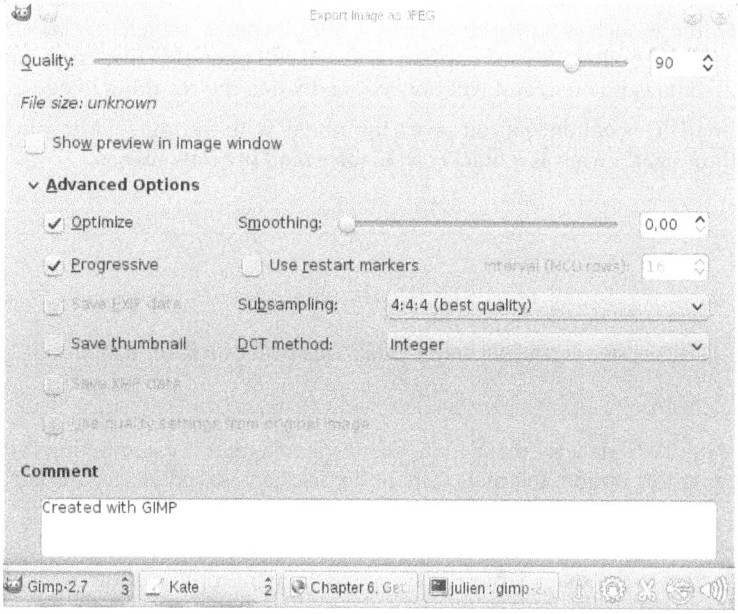

The JPEG algorithm is quite complex, and involves a bewildering number of options, whose meaning is beyond the scope of this documentation. Unless you are a JPEG expert, the Quality parameter is probably the only one you will need to adjust.

Quality When you save a file in JPEG format, a dialog is displayed that allows you to set the Quality level, which ranges from 0 to 100. Values above 95 are generally not useful, though. The default quality of 85 usually produces excellent results, but in many cases it is possible to set the quality substantially lower without noticeably degrading the image. You can test the effect of different quality settings by checking Show Preview in image window in the JPEG dialog.

> **Note**
>
> Please note, that the numbers for the JPEG quality level have a different meaning in different applications. Saving with a quality level of 80 in GIMP is not necessarily comparable with saving with a quality level of 80 in a different application.

Preview in image window Checking this option causes each change in quality (or any other JPEG parameter) to be shown in the image display. (This does not alter the image: the image reverts back to its original state when the JPEG dialog is closed.)

Advanced settings Some information about the advanced settings:

   Optimize If you enable this option, the optimization of entropy encoding parameters will be used. The result is typically a smaller file, but it takes more time to generate.

   Progressive With this option enabled, the image chunks are stored in the file in an order that allows progressive image refinement during a slow connection web download. The progressive option for JPG has the same purpose as the interlace option for GIF. Unfortunately, the progressive option produces slightly larger JPG files (than without the progressive option).

   Save EXIF data JPEG files from many digital cameras contain extra information, called EXIF data. EXIF data provides information about the image such as camera make and model, image size, image date, etc. Although GIMP uses the "libexif" library to read and write EXIF data, the library is not automatically packaged with GIMP. If GIMP was built with libexif support, then EXIF data is preserved if you open a JPEG file, work with the resulting image, and then export it as JPEG. The EXIF data is not altered in any way when you do this. The EXIF data may indicate things such as image creation time and file name, which may no longer be correct. If GIMP was not built with EXIF support, you can still open JPG files containing EXIF data, but the EXIF data is ignored, and will not be saved when the resulting image is later exported.

   Save thumbnail This option lets you save a thumbnail with the image. Many applications use the small thumbnail image as a quickly available small preview image.

> **Note**
>
> This option is present only if GIMP was built with EXIF support.

   Save XMP data XMP data is "meta" data about the image; it is a competing format with EXIF. If you enable this option, the meta data of the image is saved in an XMP-structure within the file.

   Use quality settings from original image If a particular quality setting (or "quantization table") was attached to the image when it was loaded, then this option allows you to use them instead of the standard ones.

   If you have only made a few changes to the image, then re-using the same quality setting will give you almost the same quality and file size as the original image. This will minimize the losses caused by the quantization step, compared to what would happen if you used different quality setting.

If the quality setting found in the original file are not better than your default quality settings, then the option "Use quality settings from original image" will be available but not enabled. This ensures that you always get at least the minimum quality specified in your defaults. If you did not make major changes to the image and you want to save it using the same quality as the original, then you can do it by enabling this option.

Smoothing JPG compression creates artifacts. By using this option, you can smooth the image when saving, reducing them. But your image becomes somewhat blurred.

Restart markers The image file can include markers which allow the image to be loaded as segments. If a connection is broken while loading the image in a web page, loading can resume from the next marker.

Subsampling The human eye is not sensitive in the same way over the entire color spectrum. The compression can use this to treat slightly different colors that the eye perceives as very close, as identical colors. Three methods are available :

- 1x1,1x1,1x1 (best quality): Commonly referred to as (4:4:4), this produces the best quality, preserving borders and contrasting colors, but compression is less.
- 2x1,1x1,1x1 (4:2:2): This is the standard subsampling, which usually provides a good ratio between image quality and file size. There are situations, however, in which using no subsampling (4:4:4) provides a noticeable increase in the image quality; for example, when the image contains fine details such as text over a uniform background, or images with almost-flat colors.
- 1x2,1x1,1x1 This is similar to (2x1,1x1,1x1), but the chroma sampling is in the horizontal direction rather than the vertical direction; as if someone rotated an image.
- 2x2,1x1,1x1 (smallest file): Commonly referred to as (4:1:1), this produces the smallest files. This suits images with weak borders but tends to denature colors.

DCT Method DCT is "discrete cosine transform", and it is the first step in the JPEG algorithm going from the spatial to the frequency domain. The choices are "float", "integer" (the default), and "fast integer".

- float: The float method is very slightly more accurate than the integer method, but is much slower unless your machine has very fast floating-point hardware. Also note that the results of the floating-point method may vary slightly across machines, while the integer methods should give the same results everywhere.
- integer (the default): This method is faster than "float", but not as accurate.
- fast integer: The fast integer method is much less accurate than the other two.

Image comments In this text box, you can enter a comment which is saved with the image.

6.1.2.3   Export Image as PNG

Figure 6.4 The "Export Image as PNG" dialog

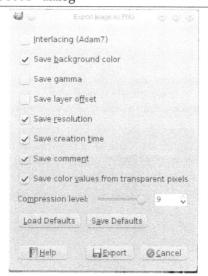

Interlacing Checking interlace allows an image on a web page to be progressively displayed as it is downloaded. Progressive image display is useful with slow connection speeds, because you can stop an image that is of no interest; interlace is of less use today with our faster connection speeds.

Save background color If your image has many transparency levels, the Internet browsers that recognize only two levels, will use the background color of your Toolbox instead. Internet Explorer up to version 6 did not use this information.

Save gamma Gamma correction is the ability to correct for differences in how computers interpret color values. This saves gamma information in the PNG that reflects the current Gamma factor for your display. Viewers on other computers can then compensate to ensure that the image is not too dark or too bright.

Save layer offset PNG supports an offset value called the "oFFs chunk", which provides position data. Unfortunately, PNG offset support in GIMP is broken, or at least is not compatible with other applications, and has been for a long time. Do not enable offsets, let GIMP flatten the layers before saving, and you will have no problems.

Save Resolution Save the image resolution, in ppi (pixels per inch).

Save creation time Date the file was saved.

Save comment You can read this comment in the Image Properties.

Save color values from transparent pixels When this option is checked, the color values are saved even if the pixels are completely transparent. But this is possible only with a single layer, not with a merged composition. When a multi-layer image gets exported to a single-layer file format, there is no way GIMP could preserve the color values in the transparent pixels.

Compression level Since compression is not lossy, the only reason to use a compression level less than 9, is if it takes too long to compress a file on a slow computer. Nothing to fear from decompression: it is as quick whatever the compression level.

Save Defaults Click to save the current settings. Latter, you can use Load Defaults to load the saved settings.

Note

The PNG format supports indexed images. Using fewer colors, therefore, results in a smaller file; this is especially useful for creating web images; see Section 16.6.6.

Computers work on 8 bits blocks named "Byte". A byte allows 256 colors. Reducing the number of colors below 256 is not useful: a byte will be used anyway and the file size will not be less. More, this "PNG8" format, like GIF, uses only one bit for transparency; only two transparency levels are possible, transparent or opaque.

If you want PNG transparency to be fully displayed by Internet Explorer, you can use the AlphaImageLoader DirectX filter in the code of your Web page. See Microsoft Knowledge Base [MSKB-294714]. Please note, that this is not necessary for InternetExplorer 7 and above.

6.1.2.4   Export Image as TIFF

Figure 6.5 The TIFF Export dialog

Compression This option allows you to specify the algorithm used to compress the image.

- None: is fast, and lossless, but the resulting file is very large.

- LZW: The image is compressed using the "Lempel-Ziv-Welch" algorithm, a lossless compression technique. This is old, but efficient and fast. More information at [WKPD-LZW].

- Pack Bits: is a fast, simple compression scheme for run-length encoding of data. Apple introduced the PackBits format with the release of MacPaint on the Macintosh computer. A PackBits data stream consists of packets of one byte of header followed by data. (Source: [WKPD-PACKBITS])

- Deflate: is a lossless data compression algorithm that uses a combination of the LZ77 algorithm and Huffman coding. It is also used in Zip, Gzip and PNG file formats. Source: [WKPD-DEFLATE].

- JPEG: is a very good compression algorithm but lossy.

- CCITT Group 3 fax; CCITT Group 4 fax is a black and white format developed to transfer images by FAX.

> **Note**
>
> These options can only be selected, if the image is in indexed mode and reduced to two colors. Use Image → Mode → Indexed to convert the image to indexed. Be certain to check "Use black and white (1-bit) palette".

Save color values from transparent pixels With this option the color values are saved even if the pixels are completely transparent.

Comment In this text box, you can enter a comment that is associated with the image.

6.1.2.5   Export Image as MNG

Figure 6.6 Export MNG File Dialog

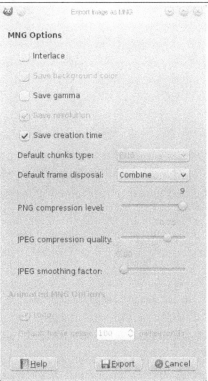

MNG is acronym for "Multiple-Image Network Graphics".

The main problem is that Konqueror is the only Web navigator that recognizes the MNG animation format. Please see http://en.wikipedia.org/wiki/Multiple-image_Network_Graphics.

6.2   Preparing your Images for the Web

One of the most common uses for GIMP, is to prepare images for web sites. This means that images should look as nice as possible while keeping the file size as small as possible. This step-by-step guide demonstrates how to create small files with minimal loss of image quality.

6.2.1   Images with an Optimal Size/Quality Ratio

An optimal image for the web depends upon the image type and the file format. Use JPEG for Photographs because they usually have many colors and great detail. An image with fewer colors, such as a button, icon, or screenshot, is better suited to the PNG format.

1. First, open the image as usual. I have opened our Wilber as an example image.

Figure 6.7 The Wilber image opened in RGBA mode

2. The image is now in RGB mode, with an additional Alpha channel (RGBA). There is usually no need to have an alpha channel for your web image. You can remove the alpha channel by flattening the image.

   A photograph rarely has an alpha channel, so the image will open in RGB mode rather than RGBA mode; and you won't have to remove the alpha channel.

Note

  If the image has a soft transition into the transparent areas, you should not remove the alpha channel, since the information used for the transition is not be saved in the file. To export an image with transparent areas that do not have a soft transition, (similar to GIF), remove the alpha channel.

---

3. After you have flattened the image, export the image in the PNG format for your web site.

Note

  You can export your image in the PNG format with the default settings. Always using maximum compression when creating the image. Maximum compression has no affect on image quality or the time required to display the image, but it does take longer to export. A JPEG image, however, loses quality as the compression is increased. If your image is a photograph with lots of colors, you should use jpeg. The main thing is to find the best tradeoff between quality and compression. You can find more information about this topic in Section 6.1.2.2.

6.2.2 Reducing the File Size Even More

If you want to reduce the size of your image a bit more, you could convert your image to Indexed mode. That means that all of the colors will be reduced to only 256 values. Do not convert images with smooth color transitions or gradients to indexed mode, because the original smooth gradients are typically converted into a series of bands. Indexed mode is not recommended for photographs because after the conversion, they typically look coarse and grainy.

Figure 6.8 The indexed image

An indexed image can look a bit grainy. The left image is Wilber in its original size, the right image is zoomed in by 300 percent.

1. Use the command described in Section 16.6.3 to convert an RGB image to indexed mode.

2. After you convert an image to indexed mode, you are once again able to export the image in PNG format.

6.2.3 Saving Images with Transparency

There are two different approaches used by graphic file formats for supporting transparent image areas: simple binary transparency and alpha transparency. Simple binary transparency is supported in the GIF format; one color from the indexed color palette is marked as the transparent color. Alpha transparency is supported in the PNG format; the transparency information is stored in a separate channel, the Alpha channel.

> **Note**
>
> The GIF format is rarely used because PNG supports all the features of GIF with additional features (e.g., alpha transparency). Nevertheless, GIF is still used for animations.

Creating an Image with Transparent Areas (Alpha Transparency)

1. First of all, we will use the same image as in the previous tutorials, Wilber the GIMP mascot.

Figure 6.9 The Wilber image opened in RGBA mode

2. To export an image with alpha transparency, you must have an alpha channel. To check if the image has an alpha channel, go to the channel dialog and verify that an entry for "Alpha" exists, besides Red, Green and Blue. If this is not the case, add a new alpha channel from the layers menu; Layer+Transparency → Add Alpha Channel.

3. The original XCF file contains background layers that you can remove. GIMP comes with standard filters that supports creating gradients; look under Filters+Light and Shadow. You are only limited by your imagination. To demonstrate the capabilities of alpha transparency, a soft glow in the background around Wilber is shown.

4. After you're done with your image, you can export it in PNG format.

Figure 6.10 The Wilber image with transparency

Mid-Tone Checks in the background layer represent the transparent region of the exported image while you are working on it in GIMP.

Chapter 7

Painting with GIMP

7.1 The Selection

Often when you operate on an image, you only want part of it to be affected. In GIMP, you make this happen by *selecting* that part. Each image has a *selection* associated with it. Most, but not all, GIMP operations act only on the selected portions of the image.

Figure 7.1 How would you isolate the tree?

There are many, many situations where creating just the right selection is the key to getting the result you want, and often it is not easy to do. For example, in the above image, suppose I want to cut the tree out from its background, and paste it into a different image. To do this, I need to create a selection that contains the tree and nothing but the tree. It is difficult because the tree has a complex shape, and in several spots is hard to distinguish from the objects behind it.

Figure 7.2 Selection shown as usual with dashed line.

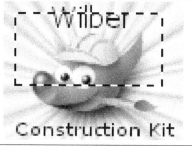

Now here is a very important point, and it is crucial to understand this. Ordinarily when you create a selection, you see it as a dashed line enclosing a portion of the image. The common, not entirely accurate, idea you could get from this, is that the selection is a sort of container, with the selected parts of the image inside, and the unselected parts outside. Although this concept of selection is okay for many purposes, it is not entirely correct.

Actually the selection is implemented as a *channel*. In terms of its internal structure, it is identical to the red, green, blue, and alpha channels of an image. Thus, the selection has a value defined at each pixel of the image, ranging between 0 (unselected) and 255 (fully selected). The advantage of this approach is that it allows some pixels to be *partially selected*, by giving them intermediate values between 0 and 255. As you will see, there are many situations where it is desirable to have smooth transitions between selected and unselected regions.

What, then, is the dashed line that appears when you create a selection?

The dashed line is a *contour line*, dividing areas that are more than half selected from areas that are less than half selected.

Figure 7.3 Same selection in QuickMask mode.

While looking at the dashed line that represents the selection, always remember that the line tells only part of the story. If you want to see the selection in complete detail, the easiest way is to click the QuickMask button in the lower left corner of the image window. This causes the selection to be shown as a translucent overlay atop the image. Selected areas are unaffected; unselected areas are reddened. The more completely selected an area is, the less red it appears.

Many operations work differently in QuickMask mode, as mentioned in the QuickMask overview. Use the QuickMask button in the lower left corner of the image window to toggle QuickMask mode on and off.

Figure 7.4 Same selection in QuickMask mode after feathering.

7.1.1   Feathering

With the default settings, the basic selection tools, such as the Rectangle Select tool, create sharp selections. Pixels inside the dashed line are fully selected, and pixels outside completely unselected. You can verify this by toggling QuickMask: you see a clear rectangle with sharp edges, surrounded by uniform red. Use the "Feather edges" checkbox in the Tool Options to toggle between graduated selections and sharp selections. The feather radius, which you can adjust, determines the distance over which the transition occurs.

If you are following along, try this with the Rectangle Select tool, and then toggle QuickMask. You will see that the clear rectangle has a fuzzy edge.

Feathering is particularly useful when you are cutting and pasting, so that the pasted object blends smoothly and unobtrusively with its surroundings.

It is possible to feather a selection at any time, even if it was originally created as a sharp selection. Use Select → Feather from the image menu to open the Feather Selection dialog. Set the feather radius and click OK. Use Select → Sharpen to do the opposite—sharpen a graduated selection into an all-or-nothing selection.

> **Note**
>
> For technically oriented readers: feathering works by applying a Gaussian blur to the selection channel, with the specified blurring radius.

7.1.2 Making a Selection Partially Transparent

You can set layer opacity, but you cannot do that directly for a selection. It is quite useful to make the image of a glass transparent. Use the following methods to set the layer opacity:

- For simple selections, use the Eraser tool with the desired opacity.

- For complex selections: use Selection → Floating to create a floating selection. This creates a new layer with the selection called "Floating Selection". Set the opacity slider in the Layer Dialog to the desired opacity. Then anchor the selection: outside the selection, the mouse pointer includes an anchor. When you click while the mouse pointer includes the anchor, the floating selection disappears from the Layer Dialog and the selection is at the right place and partially transparent (anchoring works this way only if a selection tool is activated : you can also use the Anchor Layer command in the context menu by right clicking on the selected layer in the layer dialog).

  And, if you use this function frequently: Ctrl-C to copy the selection, Ctrl-V to paste the clipboard as a floating selection, and Layer → New Layer to turn the selection into a new layer. You can adjust the opacity before, or after creating the new layer.

- Another way: use Layer → Mask → Add Layer Mask to add a layer mask to the layer with the selection, initializing it with the selection. Then use a brush with the desired opacity to paint the selection with black, i.e. paint it with transparency. Then Layer/Mask/Apply Layer Mask. See Section 15.2.1.3.

- To *make the solid background of an image transparent*, add an Alpha channel, and use the Magic Wand to select the background. Then, use the Color Picker tool to select the background color, which becomes the foreground color in Toolbox. Use the Bucket Fill tool with the selected color. Set the Bucket Fill mode to "Color Erase", which erases pixels with the selected color; other pixels are partially erased and their color is changed.

  The simplest method is to use Edit → Clear, which gives complete transparency to a selection.

7.2 Creating and Using Selections

7.2.1 Moving a Selection

Rectangular and elliptical selections have two modes. The default mode has handles on the selection. If you click the selection or press the **Enter** key, the handles disappear leaving only the dotted outline (marching ants). The other selection tools have different behaviour.

7.2.1.1 Moving rectangular and elliptical selections

If you click-and drag a selection with handles, you move the selection outline, and you don't move the contents of rectangular or elliptic selections.

Select the Move tool and set the options to move the selection; the tool supports moving the selection, path, or layer.

Figure 7.5 Moving selection outline

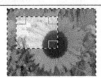

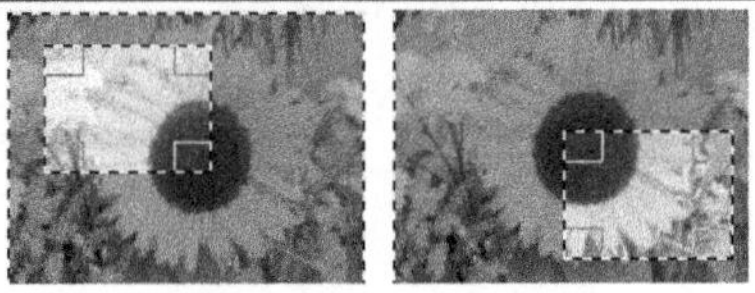

Most systems support moving the selection using the arrow keys. The precise behavior is system dependent. If the arrow keys do not cause the selection to move, try hovering the mouse cursor over the selection first. Press and hold the **Alt** (or Ctrl-Alt, Shift-Alt, or **Alt**). One combination may move the selection by one pixel, and another by 25 pixels each step. Hover the mouse cursor over a side or corner handle, and the arrow keys and combinations can change the size of the selection.

If you click-and-drag the selection without handles, you create a new selection! To move the selection contents, you have to

- hold down Ctrl-Alt keys and click-and-drag the selection. This makes the original place empty. A floating selection is created. The required key commands may differ on your system, look in the status bar to see if another combination is specified; for example, Shift-Ctrl-Alt.

Figure 7.6 Moving a selection and its content, emptying the original place

- hold down Shift-Alt keys and click-and-drag the selection to move without emptying the original place. A floating selection is created.

Figure 7.7 Moving a selection and its content without emptying the original place

Note

 On some systems, you must push **Alt** before **Shift** or **Ctrl**. On these systems, pressing **Shift** or **Ctrl** first, causes GIMP to enter a mode that adds or subtract from the current selection — after that, the **Alt** key is ineffective!

7.2.1.2   Moving the other selections

The other selections (Lasso, Magic wand, By Color) have no handle. Click-and dragging them doesn't move them. To move their contents, as with rectangular and elliptical selections, you have to hold down Ctrl-Alt keys or Shift-Alt and click-and-drag.

If you use keyboard arrow keys instead of click-and-drag, you move the outline.

7.2.1.3   Other method

> **Note**
>
> You can also use a more roundabout method to move a selection. Make it floating. Then you can move its content, emptying the origin, by click-and-dragging or keyboard arrow keys. To move without emptying, use copy-paste.

7.2.2 Adding or subtracting selections

Tools have options that you can configure. Each selection tool allows you to set the selection mode. The following selection modes are supported:

- Replace is the most used selection mode. In replace mode, a selection replaces any existing selection.

- Add mode, causes new selections to be added to any existing selection. Press and hold the **Shift** key while making a selection to temporarily enter add mode.

- Subtract mode, causes new selections to be removed from any existing selection. Press and hold the **Ctrl** key while making a selection to temporarily enter subtract mode.

- Intersect mode, causes areas in both the new and existing selection to become the new selection. Press and hold both the **Shift** and **Ctrl** key while making a selection to temporarily enter intersect mode.

Figure 7.8 Enlarging a rectangular selection with the Lasso

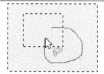

The figure shows an existing rectangular selection. Select the Lasso. While pressing the **Shift** key, make a free hand selection that includes the existing selection. Release the mouse button and areas are included in the selection.

> **Note**
>
> To correct selection defects precisely, use the Quick Mask.

7.3 The QuickMask

Figure 7.9 Image with QuickMask enabled

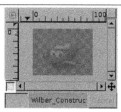

The usual selection tools involve tracing an outline around an area of interest, which does not work well for some complex selections. The QuickMask, however, allows you to paint a selection instead of just tracing its outline.

7.3.1 Overview

Normally, a selection in GIMP is represented by "marching ants" that trace the selection outline, but there may be more to a selection than the marching ants show. A GIMP selection is actually a full-fledged grayscale channel, covering the image, with pixel values ranging from 0 (unselected) to 255 (fully selected). The marching ants are drawn along a contour of half-selected pixels. Thus, what the marching ants show you as either inside or outside the boundary is really just a slice through a continuum.

The QuickMask is GIMP's way of showing the full structure of the selection. QuickMask also provides the ability to interact with the selection in new, and substantially more powerful, ways. Click the small outlined button at the lower left of the image window to toggle QuickMask on and off. The button switches between QuickMask mode, and marching ants mode. You can also use Select → Toggle QuickMask, or Shift-Q, to toggle between QuickMask and marching ants mode.

In QuickMask mode, the selection is shown as a translucent screen overlying the image, whose transparency at each pixel indicates the degree to which that pixel is selected. By default the mask is shown in red, but you can change this if another mask color is more convenient. The less a pixel is selected, the more it is obscured by the mask. Fully selected pixels are shown completely clear.

In QuickMask mode, many image manipulations act on the selection channel rather than the image itself. This includes, in particular, paint tools. Painting with white selects pixels, and painting with black unselects pixels. You can use any of the paint tools, as well as the bucket fill and gradient fill tools, in this way. Advanced users of GIMP learn that "painting the selection" is the easiest and most effective way to delicately manipulate the image.

Tip

To save a QuickMask selection to a new channel; Make sure that there is a selection and that QuickMask mode is not active in the image window. Use Select → Save to Channel. to create a new channel in the channel dialog called "SelectionMask copy" (repeating this command creates "..copy#1", "...copy#2" and so on...).

Tip

In QuickMask mode, Cut and Paste act on the selection rather than the image. You can sometimes make use of this as the most convenient way of transferring a selection from one image to another.

You can learn more on Selection masks in the section dedicated to the channel dialog.

7.3.2 Properties

There are two QuickMask properties you can change by right-clicking on the QuickMask button.

- Normally the QuickMask shows unselected areas "fogged over " and selected areas "in clear", but you can reverse this by choosing "Mask Selected Areas" instead of the default "Mask Unselected Areas".

- Use "Configure Color and Opacity" to open a dialog that allows you to set these to values other than the defaults, which are red at 50% opacity.

7.4   Using QuickMask Mode

1. Open an image or begin a new document.

2. Activate QuickMask mode using the left-bottom button in the image window. If a selection is present the mask is initialized with the content of the selection.

3. Choose any drawing tool. Paint on the QuickMask with black to remove selected areas, and paint with white to add selected areas. Use grey colors to partially select areas.

   You can also use selection tools and fill these selections with the Bucket Fill tool; this does not destroy the QuickMask selections!

4. Toggle QuickMask mode off using the left-bottom button in the image window: the selection will be displayed with marching ants.

7.5   Paths

Paths are curves (known as Bézier-curves). Paths are easy to learn and use in GIMP. To understand their concepts and mechanism, look at the glossary Bézier-curve or Wikipedia [WKPD-BEZIER]. The Paths tool is very powerful, allowing you to design sophisticated forms. To use the Paths tool in GIMP, you must first create a path, and then stroke the path.

In GIMP, the term "Stroke path" means to apply a specific style to the path (color, width, pattern...). A Path has two main purposes:

- You can convert a closed path to a selection.

- Any path, open or closed, can be *stroked*; that is, painted on the image in a variety of ways.

Figure 7.10 Illustration of four different path creating

Four examples of GIMP paths: one closed and polygonal; one open and polygonal; one closed and curved; one with a mixture of straight and curved segments.

7.5.1   Path Creation

Start by drawing the outline for your path; the outline can be modified later (see the Paths tool). To start, select the Paths tool using one of the following methods:

- Use Tools → Path from the image menu.

- Use the relevant icon ![icon] in toolbox.

- Use the hotkey **B**.

When the Paths tool is selected, the mouse cursor changes into a pointer (arrow) with a curve. Left click in the image to create the first point on the path. Move the mouse to a new point and left click the mouse to create another point linked to the previous point. Although you can create as many points as you desire, you only need two points to learn about Paths. While adding points, the mouse cursor has a little "+" next to the curve, which indicates that clicking will add a new point. When the mouse cursor is close to a line segment, the "+" changes into a cross with arrows; like the move tool.

Move the mouse cursor close to a line segment, left-click and drag the line segment. Two events occur.

- The line segment bends and curves as it is pulled.

- Each line segment has a start point and an end point that is clearly labeled. A "direction line" now projects from each end point for the line segment that was moved.

The curved line segment leaves an end point in the same direction that the "direction line" leaves the end point. The length of the "direction line" controls how far the line segment projects along the "direction line" before curving toward the other end point. Each "direction line" has an empty square box (called a handle) on one end. Click and drag a handle to change the direction and length of a "direction line".

Figure 7.11 Appearance of a path while it is manipulated
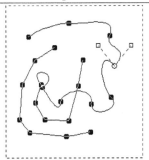

Appearance of a path while it is manipulated using the Path tool.

The path is comprised of two components with both straight and curved segments. Black squares are anchor points, the open circle indicates the selected anchor, and the two open squares are the handles associated with the selected anchor.

7.5.2 Path Properties

Paths, like layers and channels, are components of an image. When an image is saved in GIMP's native XCF file format, any paths it has are saved with it. The list of paths in an image can be viewed and operated on using the Paths dialog. You can move a path from one image to another by copying and pasting using the pop-up menu in the Paths dialog, or by dragging an icon from the Paths dialog into the destination image window.

GIMP paths belong to a mathematical type called "Bezier paths". What this means in practical terms is that they are defined by *anchors* and *handles*. "Anchors" are points the path goes through. "Handles" define the direction of a path when it enters or leaves an anchor point: each anchor point has two handles attached to it.

Paths can be very complex. If you create them by hand using the Path tool, unless you are obsessive they probably won't contain more than a few dozen anchor points (often many fewer); but if you create them by transforming a selection into a path, or by transforming text into a path, the result can easily contain hundreds of anchor points, or even thousands.

A path may contain multiple *components*. A "component" is a part of a path whose anchor points are all connected to each other by path segments. The ability to have multiple components in paths allows you to convert them into selections having multiple disconnected parts.

Each component of a path can be either *open* or *closed*: "closed" means that the last anchor point is connected to the first anchor point. If you transform a path into a selection, any open components are automatically converted into closed components by connecting the last anchor point to the first anchor point with a straight line.

Path segments can be either straight or curved. A path is called "polygonal" if all of its segments are straight. A new path segment is always created straight; the handles for the anchor points are directly on top of the anchor points, yielding handles of zero length, which produces straight-line segments. Drag a handle handle away from an anchor point to cause a segment to curve.

One nice thing about paths is that they use very few resources, especially in comparison with images. Representing a path in RAM requires storing only the coordinates of its anchors and handles: 1K of memory is enough to hold a complex path, but not enough to hold a small 20x20 pixel RGB layer. Therefore, it is possible to have literally hundreds of paths in an image without causing any significant stress to your system; the amount of stress that hundreds of paths might cause *you*, however, is another question. Even a path with thousands of segments consumes minimal resources in comparison to a typical layer or channel.

Paths can be created and manipulated using the Path tool.

7.5.3 Paths and Selections

GIMP lets you transform the selection for an image into a path; it also lets you transform paths into selections. For information about the selection and how it works, see the Selection section.

When you transform a selection into a path, the path closely follows the "marching ants". Now, the selection is a two-dimensional entity, but a path is a one-dimensional entity, so there is no way to transform the selection into a path without losing information. In fact, any information about partially selected areas (i.e., feathering) are lost when a selection is turned into a path. If the path is transformed back into a selection, the result is an all-or-none selection, similar to what is obtained by executing "Sharpen" from the Select menu.

7.5.4 Transforming Paths

Each of the Transform tools (Rotate, Scale, Perspective, etc) can be set to act on a layer, selection, or path. Select the transform tool in the toolbox, then select layer, selection, or path for the "Transform:" option in the tool's Tool Options dialog. This gives you a powerful set of methods for altering the shapes of paths without affecting other elements of the image.

By default a Transform tool, when it is set to affect paths, acts on only one path: the *active path* for the image, which is shown highlighted in the Paths dialog. You can make a transformation affect more than one path, and possibly other things as well, using the "transform lock" buttons in the Paths dialog. Not only paths, but also layers and channels, can be transform-locked. If you transform one element that is transform-locked, all others will be transformed in the same way. So, for example, if you want to scale a layer and a path by the same amount, click the transform-lock buttons so that "chain" symbols appear next to the layer in the Layers dialog, and the path in the Paths dialog; then use the Scale tool on either the layer or the path, and the other will automatically follow.

7.5.5 Stroking a Path

Figure 7.12 Stroking paths

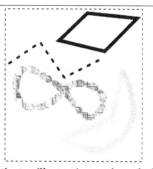

The four paths from the top illustration, each stroked in a different way.

Paths do not alter the appearance of the image pixel data unless they are *stroked*, using Edit → Stroke Path from the image menu or the Paths dialog right-click menu, or the "Stroke Path" button in the Tool Options dialog for the Path tool.

Choosing "Stroke Path" by any of these means brings up a dialog that allows you to control the way the stroking is done. You can choose from a wide variety of line styles, or you can stroke with any of the Paint tools, including unusual ones such as the Clone tool, Smudge tool, Eraser, etc.

Figure 7.13 The Stroke Path dialog

You can further increase the range of stroking effects by stroking a path multiple times, or by using lines or brushes of different widths. The possibilities for getting interesting effects in this way are almost unlimited.

7.5.6 Paths and Text

Figure 7.14 Text converted to a path

(a) *Text converted to a path and then transformed using the Perspective tool.* (b) *The path shown above, stroked with a fuzzy brush and then gradient-mapped using the Gradient Map filter with the "Yellow Contrast" gradient.*

A text item created using the Text tool can be transformed into a path using the **Path from Text** command in the the context menu of the Text tool. This can be useful for several purposes, including:

- Stroking the path, which gives you many possibilities for fancy text.

- More importantly, transforming the text. Converting text into a path, then transforming the path, and finally either stroking the path or converting it to a selection and filling it, often leads to much higher-quality results than rendering the text as a layer and transforming the pixel data.

7.5.7 Paths and SVG files

SVG, standing for "Scalable Vector Graphics", is an increasingly popular file format for *vector graphics*, in which graphical elements are represented in a resolution-independent format, in contrast to *raster graphics*; in which graphical elements are represented as arrays of pixels. GIMP is mainly a raster graphics program, but paths are vector entities.

Fortunately, paths are represented in SVG files in almost exactly the same way they are represented in GIMP. (Actually fortune has nothing to do with it: GIMP's path handling was rewritten for GIMP 2.0 with SVG paths in mind.) This compatibility makes it possible to store GIMP paths as SVG files without losing any information. You can access this capability in the Paths dialog.

It also means that GIMP can create paths from SVG files saved in other programs, such as Inkscape or Sodipodi, two popular open-source vector graphics applications. This is nice because those programs have much more powerful path-manipulation tools than GIMP does. You can import a path from an SVG file using the Paths dialog.

The SVG format handles many other graphical elements than just paths: among other things, it handles figures such as squares, rectangles, circles, ellipses, regular polygons, etc. GIMP cannot do anything with these entities, but it can load them as paths.

> **Note**
>
> Creating paths is not the only thing GIMP can do with SVG files. It can also open SVG files as GIMP images, in the usual way.

7.6 Brushes

Figure 7.15 Brush strokes example

A number of examples of brushstrokes painted using different brushes from the set supplied with GIMP. All were painted using the Paintbrush tool.

A *brush* is a pixmap or set of pixmaps used for painting. GIMP includes a set of 10 "paint tools", which not only perform operations that you would normally think of as painting, but also operations such as erasing, copying, smudging, lightening or darkening, etc. All of the paint tools, except the ink tool, use the same set of brushes. The brush pixmaps represent the marks that are made by single "touches" of the brush to the image. A brush stroke, usually made by moving the pointer across the image with the mouse button held down, produces a series of marks spaced along the trajectory, in a way specified by the characteristics of the brush and the paint tool being used.

Brushes can be selected by clicking on an icon in the Brushes dialog. GIMP's *current brush* is shown in the Brush/Pattern/Gradient area of the Toolbox. Clicking on the brush symbol there is one way of activating the Brushes dialog.

When you install GIMP, it comes with a number of basic brushes, plus a few bizarre ones that serve mainly to give you examples of what is possible (i. e., the "green pepper" brush in the illustration). You can also create new brushes, or download them and install them so that GIMP will recognize them.

GIMP can use several different types of brushes. All of them, however, are used in the same way, and for most purposes you don't need to worry about the differences when you paint with them. Here are the available types of brushes:

Ordinary brushes Most of the brushes supplied with GIMP fall into this category. They are represented in the Brushes dialog by grayscale pixmaps. When you paint using them, the current foreground color (as shown in the Color Area of the Toolbox) is substituted for black, and the pixmap shown in the brushes dialog represents the mark that the brush makes on the image.

To create such a brush: Create a small image in gray levels using zoom. Save it with the .gbr extension. Click on Refresh button in the Brush Dialog to get it in preview without it being necessary to restart GIMP.

Color brushes Brushes in this category are represented by colored images in the Brushes dialog. They can be pictures or text. When you paint with them, the colors are used as shown; the current foreground color does not come into play. Otherwise they work the same way as ordinary brushes.

To create such a brush: Create a small RGBA image. For this, open New Image, select RGB for image type and Transparent for fill type. Draw your image and and firs save it as a .xcf file to keep its properties. Then save it in *.gbr* format. Click on the *Refresh* button in Brush Dialog to get your brush without it being necessary to restart GIMP.

Tip

When you do a Copy or a Cut on a selection, you see the contents of the clipboard (that is the selection) at the first position in the brushes dialog. And you can use it for painting.

Figure 7.16 Selection to Brush after Copy or Cut

Image hoses / Image pipes Brushes in this category can make more than one kind of mark on an image. They are indicated by small red triangles at the lower right corner of the brush symbol in the Brushes dialog. They are sometimes called "animated brushes" because the marks change as you trace out a brushstroke. In principle, image hose brushes can be very sophisticated, especially if you use a tablet, changing shape as a function of pressure, angle, etc. These possibilities have never really been exploited, however; and the ones supplied with GIMP are relatively simple (but still quite useful).

You will find an example on how to create such brushes in Animated brushes

Parametric brushes These are brushes created using the Brush Editor, which allows you to generate a wide variety of brush shapes by using a simple graphical interface. A nice feature of parametric brushes is that they are *resizable*. It is possible, using the Preferences dialog, to make key presses or mouse wheel rotations cause the current brush to become larger or smaller, if it is a parametric brush.

Now, all brushes have a variable size. In fact, in the option box of all painting tools there is a slider to enlarge or reduce the size of the active brush. You can do this directly in the image window if you have set correctly your mouse wheel; see Varying brush size.

In addition to the brush pixmap, each GIMP brush has one other important property: the brush *Spacing*. This represents the distance between consecutive brush-marks when a continuous brushstroke is painted. Each brush has an assigned default value for this, which can be modified using the Brushes dialog.

7.7 Adding New Brushes

To add a new brush, after either creating or downloading it, you need to save it in a format GIMP can use. The brush file needs to be placed in the GIMP's brush search path, so that GIMP is able to index and display it in the Brushes dialog. You can hit the Refresh button, which reindexes the brush directory. GIMP uses three file formats for brushes:

GBR The .gbr ("*gimp br*ush") format is used for ordinary and color brushes. You can convert many other types of images, including many brushes used by other programs, into GIMP brushes by opening them in GIMP and saving them with file names ending in .gbr. This brings up a dialog box in which you can set the default Spacing for the brush. A more complete description of the GBR file format can be found in the file gbr.txt in the devel-docs directory of the GIMP source distribution.

Figure 7.17 Save a .gbr brush

GIH The .gih ("*gimp i*mage *h*ose") format is used for animated brushes. These brushes are constructed from images containing multiple layers: each layer may contain multiple brush-shapes, arranged in a grid. When you save an image as a .gih file, a dialog comes up that allows you to describe the format of the brush. Look at The GIH dialog box for more information about the dialog. The GIH format is rather complicated: a complete description can be found in the file gih.txt in the devel-docs directory of the GIMP source distribution.

VBR The .vbr format is used for parametric brushes, i. e., brushes created using the Brush Editor. There is really no other meaningful way of obtaining files in this format.

To make a brush available, place it in one of the folders in GIMP's brush search path. By default, the brush search path includes two folders, the system brushes folder, which you should not use or alter, and the brushes folder inside your personal GIMP directory. You can add new folders to the brush search path using the Brush Folders page of the Preferences dialog. Any GBR, GIH, or VBR file included in a folder in the brush search path will show up in the Brushes dialog the next time you start GIMP, or as soon as you press the Refresh button in the Brushes dialog.

> **Note**
>
> When you create a new parametric brush using the Brush Editor, it is automatically saved in your personal brushes folder.

There are a number of web sites with downloadable collections of GIMP brushes. Rather than supplying a list of links that will soon be out of date, the best advice is to do a search with your favorite search engine for "GIMP brushes". There are also many collections of brushes for other programs with painting functionality. Some can be converted easily into GIMP brushes, some require special conversion utilities, and some cannot be converted at all. Most fancy procedural brush types fall into the last category. If you need to know, look around on the web, and if you don't find anything, look for an expert to ask.

7.8   The GIH Dialog Box

When your new animated brush is created, it is displayed within the image window and you would like save it into a gih format. You select File → Save as... menu, name your work with the gih extension in the new window relevant field and as soon as you pressed the Save button, the following window is displayed:

Figure 7.18 The dialog to describe the animated brush

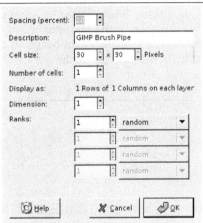

This dialog box shows up, if you save an image as GIMP image hose

---

This dialog box has several options not easy to understand. They allow you to determine the way your brush is animated.

Spacing (Percent) "Spacing" is the distance between consecutive brush marks when you trace out a brushstroke with the pointer. You must consider drawing with a brush, whatever the paint tool, like stamping. If Spacing is low, stamps will be very close and stroke look continuous. If spacing is high, stamps will be separated: that's interesting with a color brush (like "green pepper" for instance). Value varies from 1 to 200 and this percentage refers to brush "diameter": 100% is one diameter.

Description It's the brush name that will appear at the top of Brush Dialog (grid mode) when the brush is selected.

Cell Size That's size of cells you will cut up in layers... Default is one cell per layer and size is that of the layer. Then there is only one brush aspect per layer.

We could have only one big layer and cut up in it the cells that will be used for the different aspects of the animated brush.

For instance, we want a 100x100 pixels brush with 8 different aspects. We can take these 8 aspects from a 400x200 pixels layer, or from a 300x300 pixels layer but with one cell unused.

Number of cells That's the number of cells (one cell per aspect) that will be cut in every layer. Default is the number of layers as there is only one layer per aspect.

Display as This tells how cells have been arranged in layers. If, for example, you have placed height cells at the rate of two cells per layer on four layers, GIMP will display: 1 rows of 2 columns on each layer.

Dimension, Ranks, Selection There things are getting complicated! Explanations are necessary to understand how to arrange cell and layers.

GIMP starts retrieving cells from each layer and stacks them into a FIFO stack (First In First Out: the first in is at the top of the stack and so can be first out). In our example 4 layers with 2 cells in each, we'll have, from top to bottom: first cell of first layer, second cell of first layer, first cell of second layer, second cell of second layer..., second cell of fourth layer. With one cell per layer or with several cells per layer, result is the same. You can see this stack in the Layer Dialog of the resulting `.gih` image file.

Then GIMP creates a computer array from this stack with the Dimensions you have set. You can use four dimensions.

In computer science an array has a "myarray(x,y,z)" form for a 3 dimensions array (3D). It's easy to imagine a 2D array: on a paper it's an array with rows and columns

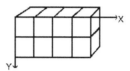

With a 3d array we don't talk rows and columns but Dimensions and Ranks. The first dimension is along x axis, the second dimension along y axis, the third along z axis. Each dimension has ranks of cells.

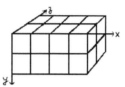

To fill up this array, GIMP starts retrieving cells from the top of stack. The way it fills the array reminds that of an odometer: right rank digits turn first and, when they reach their maximum, left rank digits start running. If you have some memories of Basic programming you will have, with an array(4,2,2), the following succession: (1,1,1),(1,1,2),(1,2,1),(1,2,2),(2,1,1),(2,1,2),(2,2,2),(3,1,1).... (4,2,2). We will see this later in an example.

Besides the rank number that you can give to each dimension, you can also give them a Selection mode. You have several modes that will be applied when drawing:

Incremental GIMP selects a rank from the concerned dimension according to the order ranks have in that dimension.

Random GIMP selects a rank at random from the concerned dimension.

Angular GIMP selects a rank in the concerned dimension according to the moving angle of the brush.

   The first rank is for the direction 0°, upwards. The other ranks are affected, clockwise, to an angle whose value is 360/number of ranks. So, with 4 ranks in the concerned dimension, the angle will move 90° clockwise for each direction change: second rank will be affected to 90° (rightwards), third rank to 180° (downwards) and fourth rank to 270° (-90°) (leftwards).[1]

Speed, Pressure, x tilt, y tilt These options are for sophisticated drawing tablets.

Examples

A one dimension image pipe Well! What is all this useful for? We'll see that gradually with examples. You can actually place in each dimension cases that will give your brush a particular action.

Let us start with a 1D brush which will allow us to study selection modes action. We can imagine it like this:

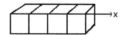

Follow these steps:

1. Open a new 30x30 pixels image, RGB with Transparent fill type. Using the Text tool create 4 layers "1", "2", "3", "4". Delete the "background" layer.

2. Save this image first with `.xcf` extension to keep its properties then save it as `.gih`.

---

[1] For previous GIMP versions you may have to replace "clockwise" with "counter-clockwise".

3. The Save As Dialog is opened: select a destination for your image. OK. The GIH dialog is opened: Choose Spacing 100, give a name in Description box, 30x30 for Cell Size, 1 dimension, 4 ranks and choose "Incremental" in Selection box. OK.

4. You may have difficulties to save directly in the GIMP Brush directory. In that case, save the `.gih` file manually into the `/usr/share/gimp/gimp/2.0/brushes` directory. Then come back into the Toolbox, click in the brush icon to open the Brush Dialog then click on Refresh 🔁 icon button. Your new brush appears in the Brush window. Select it. Select pencil tool for instance and click and hold with it on a new image:

You see 1, 2, 3, 4 digits following one another in order.

5. Take your `.xcf` image file back and save it as `.gih` setting Selection to "Random":

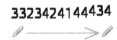

Digits will be displayed at random order.

6. Now select "Angular" Selection:

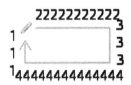

A 3 dimensions image hose We are now going to create a 3D animated brush: its orientation will vary according to brush direction, it will alternate Left/Right hands regularly and its color will vary at random between black and blue.

The first question we have to answer to is the number of images that is necessary. We reserve the first dimension (x) to the brush direction (4 directions). The second dimension (y) is for Left/Right alternation and the third dimension (z) for color variation. Such a brush is represented in a 3D array "myarray(4,2,2)":

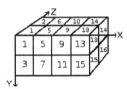

There are 4 ranks in first dimension (x), 2 ranks in second dimension (y) and 2 ranks in third dimension (z). We see that there are 4x2x2 = 16 cells. We need 16 images.

1. Creating images of dimension 1 (x)

   Open a new 30x30 pixels image, RGB with Transparent Fill Type. Using the zoom draw a left hand with fingers upwards.[2] Save it as `handL0k.xcf` (hand Left 0° Black).

   Open the Layer Dialog. Double click on the layer to open the Layer Attributes Dialog and rename it to handL0k.

   Duplicate the layer. Let visible only the duplicated layer, select it and apply a 90° rotation (Layer/Transform/ 90° rotation clockwise). Rename it to handL90k.

   Repeat the same operations to create handL180k and handL-90k (or handL270k).

2. Creating images of dimension 2 (y)

   This dimension in our example has two ranks, one for left hand and the other for right hand. The left hand rank exists yet. We shall build right hand images by flipping it horizontally.

   Duplicate the handL0k layer. Let it visible only and select it. Rename it to handR0K. Apply Layer/Transform/Flip Horizontally.

---

[2] Ok, we are cheating here: our hand is borrowed from `http://commons.wikimedia.org/wiki/File:Stop_hand.png`.

Repeat the same operation on the other left hand layers to create their right hand equivalent. Re-order layers to have a clockwise rotation from top to bottom, alternating Left and Right: handL0k, handR0k, handL90k, handR90k, ..., handR-90k.

3. Creating images of dimension 3 (z)

   Creating images of dimension 3 (z): The third dimension has two ranks, one for black color and the other for blue color. The first rank, black, exists yet. We well see that images of dimension 3 will be a copy, in blue, of the images of dimension 2. So we will have our 16 images. But a row of 16 layers is not easy to manage: we will use layers with two images.

   Select the handL0k layer and let it visible only. Using Image/Canvas Size change canvas size to 60x30 pixels.

   Duplicate hand0k layer. On the copy, fill the hand with blue using Bucket Fill tool.

   Now, select the Move tool. Double click on it to accede to its properties: check Move the Current Layer option. Move the blue hand into the right part of the layer precisely with the help of Zoom.

   Make sure only handL0k and its blue copy are visible. Right click on the Layer Dialog: Apply the Merge Visible Layers command with the option Expand as Necessary. You get a 60x30 pixels layer with the black hand on the left and the blue hand on the right. Rename it to "handsL0".

   Repeat the same operations on the other layers.

4. Set layers in order

   Layers must be set in order so that GIMP can find the required image at some point of using the brush. Our layers are yet in order but we must understand more generally how to have them in order. There are two ways to imagine this setting in order. The first method is mathematical: GIMP divides the 16 layers first by 4; that gives 4 groups of 4 layers for the first dimension. Each group represents a direction of the brush. Then, it divides each group by 2; that gives 8 groups of 2 layers for the second dimension: each group represents a L/R alternation. Then another division by 2 for the third dimension to represent a color at random between black and blue.

   The other method is visual, by using the array representation. Correlation between two methods is represented in next image:

   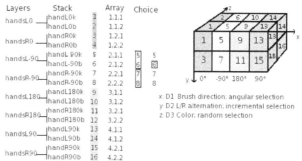

   How will GIMP read this array?: GIMP starts with the first dimension which is programmed for "angular", for instance 90°. In this 90° rank, in yellow, in the second dimension, it selects a L/R alternation, in an "incremental" way. Then, in the third dimension, in a random way, it chooses a color. Finally, our layers must be in the following order:

5. Voilà. Your brush is ready. Save it as `.xcf` first, then as `.gih` with the following parameters:

- Spacing: 100
- Description: Hands
- Cell Size: 30x30
- Number of cells: 16
- Dimensions: 3
    - Dimension 1: 4 ranks Selection: Angular
    - Dimension 2: 2 ranks Selection: Incremental
    - Dimension 3: 2 ranks Selection: Random

Place your .gih file into GIMP brush directory and refresh the brush box. You can now use your brush.

Figure 7.19 Here is the result by stroking an elliptical selection with the brush:

This brush alternates right hand and left hand regularly, black and blue color at random, direction according to four brush directions.

7.9 Varying brush size

From GIMP-2.4, all brushes have a variable size.

7.9.1 How to vary the height of a brush

You can get the brush size varying in three ways:

1. Using the Size slider of the tool options. Pencil, Paintbrush, Eraser, Airbrush, Clone, Heal, Perspective Clone, Blur/Sharpen and Dodge/Burn tools have a slider to vary the brush size.

Figure 7.20 The Size slider

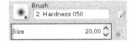

2. By programming the mouse wheel:
    (a) In the main window of GIMP, click on Edit → Preferences.
    (b) In the left column of the new window, select Input Devices → Input Controllers.
    (c) You can see Additional Input Controllers, with two columns: Available Controllers and Active Controllers.
    In the column Active Controllers, double-click the Main Mouse Wheel button.
    (d) Then, you see a new window: Configure Input Controller.
    In the left column Event, click Scroll Up to get it highlighted.
    (e) Click the Edit button (at the bottom middle of the list).

(f) You can see the window Select Controller Event Action.

Drop-down the Tools item, by clicking the small triangle on its left.

(g) In the left column Action, click Increase Brush Scale to highlight it, then click the OK button.

(h) Now, in front of Scroll Up is display tools-paint-brush-scale-increase.

(i) Close the window.

(j) With the same method, program Scroll Down with Decrease Brush Scale.

(k) Don't forget to click the OK button of the main window of Preferences.

After these somewhat long explanations, you can use your mouse wheel to vary size brush. For example, choose the pencil tool with the "Circle" brush. Set the pointer in the image window, use the mouse wheel, in the two directions, you can see the "Circle" shrinking or stretching.

3. You can program the "Up" and "Down" arrow keys of the keyboard.

The method is similar to that of the mouse wheel. The only differences are:

- In the column Active Controllers, double-click Main Keyboard.

- In the column Event, click Cursor Up for the first key, and Cursor Down for the second key.

- Then, use the two keys (Up arrow and Down arrow) and the result is the same as you got with the mouse wheel.

7.9.2 Creating a brush quickly

Two methods to create a new brush easily:

1. First, the "superfast" method. You have an image area you want make a brush from it, to be used with a tool like pencil, airbrush... Select it with the rectangular (or elliptical) select tool, then do a Copy of this selection and immediately you can see this copy in the first position of the Brush Dialog, and its name is "Clipboard". It is immediately usable.

Figure 7.21 Selection becomes a brush after copying

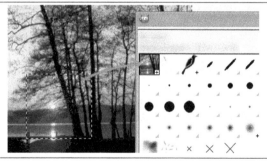

2. The second method is more elaborate.

Do File → New with, for example, a width and a length of 35 pixels and in the advanced options a Color Space in Gray Level and Fill with: white.

Zoom on this new image to enlarge it and draw on it with a black pencil.

Save it with a .gbr extension in the directory /home/name_of_user/.gimp-2.8/brushes/.

In the Brushes dialog window, click on the button Refresh brushes 🔄 .

And your marvellous brush appears right in the middle of the other brushes. You can use it immediately, without starting GIMP again.

Figure 7.22 Steps to create a brush

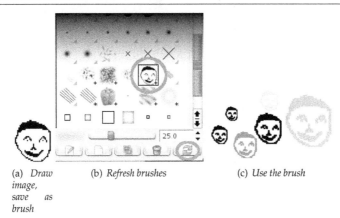

(a) *Draw image, save as brush*   (b) *Refresh brushes*   (c) *Use the brush*

7.10   Gradients

Figure 7.23 Some examples of GIMP gradients.

Gradients from top to bottom: FG to BG (RGB); Full saturation spectrum; Nauseating headache; Browns; Four bars

A *gradient* is a set of colors arranged in a linear order. The most basic use of gradients is by the Blend tool, sometimes known as the "gradient tool" or "gradient fill tool": it works by filling the selection with colors from a gradient. You have many options to choose from for controlling the way the gradient colors are arranged within the selection. There are also other important ways to use gradients, including:

Painting with a gradient Each of GIMP's basic painting tools allows you the option of using colors from a gradient. This enables you to create brushstrokes that change color from one end to the other.

The Gradient Map filter This filter is now in the Colors menu, and allows you to "colorize" an image, using the color intensity of each point with the corresponding color from the active gradient (the intensity 0, very dark, is replaced by the color at most left end of the gradient, progressively until the intensity is 255, very light, replaced by the most right color of the gradient. See Section 16.8.23 for more information.

When you install GIMP, it comes presupplied with a large number of interesting gradients, and you can add new ones that you create or download from other sources. You can access the full set of available gradients using the Gradients dialog, a dockable dialog that you can either activate when you need it, or keep around as a tab in a dock. The "current gradient", used in most gradient-related operations, is shown in the Brush/Pattern/Gradient area of the Toolbox. Clicking on the gradient symbol in the Toolbox is an alternative way of bringing up the Gradients dialog.

Many quickly examples of working with gradient (for more information see Blend Tool):

- Put a gradient in a selection:

  1. Choose a gradient.
  2. With the Blend Tool click and drag with the mouse between two points of a selection.

3. Colors will distributed perpendicularly to the direction of the drag of the mouse and according to the length of it.

Figure 7.24 How to use rapidly a gradient in a selection

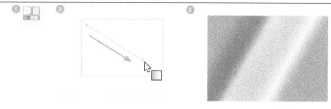

- Painting with a gradient:

You can also use a gradient with the Pencil, Paintbrush or Airbrush tools if you choose the dynamics Color From Gradient. In the next step choose a suitable gradient from Color options and in the Fade options set the gradients length and the style of the repeating. The chapter Section 14.3.2.6 describes these parameters in more detail.

The following example shows the impact on the Pencil tool. You see in the upper side of the figure the necessary settings and the lower side of the figure shows the resulting succession of the gradients colors.

Figure 7.25 How to use rapidly a gradient with a drawing tool

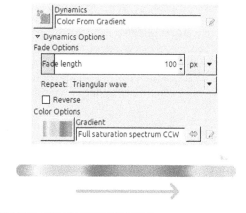

To use the Paint tools with the same settings as they were known as option Use color from gradient in GIMP up to version 2.6 open the Tool Presets Dialog. Then choose one of the items Airbrush (Color From Gradient), Paintbrush (Color From Gradient) or Pencil (Color From Gradient) from it.

- Different productions with the same gradient:

Figure 7.26 Gradient usage

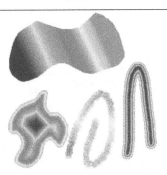

Four ways of using the Tropical Colors gradient: a linear gradient fill, a shaped gradient fill, a stroke painted using colors from a gradient, and a stroke painted with a fuzzy brush then colored using the Gradient Map filter.

A few useful things to know about GIMP's gradients:

- The first four gradients in the list are special: they use the Foreground and Background colors from the Toolbox Color Area, instead of being fixed. FG to BG (RGB) is the RGB representation of the gradient from the Foreground color to the Background color in Toolbox. FG to BG (HSV counterclockwise) represents the hue succession in Color Circle from the selected hue to 360°. FG to BG (HSV clockwise represents the hue succession in Color Circle from the selected hue to 0°. With FG to transparent , the selected hue becomes more and more transparent. You can modify these colors by using the Color Selector. Thus, by altering the foreground and background colors, you can make these gradients transition smoothly between any two colors you want.

- Gradients can involve not just color changes, but also changes in opacity. Some of the gradients are completely opaque; others include transparent or translucent parts. When you fill or paint with a non-opaque gradient, the existing contents of the layer will show through behind it.

- You can create new *custom* gradients, using the Gradient Editor. You cannot modify the gradients that are supplied with GIMP, but you can duplicate them or create new ones, and then edit those.

The gradients that are supplied with GIMP are stored in a system `gradients` folder. By default, gradients that you create are stored in a folder called `gradients` in your personal GIMP directory. Any gradient files (ending with the extension `.ggr`) found in one of these folders, will automatically be loaded when you start GIMP. You can add more directories to the gradient search path, if you want to, in the Gradients tab of the Data Folders pages of the Preferences dialog.

New in GIMP 2.2 is the ability to load gradient files in SVG format, used by many vector graphics programs. To make GIMP load an SVG gradient file, all you need to do is place it in the `gradients` folder of your personal GIMP directory, or any other folder in your gradient search path.

Tip

 You can find a large number of interesting SVG gradients on the web, in particular at OpenClipArt Gradients [OPENCLIPART-GRADIENT]. You won't be able to see what these gradients look like unless your browser supports SVG, but that won't prevent you from downloading them.

7.11 Patterns

A *pattern* is an image, usually small, used for filling regions by *tiling*, that is, by placing copies of the pattern side by side like ceramic tiles. A pattern is said to be *tileable* if copies of it can be adjoined left-edge-to-right-edge and top-edge-to-bottom-edge without creating obvious seams. Not all useful patterns are tileable, but tileable patterns are nicest for many purposes. (A *texture*, by the way, is the same thing as a pattern.)

Figure 7.27 Pattern usage

Three ways of using the "Leopard" pattern: bucket-filling a selection, painting with the Clone tool, and stroking an elliptical selection with the pattern.

In GIMP there are three main uses for patterns:

- With the Bucket Fill tool, you can choose to fill a region with a pattern instead of a solid color.

Figure 7.28 The checked box for use a pattern

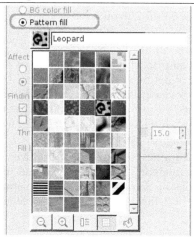

The box for pattern fill is checked and a click on the pattern shows you all patterns in grid mode.

- With the Clone tool, you can paint using a pattern, with a wide variety of paintbrush shapes.

- When you *stroke* a path or selection, you can do it with a pattern instead of a solid color. You can also use the Clone tool as your choice if you stroke the selection using a painting tool.

> **Tip**
>
> Note: Patterns do not need to be opaque. If you fill or paint using a pattern with translucent or transparent areas, then the previous contents of the area will show through from behind it. This is one of many ways of doing "overlays" in GIMP.

When you install GIMP, it comes presupplied with a few dozen patterns, which seem to have been chosen more or less randomly. You can also add new patterns, either ones you create yourself, or ones you download from the vast number available online.

GIMP's *current pattern*, used in most pattern-related operations, is shown in the Brush/Pattern/Gradient area of the Toolbox. Clicking on the pattern symbol brings up the Patterns dialog, which allows you to select a different pattern. You can also access the Patterns dialog by menu, or dock it so that it is present continuously.

To add a new pattern to the collection, so that it shows up in the Patterns dialog, you need to save it in a format GIMP can use, in a folder included in GIMP's pattern search path. There are several file formats you can use for patterns:

PAT The `.pat` format is used for patterns which were created specifically for GIMP. You can convert any image into a `.pat` file by opening it in GIMP and then saving it using a file name ending in `.pat`.

> ### Caution
>
> Do not confuse GIMP-generated `.pat` files with files created by other programs (e.g. Photoshop) – after all, `.pat` is just a part of an (arbitrary) file name.
>
> (However, GIMP *does* support Photoshop `.pat` files until a certain version.)

PNG, JPEG, BMP, GIF, TIFF Since GIMP 2.2 you can use `.png`, `.jpg`, `.bmp`, `.gif`, or `.tiff` files as patterns.

To make a pattern available, you place it in one of the folders in GIMP's pattern search path. By default, the pattern search path includes two folders, the system `patterns` folder, which you should not use or alter, and the `patterns` folder inside your personal GIMP directory. You can add new folders to the pattern search path using the Pattern Folders page of the Preferences dialog. Any PAT file (or, in GIMP 2.2, any of the other acceptable formats) included in a folder in the pattern search path will show up in the Patterns dialog the next time you start GIMP.

There are countless ways of creating interesting patterns in GIMP, using the wide variety of available tools and filters -- particularly the rendering filters. You can find tutorials for this in many locations, including the GIMP home page [GIMP]. Some of the filters have options that allows you to make their results tileable. Also, see Section 17.2.7, this filter allows you to blend the edges of an image in order to make it more smoothly tileable.

Figure 7.29 Pattern script examples

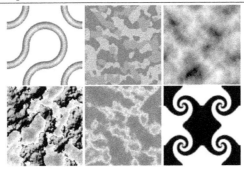

Examples of patterns created using six of the Pattern Script-Fu's that come with GIMP. Default settings were used for everything except size. (From left to right: 3D Truchet; Camouflage; Flatland; Land; Render Map; Swirly)

Also of interest are a set of pattern-generating scripts that come with GIMP: you can find them in the menu bar, through File → Create → Patterns. Each of the scripts creates a new image filled with a particular type of pattern: a dialog pops up that allows you to set parameters controlling the details of the appearance. Some of these patterns are most useful for cutting and pasting; others serve best as bumpmaps.

Figure 7.30 How to create new patterns

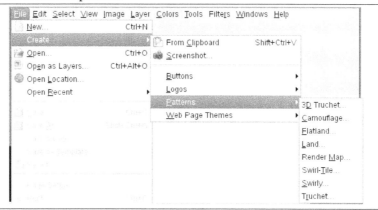

7.12   Palettes

A *palette* is a set of discrete colors. In GIMP, palettes are used mainly for two purposes:

- They allow you to paint with a selected set of colors, in the same way an oil painter works with colors from a limited number of tubes.

- They form the colormaps of indexed images. An indexed image can use a maximum of 256 different colors, but these can be any colors. The colormap of an indexed image is called an "indexed palette" in GIMP.

Actually neither of these functions fall very much into the mainstream of GIMP usage: it is possible to do rather sophisticated things in GIMP without ever dealing with palettes. Still, they are something that an advanced user should understand, and even a less advanced user may need to think about them in some situations, as for example when working with GIF files.

Figure 7.31 The Palettes dialog

When you install GIMP, it comes supplied with several dozen predefined palettes, and you can also create new ones. Some of the predefined palettes are commonly useful, such as the "Web" palette, which contains the set of colors considered "web safe"; many of the palettes seem to have been chosen more or less whimsically. You can access all of the available palettes using the Palettes dialog. This is also the starting point if you want to create a new palette.

Figure 7.32 The Palette Editor

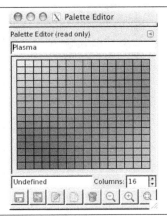

Double-clicking on a palette in the Palettes dialog brings up the Palette Editor, showing the colors from the palette you clicked on. You can use this to paint with the palette: clicking on a color sets GIMP's foreground to that color, as shown in the Color Area of the Toolbox. Holding down the **Ctrl** key while clicking, on the other hand, sets GIMP's background color to the color you click on.

You can also, as the name implies, use the Palette Editor to change the colors in a palette, so long as it is a palette that you have created yourself. You cannot edit the palettes that are supplied with GIMP; however you can duplicate them and then edit the copies.

When you create palettes using the Palette Editor, they are automatically saved as soon as you exit GIMP, in the `palettes` folder of your personal GIMP directory. Any palette files in this directory, or in the system `palettes` directory created when GIMP is installed, are automatically loaded and shown in the Palettes dialog the next time you start GIMP. You can also add other folders to the palette search path using the Palette Folders page of the Preferences dialog.

GIMP palettes are stored using a special file format, in files with the extension `.gpl`. It is a very simple format, and they are ASCII files, so if you happen to obtain palettes from another source, and would like to use them in GIMP, it probably won't be very hard to convert them: just take a look at any `.gpl` and you will see what to do.

7.12.1 Colormap

Confusingly, GIMP makes use of two types of palettes. The more noticeable are the type shown in the Palettes dialog: palettes that exist independently of any image. The second type, *indexed palettes*, form the colormaps of indexed images. Each indexed image has its own private indexed palette, defining the set of colors available in the image: the maximum number of colors allowed in an indexed palette is 256. These palettes are called "indexed" because each color is associated with an index number. (Actually, the colors in ordinary palettes are numbered as well, but the numbers have no functional significance.)

Figure 7.33 The Colormap dialog

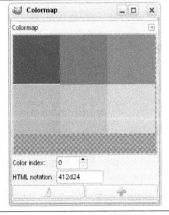

The colormap of an indexed image is shown in the Indexed Palette dialog, which should not be confused with the Palettes dialog. The Palettes dialog shows a list of all of the palettes available; the Colormap dialog shows the colormap of the currently active image, if it is an indexed image – otherwise it shows nothing.

You can, however, create an ordinary palette from the colors in an indexed image—actually from the colors in any image. To do this, choose Import Palette from the right-click popup menu in the Palettes dialog: this pops up a dialog that gives you several options, including the option to import the palette from an image. (You can also import any of GIMP's gradients as a palette.) This possibility becomes important if you want to create a set of indexed images that all use the same set of colors.

When you convert an image into indexed mode, a major part of the process is the creation of an indexed palette for the image. How this happens is described in detail in Section 16.6.6. Briefly, you have several methods to choose from, one of which is to use a specified palette from the Palettes dialog.

Thus, to sum up the foregoing, ordinary palettes can be turned into indexed palettes when you convert an image into indexed mode; indexed palettes can be turned into ordinary palettes by importing them into the Palettes dialog.

Figure 7.34 Colormap dialog (1) and Palette dialog (2)

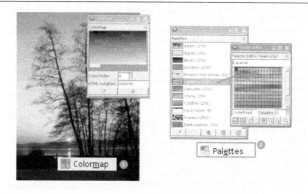

7.13   Presets

If you often use tools with particular settings, presets are for you. You can save these settings and get them back when you want.

Paint tools, which are normally in Toolbox, have a preset system that have been much improved with GIMP-2.8. Color tools (except Posterize and Desaturate), which are not normally in Toolbox, have their own preset system.

Four buttons at the bottom of all tools options dialogs allow you to save, restore, delete or reset presets.

Paint tool presets are described in Section 15.5.1.
Color tool presets are described in Section 14.5.1.1.

7.14   Drawing Simple Objects

In this section, you will learn how to create simple objects in GIMP. It's pretty easy once you figure out how to do it. GIMP provides a huge set of Tools and Shortcuts which most new users get lost in.

7.14.1   Drawing a Straight Line

Let's begin by painting a straight line. The easiest way to create a straight line is by using your favorite brush tool, the mouse and the keyboard.

Drawing a Straight Line

Figure 7.35 A new image

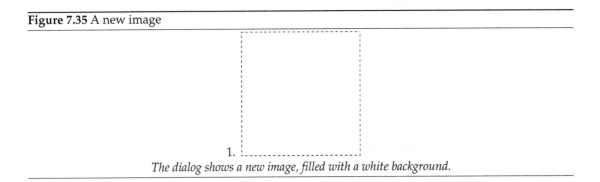

1.

The dialog shows a new image, filled with a white background.

Create a new image. Select your favorite brush tool or use the pencil, if in doubt. Select a foreground color, but be sure that the foreground and background colors are different.

Figure 7.36 The start of the straight line

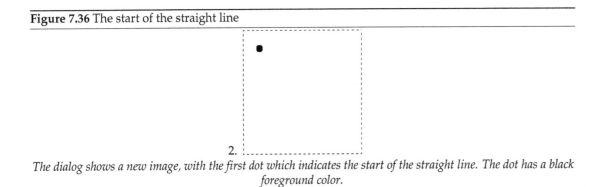

2.

The dialog shows a new image, with the first dot which indicates the start of the straight line. The dot has a black foreground color.

Create a starting point by clicking on the image display area with the left mouse button. Your canvas should look similar to Figure 7.35.

Figure 7.37 The helpline

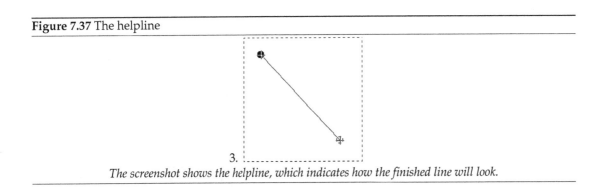

3.

The screenshot shows the helpline, which indicates how the finished line will look.

Now, hold down the **Shift** button on your keyboard and move the mouse away from the starting point you created. You'll see a thin line indicating how the line will look.

Figure 7.38 The line after the second click

*The line created appears in the image window after drawing the second point (or end point), while the **Shift** key is still pressed.*

If you're satisfied with the direction and length of the line, click the left mouse button again to finish the line. The GIMP displays a straight line now. If the line doesn't appear, check the foreground and background colors and be sure that you kept the **Shift** key pressed while painting. You can keep creating lines by continuing to hold the **Shift** key and creating additional end points.

7.14.2 Creating a Basic Shape

1. GIMP is not designed to be used for drawing.[3] However, you may create shapes by either painting them using the technique described in Section 7.14.1 or by using the selection tools. Of course, there are various other ways to paint a shape, but we'll stick to the easiest ones here. So, create a new image and check that the foreground and background colors are different.

Figure 7.39 Creating a rectangular selection

The screenshot shows how a rectangular selection is created. Press and hold the left mouse button while you move the mouse in the direction of the red arrow.

Basic shapes like rectangles or ellipses, can be created using the selection tools. This tutorial uses a rectangular selection as an example. So, choose the rectangular selection tool and create a new selection: press and hold the left mouse button while you move the mouse to another position in the image (illustrated in figure Figure 7.39). The selection is created when you release the mouse button. For more information about key modifiers see selection tools.

Figure 7.40 Rectangular selection filled with foreground color

The screenshot shows a rectangular selection filled with the foreground color.

---

[3] Try out e.g. [INKSCAPE] for this purpose.

After creating the selection, you can either create a filled or an outlined shape with the foreground color of your choice. If you go for the first option, choose a foreground color and fill the selection with the bucket fill tool. If you choose the latter option, create an outline by using the Stroke selection menu item from the Edit menu. If you're satisfied with the result, remove the selection.

Chapter 8

Combining Images

8.1 Introduction to Layers

A good way to visualize a GIMP image is as a stack of transparencies: in GIMP terminology, each individual transparency is called a *layer*. There is no limit, in principle, to the number of layers an image can have: only the amount of memory available on the system. It is not uncommon for advanced users to work with images containing dozens of layers.

The organization of layers in an image is shown by the Layers dialog, which is the second most important type of dialog window in GIMP, after the Main Toolbox. The appearance of the Layers dialog is shown in the adjoining illustration. How it works is described in detail in the Layers Dialog section, but we will touch on some aspects of it here, in relation to the layer properties that they display.

Each open image has at any time a single *active drawable*. A "drawable" is a GIMP concept that includes layers, but also several other types of things, such as channels, layer masks, and the selection mask. (Basically, a "drawable" is anything that can be drawn on with painting tools). If a layer is currently active, it is shown highlighted in the Layers dialog, and its name is shown in the status area of the image window. If not, you can activate it by clicking on it. If none of the layers are highlighted, it means the active drawable is something other than a layer.

In the menubar above an image window, you can find a menu called Layer, containing a number of commands that affect the active layer of the image. The same menu can be accessed by right-clicking in the Layers dialog.

8.1.1 Layer Properties

Each layer in an image has a number of important attributes:

Name Every layer has a name. This is assigned automatically when the layer is created, but you can change it. You can change the name of a layer either by double-clicking on it in the Layers dialog, or by right-clicking there and then selecting the top entry in the menu that appears, Edit Layer Attributes.

Presence or absence of an alpha channel An alpha channel encodes information about how transparent a layer is at each pixel. It is visible in the Channel Dialog: white is complete opacity, black is complete transparency and grey levels are partial transparencies.

The background layer is particular. If you have just created a new image, it has still only one layer which is a background layer. If the image has been created with an opaque Fill type, this one layer has no Alpha channel. If you add a new layer, even with an opaque Fill type, an Alpha channel is automatically created, which applies to all layers apart from the background layer. To get a background layer with transparency, either you create your new image with a transparent Fill type, or you use the Add an Alpha Channel.

Every layer other than the bottom layer of an image has automatically an Alpha channel, but you can't see a grayscale representation of the alpha values. See Alpha in Glossary for more information.

Example for Alpha channel

Figure 8.1 Alpha channel example: Basic image

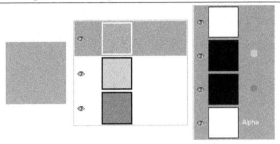

This image has three layers painted with pure 100% opaque Red, Green, and Blue. In the Channel Dialog, you can see that an alpha Channel has been added. It is white because the image is not transparent since there is at least one 100% opaque layer. The current layer is the red one : since it is painted with pure red, there is no green and no blue and the corresponding channels are black.

Figure 8.2 Alpha channel example: One transparent layer

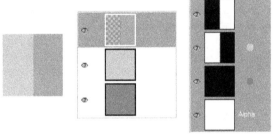

The left part of the first layer has been made transparent (Rectangular selection, Edit/Clear). The second layer, green, is visible. The Alpha channel is still white, since there is an opaque layer in this part of the image.

Figure 8.3 Alpha channel example: Two transparent layers

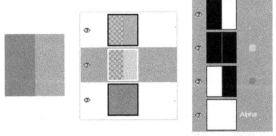

The left part of the second layer has been made transparent. The third layer, blue, is visible through the first and second layers. The Alpha channel is still white, since there is an opaque layer in this part of the image.

Figure 8.4 Alpha channel example: Three transparent layers

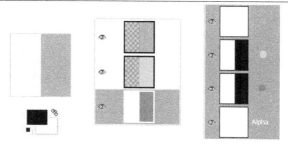

The left part of the third layer has been made transparent. The Alpha channel is still white and the left part of the layer is white, opaque! The background layer has no Alpha channel. In this case, the Clear command works like the Eraser and uses the Background color of Toolbox.

Figure 8.5 Alpha channel example: Alpha channel added to the Background

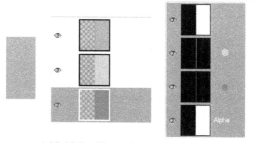

We used the Layer → Transparency → Add Alpha Channel command, on the Background layer. Now, the left part of the image is fully transparent and has the color of the page the image is lying on. The left part of the Alpha Channel thumbnail is black (transparent) in the Channel Dialog.

Layer type The layer type is determined by the image type (see previous section) and the presence or absence of an alpha channel. These are the possible layer types:

- RGB
- RGBA
- Gray
- GrayA
- Indexed
- IndexedA

The main reason this matters is that most filters (in the Filters menu) only accept a subset of layer types, and appear grayed out in the menu if the active layer does not have an acceptable type. Often you can rectify this either by changing the mode of the image or by adding or removing an alpha channel.

Visibility It is possible to remove a layer from an image, without destroying it, by clicking on the symbol in the Layers dialog. This is called "toggling the visibility" of the layer. Most operations on an image treat toggled-off layers as if they did not exist. When you work with images containing many layers, with varying opacity, you often can get a better picture of the contents of the layer you want to work on by hiding some of the other layers.

Tip

If you *Shift*-click on the eye symbol, this will cause all layers *except* the one you click on to be hidden.

Linkage to other layers If you click between the eye icon and the layer thumbnail, you get a chain icon, which enables you to group layers for operations on multiple layers (for example with the Move tool or a transform tool).

Figure 8.6 Layer Dialog

Red: Linkage to others layers. Green: Visibility.

Size and boundaries In GIMP, the boundaries of a layer do not necessarily match the boundaries of the image that contains it. When you create text, for example, each text item goes into its own separate layer, and the layer is precisely sized to contain the text and nothing more. Also, when you create a new layer using cut-and-paste, the new layer is sized just large enough to contain the pasted item. In the image window, the boundaries of the currently active layer are shown outlined with a black-and-yellow dashed line.

The main reason why this matters is that you cannot do anything to a layer outside of its boundaries: you can't act on what doesn't exist. If this causes you problems, you can alter the dimensions of the layer using any of several commands that you can find near the bottom of the Layer menu.

Note

The amount of memory that a layer consumes is determined by its dimensions, not its contents. So, if you are working with large images or images that contain many layers, it might pay off to trim layers to the minimum possible size.

Opacity The opacity of a layer determines the extent to which it lets colors from layers beneath it in the stack show through. Opacity ranges from 0 to 100, with 0 meaning complete transparency, and 100 meaning complete opacity.

Mode The Mode of a layer determines how colors from the layer are combined with colors from the underlying layers to produce a visible result. This is a sufficiently complex, and sufficiently important, concept to deserve a section of its own, which follows. See Section 8.2.

Layer mask In addition to the alpha channel, there is another way to control the transparency of a layer: by adding a *layer mask*, which is an extra grayscale drawable associated with the layer. A layer does not have a layer mask by default: it must be added specifically. Layer masks, and how to work with them, are described much more extensively in the Layer Mask section.

"Lock alpha channel" setting In the upper left corner of the Layers dialog appears a small checkbox that controls the "Lock" setting for the transparency of the layer (see the figure below). If this is checked, then the alpha channel for the layer is locked, and no manipulation has any effect on it. In particular, nothing that you do to a transparent part of the layer will have any effect.

Figure 8.7 Lock Alpha channel

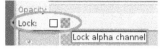

8.2 Layer Modes

GIMP has twenty-one layer modes. Layer modes are also sometimes called "blending modes". Selecting a layer mode changes the appearance of the layer or image, based on the layer or layers beneath it. If there is only one layer, the layer mode has no effect. There must therefore be at least two layers in the image to be able to use layer modes.

You can set the layer mode in the Mode menu in the Layers dialog. GIMP uses the layer mode to determine how to combine each pixel in the top layer with the pixel in the same location in the layer below it.

> **Note**
>
> There is a drop-down list in the Toolbox options box which contains modes that affect the painting tools in a similar way to the layer modes. You can use all of the same modes for painting that are available for layers, and there are two additional modes just for the painting tools. See Section 14.3.3.

Layer modes permit complex color changes in the image. They are often used with a new layer which acts as a kind of mask. For example, if you put a solid white layer over an image and set the layer mode of the new layer to "Saturation", the underlying visible layers will appear in shades of gray.

Figure 8.8 Images (masks) for layer mode examples

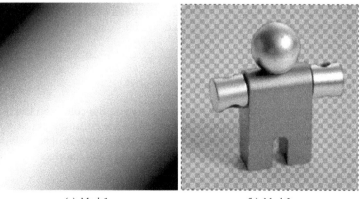

(a) *Mask 1*   (b) *Mask 2*

Figure 8.9 Images (backgrounds) for layer mode examples

(a) *Key fob*   (b) *Ducks*

In the descriptions of the layer modes below, the equations are also shown. This is for those who are curious about the mathematics of the layer modes. You do not need to understand the equations in order to use the layer modes effectively, however.

The equations are in a shorthand notation. For example, the equation

Equation 8.1 Example

$$E = M + I$$

means, " For each pixel in the upper (*Mask*)and lower (*Image*) layer, add each of the corresponding color components together to form the *E* resulting pixel's color. " Pixel color components must always be between 0 and 255.

> **Note**
>
> Unless the description below says otherwise, a negative color component is set to 0 and a color component larger than 255 is set to 255.

The examples below show the effects of each of the modes.

Since the results of each mode vary greatly depending upon the colors on the layers, these images can only give you a general idea of how the modes work. You are encouraged to try them out yourself. You might start with two similar layers, where one is a copy of the other, but slightly modified (by being blurred, moved, rotated, scaled, color-inverted, etc.) and seeing what happens with the layer modes.

Normal

Figure 8.10 Example for layer mode "Normal"

(a) Both images are blended into each other with (b) With 100% opacity only the upper layer is
the same intensity.   shown when blending with "Normal".

Normal mode is the default layer mode. The layer on top covers the layers below it. If you want to see anything below the top layer when you use this mode, the layer must have some transparent areas.

The equation is:

Equation 8.2 Equation for layer mode Normal

$$E = M$$

Dissolve

Figure 8.11 Example for layer mode "Dissolve"

(a) Both images are blended into each other with (b) With 100% opacity only the upper layer is
the same intensity.   shown when blending with "dissolve".

Dissolve mode dissolves the upper layer into the layer beneath it by drawing a random pattern of pixels in areas of partial transparency. It is useful as a layer mode, but it is also often useful as a painting mode.

This is especially visible along the edges within an image. It is easiest to see in an enlarged screenshot. The image on the left illustrates "Normal" layer mode (enlarged) and the image on the right shows the same two layers in "Dissolve" mode, where it can be clearly seen how the pixels are dispersed.

Figure 8.12 Enlarged screenshots

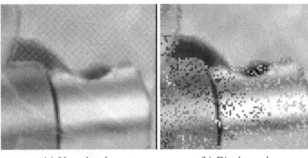

(a) *Normal mode.*   (b) *Dissolve mode.*

Multiply

Figure 8.13 Example for layer mode "Multiply"

(a) *Mask 1 is used as upper layer with 100%* (b) *Mask 2 is used as upper layer with 100%*
opacity.   *opacity.*

Multiply mode multiplies the pixel values of the upper layer with those of the layer below it and then divides the result by 255. The result is usually a darker image. If either layer is white, the resulting image is the same as the other layer (1 * I = I). If either layer is black, the resulting image is completely black (0 * I = 0).

The equation is:

Equation 8.3 Equation for layer mode Multiply

$$E = \frac{M \times I}{255}$$

The mode is commutative; the order of the two layers doesn't matter.

Divide

Figure 8.14 Example for layer mode "Divide"

(a) *Mask 1 is used as upper layer with 100% opacity.*

(b) *Mask 2 is used as upper layer with 100% opacity.*

Divide mode multiplies each pixel value in the lower layer by 256 and then divides that by the corresponding pixel value of the upper layer plus one. (Adding one to the denominator avoids dividing by zero.) The resulting image is often lighter, and sometimes looks "burned out".

The equation is:

Equation 8.4 Equation for layer mode Divide

$$E = \frac{256 \times I}{M + 1}$$

Screen

Figure 8.15 Example for layer mode "Screen"

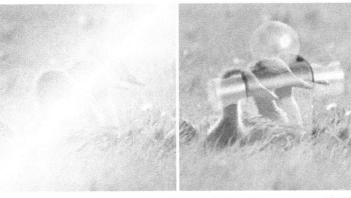

(a) *Mask 1 is used as upper layer with 100% opacity.* (b) *Mask 2 is used as upper layer with 100% opacity.*

Screen mode inverts the values of each of the visible pixels in the two layers of the image. (That is, it subtracts each of them from 255.) Then it multiplies them together, divides by 255 and inverts this value again. The resulting image is usually brighter, and sometimes "washed out" in appearance. The exceptions to this are a black layer, which does not change the other layer, and a white layer, which results in a white image. Darker colors in the image appear to be more transparent.

The equation is:

Equation 8.5 Equation for layer mode Screen

$$E = 255 - \frac{(255 - M) \times (255 - I)}{255}$$

The mode is commutative; the order of the two layers doesn't matter.

Overlay

Figure 8.16 Example for layer mode "Overlay"

(a) *Mask 1 is used as upper layer with 100% opacity.* (b) *Mask 2 is used as upper layer with 100% opacity.*

Overlay mode inverts the pixel value of the lower layer, multiplies it by two times the pixel value of the upper layer, adds that to the original pixel value of the lower layer, divides by 255, and then multiplies by the pixel value of the original lower layer and divides by 255 again. It darkens the image, but not as much as with "Multiply" mode.

The equation is: [1]

Equation 8.6 Equation for layer mode Overlay

$$E = \frac{I}{255} \times \left(I + \frac{2 \times M}{255} \times (255 - I) \right)$$

Dodge

Figure 8.17 Example for layer mode "Dodge"

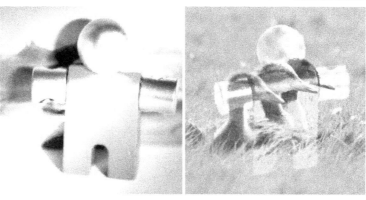

(a) *Mask 1 is used as upper layer with 100%* (b) *Mask 2 is used as upper layer with 100%*
opacity.   *opacity.*

Dodge mode multiplies the pixel value of the lower layer by 256, then divides that by the inverse of the pixel value of the top layer. The resulting image is usually lighter, but some colors may be inverted.

In photography, dodging is a technique used in a darkroom to decrease the exposure in particular areas of the image. This brings out details in the shadows. When used for this purpose, dodge may work best on Grayscale images and with a painting tool, rather than as a layer mode.

The equation is:

Equation 8.7 Equation for layer mode Dodge

$$E = \frac{256 \times I}{(255 - M) + 1}$$

Burn

---

[1] The equation is the *theoretical* equation. Due to Bug #162395 , the actual equation is equivalent to Soft light. It is difficult to fix this bug without changing the appearance of existing images.

Figure 8.18 Example for layer mode "Burn"

(a) *Mask 1 is used as upper layer with 100% opacity.* (b) *Mask 2 is used as upper layer with 100% opacity.*

Burn mode inverts the pixel value of the lower layer, multiplies it by 256, divides that by one plus the pixel value of the upper layer, then inverts the result. It tends to make the image darker, somewhat similar to "Multiply" mode.

In photography, burning is a technique used in a darkroom to increase the exposure in particular areas of the image. This brings out details in the highlights. When used for this purpose, burn may work best on Grayscale images and with a painting tool, rather than as a layer mode.

The equation is:

Equation 8.8 Equation for layer mode Burn

$$E = 255 - \frac{256 \times (255 - I)}{M + 1}$$

Hard light

Figure 8.19 Example for layer mode "Hard light"

(a) *Mask 1 is used as upper layer with 100% opacity.* (b) *Mask 2 is used as upper layer with 100% opacity.*

Hard light mode is rather complicated because the equation consists of two parts, one for darker colors and one for brighter colors. If the pixel color of the upper layer is greater than 128, the layers are combined according to the first formula shown below. Otherwise, the pixel values of the upper and lower layers are multiplied together and multiplied by two, then divided by 256. You might use this mode to combine two photographs and obtain bright colors and sharp edges.

The equation is complex and different according to the value >128 or ≤ 128:

Equation 8.9 Equation for layer mode Hard light, M > 128

$$E = 255 - \frac{(255 - 2 \times (M - 128)) \times (255 - I)}{256}, \qquad M > 128$$

Equation 8.10 Equation for layer mode Hard light, M ≤ 128

$$E = \frac{2 \times M \times I}{256}, \qquad M \leq 128$$

Soft light

Figure 8.20 Example for layer mode "Soft light"

(a) *Mask 1 is used as upper layer with 100%* (b) *Mask 2 is used as upper layer with 100%*
opacity. *opacity.*

Soft light is not related to "Hard light" in anything but the name, but it does tend to make the edges softer and the colors not so bright. It is similar to "Overlay" mode. In some versions of GIMP, "Overlay" mode and "Soft light" mode are identical.

The equation is complicated. It needs Rs, the result of Screen mode :

Equation 8.11 Equation for layer mode Screen

$$R_s = 255 - \frac{(255 - M) \times (255 - I)}{255}$$

Equation 8.12 Equation for layer mode Soft light

$$E = \frac{(255 - I) \times M + R_s}{255} \times I$$

Grain extract

119

Figure 8.21 Example for layer mode "Grain extract"

(a) *Mask 1 is used as upper layer with 100%* (b) *Mask 2 is used as upper layer with 100%*
opacity.   *opacity.*

Grain extract mode is supposed to extract the "film grain" from a layer to produce a new layer that is pure grain, but it can also be useful for giving images an embossed appearance. It subtracts the pixel value of the upper layer from that of the lower layer and adds 128.

The equation is:

Equation 8.13 Equation for layer mode Grain extract

$$E = I - M + 128$$

Grain merge There are two more layer modes, but these are available only for painting tools. See Painting Modes for detailed information.

Figure 8.22 Example for layer mode "Grain merge"

(a) *Mask 1 is used as upper layer with 100%* (b) *Mask 2 is used as upper layer with 100%*
opacity.   *opacity.*

Grain merge mode merges a grain layer (possibly one created from the "Grain extract" mode) into the current layer, leaving a grainy version of the original layer. It does just the opposite of "Grain extract". It adds the pixel values of the upper and lower layers together and subtracts 128.

The equation is:

Equation 8.14 Equation for layer mode Grain merge

$$E = I + M - 128$$

Difference

Figure 8.23 Example for layer mode "Difference"

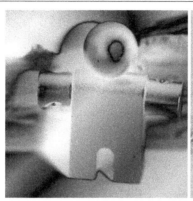

(a) *Mask 1 is used as upper layer with 100% opacity.* (b) *Mask 2 is used as upper layer with 100% opacity.*

Difference mode subtracts the pixel value of the upper layer from that of the lower layer and then takes the absolute value of the result. No matter what the original two layers look like, the result looks rather odd. You can use it to invert elements of an image.

The equation is:

Equation 8.15 Equation for layer mode Difference

$$E = |I - M|$$

The mode is commutative; the order of the two layers doesn't matter.

Addition

Figure 8.24 Example for layer mode "Addition"

(a) *Mask 1 is used as upper layer with 100% opacity.* (b) *Mask 2 is used as upper layer with 100% opacity.*

Addition mode is very simple. The pixel values of the upper and lower layers are added to each other. The resulting image is usually lighter. The equation can result in color values greater than 255, so some of the light colors may be set to the maximum value of 255.

The equation is:

Equation 8.16 Equation for layer mode Addition

$$E = \min\big((M + I), 255\big)$$

The mode is commutative; the order of the two layers doesn't matter.

Subtract

Figure 8.25 Example for layer mode "Subtract"

(a) Mask 1 is used as upper layer with 100% opacity. (b) Mask 2 is used as upper layer with 100% opacity.

Subtract mode subtracts the pixel values of the upper layer from the pixel values of the lower layer. The resulting image is normally darker. You might get a lot of black or near-black in the resulting image. The equation can result in negative color values, so some of the dark colors may be set to the minimum value of 0.

The equation is:

Equation 8.17 Equation for layer mode Subtraction

$$E = \max\big((I - M), 0\big)$$

Darken only

Figure 8.26 Example for layer mode "Darken only"

(a) *Mask 1 is used as upper layer with 100% opacity.* (b) *Mask 2 is used as upper layer with 100% opacity.*

Darken only mode compares each component of each pixel in the upper layer with the corresponding one in the lower layer and uses the smaller value in the resulting image. Completely white layers have no effect on the final image and completely black layers result in a black image.

The equation is:

Equation 8.18 Equation for layer mode Darken only

$$E = \min(M, I)$$

The mode is commutative; the order of the two layers doesn't matter.

Lighten only

Figure 8.27 Example for layer mode "Lighten only"

(a) *Mask 1 is used as upper layer with 100% opacity.* (b) *Mask 2 is used as upper layer with 100% opacity.*

Lighten only mode compares each component of each pixel in the upper layer with the corresponding one in the lower layer and uses the larger value in the resulting image. Completely black layers have no effect on the final image and completely white layers result in a white image.

The equation is:

Equation 8.19 Equation for layer mode Lighten only

$$E = \max(M, I)$$

The mode is commutative; the order of the two layers doesn't matter.

Hue

Figure 8.28 Example for layer mode "Hue"

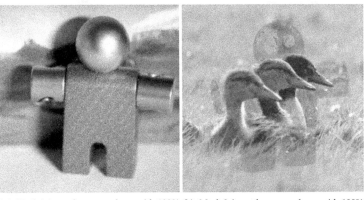

(a) *Mask 1 is used as upper layer with 100% opacity.* (b) *Mask 2 is used as upper layer with 100% opacity.*

Hue mode uses the hue of the upper layer and the saturation and value of the lower layer to form the resulting image. However, if the saturation of the upper layer is zero, the hue is taken from the lower layer, too.

Saturation

Figure 8.29 Example for layer mode "Saturation"

(a) *Mask 1 is used as upper layer with 100% opacity.* (b) *Mask 2 is used as upper layer with 100% opacity.*

Saturation mode uses the saturation of the upper layer and the hue and value of the lower layer to form the resulting image.

Color

Figure 8.30 Example for layer mode "Color"

(a) *Mask 1 is used as upper layer with 100% opacity.* (b) *Mask 2 is used as upper layer with 100% opacity.*

Color mode uses the hue and saturation of the upper layer and the value of the lower layer to form the resulting image.

Value

Figure 8.31 Example for layer mode "Value"

(a) *Mask 1 is used as upper layer with 100% opacity.* (b) *Mask 2 is used as upper layer with 100% opacity.*

Value mode uses the value of the upper layer and the saturation and hue of the lower layer to form the resulting image. You can use this mode to reveal details in dark and light areas of an image without changing the saturation.

Each layer in an image can have a different layer mode. (Of course, the layer mode of the bottom layer of an image has no effect.) The effects of these layer modes are cumulative. The image shown below has three layers. The top layer consists of Wilber surrounded by transparency and has a layer mode of "Difference". The second layer is solid light blue and has a layer mode of "Addition". The bottom layer is filled with the "Red Cubes" pattern.

Figure 8.32 Multi layer example

GIMP also has similar modes which are used for the painting tools. These are the same twenty-one modes as the layer modes, plus additionally two modes which are specific to the painting tools. You can set these modes from the Mode menu in the Tools option dialog. In the equations shown above, the layer you are painting on is the "lower layer" and the pixels painted by the tool are the "upper layer". Naturally, you do not need more than one layer in the image to use these modes, since they only operate on the current layer and the selected painting tool.

See Section 14.3.1.3 for a description of the two additional painting modes.

8.3 Creating New Layers

There are several ways to create new layers in an image. Here are the most important ones:

- Selecting Layer → New Layer in the image menu. This brings up a dialog that allows you to set the basic properties of the new layer; see the New Layer dialog section for help with it.

- Selecting Layer → Duplicate Layer in the image menu. This creates a new layer, that is a perfect copy of the currently active layer, just above the active layer.

- When you "cut" or "copy" something, and then paste it using Ctrl-V or Edit → Paste, the result is a "floating selection", which is a sort of temporary layer. Before you can do anything else, you either have to anchor the floating selection to an existing layer, or convert it into a normal layer. If you do the latter, the new layer will be sized just large enough to contain the pasted material.

8.4 Layer Groups

This possibility appeared with GIMP-2.8.

You can group layers that have similarities in a tree-like way. So, the layer list becomes easier to manage.

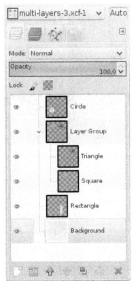

Create a Layer Group You can create a layer group by clicking on the Create a new layer group button at the bottom of the layer dialog,

through Layer → New Layer Group, or through the layer dialog context menu.

This empty layer group appears just above the current layer. It is important to give it an evocative name (double-click or **F2** on the name, or use **Edit Layer Attributes** in the context menu you get by right clicking the Layer dialog, to edit it), else you will get confused when several ones are created.

You can create several layer groups and you can **embbed** them, that is include a layer group in another one.

Adding Layers to a Layer Group You can add *existing layers* to a layer group by click-and-dragging them.

Note

The hand representing the mouse pointer must turn smaller before releasing the mouse button.

A thin horizontal line marks where the layer will be laid down.

To add a *new layer* to the current layer group, click on the Create a new layer at the bottom of the layer dialog, or use the New Layer command in the image menu.

When a layer group is not empty, a small ">" icon appears. By clicking on it, you can fold/unfold the layer list.

Layers that belong to a layer group are slightly indented to the right, allowing you know easily which layers are part of the group.

Raise and Lower Layer Groups You can raise and lower layer groups in the layer dialog as you do with normal layers: click-and-dragging, using arrow up and down keys at the bottom of the layer dialog.

Duplicate a Layer Group You can duplicate a layer group: click on the Create a duplicate of the layer button or right-click and select the **Duplicate Layer** command in the pop up context menu.

Move Layer Groups You can **move a layer group to another image** by click-and-dragging. You can also copy-paste it using Ctrl-C and Ctrl-V: then, you get a floating selection that you must anchor (anchor button at the bottom of the layer dialog).

You can also **move a layer group to the canvas**: this duplicates the group *in* the group. Chain all layers in the duplicated layer group, activate the Move tool, then, in the image, move the layer. That's a way to multiply multi-layer objects in an image.

Delete a Layer Group To delete a layer group, click on the red cross button at the bottom of the layer dialog or right-click and select **Delete layer**.

Embed Layer Groups When a layer group is activated, you can add another group inside it with the "Add New Layer Group" command. There seems to be no limit, excepted memory, to the number of embedded layer groups.

Layer Modes and Groups A layer mode applied to a layer group acts on layers that are in this group only. A layer mode above a layer group acts on all layers underneath, outside and inside the layer groups.

Original image

Figure 8.33 Layer Mode in or out Layer Group

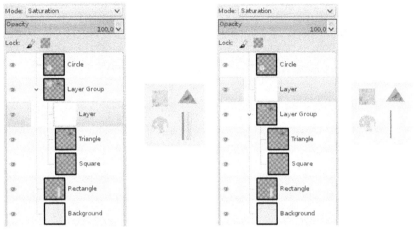

(a) *We added a white layer in the layer group with saturation mode: only square and triangle are grayed out.*
(b) *We added a white layer out of the layer group with saturation mode: all layers underneath are grayed out, background layer also.*

Opacity When a layer group is activated, opacity changes are applied to all the layers of the group.

Layer Mask You cannot add a layer mask to a layer group (the corresponding option is grayed out). But, as with normal layers, you can add a layer mask to a layer in the group to mask a part of the layer.

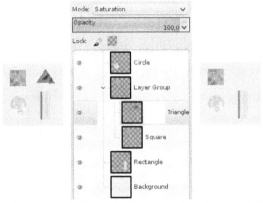

We added a white (Full opacity) layer mask to the triangle layer.

Chapter 9

Text Management

9.1 Text Management

Text is managed with the Text tool. This tool creates a new layer containing the text, above the current layer in the layer dialog, with the size of the text box. Its name is the beginning of the text.

Figure 9.1 Example of a text item

(a) *Example of a text item,* (b) *The layer dialog, with the*
showing the boundary of the *text layer above the layer which*
text layer. *(Font: Utopia* *was current.*
Bold)

The Text tool is progressively improved. With GIMP-2.8, you can now edit text directly on canvas. A text tool box has been added which overlays the canvas above the text box.

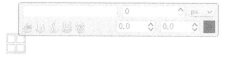

As soon as you click on the canvas with the Text tool, you get a closed text box and a semi-transparent tool box just above.

Text tool options are described in Section 14.6.6.

9.1.1 Text Area

You can start typing text at once. The text box will enlarge gradually. Press **Enter** to add a new line.

You can also **enlarge the text box** by click-and-dragging, as you do with selections. The box size appears then in the status bar at the bottom of the image:

To **edit text**, you must, first, select the part you want to edit by click-and-drag, or Shift-arrow keys and then use the options of the Section 9.1.3.

Instead of using the on-canvas text editing, you can use the text editor dialog described in Section 14.6.6.3.

You can **move the text** on the image using the Move tool: you must click on a character, not on the background.

You can get Unicode characters with Ctrl-Shift-U plus hexadecimal Unicode code of the desired char, for example:

Figure 9.2 Entering Unicode characters

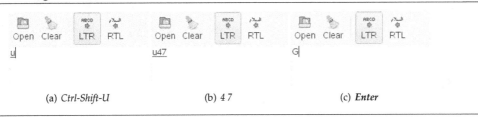

(a) *Ctrl-Shift-U*   (b) *4 7*   (c) *Enter*

Of course this feature is more useful for entering special (even exotic) characters, provided that the required glyphs for these characters are supplied by the selected font — only few fonts support Klingon. ;-)

Unicode 0x47 ("G"), 0x2665, 0x0271, 0x03C0

You can **edit the text later,** if the text layer still exists and has not been modified by another tool (see below): make the text layer active in the Layer dialog, select the Text tool and click on the text in the image window.

9.1.2 Managing Text Layer

You can operate on a text layer in the same ways as any other layer, but doing so often means giving up the ability to edit the text without losing the results of your work.

To understand some of the idiosyncrasies of text handling, it may help for you to realize that a text layer contains more information than the pixel data that you see: it also contains a representation of the text in a text-editor format. You can see this in the text-editor window that pops up while you are using the Text tool. Every time you alter the text, the image layer is redrawn to reflect your changes.

Now suppose you create a text layer, and then operate on it in some way that does not involve the Text tool: rotate it, for example. Suppose you then come back and try to edit it using the Text tool. As soon as you edit the text, the Text tool will redraw the layer, wiping out the results of the operations you performed in the meantime.

Because this danger is not obvious, the Text tool tries to protect you from it. If you operate on a text layer, and then later try to edit the text, a message pops up, warning you that your alterations will be undone, and giving you three options:

- edit the text anyway;

- cancel;

- create a new text layer with the same text as the existing layer, leaving the existing layer unchanged.

Figure 9.3 Warning lose modifications

9.1.3   Text Toolbox

Figure 9.4 Text Toolbox

You get this box, which overlays canvas, as soon as you click on canvas with the Text Tool. It allows you to edit text directly on canvas.

Apart from the usual text formatting features like font family, style and size selectors you get numeric control over baseline offset and kerning, as well as the ability to change text color for a selection.

- **Change font of selected text**: as soon as you start editing the default font name, a drop-down list appears, allowing you to select a font.

- **Change size of selected text**: self-explanatory.

- **Bold, Italic, Underline, Strikethrough** : self-explanatory.

- **Change baseline of selected text**: "In European typography and penmanship, baseline is the line upon which most letters "sit" and below which descenders extend" (Wikipedia). In HTML, there are several kinds of baselines (alphabetic, ideographic, bottom...). Here, consider that baseline is "bottom" and determines the place for descenders. The default baseline "0" gives place for descenders. You can use it to increase space between two lines only, while "Adjust line spacing" in tool options increases space between all lines.

Figure 9.5 Default Baseline

Default baseline marked with a red line.

- **Change kerning of selected text**: "In typography, kerning... is the process of adjusting the spacing between characters in a proportional font." (Wikipedia). You will probably use this setting to adjust letter spacing of a selected part of text.

  Let us look at a selected text (zoomx800 to see pixels):

We can see that the Sans font is a proportional font: letters widths are different, and "T" glyph comes over the "e". Letters widths are marked with thin vertical lines and left borders of letter width cover preceding letters by one pixel. Now we set "Change kerning of selected text" to 2 pixels:

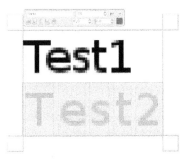

Blank spaces, 2 pixels wide, are added between all selected characters and letter widths are preserved. If no text is selected, a blank space is added at the place of the mouse pointer between two characters.

Now, we compare with the "Adjust letter spacing" option of Text tool:

The option applies to the whole text, not only to the selected text. Blank spaces are added inside letters widths and letter widths are not respected.

- You can also use Alt-arrow keys to change baseline offset and kerning.

- **Change color of selected text**: this command opens a color dialog where you choose a color for the selected text.

- **Clear style of selected text**: using this command, you can get rid of all new settings you applied to the selected text.

9.1.4   Text Context Menu

Figure 9.6 Text Editing Context Menu

You get this menu by right-clicking on text. It is somewhat different from that of the Text Editor dialog.

- Cut, Copy, Paste, Delete: these options concern a selected text. They remain grayed out as long as no text is selected. "Paste" is activated if the clipboard is full of text.

- Open text file: this command opens a file browser where you can find the wanted text file.

- Clear: this command deletes all the text, selected or not.

- Path from text: this command creates a path from the outlines of the current text. The result is not evident. You have to open the Path dialog and make path visible. Then select the Path tool and click on the text. Every letter is now surrounded with a path component. So you can modify the shape of letters by moving path control points.

  This command is similar to Layer → Text to Path.

Figure 9.7 Text to path applied

Nothing appears.

Figure 9.8 Path made visible

Path made visible in Path tab. Path appears as a red border around text.

Figure 9.9 Path tool activated

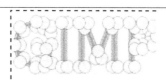

Path tool activated; click on path.

- Text along path:

  This option is enabled only if a path exists. When your text is created, then create or import a path and make it active. If you create your path before the text, the path becomes invisible and you have to make it visible in the Path Dialog.

  This command is also available from the "Layer" menu:

Figure 9.10 The Text along Path command among text commands in the Layer menu

This group of options appears only if a text layer exists.

Click on the Text along Path button. The text is bent along the path. Letters are represented with their outline. Each of them is a component of the new path that appears in the Path dialog. All path options should apply to this new path.

Figure 9.11 "Text along Path" example

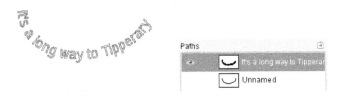

- From Left to Right / From Right to Left: fix the writing direction of your language.

- Input Methods: methods are available for some languages. For example, selecting "Inuktitut" transforms your keyboard into an Inuktitut keyboard, temporarily.

9.2 Text

9.2.1 Embellishing Text

Figure 9.12 Fancy text

Four fancy text items created using logo scripts: "alien neon", "bovination", "frosty", and "chalk". Default settings were used for everything except font size.

There are many things you can do to vary the appearance of text beyond just rendering it with different fonts or different colors. By converting a text item to a selection or a path, you can fill it, stroke the outlines, transform it, or generally apply the whole panoply of GIMP tools to get interesting effects. As a demonstration of some of the possibilities, try out the "logo" scripts at File → Create → Logos. Each of these scripts allows you to enter some text, and then creates a new image showing a logo constructed out of that text. If you would like to modify one of these scripts, or construct a logo script of your own, the Using Script-Fu and Script-Fu Tutorial sections should help you get started. Of course, you don't need Script-Fu to create these sorts of effects, only to automate them.

9.2.2 Adding Fonts

For the most authoritative and up-to-date information on fonts in GIMP, consult the "Fonts in GIMP 2.0" page [GIMP-FONTS] at the GIMP web site. This section attempts to give you a helpful overview.

GIMP uses the FreeType 2 font engine to render fonts, and a system called Fontconfig to manage them. GIMP will let you use any font in Fontconfig's font path; it will also let you use any font it finds in GIMP's font search path, which is set on the Font Folders page of the Preferences dialog. By default, the font search path includes a system GIMP-fonts folder (which you should not alter, even though it is actually empty), and a `fonts` folder inside your personal GIMP directory. You can add new folders to the font search path if it is more convenient for you.

FreeType 2 is a very powerful and flexible system. By default, it supports the following font file formats:

- TrueType fonts (and collections)

- Type 1 fonts

- CID-keyed Type 1 fonts

- CFF fonts

- OpenType fonts (both TrueType and CFF variants)

- SFNT-based bitmap fonts

- X11 PCF fonts

- Windows FNT fonts

- BDF fonts (including anti-aliased ones)

- PFR fonts

- Type42 fonts (limited support)

You can also add modules to support other types of font files. See FREETYPE 2 [FREETYPE] for more information.

Linux On a Linux system, if the Fontconfig utility is set up as usual, all you need to do to add a new font is to place the file in the directory `~/.fonts`. This will make the font available not only to GIMP, but to any other program that uses Fontconfig. If for some reason you want the font to be available to GIMP only, you can place it in the `fonts` sub-directory of your personal GIMP directory, or some other location in your font search path. Doing either will cause the font to show up the next time you start GIMP. If you want to use it in an already running GIMP, press the *Refresh* button in the Fonts dialog.

Windows The easiest way to install a font is to drag the file onto the Fonts directory and let the shell do its magic. Unless you've done something creative, it's probably in its default location of `C:\\windows\\fonts` or `C:\\winnt\\fonts`. Sometimes double-clicking on a font will install it as well as display it; sometimes it only displays it. This method will make the font available not only to GIMP, but also to other Windows applications.

Mac OS X There are several ways to install fonts on your system. You can drag-and-drop them to the "Fonts" folder in "Libraries" folder of your "Home Folder". Or you may use Font Book, invoked by double-clicking the font file icon in the Finder. You can see what the font looks like, and click your favorite fonts so that their files are to be installed on the system. These methods will make the fonts available for all applications, not only GIMP. If you want all users can use the fonts, drag-and-drop the fonts to the "Fonts" folder in "Libraries" folder of the Mac OS X Disk, or to the "Computer" folder in the Collection column of Font Book.

To install a Type 1 file, you need both the `.pfb` and `.pfm` files. Drag the one that gets an icon into the fonts folder. The other one doesn't strictly need to be in the same directory when you drag the file, since it uses some kind of search algorithm to find it if it's not, but in any case putting it in the same directory does no harm.

In principle, GIMP can use any type of font on Windows that FreeType can handle; however, for fonts that Windows can't handle natively, you should install them by placing the font files in the `fonts` folder of your personal GIMP directory, or some other location in your font search path. The support Windows has varies by version. All that GIMP runs on support at least TrueType, Windows FON, and Windows FNT. Windows 2000 and later support Type 1 and OpenType. Windows ME supports OpenType and possibly Type 1 (but the most widely used Windows GIMP installer does not officially support Windows ME, although it may work anyway).

> **Note**
>
> GIMP uses Fontconfig to manage fonts on Windows as well as Linux. The instructions above work because Fontconfig by default uses the Windows fonts directory, i. e., the same fonts that Windows uses itself. If for some reason your Fontconfig is set up differently, you will have to figure out where to put fonts so that GIMP can find them: in any case, the `fonts` folder of your personal GIMP directory should work.

9.2.3   Font Problems

Problems with fonts have probably been responsible for more GIMP 2 bug reports than any other single cause, although they have become much less frequent in the most recent releases in the 2.0 series. In most cases they have been caused by malformed font files giving trouble to Fontconfig. If you experience crashes at start-up when GIMP scans your font directories, the best solution is to upgrade to a version of Fontconfig newer than 2.2.0. As a quick workaround you can start gimp with the `--no-fonts` command-line option, but then you will not be able to use the text tool.

Another known problem is that Pango 1.2 cannot load fonts that don't provide an Unicode character mapping. (Pango is the text layout library used by GIMP.) A lot of symbol fonts fall into this category. On some systems, using such a font can cause GIMP to crash. Updating to Pango 1.4 will fix this problem and makes symbol fonts available in GIMP.

A frequent source of confusion occurs on Windows systems, when GIMP encounters a malformed font file and generates an error message: this causes a console window to pop up so that you can see the message. *Do not close that console window. It is harmless, and closing it will shut down GIMP.* When this happens, it often seems to users that GIMP has crashed. It hasn't: closing the console window causes Windows to shut GIMP down. Unfortunately, this annoying situation is caused by an interaction between Windows and the libraries that GIMP links to: it cannot be fixed within GIMP. All you need to do, though, if this happens, is minimize the console window and ignore it.

Chapter 10

Enhancing Photographs

10.1 Working with Digital Camera Photos

10.1.1 Introduction

One of the most common uses of GIMP is to fix digital camera images that for some reason are less than perfect. Maybe the image is overexposed or underexposed; maybe rotated a bit; maybe out of focus: these are all common problems for which GIMP has good tools. The purpose of this chapter is to give you an overview of those tools and the situations in which they are useful. You will not find detailed tutorials here: in most cases it is easier to learn how to use the tools by experimenting with them than by reading about them. (Also, each tool is described more thoroughly in the Help section devoted to it.) You will also not find anything in this chapter about the multitude of "special effects" that you can apply to an image using GIMP. You should be familiar with basic GIMP concepts before reading this chapter, but you certainly don't need to be an expert–if you are, you probably know most of this anyway. And don't hesitate to experiment: GIMP's powerful "undo" system allows you to recover from almost any mistake with a simple Ctrl-Z.

Most commonly the things that you want to do to clean up an imperfect photo are of four types: improving the composition; improving the colors; improving the sharpness; and removing artifacts or other undesirable elements of the image.

10.1.2 Improving Composition

10.1.2.1 Rotating an Image

It is easy, when taking a picture, to hold the camera not quite perfectly vertical, resulting in a picture where things are tilted at an angle. In GIMP, the way to fix this is to use the Rotate tool. Activate this by clicking its icon ![icon] in the Toolbox, or by pressing the Shift-R while inside the image. Make sure the Tool Options are visible, and at the top, make sure for "Transform:" that the left button ("Transform Layer") is selected. If you then click the mouse inside the image and drag it, you will see a grid appear that rotates as you drag. When the grid looks right, click Rotate or press **Enter**, and the image will be rotated.

Now as a matter of fact, it isn't so easy to get things right by this method: you often find that things are better but not quite perfect. One solution is to rotate a bit more, but there is a disadvantage to that approach. Each time you rotate an image, because the rotated pixels don't line up precisely with the original pixels, the image inevitably gets blurred a little bit. For a single rotation, the amount of blurring is quite small, but two rotations cause twice as much blurring as one, and there is no reason to blur things more than you have to. A better alternative is to undo the rotation and then do another, adjusting the angle.

Fortunately, GIMP provides another way of doing it that is considerably easier to use: in the Rotate Tool Options, for the Transform Direction you can select "Backward (Corrective)". When you do this, instead of rotating the grid to compensate for the error, you can rotate it to *line up* with the error. If this seems confusing, try it and you will see that it is quite straightforward.

Note

 Since GIMP 2.2, there is an option to preview the results of transformations, instead of just seeing a grid. This makes it easier to get things right on the first try.

After you have rotated an image, there will be unpleasant triangular "holes" at the corners. One way to fix them is to create a background that fills the holes with some unobtrusive or neutral color, but usually a better solution is to crop the image. The greater the rotation, the more cropping is required, so it is best to get the camera aligned as well as possible when you take the picture in the first place.

10.1.2.2 Cropping

When you take a picture with a digital camera, you have some control over what gets included in the image but often not as much as you would like: the result is images that could benefit from trimming. Beyond this, it is often possible to enhance the impact of an image by trimming it so that the most important elements are placed at key points. A rule of thumb, not always to be followed but good to keep in mind, is the "rule of thirds", which says that maximum impact is obtained by placing the center of interest one-third of the way across the image, both widthwise and heightwise.

To crop an image, activate the Crop tool in the Toolbox, or by pressing the "C" key (capitalized) while inside the image. With the tool active, clicking and dragging in the image will sweep out a crop rectangle. It will also pop up a dialog that allows you to adjust the dimensions of the crop region if they aren't quite right. When everything is perfect, hit the Crop button in the dialog.

10.1.3 Improving Colors

10.1.3.1 Automated Tools

In spite of sophisticated exposure-control systems, pictures taken with digital cameras often come out over- or under-exposed, or with color casts due to imperfections in lighting. GIMP gives you a variety of tools to correct colors in an image, ranging to automated tools that run with a simple button-click to highly sophisticated tools that give you many parameters of control. We will start with the simplest first.

GIMP gives you several automated color correction tools. Unfortunately they don't usually give you quite the results you are looking for, but they only take a moment to try out, and if nothing else they often give you an idea of some of the possibilities inherent in the image. Except for "Auto Levels", you can find these tools by following the menu path Colors → Auto in the image menu.

Here they are, with a few words about each:

Normalize This tool (it is really a plug-in) is useful for underexposed images: it adjusts the whole image uniformly until the brightest point is right at the saturation limit, and the darkest point is black. The downside is that the amount of brightening is determined entirely by the lightest and darkest points in the image, so even one single white pixel and/or one single black pixel will make normalization ineffective.

Equalize This is a very powerful adjustment that tries to spread the colors in the image evenly across the range of possible intensities. In some cases the effect is amazing, bringing out contrasts that are very difficult to get in any other way; but more commonly, it just makes the image look weird. Oh well, it only takes a moment to try.

Color Enhance This command increases the saturation range of the colors in the layer, without altering brightness or hue. So this command does not work on grayscale images.

Stretch Contrast This is like "Normalize", except that it operates on the red, green, and blue channels independently. It often has the useful effect of reducing color casts.

Stretch HSV Does the same as Stretch Contrast but works in HSV color space, rather than RGB color space. It preserves the Hue.

White balance This may enhance images with poor white or black by removing little used colors and stretch the remaining range as much as possible.

Auto Levels This is done by activating the Levels tool (Tools → Color Tools → Levels or Colors → Levels in the image menu), and then pressing the Auto button near the center of the dialog. You will see a preview of the result; you must press Okay for it to take effect. Pressing Cancel instead will cause your image to revert to its previous state.

If you can find a point in the image that ought to be perfect white, and a second point that ought to be perfect black, then you can use the Levels tool to do a semi-automatic adjustment that will often do a good job of fixing both brightness and colors throughout the image. First, bring up the Levels tool as previously described. Now, look down near the bottom of the Layers dialog for three buttons with symbols on them that look like eye-droppers (at least, that is what they are supposed to look like). The one on the left, if you mouse over it, shows its function to be "Pick Black Point". Click on this, then click on a point in the image that ought to be black–really truly perfectly black, not just sort of dark–and watch the image change. Next, click on the rightmost of the three buttons ("Pick White Point"), and then click a point in the image that ought to be white, and once more watch the image change. If you are happy with the result, click the Okay button otherwise Cancel.

Those are the automated color adjustments: if you find that none of them quite does the job for you, it is time to try one of the interactive color tools. All of these, except one, can be accessed via Tools->Color Tools in the image menu. After you select a color tool, click on the image (anywhere) to activate it and bring up its dialog.

10.1.3.2 Exposure Problems

The simplest tool to use is the Brightness/Contrast tool. It is also the least powerful, but in many cases it does everything you need. This tool is often useful for images that are overexposed or underexposed; it is not useful for correcting color casts. The tool gives you two sliders to adjust, for "Brightness" and "Contrast". If you have the option "Preview" checked (and almost certainly you should),you will see any adjustments you make reflected in the image. When you are happy with the results, press Okay and they will take effect. If you can't get results that you are happy with, press Cancel and the image will revert to its previous state.

A more sophisticated, and only slightly more difficult, way of correcting exposure problems is to use the Levels tool. The dialog for this tool looks very complicated, but for the basic usage we have in mind here, the only part you need to deal with is the "Input Levels" area, specifically the three triangular sliders that appear below the histogram. We refer you to the Levels Tool Help for instructions; but actually the easiest way to learn how to use it is to experiment by moving the three sliders around, and watching how the image is affected. (Make sure that "Preview" is checked at the bottom of the dialog.)

A very powerful way of correcting exposure problems is to use the *Curves* tool. This tool allows you to click and drag control points on a curve, in order to create a function mapping input brightness levels to output brightness levels. The Curves tool can replicate any effect you can achieve with Brightness/-Contrast or the Levels tool, so it is more powerful than either of them. Once again, we refer you to the Curves Tool Help for detailed instructions, but the easiest way to learn how to use it is by experimenting.

The most powerful approach to adjusting brightness and contrast across an image, for more expert GIMP users, is to create a new layer above the one you are working on, and then in the Layers dialog set the Mode for the upper layer to "Multiply". The new layer then serves as a "gain control" layer for the layer below it, with white yielding maximum gain and black yielding a gain of zero. Thus, by painting on the new layer, you can selectively adjust the gain for each area of the image, giving you very fine control. You should try to paint only with smooth gradients, because sudden changes in gain will give rise to spurious edges in the result. Paint only using shades of gray, not colors, unless you want to produce color shifts in the image.

Actually, "Multiply" is not the only mode that is useful for gain control. In fact, "Multiply" mode can only darken parts of an image, never lighten them, so it is only useful where some parts of an image are overexposed. Using "Divide" mode has the opposite effect: it can brighten areas of an image but not darken them. Here is a trick that is often useful for bringing out the maximum amount of detail across all areas of an image:

1. Duplicate the layer (producing a new layer above it).

2. Desaturate the new layer.

3. Apply a Gaussian blur to the result, with a large radius (100 or more).

4. Set Mode in the Layers dialog to Divide.

5. Control the amount of correction by adjusting opacity in the Layers dialog, or by using Brightness/Contrast, Levels, or Curves tools on the new layer.

6. When you are happy with the result, you can use Merge Down to combine the control layer and the original layer into a single layer.

In addition to "Multiply" and "Divide", you may every so often get useful effects with other layer combination modes, such as "Dodge", "Burn", or "Soft Light". It is all too easy, though, once you start playing with these things, to look away from the computer for a moment and suddenly find that you have just spent an hour twiddling parameters. Be warned: the more options you have, the harder it is to make a decision.

10.1.3.3 Adjusting Hue and Saturation

In our experience, if your image has a color cast---too much red, too much blue, etc---the easiest way to correct it is to use the Levels tool, adjusting levels individually on the red, green, and blue channels. If this doesn't work for you, it might be worth your while to try the Color Balance tool or the Curves tool, but these are much more difficult to use effectively. (They are very good for creating certain types of special effects, though.)

Sometimes it is hard to tell whether you have adjusted colors adequately. A good, objective technique is to find a point in the image that you know should be either white or a shade of gray. Activate the Color Picker tool (the eyedropper symbol in the Toolbox), and click on the aforesaid point: this brings up the Color Picker dialog. If the colors are correctly adjusted, then the red, green, and blue components of the reported color should all be equal; if not, then you should see what sort of adjustment you need to make. This technique, when well used, allows even color-blind people to color-correct an image.

If your image is washed out---which can easily happen when you take pictures in bright light---try the Hue/Saturation tool, which gives you three sliders to manipulate, for Hue, Lightness, and Saturation. Raising the saturation will probably make the image look better. In same cases it is useful to adjust the lightness at the same time. ("Lightness" here is similar to "Brightness" in the Brightness/Contrast tool, except that they are formed from different combinations of the red, green, and blue channels.) The Hue/Saturation tool gives you the option of adjusting restricted subranges of colors (using the buttons at the top of the dialog), but if you want to get natural-looking colors, in most cases you should avoid doing this.

Tip

Even if an image does not seemed washed out, often you can increase its impact by pushing up the saturation a bit. Veterans of the film era sometimes call this trick "Fujifying", after Fujichrome film, which is notorious for producing highly saturated prints.

When you take pictures in low light conditions, in some cases you have the opposite problem: too much saturation. In this case too the Hue/Saturation tool is a good one to use, only by reducing the saturation instead of increasing it.

10.1.4 Adjusting Sharpness

10.1.4.1 Unblurring

If the focus on the camera is not set perfectly, or the camera is moving when the picture is taken, the result is a blurred image. If there is a lot of blurring, you probably won't be able to do much about it with any technique, but if there is only a moderate amount, you should be able to improve the image.

The most generally useful technique for sharpening a fuzzy image is called the Unsharp Mask. In spite of the rather confusing name, which derives from its origins as a technique used by film developers, its result is to make the image sharper, not "unsharp". It is a plug-in, and you can access it as Filters->Enhance->Unsharp Mask in the image menu. There are two parameters, "Radius" and "Amount". The default values often work pretty well, so you should try them first. Increasing either the radius or the amount increases the strength of the effect. Don't get carried away, though: if you make the unsharp mask too strong, it will amplify noise in the image and also give rise to visible artifacts where there are sharp edges.

Tip

Sometimes using Unsharp Mask can cause color distortion where there are strong contrasts in an image. When this happens, you can often get better results by decomposing the image into separate Hue-Saturation-Value (HSV) layers, and running Unsharp Mask on the Value layer only, then recomposing. This works because the human eye has much finer resolution for brightness than for color. See the sections on Decompose and Compose for more information.

Next to "Unsharp Mask" in the Filters menu is another filter called Sharpen, which does similar things. It is a little easier to use but not nearly as effective: our recommendation is that you ignore it and go straight to Unsharp Mask.

In some situations, you may be able to get useful results by selectively sharpening specific parts of an image using the Blur or Sharpen tool from the Toolbox, in "Sharpen" mode. This allows you to increase the sharpness in areas by painting over them with any paintbrush. You should be restrained about this, though, or the results will not look very natural: sharpening increases the apparent sharpness of edges in the image, but also amplifies noise.

10.1.4.2   Reducing Graininess

When you take pictures in low-light conditions or with a very fast exposure time, the camera does not get enough data to make good estimates of the true color at each pixel, and consequently the resulting image looks grainy. You can "smooth out" the graininess by blurring the image, but then you will also lose sharpness. There are a couple of approaches that may give better results. Probably the best, if the graininess is not too bad, is to use the filter called Selective Blur, setting the blurring radius to 1 or 2 pixels. The other approach is to use the Despeckle filter. This has a nice preview, so you can play with the settings and try to find some that give good results. When graininess is really bad, though, it is often very difficult to fix by anything except heroic measures (i.e., retouching with paint tools).

10.1.4.3   Softening

Every so often you have the opposite problem: an image is *too* crisp. The solution is to blur it a bit: fortunately blurring an image is much easier than sharpening it. Since you probably don't want to blur it very much, the simplest method is to use the "Blur" plug-in, accessed via Filters->Blur->Blur from the image menu. This will soften the focus of the image a little bit. If you want more softening, just repeat until you get the result you desire.

10.1.5   Removing Unwanted Objects from an Image

There are two kinds of objects you might want to remove from an image: first, artifacts caused by junk such as dust or hair on the lens; second, things that were really present but impair the quality of the image, such as a telephone wire running across the edge of a beautiful mountain landscape.

10.1.5.1   Despeckling

A good tool for removing dust and other types of lens grunge is the Despeckle filter, accessed as Filters->Enhance->Despeckle from the image menu. Very important: to use this filter effectively, you must begin by making a small selection containing the artifact and a small area around it. The selection must be small enough so that the artifact pixels are statistically distinguishable from the other pixels inside the selection. If you try to run despeckle on the whole image, you will hardly ever get anything useful. Once you have created a reasonable selection, activate Despeckle, and watch the preview as you adjust the parameters. If you are lucky, you will be able to find a setting that removes the junk while minimally affecting the area around it. The more the junk stands out from the area around it, the better your results are likely to be. If it isn't working for you, it might be worthwhile to cancel the filter, create a different selection, and then try again.

If you have more than one artifact in the image, it is necessary to use Despeckle on each individually.

10.1.5.2   Garbage Removal

The most useful method for removing unwanted "clutter" from an image is the Clone ⬚ tool, which allows you to paint over one part of an image using pixel data taken from another part (or even from a different image). The trick to using the clone tool effectively is to be able to find a different part of the image that can be used to "copy over" the unwanted part: if the area surrounding the unwanted object is very different from the rest of the image, you won't have much luck. For example, if you have a lovely beach scene, with a nasty human walking across the beach who you would like to teleport away, you will probably be able to find an empty part of the beach that looks similar to the part he is walking across, and use it to clone over him. It is quite astonishing how natural the results can look when this technique works well.

Consult the Clone Tool Help for more detailed instructions. Cloning is as much an art as a science, and the more you practice at it, the better you will get. At first it may seem impossible to produce anything except ugly blotches, but persistence will pay off.

Another tool looking very much as the clone tool, but smarter, is the healing tool which also takes the area around the destination into account when cloning. A typical usage is removal of wrinkles and other minor errors in images.

In some cases you may be able to get good results by simply cutting out the offending object from the image, and then using a plug-in called "Resynthesizer" to fill in the void. This plug-in is not included with the main GIMP distribution, but it can be obtained from the author's web site [PLUGIN-RESYNTH]. As with many things, your mileage may vary.

10.1.5.3   Removing Red-eye

When you take a flash picture of somebody who is looking directly toward the camera, the iris of the eye can bounce the light of the flash back toward the camera in such a way as to make the eye appear bright red: this effect is called "red eye", and looks very bizarre. Many modern cameras have special flash modes that minimize red-eye, but they only work if you use them, and even then they don't always work perfectly. Interestingly, the same effect occurs with animals, but the eyes may show up as other colors, such as green.

From version 2.4, GIMP incorporated a special remove red eye filter. Make a selection with one of the selection tools of the red part of the eye and then choose the "Remove Red Eye" filter. Perhaps you have to fiddle around a bit with the threshold slider to get the right color.

10.1.6   Saving Your Results

10.1.6.1   Files

What file format should you use to save the results of your work, and should you resize it? The answers depend on what you intend to use the image for.

- If you intend to open the image in GIMP again for further work, you should save it in GIMP's native XCF format (i. e., name it something.xcf), because this is the only format that guarantees that none of the information in the image is lost.

- If you intend to print the image on paper, you should avoid shrinking the image, except by cropping it. The reason is that printers are capable of achieving much higher resolutions than video monitors — 600 to 1400 dpi ("dots per inch", the physical density) for typical printers, as compared to 72 to 100 pixels per inch for monitors. A 3000 x 5000-pixel image looks huge on a monitor, but it only comes to about 5 inches by 8 inches on paper at 600 ppi. There is usually no good reason to *expand* the image either: you can't increase the true resolution that way, and it can always be scaled up at the time it is printed. As for the file format, it will usually be fine to use JPEG at a quality level of 75 to 85. In rare cases, where there are large swaths of nearly uniform color, you may need to set the quality level even higher or use a lossless format such as TIFF instead.

- If you intend to display the image on screen or project it with a video projector, bear in mind that the highest screen resolution for most commonly available systems is 1600 x 1200, so there is nothing to gain by keeping the image larger than that. For this purpose, the JPEG format is almost always a good choice.

- If you want to put the image on a web page or send it by email, it is a good idea to make every effort to keep the file size as small as possible. First, scale the image down to the smallest size that makes it possible to see the relevant details (bear in mind that other people may be using different sized monitors and/or different monitor resolution settings). Second, save the image as a JPEG file. In the JPEG save dialog, check the option to "Preview in image window" , and then adjust the Quality slider to the lowest level that gives you acceptable image quality. (You will see in the image the effects of each change.) Make sure that the image is zoomed at 1:1 while you do this, so you are not misled by the effects of zooming.

See the File Formats section for more information.

10.1.6.2 Printing Your Photos

As in most softwares, in GIMP, printing needs to go to main menu File → Print. However it is very useful to keep in mind some elementary concepts to prevent some unpleasant surprises when looking at result, or to cure them if that occurs. You always must remember:

- that image displayed on the screen is in RGB mode and printing will be in CMYK mode; consequently color feature you'll get on printed sheet will not be exactly what you was waiting for. That depends on the used corresponding chart. For the curious ones some adding explanations can be got through a click on these useful Wikipedia links:

  - ICC-Profile [WKPD-ICC]
  - CMYK [WKPD-CMYK]
  - Gamut [WKPD-GAMUT]

- that a screen resolution is roughly within a range from 75 up to 100 dpi; a printer resolution is about 10x higher (or more) than a screen one; printed image size depends on available pixels and resolution; so actual printed size doesn't correspond inevitably to what is displayed on screen nor available sheet size.

Consequently, before any printing it is relevant to go to: Image → Print size and choose here your convenient output size in "print size" box adjusting either sizes or resolution. The symbol shows that the both values are linked. You can dissociate x and y resolution by clicking on that symbol, but it is risky! Probably this possibility is open because printers are built with different x vs. y resolutions. Nevertheless if you unlinked them you can be very surprised! You can try this in special effects.

Last recommendation: think of checking your margins as well as centering. It would be a pity if a too much large margin cuts off some part of your image or if an inappropriate centering damages your work especially if you use a special photo paper.

10.1.6.3 EXIF Data

Modern digital cameras, when you take a picture, add information to the data file about the camera settings and the circumstances under which the picture was taken. This data is included in JPEG or TIFF files in a structured format called EXIF. For JPEG files, GIMP is capable of maintaining EXIF data, if it is built appropriately: it depends on a library called "libexif", which may not be available on all systems. If GIMP is built with EXIF support enabled, then loading a JPEG file with EXIF data, and resaving the resulting image in JPEG format, will cause the EXIF data to be preserved unchanged. This is not, strictly speaking, the right way for an image editor to handle EXIF data, but it is better than simply removing it, which is what earlier versions of GIMP did.

If you would like to see the contents of the EXIF data, you can download from the registry an Exif Browser plug-in [PLUGIN-EXIF]. If you are able to build and install it on your system, you can access it as Filters->Generic->Exif Browser from the image menu. (See Installing New Plug-ins for help.)

Chapter 11

Color Management with GIMP

11.1 Color Management in GIMP

Many devices you use in your design or photography workflow, like digital photo cameras, scanners, displays, printers etc., have their own color reproduction characteristics. If those are not taken into account during opening, editing and saving, harmful adjustments can be done to images. With GIMP you can have reliable output for both Web and print.

Figure 11.1 Image Processing Workflow

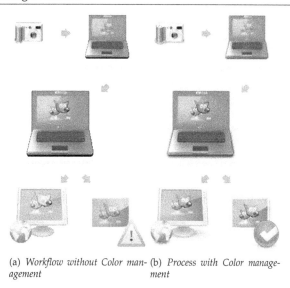

(a) *Workflow without Color man-* (b) *Process with Color manage-*
agement   *ment*

11.1.1 Problems of a non Color Managed Workflow

The basic problem of image manipulation without color management is that you do simply not see what you do. This affects two different areas:

1. There are differences in Colors caused by different color characteristics of different devices like cameras, scanners, displays or printers

2. There are differences in Colors caused by the limitations of the colorspace a specific device is able to handle

The main purpose of color management is to avoid such problems. The approach taken to do so involves the addition of a description of the color characteristic to an image or devices.

These descriptions are called *color profile*. A color profile is basically a look-up table to translate the specific color characteristic of a device to a device-independent color space - the so called working-space.

All the image manipulation is then done to images in the working-space. In addition to that the color profile of a device can be used to simulate how colors would look on that device.

The creation of color profiles is most often done by the manufacturer of the devices themselves. To make these profiles usable independent of platform and operating system, the ICC (International Color Consortium) created a standard called ICC-profile that describes how color profiles are stored to files and embedded into images.

11.1.2 Introduction to a Color Managed Workflow

> Tip
>
> Most of the parameters and profiles described here can be set in the GIMP preferences. Please see Section 12.1.14 for details.

11.1.2.1 Input

Most digital cameras embed a color profile to individual photo files without user interaction. Digital scanners usually come with a color profile, which they also attach to the scanned images.

Figure 11.2 Applying the ICC-profile

When opening an image with an embedded color profile, GIMP offers to convert the file to the RGB working color space. This is sRGB by default and it is recommended that all work is done in that color space. Should you however decide to keep the embedded color profile, the image will however still be displayed correctly.

In case for some reason a color profile is not embedded in the image and you know (or have a good guess) which one it should be, you can manually assign it to that image.

11.1.2.2 Display

For the best results, you need a color profile for your monitor. If a monitor profile is configured, either system-wide or in the Color Management section of the GIMP Preferences dialog, the image colors will be displayed most accurately.

One of the most important GIMP commands to work with color management is described in Section 16.5.8.

If you do not have a color profile for your monitor, you can create it using hardware calibration and measurement tools. On UNIX systems you will need Argyll Color Management System [ARGYLLCMS] and/or LProf [LPROF] to create color profiles.

11.1.2.2.1 Display Calibration and Profiling For displays there are two steps involved. One is called calibration and the other is called profiling. Also, calibration generally involves two steps. The first involves adjusting external monitor controls such as Contrast, Brightness, Color Temperature, etc, and it is highly dependent on the specific monitor. In addition there are further adjustments that are loaded into the video card memory to bring the monitor as close to a standard state as possible. This information is stored in the monitor profile in the so-called vgct tag. Probably under Windows XP or Mac OS, the operating system loads this information (LUT) in the video card in the process of starting your computer. Under Linux, at present you have to use an external program such as xcalib or dispwin. (If one just does a simple visual calibration using a web site such as that of Norman Koren, one might only use xgamma to load a gamma value.)

The second step, profiling, derives a set of rules which allow GIMP to translate RGB values in the image file into appropriate colors on the screen. This is also stored in the monitor profile. It doesn't change the RGB values in the image, but it does change which values are sent to the video card (which already contains the vgct LUT).

11.1.2.3   Print Simulation

Using GIMP, you can easily get a preview of what your image will look like on paper. Given a color profile for your printer, the display can be switched into Soft Proof mode. In such a simulated printout, colors that cannot be reproduced will optionally be marked with neutral gray color, allowing you to correct such mistakes before sending your images to the printer.

Chapter 12

Enrich my GIMP

12.1 Preferences Dialog

12.1.1 Introduction

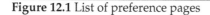

Figure 12.1 List of preference pages

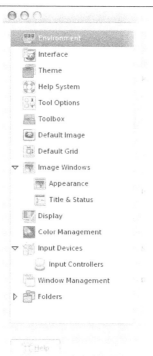

The preferences dialog can be accessed from the image menu-bar, through Edit → Preferences. It lets you customize many aspects of the way GIMP works. The following sections detail the settings that you can customize, and what they affect.

All of the Preferences information is stored in a file called `gimprc` in your personal GIMP directory, so if you are a "power user" who would rather work with a text editor than a graphical interface, you can alter preferences by editing that file. If you do, and you are on a Linux system, then **man gimprc** will give you a lot of technical information about the contents of the file and what they are used for.

12.1.2   Environment

Figure 12.2 Environment Preferences

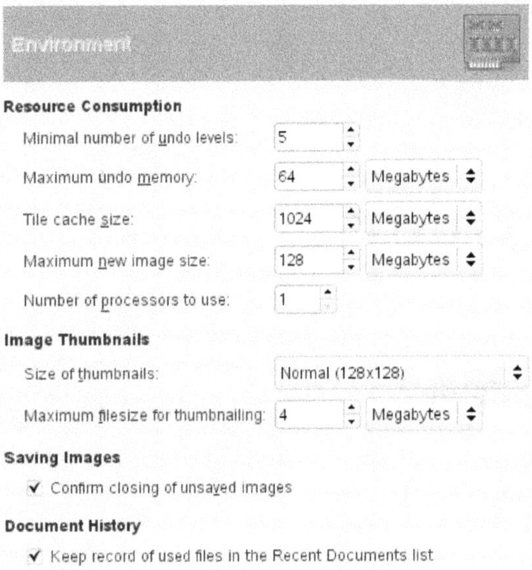

This page lets you customize the amount of system memory allocated for various purposes. It also allows you to disable the confirmation dialogs that appear when you close unsaved images, and to set the size of thumbnail files that GIMP produces.

12.1.2.1   Options

Resource Consumption

Minimal number of undo levels GIMP allows you to undo most actions by maintaining an "Undo History" for each image, for which a certain amount of memory is allocated. Regardless of memory usage, however, GIMP always permits some minimal number of the most recent actions to be undone: this is the number specified here. See Section 3.3 for more information about GIMP's Undo mechanism.

Maximum undo memory This is the amount of undo memory allocated for each image. If the Undo History size exceeds this, the oldest points are deleted, unless this would result in fewer points being present than the minimal number specified above.

Tile cache size This is the amount of system RAM allocated for GIMP image data. If GIMP requires more memory than this, it begins to swap to disk, which may in some circumstances cause a dramatic slowdown. You are given an opportunity to set this number when you install GIMP, but you can alter it here. See How to Set Your Tile Cache for more information.

Maximum new image size This is not a hard constraint: if you try to create a new image larger than the specified size, you are asked to confirm that you really want to do it. This is to prevent you from accidentally creating images much larger than you intend, which can either crash GIMP or cause it to respond verrrrrrrry slowwwwwwwly.

Number of processors to use Default is one. Your computer may have more than one processor.

Image Thumbnails

Size of thumbnails This options allows you to set the size of the thumbnails shown in the File Open dialog (and also saved for possible use by other programs). The options are "None", "Normal (128x128)", and "Large (256x256)".

Maximum filesize for thumbnailing If an image file is larger than the specified maximum size, GIMP will not generate a thumbnail for it. This options allows you to prevent thumbnailing of extremely large image files from slowing GIMP to a crawl.

Saving Images

Confirm closing of unsaved images Closing an image is not undoable, so by default GIMP asks you to confirm that you really want to do it, whenever it would lead to a loss of unsaved changes. You can disable this if you find it annoying; but then of course you are responsible for remembering what you have and have not saved.

Document history

Keep record of used files in the Recent Documents list When checked, files you have opened will be saved in the Document history. You can access the list of files with the Document history dialog from the image menu-bar : File → Open Recent → Document History.

12.1.3 Interface

Figure 12.3 Assorted Interface Preferences

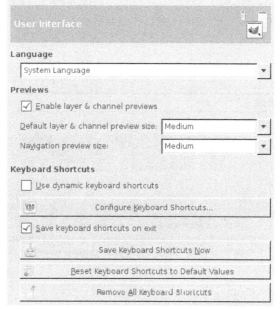

This page lets you customize language, layer/channel previews and keyboard shortcuts.

Options

Language The GIMP's default language is that of your system. You can select another language in the drop-down list. You have to start GIMP again to make this change effective. Please refer to Section 2.1.2.

Previews By default, GIMP shows miniature previews of the contents of layers and channels in several places, including the Layers dialog. If for some reason you would prefer to disable these, you can do it by unchecking Enable layer and channel previews. If you do want previews to be shown, you can customize their sizes using the menus for Default layer and channel preview size and Navigation preview size.

Keyboard Shortcuts Any menu item can be activated by holding down **Alt** and pressing a sequence of keys. Normally, the key associated with each menu entry is shown as an underlined letter in the text, called *accelerator*. If for some reason you would prefer the underlines to go away (maybe because you think they're ugly and you don't use them anyway), then you can make this happen by unchecking Show menu mnemonics.

GIMP can give you the ability to create keyboard shortcuts (key combinations that activate a menu entry) dynamically, by pressing the keys while the pointer hovers over the desired menu entry. However, this capability is disabled by default, because it might lead novice users to accidentally overwrite the standard keyboard shortcuts. If you want to enable it, check Use dynamics keyboard shortcuts here.

Pressing the button for Configure Keyboard Shortcuts brings up the Shortcut Editor, which gives you a graphical interface to select menu items and assign shortcuts to them.

If you change shortcuts, you will probably want your changes to continue to apply in future GIMP sessions. If not, uncheck Save keyboard shortcuts on exit. But remember that you have done this, or you may be frustrated later. If you don't want to save shortcuts on exit every session, you can save the current settings at any time using the Save Keyboard Shortcuts Now button, and they will be applied to future sessions. If you decide that you have made some bad decisions concerning shortcuts, you can reset them to their original state by pressing Reset Saved Keyboard Shortcuts to Default Values.

12.1.4   Theme

Figure 12.4 Theme Preference

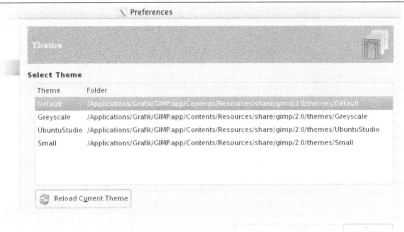

This page lets you select a theme, which determines many aspects of the appearance of the GIMP user interface, including the set of icons used, their sizes, fonts, spacing allowed in dialogs, etc. Two themes are supplied with GIMP: Default, which is probably best for most people, and Small, which may be preferable for those with small or low-resolution monitors. Clicking on a theme in the list causes it to be applied immediately, so it is easy to see the result and change your mind if you don't like it.

You can also use custom themes, either by downloading them from the net, or by copying one of the supplied themes and modifying it. Custom themes should be places in the `themes` subdirectory of your personal GIMP directory: if they are, they will appear in the list here. Each theme is actually a directory containing ASCII files that you can edit. They are pretty complicated, and the meaning of the contents goes beyond the scope of this documentation, but you should feel free to experiment: in the worst case, if you mess things up completely, you can always revert back to one of the supplied themes.

You cannot edit the supplied themes unless you have administrator permissions, and even if you do, you shouldn't: if you want to customize a theme, make a copy in your personal directory and work on it. If you make a change and would like to see the result "on the fly", you can do so by saving the edited theme file and then pressing Reload Current Theme.

12.1.5   Help System

Figure 12.5 Help System Preferences

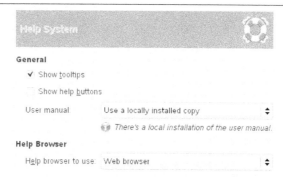

This page lets you customize the behaviour of the GIMP help system.

12.1.5.1   Options

General

Show tool tips   Tool tips are small help pop-ups that appear when the pointer hovers for a moment over some element of the interface, such as a button or icon. Sometimes they explain what the element does; sometimes they give you hints about non-obvious ways to use it. If you find them too distracting, you can disable them here by unchecking this option. We recommend that you leave them enabled unless you are a very advanced user.

Show help buttons   This option controls whether the help buttons are shown on every tool dialog, which may be used alternatively to invoke the help system.

User manual   This drop-down list lets you select between Use a locally installed copy and Use the online version. See Section 16.12.2.

Help Browser

Help browser to use   GIMP Help is supplied in the form of HTML files, i. e., web pages. You can view them using either a special help browser that comes with GIMP, or a web browser of your choice. Here you choose which option to use. Because the help pages were carefully checked to make sure they work well with GIMP's browser, whereas other web browsers are somewhat variable in their support of features, the safer option is to use the internal browser; but really any modern web browser should be okay.

> Note
>
> Note that the GIMP help browser is not available on all platforms. If it is missing, this option is hidden and the standard web browser will be used to read the help pages.

12.1.6   Tool Options

Figure 12.6 Tool Options Preferences

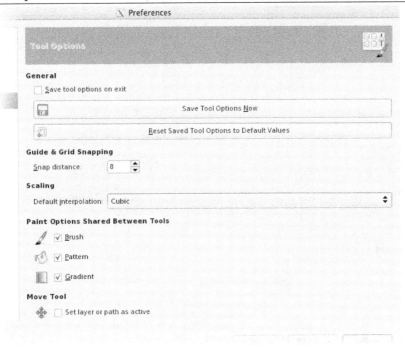

This page lets you customize several aspects of the behavior of tools.

12.1.6.1   Options

General

Save Tool Options On Exit Self explanatory

Save Tool Options Now Self explanatory

Reset Saved Tool Options To Default Values Self explanatory

Guide and Grid Snapping

Snap distance "Snapping" to guides, or to an image grid, means that when a tool is applied by clicking somewhere on the image display, if the clicked point is near enough to a guide or grid, it is shifted exactly onto the guide or grid. Snapping to guides can be toggled using View → Snap to Guides in the image menu; and if the grid is switched on, snapping to it can be toggled using View → Snap to Grid. This preference option determines how close a clicked point must be to a guide or grid in order to be snapped onto it, in pixels.

Scaling

Default interpolation When you scale something, each pixel in the result is calculated by interpolating several pixels in the source. This option determines the default interpolation method: it can always be changed, though, in the Tool Options dialog.

There are four choices:

None This is the fastest method, but it's quite crude: you should only consider using it if your machine is very seriously speed-impaired.

Linear This used to be the default, and is good enough for most purposes.

Cubic This is the best choice (although it can actually look worse than Linear for some types of images), but also the slowest. Since GIMP 2.6, this method is the default.

Sinc (Lanczos3) This method performs a high quality interpolation.

Paint Options Shared Between Tools

Brush, Pattern, Gradient You can decide here whether changing the brush etc for one tool should cause the new item to be used for all tools, or whether each individual tool (pencil, paintbrush, airbrush, etc) should remember the item that was last used for it specifically.

Move tool

Set layer or path as active You can decide here whether changing the current layer or path when using the move tool and without pressing any key.

12.1.7　Toolbox

Figure 12.7 Toolbox Preferences

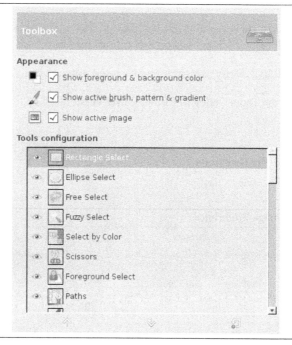

12.1.7.1　Options

Figure 12.8 Default Toolbox appearance

This page lets you customize the appearance of the Toolbox, by deciding whether the three "context information" areas should be shown at the bottom.

Appearance

Show foreground and background color Controls whether the color area on the left (2) appears in the Toolbox.

Show active brush, pattern, and gradient Controls whether the area in the center (3), with the brush, pattern, and gradient icons, appears in the Toolbox.

Show active image Controls whether a preview of the currently active image appears on the right (4).

Tools configuration

In this list, tools with an eye are present in the Toolbox. By default, color tools have no eye: you can add them to the Toolbox by clicking the corresponding checkbox.

You can also sort tools by priority using the arrow up and down buttons at the bottom of the dialog.

This option replaces the Tools Dialog of former GIMP versions.

12.1.8 Default Image Preferences

Figure 12.9 Default New Image Preferences

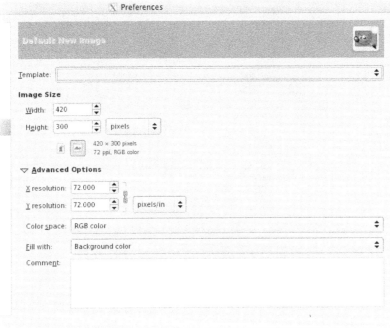

This tab lets you customize the default settings for the New Image dialog. See the New Image Dialog section for an explanation of what each of the values means.

12.1.9   Default Image Grid

Figure 12.10 Default Grid Preferences

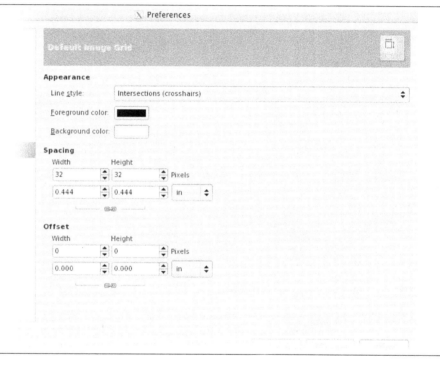

This page lets you customize the default properties of GIMP's grid, which can be toggled on or off using View → Show Grid from the image menu. The settings here match those in the Configure Image Grid dialog, which can be used to reconfigure the grid for an existing image, by choosing Image → Configure Grid from the image menu. See the Configure Grid dialog section for information on the meaning of each of the settings.

12.1.10   Image Windows

Figure 12.11 General Image Window Preference

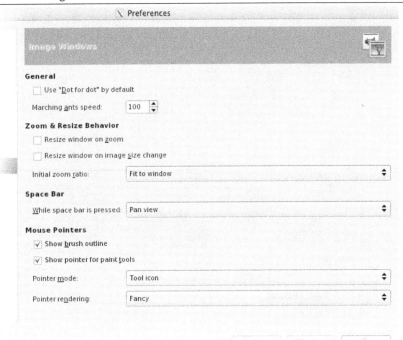

This page lets you customize several aspects of the behaviour of image windows.

12.1.10.1   Options

General

Use "Dot for dot" by default Using "Dot for dot" means that at 1:1 zoom, each pixel is the image is scaled to one pixel on the display. If "Dot for dot" is not used, then the displayed image size is determined by the X and Y resolution of the image. See the Scale Image section for more information.

Marching ants speed When you create a selection, the edge of it is shown as a dashed line with dashes that appear to move, marching slowly along the boundary: they are jokingly called "marching ants". The smaller the value entered here, the faster the ants march (and consequently the more distracting they are!).

Zoom and Resize Behavior

Resize window on zoom If this option is checked, then each time you zoom the image, the image window will automatically resize to follow it. Otherwise, the image window will maintain the same size when you zoom the image.

Resize window on image size change If this option is checked, then each time change the size of the image, by cropping or resizing it, the image window will automatically resize to follow. Otherwise, the image window will maintain the same size.

Initial zoom ratio You can choose either to have images, when they are first opened, scaled so that the whole image fits comfortably on your display, or else shown at 1:1 zoom. If you choose the second option, and the image is too large to fit on your display, then the image window will show only part of it (but you will be able to scroll to other parts).

Space bar

While space bar is pressed

- Pan view (default) or

- Toogle to Move Tool
- No action

Mouse Cursors

Show brush outline If this option is checked, then when you use a paint tool, the outline of the brush will be shown on the image as you move the pointer around. On slow systems, if the brush is very large, this could occasionally cause some lag in GIMP's ability to follow your movements: if so, switching this off might help. Otherwise, you will probably find it quite useful.

Show paint tool cursor If this is checked, a cursor will be shown. This is in addition to the brush outline, if the brush outline is being shown. The type of cursor is determined by the next option.

Cursor mode This option has no effect unless Show paint tool cursor is checked. If it is, you have three choices: Tool icon, which causes a small iconic representation of the currently active tool to be shown beside the cursor; Tool icon with crosshair, which shows the icon as well as a crosshair indicating the center of the cursor; or Crosshair only.

Cursor rendering If you choose "Fancy" here, the cursor is drawn in grayscale. If you choose "Black and White", it is drawn in a simpler way that may speed things up a little bit if you have speed issues.

12.1.11 Image Window Appearance

Figure 12.12 Image Window Appearance Defaults

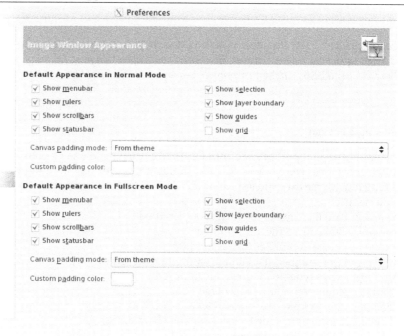

This page lets you customize the default appearance of image windows, for normal mode and for fullscreen mode. All of the settings here can be altered on an image-specific basis using entries in the View menu. See the Image Window section for information on the meaning of the entries.

The only parts that may need further explanation are the ones related to padding. "Padding" is the color shown around the edges of the image, if it does not occupy all of the display area (shown in light gray in all the figures here). You can choose among four colors for the padding color: to use the color specified by the current theme; to use the light or dark colors specified for checks, such as represent transparent parts of the image; or to use a custom color, which can be set using the color button for "Custom padding color".

12.1.12   Image Window Title and Statusbar

Figure 12.13 Image Window Title and Statusbar formats

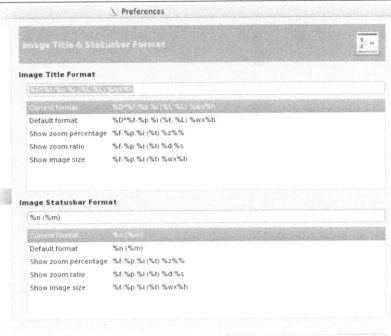

This page lets you customize the text that appears in two places: the title bar of an image, and the status bar. The title bar should appear above the image; however this depends on cooperation from the window manager, so it is not guaranteed to work in all cases. The statusbar appears underneath the image, on the right side. See the Image Window section for more information.

12.1.12.1   Choosing a Format

You can choose among several predesigned formats, or you can create one of your own, by writing a *format string* in the entry area. Here is how to understand a format string: anything you type is shown exactly as you type it, with the exception of *variables*, whose names all begin with "%". Here is a list of the variables you can use:

Variable: %f, *Meaning:* Bare filename of the image, or "Untitled"
Variable: %F, *Meaning:* Full path to file, or "Untitled"
Variable: %p, *Meaning:* Image id number (this is unique)
Variable: %i, *Meaning:* View number, if an image has more than one display
Variable: %t, *Meaning:* Image type (RGB, grayscale, indexed)
Variable: %z, *Meaning:* Zoom factor as a percentage
Variable: %s, *Meaning:* Source scale factor (zoom level = %d/%s)
Variable: %d, *Meaning:* Destination scale factor (zoom level = %d/%s)
Variable: %Dx, *Meaning:* Expands to x if the image is dirty, nothing otherwise
Variable: %Cx, *Meaning:* Expands to x if the image is clean, nothing otherwise
Variable: %l, *Meaning:* The number of layers
Variable: %L, *Meaning:* Number of layers (long form)
Variable: %m, *Meaning:* Memory used by the image
Variable: %n, *Meaning:* Name of the active layer/channel
Variable: %P, *Meaning:* id of the active layer/channel
Variable: %w, *Meaning:* Image width in pixels
Variable: %W, *Meaning:* Image width in real-world units
Variable: %h, *Meaning:* Image height in pixels
Variable: %H, *Meaning:* Image height in real-world units
Variable: %u, *Meaning:* Unit symbol (eg. px for Pixel)

Variable: %U, *Meaning:* Unit abbreviation
Variable: %%, *Meaning:* A literal "%" symbol

12.1.13   Display

Figure 12.14 Display Preferences

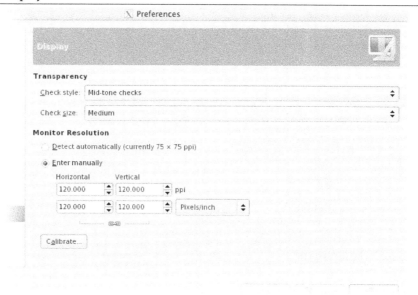

This page lets you customize the way transparent parts of an image are represented, and lets you recalibrate the resolution of your monitor.

12.1.13.1   Options

Transparency

Transparency type By default, GIMP indicates transparency using a checkerboard pattern with mid-tone checks, but you can change this if you want, either to a different type of checkerboard, or to solid black, white, or gray.

Check size Here you can alter the size of the squares in the checkerboard pattern used to indicate transparency.

Figure 12.15 The Calibration dialog

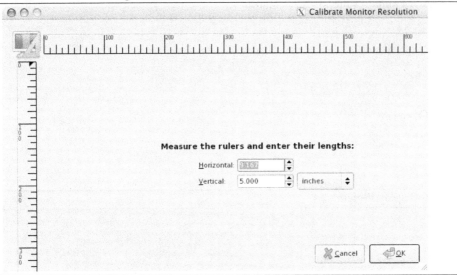

Monitor Resolution Monitor Resolution is the ratio of pixels, horizontally and vertically, to inches. You have three ways to proceed here:

- Get Resolution from windowing system. (easiest, probably inaccurate).
- Set Manually
- Push the Calibrate Button.

The Calibrate Dialog My monitor was impressively off when I tried the Calibrate Dialog. The "Calibrate Game" is fun to play. You will need a soft ruler.

12.1.14 Color Management

Figure 12.16 Color Management Preferences

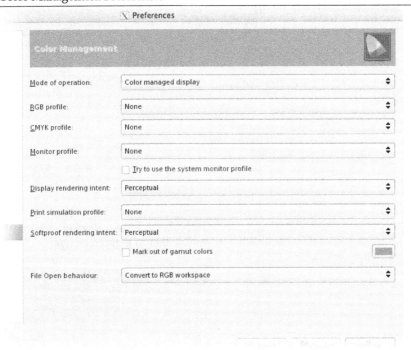

12.1.14.1 Options

This page lets you customize the GIMP color management.

Some of the options let you choose a color profile from a menu. If the desired profile is not in the menu yet, you can add it by clicking on the Select color profile from disk... item.

Tip

Files containing color profiles are easily recognizable by their `.icc` suffix. In addition to that they are usually stored all together in only a few places. If you are running GIMP on Mac OS X, you should try `/Library/ColorSync/Profiles/` and `Library/Printers/[manufacturer]/Profiles`.

Mode of operation Using this option you can decide how the GIMP color management operates. There are three modes you can choose from:

- No color management: choosing this selection shuts down the color management in GIMP completely.

- Color managed display: with this selection you can enable the GIMP color management to provide a fully corrected display of the images according to the given color profile for the display.

- Print simulation: when choosing this selection, you enable the GIMP color management not only to apply the profile for the display, but also the selected printer simulation profile. Doing so, you can preview the color results of a print with that printer.

Note

Please note, that the GIMP color management is used to enhance the display of images and the embedding of profiles to image files only. Especially are the options you choose in this dialog in no way used for printing from within GIMP. This is because the printing is a special task done by a more specialized printing engine that is no part of GIMP.

RGB profile Select the default color profile for working with RGB images.

CMYK profile Select the default color profile for conversion between RGB for the screen work and CMYK for printing.

Monitor profile This option gives you two elements for interaction:

- You should select a display profile for this option. The selected color profile is used to display GIMP on the screen.

- If you activate the Try to use the system monitor profile option, GIMP will use the color profile provided for the displays by the operating systems color management system.

Display rendering intent Rendering intents, as the one you can configure with this option, are ways of dealing with colors that are out-of- *Gamut* colors present in the source space that the destination space is incapable of producing. There are four method rendering intents to choose from:

- Perceptual

- Relative colorimetric

- Saturation

- Absolute colorimetric

A description of the individual methods can be found at *Rendering Intent* .

Print simulation mode You should select a printer profile for this option. The selected color profile is used for the print simulation mode.

Softproof rendering intent This option again provides two different elements for interaction:

- You can use the menu to select the rendering intent for the soft proof. They are the same as already described for the display rendering intent.

- If you enable the Mark out of gamut colors option, all pixels that have a color that is not printable are marked by a special color. Which color is used for this can also be chosen by you. You can do this simply by clicking on the color icon on the right besides the checkbox.

File Open behaviour Using this menu you can determine how GIMP behaves when opening a file that contains an embedded color profile that does not match the workspace sRGB. You can choose from the following entries:

- Ask what to do: if selected, GIMP will ask every time what to do.

- Keep embedded profile: if you choose this, GIMP will keep the attached profile and not convert the image to the workspace. The image is displayed correctly anyways, because the attached profile will be applied for display.

- Convert to RGB workspace: by choosing this entry GIMP will automatically use the attached color profile to convert the image to the workspace.

Note

For more explanations:

- ICC Profiles are explained in Wikipedia [WKPD-ICC].

- See OpenICC project ([OPENICC]) where GIMP and others great names of free infography contribute to.

  Many profiles to load from the web:

- ICC sRGB Workspace: ICCsRGB [ICCsRGB]

- Microsoft sRGB Workspace: MsRGB [MsRGB]

- Adobe RGB98 Workspace : Adobe RGB (1998) [AdobeRGB]

- ECI (European Color Initiative) Profiles: ECI [ECI]

12.1.15   Input Devices

Figure 12.17 Input devices preferences

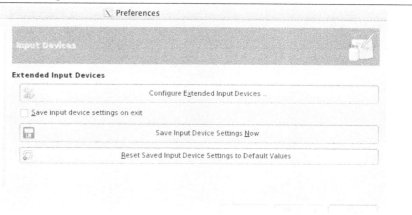

Extended Input Devices

Configure Extended Input Devices This large button allows you to set the devices associated with your computer: tablet, MIDI keyboard... If you have a tablet, you will see a dialog like this:

Figure 12.18 Preferences for a tablet

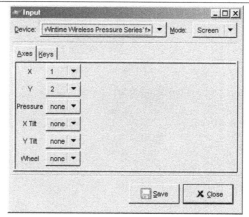

Save input device settings on exit When you check this box, GIMP remembers the tool, color, pattern and brush you were using the last time you quitted.

Save Input Device Settings Now Self explanatory.

Reset Saved Input Device Settings to Default Values Delete your settings and restore default settings.

12.1.16   Input Controllers

Figure 12.19 Input controllers preferences

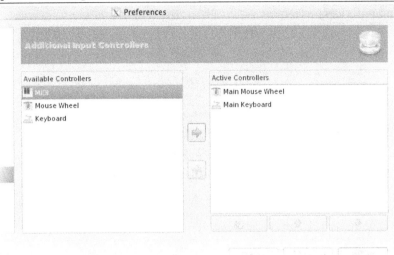

This dialog has two lists of additional input controllers: Available Controllers on the left, Active Controllers on the right.

A click on an item will highlight it and you can move the controller from one list to the other by clicking on the respective arrow key. When you try to move a controller from the list of active controllers to the available controllers, a dialog pops up and you will have the choice of removing the controller or just disabling it.

When you double click on a (typically active) controller or alternatively click on the Edit button at the bottom of the list, you can configure this controller in a dialog window:

Main Mouse Wheel

Figure 12.20 Main Mouse Wheel

General

> **Dump events from this controller** This option must be checked if you want a print on the stdout
> of the events generated by the enabled controllers. If you want to see those event you should

start GIMP from a terminal or making it to print the stdout to file by the shell redirection. The main use of this option is for debug.

Enable this controller   This option must be checked if you want to add a new actions to the mouse wheel.

Mouse Wheel Events   In this window with scroll bars you have: on the left, the possible events concerning the mouse wheel, more or less associated with control keys; on the right, the action assigned to the event when it will happen. You have also two buttons, one to Edit the selected event, the other to Cancel the action of the selected event.

Some actions are assigned to events yet. They seem to be examples, as they are not functional.

Select the action allocated to the event   After selecting an event, if you click on the Edit button, you open the following dialog:

Figure 12.21 Select Controller Event Action

If an action exists yet for this event, the window will open on this action. Else, the window will display the sections that order actions. Click on an action to select it.

Main Keyboard

You can use this dialog in the same way as that of the mouse wheel. Events are related to the arrow keys of the keyboard, combined or not with control keys.

Figure 12.22 Main Keyboard

Note

You will find an example of these notions in Creating a variable size brush.

12.1.17   Window Management

Figure 12.23 Window Management Preferences

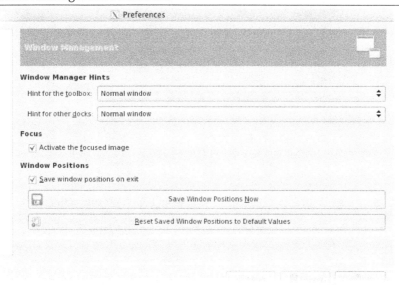

This page lets you customize the way windows are handled in GIMP. You should note that GIMP does not manipulate windows directly, instead it sends requests to the window manager (i. e., to Windows if you are running in Windows; to Metacity if you are running in a standard Gnome setup in Linux; etc). Because there are many window managers, and not all of them are well behaved, it cannot be guaranteed that the functions described here will actually work as described. However, if you are using a modern, standards-compliant window manager, they ought to.

12.1.17.1 Options

Window Manager Hints

Window type hints for the toolbox and the docks The choices you make here determine how the Toolbox, and the docks that hold dialogs, will be treated. You have three possibilities for them:

- If you choose Normal Window, they will be treated like any other windows.
- If you choose Utility Window, the reduce button in the title bar is absent and the docks will remain permanently on your screen.

Figure 12.24 Utility window title bar

(a) *Normal title bar*   (b) *The title bar in a utility window*

- If you choose Keep above, they will be kept in front of every other window at all times.

Note that changes you make here will not take effect until the next time you start GIMP.

Focus

Activate the focused image Normally, when you focus an image window (usually indicated by a change in the color of the frame), it becomes the "active image" for GIMP, and therefore the target for any image-related actions you perform. Some people, though, prefer to set up their window managers such that any window entered by the pointer is automatically focused. If you do this, you may find that it is inconvenient for focused images to automatically become active, and may be happier if you uncheck this option.

Window Positions

Save window positions on exit If this option is checked, the next time you start GIMP, you will see the same set of dialog windows, in the same positions they occupied when you last exited.

Save Window Positions Now This button is only useful if "Save window positions on exit" is unchecked. It allows you to set up your windows they way you like, click the button, and then have them come up in that arrangement each time you start GIMP.

Reset Saved Window Positions to Default Values If you decide that you are unhappy with the arrangement of windows you have saved, and would rather go back to the default arrangement than spend time moving them around, you can do so by pressing this button.

12.1.18 Folders

Figure 12.25 Basic Folder Preferences

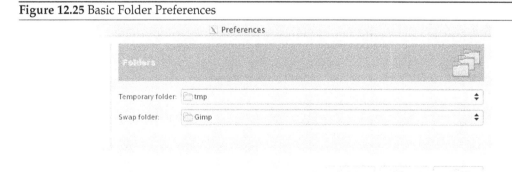

This page allows you to set the locations for two important folders used by GIMP for temporary files. The pages below it allow you to customize the locations searched for resources such as brushes etc.; see Data Folders for a description that applies to them. You can change the folders here by editing the entries, or by pressing the buttons on the right to bring up a file chooser window.

Folders

Temp folder This folder is used for temporary files: files created for temporary storage of working data, and then deleted within the same GIMP session. It does not require a lot of space or high performance. By default, a subdirectory called `tmp` in your personal GIMP directory is used, but if that disk is very cramped for space, or has serious performance issues, you can change it to a different directory. The directory must exist and be writable by you, or bad things will happen.

Swap folder This is the folder used as a "memory bank" when the total size of images and data open in GIMP exceeds the available RAM. If you work with very large images, or images with many layers, or have many images open at once, GIMP can potentially require hundreds of megabytes of swap space, so available disk space and performance are definitely things to think about for this folder. By default, it is set to your personal GIMP directory, but if you have another disk with more free space, or substantially better performance, you may see a significant benefit from moving your swap folder there. The directory must exist and be writable by you.

12.1.19 Data Folders

Figure 12.26 Preferences: Brush Folders

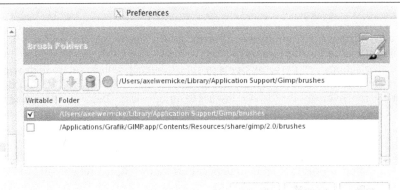

GIMP uses several types of resources – such as brushes, patterns, gradients, etc. – for which a basic set are supplied by GIMP when it is installed, and others can be created or downloaded by the user. For each such resource type, there is a Preference page that allows you to specify the *search path*: the set of directories from which items of the type in question are automatically loaded when GIMP starts. These pages all look very much the same: the page for brushes is shown to the right as an example.

By default, the search path includes two folders: a *system* folder, where items installed along with GIMP are placed, and a *personal* folder, inside your personal GIMP directory, where items added by you should be placed. The system folder should not be marked as writable, and you should not try to alter its contents. The personal folder must be marked as writable or it is useless, because there is nothing inside it except what you put there.

You can customize the search path with the buttons at the top of the dialog.

Options

Select a Folder If you click on one of the folders in the list, it is selected for whatever action comes next.

Add/Replace Folder If you type the name of a folder in the entry space, or navigate to it using the file chooser button 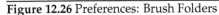 on the right, and then click the left button, this will replace the selected folder with the one you have specified. If nothing in the list is selected, the folder you specify will be added to the list. If the light-symbol to the left of the text entry area is red instead of green, it means that the folder you have specified does not exist. GIMP will not create it for you, so you should do this immediately.

Move Up/Down If you click on the up-arrow or down-arrow buttons, the selected folder will be changed to the following or preceding one in the list. Since the folders are read in order, using those buttons change the loading precedence of the items located in those folders.

Delete Folder If you click the trash-can button, the selected folder will be deleted from the list. (The folder itself is not affected; it is merely removed from the search path.) Deleting the system folder is probably a bad idea, but nothing prevents you from doing it.

12.2 Grids and Guides

You will probably have it happen many times that you need to place something in an image very pre-cisely, and find that it is not easy to do using a mouse. Often you can get better results by using the arrow keys on the keyboard (which move the affected object one pixel at a time, or 25 pixels if you hold down the **Shift** key), but GIMP also provides you with two other aids to make positioning easier: grids and guides.

Figure 12.27 Image used for examples below

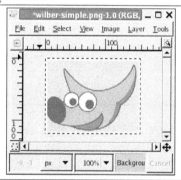

12.2.1 The Image Grid

Figure 12.28 Image with default grid

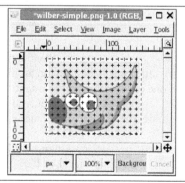

Each image has a grid. It is always present, but by default it is not visible until you activate it by toggling View → Show Grid in the image menu. If you want grids to be present more often than not, you can change the default behavior by checking "Show grid" in the Image Window Appearance page of the Preferences dialog. (Note that there are separate settings for Normal Mode and Fullscreen Mode.)

The default grid appearance, set up when you install GIMP, consists of plus-shaped black crosshairs at the grid line intersections, with grid lines spaced every 10 pixels both vertically and horizontally. You can customize the default grid using the Default Image Grid page of the Preferences dialog. If you only want to change the grid appearance for the current image, you can do so by choosing Image → Configure Grid from the image menu: this brings up the Configure Grid dialog.

Figure 12.29 A different grid style

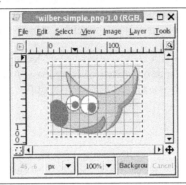

Not only can a grid be helpful for judging distances and spatial relationships, it can also permit you to align things exactly with the grid, if you toggle View → Snap to Grid in the image menu: this causes the pointer to "warp" perfectly to any grid line located within a certain distance. You can customize the snap distance threshold by setting "Snap distance" in the Tool Options page of the Preferences dialog, but most people seem to be happy with the default value of 8 pixels. (Note that it is perfectly possible to snap to the grid even if the grid is not visible. It isn't easy to imagine why you might want to do this, though.)

12.2.2   Guides

Figure 12.30 Image with four guides

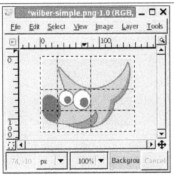

In addition to the image grid, GIMP also gives you a more flexible type of positioning aid: *guides*. These are horizontal or vertical lines you can temporarily display on an image while you are working on it.

To create a guide, simply click on one of the rulers in the image window and pull out a guide, while holding the mouse Left Button pressed. The guide is then displayed as a blue, dashed line, which follows the pointer. As soon as you create a guide, the "Move" tool is activated and the mouse pointer changes to the Move icon.

You can also create a guide with the New Guide command, which allows you to precisely place the guide on the image, the New Guide (by Percent) command, or the New Guides from Selection command.

You can create as many guides as you like, positioned wherever you like. To move a guide after you have created it, activate the Move tool in the Toolbox (or press the **M** key), you can then click and drag a guide. To delete a guide, simply drag it outside the image. Holding down the **Shift** key, you can move everything but a guide, using the guides as an effective alignment aid.

The behavior of the guides depends upon the Move (Affect) mode of the "Move" tool. When *Layer* mode is selected, the mouse pointer turns into a small hand as soon as it gets close to a guide. Then the guide is activated and it turns red, and you can move the guide or delete it by moving it back into the ruler. If *Selection* mode is selected, you can position a guide, but you cannot move it after that.

As with the grid, you can cause the pointer to snap to nearby guides, by toggling View → Snap to Guides in the image menu. If you have a number of guides and they are making it difficult for you to judge the image properly, you can hide them by toggling View → Show Guides. It is suggested that you only do this momentarily, otherwise you may get confused the next time you try to create a guide and don't see anything happening.

If it makes things easier for you, you can change the default behavior for guides in the Image Windows Appearance page of the Preferences dialog. Disabling Show guides is probably a bad idea, though, for the reason just given.

You can remove the guides with the Image → Guides → Remove all Guides command.

> **Note**
>
> Another use for guides: the Guillotine plugin can use guides to slice an image into a set of sub-images.

12.3 Rendering a Grid

How can you create a grid that is actually part of the image? You can't do this using the image grid: that is only an aid, and is only visible on the monitor or in a screenshot. You can, however, use the Grid plugin to render a grid very similar to the image grid. (Actually, the plugin has substantially more options.)

See also Grid and Guides.

12.4 How to Set Your Tile Cache

During the data processing and manipulation of pictures, GIMP becomes in the need of much main memory. The more is available the better is. GIMP uses the operating system memory available resources as effectively as possible, striving to maintain the work on the pictures fast and comfortable for the user. That Data memory, during the treatment, is organized in buffered blocks of graphic data, which could exist in two different forms of data memory: in the slow not removable disk or in the fast main RAM memory. GIMP uses preferably the RAM, and when it runs short of this memory, it uses the hard disk for the remaining data. These chunks of graphic data are commonly referred to as "tiles" and the entire system is called "tile cache".

A low value for tile cache means that GIMP sends data to the disk very quickly, not making real use of the available RAM, and making the disks work for no real reason. Too high a value for tile cache, and other applications start to have less system resources, forcing them to use swap space, which also makes the disks work too hard; some of them may even terminate or start to malfunction due lack of RAM.

How do you choose a number for the Tile Cache size? Here are some tips to help you decide what value to use, as well as a few tricks:

- The easiest method is to just forget about this and hope the default works. This was a usable method when computers had little RAM, and most people just tried to make small images with GIMP while running one or two other applications at the same time. If you want something easy and only use GIMP to make screenshots and logos, this is probably the best solution.

- If you have a modern computer with plenty of memory–say, 512 MB or more–setting the Tile Cache to half of your RAM will probably give good performance for GIMP in most situations without depriving other applications. Probably even 3/4 of your RAM would be fine.

- Ask someone to do it for you, which in the case of a computer serving multiple users at the same time can be a good idea: that way the administrator and other users do not get mad at you for abusing the machine, nor do you get a badly underperforming GIMP. If it is your machine and only serves a single user at a given time, this could mean money, or drinks, as price for the service.

- Start changing the value a bit each time and check that it goes faster and faster with each increase, but the system does not complain about lack of memory. Be forewarned that sometimes lack of memory shows up suddenly with some applications being killed to make space for the others.

- Do some simple math and calculate a viable value. Maybe you will have to tune it later, but maybe you have to tune it anyway with the other previous methods. At least you know what is happening and can get the best from your computer.

Let's suppose you prefer the last option, and want to get a good value to start with. First, you need to get some data about your computer. This data is the amount of RAM installed in your system, the operating system's swap space available, and a general idea about the speed of the disks that store the operating system's swap and the directory used for GIMP's swap. You do not need to do disk tests, nor check the RPM of the disks, the thing is to see which one seems clearly faster or slower, or whether all are similar. You can change GIMP's swap directory in the Folders page of the Preferences dialog.

The next thing to do is to see how much resources you require for other apps you want to run at the same time than GIMP. So start all your tools and do some work with them, except GIMP of course, and check the usage. You can use applications like free or top, depending in what OS and what environment you use. The numbers you want is the memory left, including file cache. Modern Unix keeps a very small area free, in order to be able to keep large file and buffer caches. Linux's *free* command does the maths for you: check the column that says "free", and the line "-/+ buffers/cache". Note down also the free swap.

Now time for decisions and a bit of simple math. Basically the concept is to decide if you want to base all Tile Cache in RAM, or RAM plus operating system swap:

1. Do you change applications a lot? Or keep working in GIMP for a long time? If you spend a lot of time in GIMP, you can consider free RAM plus free swap as available; if not, you need to go to the following steps. (If you're feeling unsure about it, check the following steps.) If you are sure you switch apps every few minutes, only count the free RAM and just go to the final decision; no more things to check.

2. Does the operating system swap live in the same physical disk as GIMP swap? If so, add RAM and swap. Otherwise go to the next step.

3. Is the disk that holds the OS swap faster or the same speed as the disk that holds the GIMP swap? If slower, take only the free RAM; if faster or similar, add free RAM and swap.

4. You now have a number, be it just the free RAM or the free RAM plus the free OS swap. Reduce it a bit, to be on the safe side, and that is the Tile Cache you could use as a good start.

As you can see, all is about checking the free resources, and decide if the OS swap is worth using or will cause more problems than help.

There are some reasons you want to adjust this value, though. The basic one is changes in your computer usage pattern, or changing hardware. That could mean your assumptions about how you use your computer, or the speed of it, are no longer valid. That would require a reevaluation of the previous steps, which can drive you to a similar value or a completely new value.

Another reason to change the value is because it seems that GIMP runs too slowly, while changing to other applications is fast: this means that GIMP could use more memory without impairing the other applications. On the other hand, if you get complaints from other applications about not having enough memory, then it may benefit you to not let GIMP hog so much of it.

If you decided to use only RAM and GIMP runs slowly, you could try increasing the value a bit, but never to use also all the free swap. If the case is the contrary, using both RAM and swap, and you have problems about lack of resources, then you should decrease the amount of RAM available to GIMP.

Another trick is to put the Swap Dir on a very fast disk, or on a different disk than the one where most of your files reside. Spreading the operating system swap file over multiple disks is also a good way to speed things up, in general. And of course, you might have to buy more RAM or stop using lots of programs at the same time: you can not expect to edit a poster on a computer with 16MB and be fast.

You can also check what memory requirements your images have. The larger the images, and the number of undoes, the more resources you need. This is another way to choose a number, but it is only good if you always work with the same kind of images, and thus the real requirements do not vary. It is also helpful to know if you will require more RAM and/or disk space.

12.5   Creating Shortcuts to Menu Functions

Many functions which are accessible via the image menu have a default keyboard shortcut. You may want to create a new shortcut for a command that you use a lot and doesn't have one or, more rarely, edit an existing shortcut. There are two methods for doing this.

Using dynamic keyboard shortcuts

1. First, you have to activate this capability by checking the Use dynamic keyboard shortcuts option in the Interface item of the Preferences menu. This option is usually not checked, to prevent accidental key presses from creating an unwanted shortcut.

2. While you're doing that, also check the Save keyboard shortcuts on exit option so that your shortcut will be saved.

3. To create a keyboard shortcut, simply place the mouse pointer on a command in the menu: it will then be highlighted. Be careful that the mouse pointer doesn't move and type a sequence of three keys, keeping the keys pressed. You will see this sequence appear on the right of the command.

4. It is best to use the Ctrl-Alt-Key sequence for your custom shortcuts.

Figure 12.31 Configure Keyboard Shortcuts

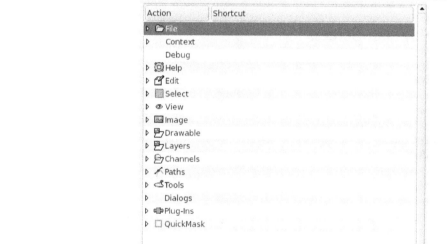

Using the Keyboard Shortcut Editor

1. You get to this Editor by clicking on Configure keyboard shortcuts in the "Interface" item of the Preferences menu.

2. As shown in this dialog, you can select the command you want to create a shortcut for, in the "Action" area. Then you type your key sequence as above. In principle, the Space bar should clear a shortcut. (In practice, it clears it, but doesn't delete it.)

3. This shortcut editor also allows you to *control the tool parameter settings* with the keyboard. At the top of this dialog, you can find a Context menu that takes you to the tool parameters. To make your work easier, tool types are marked with small icons.

Note

Custom Keyboard shortcuts are stored in one of Gimp's hidden directory (`/home/`
`[username]/.gimp-2.8/menurc`) under Linux. Under Windows, path varies
according to version:

- `C:\Documents and Settings\[Username]\.gimp-2.8\menurc`
  under Windows XP.

- `C:\Program Files\GIMP 2\etc\gimp\2.0\menurc` under Windows
  7.

- `C:\Programmes\GIMP 2\etc\gimp\2.0\menurc` under Windows 10.

More, this location may change if GIMP is installed after having already installed
Git Bash or Cygwin. In this case, they will appear in `C:\Program Files\Git\`
`.gimp-[version]\menurc`.

"menu.rc" is a simple text file that you can transport from one computer to another.

12.6   Customize Splash-Screen

When you start GIMP, you see the *splash-screen* displaying short status messages while the program is
loading all its components.

   Of course, you can customize the splash-screen: Create a `splashes` directory in your in your personal GIMP folder (`/home/user_name/.gimp-2.8` on Linux, `C:\\Documents and Settings\`
`\user_name\\.gimp-2.8\\` on Windows).

   Copy your image(s) into this `splashes` directory. On start, GIMP will read this directory and choose
one of the images at random.

Tip

Make sure that your images aren't too small.

Chapter 13

Scripting

13.1 Plugins

13.1.1 Introduction

One of the nicest things about GIMP is how easily its functionality can be extended, by using plugins. GIMP plugins are external programs that run under the control of the main GIMP application and interact with it very closely. Plugins can manipulate images in almost any way that users can. Their advantage is that it is much easier to add a capability to GIMP by writing a small plugin than by modifying the huge mass of complex code that makes up the GIMP core. Many valuable plugins have C source code that only comes to 100-200 lines or so.

Several dozen plugins are included in the main GIMP distribution, and installed automatically along with GIMP. Most of them can be accessed through the Filters menu (in fact, everything in that menu is a plugin), but a number are located in other menus. In many cases you can use one without ever realizing that it is a plugin: for example, the "Normalize" function for automatic color correction is actually a plugin, although there is nothing about the way it works that would tell you this.

In addition to the plugins included with GIMP , many more are available on the net. A large number can be found at the GIMP Plugin Registry [GIMP-REGISTRY], a web site whose purpose is to provide a central repository for plugins. Creators of plugins can upload them there; users in search of plugins for a specific purpose can search the site in a variety of ways.

Anybody in the world can write a GIMP plugin and make it available over the web, either via the Registry or a personal web site, and many very valuable plugins can be obtained in this way some are described elsewhere in the User's Manual. With this freedom from constraint comes a certain degree of risk, though: the fact that anybody can do it means that there is no effective quality control. The plugins distributed with GIMP have all been tested and tuned by the developers, but many that you can download were just hacked together in a few hours and then tossed to the winds. Some plugin creators just don't care about robustness, and even for those who do, their ability to test on a variety of systems in a variety of situations is often quite limited. Basically, when you download a plugin, you are getting something for free, and sometimes you get exactly what you pay for. This is not said in an attempt to discourage you, just to make sure you understand reality.

Warning

 Plugins, being full-fledged executable programs, can do any of the things that any other program can do, including install back-doors on your system or otherwise compromise its security. Don't install a plugin unless it comes from a trusted source.

These caveats apply as much to the Plugin Registry as to any other source of plugins. The Registry is available to any plugin creator who wants to use it: there is no systematic oversight. Obviously if the maintainers became aware that something evil was there, they would remove it. (That hasn't happened yet.) There is, however, for GIMP and its plugins the same warranty as for any other free software: namely, none.

Caution

Plugins have been a feature of GIMP for many versions. However, plugins written for one version of GIMP can hardly ever be used successfully with other versions. They need to be ported: sometimes this is easy, sometimes not. Many plugins are already available in several versions. Bottom line: before trying to install a plugin, make sure that it is written for your version of GIMP.

13.1.2 Using Plugins

For the most part you can use a plugin like any other GIMP tool, without needing to be aware that it is a plugin. But there are a few things about plugins that are useful to understand.

One is that plugins are generally not as robust as the GIMP core. When GIMP crashes, it is considered a very serious thing: it can cost the user a lot of trouble and headache. When a plugin crashes, the consequences are usually not so serious. In most cases you can just continuing working without worrying about it.

Note

Because plugins are separate programs, they communicate with the GIMP core in a special way: The GIMP developers call it "talking over a wire". When a plugin crashes, the communication breaks down, and you will see an error message about a "wire read error".

Tip

When a plugin crashes, GIMP gives you a very ominous-looking message telling you that the plugin may have left GIMP in a corrupted state, and you should consider saving your images and exiting. Strictly speaking, this is quite correct, because plugins have the power to alter almost anything in GIMP, but for practical purposes, experience has shown that corruption is actually quite rare, and many users just continue working and don't worry about it. Our advice is that you simply think about how much trouble it would cause you if something went wrong, and weigh it against the odds.

Because of the way plugins communicate with GIMP, they do not have any mechanism for being informed about changes you make to an image after the plugin has been started. If you start a plugin, and then alter the image using some other tool, the plugin will often crash, and when it doesn't will usually give a bogus result. You should avoid running more than one plugin at a time on an image, and avoid doing anything to the image until the plugin has finished working on it. If you ignore this advice, not only will you probably screw up the image, you will probably screw up the undo system as well, so that you won't even be able to recover from your foolishness.

13.1.3 Installing New Plugins

The plugins that are distributed with GIMP don't require any special installation. Plugins that you download yourself do. There are several scenarios, depending on what OS you are using and how the plugin is structured. In Linux it is usually pretty easy to install a new plugin; in Windows, it is either easy or very hard. In any case, the two are best considered separately.

13.1.3.1 Linux / Unix-sytem like systems

Most plugins fall into two categories: small ones whose source code is distributed as a single .c file, and larger ones whose source code is distributed as a directory containing multiple files including a `Makefile`.

For a simple one-file plugin, call it `borker.c`, installing it is just a matter of running the command **gimptool-2.0 --install borker.c**. This command compiles the plugin and installs it in your personal plugin directory, `~/gimp-2.4/plugins` unless you have changed it. This will cause it to be loaded automatically the next time you start GIMP. You don't need to be root to do these things; in fact, you shouldn't be. If the plugin fails to compile, well, be creative.

Once you have installed the plugin, how do you activate it? The menu path is determined by the plugin itself, so to answer this you need to either look at the documentation for the plugin (if there is any), or launch the Plugin Description dialog (from Xtns/Plugins Details) search the plug-in by its name and look of the Tree view tab. If you still don't find, finally explore the menus or look at the source code in the Register section -- whichever is easiest.

For more complex plugins, organized as a directory with multiple files, there ought to be a file inside called either `INSTALL` or `README`, with instructions. If not, the best advice is to toss the plugin in the trash and spend your time on something else: any code written with so little concern for the user is likely to be frustrating in myriad ways.

Some plugins (specifically those based on the GIMP Plugin Template) are designed to be installed in the main system GIMP directory, rather than your home directory. For these, you will need to be root to perform the final stage of installation (when issuing the **make install** command).

If you install in your personal plugin directory a plugin that has the same name as one in the system plugin directory, only one can be loaded, and it will be the one in your home directory. You will receive messages telling you this each time you start GIMP. This is probably a situation best avoided.

13.1.3.2 Windows

Windows is a much more problematic environment for building software than Linux. Every decent Linux distribution comes fully supplied with tools for compiling software, and they are all very similar in the way they work, but Windows does not come with such tools. It is possible to set up a good software-building environment in Windows, but it requires either a substantial amount of money or a substantial amount of effort and knowledge.

What this means in relation to GIMP plugins is the following: either you have an environment in which you can build software, or you don't. If you don't, then your best hope is to find a precompiled version of the plugin somewhere (or persuade somebody to compile it for you), in which case you simply need to put it into your personal plugin directory. If you do have an environment in which you can build software (which for present purposes means an environment in which you can build GIMP), then you no doubt already know quite a bit about these things, and just need to follow the Linux instructions.

13.1.3.3 Apple Mac OS X

How you install plugins on OS X mostly depends on how you installed GIMP itself. If you were one of the brave and installed GIMP through one of the package managers like fink [DARWINORTS] or darwinports, [FINK] the plugin installation works exactly the way it is described for the Linux platform already. The only difference is, that a couple of plugins might be even available in the repository of you package manager, so give it a try.

If you on the other hand are one of the Users that preferred to grab a prebuild GIMP package like GIMP.app, you most probably want to stick to that prebuild stuff. So you can try to get a prebuild version of the plugin of you dreams from the author of the plugin, but I'd not want to bet on this. Building your own binaries unfortunately involves installing GIMP through one of the package managers mentioned above.

13.1.4 Writing Plugins

If you want to learn how to write a plugin, you can find plenty of help at the GIMP Developers web site [GIMP-DEV-PLUGIN]. GIMP is a complex program, but the development team has made strenuous efforts to flatten the learning curve for plugin writing: there are good instructions and examples, and the main library that plugins use to interface with GIMP (called "libgimp") has a well-documented API.

Good programmers, learning by modifying existing plugins, are often able to accomplish interesting things after just a couple of days of work.

13.2 Using Script-Fu Scripts

13.2.1 Script-Fu?

Script-Fu is what the Windows world would call "macros" But Script-Fu is more powerful than that. Script-Fu is based on an interpreting language called Scheme, and works by using querying functions to the GIMP database. You can do all kinds of things with Script-Fu, but an ordinary GIMP user will probably use it for automating things that:

- You want to do frequently.

- Are really complicated to do, and hard to remember.

Remember that you can do a whole lot with Script-Fu. The scripts that come with GIMP can be quite useful, but they can also serve as models for learning Script-Fu, or at least as a framework and source of modification when you make your own script. Read the Script-Fu Tutorial in the next section if you want to learn more about how to make scripts.

We will describe some of the most useful scripts in this chapter, but we won't cover them all. There are simply too many scripts. Some of the scripts are also very simple and you will probably not need any documentation to be able to use them.

Script-Fu (a dialect of Scheme) isn't the only scripting language available for GIMP. But Script-Fu is the only scripting language that is installed by default.

13.2.2 Installing Script-Fus

One of the great things about Script-Fu is that you can share your script with all your GIMP friends. There are many scripts that come with GIMP by default, but there are also vast quantities of scripts that are available for download all around the Internet.

1. If you have downloaded a script, copy or move it to your scripts directory. It can be found in the Preferences: Folders → Scripts.

2. Do a refresh by using Filters → Script-Fu → Refresh Scripts from the image menubar. The script will now appear in one of your menus. If you don't find it, look for it under the root file menu filters. If it doesn't appear at all, something was wrong with the script (e.g. it contains syntax errors).

13.2.3 Do's and Don'ts

A common error when you are dealing with Script-Fus is that you simply bring them up and press the OK button. When nothing happens, you probably think that the script is broken or buggy, but there is most likely nothing wrong with it.

13.2.4 Different Kinds Of Script-Fus

There are two kinds of Script-Fus:

Standalone Script-Fus You will find the standalone variants under File → Create → Type of Script in the image menubar (see the figure below).

Figure 13.1 Script-Fus by category

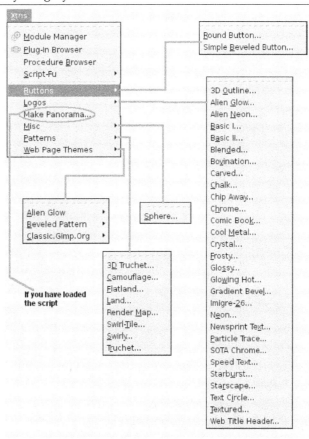

Image-dependent Script-Fus Menus have been reorganized. A new Colors-menu appears. It groups together all scripts that work on colors, for example tools that adjust hue, saturation, lightness..., filters...etc. Filters-menu and Script-Fu-menu are merged in one Filters-menu and it is organized according to new categories. Image-dependent Plug-ins and Script-Fus are now disseminated in the image-menus. For example, Color to Alpha filter is in Colors-menu. At the beginning, it's disconcerting, but you finish to get used to this because it's more logical.

The figure below show where you can find them in the image-menu.

Figure 13.2 Where find Image-dependent scripts

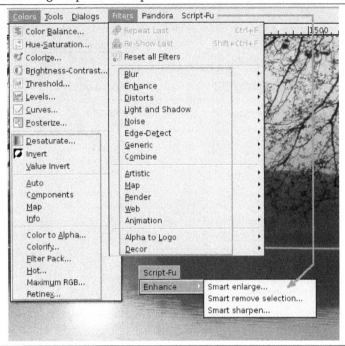

13.2.5 Standalone Scripts

We will not try to describe every script in depth. Most Script-Fus are very easy to understand and use. At the time of this writing, the following types are installed by default:

- Patterns

- Web page themes

- Logos

- Buttons

Patterns You will find all kinds of pattern-generating scripts here. Generally, they are quite useful because you can add many arguments to your own patterns.

> We'll take a look at the Land script. In this script you have to set the image/pattern size, and specify what levels of random to use for your land creation. The colors used to generate the land map are taken from the currently selected gradient in the gradient editor. You must also supply values for the level of detail, land and sea height/depth and the scale. Scale refers to the scale of your map, just as in an ordinary road map, 1:10 will be typed as 10.

Web Page Themes Here is clearly a practical use for scripts. By creating a script for making custom text, logos, buttons arrows, etc., for your web site, you will give them all the same style and shape. You will also be saving a lot of time, because you don't have to create every logo, text or button by hand.

> Most of the scripts are quite self-explanatory, but here are some hints:

- Leave all strange characters like ' and " intact.
- Make sure that the pattern specified in the script exists.
- Padding refers to the amount of space around your text.
- A high value for bevel width gives the illusion of a higher button.
- If you type TRUE for "Press", the button will look pushed down.

- Choose transparency if you don't want a solid background. If you choose a solid background, make sure it is the same color as the web page background.

Here you will find all kinds of logo-generating scripts. This is nice, but use it with care, as people might recognize your logo as being made by a known GIMP script. You should rather regard it as a base that you can modify to fit your needs. The dialog for making a logo is more or less the same for all such scripts:

Logos   1. In the Text String field, type your logo name, like Frozenriver.

        2. In the Font Size text field, type the size of your logo in pixels.

        3. In the Font text field, type the name of the font that you want to use for your logo.

        4. To choose the color of your logo, just click on the color button. This brings up a color dialog.

        5. If you look at the current command field, you can watch the script run.

Make Buttons Under this headline you'll find two scripts that makes rectangular beveled buttons, with or without round corners (Round Button or Simple Beveled Button). They have a dozen parameters or so, and most of them are similar to those in the logo scripts. You can experiment with different settings to come up with a button you like.

13.2.6 Image-Dependent Scripts

Now, scripts and filters that perform operations on an existing image are accessible directly by the appropriate menu. For example, the script New Brush (script-fu-paste-as-brush) is integrated in the Edit image menu (Edit → Paste as... → New Brush), that is more logical.

Furthermore, a new Color menu has been created that regroups together all that concern works on colors, the hue or level color adjustment tools, etc...

Filters menu and Script-Fu menu are regrouped in one Filters menu and organised according to new categories. Now if a plugin and a filter works similarly, they are nearby in the menu.

The Script-Fu menu only appears if you have loaded additional scripts: for example the gimp-resynthesizer pack corresponding to your Linux distribution (.deb, .rpm, .gz ...).

13.3 A Script-Fu Tutorial

In this training course, we'll introduce you to the fundamentals of Scheme necessary to use Script-Fu, and then build a handy script that you can add to your toolbox of scripts. The script prompts the user for some text, then creates a new image sized perfectly to the text. We will then enhance the script to allow for a buffer of space around the text. We will conclude with a few suggestions for ways to ramp up your knowledge of Script-Fu.

Note

 This section as adapted from a tutorial written for the GIMP 1 User Manual by Mike Terry.

13.3.1 Getting Acquainted With Scheme

13.3.1.1 Let's Start Scheme'ing

The first thing to learn is that:

Every statement in Scheme is surrounded by parentheses ().

The second thing you need to know is that:

The function name/operator is always the first item in the parentheses, and the rest of the items are parameters to the function.

However, not everything enclosed in parentheses is a function — they can also be items in a list — but we'll get to that later. This notation is referred to as prefix notation, because the function prefixes everything else. If you're familiar with postfix notation, or own a calculator that uses Reverse Polish Notation (such as most HP calculators), you should have no problem adapting to formulating expressions in Scheme.

The third thing to understand is that:

> Mathematical operators are also considered functions, and thus are listed first when writing mathematical expressions.

This follows logically from the prefix notation that we just mentioned.

13.3.1.2 Examples Of Prefix, Infix, And Postfix Notations

Here are some quick examples illustrating the differences between *prefix*, *infix*, and *postfix* notations. We'll add a 1 and 23 together:

- Prefix notation: **+ 1 23** (the way Scheme will want it)

- Infix notation: **1 + 23** (the way we "normally" write it)

- Postfix notation: **1 23 +** (the way many HP calculators will want it)

13.3.1.3 Practicing In Scheme

Now, let's practice what we have just learned. Start up GIMP, if you have not already done so, and choose Filters → Script-Fu → Console. This will start up the Script-Fu Console window, which allows us to work interactively in Scheme. In a matter of moments, the Script-Fu Console will appear:

13.3.1.4 The Script-Fu Console Window

At the bottom of this window is an entry-field ought to be entitled Current Command. Here, we can test out simple Scheme commands interactively. Let's start out easy, and add some numbers:

```
(+ 3 5)
```

Typing this in and hitting **Enter** yields the expected answer of 8 in the center window.

Figure 13.3 Use Script-Fu Console.

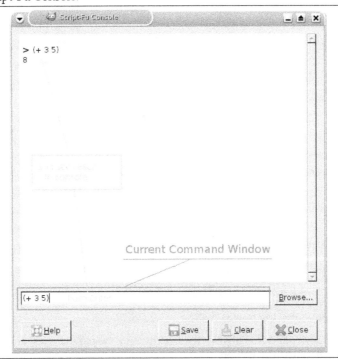

Now, what if we wanted to add more than one number? The "+" function can take two or more arguments, so this is not a problem:

```
(+ 3 5 6)
```

This also yields the expected answer of 14.

So far, so good — we type in a Scheme statement and it's executed immediately in the Script-Fu Console window. Now for a word of caution...

13.3.1.5 Watch Out For Extra Parentheses

If you're like me, you're used to being able to use extra parentheses whenever you want to — like when you're typing a complex mathematical equation and you want to separate the parts by parentheses to make it clearer when you read it. In Scheme, you have to be careful and not insert these extra parentheses incorrectly. For example, say we wanted to add 3 to the result of adding 5 and 6 together:

```
3 + (5 + 6) + 7 = ?
```

Knowing that the + operator can take a list of numbers to add, you might be tempted to convert the above to the following:

```
(+ 3 (5 6) 7)
```

However, this is incorrect — remember, every statement in Scheme starts and ends with parens, so the Scheme interpreter will think that you're trying to call a function named "5" in the second group of parens, rather than summing those numbers before adding them to 3.

The correct way to write the above statement would be:

```
(+ 3 (+ 5 6) 7)
```

13.3.1.6 Make Sure You Have The Proper Spacing, Too

If you are familiar with other programming languages, like C/C++, Perl or Java, you know that you don't need white space around mathematical operators to properly form an expression:

```
3+5, 3 +5, 3+ 5
```

These are all accepted by C/C++, Perl and Java compilers. However, the same is not true for Scheme. You must have a space after a mathematical operator (or any other function name or operator) in Scheme for it to be correctly interpreted by the Scheme interpreter.

Practice a bit with simple mathematical equations in the Script-Fu Console until you're totally comfortable with these initial concepts.

13.3.2 Variables And Functions

Now that we know that every Scheme statement is enclosed in parentheses, and that the function name/-operator is listed first, we need to know how to create and use variables, and how to create and use functions. We'll start with the variables.

13.3.2.1 Declaring Variables

Although there are a couple of different methods for declaring variables, the preferred method is to use the **let*** construct. If you're familiar with other programming languages, this construct is equivalent to defining a list of local variables and a scope in which they're active. As an example, to declare two variables, a and b, initialized to 1 and 2, respectively, you'd write:

```
(let*
    (
        (a 1)
        (b 2)
    )
    (+ a b)
)
```

or, as one line:

```
(let* ( (a 1) (b 2) ) (+ a b) )
```

> **Note**
>
> You'll have to put all of this on one line if you're using the console window. In general, however, you'll want to adopt a similar practice of indentation to help make your scripts more readable. We'll talk a bit more about this in the section on White Space.

This declares two local variables, a and b, initializes them, then prints the sum of the two variables.

13.3.2.2 What Is A Local Variable?

You'll notice that we wrote the summation `(+ a b)` within the parens of the `let*` expression, not after it.

This is because the `let*` statement defines an area in your script in which the declared variables are usable; if you type the **(+ a b)** statement after the **(let* ...)** statement, you'll get an error, because the declared variables are only valid within the context of the `let*` statement; they are what programmers call local variables.

13.3.2.3 The General Syntax Of `let*`

The general form of a `let*` statement is:

```
(let* ( variables )
  expressions )
```

where variables are declared within parens, e.g., **(a 2)**, and expressions are any valid Scheme expressions. Remember that the variables declared here are only valid within the `let*` statement — they're local variables.

13.3.2.4 White Space

Previously, we mentioned the fact that you'll probably want to use indentation to help clarify and organize your scripts. This is a good policy to adopt, and is not a problem in Scheme — white space is ignored by the Scheme interpreter, and can thus be liberally applied to help clarify and organize the code within a script. However, if you're working in Script-Fu's Console window, you'll have to enter an entire expression on one line; that is, everything between the opening and closing parens of an expression must come on one line in the Script-Fu Console window.

13.3.2.5 Assigning A New Value To A Variable

Once you've initialized a variable, you might need to change its value later on in the script. Use the `set!` statement to change the variable's value:

```
(let* ( (theNum 10) ) (set! theNum (+ theNum theNum)) )
```

Try to guess what the above statement will do, then go ahead and enter it in the Script-Fu Console window.

> **Note**
>
> The "\" indicates that there is no line break. Ignore it (don't type it in your Script-Fu console and don't hit **Enter**), just continue with the next line.

13.3.2.6 Functions

Now that you've got the hang of variables, let's get to work with some functions. You declare a function with the following syntax:

```
(define
    (
        name
        param-list
    )
    expressions
)
```

where *name* is the name assigned to this function, *param-list* is a space-delimited list of parameter names, and *expressions* is a series of expressions that the function executes when it's called. For example:

```
(define (AddXY inX inY) (+ inX inY) )
```

AddXY is the function's name and inX and inY are the variables. This function takes its two parameters and adds them together.

If you've programmed in other imperative languages (like C/C++, Java, Pascal, etc.), you might notice that a couple of things are absent in this function definition when compared to other programming languages.

- First, notice that the parameters don't have any "types" (that is, we didn't declare them as strings, or integers, etc.). Scheme is a type-less language. This is handy and allows for quicker script writing.

- Second, notice that we don't need to worry about how to "return" the result of our function — the last statement is the value "returned" when calling this function. Type the function into the console, then try something like:

  ```
  (AddXY (AddXY 5 6) 4)
  ```

13.3.3 Lists, Lists And More Lists

We've trained you in variables and functions, and now enter the murky swamps of Scheme's lists.

13.3.3.1 Defining A List

Before we talk more about lists, it is necessary that you know the difference between atomic values and lists.

You've already seen atomic values when we initialized variables in the previous lesson. An atomic value is a single value. So, for example, we can assign the variable "x" the single value of 8 in the following statement:

```
(let* ( (x 8) ) x)
```

(We added the expression x at the end to print out the value assigned to x—normally you won't need to do this. Notice how let* operates just like a function: The value of the last statement is the value returned.)

A variable may also refer to a list of values, rather than a single value. To assign the variable x the list of values 1, 3, 5, we'd type:

```
(let* ( (x '(1 3 5))) x)
```

Try typing both statements into the Script-Fu Console and notice how it replies. When you type the first statement in, it simply replies with the result:

```
8
```

However, when you type in the other statement, it replies with the following result:

```
(1 3 5)
```

When it replies with the value 8 it is informing you that x contains the atomic value 8. However, when it replies with `(1 3 5)`, it is then informing you that x contains not a single value, but a list of values. Notice that there are no commas in our declaration or assignment of the list, nor in the printed result.

The syntax to define a list is:

```
'(a b c)
```

where a, b, and c are literals. We use the apostrophe (`'`) to indicate that what follows in the parentheses is a list of literal values, rather than a function or expression.

An empty list can be defined as such:

```
'()
```

or simply:

```
()
```

Lists can contain atomic values, as well as other lists:

```
(let*
    (
        (x
            '("GIMP" (1 2 3) ("is" ("great" () ) ) )
        )
    )
    x
)
```

Notice that after the first apostrophe, you no longer need to use an apostrophe when defining the inner lists. Go ahead and copy the statement into the Script-Fu Console and see what it returns.

You should notice that the result returned is not a list of single, atomic values; rather, it is a list of a literal (`"The GIMP"`), the list (`1 2 3`), etc.

13.3.3.2   How To Think Of Lists

It's useful to think of lists as composed of a "head" and a "tail". The head is the first element of the list, the tail the rest of the list. You'll see why this is important when we discuss how to add to lists and how to access elements in the list.

13.3.3.3   Creating Lists Through Concatenation (The Cons Function)

One of the more common functions you'll encounter is the cons function. It takes a value and places it to its second argument, a list. From the previous section, I suggested that you think of a list as being composed of an element (the head) and the remainder of the list (the tail). This is exactly how cons functions — it adds an element to the head of a list. Thus, you could create a list as follows:

```
(cons 1 '(2 3 4) )
```

The result is the list (`1 2 3 4`).
You could also create a list with one element:

```
(cons 1 () )
```

You can use previously declared variables in place of any literals, as you would expect.

13.3.3.4   Defining A List Using The `list` Function

To define a list composed of literals or previously declared variables, use the `list` function:

```
(list 5 4 3 a b c)
```

This will compose and return a list containing the values held by the variables a, b and c. For example:

```
(let*  (
          (a 1)
          (b 2)
          (c 3)
        )

      (list 5 4 3 a b c)
  )
```

This code creates the list `(5 4 3 1 2 3)`.

13.3.3.5 Accessing Values In A List

To access the values in a list, use the functions `car` and `cdr`, which return the first element of the list and the rest of the list, respectively. These functions break the list down into the head::tail construct I mentioned earlier.

13.3.3.6 The **car** Function

`car` returns the first element of the list (the head of the list). The list needs to be non-null. Thus, the following returns the first element of the list:

```
(car '("first" 2 "third"))
```

which is:

```
"first"
```

13.3.3.7 The **cdr** function

`cdr` returns the rest of the list after the first element (the tail of the list). If there is only one element in the list, it returns an empty list.

```
(cdr '("first" 2 "third"))
```

returns:

```
(2 "third")
```

whereas the following:

```
(cdr '("one and only"))
```

returns:

```
()
```

13.3.3.8 Accessing Other Elements In A List

OK, great, we can get the first element in a list, as well as the rest of the list, but how do we access the second, third or other elements of a list? There exist several "convenience" functions to access, for example, the head of the head of the tail of a list (`caadr`), the tail of the tail of a list (`cddr`), etc.

The basic naming convention is easy: The a's and d's represent the heads and tails of lists, so

```
(car (cdr (car x) ) )
```

could be written as:

```
(cadar x)
```

To get some practice with list-accessing functions, try typing in the following (except all on one line if you're using the console); use different variations of `car` and `cdr` to access the different elements of the list:

```
(let* (
        (x  '( (1 2 (3 4 5) 6)  7  8  (9 10) )
        )
      )
      ; place your car/cdr code here
)
```

Try accessing the number 3 in the list using only two function calls. If you can do that, you're on your way to becoming a Script-Fu Master!

Note

In Scheme, a semicolon (;) marks a comment. It, and anything that follows it on the same line, are ignored by the script interpreter, so you can use this to add comments to jog your memory when you look at the script later.

13.3.4 Your First Script-Fu Script

Do you not need to stop and catch your breath? No? Well then, let's proceed with your fourth lesson — your first Script-Fu Script.

13.3.4.1 Creating A Text Box Script

One of the most common operations I perform in GIMP is creating a box with some text in it for a web page, a logo or whatever. However, you never quite know how big to make the initial image when you start out. You don't know how much space the text will fill with the font and font size you want.

The Script-Fu Master (and student) will quickly realize that this problem can easily be solved and automated with Script-Fu.

We will, therefore, create a script, called Text Box, which creates an image correctly sized to fit snugly around a line of text the user inputs. We'll also let the user choose the font, font size and text color.

13.3.4.2 Editing And Storing Your Scripts

Up until now, we've been working in the Script-Fu Console. Now, however, we're going to switch to editing script text files.

Where you place your scripts is a matter of preference — if you have access to GIMP's default script directory, you can place your scripts there. However, I prefer keeping my personal scripts in my own script directory, to keep them separate from the factory-installed scripts.

In the .gimp-2.8 directory that GIMP made off of your home directory, you should find a directory called scripts. GIMP will automatically look in your .gimp-2.8 directory for a scripts directory, and add the scripts in this directory to the Script-Fu database. You should place your personal scripts here.

13.3.4.3 The Bare Essentials

Every Script-Fu script defines at least one function, which is the script's main function. This is where you do the work.

Every script must also register with the procedural database, so you can access it within GIMP.

We'll define the main function first:

```
(define (script-fu-text-box inText inFont inFontSize inTextColor))
```

Here, we've defined a new function called script-fu-text-box that takes four parameters, which will later correspond to some text, a font, the font size, and the text's color. The function is currently empty and thus does nothing. So far, so good — nothing new, nothing fancy.

13.3.4.4 Naming Conventions

Scheme's naming conventions seem to prefer lowercase letters with hyphens, which I've followed in the naming of the function. However, I've departed from the convention with the parameters. I like more descriptive names for my parameters and variables, and thus add the "in" prefix to the parameters so I can quickly see that they're values passed into the script, rather than created within it. I use the prefix "the" for variables defined within the script.

It's GIMP convention to name your script functions `script-fu-abc`, because then when they're listed in the procedural database, they'll all show up under Script-Fu when you're listing the functions. This also helps distinguish them from plug-ins.

13.3.4.5 Registering The Function

Now, let's register the function with GIMP. This is done by calling the function `script-fu-register`. When GIMP reads in a script, it will execute this function, which registers the script with the procedural database. You can place this function call wherever you wish in your script, but I usually place it at the end, after all my other code.

Here's the listing for registering this function (I will explain all its parameters in a minute):

```
(script-fu-register
  "script-fu-text-box"                        ;func name
  "Text Box"                                  ;menu label
  "Creates a simple text box, sized to fit\
    around the user's choice of text,\
    font, font size, and color."              ;description
  "Michael Terry"                             ;author
  "copyright 1997, Michael Terry;\
    2009, the GIMP Documentation Team"        ;copyright notice
  "October 27, 1997"                          ;date created
  ""                      ;image type that the script works on
  SF-STRING      "Text"         "Text Box"    ;a string variable
  SF-FONT        "Font"         "Charter"     ;a font variable
  SF-ADJUSTMENT  "Font size"    '(50 1 1000 1 10 0 1)
                                              ;a spin-button
  SF-COLOR       "Color"        '(0 0 0)      ;color variable
)
(script-fu-menu-register "script-fu-text-box" "<Image>/File/Create/Text")
```

If you save these functions in a text file with a `.scm` suffix in your script directory, then choose Filters → Script-Fu → Refresh Scripts, this new script will appear as File → Create → Text → Text Box.

If you invoke this new script, it won't do anything, of course, but you can view the prompts you created when registering the script (more information about what we did is covered next).

Finally, if you invoke the Procedure Browser (Help → Procedure Browser), you'll notice that our script now appears in the database.

13.3.4.6 Steps For Registering The Script

To register our script with GIMP, we call the function `script-fu-register`, fill in the seven required parameters and add our script's own parameters, along with a description and default value for each parameter.

The Required Parameters

- The *name* of the function we defined. This is the function called when our script is invoked (the entry-point into our script). This is necessary because we may define additional functions within the same file, and GIMP needs to know which of these functions to call. In our example, we only defined one function, text-box, which we registered.

- The *location* in the menu where the script will be inserted. The exact location of the script is specified like a path in Unix, with the root of the path being image menu as `<Image>`.[1]

---

[1] Before version 2.6, `<Toolbox>` could be also used, but now the toolbox menu is removed, so don't use it.

If your script does not operate on an existing image (and thus creates a new image, like our Text Box script will), you'll want to insert it in the image window menu, which you can access through the image menu bar, by right-clicking the image window, by clicking the menu button icon at the left-top corner of the image window, or by pressing **F10**.

If your script is intended to work on an image being edited, you'll want to insert it in the image window menu. The rest of the path points to the menu lists, menus and sub-menus. Thus, we registered our Text Box script in the Text menu of the Create menu of the File menu.[2] (File → Create → Text → Text Box).

If you notice, the Text sub-menu in the File/Create menu wasn't there when we began — GIMP automatically creates any menus not already existing.

- A *description* of your script, to be displayed in the Procedure Browser.

- *Your name* (the author of the script).

- *Copyright* information.

- The *date* the script was made, or the last revision of the script.

- The *types* of images the script works on. This may be any of the following: RGB, RGBA, GRAY, GRAYA, INDEXED, INDEXEDA. Or it may be none at all — in our case, we're creating an image, and thus don't need to define the type of image on which we work.

Figure 13.4 The menu of our script.

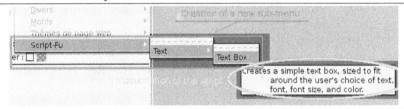

13.3.4.7   Registering The Script's Parameters

Once we have listed the required parameters, we then need to list the parameters that correspond to the parameters our script needs. When we list these params, we give hints as to what their types are. This is for the dialog which pops up when the user selects our script. We also provide a default value.

This section of the registration process has the following format:

Param Type	Description	Example
SF-IMAGE	If your script operates on an open image, this should be the first parameter after the required parameters. GIMP will pass in a reference to the image in this parameter.	3
SF-DRAWABLE	If your script operates on an open image, this should be the second parameter after the SF-IMAGE param. It refers to the active layer. GIMP will pass in a reference to the active layer in this parameter.	17

---

[2] The original, written by Mike, says put the menu entry in the Script-Fu menu of the Xtns menu at the Toolbox, but since version 2.6, the Toolbox menu had been removed and merged with the image window menubar.

Param Type	Description	Example
SF-VALUE	Accepts numbers and strings. Note that quotes must be escaped for default text, so better use SF-STRING.	42
SF-STRING	Accepts strings.	"Some text"
SF-COLOR	Indicates that a color is requested in this parameter.	'(0 102 255)
SF-TOGGLE	A checkbox is displayed, to get a Boolean value.	TRUE or FALSE

13.3.4.8 The Script-Fu parameter API[3]

> **Note**
>
>
> Beside the above parameter types there are more types for the interactive mode, each of them will create a widget in the control dialog. You will find a list of these parameters with descriptions and examples in the test script `plug-ins/script-fu/scripts/test-sphere.scm` shipped with the GIMP source code.

Param Type	Description
SF-ADJUSTMENT	Creates an adjustment widget in the dialog. SF-ADJUSTMENT "label" '(value lower upper step_inc page_inc digits type) **Widget arguments list** *Element:* "label", *Description:* Text printed before the widget. *Element:* value, *Description:* Value print at the start. *Element:* lower / upper, *Description:* The lower / upper values (range of choice). *Element:* step_inc, *Description:* Increment/decrement value. *Element:* page_inc, *Description:* Increment/decrement value using page key. *Element:* digits, *Description:* Digits after the point (decimal part). *Element:* type, *Description:* One of: SF-SLIDER or 0, SF-SPINNER or 1

---

[3] This section is not part of the original tutorial.

Param Type	Description
SF-COLOR	Creates a color button in the dialog. SF-COLOR "label" '(red green blue) or SF-COLOR "label" "color" **Widget arguments list** *Element:* "label", *Description:* Text printed before the widget. *Element:* '(red green blue), *Description:* List of three values for the red, green and blue components. *Element:* "color", *Description:* Color name in CSS notatation.
SF-FONT	Creates a font-selection widget in the dialog. It returns a fontname as a string. There are two new gimp-text procedures to ease the use of this return parameter: (gimp-text-fontname image drawable x-pos y-pos text border antialias size unit font) (gimp-text-get-extents-fontname text size unit font) where font is the fontname you get. The size specified in the fontname is silently ignored. It is only used in the font-selector. So you are asked to set it to a useful value (24 pixels is a good choice). SF-FONT "label" "fontname" **Widget arguments list** *Element:* "label", *Description:* Text printed before the widget. *Element:* "fontname", *Description:* Name of the default font.
SF-BRUSH	It will create a widget in the control dialog. The widget consists of a preview area (which when pressed will produce a popup preview) and a button with the "..." label. The button will popup a dialog where brushes can be selected and each of the characteristics of the brush can be modified. SF-BRUSH "Brush" '("Circle (03)" 100 44 0) Here the brush dialog will be popped up with a default brush of Circle (03) opacity 100 spacing 44 and paint mode of Normal (value 0). If this selection was unchanged the value passed to the function as a parameter would be '("Circle (03)" 100 44 0).

Param Type	Description
SF-PATTERN	It will create a widget in the control dialog. The widget consists of a preview area (which when pressed will produce a popup preview) and a button with the "..." label. The button will popup a dialog where patterns can be selected. SF-PATTERN "Pattern" "Maple Leaves" The value returned when the script is invoked is a string containing the pattern name. If the above selection was not altered the string would contain "Maple Leaves".
SF-GRADIENT	It will create a widget in the control dialog. The widget consists of a button containing a preview of the selected gradient. If the button is pressed a gradient selection dialog will popup. SF-GRADIENT "Gradient" "Deep Sea" The value returned when the script is invoked is a string containing the gradient name. If the above selection was not altered the string would contain "Deep Sea".
SF-PALETTE	It will create a widget in the control dialog. The widget consists of a button containing the name of the selected palette. If the button is pressed a palette selection dialog will popup. SF-PALETTE "Palette" "Named Colors" The value returned when the script is invoked is a string containing the palette name. If the above selection was not altered the string would contain "Named Colors".
SF-FILENAME	It will create a widget in the control dialog. The widget consists of a button containing the name of a file. If the button is pressed a file selection dialog will popup. SF-FILENAME "label" (string-append "" gimp-data-directory "/scripts/beavis.jpg") The value returned when the script is invoked is a string containing the filename.
SF-DIRNAME	Only useful in interactive mode. Very similar to SF-FILENAME, but the created widget allows to choose a directory instead of a file. SF-DIRNAME "label" "/var/tmp/images" The value returned when the script is invoked is a string containing the dirname.

Param Type	Description
SF-OPTION	It will create a widget in the control dialog. The widget is a combo-box showing the options that are passed as a list. The first option is the default choice. SF-OPTION "label" '("option1" "option2") The value returned when the script is invoked is the number of the chosen option, where the option first is counted as 0.
SF-ENUM	It will create a widget in the control dialog. The widget is a combo-box showing all enum values for the given enum type. This has to be the name of a registered enum, without the "Gimp" prefix. The second parameter speficies the default value, using the enum value's nick. SF-ENUM "Interpolation" '("InterpolationType" "linear") The value returned when the script is invoked corresponds to chosen enum value.

13.3.5 Giving Our Script Some Guts

Let us continue with our training and add some functionality to our script.

13.3.5.1 Creating A New Image

In the previous lesson, we created an empty function and registered it with GIMP. In this lesson, we want to provide functionality to our script — we want to create a new image, add the user's text to it and resize the image to fit the text exactly.

Once you know how to set variables, define functions and access list members, the rest is all downhill — all you need to do is familiarize yourself with the functions available in GIMP's procedural database and call those functions directly. So fire up the Section 16.12.7 and let's get cookin'!

Let's begin by making a new image. We'll create a new variable, theImage, set to the result of calling GIMP's built-in function gimp-image-new.

As you can see from the DB Browser, the function gimp-image-new takes three parameters — the image's width, height and the type of image. Because we'll later resize the image to fit the text, we'll make a 10x10 pixels RGB image. We'll store the image's width and sizes in some variables, too, as we'll refer to and manipulate them later in the script.

```
(define (script-fu-text-box inText inFont inFontSize inTextColor)
(let*
      (
        ; define our local variables
        ; create a new image:
        (theImageWidth  10)
        (theImageHeight 10)
        (theImage (car
                       (gimp-image-new
                        theImageWidth
                        theImageHeight
                        RGB
                       )
                  )
        )
        (theText)         ;a declaration for the text
                          ;we create later
```

Note: We used the value RGB to specify that the image is an RGB image. We could have also used 0, but RGB is more descriptive when we glance at the code.

You should also notice that we took the head of the result of the function call. This may seem strange, because the database explicitly tells us that it returns only one value — the ID of the newly created image. However, all GIMP functions return a list, even if there is only one element in the list, so we need to get the head of the list.

13.3.5.2   Adding A New Layer To The Image

Now that we have an image, we need to add a layer to it. We'll call the `gimp-layer-new` function to create the layer, passing in the ID of the image we just created. (From now on, instead of listing the complete function, we'll only list the lines we're adding to it. You can see the complete script here.) Because we've declared all of the local variables we'll use, we'll also close the parentheses marking the end of our variable declarations:

```
;create a new layer for the image:
    (theLayer
            (car
                  (gimp-layer-new
                   theImage
                   theImageWidth
                   theImageHeight
                   RGB-IMAGE
                   "layer 1"
                   100
                   NORMAL
                  )
             )
      )
) ;end of our local variables
```

Once we have the new layer, we need to add it to the image:

```
(gimp-image-add-layer theImage theLayer 0)
```

Now, just for fun, let's see the fruits of our labors up until this point, and add this line to show the new, empty image:

```
(gimp-display-new theImage)
```

Save your work, select Filters → Script-Fu → Refresh Scripts, run the script and a new image should pop up. It will probably contain garbage (random colors), because we haven't erased it. We'll get to that in a second.

13.3.5.3   Adding The Text

Go ahead and remove the line to display the image (or comment it out with a (;) as the first character of the line).

Before we add text to the image, we need to set the background and foreground colors so that the text appears in the color the user specified. We'll use the gimp-context-set-back/foreground functions:

```
(gimp-context-set-background '(255 255 255) )
(gimp-context-set-foreground inTextColor)
```

With the colors properly set, let's now clean out the garbage currently in the image by filling the drawable with the background color:

```
(gimp-drawable-fill theLayer BACKGROUND-FILL)
```

With the image cleared, we're ready to add some text:

```
(set! theText
            (car
                  (gimp-text-fontname
                   theImage theLayer
                   0 0
                   inText
```

```
                                0
                                TRUE
                                inFontSize PIXELS
                                "Sans")
                         )

               )
```

Although a long function call, it's fairly straightforward if you go over the parameters while looking at the function's entry in the DB Browser. Basically, we're creating a new text layer and assigning it to the variable theText.

Now that we have the text, we can grab its width and height and resize the image and the image's layer to the text's size:

```
(set! theImageWidth    (car (gimp-drawable-width  theText) ) )
(set! theImageHeight   (car (gimp-drawable-height theText) ) )

(gimp-image-resize theImage theImageWidth theImageHeight 0 0)

(gimp-layer-resize theLayer theImageWidth theImageHeight 0 0)
```

If you're like me, you're probably wondering what a drawable is when compared to a layer. The difference between the two is that a drawable is anything that can be drawn into, including layers but also channels, layer masks, the selection, etc; a layer is a more specific version of a drawable. In most cases, the distinction is not important.

With the image ready to go, we can now re-add our display line:

```
(gimp-display-new theImage)
```

Save your work, refresh the database and give your first script a run!

13.3.5.4   Clearing The Dirty Flag

If you try to close the image created without first saving the file, GIMP will ask you if you want to save your work before you close the image. It asks this because the image is marked as dirty, or unsaved. In the case of our script, this is a nuisance for the times when we simply give it a test run and don't add or change anything in the resulting image — that is, our work is easily reproducible in such a simple script, so it makes sense to get rid of this dirty flag.

To do this, we can clear the dirty flag after displaying the image:

```
(gimp-image-clean-all theImage)
```

This will set dirty count to 0, making it appear to be a "clean" image.

Whether to add this line or not is a matter of personal taste. I use it in scripts that produce new images, where the results are trivial, as in this case. If your script is very complicated, or if it works on an existing image, you will probably not want to use this function.

13.3.6   Extending The Text Box Script

13.3.6.1   Handling Undo Correctly

When creating a script, you want to give your users the ability to undo their actions, should they make a mistake. This is easily accomplished by calling the functions gimp-undo-push-group-start and gimp-undo-push-group-end around the code that manipulates the image. You can think of them as matched statements that let GIMP know when to start and stop recording manipulations on the image, so that those manipulations can later be undone.

If you are creating a new image entirely, it doesn't make sense to use these functions because you're not changing an existing image. However, when you are changing an existing image, you most surely want to use these functions.

Undoing a script works nearly flawlessly when using these functions.

13.3.6.2 Extending The Script A Little More

Now that we have a very handy-dandy script to create text boxes, let's add two features to it:

- Currently, the image is resized to fit exactly around the text — there's no room for anything, like drop shadows or special effects (even though many scripts will automatically resize the image as necessary). Let's add a buffer around the text, and even let the user specify how much buffer to add as a percentage of the size of the resultant text.

- This script could easily be used in other scripts that work with text. Let's extend it so that it returns the image and the layers, so other scripts can call this script and use the image and layers we create.

13.3.6.3 Modifying The Parameters And The Registration Function

To let the user specify the amount of buffer, we'll add a parameter to our function and the registration function:

```
(define (script-fu-text-box inTest inFont inFontSize inTextColor inBufferAmount ←
    )
  (let*
      (
        ; define our local variables
        ; create a new image:
        (theImageWidth  10)
        (theImageHeight 10)
        (theImage (car
                    (gimp-image-new
                     theImageWidth
                     theImageHeight
                     RGB
                     )
                   )
        )
        (theText)          ;a declaration for the text
                           ;we create later

        (theBuffer)        ;added

        (theLayer
               (car
                    (gimp-layer-new
                     theImage
                     theImageWidth
                     theImageHeight
                     RGB-IMAGE
                     "layer 1"
                     100
                     NORMAL
                     )
                   )
        )
      ) ;end of our local variables

  [Code here]
)

(script-fu-register
  "script-fu-text-box"                          ;func name
  "Text Box"                                    ;menu label
  "Creates a simple text box, sized to fit\
    around the user's choice of text,\
    font, font size, and color."                ;description
  "Michael Terry"                               ;author
  "copyright 1997, Michael Terry;\
```

```
   2009, the GIMP Documentation Team"          ;copyright notice
  "October 27, 1997"                           ;date created
  ""                     ;image type that the script works on
   SF-STRING      "Text"           "Text Box"  ;a string variable
   SF-FONT        "Font"           "Charter"   ;a font variable
   SF-ADJUSTMENT  "Font size"      '(50 1 1000 1 10 0 1)
                                               ;a spin-button
   SF-COLOR       "Color"          '(0 0 0)    ;color variable
   SF-ADJUSTMENT  "Buffer amount" '(35 0 100 1 10 1 0)
                                               ;a slider
 )
 (script-fu-menu-register "script-fu-text-box" "<Image>/Font/Create/Text")
```

13.3.6.4 Adding The New Code

We're going to add code in two places: right before we resize the image, and at the end of the script (to return the new image, the layer and the text).

After we get the text's height and width, we need to resize these values based on the buffer amount specified by the user. We won't do any error checking to make sure it's in the range of 0-100% because it's not life-threatening, and because there's no reason why the user can't enter a value like "200" as the percent of buffer to add.

```
        (set! theBuffer (* theImageHeight (/ inBufferAmount 100) ) )

        (set! theImageHeight (+ theImageHeight theBuffer theBuffer) )
        (set! theImageWidth  (+ theImageWidth  theBuffer theBuffer) )
```

All we're doing here is setting the buffer based on the height of the text, and adding it twice to both the height and width of our new image. (We add it twice to both dimensions because the buffer needs to be added to both sides of the text.)

Now that we have resized the image to allow for a buffer, we need to center the text within the image. This is done by moving it to the (x, y) coordinates of (theBuffer, theBuffer). I added this line after resizing the layer and the image:

```
        (gimp-layer-set-offsets theText theBuffer theBuffer)
```

Go ahead and save your script, and try it out after refreshing the database.

All that is left to do is return our image, the layer, and the text layer. After displaying the image, we add this line:

```
(list theImage theLayer theText)
```

This is the last line of the function, making this list available to other scripts that want to use it.

To use our new text box script in another script, we could write something like the following:

```
        (set! theResult (script-fu-text-box
                        "Some text"
                        "Charter" "30"
                        '(0 0 0)
                        "35"
                        )
        )
        (gimp-image-flatten (car theResult))
```

Congratulations, you are on your way to your Black Belt of Script-Fu!

13.3.7 Your script and its working

13.3.7.1 What you write

Below the complete script:

```
(script-fu-register
        "script-fu-text-box"                         ;func name
        "Text Box"                                   ;menu label
        "Creates a simple text box, sized to fit\
          around the user's choice of text,\
          font, font size, and color."               ;description
        "Michael Terry"                              ;author
        "copyright 1997, Michael Terry;\
          2009, the GIMP Documentation Team"         ;copyright notice
        "October 27, 1997"                           ;date created
        ""                          ;image type that the script works on
        SF-STRING       "Text"          "Text Box"   ;a string variable
        SF-FONT         "Font"          "Charter"    ;a font variable
        SF-ADJUSTMENT   "Font size"     '(50 1 1000 1 10 0 1)
                                                     ;a spin-button
        SF-COLOR        "Color"         '(0 0 0)     ;color variable
        SF-ADJUSTMENT   "Buffer amount" '(35 0 100 1 10 1 0)
                                                     ;a slider
)
(script-fu-menu-register "script-fu-text-box" "<Image>/File/Create/Text")
(define (script-fu-text-box inText inFont inFontSize inTextColor inBufferAmount ↩
   )
  (let*
    (
      ; define our local variables
      ; create a new image:
      (theImageWidth  10)
      (theImageHeight 10)
      (theImage)
      (theImage
              (car
                   (gimp-image-new
                     theImageWidth
                     theImageHeight
                     RGB
                   )
              )
      )
      (theText)               ;a declaration for the text
      (theBuffer)             ;create a new layer for the image
      (theLayer
              (car
                   (gimp-layer-new
                     theImage
                     theImageWidth
                     theImageHeight
                     RGB-IMAGE
                     "layer 1"
                     100
                     NORMAL
                   )
              )
      )
    ) ;end of our local variables
    (gimp-image-add-layer theImage theLayer 0)
    (gimp-context-set-background '(255 255 255) )
    (gimp-context-set-foreground inTextColor)
    (gimp-drawable-fill theLayer BACKGROUND-FILL)
    (set! theText
              (car
                   (gimp-text-fontname
                     theImage theLayer
                     0 0
```

```
                          inText
                          0
                          TRUE
                          inFontSize PIXELS
                          "Sans")
                    )
        )
    (set! theImageWidth   (car (gimp-drawable-width  theText) ) )
    (set! theImageHeight  (car (gimp-drawable-height theText) ) )
    (set! theBuffer (* theImageHeight (/ inBufferAmount 100) ) )
    (set! theImageHeight (+ theImageHeight theBuffer theBuffer) )
    (set! theImageWidth  (+ theImageWidth  theBuffer theBuffer) )
    (gimp-image-resize theImage theImageWidth theImageHeight 0 0)
    (gimp-layer-resize theLayer theImageWidth theImageHeight 0 0)
    (gimp-layer-set-offsets theText theBuffer theBuffer)
    (gimp-display-new theImage)
    (list theImage theLayer theText)
    )
)
```

13.3.7.2   What you obtain

Figure 13.5 And the result on the screen.

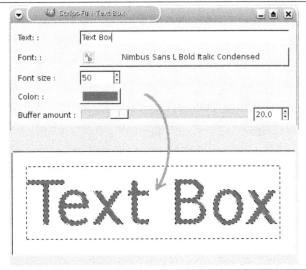

Part III

Function Reference

Chapter 14

Tools

14.1 The Toolbox

14.1.1 Introduction

GIMP provides a comprehensive toolbox in order to quickly perform basic tasks such as making selections or drawing paths. The many tools contained within GIMP's toolbox are discussed in detail here.

(In case you're curious, in GIMP lingo a "tool" is a way of acting on an image that requires access to its display, either to let you indicate what you want to do by moving the pointer around inside the display, or to show you interactively the results of changes that you have made. But if you want to think of a tool as a saw, and an image as a piece of wood, it probably won't do you a great deal of harm.)

Note

 See Main Windows: The Toolbox **for an overview of the toolbox and its components.**

GIMP has a diverse assortment of tools that let you perform a large variety of tasks. The tools can be thought of as falling into five categories:

- *Selection tools*, which specify or modify the portion of the image that will be affected by subsequent actions;

- *Paint tools*, which alter the colors in some part of the image;

- *Transform tools*, which alter the geometry of the image;

- *Color tools*, which alter the distribution of colors across the entire image;

- *Other tools*, which don't fall into the other four categories.

14.1.2 Tool Icons

Figure 14.1 The Tool Icons in the Toolbox

Most tools can be activated by clicking on an icon in the Toolbox. By default, some tools are accessible only via the menus (namely the Color tools are accessible only either as Colors or as Tools → Colors). Every tool, in fact, can be activated from the *Tools* menu; also, every tool can be activated from the keyboard using an accelerator key.

In the default setup, created when GIMP is first installed, not all tools show icons in the Toolbox: the Color tools are omitted. You can customize the set of tools that are shown in the Toolbox through Edit → Preferences → Toolbox. There are two reasons you might want to do this: first, if you only rarely use a tool, it might be easier to find the tools you want if the distracting icon is removed; second, if you use the Color tools a lot, you might find it convenient to have icons for them easily available. In any case, regardless of the Toolbox, you can always access any tool at any time using the Tools menu from an image menubar.

The shape of the cursor changes when it is inside an image, to one that indicates which tool is active (if in Preferences you have set Image Windows → Mouse Pointers → Pointer mode → Tool icon).

14.1.3 Color and Indicator Area

Figure 14.2 Color and Indicator Area in the Toolbox

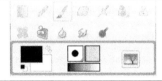

14.1.3.1 Color Area

Figure 14.3 Active Colors in the Toolbox

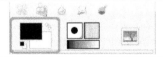

Color area This area shows GIMP's basic palette, consisting of two colors, the Foreground and Background, used for painting, filling, and many other operations. Clicking on either of the color displays brings up a Color Editor dialog, which permits you to change it.

Default colors Clicking on this small symbol resets the Foreground and Background colors to black and white, respectively. Pressing the **D** key has the same effect.

Swap FG/BG colors Clicking on the small curved line with two arrowheads causes the Foreground and Background colors to be swapped. Pressing the **X** key has the same effect.

> **Tip**
>
> You can click-and-drag one of these colors directly into a layer: it will fill the whole layer.

14.1.3.2 Tools Indicator Area

Figure 14.4 Active Brush, Pattern and Gradient in the Toolbox

This part of the Toolbox shows the currently selected brush, pattern, and gradient. Clicking on any of them brings up a dialog that allows you to change it.

14.1.3.3 Active Image Area

Figure 14.5 Active Image in the Toolbox

A thumbnail of the active image can be displayed in this area if the "Display Active Image" option is checked in Preferences/Toolbox. If you click on this thumbnail, the "Images" dialog is opened, useful if you have many images on your screen. You can also click and drag this thumbnail to an enabled XDS[1] file manager to directly save the corresponding image.

---

[1] See [XDS].

14.1.4 Tool Options

Figure 14.6 Tool Options Dialog
_____

The Tool Options dialog of the Airbrush tool.

If you have things set up like most people do, activating a tool causes its Tool Options dialog to appear below the Toolbox. If you don't have things set up this way, you probably should: it is very difficult to use tools effectively without being able to manipulate their options.

> **Tip**
>
> The Tool Options appear beneath the Toolbox in the default setup. If you lose it somehow, you can get it back by creating a new Tool Options dialog using Windows → Dockable Dialogs → Tool Options and then docking it below the Toolbox. See the section on Dialogs and Docking if you need help.

Each tool has its own specific set of options. The choices you make for them are kept throughout the session, until you change them. In fact, the tool options are maintained from session to session. The persistence of tool options across sessions can sometimes be an annoying nuisance: a tool behaves very strangely, and you can't figure out why until you remember that you were using some unusual option the last time you worked with it, two weeks ago.

At the bottom of the Tool Options dialog, four buttons appear:

 Save Options to This button allows you to save the settings for the current tool, so that you can restore them later. It brings up the Section 15.5.1 allowing you to give a name for the new preset. When you Restore options, only saved presets for the active tool are shown, so you need not worry about including the name of the tool when you assign a name here.

Restore Options This button allows you to restore a previously saved preset of options for the active tool. If no presets have ever been saved for the active tool, the button will be insensitive. Otherwise, clicking it will bring up a menu showing the names of all saved option sets: choosing a menu entry will apply those settings.

Delete Options This button allows you to delete a previously saved set of options for the active tool. If no option-sets have ever been saved for the active tool, the button will simply repeat the tool name. Otherwise, clicking it will bring up a menu showing the names of all saved presets: the selected preset will be deleted.

 Reset Options This button resets the options for the active tool to their default values.

New sliders Option sliders have changed with GIMP-2.8: it is not visible, but the slider area is now divided into upper and lower parts.

Figure 14.7 The new sliders of tool options dialogs

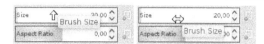

(a) *The upwards arrow pointer* (b) *The horizontal two-way ar-*
in the top half of the slider area *row pointer in the lower half of*
the slider area

- **In the top half of the slider area:** Clicking with the up arrow pointer sets slider to a value that depends on the position of the pointer (no reference, imprecise). Clicking and dragging the up arrow pointer sets the value by large amounts.
- **In the lower half of the slider area:** Clicking with the two-way arrow pointer has no effect. Clicking and dragging the two-way arrow pointer sets the value by small amounts.

Once you have set the value approximately, you can tune it precisely using the two small arrow buttons at the right of the slider.

The value area in the slider area works as a text editor: there, you can edit the value or enter a new value directly.

For some options, you can drag the pointer outside the tool dialog. For example with the size slider, whose maximum value is 10,000, you can drag the mouse pointer up to the right side of your screen.

14.2 Selection Tools

Figure 14.8 The Selection tools

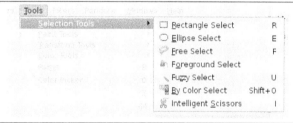

14.2.1 Common Features

Selection tools are designed to select regions from the active layer so you can work on them without affecting the unselected areas. Each tool has its own individual properties, but the selection tools also share a number of options and features in common. These common features are described here; the variations are explained in the following sections for each tool specifically. If you need help with what a "selection" is in GIMP, and how it works, see Selection.

There are seven selection tools:

- the Rectangle Select;
- the Ellipse Select;

- the Free Select (the Lasso);

- the Select Contiguous Regions (the Magic Wand);

- the Select by Color;

- the Select Shapes from Image (Intelligent Scissors) and

- the Foreground Select.

In some ways the Path tool can also be thought of as a selection tool: any closed path can be converted into a selection. It also can do a great deal more, though, and does not share the same set of options with the other selection tools.

14.2.1.1   Key modifiers (Defaults)

The behavior of selection tools is modified if you hold down the **Ctrl**, **Shift**, and/or **Alt** keys while you use them.

Note

 Advanced users find the modifier keys very valuable, but novice users often find them confusing. Fortunately, it is possible for most purposes to use the Mode buttons (described below) instead of modifier keys.

Ctrl   When creating a selection, holding down the **Ctrl** key can have two different actions according to the way you use it:

- Holding down the key *while drawing* the selection toggles the "Expand from center" option.
- If you hold down the **Ctrl** key *before drawing a selection*, this new selection switches to the Subtract mode. So, this new selection will be subtracted from an existing one as soon as you release the click, as far as they have common pixels.

Alt   Holding **Alt** will allow movement of the current selection (only its frame, not its content). If the whole image is moved instead of the selection only, try Shift-Alt. Note that the **Alt** key is sometimes intercepted by the windowing system (meaning that GIMP never knows that it was pressed), so this may not work for everybody.

Shift   When creating a selection, holding down the **Shift** key can have two different actions according to the way you use it:

- If you hold down the key *before clicking* to start the selection, this selection will be in *Addition* mode as long as you press the key.
- If you hold down the **Shift** key *after clicking* to start the selection, the effect will depend on the tool you are using: for example, the selection will be a square with the Rectangle Select tool.

Ctrl-Shift   Using Ctrl-Shift together can do a variety of things, depending on which tool is used. Common to all selection tools is that the selection mode will be switched to intersection, so that after the operation is finished, the selection will consist of the intersection of the region traced out with the pre-existing selection. It is an exercise for the reader to play with the various combinations available when performing selections while holding Ctrl-Shift and releasing either both or either prior to releasing the mouse Left Button.

Key modifiers to move selections   Ctrl-Alt-Left-click-and-drag and Shift-Alt-Left-click-and-drag are used to move selections. See Section 7.2.1.

Space bar   Pressing the **Space** bar while using a selection tool transforms this tool into the Navigation cross as long as you press the bar, allowing you to pan around the image instead of using the scrollbars when your image is bigger than the canvas. This is the default option: in Preferences/Image Windows, you can toggle the Space bar to the Move tool.

14.2.1.2 Options

Here we describe the tool options that apply to all selection tools: options that apply only to some tools, or that affect each tool differently, are described in the sections devoted to the individual tools. The current settings for these options can be seen in the Tool Options dialog, which you should always have visible when you are using tools. To make the interface consistent, the same options are presented for all selection tools, even though some of them don't have any effect for some of the tools.

Figure 14.9 Common options of selection tools

Mode This determines the way that the selection you create is combined with any pre-existing selection. Note that the functions performed by these buttons can be duplicated using modifier keys, as described above. For the most part, advanced users use the modifier keys; novice users find the mode buttons easier.

Replace mode will cause any existing selection to be destroyed or replaced when the new selection is created.

Add mode will cause the new selection to be added to any existing selection regions.

Subtract mode will remove the new selection area from any existing selection regions.

Intersection mode will make a new selection from the area where the existing selection region and the new selection region overlap.

Antialiasing This option only affects some selection tools: it causes the boundary of the selection to be drawn more smoothly.

Feather Edges This options allows the boundary of the selection to be blurred, so that points near the boundary are only partially selected. For further information regarding feathering, see the glossary entry Feathering.

14.2.2 Rectangle Selection

Figure 14.10 Rectangle Select icon in the Toolbox

The Rectangle Selection tool is designed to select rectangular regions of the active layer: it is the most basic of the selection tools, but very commonly used. For information on selections and how they are used in GIMP see Selections; for information on features common to all selection tools see Selection Tools.

This tool is also used for rendering a rectangle on an image. To render a filled rectangle, create a rectangular selection, and then fill it using the Bucket Fill tool. To create a rectangular outline, the simplest and most flexible approach is to create a rectangular selection and then stroke it.

14.2.2.1 Activating the tool

You can access the Selection Tool in different ways:

- from the image menu bar Tools → Selection Tools → Rectangle Select,

- by clicking on the tool icon in the ToolBox,

- by using the keyboard shortcut **R**.

14.2.2.2 Key modifiers

> **Note**
>
> See Selection Tools for help with modifier keys that affect all these tools in the same way. Only effects options that are specific to this tool are explained here.

Ctrl Pressing the **Ctrl** key after starting your selection, and holding it down until you are finished, causes your starting point to be used as the center of the selected rectangle, instead of a corner. Note that if you press the **Ctrl** key *before* starting to make the selection, the resulting selection will be subtracted from the existing selection. The cursor becomes

Shift If you press the **Shift** key *before* starting the selection, the resulting selection will be added to the existing one. The cursor becomes

Pressing the **Shift** key *after* starting your selection, toggles the Fixed option, and holding it down until you are finished, will constrain the selection to a square, if it is your first selection. Later, with the default Aspect Ratio , your selection will respect the aspect ratio of the previous selection.

Ctrl-Shift Pressing both keys after starting your selection combines the two effects, giving you a square selection centered on your starting point. Note that pressing these keys before starting your selection intersects the resulting selection with the existing one and the pointer change shape accordingly :

14.2.2.3 Tool manipulation

Figure 14.11 Example of Rectangle Selection.

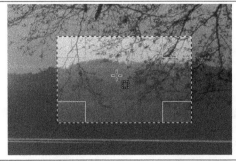

When this tool is selected the mouse pointer is displayed like this: as soon as it is over the image. A drag and drop allows to get a rectangular (or square) shape. When the mouse button is relaxed, a dotted line ("marching ants") outlines the selection. It's not necessary to adjust the selection with care; you can resize it easily later.

When the pointer is moving on the canvas, the pointer and selection aspects change:

- outside the selection it looks like previously; this allows to design a new selection but will erase the existing one if this isn't combined with an action on the relevant key to add or subtract another selection as described in the previous paragraph.

- within selection peripheral parts, the mouse pointer changes into various shapes when overflying rectangular sensitive and clearly marked areas. These *handles* allow you to resize the selection. In selection corners the pointer changes into a shape according to the context; for instance in the low right corner it becomes: . So, by click-and-dragging these areas, you can magnify or shrink the selection size. Over median selection parts, lateral, low or up, pointer is changed into appropriate shapes according to the context. For instance, when the mouse pointer is over the median right side, the pointer looks like: . So you can click-and-drag to magnify or to shrink the selection size by moving the chosen boundary.

- inside selection central area the mouse pointer looks like usual for object manipulation, i.e.: . So you can move the whole selection by a click-and-drag.

Moreover, if you have not unchecked the Highlight option, your work will be easier because what is out the selection will be darkest than what is in the selection, and then the selection seems highlighted.

> **Tip**
>
> *i*   If you use moving keys you can move the selection or modify its size by one pixel step. If you use it in combination with **Shift** you can move it by a 25 pixel step.

Figure 14.12 Sensitive selection areas

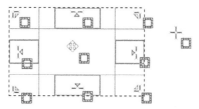

Display of all possible pointers in function of their localization with respect to the selection area.

After creating and modifying the selection, you will have to exit this editing mode (and commit any changes). You can do this with a single click inside the selection or by pressing the **Enter** key. Or you can just use a non-selection tool and, for example, fill or paint the selection.

14.2.2.4 Tool Options

Figure 14.13 Tool Options for the Rectangle Select tool

Normally, tool options are displayed in a window attached under the Toolbox as soon as you activate a tool. If they are not, you can access them from the image menu bar through Windows → Dockable Windows → Tool Options which opens the option window of the selected tool.

> **Note**
>
> See Selection Tools for help with options that are common to all these tools. Only options that are specific to this tool are explained here.

Mode; Antialiasing; Feather edges   Common select options.

Rounded corners If you enable this option, a slider appears. You can use this to adjust the radius that is used to round the corners of the selection.

Expand from center If you enable this option, the point the selection is started by pressing the mouse button is used as center of the selected area.

Fixed This menu allows you the option of constraining the shape of the rectangle in different ways.

> **Aspect ratio** This option allows you to design and resize the selection while keeping the aspect ratio fixed and written within the relevant box. By default the ratio is 1:1 (so we have a square) but it can be changed. With the two little landscape and picture icons, you can invert this ratio.
>
> **Width** With this choice you can fix the width of the selection.
>
> **Height** With this choice you can fix the height of the selection.
>
> **Size** With this choice you can fix the width and height of the selection.

Position These two text fields contain the current horizontal and vertical coordinates of the upper left corner of the selection. You can use these fields to adjust the selection position precisely.

Size These two text fields contain the current width and height of the the selection. You can use these fields to adjust the selection size precisely.

Highlight If you enable this option, the selected area is emphasized by a surrounding mask to make visual selection much easier.

Guides With this menu you can select the type of guides that is shown within the selection to make the creation of a selection easier, respecting *Photo composition rules*.

Six options are available:

- No Guides
- Center lines
- Rule of thirds
- Rule of fifths
- Golden sections
- Diagonal lines

Auto Shrink Selection This option is active when a rectangle selection is drawn. Clicking on the Auto Shrink Selection button will make the selection automatically shrink to the nearest rectangular shape including elements in the selection. The algorithm for finding the best rectangle to shrink to is "intelligent", which in this case means that it sometimes does surprisingly sophisticated things, and sometimes does surprisingly strange things. In any case, if the region that you want to select has a solid-colored surround, auto-shrinking will always pick it out correctly. Note that the resulting selection does not need to have the same shape as the one you sweep out.

Figure 14.14 Auto Shrink example

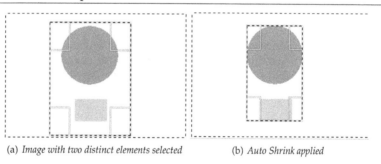

(a) *Image with two distinct elements selected*   (b) *Auto Shrink applied*

Shrink merged If Sample Merged is also enabled, then Auto Shrink will use the pixel information from the visible display of the image, rather than just from the active layer. For further information regarding Sample Merge, see the glossary entry Sample Merge.

14.2.3   Ellipse Selection

Figure 14.15 Ellipse Select icon in the Toolbox

The Ellipse Selection tool is designed to select circular and elliptical regions from an image, with high-quality anti-aliasing if you want it. For information on selections and how they are used in GIMP see Selections; for information on features common to all selection tools see Selection Tools.

This tool is also used for rendering a circle or ellipse on an image. To render a filled ellipse, create an elliptical selection, and then fill it using the Bucket Fill tool. To create an elliptical outline, the simplest and most flexible approach is to create an elliptical selection and then stroke it. However, the quality of anti-aliasing with this approach is rather crude. A higher quality outline can be obtained by creating two elliptical selections with different sizes, subtracting the inner one from the outer one; however this is not always easy to get right. The command Select → Border... makes it easy.

14.2.3.1 Activating the tool

You can access the Ellipse Selection Tool in different ways:

- From the image menu bar Tools → Selection Tools → Ellipse Select;

- By clicking on the tool icon in the ToolBox,

- By using the keyboard shortcut **E**.

14.2.3.2 Key modifiers

> **Note**
>
> See Selection Tools for help with modifier keys that affect all these tools in the same way. Only effects options that are specific to this tool are explained here.

Ctrl Pressing the key after starting your selection, and holding it down until you are finished, causes your starting point to be used as the center of the selected ellipse, instead of a corner of the rectangle that may contain it. Note that if you press the **Ctrl** key *before* starting to make the selection, the resulting selection will be subtracted from the existing selection.

Shift Pressing the **Shift** key after starting your selection, and holding it down until you are finished, constrains the selection to be a circle. Note that if you press the **Shift** key *before* starting to make the selection, the resulting selection will be added to the existing selection.

Ctrl-Shift Pressing both keys combines the two effects, giving you a circular selection centered on your starting point.

14.2.3.3 Tool handling

Figure 14.16 Example of Ellipse Selection.

When this tool is selected the mouse pointer comes with a circle icon as soon as it is over the image. A drag-and-drop allows you to get an ellipse (or a circle) within a rectangular box. When the mouse button is relaxed, a dotted line ("marching ants") outlines the elliptic selection. It's not necessary to adjust the selection with care; you can resize it easily later.

When the pointer is moving on the canvas, the pointer and selection aspects change. You can change the size of the selection by using handles. See Tool handling within the rectangular chapter.

14.2.3.4 Options

Figure 14.17 Tool Options for the Ellipse Select tool

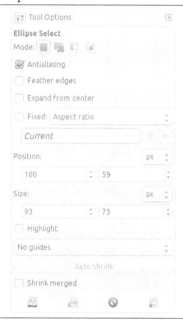

Normally, tool options are displayed in a window attached under the Toolbox as soon as you activate a tool. If they are not, you can access them from the image menu bar through Windows → Dockable Windows → Tool Options which opens the option window of the selected tool.

> **Note**
>
> See Selection Tools for help with options that are common to all these tools. Only options that are specific to this tool are explained here.

Modes; Antialiasing; Feather edges Common select options.

All other options All these options work exactly the same way, they were described for the rectangular selection already. See for Section 14.2.2.4 details.

14.2.4   Free Selection (Lasso)

Figure 14.18 Free Selection icon in the Toolbox

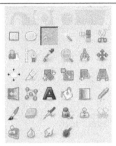

The Free Selection tool, or Lasso, lets you create a selection by drawing it free-hand with the pointer, while holding down the left mouse button (or, for a stylus, pressing it against the tablet). When you release the mouse button, the selection is closed by connecting the current pointer location to the start location with a straight line. You can go outside the edge of the image display and come back in if you want to. The Lasso is often a good tool to use for "roughing in" a selection; it is not so good for precise definition. Experienced users find that it is often convenient to begin with the lasso tool, but then switch to QuickMask mode for detail work.

For information on selections and how they are used in GIMP see Selections. For information on features common to all selection tools see Selection Tools.

Note

      The Free Selection tool is much easier to use with a tablet than with a mouse.

A new possibility came up with GIMP-2.6: the polygonal selection. Instead of click-and-dragging to draw a free hand selection, you can click only. This creates an anchor point. Then moving the mouse pointer draws a line with a new anchor point that you can move as long as you don't click again (the mouse pointer comes with the moving cross). Clicking again anchors this point and creates a segment. By pressing the **Ctrl** keyboard key while moving the mouse pointer contrains moving angles to 15°.

So, you can mix free hand segments and polygonal segments.

Figure 14.19 Mixing free hand segments and polygonal segments

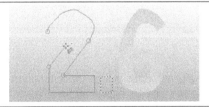

14.2.4.1   Activating the tool

You can access the Lasso Tool in different ways:

- From the image menu bar Tools → Selection Tools → Free Select,

- by clicking on the tool icon in the ToolBox,

- by using the keyboard shortcut **F**.

14.2.4.2   Key modifiers

The Free Select tool does not have any special key modifiers, only the ones that affect all selection tools in the same way. See Selection Tools for help with these.

14.2.4.3   Tool handling

To move the selection, see Moving selections.

Figure 14.20 Rough selection with the Free Selection tool.

14.2.4.4   Options

Figure 14.21 Tool Options for the Lasso tool

Normally, tool options are displayed in a window attached under the Toolbox as soon as you activate a tool. If they are not, you can access them from the image menu bar through Windows → Dockable Windows → Tool Options which opens the option window of the selected tool.

The Free Select tool has no special tool options, only the ones that affect all selection tools in the same way. See Selection Tools for help with these.

14.2.5   Fuzzy selection (Magic wand)

Figure 14.22 Magic Wand tool icon in the Toolbox

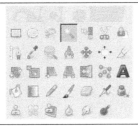

The Fuzzy Select (Magic Wand) tool is designed to select areas of the current layer or image based on color similarity.

When using this tool, it is very important to pick the right starting point. If you select the wrong spot, you might get something very different from what you want, or even the opposite.

The Wand is a good tool for selecting objects with sharp edges. It is fun to use, so beginners often start out using it a lot. You will probably find, however, that the more you use it, the more frustrated you become with the difficulty of selecting exactly what you want, no more, no less. More experienced users find that the Path and Color Select tools are often more efficient, and use the Wand less. Still, it is useful for selecting an area within a contour, or touching up imperfect selections. It often works very well for selecting a solid-colored (or nearly solid-colored) background area.

Note that as the selected area expands outward from the center, it does not only propagate to pixels that touch each other: it is capable of jumping over small gaps, depending on Threshold option. To increase/decrease Threshold, during the use of Fuzzy Selection, after the first button-press, dragging the pointer downward (or to the right) or upward (or to the left).

14.2.5.1   Activating the tool

You can access the Magic Wand Tool in different ways:

- From the image menu bar Tools → Selection Tools → Fuzzy Select,

- by clicking on the tool icon ![icon] in the ToolBox,

- by using the keyboard shortcut **U**.

14.2.5.2   Key modifiers (Defaults)

The Fuzzy Select tool does not have any special key modifiers, only the ones that affect all selection tools in the same way. See Section 14.2.1 for help with these.

14.2.5.3   Tool handling

Figure 14.23 Using Magic Wand tool: selected pixels are contiguous

It starts selecting when you click at a spot in the image, and expands outwards like water flooding low-lying areas, selecting contiguous pixels whose colors are similar to the starting pixel. You can control the threshold of similarity by dragging the mouse downward or to the right: the farther you drag it, the larger you get the selected region. And you can reduce the selection by dragging upwards or to the left.

To move the selection see Moving selections.

14.2.5.4   Options

Figure 14.24 Tool Options for the Magic Wand tool

Normally, tool options are displayed in a window attached under the Toolbox as soon as you activate a tool. If they are not, you can access them from the image menu bar through Windows → Dockable Windows → Tool Options which opens the option window of the selected tool.

> **Note**
>
> See Selection Tools for help with options that are common to all these tools. Only options that are specific to this tool are explained here.

Mode; Antialiasing; Feather edges   Common select options.

Finding Similar Colors These options affect the way the Magic Wand expands the selection out from the initial point.

Select Transparent Areas This option gives the Magic Wand the ability to select areas that are completely transparent. If this option is not checked, transparent areas will never be included in the selection.

Sample Merged This option becomes relevant when you have several layers in your image, and the active layer is either semi-transparent or is set to another Layer Mode than Normal. If this is the case, the colors present in the layer will be different from the colors in the composite image. If the "Sample Merged" option is unchecked, the wand will only react to the color in the active layer when it creates a selection. If it is checked it will react to the composite color of all visible layers. For further information, see the glossary entry Sample Merged.

Threshold This slider determines the range of colors that will be selected at the moment you click the pointer on the initial point, before dragging it: the higher the threshold, the larger the resulting selection. After the first button-press, dragging the pointer downward or to the right will increase the size of the selection; dragging upward or to the left will decrease it. Thus, you have the same set of possibilities regardless of the Threshold setting: what differs is the amount of dragging you have to do to get the result you want.

Selection by With this option you can choose which component of the image GIMP shall use to calculate the similarity.

The components you can choose from are Red, Green, Blue, Hue, Saturation and Value.

14.2.6 Select By Color

Figure 14.25 Select by Color tool icon in the Toolbox

The Select by Color tool is designed to select areas of an image based on color similarity. It works a lot like the Fuzzy Select tool ("Magic Wand"). The main difference between them is that the Magic Wand selects *contiguous* regions, with all parts connected to the starting point by paths containing no large gaps; while the Select by Color tool selects all pixels that are sufficiently similar in color to the pixel you click on, regardless of where they are located.

14.2.6.1 Activating the tool

You can access the Select by Color Tool in different ways:

- From the image menu bar Tools → Selection Tools → By Color Select,

- by clicking on the tool icon  in the ToolBox,

- by using the keyboard shortcut Shift -O.

14.2.6.2 Key modifiers (Defaults)

The select by color tool does not have any special key modifiers, only the ones that affect all selection tools in the same way. See Selection Tools for help with these.

14.2.6.3 Handling tool

Figure 14.26 Using Select by Color tool: selected pixels are not only contiguous

As with fuzzy tool, the selection starts as soon as you click and the reference is the first clicked pixel. If you click and drag, you can change the threshold by the same way as with the fuzzy tool.

To move the selection see Moving selections.

14.2.6.4 Options

Figure 14.27 Tool Options for the Select by Color tool

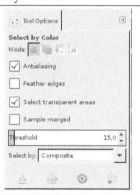

Normally, tool options are displayed in a window attached under the Toolbox as soon as you activate a tool. If they are not, you can access them from the image menu bar through Windows → Dockable Windows → Tool Options which opens the option window of the selected tool.

> **Note**
>
> See Selection Tools for help with options that are common to all these tools. Only options that are specific to this tool are explained here.

Mode; Antialiasing; Feather edges Common select options.

Similar colors All these options work exactly the same way, they were described for the fuzzy selection already. See for Section 14.2.5.4 details.

14.2.7   Intelligent Scissors

Figure 14.28 Intelligent Scissors tool icon in the Toolbox

The Intelligent Scissors tool is an interesting piece of equipment: it has some features in common with the Lasso, some features in common with the Path tool, and some features all its own. It is useful when you are trying to select a region defined by strong color-changes at the edges. To use the Scissors, you click to create a set of "control nodes", also referred to as anchors or control points, at the edges of the region you are trying to select. The tool produces a continuous curve passing through these control nodes, following any high-contrast edges it can find. If you are lucky, the path that the tool finds will correspond to the contour you are trying to select.

Unfortunately, there seem to be some problems with the edge-following logic for this tool, with the result that the selections it creates tend to be pretty crude in a lot of cases. A good way to clean them up is to switch to QuickMask mode, and use paint tools to paint in the problematic parts. On the whole, most people find the Path tool to be more useful than the Scissors, because, even though it does not have the intelligent edge-finding capability, the paths it produces persist until you delete them, and can be altered at any time.

14.2.7.1   Activating the tool

You can access the Intelligent Scissors Tool in different ways:

- From the image menu bar Tools → Selection Tools → Intelligent Scissors,

- by clicking on the tool icon <img> in the ToolBox,

- by using the keyboard shortcut **I**.

14.2.7.2   Key modifiers

The default behavior of the **Shift**, **Ctrl**, and **Alt** keys is described in Section 14.2.1.1 for all selection tools.

There is, however, one key modifier that has a special behavior if you use it while editing a selection, that is *after* you have added the first node:

Shift   By default, the *auto-edge snap feature* is enabled: whenever you click and drag the mouse pointer, the Scissors tool finds the point of the maximal gradient (where the color change is maximal) for placing a new control node or moving an existing node.

Holding down this key while clicking and dragging disables this feature, and the control node will be placed at the position of the mouse pointer.

14.2.7.3   Tool handling

Figure 14.29 Using Intelligent Scissors

Each time you left-click with the mouse, you create a new control point, which is connected to the last control point by a curve that tries to follow edges in the image. To finish, click on the first point (the cursor changes to indicate when you are in the right spot). You can adjust the curve by dragging the control nodes, or by clicking to create new control nodes. When you are satisfied, click anywhere inside the curve to convert it into a selection.

As said above when you click with this tool you drop points. The selection boundary is driven by these control points. During creation you can move each one by clicking and dragging, except the first and the last one. The selection is closed when you are clicking the last point over the first one. When

the selection is closed the pointer shape changes according to its position: inside , on the boundary , and outside . You can adjust the selection creating new points by clicking on the boundary or by moving each control points (merged first and last point). The selection is validated when you click inside.

You have to notice that you can get only one selection; if you create a second selection, the first one is erased when you validate the second one.

> **Warning**
>
> Be sure not to click inside the curve until you are completely done adjusting it. Once you have converted it into a selection, undoing takes you back to zero, and you will have to start constructing the curve again from scratch if you need to change it. Also be sure not to switch to a different tool, or again all of your carefully created control nodes will be lost. (But you still can transform your selection into a path and work it with the Path tool.)

To move the selection, see Moving selections.

14.2.7.4   Options

Figure 14.30 Tool Options for the Intelligent Scissors

Normally, tool options are displayed in a window attached under the Toolbox as soon as you activate a tool. If they are not, you can access them from the image menu bar through Windows → Dockable Windows → Tool Options which opens the option window of the selected tool.

Modes; Antialiasing; Feather edges

> **Note**
>
> See Selection Tools for help with options that are common to all these tools. Only options that are specific to this tool are explained here.

Interactive boundary If this option is enabled, dragging a control node during placement will indicate the path that will be taken by the selection boundary. If it is not enabled, the node will be shown connected to the previous node by a straight line while you are dragging it around, and you won't see the resulting path until you release the pointer button. On slow systems, if your control nodes are far apart, this may give a bit of a speed-up.

14.2.8   Foreground Select

Figure 14.31 The "Foreground Select" tool in the Toolbox

This tool lets you extract the foreground from the active layer or from a selection. It is based on the SIOX method (Simple Interactive Object Extraction). You can visit its Web page at [SIOX].

14.2.8.1   Directions for use

The creation of a selection with this tool works in a couple of steps:

1. *Roughly select the foreground* you want to extract. When you select this tool, the mouse pointer goes with the lasso icon. It actually works like the Fuzzy Select tool. Select as little as possible from the background.

As soon as you release the mouse button, the non selected part of the image is covered with a dark blue mask. If the selection is not closed, its ends will be linked automatically together by a straight line. The mouse pointer goes now with the Paint-brush icon for the next step.

Figure 14.32 The foreground is roughly selected

2. *Draw a line through the foreground*: using the paintbrush, whose size can be changed in options, draw a continuous line in the selected foreground going over colors which will be kept for the extraction. The color used to draw the line is of no importance; not using the same color as foreground is better. Be careful not painting background pixels.

Figure 14.33 The line drawn on the foreground

In this example, it is important that the line goes over the yellow capitulum of the flower.

3. When you release the mouse button, all non-selected areas are in dark:

Figure 14.34 The area which will be selected

4. You still have to press the **Enter** key to get the wanted selection:

Figure 14.35 Foreground is selected

> **Note**
>
> Until you press **Enter**, you can't undo this selection by Ctrl-Z nor by Select → None, and the Undo History is not concerned. To delete this selection, you must select another tool.

14.2.8.2   Activating the Tool

You can activate the Foreground Select tool in two ways:

- by clicking on the tool icon in the Toolbox,

- through Tools → Selection Tools → Foreground Select in the image menu.

- This tool has no shortcut, but you can set one using Edit → Preferences → Interface → Configure Keyboard Shortcuts → Tools → Foreground Select

14.2.8.3   Key modifiers (Defaults)

Ctrl   By pressing the **Ctrl** key, you can switching between foreground and background selection painting.

14.2.8.4   Options

Figure 14.36 "Foreground Select" tool options

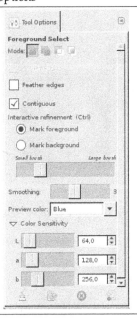

Normally, tool options are displayed in a window attached under the Toolbox as soon as you activate a tool. If they are not, you can access them from the image menu bar through Windows → Dockable Windows → Tool Options which opens the option window of the selected tool.

Mode; Antialiasing; Feather edges

Note

 See Selection Tools for help with options that are common to all these tools. Only options that are specific to this tool are explained here.

Contiguous If this option is enabled, only the area contiguous to the stroke will be selected. Otherwise all the areas with same colors will be selected.

Figure 14.37 "Contiguous" option effect

(a) Two separated ar- *(b) The Contiguous* *(c) The Contiguous*
eas with the same color. *option is checked: only* *option is not checked:*
On the left, only the left *the area close to the* *both areas, although*
area is marked. *painted line is selected.* *they are separated, are*
selected.

Interactive refinement Here are some options to work more precisely on your selection:

Mark foreground default option. The foreground color of the Toolbox is used to paint. Colors covered by the painted line will be used for extraction.

Mark background You can access this option either by clicking on the radio button or, more simply, by pressing the **Ctrl** key. The mouse pointer goes with a small eraser icon. The used color is the background color of Toolbox. The pixels of the selection which have the same color as the "erased" pixels will NOT be extracted.

Small brush / Large brush This slider lets you adapt the size of the brush used to paint the line. A small brush fits well thin details.

Smoothing Smaller values give a more accurate selection border but may introduce holes in the selection.

Preview color You can select between Red, Green and Blue to mask the image background.

Color Sensitivity This option uses the L*a*b color model. If your image contains many pixels of the same color in different tones, you can increase the sensibility of the selection for this color.

14.3 Paint Tools

Figure 14.38 The Paint Tools (Tools menu)

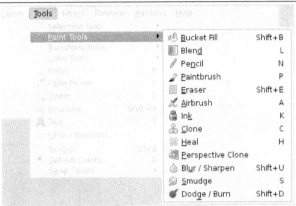

14.3.1 Common Features

The GIMP Toolbox includes thirteen "paint tools", all grouped together at the bottom (in the default arrangement).

Figure 14.39 The Paint Tools (Tools Box)

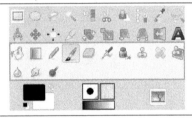

The feature they all have in common is that all of them are used by moving the pointer across the image display, creating brush-strokes. Four of them

- the Pencil,

- the Paintbrush,

- the Airbrush and

- the Ink tool

behave like the intuitive notion of "painting" with a brush. Pencil, Paintbrush, and Airbrush are called "basic painting tools" or brush tools.

The other tools use a brush to modify an image in some way rather than paint on it:

- the Bucket Fill fills with color or pattern;

- the Gradient fills with gradients;

- the Eraser erases;

- the Clone tool copies from a pattern, or image;

- the Perspective Clone tool copies into a changed perspective;

- the Heal tool corrects small defects;

- the Convolve tool blurs or sharpens;

- the Smudge tool smears;

- and the Dodge/Burn tool lightens or darkens.

The advantages of using GIMP with a tablet instead of a mouse probably show up more clearly for brush tools than anywhere else: the gain in fine control is invaluable. These tools also have special "Pressure sensitivity" options that are only usable with a tablet.

In addition to the more common "hands-on" method, it is possible to apply paint tools in an automated way, by creating a selection or path and then "stroking" it. You can choose to stroke with any of the paint tools, including nonstandard ones such as the Eraser, Smudge tool, etc., and any options you set for the tool will be applied. See the section on Stroking for more information.

14.3.1.1 Key modifiers

Ctrl Holding down the **Ctrl** key has a special effect on every paint tool. For the Pencil, Paintbrush, Airbrush, Ink, and Eraser, it switches them into "color picker" mode, so that clicking on an image pixel causes GIMP's foreground to be set to the active layer's color at that point (or, for the Eraser, GIMP's background color). For the Clone tool, the **Ctrl** key switches it into a mode where clicking sets the reference point for copying. For the Convolve tool, the **Ctrl** key switches between blur and sharpen modes; for the Dodge/Burn tool, it switches between dodging and burning.

Shift Holding down the **Shift** key has the same effect on most paint tools: it places the tool into *straight line* mode. To create a straight line with any of the paint tools, first click on the starting point, *then* press the **Shift** key. As long as you hold it down, you will see a thin line connecting the previously clicked point with the current pointer location. If you click again, while continuing to hold down the **Shift** key, a straight line will be rendered. You can continue this process to create a series of connected line segments.

Ctrl-Shift Holding down both keys puts the tool into *constrained straight line* mode. This is similar to the effect of the **Shift** key alone, except that the orientation of the line is constrained to the nearest multiple of 15 degrees. Use this if you want to create perfect horizontal, vertical, or diagonal lines.

14.3.1.2 Tool Options

Figure 14.40 Tool options shared by paint tools

Many tool options are shared by several paint tools: these are described here. Options that apply only to one specific tool, or to a small number of tools, are described in the sections devoted to those tools.

Mode The Mode drop-down list provides a selection of paint application modes. As with the opacity, the easiest way to understand what the Mode setting does is to imagine that the paint is actually applied to a layer above the layer you are working on, with the layer combination mode in the Layers dialog set to the selected mode. You can obtain a great variety of special effects in this way. The Mode option is only usable for tools that can be thought of as adding color to the image: the Pencil, Paintbrush, Airbrush, Ink, and Clone tools. For the other paint tools, the option appears for the sake of consistency but is always grayed out. A list of modes can be found in Section 8.2.

In this list, some modes are particular and are described below.

Opacity The Opacity slider sets the transparency level for the brush operation. To understand how it works, imagine that instead of altering the active layer, the tool creates a transparent layer above the active layer and acts on that layer. Changing Opacity in the Tool Options has the same effect that changing opacity in the Layers dialog would have in the latter situation. It controls the "strength" of all paint tools, not just those that paint on the active layer. In the case of the Eraser, this can come across as a bit confusing: it works out that the higher the "opacity" is, the more transparency you get.

Brush The brush determines how much of the image is affected by the tool, and how it is affected, when you trace out a brushstroke with the pointer. GIMP allows you to use several different types of brushes, which are described in the Brushes section. The same brush choices are available for all paint tools except the Ink tool, which uses a unique type of procedurally generated brush. The colors of a brush only come into play for tools where they are meaningful: the Pencil, Paintbrush, and Airbrush tools. For the other paint tools, only the intensity distribution of a brush is relevant.

Size This option lets you to modify precisely the size of the brush. You can use the arrow keys to vary by ±0.01 or the Page-Up and Page-Down keys to vary by ±1.00. You can obtain the same result if you have correctly set your mouse-wheel in the Preferences. See How to vary the size of a brush

Aspect Ratio This determines the ratio between the height and the width of the brush. The slider is scaled from -20.00 to 20.00 with the default value set to 0.00. A negative value from 0.00 to -20 will narrow the height of the brush while a positive value between 0.00 and 20.00 indicates the narrowing rate of the width of the brush.

Angle This option makes the brush turn round its center. This is visible if the brush is not circular or made from a rotated figure.

Dynamics

Figure 14.41 The Brush Dynamics in the Tool Options Dialog

Brush dynamics let you map different brush parameters to several input dynamics. They are mostly used with graphic tablets, but some of them are also usable with a mouse.

You can read more about dynamics in Dynamics

When stroking paths and selections using a paint tool there is a an option to select "Emulate brush dynamics". That means that when you stoke, brush pressure and velocity are varying along the length of the stroke. Pressure starts with zero, ramps up to full pressure and then ramps down again to no pressure. Velocity starts from zero and ramps up to full speed by the end of the stroke.

Dynamics Options These options are described in Dynamics Options

Apply Jitter You know "spacing" in brush strokes: strokes are made of successive brush marks which, when they are very near, seem to draw a continuous line. Here, instead of being aligned brush marks are scattered over a distance you can set with the Amount slider.

Figure 14.42 "Jitter" example

From top to bottom: without jitter, jitter = 1, jitter = 4.

Jitter is also available in the Paint Dynamic Editor where you can connect jitter to the behavior of the brush.

Smooth Stroke This option doesn't affect the rendering of the brush stroke but its "shape". It takes away the wobbles of the line you are drawing. It makes drawing with a mouse easier.

When this option is checked, two setting areas appear, Quality and Weight. You can change the default values to adapt them to your skill.

High weight values rigidifies the brush stroke.

Figure 14.43 "Smooth Stroke" example

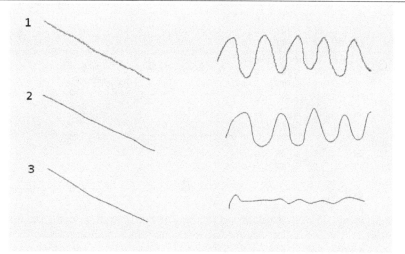

Trying to draw a straight line and a sine curve with the mouse. 1 : option unchecked 2 : default values 3 : maximum values

Incremental The incremental checkbox does not seems to work as everyone expect. If it is deactivated (the default value) the maximum effect of a single stroke is determined by the opacity set in the opacity slider. If the opacity is set to less than 100, moving the brush over the same spot will increase the opacity if the brush is lifted in the meantime. Painting over with the same stroke has no such effect. If Incremental is active the brush will paint with full opacity independent of the slider's setting. This option is available for all paint tools except those which have a "rate" control, which automatically implies an incremental effect. See also Section 8.2.

14.3.1.3 Paint Mode Examples

The following examples demonstrate some of GIMP's paint modes:

Dissolve

Figure 14.44 Dissolve mode example

Two brush-strokes made with the Airbrush, using the same fuzzy circular brush. Left: Normal mode. Right: Dissolve mode.

For any paint tool with opacity less than 100%, this very useful mode doesn't draw transparency but determines the probability of applying paint. This gives nice patterns of dots to paint-strokes or filling.

Figure 14.45 Painting in Dissolve mode

This image has only the background layer and no Alpha channel. The background color is sky blue. Three strokes with Pencil and various opacities: 100%, 50%, 25%. Foreground color pixels are scattered along brushstroke.

Behind

Figure 14.46 Example for layer mode "Behind"

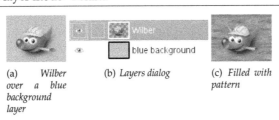

(a)   Wilber   (b) *Layers dialog*   (c) *Filled with*
over   a   blue   *pattern*
background
layer

This mode applies paint only to transparent areas of the layer: the lower the opacity, the more paint is applied. Thus, painting opaque areas has no effect; painting transparent areas has the same effect as normal mode. The result is always an increase in opacity. Of course none of this is meaningful for layers that lack an alpha channel.

In the above example image, Wilber is on the top layer, surrounded by transparency. The lower layer is solid light blue. The Bucket Fill tool was used, with the Fill Whole Selection option checked and the entire layer was selected. A pattern was used to paint with the Bucket Fill tool.

The next image (below) has two layers. The upper layer is active. Three brushtrokes with pencil, red color at 100%, 50%, 25%: only transparent or semi-transparent pixels of the layer are painted.

Figure 14.47 Painting in "Behind" mode

Painting with 100%, 50%, 25% transparency (from left to right)

Color Erase

Figure 14.48 Example for layer mode "Color erase"

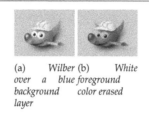

(a)   *Wilber* (b)   *White*
over   a   blue foreground
background   color erased
layer

This mode erases the foreground color, replacing it with partial transparency. It acts like the Color to Alpha filter, applied to the area under the brushstroke. Note that this only works on layers that possess an alpha channel; otherwise, this mode is identical to Normal.

In the above example image, the color of the Bucket Fill tool was white, so white parts of Wilber were erased and the blue background shows through.

This image below has only one layer, the background layer. Background color is sky blue. Three brushtrokes with pencil:

1. With the exact color of the blue area: only this blue color is erased.

2. With the exact color of the red area. Only this red color is erased, whatever its transparency. Erased areas are made transparent.

3. With the sky blue color of the layer background: only this color is erased.

Figure 14.49 Painting in "Color Erase" mode

Painted with 1. blue; 2. red; 3. background color

14.3.1.4 Further Information

Advanced users may be interested to know that paint tools actually operate at a sub-pixel level, in order to avoid producing jagged-looking results. One consequence of this is that even if you work with a hard-edged brush, such as one of the Circle brushes, pixels on the edge of the brushstroke will only be partially affected. If you need to have all-or-nothing effects (which may be necessary for getting a good selection, or for cutting and pasting, or for operating pixel-by-pixel at a high zoom level), use the Pencil tool, which makes all brushes perfectly hard and disables sub-pixel anti-aliasing.

14.3.2 Dynamics

The dynamics apply a more "real feeling" to the brush by connecting one or more of the brush parameters to the way of using the brush. You may for instance let the width of the pencil vary according to the speed of the stylus or the mouse, make the color saturation depending on the stylus pressure, make the color changing as the direction of the brush changes on the canvas, and so on. You may choose among several presets or define your own. The dynamics are created to be used together with drawing tablets, but some are available using the mouse.

The dynamics will make some of the behaviors of the drawing tools act more like the physical ("real") tools.

Figure 14.50 Dynamics in Tool Options

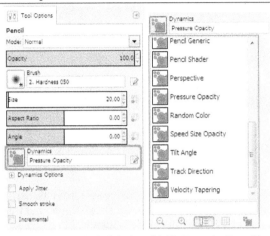

(a) *The Dynamics in Tool Options* (b) *The Dynamics Preset List Dialog*

The Dynamics area in the Tool Option dialog shows from left to right, the button to open the list containing the available dynamic presets, a field displaying the name of the current preset, and rightmost the edit button. Click on the ![icon] button to open the dialog window displaying the available dynamics presets and select another preset.

14.3.2.1   The Paint Dynamics Selection Dialog

Figure 14.51 The Paint Dynamics Selection Dialog

The Paint Dynamics dialog window can be opened

- from the image-menu: Windows → Dockable Dialogs → Paint Dynamics,

- or by clicking on the Open the dynamics selection button in the list of dynamics presets.

The Paint Dynamics dialog is a dockable dialog; please see the section Section 3.2.3 for help on manipulating it.

From this dialog you can select from all the available presets, just as from the list of dynamics presets. In addition there are five buttons:

- Edit dynamics: Click on this to edit the selected dynamics.

- Create a new dynamics: Do just that.

- Duplicate this dynamics: Make a copy of the selected dynamics.

- Delete this dynamics: Delete the selected dynamics.

- Refresh dynamics: Update the dynamics list.

14.3.2.2 Editing Paint Dynamics

Figure 14.52 Editing Paint Dynamics

The Paint Dynamics Editor can be called from:

- the edit button in the Tool Options dialog,

- the Paint Dynamics selection dialog by clicking either the Edit Dynamics button or the Create a New Dynamics button.

You select the desired behaviors by clicking in the small squares. Clicking a second time will unselect the marking.

> **Note**
>
> Pre-installed dynamics are grayed out meaning you are not allowed to change the settings. To edit the options you have to work on a copy made from one of the pre-installed dynamics or create a new dynamics.

14.3.2.3   The Paint Dynamics Matrix

The main part of the edit dialog is a table where you can decide which brush parameters should be affected by the way you use the stylus or the mouse. You can enable as many parameters and parameter combinations you want, but usually the fewer the better.

Each column in the table represents a stylus or mouse action except the random and the fade functions. All functions works with graphic tablet. Some of the functions are also available using the mouse. These functions are marked in the tables. The descriptions are using the default settings of all functions

- Pressure: It allows you to decide which aspects of the tool's action will be affected by pressing the stylus against the tablet.

- Velocity: (mouse) This is the speed of the brush.

- Direction: (mouse) This is the moving direction of the brush.

- Tilt: The behavior of the function depends on the tilting of the stylus.

- Wheel: The output depends on the rotation of the stylus or the setting of the wheel on the airbrush pen.

- Random: (mouse) The selected option will change at random.

- Fade: (mouse) The selected option will be faded in or out depending on the settings of the fade options in the Dynamic Options menu of the Tools Option dialog.

Each row shows a brush parameter and seven checkboxes, one for each action. You connect the parameters to the actions by clicking the appropriate boxes. Clicking on a selected box will unselect the connection.

Opacity Pressure: Press harder to make the drawing less transparent.

Velocity: (mouse) The opacity decreases as the speed of the stylus increases.

Direction: (mouse) The opacity depends on the direction of the stylus or the mouse. The effect seems to have a touch of randomness built in.

Tilt: The opacity depends on the tilt of the stylus.

Wheel: TO DO

Random: (mouse) The opacity changes at random in the interval set by the opacity slider in the Tool Options dialog.

Fade: (mouse) Starting with full transparency and ending with the opacity set by the opacity slider in the Tool Options dialog.

Size Pressure: Press harder to make the brush wider.

Velocity: (mouse) Increasing speed decreases the width of the brush.

Direction: (mouse) The size of the brush depends on the moving direction of the stylus or the mouse. The effect seems to have a touch of randomness built in.

Tilt: The size of the brush depends on the tilt of the stylus.

Wheel: TODO

Random: (mouse) The size of the brush changes at random up to the size set in the brush size slider in the Tool Options dialog.

Fade: (mouse) Fades from a narrow brush to the size set by the brush size slider in the Tools Options dialog.

Angle TO DO

Color By default the color is picked from the foreground color in the toolbox. However, if the color is activated in the dynamics editor, the color is instead collected from the active gradient.

Velocity: (mouse) At slow speeds the color is collected from the right side of the gradient. As the speed increase the color is picked more and more from the left side of the gradient.

Direction: (mouse) The direction determine where on the gradient the color is picked from. The effect seems to work a bit on random.

Random: (mouse) The color is picked at random from the gradient.

Fade: (mouse) The start color is collected from the left side of the gradient and then more and more from the right side during the stroke. The behavior of the fading is set in the Fade Options in the Tool Options Dialog.

Hardness The hardness option is useful only for fuzzy brushes.

Velocity: (mouse) At slow speed the brush is hard and become more fuzzy as the speed increase.

Random: (mouse) The fussiness of the brush varies at random.

Fade:(mouse) The brush become less fuzzy during the stroke. The behavior of the fading is set in the Fade Options in the Tool Options Dialog.

Force TO DO

Aspect Ratio The Aspect Ratio Slider in the Tool Options Dialog must be set to other values than the default value of 0.00 to activate the dynamics. If the aspect ratio slider is set to a negative value the width of the brush will vary while the height of the brush is constant. If the slider is set to a positive value only the height of the brush will vary.

Velocity: (mouse) The aspect ratio of the brush (width / height) varies with the speed of the brush.

Direction: (mouse) The aspect ratio of the brush varies with the moving direction of the brush. The effect seems to have a touch of randomness built in.

Random: (mouse) The aspect ratio of the brush varies at random.

Fade: (mouse) If the Aspect Ratio Slider is set to a positive value the brush will fade from full height at the start of the stroke to the height set by the aspect ratio slider. If the slider is set to a negative value the brush fades from full width to the width set by the aspect ratio slider. The behavior of the fading is set in the Fade Options in the Tool Options Dialog.

Spacing Spacing is the distance between the marks set by the brush when drawing lines. With this option set the spacing is affected by how the stylus or mouse is used.

Velocity: (mouse) The spacing between the footprints of the brush increases with increasing speed.

Direction: (mouse) The spacing varies with the moving direction of the brush. The effect seems to have a touch of randomness built in.

Random: (mouse) The spacing varies at random.

Fade: (mouse) Starting with a wide spacing and gradually make the spacing narrower. The behavior of the fading is set in the Fade Options in the Tool Options Dialog.

Rate This option applies to the Airbrush, Convolve tool, and Smudge tool, all of which have time-based effects.

The actions of these tools are more or less quick. The amount of Rate depends on the setting of the Rate slider in the Tool Options dialog.

Flow Significant only for the Airbrush: more or less paint is delivered. The amount of flow depends on the setting of the Flow slider in the Tool Options dialog.

Jitter Normally the brush draws a line by printing the brush marks close together. Adding jitter means that the brush prints are scattered along the line. The amount of scattering depends on the setting of the jitter slider in the Tool Options dialog window.

Pressure: At low pressure the brush prints are spread according to the value set in the jitter amount slider. As the pressure increases the scattering amount decreases.

Velocity: (mouse) At slow speed the brush prints are spread according to the value set in the jitter amount slider. As the speed increase the scattering amount decrease.

Direction: (mouse) The jitter effect depends on the direction of the brush. The effect seems to have a touch of randomness built in.

Random: (mouse)The jitter varies at random.

Fade: (mouse) Starting with no jitter and ending with the amount of jitter set in the jitter amount slider. The behavior of the fading is set in the fade options in the Tool Options dialog.

14.3.2.4   Customizing the Dynamics

Figure 14.53 Customizing the Dynamics

If the current options do not suits you, you may fine-tune the settings from the Paint Dynamics Editor. Click on the down arrow to open the drop down menu and then select what option to change.

Figure 14.54 The Fine Tuning Curve

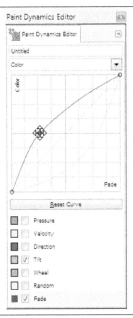

Click on one of the options to open the customizing dialog. The upper part of the dialog contains a curve where you can adjust the behaviour of the chosen parameters selected in the lower part of the dialog. You can drag the curve by pointing on it with the mouse pointer, holding down the left mouse button and the move the curve wherever you want inside the diagram.

14.3.2.5   Dynamics Examples

Figure 14.55 Dynamics Options

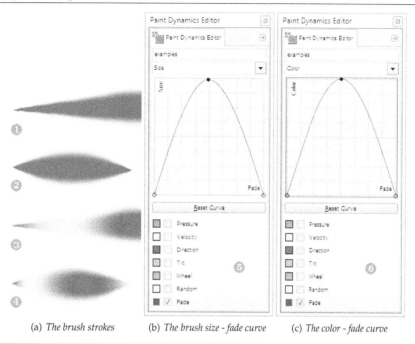

(a) *The brush strokes* (b) *The brush size - fade curve* (c) *The color - fade curve*

The examples shown are very brief, but will perhaps give you an idea of how to use this functions. Feel free to try other combinations. In these examples the foreground color is set to blue (#0000ff) and the background color to yellow (#ffff00). Fading: 200 pixels. Paintbrush size: 72. All other settings are the default values except for those values changed

- Example 1 shows the result when the brush size is connected to the fading. Default options. The brush size starts as zero and increase to the size set in the brush size slider in the Tools Options Dialog.

- In example 2 the brush size is still connected to the fade tool, but the fade curve is set as in image 5. The brush size starts at zero, fades up to full size and then fades down to zero again.

  The full fade length is set along the x-axis from left to right. The y-axis determines the size of the brush. At the bottom the brush size is zero, and at the top of the diagram the brush is set to the full size according to the size set in the slider in the Brush Options Dialog. Study the example and the curve to see the relationship.

- In example 3 the brush size is disconnected from the fade tool. The color is connected with the fade option with the curve set as in image 6. At the start of the drawing the color is picked from the left side of the gradient, then gradually more from the right side of the gradient and then finally fading back to the left side again.

  As usual the x-axis is the total fade length. When the curve is near the bottom of the diagram the color is picked from the left side of the gradient. With the curve at the top of the diagram the color is picked from the right side of the gradient.

- The last example shows a combination of these two settings. Both the size of the brush and the color are connected to the fading function with the curves set as in image 5 and 6.

14.3.2.6 Dynamics Options

Figure 14.56 Dynamics Options

Many of the dynamics behaviors also depends on the settings of the Dynamics Options in the Tool Options dialog and vice versa. For example the fading will not work if it is not applied in the Dynamics section.

Fade Options This slider determines the length of the fading. What will actually happen depends on the setting of the Dynamic. If set to act on the color for example, the color will be taken from the current gradient starting from the left side of the gradient and moving toward the right side of the gradient.

The Fade Options has a drop down list determining how the fading is repeated.

Figure 14.57 Illustration of the effects of the three gradient-repeat options, for the Abstract 2 gradient.

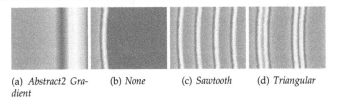

(a) *Abstract2 Gradient*   (b) *None*   (c) *Sawtooth*   (d) *Triangular*

This option determines what happens if a brush stroke extends farther than the Length specified by the slider. There are three possibilities:

- None means that the color from the end of the gradient will be used throughout the remainder of the stroke;

- Sawtooth wave means that the gradient will be restarted from the beginning, which will often produce a color discontinuity;

- Triangular wave means that the gradient will be traversed in reverse, afterwards bouncing back and forth until the end of the brush stroke.

Color Options Here you can choose the gradient to use as color source when using the brush with the color option set. Click on the box showing the gradient to change to another one from the gradient list.

If no color option is selected in the currently used dynamics, the brush will use the foreground color set in the toolbox.

14.3.3   Brush Tools (Pencil, Paintbrush, Airbrush)

Figure 14.58 Painting example

Three strokes painted with the same round fuzzy brush (outline shown in upper left), using the Pencil (left), Paintbrush (middle), and Airbrush (right).

The tools in this group are GIMP's basic painting tools, and they have enough features in common to be worth discussing together in this section. Features common to all paint tools are described in the Common Features section. Features specific to an individual tool are described in the section devoted to that tool.

The Pencil is the crudest of the tools in this group: it makes hard, non-anti-aliased brushstrokes. The Paintbrush is intermediate: it is probably the most commonly used of the group. The Airbrush is the most flexible and controllable. This flexibility also makes it a bit more difficult to use than the Paintbrush, however.

All of these tools share the same brushes, and the same options for choosing colors, either from the basic palette or from a gradient. All are capable of painting in a wide variety of modes.

14.3.3.1   Key modifiers

Ctrl   Holding down the **Ctrl** key changes each of these tools to a Color Picker: clicking on any pixel of any layer sets the foreground color (as displayed in the Toolbox Color Area) to the color of the pixel.

Shift   This key places these tools into straight line mode. Holding **Shift** while clicking the mouse left Button will generate a straight line. Consecutive clicks will continue drawing straight lines that originate from the end of the last line.

14.3.4   Bucket Fill

Figure 14.59 Toolbox Fill

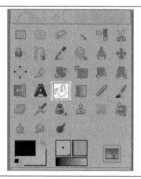

This tool fills a selection with the current foreground color. If you **Ctrl**+click and use the Bucket tool, it will use the background color instead. Depending on how the tool options are set, the Bucket Fill tool will either fill the entire selection, or only parts whose colors are similar to the point you click on. The tool options also affect the way transparency is handled.

The amount of fill depends on what Fill Threshold you have specified. The fill threshold determines how far the fill will spread (similar to the way in which the magic wand works). The fill starts at the point where you click and spreads outward until the color or alpha value becomes "too different".

When you fill objects in a transparent layer (such as letters in a text layer) with a different color than before, you may find that a border of the old color still surrounds the objects. This is due to a low fill-threshold in the Bucket Fill options dialog. With a low threshold, the bucket tool won't fill semi-transparent pixels, and they will stand out against the fill because they have kept their original color.

If you want to fill areas that are totally transparent, you have to make sure that the "Lock" option (in the Layers dialog) is unchecked. If this option is checked, only the non-transparent parts of the layer will be filled.

14.3.4.1 Activating the tool

- You can find the Bucket Fill tool from the image-menu through: Tools → Paint Tools → Bucket Fill

- You can also call it by clicking the tool icon: 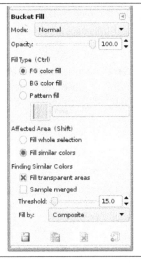 in the toolbox.

- or by pressing the Shift-B keys.

14.3.4.2 Key modifiers (Defaults)

- **Ctrl** toggles the use of BG Color Fill or FG Color Fill on the fly.

- **Shift** toggles the use of Fill Similar Color or Fill Whole Selection on the fly.

14.3.4.3 Options

Figure 14.60 "Bucket Fill" tool options

Normally, tool options are displayed in a window attached under the Toolbox as soon as you activate a tool. If they are not, you can access them from the image menu bar through Windows → Dockable Windows → Tool Options which opens the option window of the selected tool.

Mode; Opacity See Paint Tools for help with options that are common to all these tools. Only options that are specific to the Bucket Fill tool are explained here.

Fill Type GIMP provides three fill types:

    FG Color Fill sets the fill color to the currently selected foreground color.

    BG Color Fill sets the fill color to the currently selected background color.

Pattern Fill sets the fill color to the currently selected pattern. You can select the pattern to use in a drop down list.

This drop-down list allows the user to select one of many fill patterns to use on the next fill operation. The manner in which the list is presented is controlled by the four buttons at the bottom of the selector.

Affected Area

Fill whole selection This option makes GIMP fill a pre-existent selection or the whole image. A quicker approach to do the same thing could be to click and drag the foreground, background or pattern color, leaving it onto the selection.

Fill similar colors This is the default setting: the tool fills the area with a color near the pixel onto you have clicked. The color similarity is defined by a brightness threshold, that you can set by a value or by a cursor position.

Finding Similar Colors Under this section you can find two options:

Fill Transparent Areas The option Fill Transparent Areas offers the possibility of filling areas with low opacity.

Sample Merged The option Sample Merged toggles the sampling from all layers. If Sample Merged is active, fills can be made on a lower layer, while the color information used for threshold checking is located further up. Simply select the lower level and ensure that a layer above is visible for color weighting.

Threshold The Threshold slider sets the level at which color weights are measured for fill boundaries. A higher setting will fill more of a multi colored image and conversely, a lower setting will fill less area.

Fill by With this option you can choose which component of the image GIMP shall use to calculate the similarity and to determine the borders of filling.

The components you can choose from are Composite, Red, Green, Blue, Hue, Saturation and Value.

This option is not easy to understand. You have chosen, for example, the Red channel. When you click on any pixel, the tool searches for contiguous pixels similar for *the red channel* to the clicked pixel, according to the set threshold. Here is an example:

Original image: three strips with gradients of pure colors. Red (255;0;0), Green (0;255;0), Blue (0;0;255). We are going to use the Bucket-fill tool with the magenta color and a Threshold set to 15.

Image 1: Fill By = Composite. We successively clicked in the three color strips. Every strip is filled according to the threshold.

Image 2: Fill By = Red. We clicked in the red strip. The tool searches for contiguous pixels which have a similar value in the red channel, according to the set threshold. Only a narrow area corresponds to these standards. In the green and the blue strip, the value of pixels in the red channel is 0, very much different from the red channel value of the clicked pixel: the color doesn't spread to them.

Image 3: Fill By = Red. We clicked in the green strip. There, the value of the clicked pixel in the red channel is 0. All pixels in the green and the blue strips have the same red channel value (0): they are all painted.

Figure 14.61 Example for "Fill By"

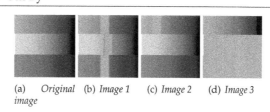

(a)   *Original*   (b) *Image 1*   (c) *Image 2*   (d) *Image 3*
image

14.3.4.4 Fill a feathered selection

By clicking repeatedly in a selection with feathered edges, you progressively fill the feathered border:

Figure 14.62 Example for "Fill a feathered Selection"

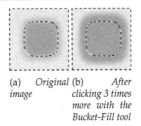

(a) Original (b) After image clicking 3 times more with the Bucket-Fill tool

14.3.5 Blend

Figure 14.63 The Blend tool in Toolbox

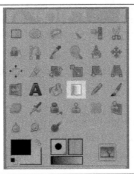

This tool fills the selected area with a gradient blend of the foreground and background colors by default, but there are many options. To make a blend, drag the cursor in the direction you want the gradient to go, and release the mouse button when you feel you have the right position and size of your blend. The softness of the blend depends on how far you drag the cursor. The shorter the drag distance, the sharper it will be.

There are an astonishing number of things you can do with this tool, and the possibilities may seem a bit overwhelming at first. The two most important options you have are the Gradient and the Shape. Clicking the Gradient button in the tool options brings up a Gradient Select window, allowing you to choose from among a variety of gradients supplied with GIMP; you can also construct and save custom gradients. Further information about gradients can be found in Section 7.10 and Section 15.3.4.

For Shape, there are 11 options: Linear, Bilinear, Radial, Square, Conical (symmetric), Conical (asymmetric), Shaped (angular), Shaped (spherical), Shaped (dimpled), Spiral (clockwise), and Spiral (counterclockwise); these are described in detail below. The Shaped options are the most interesting: they cause the gradient to follow the shape of the selection boundary, no matter how twisty it is. Unlike the other shapes, Shaped gradients are not affected by the length or direction of the line you draw: for them as well as every other type of gradient you are required to click inside the selection and move the mouse, but a Shaped appears the same no matter where you click or how you move.

> **Tip**
>
> Check out the Difference option in the Mode menu, where doing the same thing (even with full opacity) will result in fantastic swirling patterns, changing and adding every time you drag the cursor.

14.3.5.1 Activating the Tool

There are different possibilities to activate the tool:

- From the image-menu: Tools → Paint Tools → Blend.

- By clicking the tool icon  .

- By clicking on the **L** keyboard shortcut.

14.3.5.2 Key modifiers (Defaults)

Ctrl **Ctrl** is used to create straight lines that are constrained to 15 degree absolute angles.

14.3.5.3 Options

Figure 14.64 "Blend" tool options

Normally, tool options are displayed in a window attached under the Toolbox as soon as you activate a tool. If they are not, you can access them from the image menu bar through Windows → Dockable Windows → Tool Options which opens the option window of the selected tool.

Mode; Opacity See the Common Paint Tool Options for a description of tool options that apply to many or all paint tools.

Gradient A variety of gradient patterns can be selected from the drop-down list. The tool causes a shading pattern that transitions from foreground to background color or introduces others colors, in the direction the user determines by drawing a line in the image. For the purposes of drawing the gradient, the Reverse checkbox reverses the gradient direction with the effect, for instance, of swapping the foreground and background colors.

Offset The Offset value permits to increase the "slope" of the gradient. It determines how far from the clicked starting point the gradient will begin. Shaped forms are not affected by this option.

Figure 14.65 "Blend" tool: Offset example

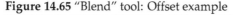
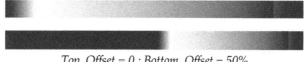

Top, Offset = 0 ; Bottom, Offset = 50%

Shape The GIMP provides 11 shapes, which can be selected from the drop-down list. Details on each of the shapes are given below.

Figure 14.66 Examples of gradient shapes

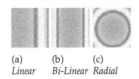

(a)   (b)   (c)
Linear   Bi-Linear Radial

Linear This gradient begins with the foreground color at the starting point of the drawn line and transitions linearly to the background color at the ending point.

Bi-Linear This shape proceeds in both directions from the starting point, for a distance determined by the length of the drawn line. It is useful, for example, for giving the appearance of a cylinder.

Radial This gradient gives a circle, with foreground color at the center and background color outside the circle. It gives the appearance of a sphere without directional lighting.

Square; Shaped

Figure 14.67 Square-shaped gradient examples

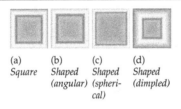

(a)   (b)   (c)   (d)
Square   Shaped   Shaped   Shaped
          (angular) (spheri-   (dimpled)
                     cal)

There are four shapes that are some variant on a square: Square, Shaped (angular), Shaped (spherical), and Shaped (dimpled). They all put the foreground color at the center of a square, whose center is at the start of the drawn line, and whose half-diagonal is the length of the drawn line. The four options provide a variety in the manner in which the gradient is calculated; experimentation is the best means of seeing the differences.

Conical (symmetric); Conical (asymmetric)

Figure 14.68 Conical gradient examples

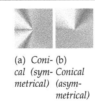

(a) Coni- (b)
cal (sym- Conical
metrical) (asym-
          metrical)

The Conical (symmetrical) shape gives the sensation of looking down at the tip of a cone, which appears to be illuminated with the background color from a direction determined by the direction of the drawn line.

Conical (asymmetric) is similar to Conical (symmetric) except that the "cone" appears to have a ridge where the line is drawn.

Spiral (clockwise); Spiral (counterclockwise)

Figure 14.69 Spiral gradient examples

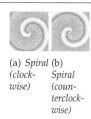

(a) *Spiral* (b)
(clock- *Spiral*
wise) *(coun-*
terclock-
wise)

The Spiral shape provide spirals whose repeat width is determined by the length of the drawn line.

Repeat There are two repeat modes: Sawtooth Wave and Triangular Wave. The Sawtooth pattern is achieved by beginning with the foreground, transitioning to the background, then starting over with the foreground. The Triangular starts with the foreground, transitions to the background, then transitions back to the foreground.

Dithering Dithering is fully explained in the Glossary

Adaptive Supersampling This a more sophisticated means of smoothing the "jagged" effect of a sharp transition of color along a slanted or curved line. Only tests can allow you to choose.

14.3.6 Pencil

Figure 14.70 Pencil tool

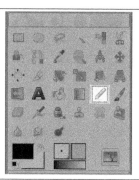

The Pencil tool is used to draw free hand lines with a hard edge. The pencil and paintbrush are similar tools. The main difference between the two tools is that although both use the same type of brush, the pencil tool will not produce fuzzy edges, even with a very fuzzy brush. It does not even do anti-aliasing.

Why would you want to work with such a crude tool? Perhaps the most important usage is when working with very small images, such as icons, where you operate at a high zoom level and need to get every pixel exactly right. With the pencil tool, you can be confident that every pixel within the brush outline will be changed in exactly the way you expect.

Tip

 If you want to draw straight lines with the Pencil (or any of several other paint tools), click at the starting point, then hold down **Shift** and click at the ending point.

14.3.6.1 Activating the Tool

- The Pencil Tool can be called from the image-menu: Tools → Paint Tools → Pencil

- The Tool can also be called by clicking the tool icon:

- or by clicking on the **N** keyboard shortcut.

14.3.6.2 Key modifiers (Defaults)

Ctrl This key changes the pencil to a Color Picker.

Shift This key places the pencil tool into straight line mode. Holding **Shift** while clicking the mouse Left Button will generate a straight line. Consecutive clicks will continue drawing straight lines that originate from the end of the last line.

14.3.6.3 Options

Figure 14.71 "Pencil" Tool options

Normally, tool options are displayed in a window attached under the Toolbox as soon as you activate a tool. If they are not, you can access them from the image menu bar through Windows → Dockable Windows → Tool Options which opens the option window of the selected tool.

Mode; Opacity; Brush; Dynamics; Dynamics Options; Apply Jitter; Smooth Stroke; Incremental See the Common Paint Tool Options for a description of tool options that apply to many or all paint tools.

14.3.7 Paintbrush

Figure 14.72 Paintbrush

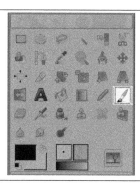

The paintbrush tool paints fuzzy brush strokes. All strokes are rendered using the current brush.

14.3.7.1 Activating the Tool

- You can call the Paintbrush Tool in the following order, from the image-menu: Tools → Paint Tools → Paintbrush.

- The Tool can also be called by clicking the tool icon:

- or by using the **P** keyboard shortcut.

14.3.7.2 Key modifiers (Defaults)

Ctrl This key changes the paintbrush to a Color Picker.

Shift This key places the paintbrush into straight line mode. Holding **Shift** while clicking Button 1 will generate a straight line. Consecutive clicks will continue drawing straight lines that originate from the end of the last line.

14.3.7.3 Options

Figure 14.73 Paintbrush tool options

Normally, tool options are displayed in a window attached under the Toolbox as soon as you activate a tool. If they are not, you can access them from the image menu bar through Windows → Dockable Windows → Tool Options which opens the option window of the selected tool.

Mode; Opacity; Brush; Dynamics; Dynamics Options; Apply Jitter; Smoot Stroke; Incremental: See the Common Paint Tool Options for a description of tool options that apply to many or all paint tools.

14.3.8 Eraser

Figure 14.74 Eraser tool icon in the Toolbox

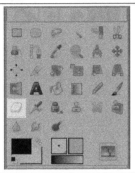

The Eraser is used to remove areas of color from the current layer or from a selection of this layer. If the Eraser is used on something that does not support transparency (a selection mask channel, a layer mask, or the Background layer if it lacks an alpha channel), then erasing will show the background color, as displayed in the Color Area of the Toolbox (in case of a mask, the selection will be modified). Otherwise, erasing will produce either partial or full transparency, depending on the settings for the tool options. You can learn more on how to add an alpha channel to a layer in Section 16.7.33.

Figure 14.75 Eraser and Alpha channel

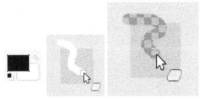

(a) *The Background Color* (b) *The image has is White. The image has no an Alpha channel. Alpha channel. The Eraser The Eraser shows (Opacity 100%) shows the transparency. BG color.*

If you need to erase some group of pixels completely, leaving no trace behind of their previous contents, you should check the "Hard edge" box in the Tool Options. Otherwise, sub-pixel brush placement will cause partial erasure at the edges of the brush-stroke, even if you use a hard-edged brush.

Tip

If you use GIMP with a tablet, you may find it convenient to treat the reverse end of the stylus as an eraser. To make this work, all you need to do is click the reverse end on the Eraser tool in the Toolbox. Because each end of the stylus is treated as a separate input device, and each input device has its own separate tool assignment, the reverse end will then continue to function as an Eraser as long as you don't select a different tool with it.

14.3.8.1 Activating the tool

You can activate this tool in several ways:

- From the image menu through Tools → Paint Tools → Eraser;

- from the Toolbox by clicking on the tool icon ;

- or from the keyboard using the shortcut Shift-E.

14.3.8.2 Key modifiers

See the Section 14.3.1 for a description of key modifiers that have the same effect on all paint tools.

Ctrl For the Eraser, holding down the **Ctrl** key puts it into "color picker" mode, so that it selects the color of any pixel it is clicked on. Unlike other brush tools, however, the Eraser sets the *background* color rather than the foreground color. This is more useful, because on drawables that don't support transparency, erasing replaces the erased areas with the current background color.

Alt For the Eraser, holding down the **Alt** key switches it into "anti-erase" mode, as described below in the Tool Options section. Note that on some systems, the **Alt** key is trapped by the Window Manager. If this happens to you, you may be able to use Alt-Shift instead.

14.3.8.3 Tool Options

Figure 14.76 Tool Options for the Eraser tool

Normally, tool options are displayed in a window attached under the Toolbox as soon as you activate a tool. If they are not, you can access them from the image menu bar through Windows → Dockable Windows → Tool Options which opens the option window of the selected tool.

Brush; Size; Brush Dynamics; Dynamic Options; Apply Jitter; Incremental   See the Common Paint Tool Options for a description of tool options that apply to many or all paint tools.

Opacity The Opacity slider, in spite of its name, in this tool determines the "strength" of the tool. Thus, when you erase on a layer with an alpha channel, the higher the opacity you use, the more transparency you get!

Hard Edge This option avoids partial erasure at the edges of the brush-stroke. See above.

Anti Erase The Anti Erase option of the Erase tool can un-erase areas of an image, even if they are completely transparent. This feature only works when used on layers with an alpha channel. In addition to the check-button in the Tool Options, it can also be activated on-the-fly by holding down the **Alt** key (or, if the **Alt** key is trapped by the Window Manager, by holding down Alt-Shift).

Note

 To understand how anti-erasing is possible, you should realize that erasing (or cutting, for that matter) only affects the alpha channel, not the RGB channels that contain the image data. Even if the result is completely transparent, the RGB data is still there, you simply can't see it. Anti-erasing increases the alpha value so that you can see the RGB data once again.

Tip

 You can use the Eraser tool to change the shape of a floating selection. By erasing, you can trim the edges of the selection.

14.3.9   Airbrush

Figure 14.77 The Airbrush tool in Toolbox

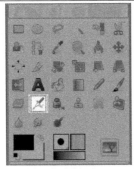

The Airbrush tool emulates a traditional airbrush. This tool is suitable for painting soft areas of color.

14.3.9.1   Activating the Tool

You can activate the Airbrush tool in several ways :

- From the image-menu, through : Tools → PaintTools → Airbrush

- By clicking on the tool icon: 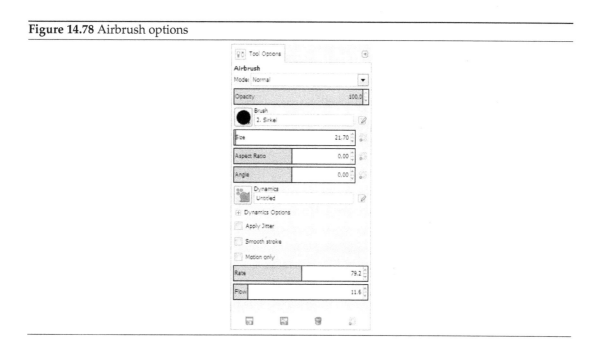 in the Toolbox,

- By using the **A** keyboard shortcut.

14.3.9.2   Key modifiers (Defaults)

Ctrl   **Ctrl** changes the airbrush to a Color Picker.

Shift   **Shift** places the airbrush into straight line mode. Holding **Shift** while clicking the mouse Left Button will generate a straight line. Consecutive clicks will continue drawing straight lines that originate from the end of the last line.

14.3.9.3   Options

Figure 14.78 Airbrush options

Normally, tool options are displayed in a window attached under the Toolbox as soon as you activate a tool. If they are not, you can access them from the image menu bar through Windows → Dockable Windows → Tool Options which opens the option window of the selected tool.

Mode; Opacity; Brush; Size; Dynamics; Dynamic Options; Fade Options; Color Options; Apply Jitter See the Common Paint Tool Options for a description of tool options that apply to many or all paint tools.

Rate The Rate slider adjusts the speed of color application that the airbrush paints. A higher setting will produce darker brush strokes in a shorter amount of time.

Flow This slider controls the amount of color that the airbrush paints. A higher setting here will result in darker strokes.

14.3.10 Ink

Figure 14.79 The "Ink" tool in Toolbox

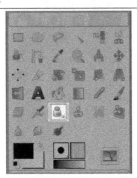

The Ink tool uses a simulation of an ink pen with a controllable nib to paint solid brush strokes with an antialiased edge. The size, shape and angle of the nib can be set to determine how the strokes will be rendered.

14.3.10.1 Activating the Tool

You can find the Ink tool in several ways :

- In the image-menu through: Tools → Paint Tools → Ink.

- By clicking on the tool icon: in Toolbox,

- or by using the **K** keyboard shortcut.

14.3.10.2 Key modifiers (Defaults)

Ctrl This key changes the nib to a Color Picker.

14.3.10.3 Options

Figure 14.80 Ink Tool options

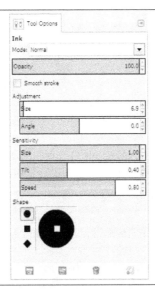

Normally, tool options are displayed in a window attached under the Toolbox as soon as you activate a tool. If they are not, you can access them from the image menu bar through Windows → Dockable Windows → Tool Options which opens the option window of the selected tool.

Mode; Opacity See the Common Paint Tool Options for a description of tool options that apply to many or all paint tools.

Adjustment

> **Size** Controls the apparent width of the pen's nib with values that ranges from 0 (very thin) to 20 (very thick).

> **Angle** This controls the apparent angle of the pen's nib relative to horizontal.

Sensitivity

> **Size** This controls the size of the nib, from minimum to maximum. Note that a size of 0 does not result in a nib of size zero, but rather a nib of minimum size.

> **Tilt** Controls the apparent tilt of the nib relative to horizontal. This control and the Angle control described above are interrelated. Experimentation is the best means of learning how to use them.

> **Speed** This controls the effective size of the nib as a function of drawing speed. That is, as with a physical pen, the faster you draw, the narrower the line.

Type and Shape

> **Type** There are three nib shapes to choose from: circle, square, and diamond.

> **Shape** The geometry of the nib type can be adjusted by holding button 1 of the mouse on the small square at the center of the Shape icon and moving it around.

14.3.11 Clone

Figure 14.81 Clone tool icon in the Toolbox

The Clone tool uses the current brush to copy from an image or pattern. It has many uses: one of the most important is to repair problem areas in digital photos, by "painting over" them with pixel data from other areas. This technique takes a while to learn, but in the hands of a skilled user it is very powerful. Another important use is to draw patterned lines or curves: see Patterns for examples.

If you want to clone from an image, instead of a pattern, you must tell GIMP which image you want to copy from. You do this by holding down the **Ctrl** key and clicking in the desired source image. Until you have set the source in this way, you will not be able to paint with the Clone tool: the tool cursor tells you this by showing ✎.

If you clone from a pattern, the pattern is *tiled*; that is, when the point you are copying from moves past one of the edges, it jumps to the opposite edge and continues, as though the pattern were repeated side-by-side, indefinitely. When you clone from an image this does not happen: if you go beyond the edges of the source, the Clone tool stops producing any changes.

You can clone from any drawable (that is, any layer, layer mask, or channel) to any other drawable. You can even clone to or from the selection mask, by switching to QuickMask mode. If this means copying colors that the target does not support (for example, cloning from an RGB layer to an Indexed layer or a layer mask), then the colors will be converted to the closest possible approximations.

14.3.11.1   Activating the tool

You can activate this tool in several ways:

- From the image menu through Tools → Paint Tools → Clone.

- By clicking on the tool icon  in Toolbox.

- By pressing the **C** keyboard shortcut.

14.3.11.2   Key modifiers (default)

See the Paint tools key modifiers for a description of key modifiers that have the same effect on all paint tools.

Ctrl   The **Ctrl** key is used to select the source, if you are cloning from an image: it has no effect if you are cloning from a pattern. You can clone from any layer of any image, by clicking on the image display, with the **Ctrl** key held down, while the layer is active (as shown in the Layers dialog). If Alignment is set to None, Aligned, or **Fixed** in tool options, then the point you click on becomes the origin for cloning: the image data at that point will be used when you first begin painting with the Clone tool. In source-selection mode, the cursor changes to a reticle cross symbol ⁺ᵢ .

14.3.11.3   Options

Figure 14.82 Tool Options for the Clone tool

Normally, tool options are displayed in a window attached under the Toolbox as soon as you activate a tool. If they are not, you can access them from the image menu bar through Windows → Dockable Windows → Tool Options which opens the option window of the selected tool.

Mode; Opacity; Brush; Dynamics; Dynamics Options; Fade Options; Apply Jitter; Smooth Stroke; Hard Edge
See the Common Paint Tool Options for a description of tool options that apply to many or all paint tools.

Source The choice you make here determines whether data will be copied from the pattern shown above, or from one of the images you have open.

Image If you choose Image source, you must tell GIMP which layer to use as the source, by **Ctrl**-clicking on it, before you can paint with the tool.

If you check Sample merged it's what you "see" (color made with all the layers of a multi-layer image) that's cloned. If it's unchecked, only the selected layer is cloned. For more information see the glossary entry Sample Merge.

Pattern Clicking on the pattern symbol brings up the Patterns dialog, which you can use to select the pattern to paint with. This option is only relevant if you are cloning from a Pattern source.

Alignment The Alignment mode defines the relation between the brush position and the source position.

In the following examples, we will use a source image where the sample to be cloned will be taken, and a destination image where the sample will be cloned (it could be a layer in the source image)

Figure 14.83 Original images for clone alignment

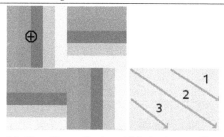

(a) We will use the largest brush with the Pencil tool. The solid source is represented here with a ringed cross.

(b) An image with a background only. We shall draw three cloning strokes successively.

None In this mode, each brushstroke is treated separately. For each stroke, the point where you first click is copied from the source origin; there is no relationship between one brush stroke and another. In non-aligned mode, different brush strokes will usually clash if they intersect each other.

Example below: At every new brush stroke, the source goes back to its first position. The same sample is always cloned.

Figure 14.84 "None" clone alignment

Aligned In this mode, the first click you make when painting sets the offset between the source origin and the cloned result, and all subsequent brushstrokes use the same offset. Thus, you can use as many brushstrokes as you like, and they will all mesh smoothly with one another.

If you want to change the offset, select a new source origin by clicking with the **Ctrl** key pressed.

In the example below, at every new brush stroke, the source keeps the same offset it had with the previous brush stroke. So, there is no cloning offset for the first brush stroke. Here, for the following strokes, the source ends up out of the source image canvas; hence the truncated aspect.

Figure 14.85 "Aligned" clone alignment

Registered The "Registered" mode is different from the other alignment modes. When you copy from an image, a **Ctrl**-click will register a source layer. Then painting in a target layer will clone each corresponding pixel (pixel with the same offset) from the source layer. This is useful when you want to clone parts of an image from one layer to another layer within the same image. (But remember that you can also clone from one image to another image.)

At every brush stroke, the source adopts the position of the mouse pointer in the destination layer. In the following example, the destination layer is smaller than the source layer; so, there is no truncated aspect.

Figure 14.86 "Registered" clone alignment

Fixed Using this mode you will paint with the source origin, unlike the modes None or Aligned even when drawing a line. The source will not be moved.

See that the source remains fixed. The same small sample is reproduced identically in a tightened way:

Figure 14.87 "Fixed" clone alignment

14.3.11.4 Further Information

Transparency The effects of the Clone tool on transparency are a bit complicated. You cannot clone transparency: if you try to clone from a transparent source, nothing happens to the target. If you clone from a partially transparent source, the effect is weighted by the opacity of the source. So, assuming 100% opacity and a hard brush:

- Cloning translucent black onto white produces gray.
- Cloning translucent black onto black produces black.
- Cloning translucent white onto white produces white.
- Cloning translucent white onto black produces gray.

Cloning can never increase transparency, but, unless "keep transparency" is turned on for the layer, it can reduce it. Cloning an opaque area onto a translucent area produces an opaque result; cloning a translucent area onto another translucent area causes an increase in opacity.

"Filter" brushes There are a few non-obvious ways to use the Clone tool to obtain powerful effects. One thing you can do is to create "Filter brushes", that is, create the effect of applying a filter with a brush. To do this, duplicate the layer you want to work on, and apply the filter to the copy. Then activate the Clone tool, setting Source to "Image source" and Alignment to "Registered". **Ctrl**-click on the filtered layer to set it as the source, and paint on the original layer: you will then in effect be painting the filtered image data onto the original layer.

History brush You can use a similar approach to imitate Photoshop's "History brush", which allows you to selectively undo or redo changes using a brush. To do this, start by duplicating the image; then, in the original, go back to the desired state in the image's history, either by undoing or by using the Undo History dialog. (This must be done in the original, not the copy, because duplicating an image does not duplicate the Undo history.) Now activate the Clone tool, setting Source to "Image source" and Alignment to "Registered". **Ctrl**-click on a layer from one image, and paint on the corresponding layer from the other image. Depending on how you do it, this gives you either an "undo brush" or a "redo brush".

14.3.12   Heal

Figure 14.88 The "Heal tool" in the Toolbox

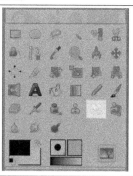

This tool was once described as "The healing brush looks like a smart clone tool on steroids". And indeed the Healing Tool is a close relative to the Clone Tool, but it is more smart to remove small failures in images. A typical usage is the removal of wrinkles in photographs. To do so, pixels are not simply copied from source to destination, but the area around the destination is taken into account before cloning is applied. The algorithm used for this, is described in a scientific paper by Todor Georgiev [GEORGIEV01].

To use it, first choose a brush with a size adapted to the defect. Then **Ctrl**-click on the area you want to reproduce. Release the **Ctrl** key and drag the sample to the defect. Click. If the defect is slight, not very different from its surrounding, it will be corrected as soon. Else, you can correct it with repeated clicks, but with a risk of daubing

14.3.12.1   Activating the Tool

There are different possibilities to activate the tool:

- From the image-menu: Tools → Paint tools → Heal,

- or by clicking the tool icon: ![icon] in the Toolbox,

- or by clicking on the **H** keyboard shortcut.

14.3.12.2   Key modifiers (Defaults)

Ctrl   The **Ctrl** key is used to select the source. You can heal from any layer of any image, by clicking on the image display, with the **Ctrl** key held down, while the layer is active (as shown in the Layers dialog). If Alignment is set to "Non-aligned" or "Aligned" in Tool Options, then the point you click on becomes the origin for healing: the image data at that point will be used when you first begin painting with the Heal tool. In source-selection mode, the cursor changes to a crosshair-symbol.

Shift Once the source is set, if you press this key, you will see a thin line connecting the previously clicked point with the current pointer location. If you click again, while going on holding the **Shift** key down, the tool will "heal" along this line.

14.3.12.3 Options

Figure 14.89 Heal Tool options

Normally, tool options are displayed in a window attached under the Toolbox as soon as you activate a tool. If they are not, you can access them from the image menu bar through Windows → Dockable Windows → Tool Options which opens the option window of the selected tool.

Mode; Opacity; Brush; Dynamics; Dynamics Options; Apply Jitter; Smoot Stroke; Hard Edge See the Common Paint Tool Options for a description of tool options that apply to many or all paint tools.

Sample merged If you enable this option, healing is not calculated only from the values of the active layer, but from all visible layers.

Alignment This option is described in Clone tool.

14.3.12.4 Healing is not cloning

Although the Heal tool has common features with the Clone tool on using, the result is quite different.

Figure 14.90 Comparing "Clone" and "Heal"

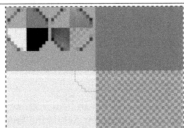

Two black spots in the red area. Zoom x800. The source is where the four colors meet. Cloning on the left spot. Healing on the right spot.

14.3.13   Perspective Clone

Figure 14.91 The "Perspective Clone" tool in the Toolbox

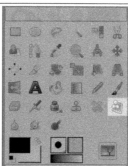

This tool allows you to clone according to the perspective you want. First, set the wanted vanishing lines in the same way as with the Perspective tool. Then copy the source area in the same way as with the Clone tool.

14.3.13.1   Activating the Tool

There are different possibilities to activate the tool:

- From the image-menu: Tools → Paint tools → Perspective Clone.

- The Tool can also be called by clicking the tool icon: in the Toolbox.

14.3.13.2   Key modifiers (Defaults)

Ctrl   **Ctrl**-click allows you to select a new clone source.

Shift   When the source is set and you press this key, you will see a thin line connecting the previously clicked point with the current pointer location. If you click again, while continuing to hold down the **Shift** key, the tool will clone along this line. Particularly useful when cloning from a pattern.

14.3.13.3 Options

Figure 14.92 Perspective Clone tool options

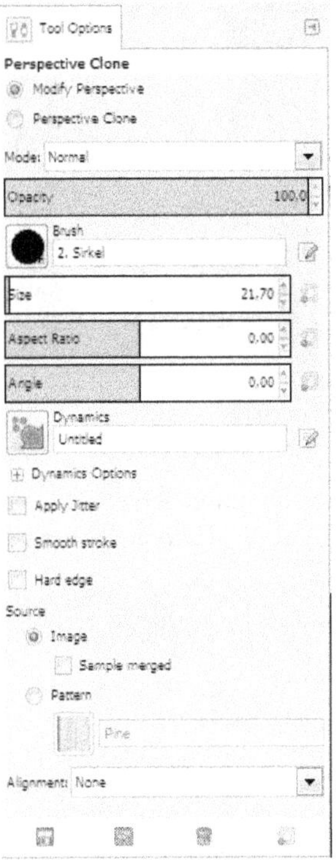

Normally, tool options are displayed in a window attached under the Toolbox as soon as you activate a tool. If they are not, you can access them from the image menu bar through Windows → Dockable Windows → Tool Options which opens the option window of the selected tool.

Operating mode When using this tool you first have to choose Modify Perspective. This works like the tool perspective. Then you choose Perspective Clone and use this in the same way as the Clone tool.

Mode; Opacity; Brush; Dynamics; Dynamics Options; Fade Options; Apply Jitter; Smooth Stroke; Hard Edge See the Common Paint Tool Options for a description of tool options that apply to many or all paint tools.

Source, Alignment This are the same as in the tool Clone.

14.3.13.4   Example

Figure 14.93 "Perspective Clone" example

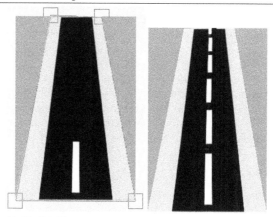

(a) The "Modify Perspective Plane" is checked. Vanishing lines have been placed.

(b) The "Perspective Clone" option is checked. The white rectangle has been cloned. You see it goes smaller going away.

14.3.14   Blur/Sharpen

Figure 14.94 Blur/Sharpen tool icon in the Toolbox

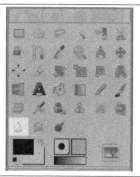

The Blur/Sharpen tool uses the current brush to locally blur or sharpen your image. Blurring with it can be useful if some element of your image stands out too much, and you would like to soften it. If you want to blur a whole layer, or a large part of one, you will probably be better off using one of the Blur Filters. The direction of a brushstroke has no effect: if you want directional blurring, use the Smudge tool.

In "Sharpen" mode, the tool works by increasing the contrast where the brush is applied. A little bit of this may be useful, but over-application will produce noise. Some of the Enhancement Filters, particularly the Unsharp Mask, do a much cleaner job of sharpening areas of a layer.

Tip

You can create a more sophisticated sharpening brush using the Clone tool. To do this, start by duplicating the layer you want to work on, and run a sharpening filter, such as Unsharp Mask, on the copy. Then activate the Clone tool, and in its Tool Options set Source to "Image source" and Alignment to "Registered". Set the Opacity to a modest value, such as 10. Then **Ctrl**-click on the copy to make it the source image. If you now paint on the original layer, you will mix together, where the brush is applied, the sharpened version with the unsharpened version.

Both blurring and sharpening work incrementally: moving the brush repeatedly over an area will increase the effect with each additional pass. The Rate control allows you to determine how quickly the modifications accumulate. The Opacity control, however, can be used to limit the amount of blurring that can be produced by a single brushstroke, regardless of how many passes are made with it.

14.3.14.1   Activating the Tool

There are different possibilities to activate the tool:

- From the image-menu: Tools → Paint tools → Blur/Sharpen.

- The Tool can also be called by clicking the tool icon: in the Toolbox.

- By using the keyboard shortcut Shift-U.

14.3.14.2   Key modifiers (Defaults)

See the Paint Tools' Common Features for a description of key modifiers that have the same effect on all paint tools.

Ctrl Holding down the **Ctrl** key toggles between Blur and Sharpen modes; it reverses the setting shown in the Tool Options.

14.3.14.3   Options

Figure 14.95 Tool Options for the Blur/Sharpen tool

Normally, tool options are displayed in a window attached under the Toolbox as soon as you activate a tool. If they are not, you can access them from the image menu bar through Windows → Dockable Windows → Tool Options which opens the option window of the selected tool.

Opacity; Brush; Dynamics; Dynamics Options; Apply Jitter; Hard Edges See the Common Paint Tool Options for a description of tool options that apply to many or all paint tools.

Convolve Type *Blur* mode causes each pixel affected by the brush to be blended with neighboring pixels, thereby increasing the similarity of pixels inside the brushstroke area. *Sharpen* mode causes each pixel to become more different from its neighbors than it previously was: it increases contrast inside the brushstroke area. Too much Sharpen ends in an ugly flocculation aspect. Whatever setting you choose here, you can reverse it on-the-fly by holding down the **Ctrl** key.

"Convolve" refers to a mathematical method using matrices.

Rate The Rate slider sets the strength of the Blur/Sharpen effect.

14.3.15 Smudge

Figure 14.96 Smudge tool

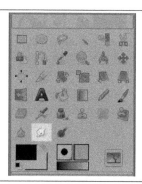

The Smudge tool uses the current brush to smudge colors on the active layer or a selection. It takes color in passing and uses it to mix it to the next colors it meets, on a distance you can set.

14.3.15.1 Activating the Tool

You can find the Smudge tool in various ways :

- through Tools → Paint Tools → Smudge. in the image menu,

- by clicking on the tool icon: in Toolbox,

- or by pressing the **S** key on keyboard.

14.3.15.2 Key modifiers (Defaults)

Shift The **Shift** key places the smudge tool into straight line mode. Holding **Shift** while clicking the mouse Left Button will smudge in a straight line. Consecutive clicks will continue smudging in straight lines that originate from the end of the last line.

Ctrl Using **Ctrl** with **Shift**, you can constrain the angle between two successive lines to vary by steps of 15°.

14.3.15.3   Options

Figure 14.97 The Smudge tool in Toolbox

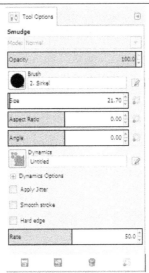

Normally, tool options are displayed in a window attached under the Toolbox as soon as you activate a tool. If they are not, you can access them from the image menu bar through Windows → Dockable Windows → Tool Options which opens the option window of the selected tool.

Opacity; Brush; Dynamics; Dynamics Options; Fade Options; Apply Jitter; Hard Edge; Rate   See the Common Paint Tool Options for a description of tool options that apply to many or all paint tools.

14.3.16   Dodge/Burn

Figure 14.98 Dodge tool

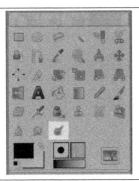

The Dodge or Burn tool uses the current brush to lighten or darken the colors in your image. The mode will determine which type of pixels are affected.

14.3.16.1   Activating the Tool

There are different possibilities to activate the tool:

- From the image-menu: Tools → Paint Tools → Dodge / Burn.

- The Tool can also be called by clicking the tool icon: ,

- or by using the Shift-D keyboard shortcut.

14.3.16.2 Key modifiers (Defaults)

Ctrl Toggle between dodge or burn types. The type will remain switched until **Ctrl** is released.

Shift **Shift** places the Dodge or Burn tool into straight line mode. Holding **Shift** while clicking the mouse Left Button will Dodge or Burn in a straight line. Consecutive clicks will continue Dodge or Burn in straight lines that originate from the end of the last line.

14.3.16.3 Options

Figure 14.99 "Dodge/Burn" tool options

Normally, tool options are displayed in a window attached under the Toolbox as soon as you activate a tool. If they are not, you can access them from the image menu bar through Windows → Dockable Windows → Tool Options which opens the option window of the selected tool.

Opacity; Brush; Dynamics; Size; Aspect Ratio; Angle; Dynamics Options; Apply Jitter; Smooth stroke; Hard
See the Common Paint Tool Options for a description of tool options that apply to many or all paint tools.

Type The dodge effect lightens colors.

The burn effect darkens colors.

Range There are three modes:

- Shadows restricts the effect to darkest pixels.

- Midtones restricts the effect to pixels of average tone.

- Highlights restricts the effect to lightest pixels.

Exposure Exposure defines how much the tool effect will be strong, as a more or less exposed photograph. Default slider is 50 but can vary from 0 to 100.

14.4 Transform Tools

Figure 14.100 An overview of the transform tools

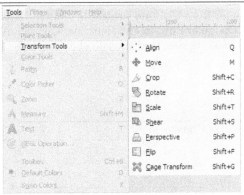

14.4.1 Common Features

Inside the Transformation tool dialog, you will find eight tools to modify the presentation of the image or the presentation of an element of the image, selection, layer or path. Each transform tool has an Option dialog and an Information dialog to set parameters.

14.4.1.1 Tool Options

Figure 14.101 Common options of transform tools

Some options are shared by several transform tools. We will describe them here. More specific options will be described with their tool.

Transform GIMP offers you three buttons which let you select which image element the transform tool will work on.

> **Note**
>
> Remember that the Transform option persists when you quit the tool.

- When you activate the first button 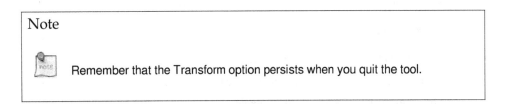 the tool works on the active layer. If no selection exists in this layer, the whole layer will be transformed.

- When you activate the second button ![icon] the tool works on the selection contour only (the whole layer contour if no selection).

- When you activate the third button, ![icon] the tool works on the path only.

Direction This option sets which way or direction a layer is transformed:

The "Normal (Forward)" mode will transform the image or layer as one might expect. You just use the handles to perform the transformation you want. If you use a grid (see below), the image or layer is transformed according to the shape and position you put the grid into.

"Corrective (Backward)" inverts the direction. Primarily used with the Rotation tool to repair digital images that have some geometric errors (a horizon not horizontal, a wall not vertical...). See Section 14.4.5.

Interpolation This drop-down list lets you choose the method and thus the quality of the transformation:

None The color of each pixel is copied from its closest neighboring pixel in the original image. This often results in aliasing (the "stair-step" effect) and a coarse image, but it is the fastest method. Sometimes this method is called "Nearest Neighbor".

Linear The color of each pixel is computed as the average color of the four closest pixels in the original image. This gives a satisfactory result for most images and is a good compromise between speed and quality. Sometimes this method is called "Bilinear".

Cubic The color of each pixel is computed as the average color of the eight closest pixels in the original image. This usually gives a good result, but it naturally takes more time. Sometimes this method is called "Bicubic".

Sinc (Lanczos3) The Lanczos3 method uses the Sinc mathematical function and performs a high quality interpolation. This is usually the best method but if you are not satisfied with the result, you may give "Cubic" a try.

You can set the default interpolation method in the Tools Options Preferences dialog.

Clipping After transformation, the image can be bigger. This option will clip the transformed image to the original image size.

You can choose between several ways to clip:

Adjust

Figure 14.102 Original image for examples

(a) *Original image* (b) *Rotation applied with* *"Adjust"* (c) *Rotation applied with* *"Adjust" and canvas en-* *larged to layer size*

With Adjust: the layer is enlarged to contain all the rotated layer. The new layer border is visible; the whole layer becomes visible by using the Image → Fit Canvas to Layers command.

Clip

Figure 14.103 Example for Clip

Clip

With Clip: all what exceeds image limits is deleted.

Crop to result

Figure 14.104 Example for Crop to result

(a) Rotation 45° (b) *The crop limit is marked with red. No trans-*
with Crop to result parent area is included.

If this option is selected, the image is cropped so that the transparent area, created by the transform operation in corners, will not be included in the resulting image.

Crop with aspect

Figure 14.105 Example for Crop with aspect

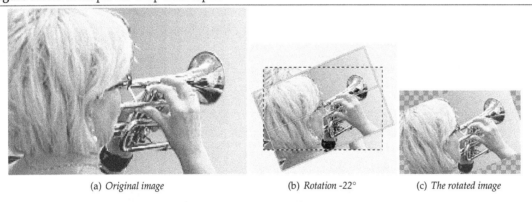

(a) *Original image*   (b) *Rotation -22°*   (c) *The rotated image*

This option works like the one described before, but makes sure, that the aspect ratio is maintained.

If this is marked, which is the default setting, the transformed image will be visible on top of the original image or layer. There will also be a slider with which you may select the preview opacity.

Prev Guides This is a drop down list where you select the type of guide lines which suits your transforming. All the guides uses a frame to mark the image's outline in addition to the lines used by the different selections.

No guides As the name tells you, there are no guides used.

Center lines Uses one vertical line and one horizontal line crossing each other in the center of the image or layer.

Rule of thirds Divides the transforming area in nine equal parts by adding two horizontal lines and two vertical lines equally spaced. According to this rule the most interesting parts of the image should be placed at the intersection points.

Rule of fifths Just as the "Rules of thirds" but divides the area in five by five parts.

Golden sections Also called "The Golden Ratio". This divides the transforming area in nine parts using a mathematical formula proportioning the parts to each others and to the area to be transformed.

Diagonal lines Divide the transforming area using diagonally lines.

Number of lines Puts a rectangular grid with equal numbers of vertically and horizontally lines. The number of lines is set in the slider popping up when this guide is selected.

Line spacing Puts a rectangular grid on the transforming area using the spacing between the lines set in the slider.

14.4.1.2 Transforming Paths

If you for some reason want to transform paths, it is possible to do this using the transform tools.

Figure 14.106 Rotating paths

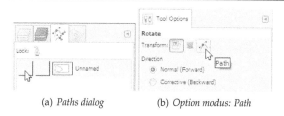

(a) *Paths dialog*   (b) *Option modus: Path*

When the path is drawn go to the path dialog and click on the first field before the path outline in the dialog window to get the eye icon visible. Then choose the transformation tool and in the upper part of the option dialog click on the path icon to tell the tool to act on the path.

Do the transformation the usual way and confirm it when finished. It could be a good idea to set the Guides to "No guides" to get the path more recognizable.

When the transformation is finished, choose the path tool and click on the changed path to activate it again for further working on it.

14.4.2 Align

Figure 14.107 The Align tool in the toolbox

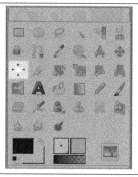

The Align tool is useful to align the image layers with various image objects. When this tool is selected, the mouse pointer turns to a small hand. By clicking on an element of a layer in the image, you choose the layer which will be moved (with **Shift** + click, you can choose several layers to be aligned); this focalised layer has small squares in corners. Various buttons in the dialog allow you to select how the layer will be moved. And you can select the image object (other layer, selection, path...) the selected layer will be aligned on. This object is called *target*.

14.4.2.1 Activating the Tool

You can activate the Align tool in several ways :

- From the image-menu, through: Tools → Transform Tools → Align,

- by clicking on the tool icon: in the toolbox,

- by using the **Q** keyboard shortcut.

14.4.2.2 Key modifiers (Defaults)

Shift You can select several layers by holding **Shift** when clicking the layers.

> **Tip**
>
> Sometimes it's easier to choose multiple layers using rubber-banding: click somewhere outside an imaginary rectangular region covering the layers you want to choose. Then drag out that region by moving the pointer, and release the mouse button. Now every layer, which is completely inside the dragged rectangle, is selected.
>
> Note that now there is no target "first item" the selected layers can be aligned on.

14.4.2.3 Tool Options

Figure 14.108 Tool Options for the Align tool

Normally, tool options are displayed in a window attached under the Toolbox as soon as you activate a tool. If they are not, you can access them from the image menu bar through Windows → Dockable Windows → Tool Options which opens the option window of the selected tool.

Align

Relative to: This is the target - the image object the selected layer will be aligned on.

- First item: the first selected item when selecting multiple layers holding the **Shift** key. Note that there is no "first item" when you select multiple layers using rubber-banding.
- Image: the image is used as a target.
- Selection: the minimal rectangular region covering the active selection.
- Active layer:
- Active Channel:
- Active Path:

⊩ ⑭ ⊲ 〒 ⅔ ⅄ These buttons become active when a layer is selected. When you click on one of these buttons, you align the selected layer with left edge, horizontal middle, right edge, top edge, vertical middle, or bottom of the target.

Distribute

⊩ ⑭ ⊲ 〒 ⅔ ⅄ These options seem to differ from the "Related to " options only by the possibility to set an offset. This offset is the distance which will separate the selected layer(s) from the target once the alignment is performed. It can be positive or negative and is expressed in pixel. Distribute add this offset to the left edges, horizontal centers, right edges, top edges, vertical centers, or bottoms of targets.

Offset This entry controls the amount of displacement that could be given to the desired alignment effect (in pixel) regarding the target. The default value is 0; it can be positive or negative.

14.4.2.4   Example for the "Align" command

Figure 14.109 Base image

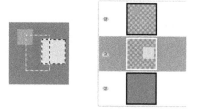

This image has three layers with different sizes and a rectangular selection. The yellow layer is active.

Figure 14.110 Red layer selected

Click on red: the red layer is selected, with a small square in every corner.

Figure 14.111 Red layer aligned

We chose "Selection" as a target and we clicked on the ⊲ button (Related to). The red layer alignes with the right side of the selection.

Figure 14.112 Distribute with offset

We set Offset to -5, we chose "Active layer" as a target and we clicked on the *button (Distribution). The layer is aligned 5 pixels before the right side of the yellow active layer.*

Figure 14.113 Align using rubber-band box

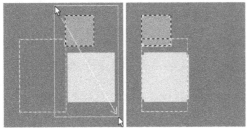

(a) *We clicked left from and above the red layer, and dragged out a region covering the red and the yellow layer by moving the pointer towards the bottom right corner.*

(b) *Again, Selection is the target. After a click on the* *button, both layers aligne with the left side of the selection.*

14.4.3 Move

Figure 14.114 The Move tool in Toolbox

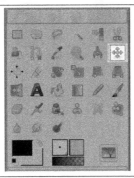

The Move Tool is used to move layers, selections, paths or guides. It works also on texts.

14.4.3.1 Activating the Tool

You can access the Move Tool in different ways:

- From the image menu bar Tools → Transform Tools → Move,

- By clicking the tool icon: .

- By using the keyboard shortcut **M**.

- The Move tool is automatically activated when you create a guide.

> **Note**
>
> Holding down the **Space** bar changes the active tool to Move temporarily. The Move tool remains active as long as the space bar is held down. The original tool is reactivated after releasing the space bar. This behaviour exists only if the Switch to Move tool option is enabled in Edit → Preferences → Image Windows → Space Bar.

14.4.3.2 Options

Figure 14.115 Move Tool options

Normally, tool options are displayed in a window attached under the Toolbox as soon as you activate a tool. If they are not, you can access them from the image menu bar through Windows → Dockable Windows → Tool Options which opens the option window of the selected tool.

Move

> **Note**
>
> These options are described in Transform tools common options.

Keep in mind that your Move choice persists after quitting the tool.

Tool toggle (Shift) If Move is on "Layer"

Pick a layer or guide On an image with several layers, the mouse pointer turns to a crosshair when it goes over an element belonging to the current layer. Then you can click-and-drag it. If the mouse pointer has a small hand shape (showing that you do *not* pick an element of the active layer), you will move a non-active layer instead (it becomes the active layer while moving).

If a guide exists on your image, it will turn to red when the mouse pointer goes over. Then it is activated and you can move it.

Move the active layer Only the current layer will be moved. This may be useful if you want to move a layer with transparent areas, where you can easily pick the wrong layer.

If Move is on "Selection"

The selection's outline will be moved (see Section 7.2.1).

If Move is on "Path"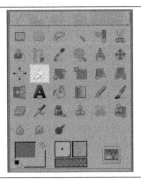

Pick a path That's the default option. The mouse pointer turns to a small hand when it goes over a visible path. Then you can move this path by click-and-dragging it (it will be the active path while moving).

Move the active path Only the current path will be moved. You can change the current path in the Path Dialog.

14.4.3.3 Summary of Move tool actions

Moving a selection The Move tool allows to move the selection outline only. If the Move Mode is "Layer", you must hold down Ctrl-Alt keys.

If the Move Mode is Selection, you can click-and-drag any point in canvas to move the selection outline. You can also use the arrow keys to move selections precisely. Then, holding down the **Shift** key moves then by increments of 25 pixels.

When you move a selection with the Move tool, the center of the selection is marked with a small cross. This cross and selection boundaries snap to guides or grid if the View → Snap to Guides (or Grid) option is checked: this makes aligning selections easier.

See Moving selections for other possibilities.

Moving a layer The Move Mode must be "Layer". Then you can choose between Move the Active Layer and, if you have one or more layers, Point to Layer (or Guide).

Moving Grouped Layers If layers are grouped (with the little chain symbol) they will all move, regardless of which layer is currently active.

Moving a guide When you pull a guide from a ruler, the Move tool is automatically activated. That's not the case after using another tool, and you have to activate it by yourself. When the mouse pointer goes over a guide, this guide turns to red and you can click-and-drag to move it.

Moving a path The Path Tool dialog has its own moving function: see Section 14.6.2. But you can also use the Move Tool. The Move Mode must be set to "Path". Note that the path becomes invisible; make it visible in the Path Dialog. You can choose the path to be moved or move the active path.

Moving a text Every text has its own layer and can be moved as layers. See Section 14.6.6.

14.4.4   Crop

Figure 14.116 Crop tool

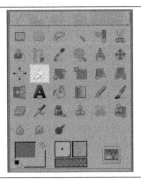

The Crop Tool is used to crop or clip an image. It works on all the layers of the image, visible and invisible. This tool is often used to remove borders, or to eliminate unwanted areas to provide you with a more focused working area. It is also useful if you need a specific image size that does not match the original dimensions of your image.

Just like the selection tools, the new crop tool has been enhanced with the v2.4 release. The resize handles actually resize the crop rectangle instead of providing both resize and move functionality. The tool behaves more naturally and consistently with other GIMP tools. To move, simply drag the rectangle clicking within the area. Resizing is possible in one or two axes at the same time dragging the handle-bars on the sides and corners. The outside area can be darkened with a nice passepartout effect to better get the idea of how the final crop will look like. To validate cropping, click inside the crop rectangle or press the **Enter** key.

When the mouse becomes the moving cross-hair, you can use the keyboard arrow keys to move the crop rectangle. Holding the **Shift** key down allows to move by increments of 25 pixels.

You can use Guides to position the crop area. Make sure that the View → Snap to Guides option is checked.

Note

You can see the aspect ratio in the status bar:

124.75   px ↕   100 % ▼ ✎ Rectangle: 79 × 48 (1.65:1)

14.4.4.1   Activating the Tool

You can activate this tool in different ways:

- From the image menu bar Tools → Transform tools → Crop,

- by clicking the tool icon: in the ToolBox,

- by using the keyboard shortcut Shift-C.

14.4.4.2   Key modifiers (Defaults)

When you maintain click on the crop rectangle, handles disappear and

- holding down the **Ctrl** key toggles to the Extend from Center option,

- holding down the **Shift** key toggles to the Fixed option, which makes some dimensions fixed.

14.4.4.3   Tool Options

Figure 14.117 Tool Options for the "Crop" tool

Normally, tool options are displayed in a window attached under the Toolbox as soon as you activate a tool. If they are not, you can access them from the image menu bar through Windows → Dockable Windows → Tool Options which opens the option window of the selected tool.

Current Layer Only This option will make crop affect only the active layer.

Allow Growing This option allows the crop or resize to take place outside the image (or layer), and even the canvas. So, you can give the size you want to the resulting image. Transparency will be used if there is no material to crop.

Figure 14.118 Example for "Allow Growing"

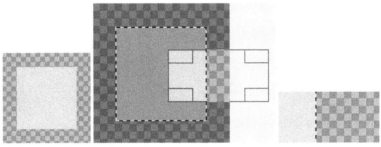

(a) *An image on a big* (b) *The option is checked. The crop rectangle* (c) *The resulting image.*
canvas   *extends outside the canvas.*

Expand from Center When this option is checked, the crop rectangle expands from the first pixel you clicked taken for center. You can toggle this option with **Ctrl** while drawing the crop rectangle.

Fixed You can also access this option by holding down the **Ctrl** key while drawing the crop rectangle. This option offers you several to make drawing the crop rectangle respect fixed dimensions, or their ratio:

- Aspect ratio: That's the default possibility. Width and Height keep the same ratio they have in the original image, when drawing the crop rectangle.

- Width / Height: Only Width or Height will remain fixed. The value of this dimension can be set in the text box below; it defaults to 100 pixels.

- Size: Both Width and Height will be fixed. Their values can be set in the text box below, in the form "150x100" for example. The crop rectangle will adopt this values as soon as you click the image. On the right, two buttons let you choose a Landscape (widthwise) or Portrait (upright) format for the crop rectangle.

Position These two text boxes show the position (horizontal on the left, vertical on the right) of the upper left corner of the crop rectangle in real time and you can change it manually too. It is stated in pixels, but you can change the unit thanks to the drop-down list of the px button. The coordinate origin is the upper left corner of the canvas (not of the image).

Size These two text boxes show the size (horizontal on the left, vertical on the right) of the crop-rectangle in real time and you can change it manually too. It is stated in pixels, but you can change the unit thanks to the drop-down list of the px button.

Highlight This option toggles the dark outside area intended for highlighting the crop rectangle.

Guides All kinds of guides are described in Section 14.2.2

Autoshrink The Auto Shrink button will attempt to locate a border, in the active layer, from which to draw dimensions from. This option only works well with isolated objects contrasting sharply with background.

Figure 14.119 Example for "Autoshrink"

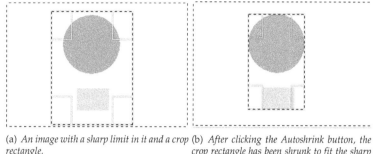

(a) *An image with a sharp limit in it and a crop rectangle.* (b) *After clicking the Autoshrink button, the crop rectangle has been shrunk to fit the sharp limits.*

Shrink Merged This option works the same, with Auto Shrink or not. It uses the pixel information from all *visible* layers, rather than just from the active layer.

14.4.5 Rotate

Figure 14.120 The Rotate tool in Toolbox

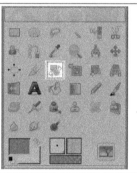

14.4.5.1 Overview

This tool is used to rotate the active layer, a selection or a path. When you click on the image or the selection with this tool a *Rotation Information* dialog is opened. There, you can set the rotation axis, marked with a point, and the rotation angle. You can do the same by dragging the mouse pointer on the image or the rotation point.

14.4.5.2 Activating the Tool

You can access the Selection Tool in different ways:

- from the image menu bar Tools → Transform Tools → Rotate,

- by clicking the tool icon: ⬛ in the Toolbox,

- by using the Shift-R key combination.

14.4.5.3 Key modifiers (Defaults)

Ctrl Holding **Ctrl** will constrain the rotation angle to 15 degrees increments.

14.4.5.4 Options

Figure 14.121 Rotation tool options

Normally, tool options are displayed in a window attached under the Toolbox as soon as you activate a tool. If they are not, you can access them from the image menu bar through Windows → Dockable Windows → Tool Options which opens the option window of the selected tool.

Transform; Direction, Interpolation; Clipping; Preview; Guides

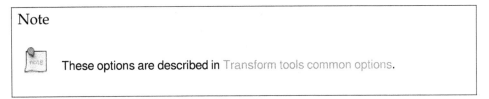

Note

These options are described in Transform tools common options.

Transform Direction The Transform Direction sets which way or direction a layer is rotated. The Normal mode will rotate the layer as one might expect. If a layer is rotated 10 degrees to the right, then the layer will be rendered as such. This behaviour is contrary to Corrective rotation.

Corrective Rotation is primarily used to repair digital images that are not straight. If the image is 13 degrees askew then you need not try to rotate by that angle. By using Corrective Rotation you can rotate visually and line up the layer with the image. Because the transformation is reversed, or performed backwards, the image will be rotated with sufficient angle to correct the error.

Constraints 15 Degrees (Ctrl) will constrain the rotation to angles divisible by 15 degrees.

14.4.5.5 The Rotation Information window

Figure 14.122 The Rotation Information dialog window

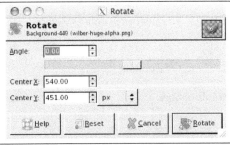

Angle Here you can set the rotation angle, from -180° to +180°, i.e. 360°.

Center X/Y This option allows you to set the position of the rotation center, represented by a cross surrounded by a circle in the image. A click-and-drag on this point also allows you to move this center
even outside the image. Default unit of measurement is pixel, but you can change it by using the
drop-down list.

Figure 14.123 The rotating center

The layer rotated around the rotating center outside the image

---

<table>
<tr><td>

Note

  You can also rotate layers with Layer → Transform → Arbitrary Rotation...

</td></tr>
</table>

14.4.6   Scale

Figure 14.124 The Scale tool in Toolbox

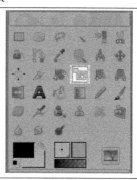

14.4.6.1   Overview

The Scale Tool is used to scale layers, selections or paths (the Object).

When you click on image with the tool the Scaling Information dialog box is opened, allowing to
change separately Width and Height. At the same time a Preview (possibly with a grid or an outline) is
superimposed on the object and handles appear on corners and borders that you can click and drag to
change dimensions. A small circle appears at center of the Preview allowing to move this preview.

14.4.6.2   Activating the Tool

You can access the Scale Tool in different ways:

- from the image menu bar Tools → Transform Tools → Scale,

- by clicking the tool icon: in the Toolbox,

- by using the Shift-T key combination.

14.4.6.3 Key modifiers (Defaults)

Ctrl Holding the **Ctrl** key down will toggle the Keep Aspect option.

14.4.6.4 Tool Options

Figure 14.125 Tool options for the Scale tool

Normally, tool options are displayed in a window attached under the Toolbox as soon as you activate a tool. If they are not, you can access them from the image menu bar through Windows → Dockable Windows → Tool Options which opens the option window of the selected tool.

Transform; Interpolation; Direction; Clipping; Preview; Guides

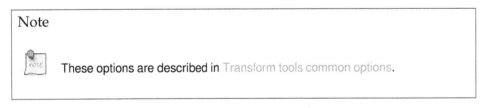

> **Note**
>
> These options are described in Transform tools common options.

> **Note**
>
> The Transform mode works on the active layer only. To work on all layers of the image, use Scale Image.

Keep Aspect (Ctrl) When you move a corner of the selection frame, this option will constrain the scale such as the Height/Width ratio of the layer will remain constant. Note that this doesn't work with border handles. Note also that it toggles the linking chain in the dialog.

14.4.6.5 The Scaling Information dialog window

Figure 14.126 The Scaling Information dialog window

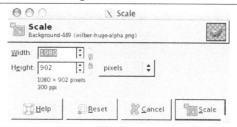

Width/Height Here, you can set Width and Height you want to give to the object. The default unit of measurement is pixel. You can change it by using the drop-down list. These values are also automatically changed when you drag handles in the image. If the associated linking chain is broken, you can change Width and Height separately.

14.4.7 Shear

Figure 14.127 The Shear tool in Toolbox

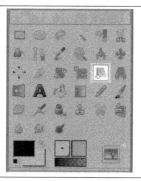

Shear tool is used to shift one part of an image, a layer, a selection or a path to a direction and the other part to the opposite direction. For instance, a horizontal shearing will shift the upper part to the right and the lower part to the left. A rectangle becomes a diamond. This is not a rotation: the image is distorted. To use this tool after selecting, click on the image or the selection: a grid is possibly surperimposed and the Shearing Information dialog is opened. By dragging the mouse pointer on the image you distort the image, horizontally or vertically according to the direction given to the pointer. When you are satisfied, click on the Shear button in the info dialog to validate.

Figure 14.128 Shear example

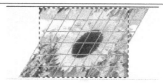

Note

  You can't shear both ways at the same time, you have to use the shear tool twice on end.

14.4.7.1 Activating the Tool

You can access the Shear Tool in different ways:

- from the image menu bar Tools → Transform Tools → Shear,

- by clicking on the tool icon: 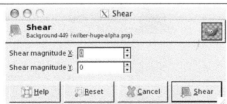 in Toolbox,

- by using the Shift-S key combination.

14.4.7.2 Options

Figure 14.129 Shear tool options

Normally, tool options are displayed in a window attached under the Toolbox as soon as you activate a tool. If they are not, you can access them from the image menu bar through Windows → Dockable Windows → Tool Options which opens the option window of the selected tool.

Transform Direction; Interpolation; Clippping; Preview; Guides

> **Note**
>
> **These options are described in** Transform tools common options.

14.4.7.3 Shearing Information

Figure 14.130 Shearing Information window

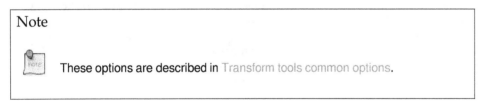

Shear magnitude X Here, you can set the horizontal shearing amplitude. A positive value produces a clock-wise tilt. A negative value gives a counter-clock-wise tilt. The unit used by shearing are half-pixels.

Shear magnitude Y As above, in the vertical direction.

14.4.8 Perspective

Figure 14.131 Perspective tool

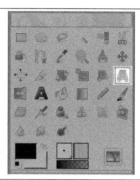

The Perspective Tool is used to change the "perspective" of the active layer content, of a selection content or of a path. When you click on the image, according to the Preview type you have selected, a rectangular frame or a grid pops up around the selection (or around the whole layer if there is no selection), with a handle on each of the four corners. By moving these handles by click-and-drag, you can modify the perspective. At the same time, a "Transformation information" pops up, which lets you valid the transformation. At the center of the element, a circle lets you move the element by click-and-drag.

> **Note**
>
> This tool is not actually a perspective tool, as it doesn't impose perspective rules. It is better described as a distort tool.

14.4.8.1 Activating the Tool

You can access the Perspective tool in different ways:

- From the image menu bar Tools/ Transform Tools Perspective,

- By clicking the tool icon: in Toolbox,

- By using the Shift-P key combination.

14.4.8.2   Options

Figure 14.132 "Perspective" tool options

Normally, tool options are displayed in a window attached under the Toolbox as soon as you activate a tool. If they are not, you can access them from the image menu bar through Windows → Dockable Windows → Tool Options which opens the option window of the selected tool.

Transform; Interpolation; Direction; Clipping; Preview; Guides

Note

These options are described in Transform tools common options.

14.4.8.3   The information window for perspective transformation

Figure 14.133 The information window of the "Perspective" tool

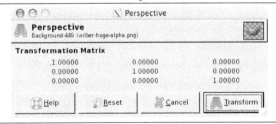

Matrix The information window shows a mathematical representation of the perspective transformation. You can find more information about transformation matrices on Wikipedia.

14.4.9 Flip

Figure 14.134 Flip tool

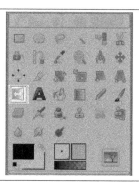

The Flip tool provides the ability to flip layers or selections either horizontally or vertically. When a selection is flipped, a new layer with a Floating Selection is created. You can use this tool to create reflections.

14.4.9.1 Activating the Tool

You can access the Flip Tool in different ways:

- From the image menu bar Tools/ Transform Tools Flip,

- By clicking the tool icon: ![icon] in Toolbox,

- by using the Shift-F key combination.

14.4.9.2 Key modifiers (Defaults)

Ctrl Ctrl lets you change the modes between horizontal and vertical flipping.

14.4.9.3 Options

Figure 14.135 "Flip Tool" Options

Normally, tool options are displayed in a window attached under the Toolbox as soon as you activate a tool. If they are not, you can access them from the image menu bar through Windows → Dockable Windows → Tool Options which opens the option window of the selected tool.

Affect

> **Note**
>
>
>
> **These options are described in** Transform tools common options.

Flip Type The Tool Toggle settings control flipping in either a Horizontal or Vertical direction. This toggle can also be switched using a key modifier.

14.4.10 The Cage Tool

Figure 14.136 The Cage Tool in the Toolbox

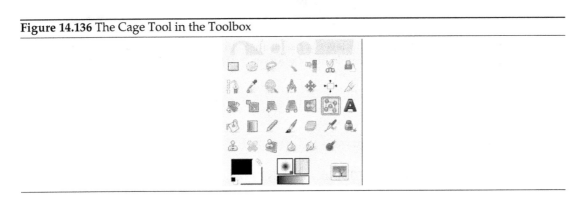

The Cage tool is a special transforming tool allowing you to select the transforming area by setting anchor points by free hand drawing similar to the way you do it with the Free Selection (Lasso) tool. The tool adds nothing to the image until you confirm the transformation by pressing the **Enter** key.

14.4.10.1 Activating the Tool

You can activate the Cage tool in several ways:

- From the image-menu, through: Tools → Transform Tools → Cage Transform

- by clicking on the tool icon: ![icon] in the toolbox

- or by using the **Shift G** keyboard shortcut.

14.4.10.2 Tool Options

Figure 14.137 Cage Tool options

Normally, tool options are displayed in a window attached under the Toolbox as soon as you activate a tool. If they are not, you can access them from the image menu bar through Windows → Dockable Windows → Tool Options which opens the option window of the selected tool.

Create or adjust the cage When activating the Cage Tool this option is selected. You can now click in the image to make anchor points around the desired area. If you need to add anchor points at a later stage, you click on this option.

Deform the cage to deform the image GIMP switch to this option automatically when the cage outline is finished. Now you are able to drag the anchor points around in the image and even outside it to transform the picture. The transforming starts when you release the mouse button.

You can activate more than one anchor point by holding down the **Shift** key while clicking on the points. You can also select more points by holding down the mouse button while drawing a rectangle around the desired points.

Fill the original position of the cage with a plain color If the transforming action results in empty areas these areas will be filled with color if this option is checked. It looks like the color is picked from the start pixel of the cage line.

14.4.10.3 Example for the "Cage" tool

Figure 14.138 Cage Tool example

(a) *The cage area selected*   (b) *Transformed*

When clicking on the cage icon in the toolbox the cage option is set to "Create or adjust the cage". You are now able to draw a cage outline in the image by successively clicking around the area you want to transform. Click on the starting point to finish the selection. GIMP will then do some mathematics and activate the "Deform the cage to deform the image" to allow you to drag the points on the line to deform the cage and the image.

The selected point(s) turns to a square. Drag the points around in the image to transform it. The transforming will occur every time you release the press on the mouse button. The transforming may take some time so be patient especially when working with large images.

If you desire to add more points to the line you have to select the "Create or adjust the cage" in the tool options dialog. Put the points on the line and switch back to the "Deform the cage to deform the image" to transform the image or layer.

When the work is done, press the **Enter** key to confirm it.

14.5 Color Tools

14.5.1 Overview

Figure 14.139 The Color tools in the Tools menu

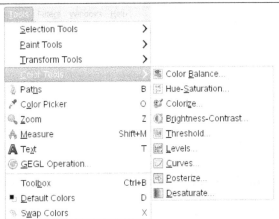

Access to the Color tools through the "classical" Tools menu.

Figure 14.140 The Color tools in the Colors menu

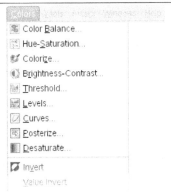

Access through the Colors menu is easier and faster.

With the Color tools you can manipulate image colors in several ways:

- Modify the color balance: Section 14.5.2

- Adjust hue, saturation and lightness levels: Section 14.5.3

- Render into a greyscale image seen through a colored glass: Section 14.5.4

- Adjust brightness and contrast levels: Section 14.5.5

- Transform into a black and white image depending on pixel value: Section 14.5.6

- Change the intensity range in a channel: Section 14.5.7

- Change color, brightness, contrast or transparency in a sophisticated way: Section 14.5.8

- Reduce the number of colors: Section 14.5.9

- Convert all colors to corresponding shades of gray: Section 14.5.10

14.5.1.1 Color Tool Presets

Except Desaturate and Posterize, color tools have *presets*: saved tool settings that you can retrieve later.

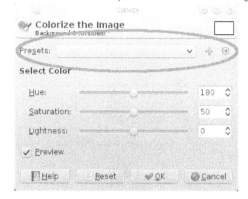

Three elements:

- **Presets**: this drop-down list shows you the existing presets. *Every time you change tool settings, a new preset is automatically saved, with date and hour*; you must be aware of that, to preserve your computer memory.

- **The cross**: clicking on this cross opens a window where you can save current settings under the name you want.

- **The small triangle**: clicking on this triangle opens a small menu:

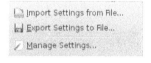

Three options:

  - Import settings from file

  - Export settings to file

  - Manage settings

14.5.2 Color Balance

The color balance tool modifies the color balance of the active selection or layer. Changes are not drastic. This tool is suitable to correct predominant colors in digital photos.

14.5.2.1   Activating the Tool

You can get to the Color balance tool in several ways :

- In the image-menu through: Tools → Color Tools → Color Balance..., or Colors → Color Balance...,

- by clicking the tool icon:  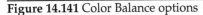 in Toolbox, provided that you have installed color tools in Toolbox. For this, please refer to Section 12.1.7.

14.5.2.2   Options

Figure 14.141 Color Balance options

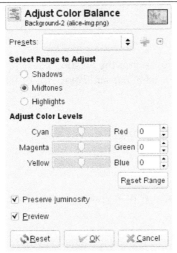

Presets You can save the color settings of your image by clicking the Add settings to favourites button

The  button opens a menu:

Figure 14.142 Preset Menu

which lets you Import Settings from File or Export Settings to File, and gives you access to the Manage Save Settings dialog:

Figure 14.143 Manage saved Settings Dialog

Select range to adjust Selecting one of these options will restrict the range of colors which are changed with the sliders or input boxes for Shadows (darkest pixels), Midtones (medium pixels) and Highlights (brightest pixels).

Adjust color levels Sliders and range from the three RGB colors to their complementary colors (CMY). The zero position corresponds to the current level value of pixels in the original image. You can change the pixel color either towards Red or Cyan, Green or Magenta, Blue or Yellow.

Reset Range This button sets color levels of the selected range back to the zero position (original values).

Preserve Luminosity This option ensures that brightness of the active layer or selection is maintained. The Value of brightest pixels is not changed.

Preview The Preview checkbox toggles dynamic image updating. If this option is on, any change made to the RGB levels are immediately seen on the active selection or layer.

14.5.3 Hue-Saturation

The Hue-Saturation tool is used to adjust hue, saturation and lightness levels on a range of color weights for the selected area or active layer.

14.5.3.1 Activating the Tool

You can get to the Hue-Saturation tool in two ways :

- In the image-menu through: Tools → Color Tools → Hue-Saturation..., or Colors → Hue-Saturation...

- By clicking the tool icon: in Toolbox, provided that you have installed color tools in Toolbox. For this, please refer to Section 12.1.7.

14.5.3.2 Options

Figure 14.144 Hue-Saturation tool options

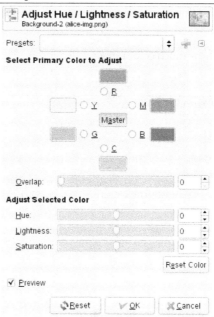

Presets You can save the color settings of your image by clicking the Add settings to favourites button

The  button opens a menu:

Figure 14.145 Preset Menu

📂 Import Settings from File...
💾 Export Settings to File...
⚙ Manage Settings...

which lets you Import Settings from File or Export Settings to File, and gives you access to the Manage Save Settings dialog:

Figure 14.146 Manage saved Settings Dialog

Select Primary Color to Adjust You can choose, between six, the three primary colors (Red, Green and Blue) and the three complementary colors (Cyan, Magenta and Yellow), the color to be modified. They are arranged according to the color circle. When hue increases, hue goes counter-clockwise. When it decreases, it goes clockwise. If you click on the Master button, all colors will be concerned with changes. GIMP standard is to set Red as 0. Note that this colors refer to color ranges and not to color channels.

Hue changes are shown in color swatches and the result is visible in the image if the "Preview" option is enabled.

Overlap This slider lets you set how much color ranges will overlap. This effect is very subtle and works on very next colors only:

Figure 14.147 Example for the "Overlap" option

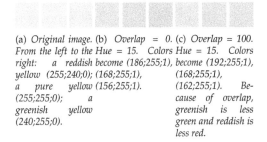

(a) *Original image.* (b) *Overlap = 0.* (c) *Overlap = 100.* *From the left to the Hue = 15. Colors Hue = 15. Colors right: a reddish become (186;255;1), become (192;255;1), yellow (255;240;0); (168;255;1), (168;255;1), a pure yellow (156;255;1). (162;255;1). Be- (255;255;0); a cause of overlap, greenish yellow greenish is less (240;255;0). green and reddish is less red.*

Adjust Selected Color

- Hue: The slider and the input box allow you to select a hue in the color circle (-180, 180).

- Lightness: The slider and the input box allow you to select a value (luminosity): -100, 100.

> **Note**
>
>
> Lightness changes here concern a color range, while they concern a color tone with Curves and Levels tools, which work on color channels. If you change the Yellow lightness with Hue-Saturation, all yellow pixels will be changed, while only dark, bright or medium pixels luminosity will be changed with Curves or Levels tools.

- Saturation: The slider and the input box allow you to select a saturation: -100, 100.

The Initialize Color button deletes changes to hue, lightness and saturation of the selected color.

Preview The Preview button makes all changes dynamically so that they can be viewed straight away.

14.5.4   Colorize

The Colorize tool renders the active layer or selection into a greyscale image seen through a colored glass. You can use it to give a "Sepia" effect to your image. See *Color model* for Hue, Saturation, Luminosity.

14.5.4.1   Activating tool

You can get to the Colorize tool in two ways:

- In the image-menu through: Tools → Color Tools → Colorize... or Colors → Colorize...,

- or by clicking the tool icon: in Toolbox, provided that you have installed color tools in Toolbox. For this, please refer to Section 12.1.7.

14.5.4.2   Options

Figure 14.148 Colorize options

Presets You can save the color settings of your image by clicking the Add settings to favourites button

The  button opens a menu:

Figure 14.149 Preset Menu

which lets you Import Settings from File or Export Settings to File, and gives you access to the Manage Save Settings dialog:

Figure 14.150 Manage saved Settings Dialog

Select Color

- Hue: The slider and the numeric text box allow you to select a hue in the HSV color circle (0 - 360).

- Saturation: The slider and the input box allows you to select a saturation: 0 through 100.

- Lightness : The slider and the text box allow you to select a value: -100 (dark) through 100 (light).

Preview The Preview button makes all changes dynamically so that they can be viewed immediately.

14.5.5 Brightness-Contrast

The Brightness-Contrast tool adjusts the brightness and contrast levels for the active layer or selection. This tool is easy to use, but relatively unsophisticated. The Levels and Curve tools allow you to make the same types of adjustments, but also give you the ability to treat bright colors differently from darker colors. Generally speaking, the BC tool is great for doing a "quick and dirty" adjustment in a few seconds, but if the image is important and you want it to look as good as possible, you will use one of the other tools.

In GIMP 2.4, a new way of operating this tool has been added: by clicking the mouse inside the image, and dragging while keeping the left mouse button down. Moving the mouse vertically changes the brightness; moving horizontally changes the contrast. When you are satisfied with the result, you can either press the OK button on the dialog, or hit the **Return** key on your keyboard.

14.5.5.1 Activating the Tool

You can get to the Brightness-Contrast tool in two ways:

- In the image-menu through: Tools → Color Tools → Brightness-Contrast... or Colors → Brightness-Contrast...,

- by clicking the tool icon: in Toolbox, provided that you have installed color tools in Toolbox. For this, please refer to Section 12.1.7.

14.5.5.2 Options

Figure 14.151 Brightness-Contrast options dialog

Presets You can save the color settings of your image by clicking the Add settings to favourites button

The  button opens a menu:

Figure 14.152 Preset Menu

which lets you Import Settings from File or Export Settings to File, and gives you access to the Manage Save Settings dialog:

Figure 14.153 Manage saved Settings Dialog

Brightness This slider sets a negative (to darken) or positive (to brighten) value for the brightness, decreasing or increasing bright tones.

Contrast This slider sets a negative (to decrease) or positive (to increase) value for the contrast.

Edit these settings as Levels To make your work easier, this button lets you turn to the Levels tool with the same settings.

Preview The Preview checkbox enables the rendering of all changes to the brightness and contrast on the canvas for immediate evaluation.

14.5.6 Threshold

The Threshold tool transforms the current layer or the selection into a black and white image, where white pixels represent the pixels of the image whose Value is in the threshold range, and black pixels represent pixels with Value out of the threshold range.

You can use it to enhance a black and white image (a scanned text for example) or to create selection masks.

> **Note**
>
> As this tool creates a black and white image, the anti-aliasing of the original image disappears. If this poses a problem, rather use the Levels tool.

14.5.6.1 Activating the Tool

There are different possibilities to activate the tool:

- You can access this tool from the image menu through Tools → Color Tools → Threshold...,

- or through Colors → Threshold...,

- or by clicking on the <image> icon in Toolbox if this tool has been installed in it. For this, please refer to Section 12.1.7.

14.5.6.2 Options

Figure 14.154 Threshold tool options

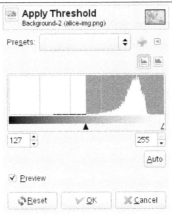

Presets You can save the color settings of your image by clicking the Add settings to favourites button

The <image> button opens a menu:

Figure 14.155 Preset Menu

---

which lets you Import Settings from File or Export Settings to File, and gives you access to the Manage Save Settings dialog:

Figure 14.156 Manage saved Settings Dialog

Threshold range The Threshold tool provides a visual graph, a histogram, of the intensity value of the active layer or selection. You can set the threshold range either using the input boxes or clicking button 1 and dragging on the graph. It allows you to select a part of the image with some intensity from a background with another intensity. Pixels inside the range will be white, and the others will be black. Adjust the range to get the selection you want in white on black background.

Preview The Preview toggle allows dynamic updating of the active layer or selection while changes are made to the intensity level.

14.5.6.3 Using Threshold and Quick Mask to create a selection mask

That's not always the case, but an element you want to extract from an image can stand out well against the background. In this case, you can use the Threshold tool to select this element as a whole. Grokking the GIMP described a method based on a channel mask, but now, using the Quick mask is easier.

1. First start decomposing you image into its RGB and HSV components by using the Decompose filter. A new grey-scaled image is created and the components are displayed as layers in the Layer Dialog. These layers come with a thumbnail but it is too small for an easy study. You can, of course, increase the size of this preview with the dialog menu (the small triangular button), but playing with the "eyes " is more simple to display the wanted layer in the decompose image. Select the layer that isolates the element the best.

Figure 14.157 The original image, the decompose image and its Layer Dialog

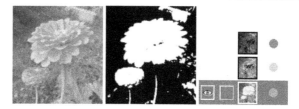

2. Call the Threshold tool from the decompose image. By moving the black cursor, fit threshold to isolate the best the element you want to extract. This will probably not be perfect: we will enhance the result with the selection mask we are going to create.

Warning

  Make sure you have selected the right layer when you call the Threshold tool: when it is opened, you can't change to another layer.

Figure 14.158 The selected layer after threshold fit

We got the best outline for our flower. There are several red objects which we must remove.

3. Make sure the image displaying the selected layer is active and copy it to the clipboard with Ctrl-C.

4. Now, make the original image active. Click on the Quick Mask button at the bottom-left corner of the image window: the image gets covered with a red (default) translucent mask. This red color does not suit well to our image with much red: go to the Channel Dialog, activate the "Quick mask" channel and change this color with the Edit Channel Attributes. Come back to the original image. Press Ctrl-V to paste the previously copied layer.

Figure 14.159 The mask

5. Voilà. Your selection mask is ready: you can improve the selection as usually. When the selection is ready, disable the Quick mask by clicking again on its button: you will see the marching ants around the selection.

Figure 14.160 The result

We used the Zoom to work at a pixel level, the Lasso to remove large unwanted areas, the pencil (to get hard limits), black paint to remove selected areas, white paint to add selected areas, especially for stem.

14.5.7 Levels

The Level tool provides features similar to the Histogram dialog but can also change the intensity range of the active layer or selection in every channel. This tool is used to make an image lighter or darker, to change contrast or to correct a predominant color cast.

14.5.7.1 Activating the Tool

You can get to this tools in several ways:

- In the image menu through Tools → Color Tools → Levels....

- In the image menu through Colors → Levels....

- By clicking on the tool icon in the toolbox if this tool has been installed there. For this, please refer to Section 12.1.7.

14.5.7.2 Options

Figure 14.161 Level tool options

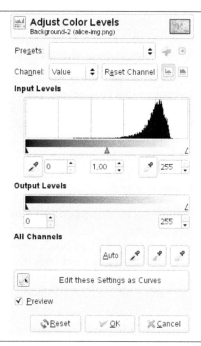

Presets You can save the color settings of your image by clicking the Add settings to favourites button

The 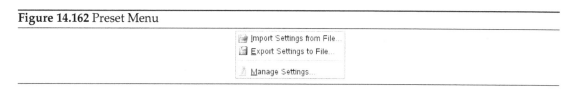 button opens a menu:

Figure 14.162 Preset Menu

which lets you Import Settings from File or Export Settings to File, and gives you access to the Manage Save Settings dialog:

Figure 14.163 Manage saved Settings Dialog

Channel You can select the specific channel which will be modified by the tool:

- Value makes changes to the value of all RGB channels in the image: the image becomes darker or lighter.

- Red, Green and Blue work on a particular color channel: the image gets more or less color. Remember that adding or removing a color result in removing or adding the complementary color

- Alpha works on semi-transparent layers or selections: here, dark means more transparency, and white is fully opaque. Your image must have an Alpha Channel, otherwise this option is disabled.

- Initialize channel cancels changes to the selected channel.

Input Levels The main area is a graphic representation of the active layer or selection dark (Shadows), mid and light (Highlight)tones content (the Histogram). They are on abscissa from level 0 (black) to level 255 (white). Pixel number for a level is on ordinate axis. The curve surface represents all the pixels of the image for the selected channel. A well balanced image is an image with levels (tones) distributed all over the whole range. An image with a blue predominant color, for example, will produce a histogram shifted to the left in Green and Red channels, signified by green and red lacking on highlights.

Level ranges can be modified in three ways:

- Three triangles as sliders: one black for dark tones (Shadows), one grey for midtones (Gamma), one white for light (Highlights) tones.
  The black slider determines the *black point* : all pixels with this value or less will be black (no color with a color channel selected / transparent with the Alpha channel selected).
  The white slider determines the *white point* : all pixels with this value or higher, will be white (fully colored with a color channel selected / fully opaque with the Alpha channel selected).
  The gray slider determines the *mid point*. Going to the left, to the black, makes the image lighter (more colored / more opaque) . Going to the right, to the white, makes the image darker (less colored / more transparent).

- Two eye-droppers: when you click them, the mouse pointer becomes an eye-dropper. Then clicking on the image determines the black or the white point according to the chosen eye-dropper. Use the left, dark one ![dropper] to determine the black-point; use the right, white one ![dropper] to determine the white point.

- Three numeric text boxes to enter values directly.

Input Levels are used to lighten highlights (bright tones), darken shadows (dark tones), change the balance of bright and dark tones. Move sliders to the left to increase lightness (increase the chosen color / increase opacity). Move the sliders to the right to lessen lightness (lessen the chosen color / lessen opacity).

Examples for Input Levels

The original image is a gray-scaled image with three stripes: Shadows (64), Mid Tones (127), Highlights (192). The histogram shows three peaks, one for each of the three tones.

Original image

1. The Value channel is selected. The black slider (Shadows) has been moved up to the Shadows peak. The 64 value became 0 and the Shadows stripe became black (0). The Gamma (mid tones) slider is automatically moved to the middle of the tone range. Mid tones are made darker to 84 and Highlights to 171.

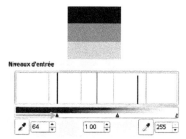

Black slider has been moved

2. The white slider (highlights) has been moved up to the highlight peak. The 192 value became 255 and the highlight stripe became white. The Gamma (mid tones) slider is automatically moved to the middle of the tone range. Mid tones are made lighter to 169 and Shadows to 84.

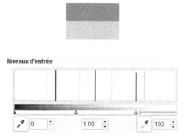

White slider has been moved

Output Levels Output levels allows manual selection of a constrained output level range. There are also numeric text boxes with arrow-heads located here that can be used to interactively change the Output Levels.

Output levels force the tone range to fit the new limits you have set.

- Working with Value: values are compressed and look more alike; so contrast is reduced. Shadows are made lighter: new details can show up but contrast is less; a compromise is necessary. Highlights are made darker.

- Working with Color channels: if you the use the green channel for example and set the output levels between 100 and 140, all pixels with some green, even a low value, will have their green channel value shifted between 100 and 140.

- Working with Alpha channel: all Alpha values will be shifted to the range you have set.

Example for Output Levels

1. The original image is a RGB gradient from black (0;0;0) to white (255;255;255). Output Levels has no histogram; here, we used Windows → Dockable Dialogs → Histogram.

Original image (a gradient)

2. Value channel selected. The black slider has been moved to 63 and the white slider to 189. The Histogram shows the compression of pixels. No pixel is less than 63, and no pixel is more than 189. In the image, Shadows are lighter and Highlights are darker: contrast is reduced.

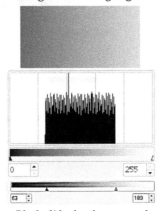

Black slider has been moved

All Channels Auto: Performs an automatic setting of the levels.

> **Three eyedroppers , , .** These three buttons respectively represent a white, a gray and a black eye-dropper. When you click one of these buttons, the mouse pointer takes the form of the eye-dropper it represents. Then, when clicking the image, the clicked pixel determines the *white point* , the *black point* or the *mid point* according to the eye-dropper you chose. Works on all channels, even if a particular channel is selected.

Figure 14.164 Example for Levels eye-droppers

Above is original gradient from black to white. Below is the result after clicking with the white eye-dropper: all pixels with a value higher than that of the clicked pixel turned to white.

Edit these settings as Curves To make your work easier, this button lets you turn to the Curves tool with the same settings.

Preview The Preview button makes all changes to the levels dynamically so that the new level settings can be viewed straight away.

14.5.7.3   Tool Options dialog

Figure 14.165 "Levels" tool options

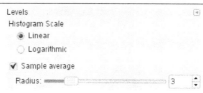

Although this tool is not present in the Toolbox by default (please refer to Section 12.1.7 if you want to add it), nevertheless it has a Tool Option Dialog under the Toolbox. These options are described here:

Histogram Scale   These two options have the same action as the Logarithmic and Linear buttons in the Levels dialog.

Sample Average   This slider sets the "radius" of the color-picking area. This area appears as a more or less enlarged square when you maintain the click on a pixel.

14.5.7.4   Actual practice

Figure 14.166 A very under-exposed image

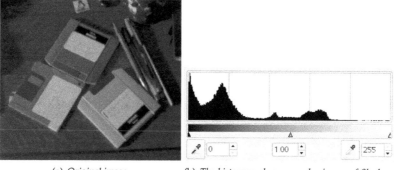

(a) *Original image*   (b) *The histogram shows a predominance of Shadows and missing Highlights.*

Figure 14.167 Setting the white point

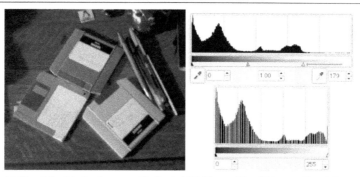

(a) *The white slider has been moved to the start of well marked Highlights. The image lightens up.*   (b) *The resulting histogram (down) shows Highlights now, but Shadows are still predominant.*

Figure 14.168 Setting the balance between Shadows and Highlights

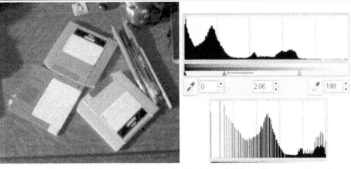

(a) *The mid slider has been moved to the left. This results in reducing the proportion of Shadows and increasing the proportion of Highlights.* (b) *The resulting histogram (down) confirms the reduction of Shadows.*

14.5.8   Curves

The Curves tool is the most sophisticated tool for changing the color, brightness, contrast or transparency of the active layer or a selection. While the Levels tool allows you to work on Shadows and Highlights, the Curves tool allows you to work on any tonal range. It works on RGB images.

14.5.8.1   Activating the Tool

You can get to this tool in several ways:

- In the image menu through Tools → Color Tools → Curves… or Colors → Curves….

- By clicking on the tool icon in Toolbox, if this tool has been installed there. For this, please refer to Section 12.1.7.

14.5.8.2   "Curves" options

Figure 14.169 The "Curves" dialog

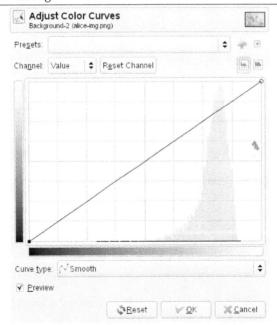

Presets You can save the color settings of your image by clicking the Add settings to favourites button

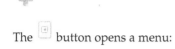

The ▣ button opens a menu:

Figure 14.170 Preset Menu

which lets you Import Settings from File or Export Settings to File, and gives you access to the Manage Save Settings dialog:

Figure 14.171 Manage saved Settings Dialog

Channel There are five options:

Value The curve represents the Value, i.e. the brightness of pixels as you can see them in the composite image.

Red; Green; Blue The curve represents the quantity of color in each of the three RGB channels. Here, *dark* means *little* of the color. *Light* means *a lot* of the color.

Alpha The curve represents the opacity of the pixels. *Dark* means *very transparent*. *Light* means *very opaque*. Your image or active layer must have an Alpha channel for this option to be enabled.

Reset Channel This button deletes all changes made to the selected channel and returns to default values.

Linear and Logarithmic buttons These buttons allow to choose the Linear or Logarithmic type of the histogram. You can also use the same options in Tool Options dialog. This grayed out histogram is not displayed by default.

Main Editing Area

- *The horizontal gradient*: it represents the input tonal scale. It, too, ranges from 0 (black) to 255 (white), from Shadows to Highlights. When you adjust the curve, it splits up into two parts; the upper part then represents the *tonal balance* of the layer or selection.

- *The vertical gradient*: it represents the destination, the output tonal scale. It ranges from 0 (black) to 255 (white), from Shadows to Highlights.

- *The chart*: the curve is drawn on a grid and goes from the bottom left corner to the top right corner. The pointer x/y position is permanently displayed in the top left part of the grid. By default, this curve is straight, because every input level corresponds to the same ouput tone. GIMP automatically places an anchor at both ends of the curve, for black (0) and white (255).

  If you click on the curve, a new *anchor* is created. When the mouse pointer goes over an anchor, it takes the form of a small hand. You can click-and-drag the anchor to bend the curve. If you click outside of the curve, an anchor is also created, and the curve includes it automatically.

Unactive anchors are black. The active anchor is white. You can activate an anchor by clicking on it. You can also swap the anchor activation by using the Left and Right arrow keys of your keyboard. You can move the anchor vertically with the Up and Down arrow keys. This allows you to fine tune the anchor position. Holding the **Shift** down lets you move it by increments of 15 pixels.

Two anchors define a *curve segment* which represents a tonal range in the layer. You can click-and-drag this segment (this creates a new anchor). Of course, you can't drag it beyond the end anchors.

To delete all anchors (apart from both ends), click on the Reset Channel button. To delete only one anchor, move beyond any adjacent anchor on horizontal axis.

Meanwhile, on the canvas, the mouse pointer has the form of an eye-dropper. If you click on a pixel, a vertical line appears on the chart, positioned to the source value of this pixel in the selected channel. If you **Shift**-click, you create an anchor in the selected channel. If you **Ctrl**-click, you create an anchor in all channels, possibly including the Alpha channel. You can also **Shift**-drag and **Ctrl**-drag: this will move the vertical line and the anchor will show up when releasing the mouse left button.

The histogram of the active layer or selection for the selected channel is represented grayed out in the chart. It's only a reference.

Curve type

Smooth This the default mode. It constrains the curve type to a smooth line with tension. It provides a more realistic render than the following.

Free Hand With this mode, you can draw a broken line that you can smooth by clicking the Curve Type button again.

Preview The Preview button makes all changes to the levels dynamically so that the new level settings can be viewed immediately.

Tool Options dialog

Although this tool is not present in the Toolbox by default (For this, please refer to Section 12.1.7 if you want to add it), nevertheless it has a Tool Option Dialog under the Toolbox. These options are described here:

Histogram Scale These two options have the same action as the Logarithmic 📈 and Linear 📉 buttons in the Curves dialog.

Sample Average This slider sets the "radius" of the color-picking area. This area appears as a more or less enlarged square when you maintain the click on a pixel. Here, the eye-dropper is used to locate a pixel: radius = 1 seems the best.

14.5.8.3 Using the "Curves" tool

14.5.8.3.1 Summary and basic shapes We create anchors and segments on the curve and we move them to shape the curve. This curve maps "input" tones of the active layer or selection to "output" tones.

14.5.8.3.1.1 How the Curves tool works Moving the anchor of a pixel upwards makes this pixel brighter.

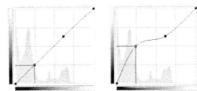

Moving the anchor upwards

14.5.8.3.1.2 Making the curve more horizontal Making the curve more horizontal forces all the input tonal range to occupy a shrunk output tonal range.

The histogram shows the compression of pixels into the output range. Darkest and brightest pixels disappeared: contrast decreases.

Figure 14.172 Making the curve more horizontal

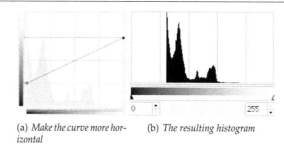

(a) *Make the curve more hor-*   (b) *The resulting histogram*
izontal

14.5.8.3.1.3   Making the curve more vertical   Moving the upper end point to the left and the lower end point to the right is the same as moving the white slider to the left and the black slider to the right in the Levels tool: all pixels whose value is more than the white point (the flat part of the curve) are made white (more colored / more opaque according to the selected channel). All pixels whose value is less than the black point (the lower flattened curve) are made black (black / completely transparent). Pixels corresponding to points of the curve that have moved up are made lighter. Pixels corresponding to points of the curve that have moved down are made darker (green arrows). All these pixels will be extended to the whole output tonal range.

The histogram shows the extension of values, from black (0) to White (255): contrast is increased. Since the Value channel is selected, changes affect all color channels and colors increase.

Figure 14.173 Making the curve more vertical

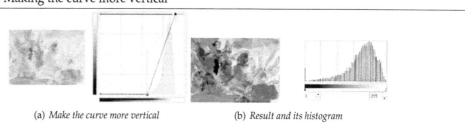

(a) *Make the curve more vertical*   (b) *Result and its histogram*

14.5.8.3.2   Practical cases

14.5.8.3.2.1   Invert colors

Inverted curve

Black is made White (fully colored / fully opaque). White is made black (black, fully transparent). All pixels adopt the complementary color. Why that? Because subtracting the channel values from 255 gives the complementary color. For example: 19;197;248 a sky blue gives 255-19; 255-197; 255-248 = 236;58;7, a bright red.

14.5.8.3.2.2 Enhance contrast

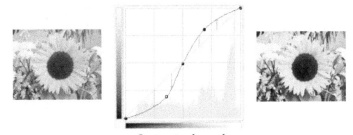

Contrast enhanced

Contrast is increased in mid tones because the curve is steeper there. Highlights and Shadows are increased but contrast is slightly less in these areas because the curve is flatter.

14.5.8.3.2.3 Working on color channels

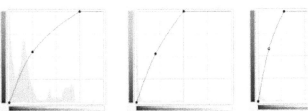

For every channel, we moved the white point horizontally to the left, to the first Highlights. This lightens Highlights up. Then we shaped the curve to lighten Mid tons and Shadows while keeping black.

The original image and the result

14.5.9 Posterize

This tool is designed to intelligently weigh the pixel colors of the selection or active layer and reduce the number of colors while maintaining a semblance of the original image characteristics.

14.5.9.1 Activating the Tool

You can get to this tool in several ways:

- In the image menu through Tools → Color Tools → Posterize... or Colors → Posterize....

- By clicking on the tool icon in Toolbox, if this tool has been installed there. For this, please refer to Section 12.1.7.

14.5.9.2 Options

Figure 14.174 Posterize tool options

Posterize Levels This slider and the input boxes with arrow-heads allow you to set the number of levels (2-256) in each RGB channel that the tool will use to describe the active layer. The total number of colors is the combination of these levels. A level to 3 will give $2^3 = 8$ colors.

Preview The Preview checkbox enables the rendering of changes right on the canvas for immediate evaluation.

14.5.9.3   Example

Figure 14.175 Example for the "Posterize" tool

Image posterized in 4 levels. The histogram shows the 4 levels and 10 colors, counting black and white also.

14.5.10   Desaturate

By using the Desaturate command, you can convert all of the colors on the active layer to corresponding shades of gray. This differs from converting the image to grayscale in two respects. First, it only operates on the active layer and second, the colors on the layer are still RGB values with three components. This means that you can paint on the layer, or individual parts of it, using color at a later time.

Note

 This command only works on layers of RGB images. If the image is in Grayscale or Indexed mode, it can do nothing.

14.5.10.1   Activating the Command

You can get to this tools in several ways:

- In the image menu through Tools → Color Tools → Desaturate... or Colors → Desaturate...,

- by clicking on the tool icon ▓ in Toolbox, if this tool has been installed there. For this, please refer to Section 12.1.7.

14.5.10.2   Options

Figure 14.176 The "Desaturate" option dialog

Three options are available:
   Choose shade of gray based on

Lightness The graylevel will be calculated as

$$\text{Lightness} = \frac{1}{2} \times (\max(R,G,B) + \min(R,G,B))$$

Luminosity The graylevel will be calculated as

$$\text{Luminosity} = 0.21 \times R + 0.72 \times G + 0.07 \times B$$

Average The graylevel will be calculated as

$$\text{Average Brightness} = (R + G + B) \div 3$$

Figure 14.177 Comparing the three options

(a) *Original image* (b)   *"Lightness"* (c) *"Luminosity"* ap- (d) *"Average" applied.*
              applied   *plied.*

14.6 Other

14.6.1 Overview

Figure 14.178 Other Tools in the Tools Menu

"Other" tools are simply those tools which don't belong to any main group of tools. You will find here, for example, the important and powerful Path tool as well as useful helper tools like the Color Picker:

- Section 14.6.2

- Section 14.6.3

- Section 14.6.4

- Section 14.6.5

- Section 14.6.6

- Section 14.6.7

14.6.2 Paths

Figure 14.179 Paths tool

The Paths tool allows to create complex selections called Bézier Curves, a bit like Lasso but with all the adaptability of vectorial curves. You can edit your curve, you can paint with your curve, or even save, import, and export the curve. You can also use paths to create geometrical figures. Paths have their own dialog box: Dialog.

14.6.2.1 Activating the Tool

You can get this tool in several ways:

- In the image menu through Tools → Paths,

- By clicking the tool icon: in Toolbox,

- or by using the **B** keyboard shortcut.

14.6.2.2 Key modifiers (Defaults)

> **Note**
>
> Help messages pop up at the bottom of the image window to help you about all these keys.

Shift This key has several functions depending on context. See Options for more details.

Ctrl ; Alt Three modes are available to work with the Paths tool: Design,Edit and Move. **Ctrl** key toggles between Design and Edit. **Alt** (or Ctrl-Alt) key toggles between Design and Move.

14.6.2.3   Options

Figure 14.180 "Path" tool options

Normally, tool options are displayed in a window attached under the Toolbox as soon as you activate a tool. If they are not, you can access them from the image menu bar through Windows → Dockable Windows → Tool Options which opens the option window of the selected tool.

Design Mode By default, this tool is in Design mode. You draw the path by clicking successively. You can move control points by clicking on them and dragging them. Between control points are segments.

Numbers are steps to draw a two segments straight path.

Curved segments are easily built by dragging a segment or a new node. Blue arrows indicate curve. Two little handles appear that you can drag to bend the curve.

Tip

To quickly close the curve, press **Ctrl** key and click on the initial control point. In previous versions, clicking inside a closed path converted it into Selection.

Now, you can use the Create selection from path button or ▦ the *Path to Selection* button in the Path Dialog.

Tip

When you have two handles, they work symmetrically by default. Release the pressure on the mouse button to move handles individually. The **Shift** key will force the handles to be symmetrical again.

Several functions are available with this mode:

Add a new node: If the active node (a small empty circle after clicking on a node) is at the end of the path, the mouse pointer is a '+' sign and a new node is created, linked to the previous one by a segment. If the active node is on the path, the pointer is a square and you can create a new component to the path. This new component is independent from the other, but belongs to the path as you can see on the Path dialog. Pressing **Shift** forces the creation of a new component.

Move one or several nodes: On a node, the mouse pointer becomes a 4-arrows cross. You can click and drag it. You can select several nodes by **Shift** and click and move them by click and drag. Pressing Ctrl-Alt allows to move all the path, as a selection.

Modify handles: You have to Edit a node before. A handle appears. Drag it to bend the curve. Pressing **Shift** toggles to symmetric handles.

Modify segment: When the mouse pointer goes over a segment, it turns to a 4-arrows cross. Click-and-drag it to bend the segment. As soon as you move, handles appear at both ends of the segment. Pressing **Shift** key toggles to symmetric handles.

Edit Mode Edit performs functions which are not available in Design mode. With this mode, you can work only on the existing path. Outside, the pointer is a small crossed circle (on the whole image if there is no path!) and you can do nothing.

Add a segment between two nodes: Click on a node at one end of the path to activate it. The pointer is like a union symbol. Click on an other node to link both nodes. This is useful when you have to link unclosed components.

Remove a segment from a path: While pressing Shift-Ctrl key combination, point to a segment. Pointer turns to -. Click to delete the segment.

Add a node to a path: point to a segment. Pointer turns to +. Click where you want to place the new control point.

Remove a node: While pressing Shift-Ctrl key combination, point to a node. Pointer turns to -. Click to delete the node.

Add a handle to a node: Point to a node. Pointer turns to small hand. Drag the node: handle appears. Pressing **Shift** toggles to symmetric handles.

Remove a handle from a node: While pressing Shift-Ctrl key combination, point to a handle. The pointer doesn't turn to the expected - and remains a hand. Click to delete the handle.

Caution

 No warning before removing a node, a segment or a handle.

Move Mode Move mode allows to move one or all components of a path. Simply click on the path and drag it.

If you have several components, only the selected one is moved. If you click and drag outside the path, all components are moved. Pressing **Shift** key toggles to move all components also.

Polygonal With this option, segments are linear only. Handles are not available and segments are not bent when moving them.

Create selection from path This button allows creation of a selection that is based on the path in its present state. This selection is marked with the usual "marching ants". Note that the path is still present: current tool is still path tool and you can modify this path without modifying the selection that has become independent. If you change tool, the path becomes invisible, but it persists in Path Dialog and you can re-activate it.

If the path is not closed, GIMP will close it with a straight line.

As the help pop-up tells, pressing **Shift** when clicking on the button will add the new selection to an eventually pre-existent. Pressing the **Ctrl** will subtract the selection from the pre-existent and the Shift-Ctrl key combination will intersect the two selections.

Stroke path In previous versions, you could access to this command only by the Edit sub-menu in the Image Menu. Now you can access to it also via this button. See Section 16.3.18 and Section 7.5.

See the Path concept.

14.6.3 Color Picker

Figure 14.181 The Color Picker in the toolbox (eye dropper icon)

The Color Picker Tool is used to select a color on any image opened on your screen. By clicking a point on an image, you can change the active color to that which is located under the pointer. By default, the tool works on the active layer, but the Sample Merge option lets you grab the color as it is in the image, resulting of the combination of all layers. *Only colors in visible layers are used.* An Info window opens when you click on the image.

14.6.3.1 Activating the Tool

You can get to this tool in several ways :

- In the image menu through Tools → Color Picker.,

- by clicking the tool icon ✎ in Toolbox,

- by pressing the **O** keyboard shortcut,

- by pressing the **Ctrl** key while using a paint tool. The Color-picker dialog is not opened during this operation and the tool remains unchanged after releasing the key. Nevertheless, you can get information by using the Pointer window.

14.6.3.2 Key modifiers (Defaults)

Ctrl If the pick mode is set to Set foreground color, then pressing the **Ctrl** key switches the tool into the Set background color mode. If the pick mode is set to Set background color then the key switches the mode to Set foreground color. When the pick mode is Pick only, the key doesn't do anything.

Shift By pressing the **Shift** key, the Color Picker Information window is opened when you click on a pixel.

Note

 The Pointer Information gives you the same information permanently. But be warned, it defaults to Sample merged.

14.6.3.3 Options

Figure 14.182 Color Picker Options

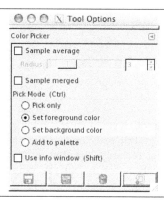

Normally, tool options are displayed in a window attached under the Toolbox as soon as you activate a tool. If they are not, you can access them from the image menu bar through Windows → Dockable Windows → Tool Options which opens the option window of the selected tool.

Sample Merged When enabled, the Sample Merged checkbox will take color information as a composite from all the visible layers. Further information regarding Sample Merge is available in the glossary entry, Sample Merge.

Sample Average The Radius slider adjusts the size of the square area that is used to determine an average color for the final selection. When you keep clicking the layer, the mouse pointer shows the size of the square or radius.

Pick Mode

> **Pick Only** The color of the selected pixel will be shown in an Information Dialog, but not otherwise used.

> **Set Foreground Color** The Foreground color, as shown in the Toolbox Color Area, will be set to the color of the pixel you click on.

> **Set Background Color** The Background color, as shown in the Toolbox Color Area, will be set to the color of the pixel you click on.

> **Add to Palette** When this option box is checked, the picked color is sent to the active color palette. See Palette Editor.

Use info window When this option is checked, the information window is opened automatically. The **Shift** key allows you to toggle this possibility temporarily.

Figure 14.183 Color Picker Info Window

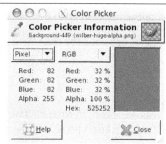

14.6.4   Zoom

Figure 14.184 The "Zoom" tool in Toolbox

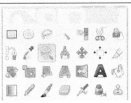

The Zoom Tool is used to change the zoom level of your working image. If you only click on the image, the zoom is applied to the whole image. But you can also click-and-drag the mouse pointer to create a zoom rectangle. Then, the action of this rectangle is better understood if the "Allow window resizing" option is unchecked: you can see that the content of this rectangle will be enlarged or reduced so that its biggest dimension fit the corresponding dimension of the image window (if the biggest dimension of the rectangle is width, then it will fit the width of the image window).

14.6.4.1   Activating the Tool

- You can get to the Zoom Tool from the image-menu through : Tools → Zoom,

- or by clicking the tool icon: ⌕ in Toolbox.

14.6.4.2   Key modifiers (Defaults)

Ctrl Holding **Ctrl** when clicking on a point of your image will change the zoom direction from zooming in to zooming out.

Ctrl-Mouse wheel Spinning the mouse wheel, while pressing **Ctrl**, varies the zoom level.

14.6.4.3   Options

Figure 14.185 Zoom tool options

Auto-resize window This option will allow the canvas to be resized if the zoom level dictates it.

Tool Toggle The two available tool toggles are used for changing the zoom direction between zooming in and zooming out.

14.6.4.4   Zoom menu

Using the Zoom tool is not the only way to zoom an image. The Zoom menu provides access to several functions for changing the image magnification level. For example, you can easily choose an exact magnification level from this menu.

14.6.5 Measure

Figure 14.186 Measure tool

The Measure Tool is used to gain knowledge about pixel distances in your working image. By clicking and holding the mouse button, you can determine the angle and number of pixels between the point of click and where the mouse pointer is located. The information is displayed on the status bar or can also be displayed in the Info Window.

When you pass the mouse pointer over the end point it turns to a move pointer. Then if you click you can resume the measure.

14.6.5.1 Status Bar

Information is displayed in the status bar, at the bottom of the Image window:

- Distance between the original point and the mouse pointer, in pixels.

- Angle, in every quadrant, from 0° to 90°.

- Pointer coordinates relative to the original point.

14.6.5.2 Activating the Tool

- You can get to the Measure Tool from the image-menu through: Tools → Measure,

- or by clicking the tool icon: in Toolbox.

14.6.5.3 Key modifiers (Defaults)

Shift Holding down the **Shift** allows to start a new measure from the pointed point without deleting the previous measure. Angle is measured from the previous line and not from the default horizontal. The mouse pointer goes with a "+" sign. So, you can *measure any angle* on the image.

Ctrl Holding down the **Ctrl** key puts the tool into constrained straight line mode. The orientation of the line is constrained to the nearest multiple of 15 degrees.

Ctrl key pressed and click on an end point creates a horizontal guide. The mouse pointer goes with the icon.

Alt **Alt** key and click on an end point creates a vertical guide. The mouse pointer goes with the icon.

Ctrl-Alt This key combination and click on a measure line allows to move the measure.

Ctrl-Alt key combination and click on an end point creates a vertical and a horizontal guides.

14.6.5.4 Options

Figure 14.187 "Measure" tool options

Use Info Window This option will display an Info Window dialog that details the measure tool results. The results are more complete on the status bar.

14.6.5.5 Measuring surfaces

You can't measure surfaces directly, but you can use the Histogram that gives you the number of pixels in a selection.

14.6.6 Text

Figure 14.188 The Text tool in Toolbox

The Text tool places text into an image. With GIMP-2.8, you can write your text directly on the canvas. No Text Editor is needed anymore (although you can still use it if you want by checking the Use editor option in the Tool Options dialog. A text toolbar has been added which allows you to edit text in different ways but you can still go on using the *Text Option dialog*, to change the font, color and size of your text, and justify it, interactively. Right clicking on the frame opens a context menu that allows you to copy, cut, paste, load a text...

As soon as you type your text, it appears on the canvas in a rectangular frame. If you draw the rectangular frame first, the text is automatically adapted to the frame size. You can enlarge this frame as you do with rectangular selections.

In this chapter, tool options will be described. To know how to use the Text tool, please refer to text management.

14.6.6.1 Activating the Tool

You can access this tool in several ways:

- In the image menu through Tools → Text,

- by clicking the tool icon in Toolbox,

- or by using the **T** keyboard shortcut.

14.6.6.2 Options

Figure 14.189 Text tool options

Normally, tool options are displayed in a window attached under the Toolbox as soon as you activate a tool. If they are not, you can access them from the image menu bar through Windows → Dockable Windows → Tool Options which opens the option window of the selected tool.

Font Click on the fonts button A to open the font selector of this tool, which offers you a list of installed X fonts.

    At the bottom of the font selector you find some icons which act as buttons for:

- resizing the font previews,

- selecting *list view* or *grid view*,

- opening the font dialog.

    Choose a font from the installed fonts. When you select a font it is interactively applied to your text.

> **Tip**
>
> You can use the scroll wheel of your pointing device (usually your mouse) on the fonts button in order to quickly change the font of your text (move the pointer on the fonts button, and don't click, just use the wheel button).

Size This control sets the size of the font in any of several selectable units.

Use editor Use an external editor window for text editing instead of direct-on-canvas editing.

Antialiasing Antialiasing will render the text with much smoother edges and curves. This is achieved by slight blurring and merging of the edges. This option can radically improve the visual appearance of the rendered typeface. Caution should be exercised when using antialiasing on images that are not in RGB color space.

Hinting Uses the index of adjustment of the font to modify characters in order to produce clear letters in small font sizes.

Color Color of the text that will be drawn next. Defaults to black. Selectable from the color picker dialog box that opens when the current color sample is clicked.

Tip

 You can also click-and-drag the color from the Toolbox color area onto the text.

Justify Causes the text to be justified according to any of four rules selectable from the associated icons.

Indent Controls the indent spacing from the left margin, for the first line.

Line Spacing Controls the spacing between successive lines of text. This setting is interactive: it appears at the same time in image text. The number is not the space between lines itself, but how many pixels must be added to or subtracted from this space (the value can be negative).

Letter Spacing Controls the spacing between letters. Also in this case the number is not the space itself between letters, but how many pixels must be added to or subtracted from this space (the value can be negative).

Box Concerns the text box. The associated drop down list offers two options:

Dynamic: default option. The size of the text box increases as you type. Text may go out of the image. You have to press the **Enter** key to add a new line. The indent option indents all lines. If you increase the box size, the option turns to "Fixed".

Fixed: you must enlarge the text box first. Else, usual shortcuts are active! The text is limited by the right side of the box and continues on next line. This is not true new line: you must press the **Enter** key to add a real new line. The text may go out the lower border of the image. The indent option works on the first line only.

14.6.6.3 Text Editor

Figure 14.190 The Text Editor

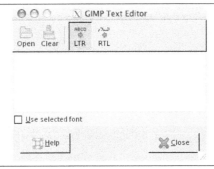

With GIMP-2.8, this text editor is available only if the Use editor option is checked. It persists probably because all its functions are not transferred to the direct-on-canvas mode. We will limit description to commands that has not been transferred.

As soon as you start writing, a Text layer is created in the Layer Dialog. On an image with such a layer (the image you are working on, or a .xcf image), you can resume text editing by activating this text layer then clicking on it (double click). Of course, you can apply to this text layer the same functions you use with other layers.

To add another text to your image click on a non-text layer: a new Text Editor will appear and a new text layer will be created. To pass from a text to another one activate the corresponding text layer and click on it to activate the editor.

The Text Editor options

Load Text from file Text can be loaded from a text file by clicking the folder icon in the text editor. All the text in the file is loaded.

This option is also in the text context menu.

From left to right This option causes text to be entered from left to right, as is the case with most Western languages and may Eastern languages.

This option is also in the text context menu.

From right to left This option allows text to be entered from right to left, as is the case with some Eastern languages, such as Arabic (illustrated in the icon).

This option is also in the text context menu.

Use selected font Default doesn't use the font you have selected in the Options dialog. If you want to use it, check this option.

Note

 See also Section 9.2.

14.6.7 GEGL Operation

Figure 14.191 GEGL Operation tool

GEGL ("Generic Graphical Library") is a graph based image processing library designed to handle various image processing tasks needed in GIMP.

The GEGL Operation tool has been added in GIMP 2.6 and was originally meant as an useful experimental tool for GIMP developers. The GEGL Operation tool enables applying GEGL operations to the image and gives on-canvas previews of the results.

Warning

GEGL is in a very early phase and still under construction.

The GEGL Operation tool is *experimental*.

14.6.7.1 Activating the Tool

You can get to this tool only from the image menu: Tools → GEGL Operation.

> **Tip**
>
>
>
> In addition to this tool for performing special GEGL operations you can configure GIMP to use GEGL for all color operations.

14.6.7.2 Options

Figure 14.192 GEGL Operation tool options

GEGL Operation tool with no operation selected.

Operation Click on this button to select the operation you want to apply to the active selection or, if there is no selection, to the active layer.

Some of these operations are very basic operations like "color" which fills the active selection or layer with the specified color, while operations like "fractal-explorer" produce fairly complex patterns — just like a rendering filter.

Remember that this is an experimental tool, so some operations may not work or even crash GIMP. As a consquence, it doesn't make sense to describe the operations here as long as the GEGL Operation tool is experimental

Operation Settings The operation settings depend on the selected Operation:

Figure 14.193 "Operation Settings" example

GEGL operation "Gaussian Blur" selected.

If the options of the selected GEGL operation are not self-explanatory (guess what's the purpose of the "color" operation's "Color" option) you can look for a corresponding non-GEGL tool. For example, the Fractal Explorer filter may have the same or similar options as the "fractal-explorer" operation.

Or you can make use of the nice realtime preview feature and just experiment with different settings.

Preview If this options is checked, as it is by default, you will get an on-canvas preview of the selected operation as soon as the operation in finished. You will have to press the OK button to actually apply the operation to the image.

The tool buttons

Reset Pressing this button resets the operation settings the to their defaults.

Cancel Clicking on this button aborts the GEGL operation tool and leaves your image untouched. This is equivalent to close the dialog window using the usual Close button provided by your window manager.

OK You have to press this button to apply the selected operation to the image. Then the dialog window will be closed.

Chapter 15

Dialogs

15.1 Dialog Introduction

Dialogs are the most common means of setting options and controls in the GIMP. The most important dialogs are explained in this section.

15.2 Image Structure Related Dialogs

The following dialogs let you control and manipulate image structures, such as layers, channels, or paths.

15.2.1 Layers Dialog

Figure 15.1 Layers Dialog

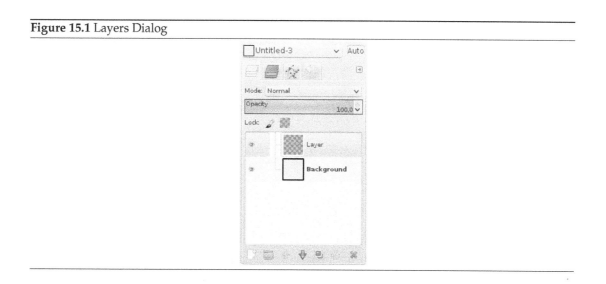

The "Layers" dialog is the main interface to edit, modify and manage your layers. You can think of layers as a stack of slides or clothes on your body. Using layers, you can construct an image of several conceptual parts, each of which can be manipulated without affecting any other part of the image. Layers are stacked on top of each other. The bottom layer is the background of the image, and the components in the foreground of the image come above it.

Figure 15.2 An image with layers

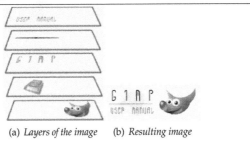

(a) *Layers of the image*   (b) *Resulting image*

15.2.1.1 Activating the dialog

The "Layers" dialog is a dockable dialog; see the section Section 3.2.3 for help on manipulating it. You can access it:

- from the image menu: Windows → Dockable Dialogs → Layers;

- from the Tab menu in any dockable dialog by clicking on ◁ and selecting Add Tab → Layers,

- from the (default) shortcut: Ctrl-L.

In the Windows menu, there is a list of detached windows which exists only if at least one dialog remains open. In this case, you can raise the "Layers" dialog from the image-menu: Windows → Layers.

15.2.1.2 Using the Layer dialog

Overview Every layer appears in the dialog in the form of a thumbnail. When an image has multiple layers as components, they appear as a list. The upper layer in the list is the first one visible, and the lowest layer the last visible, the background. Above the list one can find characteristics related individually to each layer. Under the list one can find management buttons for the layer list. A right-click in a layer thumbnail opens the Layer context menu.

Layer attributes Every layer is shown in the list along with its attributes:

    Layer visibility In front of the thumbnail is an icon showing an eye. By clicking on the eye, you toggle whether the layer is visible or not. (**Shift**-clicking on the eye causes all *other* to be hidden.)

Chain layers Another icon, showing a chain, allows you to group layers for operations on more than one layer at a time (for example with the Move tool).

Layer thumbnail The layer content is represented in a thumbnail. Maintaining left-click for a second on this thumbnail makes it larger. When the layer is active, the thumbnail has a white border. The border is black if the layer is inactive. When the layer has a mask, the inactive element takes a black border.

Layer name The main attribute is the name of the layer. You can edit this by a double-click on the name of the layer. You can also use the "Edit Layer Attributes" dialog you get by double-clicking on the thumbnail (or the mask), or through right-click on the layer and select "Edit Layer Attributes...".

Note

In the case of an animation layer (GIF or MNG), the name of the layer can be used to specify certain parameters : Layer_name (delay in ms) (combination mode), for example Frame-1 (100 ms) (replace). The delay sets the time during which the layer is visible in the animation. The combination mode sets whether you combine the layer with the previous layer or replace it: the two modes are (combine) or (replace).

Layers characteristics Above the layer list, it is possible to specify some properties for the active layer. The active layer is the one highlighted in blue. The properties are: "Layer mode", "Opacity", "Lock pixels" and "Lock Alpha channel".

Mode The layer mode determines how the layer interacts with the other layers. From the combo box you can access all the modes provided by GIMP. The layer modes are fully detailed in Section 8.2.

Opacity By moving the slider you give more or less opacity to the layer. With a 0 opacity value, the layer is transparent and completely invisible. Don't confuse this with a Layer Mask, which sets the transparency pixel by pixel.

Lock You have two possibilities:

- **Lock pixels**: when this option is checked, you can't modify layer pixels. This may be necessary to protect them from unwanted changes.
- **Lock alpha channel**: if you check this option the transparent areas of the layer will be kept, even if you have checked the Fill transparent areas option for the Bucket fill tool.

Figure 15.3 Example for Locking Alpha Channel

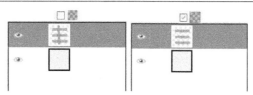

(a) *The active layer has three horizontal, opaque, green stripes on a transparent back-ground. We paint a vertical red stripe. "Lock" unchecked: Opaque and transparent areas of the active layer are painted with red.*

(b) *"Lock" checked: Only opaque areas of the active layer are painted with red. Transparent areas are preserved.*

Tip

If a layer name in the Layer Dialog is in bold, then this layer has no Alpha channel.

Layer management Under the layer list a set of buttons allows you to perform some basic operations on the layer list.

New layer Here you can create a new layer. A dialog is opened where you can enter the Layer name, perhaps change the default Height and Width, and choose the Layer fill type that will be the new layer's background.

Raise layer Here you can move the layer up a level in the list. Press the **Shift** key to move the layer to the top of the list.

Lower layer Here you can move the layer down a level in the list. Press the **Shift** key to move the layer to the bottom of the list.

> **Tip**
>
> (i) To move a layer at the bottom of the list, it may first be necessary to add a transparency channel (also called Alpha channel) to the Background layer. To do this, right click on the Background layer and select Add Alpha channel from the menu.

Duplicate layer Here you can create a copy of the active layer. Name of new layer is suffixed with a number.

Anchor layer When the active layer is a temporary layer (also called floating selection) shown by this icon , this button anchors it to the previous active layer.

Delete layer Here you can delete the active layer.

More layer functions Other functions about *layer size* are available in the Layer Drop down menu you get by right clicking on the Layer Dialog. You can find them also in the Layer sub-menu of the image menu.

You will find *merging layers functions* in the Image menu.

Clicking-and-dragging layers Click and hold on layer thumbnail: it enlarges and you can move it by dragging the mouse.

- So you can put this layer down *somewhere else in the layer list*.

- You can also *put the layer down into Toolbox*: a new image is created that contains this layer only.

- Finally, you can *put the layer down into another image*: this layer will be added to the layer list, above existing layers.

15.2.1.3 Layer masks

Figure 15.4 "Add mask" dialog

Overview A transparency mask can be added to each layer, it's called Layer mask. A layer mask has the same size and same number of pixels as the layer to which it is attached. Every pixel of the mask can then be coupled with a pixel at the same location in the layer. The mask is a set of pixels in gray-tone on a value scale from 0 to 255. The pixels with a value 0 are black and give a full transparency to the coupled pixel in the layer. The pixels with a value 255 are white and give a full opacity to the coupled pixel in the layer.

To create a layer mask start with a right click on the layer to call the context menu and select Add layer mask in the menu. A dialog appears where you can initialize the content of the mask:

- White (full opacity): the mask is white in the Layer Dialog. So, all pixels of the layer are visible in the image window since painting the mask with white makes layer pixels fully visible. You will paint with black to make layer pixels transparent.

- Black (full transparency): the mask is black in the Layer Dialog. So, the layer is fully transparent since painting the mask with black makes layer pixels transparent. Painting with white will remove the mask and make layer pixels visible.

- Layer's alpha channel: the mask is initialized according to the content of layer Alpha channel. If the layer still contains transparency it's copied in the mask.

- Transfer layer's alpha channel: Does the same thing as the previous option, except that it also resets the layer's alpha channel to full opacity.

- Selection : the mask is initialized according to pixel values found in the selection.

- Grayscale copy of layer: the mask is initialized according to pixel values of the layer.

- Channel: The layer mask is initialized with a selection mask you have created before, stored in the Channel dialog.

- Invert mask : This checkbox allows you to invert : black turns to white and white turns to black.

When the mask is created it appears as a thumbnail right to the layer thumbnail. By clicking alternatively on the layer and mask thumbnail you can enable one or other. The active item has a white border (which is not well visible around a white mask). That's an important point. Always keep the Layers Dialog prominently when working with masks, because you can't see, looking at the canvas, which of the layer or the mask is active.

Pressing **Alt** (or Ctrl-Alt and click on the layer mask thumbnail) is equivalent to the Show Layer Mask command : the layer mask border turns to green. If you press **Ctrl** the border is red and the result is equivalent to the Disable Layer Mask command. To return to normal view redo last operation. These options are for greater convenience in your work.

Layer Mask example

Figure 15.5 A layer with layer mask

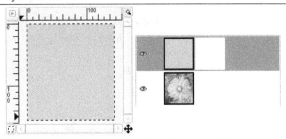

This image has a background layer with a flower and another blue one, fully opaque. A white layer mask has been added to the blue layer. In the image window, the blue layer remains visible because a white mask makes layer pixels visible.

Figure 15.6 Painting the layer mask

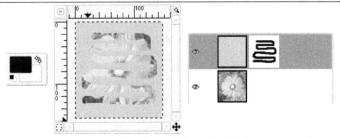

The layer mask is active. You paint with black color, which makes the layer transparent: the underlying layer becomes visible.

15.2.2 Channels Dialog

Figure 15.7 The Channels dialog

The Channels dialog is the main interface to edit, modify and manage your channels. Channels have a double usage. This is why the dialog is divided into two parts: the first part for color channels and the second part for selection masks.

Color channels apply to the image and not to a specific layer. Basically, three primary colors are necessary to render all the wide range of natural colors. As other digital software, GIMP uses Red, Green, and Blue as primary colors. The first and primary channels display the Red, Green, and Blue values of each pixel in your image. Next to the channel name is a thumbnail displaying a grayscale representation of each channel, where white is 100% and black is 0% of the primary color. Alternatively, if your image is not a colored but a Grayscale image, there is only one primary channel called Gray. For an Indexed image with a fixed number of known colors there is also only one primary channel called Indexed. Then there is a optional channel called Alpha. This channel displays transparency values of each pixel in your image (See Alpha Channel in Glossary). In front of this channel is a thumbnail displaying a grayscale representation of the transparency where white is opaque and visible, and black is transparent and invisible. If you create your image without transparency then the Alpha channel is not present, but you can add it from the Layers dialog menu. Also, if you have more than one layer in your image, GIMP automatically creates an Alpha channel.

Note

 GIMP doesn't support CMYK or YUV color models.

Figure 15.8 Representation of an image with channels

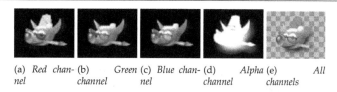

(a) Red chan- (b)   Green (c) Blue chan- (d)   Alpha (e)   All
nel   channel   nel   channel   channels

The right image is decomposed in three color channels (red, green, and blue) and the Alpha channel for transparency. On the right image the transparency is displayed as a gray checkerboard. In the color channel white is always white because all the colors are present and black is black. The red hat is visible in the red channel but quite invisible in the other channels. This is the same for plain green and blue which are visible only in their own channels and invisible in others.

15.2.2.1 Activating the Dialog

The "Channels" dialog is a dockable dialog; see Section 3.2.3 for help on manipulating it.
You can access it:

- from an image menu: Windows → Dockable Dialogs → Channels;

- from the Tab menu in any dockable dialog by clicking on ◀ and selecting Add Tab → Channels.

In the Windows menu, there is a list of detached windows which exists only if at least one dialog remains open. In this case, you can raise the "Channels" dialog from the image-menu: Windows → Channels.

15.2.2.2 Using the Channel dialog

15.2.2.2.1 Overview   The top channels are the color channels and the optional Alpha channel. They are always organized in the same order and they cannot be erased. Selection masks are described below and displayed as a list in the dialog. Every channel appears in the list with its attributes, including a thumbnail and its name. A right-click in a channel list entry opens the channel context menu.

15.2.2.2.2 Channel attributes   Every channel is shown in the list with its own attributes, which are very similar to the layer attributes:

Channel visibility   By default every channel and thus every color value is visible. This is indicated by an "open eye" icon. Clicking on the eye-symbol (or the space if the channel is not visible) will toggle the visibility of the channel.

Chain channels The channels representing selection masks (the new channels in the lower part of the channel list) may be grouped using the button with the "chain" symbol. Then these channels are all affected in the same way by operations applied to any one of them.

Primary color channels (the default channels in the upper part of the channel list) may be grouped too. By default, all color channels (and the alpha channel) are selected, their list entries are highlighted. Operations will be performed on all channels. By clicking on a channel list entry you can deactivate this channel. Operations like colorizing a layer will then be applied to the selected ("grouped") channels only. Clicking again on the list entry will activate the channel.

Thumbnail A small preview-icon represents the effect of the channel. On a selection mask, this preview can be enlarged by holding click down on it.

Channel name The name of the channel, which must be unique within the image. Double-clicking on the name of a selection mask channel will allow you to edit it. The names of the primary channels (Red, Green, Blue, Alpha) can not be changed.

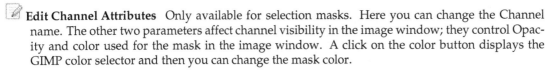

Caution

Activated channels appear highlighted (generally) in blue in the dialog. If you click on a channel in the list you toggle activation of the corresponding channel. Disabling a color channel red, blue, or green has severe consequences. For instance if you disable the blue channel, all pixels from now on added to the image will not have blue component, and so a white pixel will have the yellow complementary color.

15.2.2.2.3 Managing channels Under the channel list is a set of buttons allowing you to perform some basic operations on channel list.

Edit Channel Attributes Only available for selection masks. Here you can change the Channel name. The other two parameters affect channel visibility in the image window; they control Opacity and color used for the mask in the image window. A click on the color button displays the GIMP color selector and then you can change the mask color.

New Channel You can create here a new channel. The displayed dialog lets you set Opacity and mask color used in the image to represent the selection. (If you use the New Channel button in Channel Menu, you can create this new channel with the options previously used by pressing the **Shift** key when clicking). This new channel is a channel mask (a selection mask) applied over the image. See Selection Mask

Raise Channel Only available for selection masks: you can here put the channel up a level in the list. Press **Shift** key to move channel to top of the list.

Lower Channel You can here put the channel down a level in the list. Press the **Shift** key to move the channel to bottom of the list.

Duplicate Channel You can create here a copy of the active channel. Name of new channel is suffixed with a number.

Tip

 You can also duplicate a color channel or the Alpha channel. It's an easy way to keep a copy of them and to use them later as a selection in an image.

Channel to Selection Here you can transform the channel to become a selection. By default the selection derived from a channel replaces any previous active selection. It's possible to change this by clicking on control keys.

- **Shift**: the selection derived from a channel is added to the previous active selection. The final selection is merged from both.

- **Ctrl**: the final selection is the subtraction of selection derived from a channel from the previously active one.

- Shift-Ctrl: the final selection is the intersection of selection derived from a channel with the previously active one. Only common parts are kept.

Delete Channel Only available for selection masks: you can here delete the active channel.

Figure 15.9 Channel Context Menu

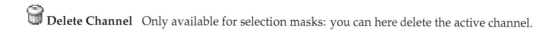

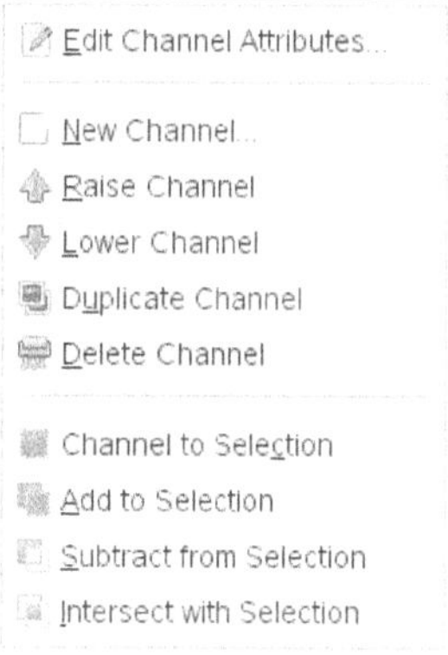

15.2.2.2.4   Channels Context Menu

Overview You can get the channel context menu by right clicking on a channel thumbnail. This menu gives the same operations on channels as those available from dialog buttons. The only difference concerns transformation to selection operations, each of them having its own entry in the menu.

Edit Channel Attributes, New Channel, Raise Channel, Lower Channel, Duplicate Channel, Delete Cha
   See Managing channels.

Channel to Selection Selection derived from channel replaces any previous active selection.

Add to Selection Selection derived from channel is added to previous active selection. Final selection is merging of both.

Subtract from Selection Final selection is subtraction of selection derived from a channel from previous active selection.

Intersect with Selection Final selection is intersection of selection derived from a channel with the previous active selection. Only common parts are kept.

15.2.2.3   Selection masks

Figure 15.10 A selection composed out of channels.

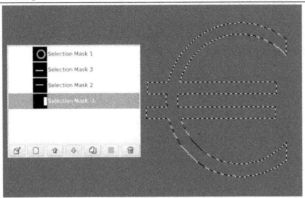

Channels can be used to save and restore your selections. In the channel dialog you can see a thumbnail representing the selection. Selection Masks are a graphical way to build selections into a gray level channel where white pixels are selected and black pixels are not selected. Therefore gray pixels are partially selected. You can think of them as feathering the selection, a smooth transition between selected and not selected. This is important to avoid the ugly pixelization effect when you fill the selection or when you erase its content after isolating a subject from background.

Creating Selection Masks There are several ways to initialize a selection mask.

- From the image window menu Select → Save to Channel if there is an active selection.

- In the image window the bottom-left button creates a Quick Mask; the content will be initialized with the active selection.

- From the channel dialog, when you click on the New channel button or from the context menu. When created, this Selection mask appears in the Channel dialog, named "Selection maskcopy" with a queuing number. You can change this by using the context menu that you get by right-clicking on the channel.

15.2.2.3.1   Using Selection Masks Once the channel is initialized, selected (highlighted in blue), visible (eye-icon in the dialog), and displayed as you want (color and opacity attributes), you can start to work with all the paint tools. The colors used are important. If you paint with some color other than white, grey, or black, the color Value (luminosity) will be used to define a gray (medium, light, or dark).

When your mask is painted, you can transform it to a selection by clicking on the button (Channel to Selection) or from the context menu.

You can work in selection masks not only with the paint tool but also with other tools. For instance, you can use the selection tools to fill areas uniformly with gradients or patterns. By adding many selection masks in your list you can easily compose very complex selections. One can say that a selection mask is to a selection as a layer is to an image.

Caution

⚠   As long as a selection mask is activated you are working in the mask and not in the image. To work in the image you have to deactivate all selection masks. Don't forget also to stop displaying masks in the image by removing the eye icon. Check also that all RGB and Alpha channels are activated and displayed in the image.

15.2.2.4   Quick Mask

Figure 15.11 Dialog Quick Mask

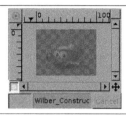

A Quick Mask is a Selection Mask intended to be used temporarily to paint a selection. Temporarily means that, unlike a normal selection mask, it will be deleted from the channel list after its transformation to selection. The selection tools sometimes show their limits when they have to be used for doing complex drawing selection, as progressive. In this case, using the QuickMask is a good idea which can give very good results.

15.2.2.4.1   Activating the dialog   The QuickMask can be activated in different ways:

- From the image menu: Select → Toggle QuickMask.

- By clicking the left-bottom button showed in red on the screenshot.

- By using the Shift-Q shortcut.

15.2.2.4.2   Creating a Quick Mask   To initialize a Quick Mask, click the bottom-left button in the image window. If a selection was active in your image, then its content appears unchanged while the border is covered with a translucent red color. If no selection was active then all the image is covered with a translucent red color. Another click on the bottom-left button will deactivate the quick mask.

From the channel dialog you can double click on the name or the thumbnail to edit the QMask attributes. Then you can change the Opacity and its filling color. At every moment you can hide the mask by clicking on the eye icon 👁 in front of the QMask.

The mask is coded in gray tones, so you must use white or gray to decrease the area limited by the mask and black to increase it. The area painted in light or dark gray will be transition areas for the selection like feathering. When your mask is ready, click again on the bottom-left button in the image window and the quick mask will be removed from the channel list and converted to a selection.

Quick mask's purpose is to paint a selection and its transitions with the paint tools without worrying about managing selection masks. It's a good way to isolate a subject in a picture because once the selection is made you only have to remove its content (or inverse if the subject is in the selection).

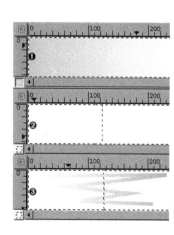

15.2.2.4.3   Using Quick Mask with a gradient

Description

1. Screenshot of the image window with activated QuickMask. As long as the Quickmask is activated, all operations are done on it. A gradient from black (left) to white (right) has been applied to the mask.

2. The QuickMask is now disabled. The selection occupies the right half part of the image (marching ants) because the limit of the selection is at the middle of the gradient.

3. A stroke is now added during the enabled selection. Weird! The gradient, although not visible, remains active all over the image, in selected and non selected areas!

After the QuickMask Button is pressed, the command generates a temporary 8-bit (0-255) channel, on which the progressive selection work is stored. If a selection is already present the mask is initialized with the content of the selection. Once QuickMask has been activated, the image is covered by a red semi-transparent veil. This one represents the non-selected pixels. Any paint tool can be used to create the selection on the QuickMask. They should use only grayscale color, conforming the channel properties, white enabling to define the future selected place. The selection will be displayed as soon as the QuickMask will be toggled but its temporary channel will not be available anymore.

> **Tip**
>
> To save in a channel the selection done with the Quickmask select in the image menu Select/Save to Channel

15.2.2.4.4 Usage

1. Open an image or begin a new document.

2. Activate the Quickmask using the left-bottom button in the image window. If a selection is present the mask is initialized with the content of the selection.

3. Choose a drawing tool and use it with grayscale colors on the QuickMask.

4. Deactivate the Quickmask using the left-bottom button in the image window.

15.2.3 Paths Dialog

Please see Section 7.5 if you don't know what a path is.

Figure 15.12 The "Paths" dialog

The "Paths" dialog is used to manage paths, allowing you to create or delete them, save them, convert them to and from selections, etc.

15.2.3.1   Activating the dialog

The "Paths" dialog is a dockable dialog; see the section Section 3.2.3 for help on manipulating it.
You can access it:

- from the image menu: Windows → Dockable Dialogs → Paths.

- from the Tab menu in any dockable dialog by clicking on  and selecting Add Tab → Paths,

In the Windows menu, there is a list of detached windows which exists only if at least one dialog remains open. In this case, you can raise the "Paths" dialog from the image-menu: Windows → Paths.

15.2.3.2   Using the Paths dialog

Each path belongs to one image: paths are components of images just like layers. The Paths dialog shows you a list of all paths belonging to the currently active image: switching images causes the dialog to show a different list of paths. If the Paths dialog is embedded in a "Layers, Channels, and Paths" dock, you can see the name of the active image in the Image Menu at the top of the dock. (Otherwise, you can add an Image Menu to the dock by choosing "Show Image Menu" from the Tab menu.)

If you are familiar with the Layers dialog, you have a head start, because the Paths dialog is in several ways similar. It shows a list of all paths that exist in the image, with four items for each path:

Path visibility   An "open eye" icon if the path is visible, or a blank space if it is not. "Visible" means that a trace of the path is drawn on the image display. The path is not actually shown in the image pixel data unless it has been stroked or otherwise rendered. Clicking in the eye-symbol-space toggles the visibility of the path.

Chain paths   A "chain" symbol is shown to the right of the eye-symbol-space if the path is transform-locked, or a blank space if it is not. "Transform-locked" means that it forms part of a set of elements (layers, channels, etc) that are all affected in the same way by transformations (scaling, rotation, etc) applied to any one of them. Clicking in the chain-symbol-space toggles the transform-lock status of the path.

Preview image   A small preview-icon showing a sketch of the path. If you click on the icon and drag it into an image, this will create a copy of the path in that image.

Path Name   The name of the path, which must be unique within the image. Double-clicking on the name will allow you to edit it. If the name you create already exists, a number will be appended (e.g., "#1") to make it unique.

If the list is non-empty, at any given moment one of the members is the image's *active path*, which will be the subject of any operations you perform using the dialog menu or the buttons at the bottom: the active path is shown highlighted in the list. Clicking on any of the entries will make it the active path.

Right-clicking on any entry in the list brings up the Paths Menu. You can also access the Paths Menu from the dialog Tab menu.

15.2.3.3   Buttons

The buttons at the bottom of the Paths dialog all correspond to entries in the Paths menu (accessed by right-clicking on a path list entry), but some of them have extra options obtainable by holding down modifier keys while you press the button.

New Path   See New Path. Holding down the **Shift** key brings up a dialog that allows you to assign a name to the new (empty) path.

Raise Path   See Raise Path.

Lower Path   See Lower Path.

Duplicate Path See Duplicate Path.

Path to Selection Converts the path into a selection; see Path to Selection for a full explanation. You can use modifier keys to set the way the new selection interacts with the existing selection:

> *Modifiers:* None, *Action:* Replace existing selection
> *Modifiers:* **Shift** , *Action:* Add to selection
> *Modifiers:* **Ctrl** , *Action:* Subtract from selection
> *Modifiers:* Shift-Ctrl , *Action:* Intersect with selection.

Selection to Path Holding down the **Shift** key brings up the Advanced Options dialog, which probably is only useful to GIMP developers.

Paint along the path See Stroke Path.

Delete Path Delete Path deletes the current selected path.

15.2.3.4 The "Paths" context menu

Figure 15.13 The "Paths" context menu

The Paths menu can be brought up by right-clicking on a path entry in the list in the Paths dialog, or by choosing the top entry ("Paths Menu") from the Paths dialog Tab menu. This menu gives you access to most of the operations that affect paths.

Path Tool Path Tool is an alternative way to activate the Path tool, used for creating and manipulating paths. It can also be activated from the Toolbox, or by using the keyboard shortcut **B** (for *Bézier*).

Edit Path Attributes Edit Path Attributes brings up a small dialog that allows you to change the name of the path. You can also do this by double-clicking on the name in the list in the Paths dialog.

New Path New Pathcreates a new path, adds it to the list in the Paths dialog, and makes it the active path for the image. It brings up a dialog that allows you to give a name to the path. The new path is created with no anchor points, so you will need to use the Path tool to give it some before you can use it for anything.

Raise Path Raise Path moves the path one slot higher in the list in the Paths dialog. The position of a path in the list has no functional significance, so this is simply a convenience to help you keep things organized.

Lower Path Lower Pathmoves the path one slot lower in the list in the Paths dialog. The position of a path in the list has no functional significance, so this is simply a convenience to help you keep things organized.

Duplicate Path "Duplicate Path" creates a copy of the active path, assigns it a unique name, adds it to the list in the Paths dialog, and makes it the active path for the image. The copy will be visible only if the original path was visible.

Delete Path Delete Path deletes the current selected path.

Merge Visible Paths Merge Visible Paths takes all the paths in the image that are visible (that is, all that show "open eye" symbols in the Paths dialog), and turns them into components of a single path. This may be convenient if you want to stroke them all in the same way, etc.

Path to Selection; Add to Selection; Subtract from Selection; Intersect with Selection These commands all convert the active path into a selection, and then combine it with the existing selection in the specified ways. ("Path to Selection" discards the existing selection and replaces it with one formed from the path.) If necessary, any unclosed components of the path are closed by connecting the last anchor point to the first anchor point with a straight line. The "marching ants" for the resulting selection should closely follow the path, but don't expect the correspondence to be perfect.

Selection to Path This operation can be accessed in several ways:

- From an image menubar, as Select → To Path
- From the Paths dialog menu, as Selection to Path.
- From the Selection to Path button ⬚ at the bottom of the Paths dialog.

Selection to Path creates a new path from the image's selection. In most cases the resulting path will closely follow the "marching ants" of the selection, but the correspondence will not usually be perfect.

Converting a two-dimensional selection mask into a one-dimensional path involves some rather tricky algorithms: you can alter the way it is done using the Advanced Options, which are accessed by holding down the **Shift** key while pressing the Selection to Path button ⬚ at the bottom of the Paths dialog. This brings up the Advanced Options dialog, which allows you to set 20 different options and variables, all with cryptic names. The Advanced Options are really intended for developers only, and help with them goes beyond the scope of this documentation. Generally speaking, Selection to Path will do what you expect it to, and you don't need to worry about how it is done (unless you want to).

Stroke Path This operation can be accessed in several ways:

- From an image menubar, as Edit → Stroke Path
- From the Paths dialog menu, as Stroke Path.
- From the Paint along the path button ✎ at the bottom of the Paths dialog.
- From the Stroke Path button in the Tool Options for the Path tool.

"Stroke Path" renders the active path on the active layer of the image, permitting a wide variety of line styles and stroking options. See the section on Stroking for more information.

Copy Path Copy Path copies the active path to the Paths Clipboard, enabling you to paste it into a different image.

Tip

  You can also copy and paste a path by dragging its icon from the Paths dialog into the target image's display.

Note

When you copy a path to an image, it is not visible. You have to make it visible in the Path dialog.

Paste Path Paste Path creates a new path from the contents of the Path Clipboard, adds it to the list in the Paths dialog, and makes it the active path for the image. If no path has previously been copied into the clipboard, the menu entry will be insensitive.

Import Path Import Path creates a new path from an SVG file: it pops up a file chooser dialog that allows you to navigate to the file. See the Paths section for information on SVG files and how they relate to GIMP paths.

Export Path Export Path allows you to save a path to a file: it pops up a file save dialog that allows you to specify the file name and location. You can later add this path to any GIMP image using the Import Path command. The format used for saving paths is SVG: this means that vector-graphics programs such as Sodipodi or Inkscape will also be able to import the paths you save. See the Paths section for more information on SVG files and how they relate to GIMP paths.

15.2.4   Colormap Dialog

Figure 15.14 An indexed image with 6 colors and its Colormap dialog

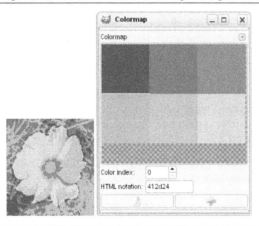

The Colormap (Indexed Palette is a better name) dialog allows you to edit the colormap of an indexed image. (If the mode of the active image is RGB or Grayscale instead of Indexed, the dialog is empty and unusable.) This is a dockable dialog; see the section on Dialogs and Docking for help on manipulating it.

15.2.4.1   Activating the dialog

The "Colormap" dialog is a dockable dialog; see the section Section 3.2.3 for help on manipulating it. You can access it:

- from the image menu: Windows → Dockable Dialogs → Colormap;

- from the Tab menu in any dockable dialog by clicking on ◁ and selecting Add Tab → Colormap.

In the Windows menu, there is a list of detached windows which exists only if at least one dialog remains open. In this case, you can raise the "Colormap" dialog from the image-menu: Windows → Colormap.

15.2.4.2 Colormaps and Indexed Images

In an Indexed image, instead of being assigned a color directly (as happens in RGB and Grayscale images), colors are assigned to pixels by an indirect method, using a look-up table called a *colormap*.

To determine the color that should be shown for that pixel, GIMP looks up the index in the image's colormap. Each indexed image has its own private colormap. In GIMP, the maximum number of entries in a colormap is 256. For a maximum-sized colormap, each index from 0 to 255 is assigned an arbitrary RGB color. There are no rules restricting the colors that can be assigned to an index or the order they appear in: any index can be assigned any color.

It is important to realize that the colors in the colormap are the *only colors available* for an indexed image (that is, unless you add new colors to the colormap). This has a major effect on many GIMP operations: for example, in a pattern fill, GIMP will usually not be able to find exactly the right colors in the colormap, so it will approximate them by using the nearest color available. This is sometimes referred to as Quantization. If the colormap is too limited or poorly chosen, this can easily produce very poor image quality.

The Colormap dialog allows you to alter the colormap for an image, either by creating new entries, or by changing the colors for the existing entries. If you change the color associated with a given index, you will see the changes reflected throughout the image, as a color shift for all pixels that are assigned that index. The entries are numbered with 0 in the upper left corner, 1 to its right, etc.

15.2.4.3 Using the Colormap dialog

Here are the operations you can perform using this dialog:

Click on a color entry This sets GIMP's foreground color to the color you click on, as shown in the Toolbox color area. As a result, this color will be used for the next painting operation you do.

Ctrl-click on a color entry This sets GIMP's background color to the color you **Ctrl**-click on, as shown in the Toolbox color area.

Double-click on a color entry This sets GIMP's foreground color to the color you click on, and also brings up a Color Editor that allows you to change that colormap entry to a new color.

Color index You can select a different colormap entry by typing its index here, or clicking the spinbutton to the right.

HTML-Notation This area shows a hex-code representation (such as is used in HTML) for the color assigned to the currently selected colormap entry. You can edit the color here, instead of using a Color Editor, if you want to. See HTML notation

Edit color This button (in the lower left corner of the dialog) brings up a Color Editor that allows you to change the color for the currently selected colormap entry. The effect is similar to double-clicking on the entry, except that it does not set GIMP's foreground color.

 Add color This button (in the lower right corner of the dialog) allows you to add new colors to the colormap. If you click on the button, the current foreground color, as shown in the Toolbox, will be tacked on to the end of the colormap. If instead you hold down **Ctrl** and click, the background color from the Toolbox will be added. (If the colormap contains 256 entries, it is full, and trying to add more will have no effect.)

Tip

> If you make a mistake, you can undo it by focusing the pointer in the image whose colormap you have changed, and then pressing Ctrl-Z or choosing Edit → Undo in the image menu.

Note

This dialog provides the most commonly used methods for altering the colormap for an indexed image. The color tools, such as Brightness/Contrast, Hue/Saturation, etc, do not operate on indexed images. There are a few plug-ins that do so, including the "Normalize", "VColor Enhance", and "Stretch Contrast" operations, and it is possible to create others as well.

Note

If you paint an indexed image with a color which is not in the Colormap, GIMP will use the most similar color of the Colormap.

15.2.4.4 The Colormap context menu

Right-clicking on a color in the Colormap selects this color and opens a pop-up submenu:

Figure 15.15 The Colormap context menu

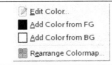

Edit color This command opens a color selector which allows you to modify the color.

Add Color from FG This command is enabled only if the indexed palette contains less than 256 colors. The background color of the Toolbox is appended to the color map.

Add Color from BG This command is enabled only if the indexed palette contains less than 256 colors. The background color of the Toolbox is appended to the color list.

Rearrange Colormap Rearrange Colormap: This command is described in Section 16.8.19.

15.2.5 Histogram dialog

Figure 15.16 The Histogram dialog

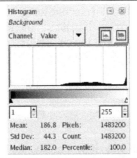

The Histogram dialog shows you information about the statistical distribution of color values in the active layer or selection. This information is often useful when you are trying to *color balance* an image.

However, the Histogram dialog is purely informational: nothing you do with it will cause any change to the image. If you want to perform a histogram-based color correction, use the Levels tool.

15.2.5.1 Activating the dialog

The "Histogram" dialog is a dockable dialog; see the section Section 3.2.3 for help on manipulating it. You can access it:

- from the image menu: Windows → Dockable Dialogs → Histogram.

- from the Tab menu in any dockable dialog by clicking on ◁ and selecting Add Tab → Histogram,

- from the image menu: Colors → Info → Histogram.

In the Windows menu, there is a list of detached windows which exists only if at least one dialog remains open. In this case, you can raise the "Histogram" dialog from the image-menu: Windows → Histogram.

15.2.5.2 About Histograms

In GIMP, each layer of an image can be decomposed into one or more color channels: for an RGB image, into R, G, and B channels; for a grayscale image, into a single Value channel. Layers that support transparency have an additional channel, the alpha channel. Each channel supports a range of intensity levels from 0 to 255 (integer valued). Thus, a black pixel is encoded by 0 on all color channels; a white pixel by 255 on all color channels. A transparent pixel is encoded by 0 on the alpha channel; an opaque pixel by 255.

For RGB images, it is convenient to define a Value "pseudochannel". This is not a real color channel: it does not reflect any information stored directly in the image. Instead, the Value at a pixel is given by the equation V =max(R, G, B). Essentially, the Value is what you would get at that pixel if you converted the image to Grayscale mode.

For more information on channels, please consult the Section 5.1.

15.2.5.3 Using the Histogram dialog

The active layer name is shown at the top of the dialog.

Channel

Figure 15.17 Channel options for an RGB layer with alpha channel

---

This allows you to select which channel to use. The possibilities depend on the layer type of the active layer. Here are the entries you might see, and what they mean:

Value For RGB and Grayscale images, this shows the distribution of brightness values across the layer. For a grayscale image, these are read directly from the image data. For an RGB image, they are taken from the Value pseudochannel.

For an indexed image, the "Value" channel actually shows the distribution of frequencies for each colormap index: thus, it is a "pseudocolor" histogram rather than a true color histogram.

Red, Green, Blue These only appear for layers from RGB images. They show the distribution of intensity levels for the Red, Green, or Blue channels respectively.

Alpha This shows the distribution of opacity levels. If the layer is completely transparent (alpha = 0) or completely opaque (alpha = 255), the histogram will consist of a single bar on the left or right edge.

RGB

Figure 15.18 Combined histograms of R, G, and B channels.

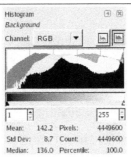

This entry, only available for RGB layers, shows the R, G, and B histograms superimposed, so that you can see all of the color distribution information in a single view.

Linear ⬚ / Logarithmic ⬚ buttons

Figure 15.19 The histogram shown at the top, changed to logarithmic mode.

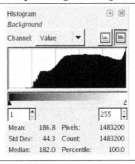

These buttons determine whether the histogram will be displayed using a linear or logarithmic Y axis. For images taken from photographs, the linear mode is most commonly useful. For images that contain substantial areas of constant color, though, a linear histogram will often be dominated by a single bar, and a logarithmic histogram will often be more useful.

Range Setting

Figure 15.20 Dialog aspect after range fixing.

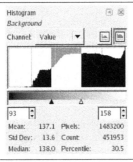

You can restrict the analysis, for the statistics shown at the bottom of the dialog, to a limited range of values if you wish. You can set the range in one of three ways:

- Click and drag the pointer across the histogram display area, from the lowest level to the highest level of the range you want.

- Click and drag the black or white triangles on the slider below the histogram.

- Use the spinbutton entries below the slider (left entry: bottom of range; right entry: top of range).

Statistics At the bottom of the dialog some basic statistics are shown describing the distribution of channel values, restricted to the selected range:

- Mean : the mean value of the interval in the selected channel.

- Std Dev : Standard deviation. Gives an idea about how homogeneous the distribution of values in the interval is.

- Median : For example, the value of the fiftieth peak in a 100 peaks interval.

- Pixels : The number of pixels in the active layer or selection.

- Count : The number of pixels in a peak (when you click on the histogram) or in the interval.

- Percentile : The ratio between the number of pixels in the interval and the total number of pixels in the active layer or selection.

15.2.6   Navigation Dialog

Figure 15.21 Navigation Dialog

The Navigation dialog is designed to offer easy movement around the active image if the zoom is set higher than what the image window can display. If this is the case, there is an inversely colored rectangle that shows the location of the current view area in respect to the image.

To change the viewing region:

- Click and drag the rectangular area.

- Use **Shift** and mouse-wheel to move horizontally, **Alt** and mouse-wheel to move vertically. The mouse pointer must be on the rectangular area in the shape of a grabbing hand.

15.2.6.1   Activating the dialog

The "Navigation" dialog is a dockable dialog; see the section Section 3.2.3 for help on manipulating it. You can access it:

- from the image menu: Windows → Dockable Dialogs → Navigation;

- from the Tab menu in any dockable dialog by clicking on [icon] and selecting Add Tab → Navigation,

- from the image-menu: View → Navigation window.

- You can access more quickly to it (but without the zoom functions) by clicking on the icon at the right bottom corner of the image window:

15.2.6.2   Using the Navigation Dialog

The slider It allows easy zoom level control, more precise than with the Zoom command. This slider can also be moved using the mouse wheel when the mouse pointer is on the slider, or **Ctrl** and mouse wheel when the mouse pointer is on the rectangular area.

The buttons *Zoom Out* ✎ *Zoom In* ✎ and *Zoom 1:1* ✎ are self explanatory.

> **Adjust the zoom ratio so that the image becomes fully visible**   The zoom ratio is adjusted so that the whole image becomes visible in the window as it is.

> **Adjust the zoom ratio so that the window is used optimally**   The image size and the zoom are adjusted so that the image is fully displayed with the lesser zoom.

> **Reduce the image window to the size of the image display**   Restore the image window to the size which allows the image to be fully displayed with the zoom unchanged. This command is also as menu entry available. See Section 16.5.5 for the details.

15.2.7   Undo History Dialog

Figure 15.22 The Undo History dialog

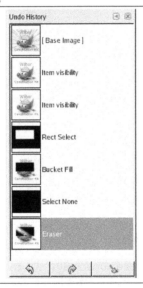

This dialog shows you a list of the actions you have most recently performed on an image, with a small sketch that attempts to illustrate the changes produced by each. You can revert the image to any point in its Undo History simply by clicking on the right entry in the list. For more information on GIMP's Undo mechanism and how it works, see the section on Undoing.

15.2.7.1   Activating the dialog

The "Undo History" dialog is a dockable dialog; see the section Section 3.2.3 for help on manipulating it.

You can access it:

- from the image menu: Windows → Dockable Dialogs → Undo History.

- from the Tab menu in any dockable dialog by clicking on ◁ and selecting Add Tab → Undo History.

15.2.7.2   Using the Undo History dialog

The most basic thing you can do is to select a point in the Undo History by clicking on it in the list. You can go back and forth between states in this way as much as you please, without losing any information or consuming any resources. In most cases, the changes are very fast.

Tip

   Ctrl-F opens a search field. See View as List; View as Grid

---

At the bottom of the dialog are three buttons:

Undo   This button has the same effect as choosing Edit → Undo from the menu, or pressing Ctrl-Z; it reverts the image to the next state back in the undo history.

Redo   This button has the same effect as choosing Edit → Redo from the menu, or pressing Ctrl-Y; it advances the image to the next state forward in the Undo History.

Clear Undo History   This button removes all contents from the undo history except the current state. If you press it, you are asked to confirm that you really want to do this. The only reason for doing it would be if you are very constrained for memory.

Note

   In a tab, this dialog is represented by

Note

   You can set the number of undo levels in Preferences/Environment.

15.3   Image-content Related Dialogs

15.3.1   FG/BG Color Dialog

Figure 15.23 The FG/BG Color dialog

The Color dialog lets you manage and pick up new colors. You can use it into five different modes: GIMP, CMYK, Triangle, Watercolor and Scales. It has an interesting eyedropper to pick up a color anywhere on your screen.

The dialog called from the FG/BG area in the toolbox is a bit different compared to the one called from the image menu:

- the sliders are permanently visible instead of selected from the scale menu,

- twelve buttons show the last used colors. You may choose a color by clicking on one of these buttons or add the current FG or BG color to this history list.

This dialog works either on the foreground or the background color.

15.3.1.1   Activating the Dialog

The "Colors" dialog is a dockable dialog; see the section Section 3.2.3 for help on manipulating it.
    You can access it:

- from an image menu: Windows → Dockable Dialogs → Colors;

- from the Tab menu in any dockable dialog by clicking on ◁ and selecting Add Tab → Colors,

- from the toolbox: click on the current Foreground or Background color.

In the Windows menu, there is a list of detached windows which exists only if at least one dialog remains open. In this case, you can raise the "Colors" dialog from the image-menu: Windows → Colors.

15.3.1.2   Using the "FG/BG color" dialog

GIMP Selector With the GIMP Color Selector, you select a color by clicking on a one-dimensional strip located at the right edge, and then in a two-dimensional area located on the left. The one-dimensional strip can encode any of the color parameters H, S, V, R, G, or B, as determined by which of the adjoining buttons is pressed. The two-dimensional area then encodes the two complementary color parameters.

CMYK

Figure 15.24 CMYK

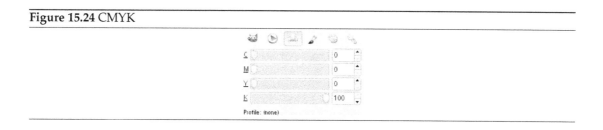

You get to this selector by clicking on the printer icon. The CMYK view gives you the possibility to manage colors from the CMYK color model.

Triangle

Figure 15.25 The triangle selector

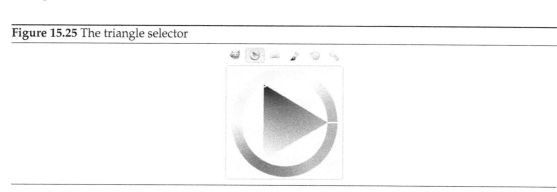

This selector uses the HSV color model. Click in the *chromatic circle* and drag the mouse pointer to select the Hue. Click-and-drag in the *triangle* to vary intuitively Saturation (vertically) and Value (horizontally).

Watercolor

Figure 15.26 Watercolor Color Selector

This color selector is symbolized by a brush. The function mode of this selector is a little different from that of models presented so far. The principle consists in changing the current foreground color by clicking in the rectangular palette. If the current foreground color is for example white, then it turns to reddish by clicking in the red color area. Repeated clicking strengthens the effect. With the slider, which is right apart from the color palette, you can set the color quantity per every mouse click. The higher the sliding control is, the more color is taken up per click.

Palette

Figure 15.27 Palette Color Selector

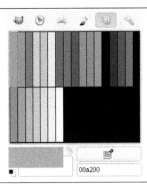

This color selector brings up a list of the colors of the current palette in the Palettes dialog. You can set GIMP's foreground or background colors by clicking on colors in the colors display. You can also use the arrow keys to move within the list of colors.

Scales

Figure 15.28 The Scales selector

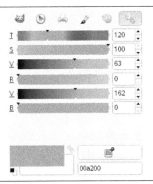

This selector displays a global view of R, G, B channels and H, S, V values, placed in sliders.

Color picker The color picker has a completely different behavior, than the color picker tool. Instead of picking the colors from the active image, you're able to pick colors from the entire screen.

HTML Notation See HTML notation. You can also use the CSS keywords; enter the first letter of a color to get a list of colors with their keyword :

Figure 15.29 CSS keywords example

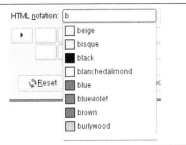

Right-clicking in the HTML Notation text box opens a context menu that allows you to edit your notation, particularly to paste a complex notation you have copied elsewhere. This menu leads to various Input Methods that allow you to use foreign characters, and to the possibility to Insert Unicode Control Characters. This is a vast field, beyond this help. Please see [UNICODE].

Figure 15.30 The HTML Notation context menu

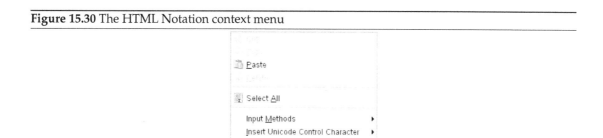

Right up you find a symbol, consisting of two arrows, with which you can exchange the foreground and background color. At the bottom left of the dialog, just below the foreground color block, you find a switching surface with two small, one black and the other white, partially overlapping squares. If you click on these, the front and background color are put back to black and white respectively.

15.3.2 Brushes Dialog

Figure 15.31 The Brushes dialog

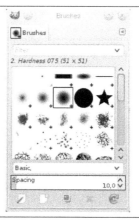

The "Brushes" dialog is used to select a brush, for use with painting tools: see the Brushes section for basic information on brushes and how they are used in GIMP. The dialog also gives you access to several functions for manipulating brushes. You can select a brush by clicking on it in the list: it will then be shown in the Brush/Pattern/Gradient area of the Toolbox. GIMP comes now with 56 brushes, different from each other, because the size, the ratio and the angle of every brush can be set in the tool options dialog. You can also create custom brushes using the Brush Editor, or by saving images in a special brush file format.

15.3.2.1 Activating the Dialog

The "Brushes" dialog is a dockable dialog; see the section Section 3.2.3 for help on manipulating it. You can access it:

- from the Toolbox, by clicking on the brush symbol in the Brush/Pattern/Gradient area (if you have checked the "Show active brush, pattern and gradient" option in the toolbox preferences).

- From an image menu: Windows → Dockable Dialogs → Brushes;

- from the Tab menu in any dockable dialog by clicking on ⊲ and selecting Add Tab → Brushes.

- from the Tool Options dialog for any of the paint tools, by clicking on the Brush icon button, you get a popup with similar functionality that permits you to quickly choose a brush from the list; if you click on the button present on the right bottom of the popup, you open the real brush dialog.

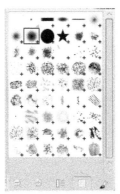

The simplified "Brushes" dialog

This window has five buttons, clearly explained by help pop-ups:

- Smaller previews
- Larger previews
- View as list
- View as Grid
- Open the brush selection dialog

Note that, depending on your Preferences, a brush selected with the popup may only apply to the currently active tool, not to other paint tools. See the Tool Option Preferences section for more information.

15.3.2.2   Using the "Brushes" dialog

15.3.2.2.1   Grid/List mode   In the Tab menu, you can choose between View as Grid and View as List. In Grid mode, the brush shapes are laid out in a rectangular array, making it easy to see many at once and find the one you are looking for. In List mode, the shapes are lined up in a list, with the names beside them.

In the Tab menu, the option Preview Size allows you to adapt the size of brush previews to your liking.

Figure 15.32 Grid/List view

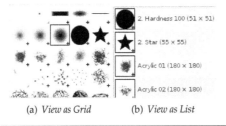

(a) *View as Grid*   (b) *View as List*

Grid mode At the top of the dialog appears the name of the currently selected brush, and its size in pixels.

In the center a grid view of all available brushes appears, with the currently selected one outlined.

List mode For the most part, the dialog works the same way in List mode as in Grid mode, with one exception:

If you double-click on the *name* of a brush, you will be able to edit it. Note, however, that you are only allowed to change the names of brushes that you have created or installed yourself, not the ones that come pre-installed with GIMP. If you try to rename a pre-installed brush, you will be able to edit the name, but as soon as you hit return or click somewhere else, the name will revert to its original value. It is a general rule that you cannot alter the resources that GIMP pre-installs for you: brushes, patterns, gradients, etc; only ones that you create yourself.

Figure 15.33 The "Brushes" dialog

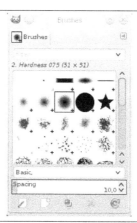

15.3.2.2.2   Brush previews   When you click on a brush preview, it becomes the current brush and it gets selected in the brush area of Toolbox and the Brush option of painting tools. When you double-click on a brush preview, you will activate the Brush Editor. You can also click on buttons at the bottom of the dialog to perform various actions.

Meaning of the small symbols at the bottom right corner of every brush preview:

- A blue corner is for brushes in normal size. You can duplicate them.

- A small cross means that the brush preview is in a reduced size. You can get it in normal size by maintaining left click on it.

- A red corner is for animated brushes. If you maintain left click on the thumbnail, the animation is played.

15.3.2.2.3   Tagging   You can use tags to reorganize the brushes display. See Section 15.3.6.

15.3.2.2.4   Buttons at the bottom   At the bottom of the dialog you find a slider and some buttons:

Spacing   This slider lets you set the distance between consecutive brush marks when you trace out a brushstroke with the mouse pointer. Spacing is a percentage of the brush width.

Edit Brush   This activates the Brush Editor. Pressing the button will open the Editor for any brush. It only works, however, for parametric brushes: for any other type, the Editor will show you the brush but not allow you to do anything with it.

New Brush   This creates a new parametric brush, initializes it with a small fuzzy round shape, and opens the Brush Editor so that you can modify it. The new brush is automatically saved in your personal `brushes` folder.

Duplicate Brush   This button is only enabled if the currently selected brush is a parametric brush. If so, the brush is duplicated, and the Brush Editor is opened so that you can modify the copy. The result is automatically saved in your personal `brushes` folder.

Delete Brush   This option is active for parametric brushes only. This removes all traces of the brush, both from the dialog and the folder where its file is stored, if you have permission to do so. It asks for confirmation before doing anything.

Refresh Brushes   If you add brushes to your personal `brushes` folder or any other folder in your brush search path, by some means other than the Brush Editor, this button causes the list to be reloaded, so that the new entries will be available in the dialog.

The functions performed by these buttons can also be accessed from the dialog pop-up menu, activated by right-clicking anywhere in the brush grid/list, or by choosing the top item, Brushes menu, from the dialog Tab menu.

Figure 15.34 The "Brushes" context menu

15.3.2.2.5 The "Brushes" context menu Right clicking on a brush preview opens a context menu. This menu has now some options which let you create elliptical and rectangular brushes. These brushes can be feathered, but they are not parametric brushes.

The other commands of this submenu are described with the Buttons, except for Copy Brush Location which allows to copy brush path into clipboard. By using the File → Open Location, command, you can open the brush as a new image.

15.3.2.3 Brush Editor

Figure 15.35 The "Brushes" Editor dialog

The Brush Editor, activated for a new brush.

The Brush Editor allows you to view the brush parameters of a brush supplied by GIMP, and you can't change them. You can also create a custom brush: click on the New Brush button to activate the functions of the brush editor; you can select a geometrical shape, a circle, a square or a diamond. This editor has several elements:

The dialog bar: As with all dialog windows, a click on the small triangle prompts a menu allowing you to set the aspect of the Brush Editor.

The title bar: To give a name to your brush.

The preview area: Brush changes appear in real time in this preview.

Settings:

Shape A circle, a square and a diamond are available. You will modify them by using the following options:

Radius Distance between brush center and edge, in the width direction. A square with a 10 pixels radius will have a 20 pixels side. A diamond with a 5 pixels radius will have a 10 pixels width.

Spikes This parameter is useful only for square and diamond. With a square, increasing spikes results in a polygon. With a diamond, you get a star.

Hardness This parameter controls the feathering of the brush border. Value = 1.00 gives a brush with a sharp border (0.00-1.00).

Aspect ratio This parameter controls the brush Width/Height ratio. A diamond with a 5 pixels radius and an Aspect Ratio = 2, will be flattened with a 10 pixels width and a 5 pixels height (1.0-20.0).

Angle This angle is the angle between the brush width direction, which is normally horizontal, and the horizontal direction, counter-clock-wise. When this value increases, the brush width turns counter-clock-wise (0° to 180°).

Spacing When the brush draws a line, it actually stamps the brush icon repeatedly. If brush stamps are very close, you get the impression of a solid line: you get that with Spacing = 1. (1.00 to 200.0).

15.3.2.4   The Clipboard Brush

When you use the Copy or Cut command on an image or a selection of it, a copy appears as a new brush in the upper left corner of the "Brushes" dialog. This brush will persist until you use the Copy command again. It disappears when you close GIMP.

Figure 15.36 A new "Clipboard Brush"

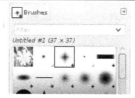

> **Note**
>
> You can save this clipboard brush by using the Edit → Paste as → New brush as soon as it appears in the "Brushes" dialog. (See Section 16.3.11.3.)

15.3.3   Patterns Dialog

In GIMP, a *pattern* is a small image used to fill areas by placing copies of side by side. See the Patterns section for basic information on patterns and how they can be created and used.

You can use them with the Bucket Fill and Clone tools and the Fill with pattern command.

The "Patterns" dialog is used to select a pattern, by clicking on it in a list or grid view: the selected pattern will then be shown in the Brush/Pattern/Gradient area of the Toolbox. A few dozen more or less randomly chosen patterns are supplied with GIMP, and you can easily add new patterns of your own.

15.3.3.1   Activating the dialog

The "Patterns" dialog is a dockable dialog; see the section Section 3.2.3 for help on manipulating it.

You can access it:

- From the Toolbox, by clicking on the pattern symbol in the Brush/Pattern/Gradient area (if you have checked the "Show active brush, pattern and gradient" option in the toolbox preferences).

- from the image menu: Windows → Dockable Dialogs → Patterns;

- from the Tab menu in any dockable dialog by clicking on and selecting Add Tab → Patterns.

- From the Tool Options dialog of the Clone tool and the Bucket Fill tool, by clicking on the pattern source button, you get a pop-up with similar functionality that permits you to quickly choose a pattern from the list; if you clic on the Bucket Fill button present on the right bottom of the pop-up, you open the real pattern dialog. Note that, depending on your Preferences, a pattern selected with the pop-up may only apply to the currently active tool, not to other paint tools. See the Tool Option Preferences section for more information.

15.3.3.2 Using the pattern dialog

Grid/List modes In the Tab menu, you can choose between View as Grid and View as List. In Grid mode, the patterns are laid out in a rectangular array, making it easy to see many at once and find the one you are looking for. In List mode, the patterns are lined up in a list, with the names beside them.

> **Tip**
>
> Independent of the real size of a pattern all patterns are shown the same size in the dialog. So for larger patterns this means that you see only a small portion of the pattern in the dialog at all - no matter whether you view the dialog in the list or the grid view. To see the full pattern you simply click on the pattern *and hold the mouse button* for a second.

> **Note**
>
> In the Tab menu, the option Preview Size allows you to adapt the size of pattern previews to your liking.

Figure 15.37 The Patterns dialog

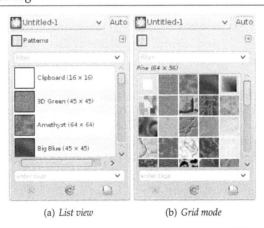

(a) *List view*   (b) *Grid mode*

Using the Patterns dialog (Grid mode) At the top appears the name of the currently selected patterns, and its dimensions in pixels.

In the center appears a grid view of all available patterns, with the currently selected one outlined. Clicking on one of them sets it as GIMP's current pattern, and causes it to appear in the Brush/Pattern/Gradient area of the Toolbox.

Using the Patterns dialog (List view) In this view, instead of a grid, you see a list of patterns, each labeled with its name and size. Clicking on a row in the list sets that pattern as GIMP's current pattern, just as it does in the grid view.

If you *double-click* on the name of a pattern, you will be able to edit the name. Note that you are only allowed to rename patterns that you have added yourself, not the ones that are supplied with GIMP. If you edit a name that you don't have permission to change, as soon as you hit return or move to a different control, the name will revert back to its previous value.

Everything else in the List view works the same way as it does in the Grid view.

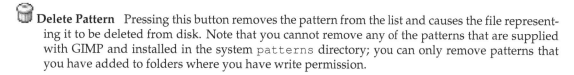 **Delete Pattern** Pressing this button removes the pattern from the list and causes the file representing it to be deleted from disk. Note that you cannot remove any of the patterns that are supplied with GIMP and installed in the system `patterns` directory; you can only remove patterns that you have added to folders where you have write permission.

Refresh Patterns Pressing this button causes GIMP to rescan the folders in your pattern search path, adding any newly discovered patterns to the list. This button is useful if you add new patterns to a folder, and want to make them available without having to restart GIMP.

Open pattern as image If you click on this button, the current pattern is opened in a new image window. So, you can edit it. But if you try to save it with the `.pat`, even with a new name, you will bang into a "Denied permission" problem because this image file is "root". But this is possible under Windows, less protected.

15.3.3.3 Tagging

You can use tags to reorganize the patterns display. See Section 15.3.6.

15.3.3.4 The Pattern context menu

You get it by right-clicking on the "Patterns" dialog. The commands of this menu are described with Buttons, except for Copy Location which allows to copy the path to pattern into clipboard.

15.3.3.5 The Clipboard pattern

When you use the Copy or Cut command, a copy appears as a new pattern in the upper left corner of the Patterns dialog. This brush will persist until you use the Copy (or Cut) command again. It will disappear when you close GIMP.

Figure 15.38 A new "Clipboard Pattern"

Note

 You can save this clipboard pattern by using the Edit → Paste as → New pattern as soon as it appears in the Patterns dialog.

15.3.4   Gradients Dialog

Figure 15.39 The screenshot illustrates the Gradients dialog

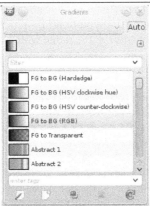

The "Gradients" dialog offers a gradient palette which is used to select a gradient — a set of colors arranged in a linear scale — for use with the Blend tool and numerous other operations. It also gives you access to several functions for manipulating gradients. You can select a gradient by clicking on it in the list: it will then be shown in the Brush/Pattern/Gradient area of the Toolbox. A few dozen nice gradients come pre-installed with GIMP. You can create more using the Gradient Editor. General information about gradients and how they are used in GIMP can be found in the Gradients section.

The first five gradients are particular: they reproduce the gradient between Foreground and background colors of toolbox in different ways.

- FG to BG (Hardedge): only black and white with a sharp limit.

- FG to BG (HSV clock-wise/counter-clockwise Hue): all hues in the color circle between the Foreground and the background color, clockwise or counter-clockwise.

- FG to BG (RGB): default gradient, between the Foreground and the background colors of the Toolbox, in the RGB mode.

- FG to Transparent: only uses one color (the Foreground color) from complete opacity to complete transparency. This gradient is very useful when you work with softly blended collages or fog effects.

15.3.4.1   Activating the Dialog

The "Gradients" dialog is a dockable dialog; see the section Section 3.2.3 for help on manipulating it. You can access it:

- from an image menu: Windows → Dockable Dialogs → Gradients;

- from the Tab menu in any dockable dialog by clicking on ◁ and selecting Add Tab → Gradients,

- from the Toolbox, by clicking on the current gradient in the Brush/Pattern/Gradient area (if you have checked the "Show active brush, pattern and gradient" option in the toolbox preferences).

- From the image by using the Ctrl-G shortcut.

In the Windows menu, there is a list of detached windows which exists only if at least one dialog remains open. In this case, you can raise the "Gradients" dialog from the image-menu: Windows → Gradients.

15.3.4.2 Using the "Gradients" dialog

The most basic, and most commonly used, operation with the dialog is simply to click on one of the gradients in the scrollable list, in order to make it GIMP's current gradient, which will then be used by any operation that involves a gradient.

If you *double-click* on a gradient, you open the Gradient Editor where you will be able to edit its name. Note, however, that you are only allowed to change the names of gradients that you have created yourself, not the ones that come pre-installed with GIMP. If you try to rename a pre-installed gradient, you will be able to edit the name, but as soon as you hit return or click somewhere else, the name will revert to its original value. It is a general rule that you cannot alter the resources that GIMP pre-installs for you: brushes, patterns, gradients, etc; only ones that you create yourself.

Grid/List modes In the Tab menu, you can choose between View as Grid and View as List. In Grid mode, the gradients are laid out in a rectangular array. They look quite dazzling when viewed this way, but it is not very easy to pick the one you want, because of visual interference from the neighboring ones. In List mode, the more usable default, the gradients are lined up vertically, with each row showing its name.

In the Tab menu, the option Preview Size allows you to adapt the size of gradient previews to your liking.

The buttons at the bottom of the dialog allow you to operate on gradients in several ways:

Edit Gradient This button activates the Gradient Editor.

New Gradient This creates a new gradient, initialized as a simple grayscale, and activates the Gradient Editor so that you can alter it. Gradients that you create are automatically saved in the `gradients` folder of your personal GIMP directory, from which they are automatically loaded when GIMP starts. (You can change this folder, or add new ones, using the Preferences dialog.)

Duplicate Gradient This creates a copy of the currently selected gradient. You will be able to edit the copy even if you cannot edit the original.

Delete Gradient This removes all traces of the gradient, if you have permission to do so. It asks for confirmation before doing anything.

Refresh Gradients If you add gradients to your personal `gradients` folder by some means other than this dialog, this button causes the list to be reloaded, so that the new entries will be available.

The functions performed by these buttons can also be accessed from the dialog pop-up menu, activated by right-clicking anywhere in the gradient list, or via Gradient Menu in the Tab menu:

Figure 15.40 The Gradients Menu

The gradient menu also gives you some additional functions:

Save as POV-Ray... This allows you to save the gradient in the format used by the POV-Ray 3D ray-tracing program.

Copy Gradient Location This command allows you to copy the gradient file location to the clipboard. You can then use it in a text editor.

Custom Gradient... This command creates a sample image filled with the selected gradient. You can select width and height of the image as well as the gradient direction in the dialog window.

Save as CSS The CSS (Cascading Style Sheets) language is used to format the display of HTML and XML files, for instance background color, font size... and background gradient. The "CSS Save" plugin is a CSS3 linear gradient generator that allows you to save a CSS3 code snippet, containing the gradient data for a given GIMP gradient. This code snippet is a text file: you can copy-paste it to the stylesheet related to your HTML file, to get a gradient background on opening the HTML file in Firefox, Chrome or Safari web navigators. This CSS3 code snippet can also be used as a gradient in SVG files.

Here is an example of code snippet, got using the Blue Green gradient:

A CSS snippet created with Save as CSS

```
background-image: linear-gradient(top, rgb(0,123,255) 0%, rgb ↩
    (72,226,255), 56%,
      rgb(0,255,161) 100%);
background-image: -moz-linear-gradient(center top, rgb(0,123,255)  ↩
    0%,rgb(72,
    226,255) 56%,rgb(0,255,
    161) 100%);
background-image: -webkit-gradient(linear, left top, left bottom,
      color-stop(0.000, rgb(0,123,255)),color-stop(0.566, rgb ↩
        (72,226,255)),
    color-stop(1.000, rgb(0,255,161)));
```

15.3.4.2.1   Tagging   You can use tags to reorganize the gradients display. See Section 15.3.6.

15.3.4.3   The Gradient Editor

Figure 15.41 The gradient editor

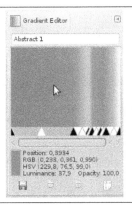

The Gradient Editor allows you to edit the colors in a gradient. It can only be used on gradients you have created yourself (or on a copy of a system gradient), not on system gradients that come pre-installed with GIMP. This is a sophisticated tool that may take a bit of effort to understand. The concept behind it is that a gradient can be decomposed into a series of adjoining *segments*, with each segment consisting of a smooth transition from the color on the left edge to the color on the right edge. The Gradient Editor allows you to pack together any number of segments, with any colors you want for the left and right edges of each segment, and with several options for the shape of the transition from left to right.

15.3.4.3.1   How to Activate the Gradient Editor   You can activate the Gradient Editor in several ways:

- by double-clicking on the gradient stripe in the Gradient dialog,

- from the context menu you get by right clicking on the selected gradient name,

- by clicking on the Edit gradient ![button] button in the Gradient Dialog,

- from the Gradient Menu you get by clicking on ![icon] in the Gradient Dialog.

15.3.4.3.2 Display

Name In the name area, you have the tab menu button (the small triangle).

The Gradient Preview Window Below the name, you see the current result of your work if the Instant update option is checked; else, changes will appear only when you release the mouse button.

If you simply move the mouse pointer on this display, it works somewhat as a color-picker. Values of the pointed pixel are displayed in a rather odd way. *Position* is a number given to 3 decimal places, from 0.000 on the left to 1.000 on the right of the whole gradient. *RGB, HSV, Intensity and Opacity* are also a ratio...

If you click-n-drag on display, then only position and RGB data are displayed. But they are passed on to the Foreground color in the Toolbox and to the four first gradients of the list (by pressing the **Ctrl** key, the Color is sent to the Background color of the Toolbox).

Range Selection/Control Sliders Below the gradient display, you see a set of black and white triangles lined up in row which allow you to adjust endpoints and midpoints in the gradient preview. A *segment* is the space between two consecutive *black* triangles. Inside each segment is a white triangle, which is used to "warp" the colors in the segment, in the same way that the middle slider in the Levels tool warps the colors there. You can select a segment by clicking between the two black triangles that define it. It turns from white to blue. You can select a range of segments by shift-clicking on them. The selected range always consists of a set of *consecutive* segments, so if you skip over any when shift-clicking, they will be included automatically. If "Instant update" is checked, the display is updated immediately after any slider movement; if it is unchecked, updates only occur when you release the mouse button.

You can move sliders, segments and selections. If you simply *click-n-drag a slider*, you only move the corresponding transition. By *click-n-drag on a segment* you can move this segment up to the next triangle. By *Shift+click-n-drag on a segment/selection*, you can move this segment/selection and compress/ dilate next segments.

Scrollbar Below the sliders is a scrollbar. This only comes into play if you zoom in using the buttons at the bottom.

Feedback Area Below, a color swatch shows the color pointed by the mouse cursor. Informations about this color and helpful hints or feedback messages may appear here.

Buttons At the bottom of the dialog appear five buttons:

> **Save** Clicking this button causes the gradient, in its current state, to be saved in your personal `gradients` folder, so that it will automatically be loaded the next time you start GIMP.

> **Revert** Clicking this button undoes all of your editing. (However, at the time this is being written, this function is not yet implemented.)

> **Zoom Out** Clicking this button shrinks the gradient display horizontally.

> **Zoom In** Clicking this button expands the gradient display horizontally. You can then use the scrollbar to pan the display left or right.

> **Zoom All** Clicking this button resizes the display horizontally so that it fits precisely into the window.

Figure 15.42 The Gradient Editor pop-up menu

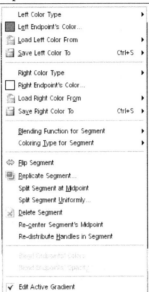

15.3.4.3.3   The Gradient Editor pop-up Menu   You can access the Gradient Editor menu either by right-clicking on the gradient display, or by choosing the top item in the dialog's tab menu. The menu allows you to edit endpoint's color (set the left and right edge colors for each segment), blend colors, select a color model and edit segments. This editor works only with custom gradients or a copy of a system gradient.

The following commands can be found in the menu:

Editing endpoint's color

Left/Right color type   This command opens a submenu:

Figure 15.43 The Left/Right color type sub-menu

This submenu allows you to select the endpoint color from the toolbox foreground and background colors. Whenever you change the foreground or background color, this endpoint color may be changed as well. The alternative is to select a Fixed endpoint color.

Left [Right] Endpoint's Color   These options allow you to choose a color for the respective endpoint using a Color Editor.

> **Note**
>
> This command is related to the previous one and becomes inactive if you have selected any other value than Fixed for the corresponding Left [Right] Color Type.

Figure 15.44 The "Load Color From" submenu

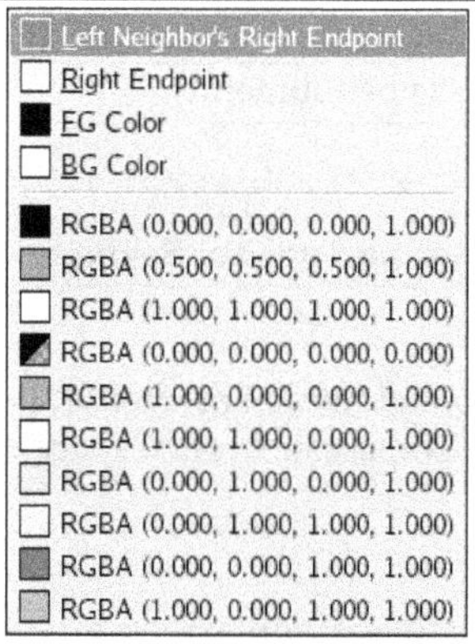

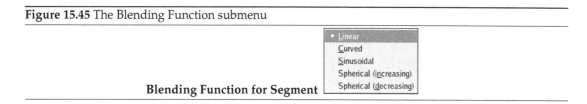

Load Left [Right] Color From

These options give you a number of alternative ways of assigning colors to the endpoints. From the submenu you can choose (assuming we're dealing with the left endpoint):

Left Neighbor's Right Endpoint This choice will cause the color of the right endpoint of the segment neighboring on the left to be assigned to the left endpoint of the selected range.

Right Endpoint This choice will cause the color of the right endpoint of the selected range to be assigned to the left endpoint.

FG/BG color This choice causes GIMP's current foreground or background color, as shown in the Toolbox, to be assigned to the endpoint. Note that changing foreground or background color later will not change the endpoint's color.

RGBA slots At the bottom of the menu are 10 "memory slots". You can assign colors to them using the "Save" menu option described below. If you choose one of the slots, the color in it will be assigned to the endpoint.

Save Left [Right] Color To These options cause the color of the endpoint in question to be assigned to the "memory slot" selected from the submenu.

Click and drag colors You can also click and drag a color from the toolbox FG-BG colors or from a palette

- to an endpoint (a black triangle), to set left [right] colors,
- to the gradient display area, to add a new endpoint with this color on both sides.

Blending and coloring functions for segment

Figure 15.45 The Blending Function submenu

Blending Function for Segment

This option determines the course of the transition from one endpoint of the range (segment or selection) to the other, by fitting the specified type of function to the endpoints and midpoint of the range:

Linear Default option. Color varies linearly from one endpoint of the range to the other.

Curved Gradient varies more quickly on ends of the range than on its middle.

Sinusoidal The opposite of the curved type. Gradients varies more quickly on center of the range than on its ends.

Spherical (increasing) Gradient varies more quickly on the left of the range than on its right.

Spherical (decreasing) Gradient varies more quickly on the right than on the left.

Figure 15.46 The Coloring Type submenu

Coloring Type for Segment

This option gives you additional control of the type of transition from one endpoint to the other: as a line either in RGB space or in HSV space.

Modifying segments

Flip Segment This option does a right-to-left flip of the selected range (segment or selection), flipping all colors and endpoint locations.

Replicate Segment This option splits the selected range (segment or selection) into two parts, each of which is a perfect compressed copy of the original range.

Split Segment at Midpoint This option splits each segment in the selected range in into two segments, splitting at the location of the white triangle.

Split Segment Uniformly This option is similar to the previous one, but it splits each segment halfway between the endpoints, instead of at the white triangle.

Delete Segment This option deletes all segments in the selected range, (segment or selection) replacing them with a single black triangle at the center, and enlarging the segments on both sides to fill the void.

Re-center Segment's midpoint This option moves the white triangle for each segment in the selected range to a point halfway between the neighboring black triangles.

Re-distribute Handles in Segment This option causes the black and white triangles in the selected range to be shifted so that the distances from one to the next are all equal.

Blending colors
These options are available only if more than one segment are selected.

Blend Endpoints' Colors This option causes the colors at interior endpoints in the range to be averaged, so that the transition from each segment to the next is smooth.

Blend Endpoints' Opacity This option does the same thing as the previous option, but with opacity instead of color.

Caution

There is no "undo" available within the Gradient Editor, so be careful!

15.3.4.3.4 Using example for the Gradient Editor All these options can seem somewhat boring. Here is an example to clear ideas:

1. Open the Gradient Dialog. Click the New Gradient . The Gradient Editor is opened and shows a gradient from black to white.

Figure 15.47 New gradient

2. Right click in this new gradient and click the Split Segment Uniformly. Fix the number of segments you want.

Figure 15.48 Gradient with three segments

*Every segment is limited with two black triangular sliders. Click a segment to activate it. By pressing the **Shift** key, you can select several contiguous segments.*

3. In the context menu you get by right-clicking in the gradient, set Left Endpoint Color and Right Endpoint Color for the selected segment or segment group.

Figure 15.49 First segment colored

Red has been chosen for left endpoint and yellow for the right enpoint.

4. Go on the same way for other segments. Then use the Blending functions for segment to achieve various effects.

15.3.5 Palettes Dialog

A *palette* is a set of discrete colors, in no particular order. See the Palettes section for basic information on palettes and how they can be created and used.

The "Palettes" dialog is used to select a palette, by clicking on it in a list or grid view. A few dozen more or less randomly chosen palettes are supplied with GIMP, and you can easily add new palettes of your own. The "Palettes" dialog also give you access to several operations for creating new palettes or manipulating the ones that already exist.

Note

 The "Palettes" dialog is not the same thing as the Index Palette dialog, which is used to manipulate the colormaps of indexed images.

15.3.5.1 Activating the dialog

The "Palettes" dialog is a dockable dialog; see the section Section 3.2.3 for help on manipulating it. You can access it:

- from the image menu: Windows → Dockable Dialogs → Palettes;

- from the Tab menu in any dockable dialog by clicking on ⬕ and selecting Add Tab → Palettes.

15.3.5.2   Using the Palettes dialog

Clicking on a palette in the dialog selects this palette and brings up the Palette Editor, which allows you to set GIMP's foreground or background colors by clicking on colors in the palette display. You can also use the arrow keys to select a palette.

Double-clicking on a palette *name* (in List View mode) lets you to edit the name. Note that you are only allowed to change the names of palettes that you have added yourself, not those that are supplied with GIMP. If you edit a name that you are not allowed to change, it will revert back to its previous value as soon as you hit return or move the pointer focus elsewhere.

Grid/List modes

Figure 15.50 The "Palettes" dialog

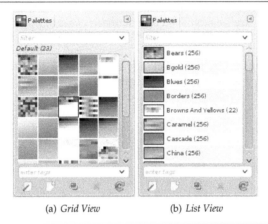

(a) *Grid View*   (b) *List View*

In the Tab menu, you can choose between View as Grid and View as List. In Grid mode, the palettes are laid out in a spectacular rectangular array, making it easy to see many at once and find the one you are looking for. In List mode (the default), the palettes are lined up in a list, with the names beside them.

The option Preview Size allows you to adapt the size of color cell previews to your liking.

Tagging You can use tags to reorganize the palettes display. See Section 15.3.6.

The buttons of the Palettes Dialog
Below the palettes view, at the bottom of the dialog window, there are several buttons:

🖋 **Edit Palette**   This button brings up the Section 15.3.5.4.

🗋 **New Palette**   For more information on this button please refer to New Palette.

🗐 **Duplicate Palette**   For more information on this button please refer to Duplicate Palette.

🗑 **Delete Palette**   For more information on this button please refer to Delete Palette.

🔄 **Refresh Palettes**   For more information on this button please refer to Refresh Palettes.

15.3.5.3 The "Palettes" pop-menu

Figure 15.51 The "Palettes" pop-menu

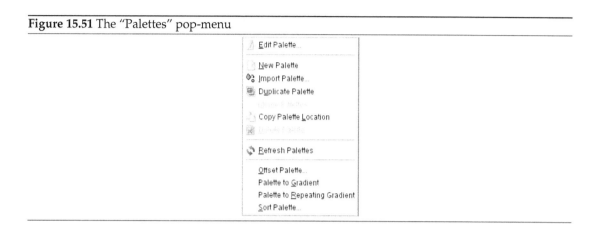

The "Palettes" pop-menu can be accessed by right-clicking in the Palettes dialog, or by choosing the top item from the dialog Tab menu ( ).

> **Note**
>
> Some of the listed pop-menu entries are installation dependend and need the Python language interpreter to be installed. This includes at the time of writing: Offset Palette..., Palette to gradient, Palette to Repeating Gradient and Sort Palette....

Edit Palette "Edit Palette" is an alternative way of activating the Palette Editor: it can also be activated by double-clicking on a palette in the Palettes dialog, or by pressing the "Edit Palette" button at the bottom of the dialog.

New Palette "New Palette" creates a new, untitled palette, initially containing no color entries, and pops up the Palette Editor so that you can add colors to the palette. The result will automatically be saved in your personal `palettes` folder when you quit GIMP, so it will be available from the Palettes dialog in future sessions.

Import Palette

Figure 15.52 The Import Palette dialog

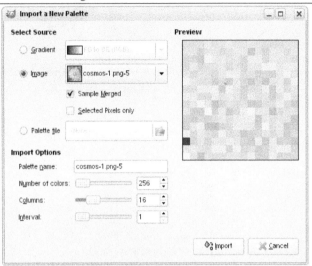

"Import Palette" allows you to create a new palette from the colors in a gradient, an image or a palette file. Choosing it brings up the "Import Palette" dialog, which gives you the following options:

Note

 Former versions of GIMP had a "Save palette" command. It no longer exists. To save the palette of an image, indexed or not, you must *import* it in fact from the image.

Select Source You can import a palette either from any of GIMP's gradients (choosing one from the adjoining menu), or from any of the currently open images (chosen from the adjoining menu). Since GIMP 2.2, you can also import a RIFF palette file (with extension .pal), of the type used by several Microsoft Windows applications.

Two options concerning image as source, available for RGB images only:

- Sample merged: When this option is checked, colors are picked from all visible layers. If unchecked, pixels are picked from the active layer only, even though not visible.

- Selected pixels only: As the name says, pixels are picked from the selected area only, in the active layer or all visible layers according to the status of the previous option.

Palette name You can give a name to the new palette here. If the name you choose is already used by an existing palette, a unique name will be formed by appending a number (e. g., "#1").

Number of colors Here you specify the number of colors in the palette. The default is 256, chosen for three reasons: (1) every gradient contains 256 distinct colors; (2) GIF files can use a maximum of 256 colors; (3) GIMP indexed images can contain a maximum of 256 distinct colors. You can use any number you like here, though: GIMP will try to create a palette by spacing the specified number of colors even across the color range of the gradient or image.

Columns Here you specify the number of columns for the palette. This only affects the way the palette is displayed, and has no effect on the way the palette is used.

Interval Even setting "Number of colors" to maximum, the number of colors can't exceed 10000 in the palette. RGB images have much more colors. Interval should allow to group similar colors around an average and so get a better palette. This problem doesn't exist with 256 colors indexed images: Interval to 1 allows picking 256 colors (this option is grayed out with more than 256 colors indexed palettes too).

The imported palette will be added to the Palettes dialog, and automatically saved in your personal `palettes` folder when you quit GIMP, so it will be available in future sessions.

Duplicate Palette Duplicate Palette creates a new palette by copying the palette that is currently selected, and brings up a Palette Editor so that you can alter the palette. The result will automatically be saved in your personal `palettes` folder when you quit GIMP, so it will be available from the Palettes dialog in future sessions.

Merge Palettes Currently this operation is not implemented, and the menu entry will always be insensitive.

Copy Palette Location This command allows you to copy the palette file location to clipboard. You can then paste it in a text editor.

Delete Palette Delete Palette removes the palette from the "Palettes "dialog, and deletes the disk file in which it is stored. Before it acts, it asks you confirm that you really want to do these things. Note that you cannot remove any of the palettes that are supplied with GIMP, only palettes you have added yourself.

Refresh Palettes Refresh Palettes rescans all of the folders in your palette search path, and adds any newly discovered palettes to the list in the Palettes dialog. This may be useful if you obtain palette files from some external source, copy them into one of your palettes folders, and want to make them available during the current session.

Offset Palette... This command opens a dialog window:

Figure 15.53 The "Offset Palette"dialog

This command takes the last color of the palette and puts it at the first place. The Offset parameter lets you set how many times this action must be performed.

With negative "Offsets" colors are put from the first position to the end of the colors list.

Figure 15.54 "Offset Palette" examples

From top to bottom: original palette, Offset = 1, Offset = 2.

Palette to gradient With this command, all the colors of the palette are used to form the current gradient which is saved in the Gradient Dialog. The created gradient is build with segments just as much as the number of colors on the given palette.

Palette to Repeating Gradient This command creates a repeating gradient, using all the colors of the palette. This gradient appears in the Gradient Dialog and becomes the current gradient. The gradient is created with segments one more than the number of colors on the given palette. The left side color at the leftmost segment will be the same color on the right side at the rightmost segment.

Figure 15.55 "Palette to repeating gradient" examples

Top: palette. Bottom: the gradient created with the command.

Sort Palette... This command opens a dialog window which allows you to sort the colors of the palette according to certain criterions:

Figure 15.56 The "Sort Palette"dialog

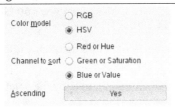

- Color model: you can choose between *RGB* and *HSV*

- Channel to sort: you can choose between the three RGB channels if the RGB model is selected, or the three HSV channels if the HSV channel is selected.

- Ascending (default is Yes): values are sorted from the lower to the upper. By clicking on this Yes you can toggle to No and values will be sorted in descending order.

15.3.5.4 Palette Editor

Figure 15.57 The Palette Editor

The Palette Editor is used mainly for two purposes: first, for setting GIMP's foreground or background colors (as shown in the Color Area of the Toolbox) to selected colors from the palette; second, for modifying the palette. You can activate the Palette Editor for any palette in the Palettes dialog, but you can only modify palettes that you have created yourself, not the palettes that are supplied when you install GIMP. (You can, however, duplicate any palette and then edit the newly created copy.) If you modify a palette, the results of your work will automatically be saved when you exit from GIMP.

15.3.5.4.1 How to Activate the Palette Editor   The Palette Editor is only accessible from the Palettes

dialog: you can activate it by double-clicking on a palette, or by pressing the [image: Edit Palette icon] "Edit Palette" button at the bottom, or by choosing "Edit Palette" from the "Palettes" Menu.

The Palette Editor is a dockable dialog; see the section on Dialogs and Docking for help on manipulating it.

15.3.5.4.2 Using the Palette Editor   If you click on a color box in the palette display, GIMP's foreground color will be set to the selected color: you can see this in the Color Area of the Toolbox. If you hold down the **Ctrl** key while clicking, GIMP's background color will be set to the selected color.

If the palette is a custom palette, double-clicking on a color not only sets the foreground, it also brings up a color editor that allows you to modify the selected palette entry.

Right-clicking in the palette display area brings up the Palette Editor menu. It's functions are mainly the same as those of the buttons at the bottom of the dialog.

Below the palette display area, at the left, appears a text entry area that shows the name of the selected color (or "Untitled " if it does not have one). This information has no functional significance, and is present only to serve you as a memory aid.

To the right of the name entry is a spinbutton that allows you to set the number of columns used to display the palette. This only affects the display, not how the palette works. If the value is set to 0, a default will be used.

At the bottom of the dialog are a set of buttons, which mostly match the entries in the Palette Editor menu, accessible by right-clicking in the palette display area. Here are the buttons:

Save This button causes the palette to be saved in your personal `palettes` folder. It would be saved automatically when GIMP exits in any case, but you might want to use this button if you are concerned that GIMP might crash in the meantime.

Revert This operation has not yet been implemented.

Edit Color Pops up a color editor allowing you to alter the color. If the palette is one you aren't allowed to alter, this button will be insensitive. See below

New Color from FG For more information on this button please refer to below.

Delete Color For more information on this button please refer to below.

Zoom Out For more information on this button please refer to below.

Zoom In For more information on this button please refer to below.

Zoom All For more information on this button please refer to below.

15.3.5.5 The Palette Editor pop-menu

Figure 15.58 The Palette Editor pop-menu

The Palette Editor Menu can be accessed by right-clicking on the palette display in the Palette Editor, or by choosing the top entry from the dialog Tab menu. The operations in it can also be executed using the buttons at the bottom of the Palette Editor dialog.

Edit Color "Edit Color" brings up a color editor that allows you to modify the color of the selected palette entry. If the palette is one that you are not allowed to edit (that is, one supplied by GIMP when it is installed), then the menu entry will beinsensitive.

New Color from FG; New Color from BG These commands each create a new palette entry, using either GIMP's current foreground color (as shown in the Color Area of the Toolbox), or the current background color.

Delete Color "Delete Color" removes the selected color entry from the palette. If the palette is one that you are not allowed to edit, then the menu entry will be insensitive.

Zoom Out "Zoom Out" reduces the vertical scale of the entries in the palette display.

Zoom In "Zoom In" increases the vertical scale of the entries in the palette display.

Zoom All "Zoom All" adjusts the vertical size of the entries in the palette display so that the entire palette fits into the display area.

Edit Active Palette When this option is checked (default), you can edit another palette by clicking on it in the "Palettes" dialog.

15.3.6 Tagging

In Brushes, Gradients, Patterns and Palettes dialogs and some other dockable dialogs, you can define tags and then, you can reorganize items according to chosen tags only.

You have two input fields:

Figure 15.59 Tagging

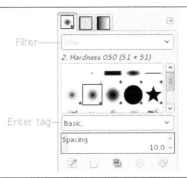

- "Filter" field: There, you can enter a tag previously defined or select a tag in the pop list you get by clicking on the arrow head at the right end of the field. Brushes, gradients, patterns, or palettes are filtered and only these that have this chosen tag will be displayed. You can enter several tags, separated with commas.

- "Enter tag" field: There, tags belonging to the current brush, gradient, pattern, or palette are displayed. You can add another tag to the current item by clicking on one of the defined tag in the pop up list of the field. You can also create your own tag for this item by typing its name in the field. Then the new tag appears in the tag pop up list.

Figure 15.60 Example

In this example, we defined a "green" tag for the Pepper and Vine brushes. Then, we entered "green" in the Filterinput field and so, only brushes with the green tag are displayed.

Tip

 To give several brushes the same tag at once, display brushes in List Mode, and use Ctrl-Mouse Left Button on the brushes you want to select.

You can delete tags: select a brush, then select a tag in the "Enter tag" field and press the **Delete** key. When this tag has been removed from all brushes, it disappears from the list.

15.3.7 Fonts Dialog

Figure 15.61 The Fonts dialog

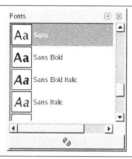

The "Fonts" dialog is used for selecting fonts for the Text tool. It also allows you to refresh the list of available fonts, if you add new ones to your system while GIMP is running.

15.3.7.1 Activating the Dialog

The "Fonts" dialog is a dockable dialog; see the section Section 3.2.3 for help on manipulating it.
You can access it:

- from an image menu: Windows → Dockable Dialogs → Fonts;

- from the Tab menu in any dockable dialog by clicking on ▣ and selecting Add Tab → Fonts,

- from the Tool Options for the Text tool. If you click on the "Font" button, a Font-selector pops up. In the lower right corner is a button that, if pressed, brings up the "Fonts" dialog.

In the Windows menu, there is a list of detached windows which exists only if at least one dialog remains open. In this case, you can raise the "Fonts" dialog from the image-menu: Windows → Fonts.

15.3.7.2 Using the Fonts dialog

The most basic thing you can do is to select a font by clicking on it: this font will then be used by the Text tool. If instead of clicking and releasing, you hold down the left mouse button with the pointer positioned over the font example ("Aa"), a window showing a larger text example will pop up ("Pack my box with five dozen liquor jugs").

Grid/List modes

Figure 15.62 The Fonts dialog

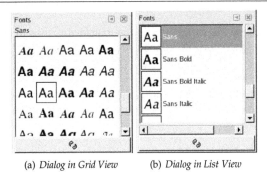

(a) *Dialog in Grid View*   (b) *Dialog in List View*

Tip

 Ctrl-F opens a search field. See View as List; View as Grid

In the Tab menu for the Fonts dialog, you can choose between View as Grid and View as List. In Grid mode, the fonts are laid out in a rectangular array. In List mode, they are lined up vertically, with each row showing an example of the appearance of the font ("Aa"), followed by the name of the font.

 Refresh font list Pressing this button at the bottom of the dialog causes the system font list to be rescanned. This may be useful if you add new fonts while GIMP is running, and want to make them accessible for the Text tool. You can also cause the font list to be rescanned by right-clicking in the font display, and selecting "Rescan Font List" from the menu that pops up (it is actually the only option in the menu).

Tip

 You can change the size of the font previews in the dialog using the "Preview Size" submenu of the dialog's Tab menu.

15.4   Image Management Related Dialogs

15.4.1   Buffers Dialog

Figure 15.63 The Buffers dialog (as a list)

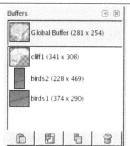

Buffers are temporary repositories for image data, created when you cut or copy part of a drawable (a layer, layer mask, etc.). You can save a document in this buffer in two ways: Edit → Buffer → Copy Named or Edit → Buffer → Cut Named A dialog pops up asking you to name a buffer to store the data in. There is no hard limit on the number of named buffers you can create, although, of course, each one consumes a share of memory.

The "Buffers" dialog shows you the contents of all existing named buffers, and allows you to operate on them in several ways. It also shows you, at the top, the contents of the Global Buffer, but this is merely a display: you can't do anything with it.

> ### Caution
>
> Named buffers are not saved across sessions. The only way to save their contents is to paste them into images.

15.4.1.1   Activating the Dialog

This dialog is a dockable dialog; see the section Section 3.2.3 for help on manipulating it.

You can access it:

- from an image menu: Windows → Dockable Dialogs → Buffers;

- from the Tab menu in any dockable dialog by clicking on ⊲ and selecting Add Tab → Buffers.

In the Windows menu, there is a list of detached windows which exists only if at least one dialog remains open. In this case, you can raise the "Buffers" dialog from the image-menu: Windows → Buffers.

15.4.1.2   Using the Buffers dialog

Figure 15.64 The Buffers Menu

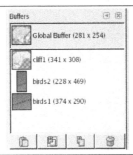

Clicking on a buffer in the display area makes it the active buffer, i. e., the one that will be used for paste commands executed with the Buffers Menu or the buttons at the bottom of the dialog. Double-clicking on a buffer causes its contents to be pasted to the active image as a floating selection; this is a quick way of executing the "Paste Buffer" command.

At the bottom of the dialog are four buttons. The operations they perform can also be accessed from the Buffers Menu that you get by right clicking on the active buffer.

Figure 15.65 The Buffers dialog (Grid View)

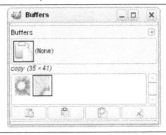

In the Tab menu for the "Buffers" dialog, you can choose between View as Grid and View as List. In Grid mode, the buffers are laid out in a rectangular array. In List mode, they are lined up vertically, with each row showing a thumbnail of the contents of the buffer, its name, and its pixel dimensions.

Tip

  Ctrl-F opens a search field. See View as List; View as Grid

---

You can change the size of the buffer previews in the dialog using the "Preview Size" submenu of the dialog's Tab menu.

15.4.1.2.1   Buttons at the bottom   At the bottom of the dialog you find a couple of buttons:

Paste Buffer This command pastes the contents of the selected buffer into the active image, as a floating selection. The only difference between this and the ordinary Paste command is that it uses the selected buffer rather than the global clipboard buffer.

Paste Buffer Into This command pastes the contents of the selected buffer into the active image's selection, as a floating selection. The only difference between this and the ordinary Paste Into command is that it uses the selected buffer rather than the global clipboard buffer.

Paste Buffer as New This command creates a new single-layer image out of the contents of the selected buffer. The only difference between this and the ordinary Paste as New command is that it uses the selected buffer rather than the content of the global clipboard buffer.

Delete Buffer This command deletes the selected named buffer, no questions asked. You cannot delete the Global Buffer.

Figure 15.66 The "Buffers" context menu

15.4.1.2.2   Context menu   These commands are explained above with Buttons.

15.4.2   Images Dialog

Figure 15.67 The Images dialog

The "Images" Dialog displays the list of open images on your screen; each of them is represented with a thumbnail. This dialog is useful when you have many overlapping images on your screen: thus, you can raise the wanted image to foreground.

15.4.2.1   Activating the dialog

The "Images" dialog is a dockable dialog; see the section Section 3.2.3 for help on manipulating it.
  You can access it:

- from the image menu: Windows → Dockable Dialogs → Images;

- from the Tab menu in any dockable dialog by clicking on  and selecting Add Tab → Images.

In the Windows menu, there is a list of detached windows which exists only if at least one dialog remains open. In this case, you can raise the "Images" dialog from the image-menu: Windows → Images.

15.4.2.2   Using the Images dialog

In multi-window mode, at the top of the dialog, a drop-list of open images appears if the "Show Image Selection" option is checked in the Tab Menu.
  At center, open images appear, as a list or a grid, according to the selected mode. The current image is highlighted in list mode, outlined in grid mode. With a double click on an image name, you raise this image to the foreground of your screen. With a simple click you select this image so that the buttons of the dialog can act on it.

Grid and List modes, preview size In the Tab menu for the "Images" dialog, you can choose between View as Grid and View as List. In Grid mode, the images are laid out in a rectangular array. In List mode, they are lined up vertically, with each row showing a thumbnail of the contents of the image, its name, and its pixel dimensions.

Tip

 Ctrl-F opens a search field. See View as List; View as Grid

You can change the size of the image previews in the dialog using the "Preview Size" submenu of the dialog's Tab menu.

Buttons Three buttons at the bottom of the dialog allow you to operate on the selected image. These buttons are present if the "Show button bar" is checked in the tab dialog. You can get the same commands through the pop menu by right-clicking on the dialog.

Raise this image displays The selected image appears at the foreground of your screen. If this image has another view, this view also is raised but remains behind the original. The same option in the pop-up menu, that you get by right-clicking, is called "Raise views "

Create a new display for this image Duplicates the image window (not the image) of the selected image.

Delete This command works only on a image which is loaded without any window. Though images can be opened by the New Window command, if the image has been already loaded without window by a primitive procedure command (such as gimp-image-new, file-png-load, etc.), it can not be unloaded even if its windows are closed to the last. Then use this command to close it.

15.4.3 Document History Dialog

Figure 15.68 Document History dialog

The History Dialog displays the list of the documents you have opened in previous sessions. It is more complete than the list you get with the "Open Recent" command.

15.4.3.1 Activating the Dialog

The "History" dialog is a dockable dialog; see the section Section 3.2.3 for help on manipulating it. You can access it:

- From an image menu: Windows → Dockable Dialogs → Document History.

- From the Tab menu in any dockable dialog by clicking on ◁ and selecting Add Tab → Document History.

- From the image Menu bar through: File → Open Recent → Document History.

15.4.3.2 Using the Document History dialog

The scroll bar allows you to browse all images you have opened before.

In the Tab menu for the "Document History" dialog, you can choose between View as Grid and View as List. In Grid mode, the documents are laid out in a rectangular array. In List mode, they are lined up vertically, with each row showing a thumbnail of the contents of the image, its name, and its pixel dimensions.

Tip

   Ctrl-F opens a search field. See View as List; View as Grid

---

Use the *Open the selected entry* button or Open Image command of the dialog's context menu, to open the image you have selected. With the **Shift** key pressed, it raises an image hidden behind others. With the **Ctrl** key pressed, it opens the Open Image dialog.

Use the *Remove the selected entry* = button or Remove Entry command of the dialog's context menu, to remove an image from the History dialog. The image is removed from the recently open images list also. But the image itself is not deleted.

Use the *Clear the entire file history* button or Clear History command of the dialog's context menu, to remove all the files from the history.

Use the *Recreate Preview* button or Recreate Preview command of the dialog's context menu, to update preview in case of change. With **Shift** key pressed, it acts on all previews. With **Ctrl** key pressed, previews that correspond to files that can't be found out, are deleted.

15.4.4 Templates Dialog

Figure 15.69 The Templates dialog

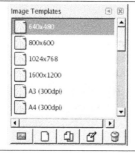

Templates are templates for an image format to be created. GIMP offers you a lot of templates and you can create your owns. When you create a New image, you can access to the list of existing templates but you can't manage them. The "Templates" dialog allows you to manage all these templates.

15.4.4.1 Activating the dialog

The "Templates" dialog is a dockable dialog; see the section Section 3.2.3 for help on manipulating it. You can access it:

- from the image menu: Windows → Dockable Dialogs → Templates.

- from the Tab menu in any dockable dialog by clicking on and selecting Add Tab → Templates.

15.4.4.2 Using the Templates dialog

You select a template by clicking on its icon. Right clicking reveals a local menu that offers the same functions as buttons.

15.4.4.2.1 Grid/List modes In the Tab menu for the "Templates" dialog, you can choose between View as Grid and View as List. In Grid mode, templates are laid out in a rectangular array of identical icons (unless you gave them a particular icon, as we will see later). Only the name of the selected template is displayed. In List mode, they are lined up vertically; icons are identical too; all names are displayed.

In this Tab menu, the Preview Size option allows you to change the size of thumbnails.

Tip

 Ctrl-F in a list view opens a search field. See View as List; View as Grid

---

15.4.4.2.2 Buttons at the bottom The buttons at the bottom of the dialog allow you to operate on templates in several ways:

Create a new image from the selected template Clicking on this button opens the dialog Create a new image on the model of the selected template.

Create a new template Clicking on this button opens the New template dialog, identical to the Edit Template dialog, that we will see below.

Duplicate the selected template Clicking on this button opens the Edit Template dialog that we are going to study now.

Edit the selected template Clicking on this button opens the Edit Template dialog.

Delete the selected template Guess what?

Tip

 Every template is stored in a `templaterc` file at your personal GIMP directory. If you want to restore some deleted templates, you can copy or append template entries to your file from the master `templaterc` file at the `etc/gimp/2.0` directory of the GIMP's system folder.

15.4.4.3 Edit Template

Figure 15.70 The Edit Template dialog

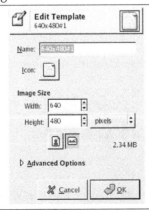

The dialog allows you to set the specifications of the selected template.

You can access this editor by clicking on the Edit Template button at the bottom of the dialog. Options

Name In this text box, you can modify the displayed template name.

Icon By clicking on this icon, you open a list of icons. You can choose one of them to illustrate the selected template name.

Image size Here you set the width and height of the new image. The default units are pixels, but you can switch to some other unit if you prefer, using the adjoining menu. If you do, note that the resulting pixel size will be determined by the X and Y resolution (which you can change in the Advanced Options), and by the setting of "Dot for Dot", which you can change in the View menu.

Note

 Please keep in mind, that every Pixel of an image is stored in the memory. If you're creating large files with a high density of pixels, GIMP will need some time for every function you're applying to the image.

Portrait/Landscape buttons These buttons toggle between Portrait and Landscape mode. Concretely, their effect is to exchange the values for Width and Height. If the X and Y resolutions are different (in Advanced Options), then these values are exchanged also. On the right, image size, image resolution and color space are displayed.

Advanced Options

Figure 15.71 The "Advanced Options" dialog

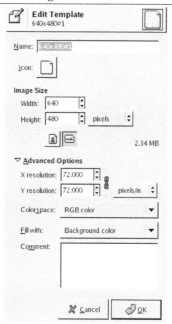

These are options that will mainly be of interest to more advanced users.

X and Y resolution These values come into play mainly in relation to printing: they do not affect the size of the image in pixels, but they determine its size on paper when printed. They can also affect the way the image is displayed on the monitor: if "Dot for Dot" is switched off in the View menu, then at 100% zoom, GIMP attempts to display the image on the monitor at the correct physical size, as calculated from the pixel dimensions and the resolution. The display may not be accurate, however, unless the monitor has been calibrated. This can be done either when GIMP is installed, or from the Display tab of the Preferences dialog.

Colorspace You can create the new image as either an RGB image or a grayscale image. You cannot create an indexed image directly in this way, but of course nothing prevents you from converting the image to indexed mode after it has been created.

Fill You have four choices for the solid color that will fill the new image's background layer:

- Foreground color, as shown in the Main Toolbox.
- Background color, as shown in the Main Toolbox.
- White, the more often used.
- Transparent. If this option is chosen, then the Background layer in the new image will be created with an alpha channel; otherwise not.

Comment You can write a descriptive comment here. The text will be attached to the image as a "parasite", and will be saved along with the image by some file formats (but not all of them).

15.5 Misc. Dialogs

15.5.1 Tool Presets Dialog

In GIMP-2.6, tool presets were not easy to use. You had to click on a tool first, and then click on the Restore Presets... button in the button bar at the bottom of the Tool options dialog... if you had not disabled this button bar in the Tab menu to make place on your desk! Now, with GIMP-2.8, a dockable Tool Presets Dialog is available where you just have to click on a preset to open the corresponding tool with its saved options.

Figure 15.72 The Tool Presets Dialog

15.5.1.1 Activating the Dialog

The "Tool Presets Dialog" is a dockable dialog; see the section Section 3.2.3 for help on manipulating it. You can access it:

- from an image menu: Windows → Dockable Dialogs → Tool Presets;
- or, as a tab in Toolbox window, through Tab Menu → Add Tab → Tool Presets.

15.5.1.2 Using the Tool Presets Dialog

This dialog comes with a list of predefined presets. Each of them has an icon representing the tool presets will be applied to and a name.

Presets can be tagged so that you can arrange presets display as you want. Please see Section 15.3.6 for more information about tagging.

Double-clicking on a preset icon opens the Tool Preset Editor.
Double-clicking on preset name allows you to edit this name.
At the bottom of the dialog appear four buttons:

- Edit this tool preset: clicking on this button opens the Tool Preset Editor for the selected preset. You can actually edit presets you have created; predefined presets options are all grayed out and inactive. But you can create a new preset from a predefined preset and edit its options.

The Tool Preset Editor is described in Section 15.5.2.

- Create a new tool preset: before clicking on this button, you can either select an existing preset, or select a tool in Toolbox, for example the Healing Tool which is not in the presets list. A new preset is created at the top of the dialog and the Tool Preset Editor is opened. Please see Section 15.5.2.

- Delete this tool preset: this button is active only for presets you have created.

- Refresh tool presets: If you have added a preset manually in gimp/2.0/tool-presets folder, you have to click on this button to include it in the presets list.

Note

 With GIMP-2.8, tool presets are saved in a new format (.gtp). To use your 2.6 presets, you have to convert them using http://wiki.gimp.org/index.php/Mindstorm:Preset_converter, until it is included in GIMP.

15.5.1.3   The Tool Presets Dialog Context Menu

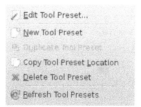

Right-clicking on the Presets Dialog opens a context menu where you find some commands already described with buttons: Edit tool preset, New tool preset, Refresh tool presets. You also find two new commands:

- Duplicate Tool Preset: this command is always disabled. It is not necessary since, as we saw above, a duplicate is automatically created when you create a new preset from an existing preset.

- Copy Tool Preset Location: this command copies the path to the tool preset file into clipboard.

15.5.2   Tool Preset Editor

Figure 15.73 The Tool Preset Editor

15.5.2.1   Activating the Dialog

You can access this dialog through:

- a click on the Edit this tool preset button in the button bar of the Tool Presets Dialog.

- a double-click on a preset icon in the Tool Presets Dialog.

- a right-click on a preset in the Tool Presets Dialog to open a context menu and then click on the Edit Tool Preset command.

15.5.2.2   Using the Tool Preset Editor

You can edit presets you have created only; all options of predefined presets are grayed out and disabled. In this dialog you can:

- **edit preset name** in text box,

- **change preset icon** by clicking on preset icon. This opens a window where you can choose a new icon.

- **select resources to be saved** by clicking on check boxes.

15.5.3   Device Status Dialog

Figure 15.74 The "Device Status" Dialog

This window gathers together the current options of Toolbox, for each of your input devices: the mouse (named "Core pointer") or either the tablet, if you have one. These options are represented by icons: foreground and background colors, brush, pattern and gradient. Excepted for colors, clicking on an icon opens the window which lets you select another option; the tool-box will be updated when changing. You can drag and drop items to this dialog.

The "Save device status" button ▒ at the bottom of the window, seems to have the same action as the "Record device status now" option in the Input Devices section in preferences.

15.5.3.1 Activating the Dialog

The device status dialog is a dockable dialog; see the section Section 3.2.3 for help on manipulating it. It can be activated in two ways:

- From an image menu : Windows → Dockable Dialogs → Device Status.

- From the Tab menu in any dialog : Add a Dock → Device Status

15.5.4 Error Console

The Error console offers more possibilities than the single "GIMP Message". This is a log of all errors occurring while GIMP is running. You can save all this log or only a selected part.

15.5.4.1 Activating the Dialog

The "Error Console" dialog is a dockable dialog; see the section Section 3.2.3 for help on manipulating it.

You can access it:

- from an image menu: Windows → Dockable Dialogs → Error Console;

- from the Tab menu in any dockable dialog by clicking on ◁ and selecting Add Tab → Error Console.

15.5.4.2 The "Error Console" Dialog

Figure 15.75 "Error Console" Dialog window

Clear errors This button lets you delete all errors in the log.

Save all errors This button lets you save the whole log. You can also select a part of the log (by click-and-dragging the mouse pointer or by using the Shift-arrow keys key combination) and save only this selected part by pressing the **Shift** key.

A dialog window Save Error Log to File lets you choose the name and the destination directory of this file:

Figure 15.76 "Save Error Log to file" Dialog window

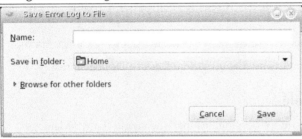

> ### Tip
>
> You will as well find these button actions in the dialog tab menu by clicking on ,
> or in the context menu you get by right-clicking on the dialog window.

15.5.5 Save File

The Save command saves your image to disk. With GIMP-2.8, this command saves in XCF format only. If you try to save to a format other than XCF, you get an error message:

Starting from GIMP-2.8.8, the error dialog sports a link that jumps directly to the export command dialog. Please see Section 6.1.1.

If you have already saved the image, the previous image file is overwritten with the current version. If you have not already saved the image, the Save command opens the Save Image dialog.

If you quit without having saved your image, GIMP asks you if you really want to do so, if the "Confirm closing of unsaved images" option is checked in the Environment page of the Preferences dialog.

Figure 15.77 Save Image Dialog

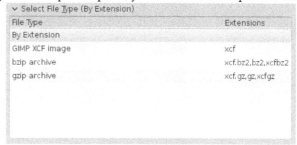

15.5.5.1 Activate the Dialog

- You can access this command in the image menu bar through File → Save,

- or from the keyboard by using the shortcut Ctrl-S.

- Use Ctrl-Shift-S to save the opened image with a different name.

15.5.5.2 The Save Image Dialog

With this file browser, you can edit filename directly in name box (default is "Untitled.xcf") or by selecting a file in name list. We repeat that only XCF format is permitted. You must also fix the image destination in Save in Folder. You can create a new folder if necessary.

Select File Type If you develop this option, you can select a compressed format for your XCF file:

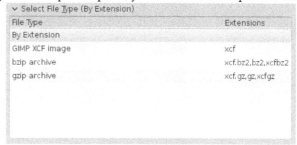

15.5.6 Export File

With GIMP-2.8, the Save command saves images in XCF format only. The Export command is now used to store images to various file formats.

You can access to this command through File → Export As..., or from the keyboard by using the shortcut Ctrl-Shift-E.

Figure 15.78 Export Image Dialog

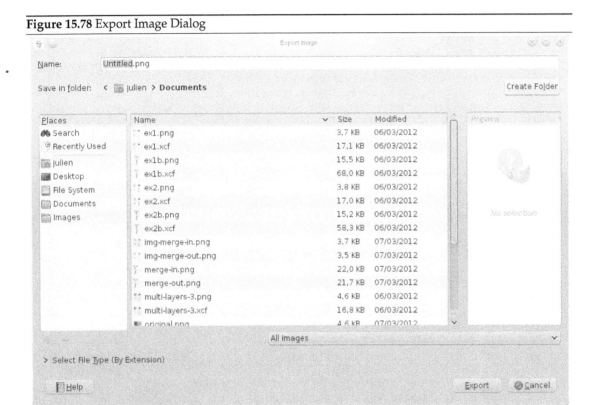

15.5.6.1 The Export Image Dialog

With this file browser, you can edit filename and extension directly in name box (default is "Untitled.png") or by selecting a file in name list. You must also fix the image destination in Save in Folder. You can create a new folder if necessary.

Select File Type If you develop this option, you can select an extension in the drop-down list for your file:

File formats dialogs are described in Section 6.1.

15.5.6.2 Exporting

When file name and destination are set, click on Export. This opens the export dialog for the specified file format.

If you have loaded a non-XCF file, a new item appears in File menu, allowing you to to export file in the same format, overwriting the original file.

If you modify an image that you already have exported, the **Export** command in File menu is changed, allowing you to export file again in the same format.

15.5.7   Sample Points Dialog

While the Color Picker can display color information about one pixel, the "Sample Points" dialog can display the data of four pixels of the active layer or the image, at the same time. Another important difference is that the values of these points are changed in real time as you are working on the image.

15.5.7.1   Activating the dialog

The "Sample Points" dialog is a dockable dialog; see the section Section 3.2.3 for help on manipulating it.

You can access it:

- from the image menu: Windows → Dockable Dialogs → Sample Points.

- from the Tab menu in any dockable dialog by clicking on ◁ and selecting Add Tab → Sample Points.

15.5.7.2   Using sample points

To create a sample point, **Ctrl**-click on one of the two measure rules of the image window and drag the mouse pointer. Two perpendicular guides appear. The sample point is where both guides intersect. You can see its coordinates in the lower left corner and the information bar of the image window. Release the mouse button.

The reticle you get Ctrl + click-and-dragging from a rule.

By default, this sample point comes with a round mark and an order number. You can cancel these marks by unchecking the Show Sample Points option in the View menu.

The "Sample Points" dialog should automatically open when you create a sample point. This is not the case; you have to open it manually.

You can delete a sample point, as you do with guides, by click-and-dragging it up to a rule. Order numbers are automatically re-arranged in the dialog window; the most recent are moved one rank up.

By default, sampling is performed on all layers. If you want to sample on the active layer only, uncheck the Sample merged option in the tab menu:

Figure 15.79 The "Sample Point" menu

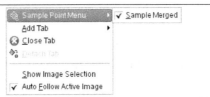

15.5.7.3 "Sample Points" dialog description

Figure 15.80 Sample points dialog

The information about four sample points is displayed in this window. You can create more, which will be existing and not shown. To show them, you have to delete displayed points.

The color of the sampled point is displayed in a swatch box.

In the drop-down list, you can choose between:

Pixel This choice displays the *Red, Green, Blue* and *Alpha* values of the pixel, as numbers between 0 and 255.

RGB This choice displays the *Red, Green, Blue* and *Alpha* values of the pixel, as percentages. It also shows the hexadecimal value of the pixel's color.

HSV This choice displays the *Hue*, in degrees, as well as the *Saturation, Value* and *Alpha* of the pixel, as percentages.

CMYK This choice displays the *Cyan, Magenta, Yellow, Black* and *Alpha* values of the pixel, as percentages.

Data are supplied for every channel in the chosen color model. The Alpha is present only if the image holds an Alpha channel.

Hexa appears only with the RGB mode. That's the hexadecimal code of the HTML Notation.

15.5.8 Pointer Dialog

Figure 15.81 Pointer dialog

This dialog offers you, in a same window, in real time, the position of the mouse pointer, and the channel values of the pointed pixel, in the chosen color model.

15.5.8.1 Activating the dialog

The "Pointer" dialog is a dockable dialog; see the section Section 3.2.3 for help on manipulating it. You can access it:

- from the image menu: Windows → Dockable Dialogs → Pointer.

- from the Tab menu in any dockable dialog by clicking on ◁ and selecting Add Tab → Pointer.

15.5.8.2 "Pointer" dialog options

Pixels Shows the position of the pointed pixel, in X (horizontal) and Y (vertical) coordinates, stated in pixels from the origin (the upper left corner of the canvas).

Units Shows the distance from the origin, in inches.

Pointer Bounding Box This information is active when a selection exists. X and Y are the coordinates of the upper left corner of the rectangular frame that bounds rectangular and ellipse selections. H and W are the height and width of this box.

This information also exits for the other selections, but they are of less interest and the bounding box is not visible.

This information concerning the selection remains unchanged when you use another tool, while pointer coordinates vary.

Channel values The channel values for the selected color model are shown below. Both pulldown menus contain the same choices, which makes it easier for you to compare the color values of a particular pixel using different color models. "Hex" is the HTML Notation of the pixel color, in hexadecimal. The choices on the pulldown menus are (Pixel is the default):

Pixel The RGB channel values. This choice displays the *Red, Green, Blue* and *Alpha* values of the pixel, as numbers between 0 and 255.

RGB The RGB channel values. This choice displays the *Red, Green, Blue* and *Alpha* values of the pixel, as percentages. It also shows the hexadecimal value of the pixel's color.

HSV The HSV components. This choice displays the *Hue*, in degrees, as well as the *Saturation, Value* and *Alpha* of the pixel, as percentages.

CMYK The CMYK channel values. This choice displays the *Cyan, Magenta, Yellow, Black* and *Alpha* values of the pixel, as percentages.

Sample Merged If this option is checked (default), sampling is performed on all layers. If it is unchecked, sampling is performed on the active layer only.

Chapter 16

Menus

16.1 Introduction to Menus

There are many places in GIMP where you can find menus. The aim of this chapter is to explain all the commands that are accessible from the image menu bar and the image menu you can get by right clicking in the canvas. All the context menus and the menu entries for the other dialogs are described elsewhere in the chapters that describe the dialogs themselves.

16.1.1 The Image Menu Bar

This menu bar may contain other entries if you have added script-fus, python-fus or videos to your GIMP.

16.1.2 Context Menus

If you right-click on certain parts of the GIMP interface, a "context menu" opens, which leads to a variety of functions. Some places where you can access context menus are:

- Clicking on an image window displays the Image menu. This is useful when you are working in full-screen mode, without a menubar.

- Clicking on a layer in the Layers Dialog or on a channel in the Channels Dialog displays functions for the selected layer or channel.

- Right-clicking on the image menubar has the same effect as left-clicking.

- Right-clicking on the title bar displays functions which do not belong to GIMP, but to the window manager program on your computer.

16.1.3 Tear-off menus

There is an interesting property associated with some of the menus in GIMP. These are any of the menus from the Image context menu you get by right-clicking on the canvas and any of its submenus. (You can tell that a menu item leads to a submenu because there is an ▶ icon next to it.) When you bring up any of these menus, there is a dotted line at the top of it (tear-off line). By clicking on this dotted line, you detach the menu under it and it becomes a separate window.

Figure 16.1 The "windows" submenu and its tear-off submenu

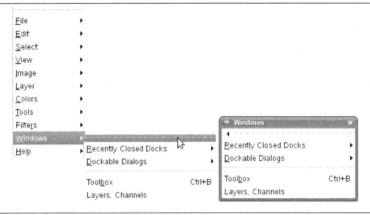

Tear-off menus are actually independent. They are always visible, their functions always apply to the current image, and they persist when all of the images are closed. You can close a tear-off submenu by clicking on the dotted line again or closing the window from the window manager on your computer (often by clicking on an X icon in the upper right corner of the window).

These tear-off submenus are also created in single-window mode, but are of less interest since they are masked by the window as soon as you click on it.

16.1.4   Tab menus

The following type of menus is not related to the image menu bar, but for the sake of completeness:

Every dockable dialog contains a Tab Menu button, as highlighted below. Pressing this Tab Menu button opens a special menu of tab-related operations, with an entry at the top that opens into the dialog's context menu.

Figure 16.2 A dockable dialog.

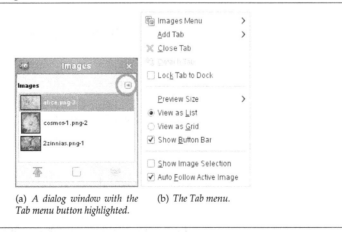

(a) *A dialog window with the Tab menu button highlighted.*   (b) *The Tab menu.*

See Section 3.2.3.2 to learn more about Tab menus.

16.2   The "File" Menu

16.2.1   Overview

Figure 16.3 The File menu

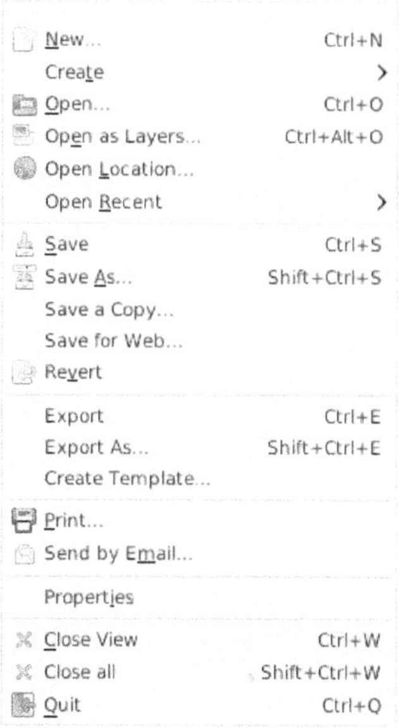

New...	Ctrl+N
Create	>
Open...	Ctrl+O
Open as Layers...	Ctrl+Alt+O
Open Location...	
Open Recent	>
Save	Ctrl+S
Save As...	Shift+Ctrl+S
Save a Copy...	
Save for Web...	
Revert	
Export	Ctrl+E
Export As...	Shift+Ctrl+E
Create Template...	
Print...	
Send by Email...	
Properties	
Close View	Ctrl+W
Close all	Shift+Ctrl+W
Quit	Ctrl+Q

> **Note**
>
> Besides the commands described here, you may also find other entries in the menu. They are not part of GIMP itself, but have been added by extensions (plug-ins). You can find information about the functionality of a Plugin by referring to its documentation.

16.2.2   New...

Using the "Create a New Image" dialog, you can create a new empty image and set its properties. The image is shown in a new image window. You may have more than one image on your screen at the same time.

16.2.2.1   Activate the command

- You can access the command in the Image menu through: File → New...,

- or by using the keyboard shortcut Ctrl-N.

16.2.2.2   Basic Options

Figure 16.4 The "Create a New Image" dialog

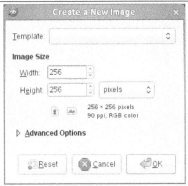

Template

Figure 16.5 The "Template" dialog

Rather than entering all the values by hand, you can select some predefined values for your image from a menu of templates, which represent image types that are somewhat commonly useful. The templates set values for the size, resolution, comments, etc. If there is a particular image shape that you use often and it does not appear on the list, you can create a new template, using the Templates dialog.

Image Size Here you set the Width and Height of the new image. The default units are pixels, but you can choose a different unit if you prefer, using the adjoining menu. If you do, note that the resulting pixel size is determined by the X and Y resolution (which you can change in the Advanced Options), and by setting "Dot for Dot" in the View menu.

If no image is open, the "New" image is opened in the empty image window, with the default size you have determined. If you open the "New" image when another is open (or has been), then it is opened in another window, with the same size as the first image.

Note

 Keep in mind that every pixel of an image is stored in memory. If you create large files with a high pixel density, GIMP will need a lot of time and memory for every function you apply to the image.

Portrait/Landscape buttons There are two buttons which toggle between Portrait and Landscape mode. What they actually do is to exchange the values for Width and Height. (If the Width and Height are the same, these buttons are not activated.) If the X and Y resolutions are not the same (which you can set in Advanced Options), then these values are also exchanged. On the right of the dialog, image size, screen resolution and color space are displayed.

16.2.2.3 Advanced Options

Figure 16.6 New Image dialog (Advanced Options)

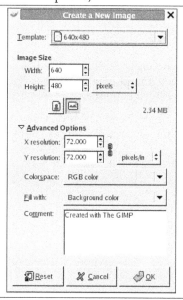

The Advanced Options are mostly of interest to more advanced GIMP users. You can display these options by clicking on the small triangle on the lower edge of the dialog window.

X and Y resolution The values in the X resolution and Y resolution fields relate mainly to printing: they do not affect the size of the image in pixels, but they may determine its physical size when it is printed. The X and Y resolution values can determine how pixels are translated into other measurement units, such as millimeters or inches.

Tip

 If you want to display the image on the screen at the correct dimensions, select View → Dot for Dot Set the zoom factor to 100% to see the image at its true screen size. The calibration of the screen size is normally done when GIMP is installed, but if the image does not display at the correct size, you may have to adjust the screen parameters in the GIMP. You can do this in the Preferences dialog.

Colorspace You can create the new image in different color modes, as either an RGB image or a grayscale image.

RGB color The image is created in the Red, Green, Blue color system, which is the one used by your monitor or your television screen.

Grayscale The image is created in black and white, with various shades of gray. Aside from your artistic interests, this type of image may be necessary for some plug-ins. Nevertheless, the GIMP allows you to change an RGB image into grayscale, if you would like.

You cannot create an indexed image directly with this menu, but of course you can always convert the image to indexed mode after it has been created. To do that, use the Image → Mode → Indexed command.

Fill Here, you specify the background color that is used for your new image. It is certainly possible to change the background of an image later, too. You can find more information about doing that in the Layer dialog.

There are several choices:

- Fill the image with the current Foreground color, shown in the Toolbox.
  Note that you can change the foreground color while the "New Image" dialog window is open.
- Fill the image with the current Background color, shown in the Toolbox. (You can change the background color too, while the dialog window is open.)
- Fill the image with White.
- Fill the image with Transparency. If you choose this option, the image is created with an alpha channel and the background is transparent. The transparent parts of the image are then displayed with a checkered pattern, to indicate the transparency.

You can write a descriptive comment here. The text is attached to the image as a parasite, and is saved with the image by some file formats (PNG, JPEG, GIF).

Note

 You can view and edit this comment in the Image Properties dialog.

16.2.3 Create

Figure 16.7 The "Create" submenu

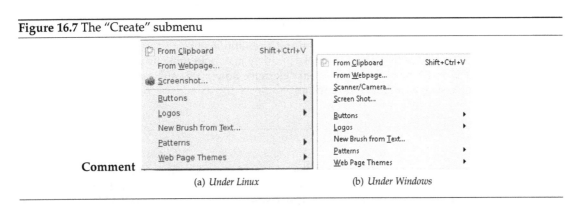

(a) *Under Linux*   (b) *Under Windows*

This menu item replaces the "Acquire" menu which existed in GIMP previous versions in the Toolbox Menu and contains a lot of logos, buttons, patterns...

These commands vary somewhat, depending upon your system, since the GIMP makes calls to system functions.

16.2.3.1   Activate the Submenu

- You can access this submenu from the Image menu bar through File → Create

16.2.3.2   From Clipboard

When you copy a selection, it goes into the clipboard. Then you can create a new image with it.

This command has the same action as the Paste as new command.

The **Print Screen** keyboard key captures the screen and puts it in the clipboard. This command has the same action as "taking a screenshot of the entire screen" in the Screenshot dialog window. The Alt-Print Screen key combination grabs the active window in the screen with its decorations and puts it in the clipboard.

16.2.3.3   From Web page

This command opens a dialog where you can enter the URL of a Web page and get the image in GIMP.

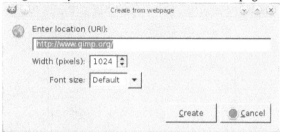

The command defaults to gimp.org. Please have a try to it.

16.2.3.4   Screenshot

Figure 16.8 The "Screenshot" window

The Screenshot command opens a dialog with two parts:

Area

> **Take a screenshot of a single window**   The mouse pointer becomes a cross. Click in the image window you want to capture. A new image is created. If the Include window decoration option is unchecked, the title bar and the blue frame around the image will be removed.

> **Take a screenshot of the entire screen**   This is useful if you want to capture a pop menu. A delay is then necessary, so that you have time to pull the pop menu down.

> If the Include mouse pointer option is checked, then the mouse pointer and its coming with icon are also captured. The mouse pointer is captured in a separate layer. So you can move it to another place in the image.

403

Select a region to grab The mouse pointer becomes a cross. Click and drag to create a rectangular selection in the image window. This selection will be opened as a new image. Its size is adapted to the selection size.

Delay When taking a screenshot of the entire screen, the screen is captured after this delay. In the other cases, the mouse pointer turns to a cross after this delay.

16.2.3.5   Scanner/Camera

This item is present in Windows operating system, using TWAIN. Image input devices appear in dialog if they are plugged-in.

Figure 16.9 Scanner and Camera

The kinds of devices used to take pictures are too varied to be described here. Fortunately, their use is fairly intuitive. In the example shown (under Windows 7), you can start a scanner or load an image from a camera card.

16.2.3.6   Buttons, Logos, Patterns, Web Page Themes

An impressive list of Script-Fus. Have a look at it!

16.2.3.7   New brush from text...

TODO (this command fails on my system)

16.2.4   Open...

The Open... command activates a dialog that lets you load an existing image from your hard-drive or an external medium. For alternative, and sometimes more convenient, ways of opening files, see the following commands (Section 16.2.5 etc.).

16.2.4.1   Activate Dialog

- You can access the Open dialog from an image window through: File → Open....

- You can also open this dialog by using the keyboard shortcut Ctrl-O.

16.2.4.2   File browsing

Figure 16.10 The Open Image Dialog

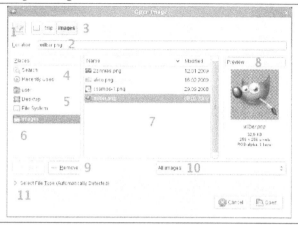

This browser looks like other browsers and it is mostly self-explanatory. It has some particuliar features nevertheless.

1. The button Type a file name toggles between add and remove the Location text box.

   The Ctrl-L key combination has the same action as this button.

2. In the Location text box you can type a path to an image file. If you don't type any path, the name of the selected file will be displayed. You can also type the first letters of the name: it will be auto-completed and a list of file names beginning with these letters will be displayed.

   When you search for a file or directory using the Search feature (see below, item 4), the label changes to Search and you can enter the name in this text box.

3. The path to the current folder is displayed. You can navigate along this path by clicking on an element.

4. With Search you can look for a file (or directory), even if you don't know the exact name of that file. Click on Search, type a file name or just a part of a file name in the text box above, and press **Enter**. Then the central frame (7) will list all files and directories of your home directory with names containing the text you typed in. Unfortunately you can't restrict the results to files of a specified type (10).

   Recently used is self-explanatory.

5. Here, you can access to your main folders and to your store devices.

6. Here, you can add bookmarks to folders, by using the Add or the Add to Bookmarks option you get by right-clicking a folder in the central panel, and also remove them.

7. The contents of the selected folder is displayed here. Change your current folder by double left clicking on a folder in this panel. Select a file with a single left click. You can then open the file you have selected by clicking on the Open button. A double left click opens the file directly. Please note that you can open image files only.

   Right-clicking a folder name opens a context menu:

The folder context menu

8. The selected image is displayed in the Preview window. If it is an image created by GIMP, file size, resolution and image composition are displayed below the preview window.

> **Tip**
>
> If your image has been modified by another program, click on the Preview window to update it.

9. By clicking the Add button, you add the selected folder to bookmarks.

   By clicking the Remove, you remove the selected bookmark from the list.

10. You will generally prefer to display the names of All images. You can also select All files. You can also limit yourself to a particular type of image (GIF, JPG, PNG ...).

11. Select File Type: In most cases you don't need to pay any attention to this, because GIMP can determine the file type automatically. In a few rare situations, neither the file extension nor internal information in the file are enough to tell GIMP the file type. If this happens, you can set it by selecting it from the list.

16.2.5   Open as Layers...

The Open Image as layers command opens the Open Image dialog. The layers of the selected file are added to the current image as the top layers in the stack.

16.2.5.1   Activate Command

- You can access this command from the image menubar through File → Open as layers...,

- or by using the keyboard shortcut Ctrl-Alt-O.

16.2.6   Open Location...

This command opens the "Open Location" dialog that lets you load an image from a network location, specified by a URI, in any of the formats that GIMP supports.

16.2.6.1   Activate Command

- You can access this command from the Toolbox menubar or the image menubar through File → Open Location....

16.2.6.2   Description of the dialog window

Figure 16.11 The "Open Location" dialog window

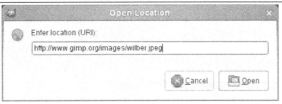

The most typical schemes to open images with are:

file:// to open an image from a local drive

   You can omit the "file://" prefix and open images simply by putting an absolute or relative path and filename in here.

The default base directory for relative paths depends on your operating system. It is typically
`/home/<username>/` on Linux, `C:\\Documents and                Settings\\<username>`
`\\My Documents\\My Images\\` on Windows and `/Users/<username>/` on Mac OS X.

ftp:// to open an image from a ftp server

http:// to load an image from a website

Tip

When you are visiting an Internet site, you can right-click on an image and choose "Copy link address" in the drop-down menu. Then paste it in the "Open Location" dialog to open it in GIMP.

Even if this command makes it very easy to grab images from web sites: *Please respect the copyright! Images, even if published on the Internet are not always free to be used for you.*

16.2.7 Open Recent

Selecting Open Recent displays a submenu with the names of the files that you have opened recently in GIMP. Simply click on a name to reopen it. See the Document History dialog at the bottom of the Open Recent submenu, if you cannot find your image.

16.2.7.1 Activate Command

- You can access this command from the image menubar through File → Open Recent,

16.2.8 Save

This command opens Section 15.5.5.

16.2.9 Save as...

The Save as command displays the "Save Image" dialog. Since GIMP-2.8, the file is automatically saved in the XCF format and you can't *save* in another file format (for this, you have to *export* the file). The Save as dialog allows you to save with another name and/or to another folder.

16.2.9.1 Activating the Command

- You can access this command from the image menubar through File → Save As...,

- or by using the keyboard shortcut Shift-Ctrl-S.

16.2.9.2   The "Save Image" dialog

Figure 16.12 The "Save Image" dialog

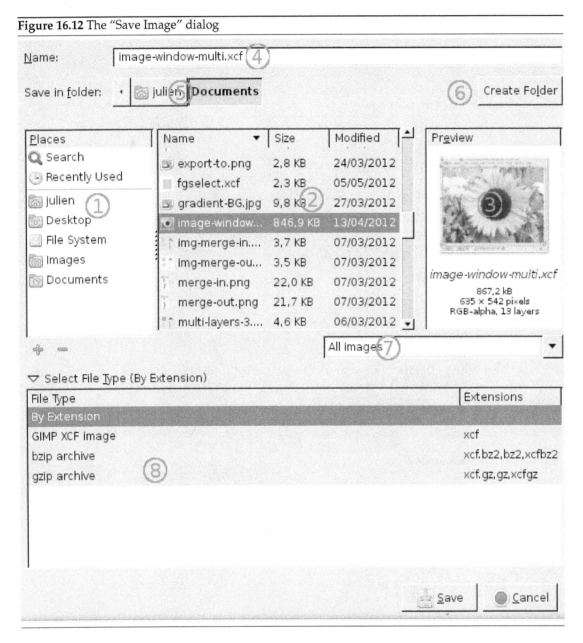

1. The left panel is divided into two parts. The upper part lists your main directories and your storage devices; you cannot modify this list. The lower part lists your bookmarks; you can add or remove *bookmarks*. To add a bookmark, select a directory or a file in the middle panel and click on the Add button at the bottom of the left panel. You can also use the Add to bookmarks command in the context menu, which you get by clicking the right mouse button. You can delete a bookmark by selecting it and clicking on the Remove button.

2. The middle panel displays a list of the files in the current directory. Change your current directory by double left-clicking on a directory in this panel. Select a file with a single left click. You can then save to the file you have selected by clicking on the Save button. Note that a double left click saves the file directly.

   You can right click on the middle panel to access the *Show Hidden Files* command.

3. The selected image is displayed in the Preview window. File size, resolution and image composition are displayed below the preview window.

If your image has been modified by another program, click on the preview to update it.

4. Enter the filename of the new image file here.

> ### Note
>
> If the image has already been saved, GIMP suggests the same filename to you. If you click on *Save*, the file is overwritten.

5. Above the middle panel, the path of the current directory is displayed. You can navigate along this path by clicking on one of the buttons.

6. If you want to save the image into a folder that doesn't yet exist, you can create it by clicking on Create Folder and following the instructions.

7. This button shows All Images by default. This means that all images will be displayed in the middle panel, whatever their file type. By developing this list, you can choose to show only one type of file.

8. At Select File Type, you can select a compressed format for your XCF file.

16.2.10   Save a Copy...

The Save a Copy command does the same thing as the Save command, but with one important difference. It always asks for a file name and saves the image into the XCF file format, but it does not change the name of the active image or mark it as "clean". As a result, if you try to delete the image, or exit from GIMP, you are informed that the image is "dirty" and given an opportunity to save it.

This command is useful when you want to save a copy of your image in its current state, but continue to work with the original file without interruption.

16.2.10.1   Activate Command

- You can access this command from the image menubar through File → Save a Copy.... There is no default keyboard shortcut.

16.2.11   Revert

The Revert command reloads the image from disk, so that it looks just like it did the last time it was saved — unless, that is, you or some application other than GIMP have modified the image file, in which case, the new contents are loaded.

> ### Warning
>
> When GIMP reverts a file, it actually closes the existing image and creates a new image. Because of this, reverting an image is not undoable, and causes the undo history of the image to be lost. GIMP tries to protect you from losing your work in this way by asking you to confirm that you really want to revert the image.

16.2.11.1   Activate Command

- You can access this command from the image menubar through File → Revert. There is no default keyboard shortcut.

16.2.12 Export...

This command is called "Export" for a native XCF file. Then, it does the same thing as **Export As...**.
At early GIMP 2.8 releases, this menu label was "Export to". Since the version 2.8.10, "Export to" and "Export" have been renamed to "Export" and "Export As" after the manner of "Save" and "Save As".

The name becomes "Overwriting name.extension" for an imported image. So, you can export the imported image directly in its original file format, without going through the export dialog.

16.2.13 Export As...

The **Export As...** command allows you to store your image in a format other than XCF.

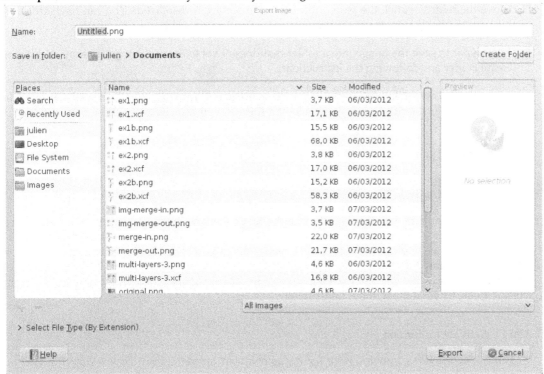

Note

 Please refer to Section 6.1 for information about exporting in different file formats.

16.2.13.1 Activating the Command

- You can access this command from the image menubar through File → Export As...,

- or by using the keyboard shortcut Shift-Ctrl-E.

16.2.14 Create Template...

The Create Template... command opens the "Create New Template" dialog that allows you to create a template with the same dimensions and color space as the current image. A dialog pops up, which asks you to name the new template. Then the template is saved and becomes available in the New Image dialog. If you give a name that already exists, GIMP generates a unique name by appending a number to it. You can use the Templates dialog to modify or delete templates.

16.2.14.1 Activating the Command

- You can access this command from the image menu through File → Create Template.... There is no default keyboard shortcut.

16.2.15 Print

Since the 2.4.0 release, GIMP has its own printing module. You can set page and image up. A preview button allows you to verify the result before printing.

Figure 16.13 The "Print" dialog

Note
See Printing your photos.

16.2.15.1 Activate Command

You can access this command from the image menubar through File → Print, or by using Ctrl-P.

16.2.16 Close

The Close command closes the active image.It is disabled if no image is open.

Closing an image is not undoable: once it is closed, everything is gone, including the undo history. If the image is not "clean" — that is, if you have changed it since the last time you saved it — you are asked to confirm that you really want to close it. Note that an image is marked as clean when it is saved to a file, even if the file format chosen does not preserve all the information in the image, so it is a good idea to think for a moment about what you are doing before closing an image. If there is the slightest possibility that you will regret it, save the file (automatically in the XCF file format since GIMP-2.8).

16.2.16.1 Activating the Command

- You can access this command from the image menu through File → Close,

- or by using the keyboard shortcut Ctrl-W.

- For most systems on which the GIMP runs, you can also execute it by clicking on a "Close" button somewhere on the image window titlebar. The location and appearance of this button are determined by the windowing system and the window manager. If no image is open, clicking on this button closes GIMP.

16.2.17 Close all

This command closes all images you have opened.

16.2.17.1 Activate the Command

- You can access this command from the image menubar through File → Close All,

- or by using the keyboard shortcut Shift-Ctrl-W.

16.2.18 Quit

The Quit command causes GIMP to close all images and exit. If there are any open images which contain unsaved changes (that is, they are not marked as "clean"), GIMP notifies you and displays a list of the unsaved images. You can then choose which images you would like to save, or you can cancel the command. Note that if you have a large number of images open, or are using a large part of the RAM on your system, it may take a little while for everything to shut down.

16.2.18.1 Activate Command

- You can access this command from the image menubar through File → Quit,

- or by using the keyboard shortcut Ctrl-Q.

- For most systems on which the GIMP runs, you can also execute it by clicking on a "Close" button somewhere on the main image window's titlebar. The location and appearance of this button are determined by the windowing system and the window manager. Clicking on this button closes GIMP when no image is open.

16.3 The "Edit" Menu

16.3.1 "Edit" Menu Entries

Figure 16.14 Contents of the Edit Menu

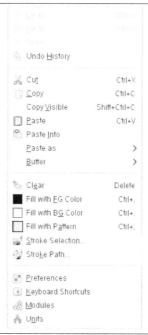

In this section, you will find help for commands in the Edit menu item.

> **Note**
>
> Besides the commands described here, you may also find other entries in the menu. They are not part of GIMP itself, but have been added by extensions (plug-ins). You can find information about the functionality of a Plugin by referring to its documentation.

16.3.2 Undo

If you have made drawing or editing changes to the image which you don't want to keep, the Undo command allows you to undo the last change and return the image to its previous state. Almost anything you do to an image can be undone in this way (with the exception of scripts, which deactivate this function). Further Undo operations may be performed, depending upon the number of Undo levels configured in the Environment page of the Preferences Dialog. See the section on Undoing for more information about GIMP's very sophisticated "Undo" functions.

The operation that has been "undone" is not lost immediately: you can get it back by using the Redo command right away. But if you perform another operation, the ability to "Redo" will be irretrievably lost.

16.3.2.1 Activate the Command

- You can access this command from the image menubar through Edit → Undo,

- by using the keyboard shortcut Ctrl-Z,

- or by simply clicking on the status you want in the Undo History dialog.

16.3.3 Redo

The Redo command reverses the effects of the Undo command. Each "Undo" action can be reversed by a single "Redo" action. You can alternate "Undo" and "Redo" as many times as you like. Note that you can only "Redo" an operation if the last action you did was an "Undo". If you perform any operation on the image after Undoing something, then the former Redo steps are lost, and there is no way to recover them. See the Undoing section for more information.

To see the operations which you have done and undone, use the Undo History dialog.

16.3.3.1 Activating the Command

- You can access this command from the image menubar through Edit → Redo,

- by using the keyboard shortcut Ctrl-Y,

- or by simply clicking on the status you want in the Undo History dialog.

16.3.4 Fade

This command is usually grayed out. It becomes active if you use the Fill function or the Blend tool, or if you apply some filters.

It allows you to modify the paint mode and opacity of the *last* drawable operation (Fill, Blend, Filter) by creating a blend between the current state of the layer and the previous state. It performs the following operations: copy the active drawable, undo the last action, paste the copy as a new layer, set its "Opacity", and merge both new layer and previously active drawable.

16.3.4.1 Activate the command

You can get to this command from the image Menu bar through: Edit → Fade...

16.3.4.2 Options

This command brings up a dialog window:

Figure 16.15 The "Fade" dialog

Mode This drop-down list allows you to choose a Layer merge mode.

Opacity This slider value is initially set to the opacity of the color you used with the Fill or Blend tool, which corresponds to the current state. Lowering the opacity to 0 changes the drawable to its previous state. Intermediate values produce a mixture of the two according to the mode you have chosen. The effect of this setting is visible in real time in the image, but you have to click on the Fade button to validate it.

16.3.5 Undo History

The Undo History command activates the Undo History dialog, which shows you thumbnails representing the operations you have done so far on the current image. This overview makes it easier for you to undo steps or to redo them.

Use the arrows for Undo and Redo, or simply click on the thumbnail, to bring the image back to a previous state. This is especially useful when you are working on a difficult task, where you often need to undo several steps at once. It is much easier to click on step 10 than to type Ctrl-Z ten times.

The "Clear undo History" command may be useful if you are working on a complex image and you want to free some memory.

16.3.5.1   Activating the Command

- You can access this command from the image menubar through Edit → Undo History. There is no default keyboard shortcut.

16.3.6   Cut

The Cut command deletes the contents of the image's selections, and saves them in a clipboard so that they can later be pasted using the "Paste", "Paste Into", or "Paste As New" commands. If there is no selection, the entire current layer is cut. The areas whose contents are cut are left transparent, if the layer has an alpha channel, or filled with the layer's background color, otherwise.

Note

 The Cut command only works on the current active layer. Any layers above or below the active layer are ignored.

16.3.6.1   Activate the Command

- You can access this command from the image menubar through Edit → Cut,

- or by using the keyboard shortcut Ctrl-X.

16.3.7   Copy

The Copy command makes a copy of the current selection and stores it in the Clipboard. The information can be recalled using the Paste, Paste Into, or Paste As New commands. If there is no selection, the entire current layer is copied. "Copy" only works on the current active layer. Any layers above or below it are ignored.

16.3.7.1   Activate the Command

- You can access this command from the image menubar through Edit → Copy,

- or by using the keyboard shortcut Ctrl-C.

16.3.8   Copy Visible

The Copy Visible command is similar to the Copy command. However, it does not just copy the contents of the current layer; it copies the contents of the visible layers (or the selection of the visible layers), that is, the ones that are marked with an "eye".

Note

 Please note that the information about the layers is lost when the image data is put in the clipboard. When you later paste the clipboard contents, there is only one layer, which is the fusion of all the marked layers.

16.3.8.1 Activating the Command

You can access this command from the image menubar through Edit → Copy Visible.

16.3.9 Paste

The Paste command puts whatever is in the Clipboard from the last "Copy" or "Cut" command into the current image. The pasted section becomes a "floating selection" and is shown as a separate layer in the Layers Dialog.

   If there is an existing selection on the canvas, it is used to align the pasted data. If there is already a selection, the data is pasted using the selection as a center point. If you want the selection to be used as a clipping region for the pasted data, you should use the "Paste Into" command.

Note

 You can have only *one* floating selection at any one time. You cannot work on any other layer while there is a floating selection; you have to either anchor it or remove it.

16.3.9.1 Activate the Command

- You can access this command from the image menubar through Edit → Paste.

- or by using the keyboard shortcut Ctrl-V.

16.3.10 Paste Into

The Paste Into command acts in a similar way to the Paste command. The primary difference becomes apparent if there is a selection within the canvas. Unlike the "Paste" command, which simply centers the pasted image data over the selection and replaces the selection with its own, "Paste Into" clips the pasted image data by the existing selection. The new selection can be moved as usual, but it is always clipped by the original selection area.

   If no selection exists, the "Paste Into" command places the data from the Clipboard into the center of the canvas, as the "Paste" command does.

16.3.10.1 Activate the Command

You can access this command from the image menubar through Edit → Paste Into.

16.3.11 Paste as

This command pastes the clipboard contents. Of course, you must use the "Copy" command before, so that you have something in the clipboard. Else you will be prompted a warning:

or, if there is something you have forgotten, it will be pasted! There is no way to empty the clipboard. This command leads to the sub-menu:

Figure 16.16 The "Paste as" sub-menu

New Image   Shift+Ctrl+V
New Layer
New Brush...
New Pattern...

- Section 16.3.11.1

- Section 16.3.11.2

- Section 16.3.11.3

- Section 16.3.11.4

16.3.11.1   Paste as New Image

The Paste As New Image command creates a new image and pastes the image data from the Clipboard into it. If the data is not rectangular or square in shape, any regions outside the selection are left transparent (an alpha channel is automatically created). Of course, you have to copy your selection before you use this command, so that you get an image with the same dimensions as the selection.
  This command has the same action as the File → Create → From Clipboard command.

16.3.11.1.1   Activate the Command   You can access this command from the image menubar through Edit → Paste as → New Image.

16.3.11.2   Paste as New Layer

The Paste As New Layer command creates a new layer in the active image and pastes the image data from the Clipboard into it. If the data are not rectangular or square in shape, any regions that do not extend to the edge of the canvas are left transparent (an Alpha channel is automatically created). Of course, you have to Copy your selection before you use this command.

16.3.11.2.1   Activate the Command   You can access this command from the image menubar through Edit → Paste as → New Layer.

16.3.11.3   Paste as New Brush

This command opens a dialog window which lets you name the new brush. The brush appears in the Brushes dialog.

Figure 16.17 The "New Brush"dialog

16.3.11.3.1   Options

Brush name   Brush name is the name as it will be in the "Brushes" Dialog.

File name   The new brush is saved as File name (with extension .gbr) in your personal brushes folder.

Spacing   Spacing: When the brush draws a line, it actually stamps the brush icon repeatedly. If brush stamps are very close, you get the impression of a solid line.

16.3.11.3.2   Activate the Command

- You can access this command from the image menubar through Edit → Paste as → New Brush....

16.3.11.4   Paste as New Pattern

This command opens a dialog window which allows you to name your new pattern. The pattern appears in the Patterns dialog.

Figure 16.18 The "New Pattern"dialog

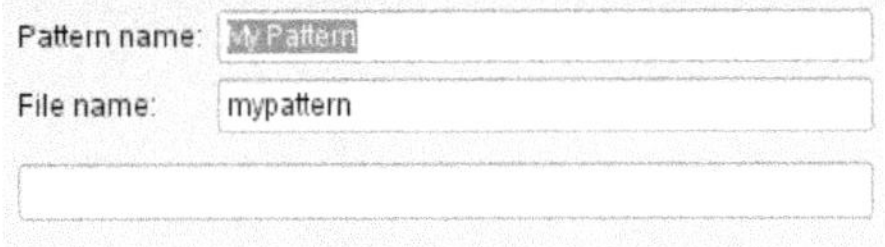

Pattern name: My Pattern

File name: mypattern

16.3.11.4.1 Options

Pattern name Pattern name is the name as it will be in the Pattern Dialog.

File name The new pattern is saved as File name (with extension .pat) in your personal patterns folder.

16.3.11.4.2 Activate the Command You can access this command from the image menubar through Edit → Paste as → New Pattern....

16.3.12 Buffer

Figure 16.19 The "Buffer" submenu of the "Edit" menu

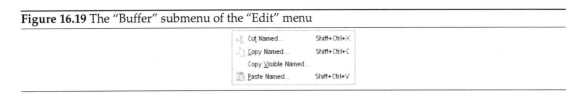

The commands in this submenu operate on *named buffers*. You can use the Buffers dialog to view and manage any named buffers you have created.

16.3.12.1 Activate the Submenu

You can access this submenu from the image menubar through Edit → Buffer.

16.3.12.2 Sub-menu entries

Cut Named The Cut Named command cuts the content of the selection from the active layer in the usual way, but instead of storing the contents in the global clipboard, it stores it in a special buffer that you name using a pop-up dialog.

Copy Named The Copy Named command copies the contents of the selection from the active layer in the usual way, but instead of storing the content in the global clipboard, it stores it in a special buffer that you name using a pop-up dialog.

Copy Visible Named The Copy Visible Named command copies the content of the selection from all the visible layers in the usual way, but instead of storing the content in the global clipboard, it stores it in a special buffer that you name using a pop-up dialog.

Paste Named The Paste Named command simply brings up the Buffers dialog. By selecting one of the listed buffers, and pressing one of the buttons at the bottom, you can either Paste Buffer, Paste Buffer Into, or Paste Buffer as New.

16.3.13 Clear

The Clear command deletes everything in the current selection. If there is no current selection, the contents of the active layer are removed. If the active layer has an alpha channel, the deleted selection is made transparent. You can restore the original color to the transparent area using the Eraser tool, by setting it to Anti-Erase. If the layer does not have an alpha channel, the deleted area is filled using the current background color.

Clearing a selection does not delete the selection itself. Unlike "Cut", "Clear" does not place the deleted contents in the Clipboard and the contents of the clipboard are unaffected.

16.3.13.1 Activate the Command

- You can access this command from the image menubar through Edit → Clear,

- or by using the keyboard shortcut **Delete**.

16.3.14 Fill with FG Color

The Fill with FG Color command fills the image's selection with the solid color shown in the foreground part of the Color Area of the Toolbox. (The color is also shown to the left of the menu entry.) If some areas of the image are only partially selected (for example, as a result of feathering the selection), they are filled in proportion to how much they are selected.

> Note
>
> Please note that if the image has no selection, the whole active layer is filled.

16.3.14.1 Activate the Command

- You can access this command from the image menubar through Edit → Fill with FG Color,

- or by using the keyboard shortcut Ctrl-,.

> Note
>
> You can also fill a selection by click-and-dragging from the Toolbox foreground color.

16.3.15 Fill with BG Color

The Fill with BG Color command fills the active layer selection with the solid color shown in the Background part of the Color Area of the Toolbox. (The color is also shown to the left of the menu entry.) If some areas of the image are only partially selected (for example, as a result of feathering the selection), they are filled in proportion to how much they are selected.

> Note
>
> Please note that if the image has no selection, the whole active layer is filled.

16.3.15.1 Activate the Command

- You can access this command from the image menubar through Edit → Fill with BG Color,

- or by using the keyboard shortcut Ctrl-..

> **Note**
>
> You can also fill a selection by click-and-dragging from the Toolbox background color.

16.3.16 Fill with Pattern

The Fill with Pattern command fills the image's selection with the pattern shown in the Brush/Pattern/-Gradient area of the Toolbox. (The pattern is also shown to the left of the menu entry.) If some areas of the image are only partially selected (for example, as a result of feathering the selection), they are filled in proportion to how much they are selected.

You can select another pattern by using the Pattern Dialog.

> **Note**
>
> Please note that if the image has no selection, the whole active layer is filled.

16.3.16.1 Activate the Command

- You can access this command from the image menubar through Edit → Fill with Pattern,

- or by using the keyboard shortcut Ctrl-;.

16.3.17 Stroke Selection

The Stroke Selection command strokes a selection in the image. There are two ways you can stroke the selection, either by using a paint tool or without using one. This means that the selection border, which is emphasized in the image with a dotted line, can be drawn with a stroke. There are various options which you can use to specify how this stroke should look.

> **Note**
>
> This command is only active if the image has an active selection.

16.3.17.1 Activate the Command

- You can access this command from the image menubar through Edit → Stroke Selection.

- You can also access it through the Selection Editor.

16.3.17.2 The "Stroke Selection" dialog

> **Note**
>
> The options for stroking selections and for stroking paths are the same. You can find the documentation about the options in the dialog box in the Stroke Path section.

16.3.18 Stroke Path

The Stroke Path command strokes a path in the image. There are two ways you can stroke the path, either by using a paint tool, or without using one. There are various options which you can use to specify how this stroke should look.

> **Note**
>
> This command is active only if there is a path in your image.

16.3.18.1 Activating the Command

- You can access this command from the image menubar through Edit → Stroke Path.

- You can also access it by clicking on the button with the same name in the Path dialog.

16.3.18.2 Description of the Dialog Window

Figure 16.20 The "Choose Stroke Style" dialog window

The Choose Stroke Style dialog box allows you to choose between stroking the path with the options you specify or stroking it with a paint tool. If you stroke the path with a paint tool, the current paint tool options are used to draw the stroke.

Stroke line

The stroke is drawn with the current foreground color, set in the Toolbox. By clicking on the triangle next to Line Style however, the dialog expands and you can set several additional options:

Line Width You can set the width of the stroke using the text box. The default unit is pixels, but you can choose another unit with the drop-down list button.

Solid color / Pattern You can choose whether the line is drawn in the *Solid* or the *Pattern* style. Here, Solid and Pattern are distinct from the dash pattern. If you select a Solid line with no dash pattern, an unbroken line is drawn in the foreground color set in the Toolbox. If you select a Patterned line with no dash pattern, an unbroken line is drawn with the pattern set in the Toolbox. If you select a line with a dash pattern, the color or pattern is still determined by the foreground color or pattern set in the Toolbox. That is, if you select a marbled pattern and Patterned, dashed lines, the dashes are drawn in the marbled pattern

Line Style This drop-list brings some detailed options :

- Cap Style : You can choose the shape of the ends of an unclosed path, which can be *Butt*, *Round* or *Square*.

- Join Style : You can choose the shape of the path corners by clicking on *Miter*, *Round* or *Bevel*.

- Miter limit : When two segments of a path come together, the mitering of the corner is determined by the Miter Limit. If the strokes were wide, and no mitering were done, there would be pointed ends sticking out at the corner. The Miter Limit setting determines how the gap, formed when the outer edges of the two lines are extended, will be filled. You can set it to a value between 0.0 and 100.0, by using the slider or the associated text box and its arrows.

Figure 16.21 Example of miter limit

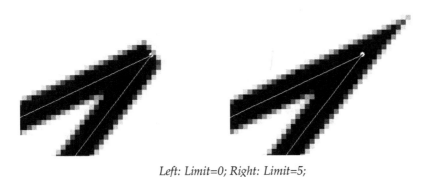

Left: Limit=0; Right: Limit=5;

- Dash Pattern : On the pixel level, a dashed line is drawn as a series of tiny boxes. You can modify the pattern of these boxes. The black area with thin vertical lines represents the pixels of the dash. If you click on a black pixel, you remove it from the dash. If you click on a white pixel, you add it to the dash. The gray areas indicate how the pattern will be repeated when a dashed line is drawn.

- Dash Preset : Instead of making your own dash pattern, you can choose one from the drop-down box. This pattern will then be displayed in the Dash pattern area, so you can get an idea of how it will look.

- Anti-aliasing : Curved strokes or strokes drawn at an angle may look jagged or stair-stepped. The anti-aliasing option smooths them out.

Stroking with a Paint Tool

    Paint Tool You can select a paint tool to use to draw the stroke from the drop-down box. If you do that, the currently-selected options of the paint tool are used, rather than the settings in the dialog.

    Emulate Brush Dynamics See Brush Dynamics.

16.3.19 The "Preferences" Command

This command displays the Preferences dialog, which lets you alter a variety of settings that affect the look, feel, and performance of the GIMP.

16.3.19.1 Activate Command

You can access this command in the image menu bar through Edit → Preferences

16.3.20 Keyboard Shortcuts

How to use this command is described in Section 12.5.

16.3.20.1 Activate the Command

You can access this command from the image menubar through Edit → Keyboard Shortcuts....

16.3.21 Modules

With the Modules command, you can show the various extension modules which are available and control which of them should be loaded. Modules perform functions such as choosing colors and display filtering. Any changes you make to the settings with the Module Manager command will take effect the next time you start GIMP. These changes affect GIMP's functional capabilities, its size in memory and its start-up time.

16.3.21.1 Activating the Command

You can access this command from the image menubar through Edit → Modules

16.3.21.2 Description of the "Module Manager" Dialog

Figure 16.22 The "Module Manager" dialog window

The window of the Module Manager shows the loadable modules.

Clicking on the boxes in the first column of the modules list will check or uncheck the modules. The next time you start GIMP, any checked module will be loaded.

You will notice the difference only when you try to use the modules. For example, there are several color selectors to select the foreground or background color. Some of these selectors are modules and will only be available when you check the respective option in the module manager:

Figure 16.23 Loaded modules example: Color selector modules

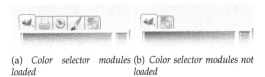

(a) *Color selector modules* (b) *Color selector modules not*
loaded   *loaded*

For loaded modules, information about the selected module is displayed at the bottom of the dialog.

In the second column, for each loaded module the purpose of the module is shown. For any module, that is not loaded, the directory path of this module is shown.

When you click on the Refresh button, the list of modules will be updated: modules no longer on disk will be removed, and new modules found will be added.

16.3.22 Units

The Units command displays a dialog which shows information about the units of measurement that are currently being used by GIMP. It also allows you to create new units which can be used by GIMP in a variety of situations.

16.3.22.1 Activate the Command

You can access this command from the image menubar through Edit → Units.

16.3.22.2 Description of the "Unit Editor" dialog window

Figure 16.24 The "Unit Editor" dialog window

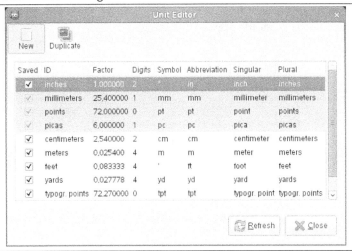

The figure above shows the "Unit Editor" dialog window. The list shows the units of measurement which are currently defined. You can click on the New button or the Duplicate button to create a new measurement unit, as described below.

Description of the list elements

- *Saved*: If this column is checked, a unit definition will be saved when GIMP exits. Some units are always kept, even if they are not marked with a check. These are highlighted in the list.

- *ID*: The string GIMP uses to identify the unit in its configuration files.

- *Factor*: How many units make up an inch.

- *Digits*: This field is a hint for numerical input fields. It specifies how many decimal digits the input field should provide to get approximately the same accuracy as an "inch" input field with two decimal digits.

- *Symbol*: The unit's symbol if it has one (e.g. ″ for inches). The unit's abbreviation is used if doesn't have a symbol.

- *Abbreviation*: The unit's abbreviation (e.g. "cm" for centimeters).

- *Singular*: The unit's singular form, which GIMP can use to display messages about the unit.

- *Plural*: The unit's plural form, which GIMP can use to display messages about the unit.

16.3.22.3 Defining New Units

Figure 16.25 The "New Unit" dialog

Adding the new unit "wilbers"

You can display the dialog shown above by clicking on either the New button or the Duplicate button on the Unit Editor dialog. The input fields on the dialog are described above.

If you click on the New button, most input fields are empty. If you click on the Duplicate button, the values initially displayed in the input fields of the dialog are the values of the unit you have currently selected in the Unit Editor dialog. You can then edit the values to create your new unit.

16.4 The "Select" Menu

16.4.1 Introduction to the "Select" Menu

Figure 16.26 The Contents of the "Select" menu

	All	Ctrl+A
✕	None	Shift+Ctrl+A
	Invert	Ctrl+I
	Float	Shift+Ctrl+L
	By Color	Shift+O
	From Path	Shift+V
	Selection Editor	
	Feather...	
	Sharpen	
	Shrink...	
	Grow...	
	Border...	
	Distort...	
	Rounded Rectangle...	
	Toggle Quick Mask	Shift+Q
	Save to Channel	
	To Path	

This section explains the commands on the Select menu of the image menubar.

Note

 Besides the commands described here, you may also find other entries in the menu. They are not part of GIMP itself, but have been added by extensions (plug-ins). You can find information about the functionality of a Plugin by referring to its documentation.

16.4.2   Select All

The Select All command creates a new selection which contains everything on the current layer.

16.4.2.1   Activate the Command

- You can access this command from the image menubar through Select → All,

- or by using the keyboard shortcut Ctrl-A.

- In addition, at the Selection Editor, you can access it through the Tab menu: Selection Editor Menu → All, or by clicking on the ⌐ ¬ icon button on the bottom of this dialog.

16.4.3   None

The None command cancels all selections in the image. If there are no selections, the command doesn't do anything. Floating selections are not affected.

16.4.3.1   Activating the Command

- You can access this command from the image menubar through Select → None.

- You can also use the keyboard shortcut Shift-Ctrl-A.

- In addition, at the Selection Editor, you can access it through the Tab menu: Selection Editor Menu → None, or by clicking on the ✖ icon button on the bottom of this dialog.

16.4.4   Invert

The Invert command inverts the selection in the current layer. That means that all of the layer contents which were previously outside of the selection are now inside it, and vice versa. If there was no selection before, the command selects the entire layer.

Warning

 Do not confuse this command with the Invert colors command.

16.4.4.1   Activate the Command

- You can access this command from the image menubar through Select → Invert.

- You can also use the keyboard shortcut Ctrl-I,

- or click on the corresponding icon in the Selection Editor

16.4.5 Float

The Float command converts a normal selection into a "floating selection".

A floating selection (sometimes called a "floating layer") is a type of temporary layer which is similar in function to a normal layer, except that before you can resume working on any other layers in the image, a floating selection must be *anchored*. That is, you have to attach it to a normal (non-floating) layer, usually the original layer (the one which was active previously), for instance, by clicking on the image outside of the floating selection (see below).

Important

 You cannot perform any operations on other layers while the image has a floating selection!

You can use various operations to change the image data on the floating selection. There can only be one floating selection in an image at a time.

Tip

 If you display the layer boundary by using the Show Layer Boundary command, you may have difficulty selecting a precise area of the image which you want in a layer. To avoid this problem, you can make a rectangular selection, transform it into a floating selection and anchor it to a new layer. Then simply remove the original layer.

In early versions of GIMP, floating selections were used for performing operations on a limited part of an image. You can do that more easily now with layers, but you can still use this way of working with images.

16.4.5.1 Activate the Command

- You can access this command from the image menubar through Select → Float,

- or by using the keyboard shortcut Shift-Ctrl-L.

16.4.5.2 Creating a Floating Selection Automatically

Some image operations create a floating selection automatically:

- The "paste" operations, Paste Named Buffer, Paste or Paste Into, also create a floating selection.

- In addition, the Transform tools, Flip, Shear, Scale, Rotate and Perspective, create a floating selection when they are used on a selection, rather than a layer. When the Affect mode is *Transform Layer* and a selection already exists, these tools transform the selection and create a floating selection with the result. If a selection does not exist, they transform the current layer and do not create a floating selection. (If the Affect mode is *Transform Selection*, they also do not create a floating selection.)

- By click-and-dragging a selection while pressing the Ctrl-Alt keys (see Section 7.2.1) you also automatically create a floating selection.

16.4.5.3 Anchor a Floating Selection

You can anchor a floating selection in various ways:

- You can anchor the floating selection to the current layer the selection is originating from. To do this, click anywhere on the image except on the floating selection. This merges the floating selection with the current layer.

- Or you can use the Anchor layer command (Ctrl-H).

- You can also anchor the floating selection to the current layer by clicking on the anchor button of the Layers dialog.

- If you create a New Layer while there is a floating selection, the floating selection is anchored to this newly created layer.

16.4.6 By Color

The Select By Color command is an alternate way of accessing the "Select By Color" tool, one of the basic selection tools. You can find more information about using this tool in Select By Color.

16.4.6.1 Activating the Command

- You can access this command from the image menubar through Select → By Color,

- or by using the keyboard shortcut Shift-O.

16.4.7 From Path

The From Path command transforms the current path into a selection. If the path is not closed, the command connects the two end points with a straight line. The original path is unchanged.

16.4.7.1 Activating the Command

- You can access this command from the image menubar through Select → From Path.

- In addition, you can click on the Path to Selection button ▨ in the Path dialog to access the command.

- You can also use the keyboard shortcut Shift-V.

16.4.8 Selection Editor

The Selection Editor command displays the "Selection Editor" dialog window. This dialog window displays the active selection in the current image and gives you easy access to the selection-related commands. It is not really intended for editing selections directly, but if you are working on a selection, it is handy to have the selection commands all together, since it is easier to click on a button than to search for commands in the command tree of the menubar. The "Selection Editor" also offers some advanced options for the "Select to Path" command.

16.4.8.1 Activating the Command

You can access this command from the image menubar through Select → Selection Editor.

16.4.8.2   Description of the "Selection Editor" dialog window

Figure 16.27 The "Selection Editor" dialog window

The Buttons The "Selection Editor" dialog window has several buttons which you can use to easily access selection commands:

- The Select All button.

- The Select None button.

- The Select Invert button.

- The Save to Channel button.

- The To Path button. If you hold the **Shift** key while clicking on this button, the "Advanced Settings" dialog is displayed. Please see the next section for details about these options.

- The Stroke Selection button.

The display window In the display window, selected areas of the image are white, non-selected areas are black, and partially selected areas are in shades of gray. Clicking in this window acts like Select by Color. See the example below.

Figure 16.28 Example of clicking in the "Selection Editor" display window

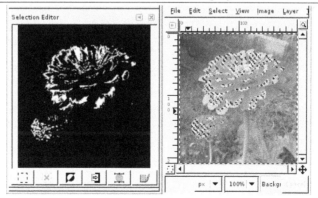

Clicking in the "Selection Editor" display window to "Select By Color". Note that this figure could just as well show the appearance of the "Selection Editor" display window when "Select By Color" is used in the image window.

16.4.8.3 The "Selection to Path Advanced Settings" dialog

Figure 16.29 The "Advanced Settings" dialog window

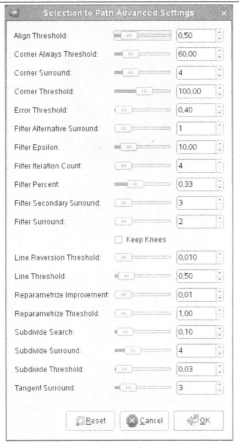

The "Selection to Path Advanced Settings" dialog, that you get by **Shift** clicking on the Selection to Path button, contains a number of options, most of which you can set with either a slider bar or a text box. There is also one check box. These options are mostly used by advanced users. They are:

- *Align Threshold*: If two endpoints are closer than this value, they are made to be equal.

- *Corner Always Threshold*: If the angle defined by a point and its predecessors and successors is smaller than this, it is a corner, even if it is within *Corner Surround* pixels of a point with a smaller angle.

- *Corner Surround*: Number of points to consider when determining if a point is a corner or not.

- *Corner Threshold*: If a point, its predecessors, and its successors define an angle smaller than this, it is a corner.

- *Error Threshold*: Amount of error at which a fitted spline[1] is unacceptable. If any pixel is further away than this from the fitted curve, the algorithm tries again.

---

[1] "Spline" is a mathematical term for a function which defines a curve by using a series of control points, such as a Bézier curve.

See Wikipedia for more information.

- *Filter Alternative Surround*: A second number of adjacent points to consider when filtering.

- *Filter Epsilon*: If the angles between the vectors produced by *Filter Surround* and *Filter Alternative Surround* points differ by more than this, use the one from *Filter Alternative Surround*.

- *Filter Iteration Count*: The number of times to smooth the original data points. Increasing this number dramatically, to 50 or so, can produce vastly better results. But if any points that "should" be corners aren't found, the curve goes wild around that point.

- *Filter Percent*: To produce the new point, use the old point plus this times the neighbors.

- *Filter Secondary Surround*: Number of adjacent points to consider if *Filter Surround* points defines a straight line.

- *Filter Surround*: Number of adjacent points to consider when filtering.

- *Keep Knees*: This check box says whether or not to remove "knee" points after finding the outline.

- *Line Reversion Threshold*: If a spline is closer to a straight line than this value, it remains a straight line, even if it would otherwise be changed back to a curve. This is weighted by the square of the curve length, to make shorter curves more likely to be reverted.

- *Line Threshold*: How many pixels (on the average) a spline can diverge from the line determined by its endpoints before it is changed to a straight line.

- *Reparametrize Improvement*: If reparameterization doesn't improve the fit by this much percent, the algorithm stops doing it.

- *Reparametrize Threshold*: Amount of error at which it is pointless to reparameterize. This happens, for example, when the algorithm is trying to fit the outline of the outside of an "O" with a single spline. The initial fit is not good enough for the Newton-Raphson iteration to improve it. It may be that it would be better to detect the cases where the algorithm didn't find any corners.

- *Subdivide Search*: Percentage of the curve away from the worst point to look for a better place to subdivide.

- *Subdivide Surround*: Number of points to consider when deciding whether a given point is a better place to subdivide.

- *Subdivide Threshold*: How many pixels a point can diverge from a straight line and still be considered a better place to subdivide.

- *Tangent Surround*: Number of points to look at on either side of a point when computing the approximation to the tangent at that point.

16.4.9 Feather

The Feather command feathers the edges of the selection. This creates a smooth transition between the selection and its surroundings. You normally feather selection borders with the "Feather Edges" option of the selection tools, but you may feather them again with this command.

16.4.9.1 Activating the Command

You can access this command from the image menubar through Select → Feather.

16.4.9.2   Description of the "Feather Selection" dialog window

---

Figure 16.30 The "Feather Selection" dialog

Feather selection by Enter the width of the selection border feathering. The default units are pixels, but you can also choose other units with the drop-down menu.

16.4.10   Sharpen

The Sharpen command reduces the amount of blur or fuzziness around the edge of a selection. It reverses the effect of the Feather Selection command. The new edge of the selection follows the dotted line of the edge of the old selection. Anti-aliasing is also removed.

Note

      Please do not confuse this command with the Sharpen filter.

16.4.10.1   Activating the Command

You can access this command from the image menubar through Select → Sharpen.

16.4.11   Shrink

The Shrink command reduces the size of the selected area by moving each point on the edge of the selection a certain distance further away from the nearest edge of the image (toward the center of the selection). Feathering is preserved, but the shape of the feathering may be altered at the corners or at points of sharp curvature.

16.4.11.1   Activating the Command

You can access this command from the image menubar through Select → Shrink....

16.4.11.2   Description of the "Shrink" dialog

Figure 16.31 The "Shrink Selection" dialog

Shrink selection by Enter the amount by which to reduce the selection in the text box. The default unit is pixels, but you can choose a different unit of measurement from the drop-down menu.

Shrink from image border This option is only of interest if the selection runs along the edge of the image. If it does and this option is checked, then the selection shrinks away from the edge of the image. If this option is not checked, the selection continues to extend to the image border.

16.4.12   Grow

The Grow command increases the size of a selection in the current image. It works in a similar way to the Shrink command, which reduces the size of a selection.

16.4.12.1   Activating the Command

You can access this command from the image menubar through Select → Grow.

16.4.12.2   Description of the "Grow Selection" dialog

Figure 16.32 The "Grow Selection" dialog window

Grow selection by You can enter the amount by which to increase the selection in the text box. The default unit of measurement is pixels, but you can choose a different unit by using the drop-down menu.

16.4.12.3   A Peculiarity of Rectangular Selections

When you grow a rectangular selection, the resulting selection has rounded corners. The reason for this is shown in the image below:

Figure 16.33 Why growing a rectangular selection results in rounded corners

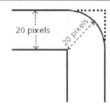

If you do not want rounded corners, you can use the Rounded Rectangle command with a 0% radius.

16.4.13   Border

Figure 16.34 Example of creating a border from a selection

(a) *An image with a selection*   (b) *After "Select Border"*

The Select Border command creates a new selection along the edge of an existing selection in the current image. The edge of the current selection is used as a form and the new selection is then created around it. You enter the width of the border, in pixels or some other unit, in the dialog window. Half of the new border lies inside of the selected area and half outside of it.

16.4.13.1   Activating the Command

You can access this command from the image menubar through Select → Border.

16.4.13.2   Description of the "Border" dialog window

Figure 16.35 The "Border" dialog window

Border selection by   Enter the width of the border selection in the box. The default units are pixels, but you can also choose the units with the drop-down menu.

Feather border   If this option is checked, the edges of the selection will be feathered. This creates a smooth transition between the selection and its surroundings. Note than you can't use the Feather Edges option of the selection tools for this purpose.

Lock selection to image edges   With this option enabled, an edge of an (usually rectangle) selection remains unchanged if it is aligned with an edge of the image; no new selection will be created around it.

Figure 16.36 Select border with and without "Lock to image edges"

(a) *Select border without (middle) and with (right) locked selection.*   (b) *Same selections filled with red.*

16.4.14   Distort

Figure 16.37 Example of using Distort on a selection

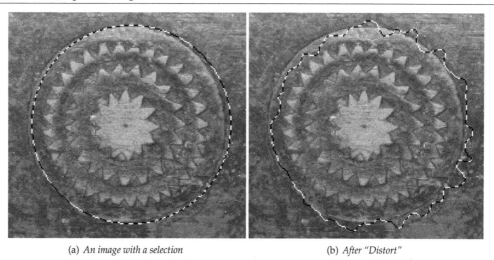

(a) *An image with a selection*   (b) *After "Distort"*

The "Distort" command deforms the selection contour.

16.4.14.1   Activating the Command

You can access this command from the image menu bar through Select → Distort....

16.4.14.2   Description of the "Distort" Dialog Window

Figure 16.38 The "Distort" dialog

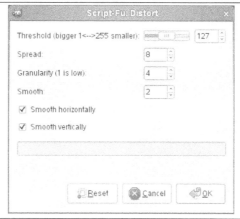

This command has several options which allow to increase or reduce the deformation. It is not possible to foresee the result and you have to experiment.

Threshold A higher threshold shrinks the distorted selection. A lower threshold makes the selection bigger.

If the active selection has a regular shape (e.g. rectangle or ellipse selection), this option controls if the new outline is more inside the original selection or more outside the original selection.

Spread A higher "Spread" increases the deformation.

Granularity A higher "Granularity" increases the deformation.

Smooth A higher "Smooth" decreases the deformation.

Deactivating Smooth horizontally or Smooth vertically increases the deformation.

16.4.15 Rounded Rectangle

Figure 16.39 Example of using Rounded rectangle on a selection

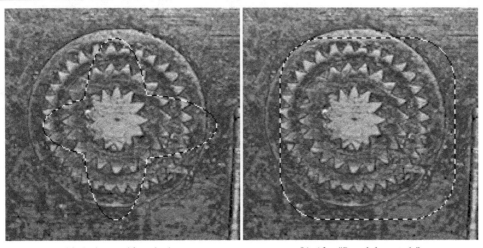

(a) *An image with a selection*   (b) *After "Rounded rectangle"*

The "Rounded Rectangle" Script-Fu command converts an existing selection (rectangular, elliptical or other shape) into a rectangular selection with rounded corners. The corners can be curved toward the inside (concave) or toward the outside (convex). To do this, the command adds or removes circles at the corners of the selection.

16.4.15.1 Activating the Command

You can access this command from the image menu bar through Select → Rounded Rectangle….

16.4.15.2 Description of the "Rounded Rectangle" Dialog Window

Figure 16.40 The "Rounded Rectangle" dialog

Radius (%) You can enter the radius of the rounded corner in percent by using a slider or a text field. This value is a percentage of the height or the width, whichever is less.

Concave If you check this box, the corners will be concave (curving toward the inside), rather than convex (curving toward the outside).

16.4.16   Toggle QuickMask

This command has the same action as clicking on the small button in the bottom left corner of the image. See Quick Mask

16.4.16.1   Activate Dialog

- You can access this command through Select → Toggle QuickMask.

- Default shortcut is Shift-Q

16.4.17   Save to Channel

The Save to Channel command saves the selection as a channel. The channel can then be used as a channel selection mask. You can find more information about them in the Channel Dialog section.

You will find a simple example how to use this command in the introduction of Section 17.16. It shows how to convert a selection to an alpha channel so that you can apply an alpha to logo filter to this selection.

16.4.17.1   Activate the Command

- You can access this command from the image menubar through Select → Save to Channel.

- You can also access it from the Selection Editor.

16.4.18   To Path

The To Path command converts a selection into a path. The image does not seem to change, but you can see the new path in the Paths Dialog. By using the Path tool in the Toolbox, you can precisely adapt the outline of the selection. You can find further information regarding paths in the Paths dialog section.

16.4.18.1   Activating the Command

- You can access this command from the image menu bar through Select → To Path.

- You can also access it from the Selection Editor or from the Paths Dialog which offers you a lot of Advanced Options.

16.5   The "View" Menu

16.5.1   Introduction to the "View" Menu

Figure 16.41 Contents of the View menu

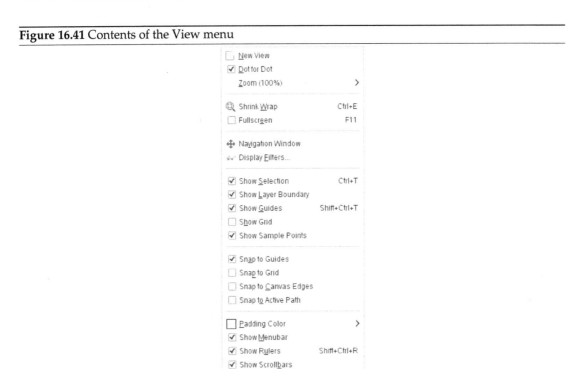

This section describes the View menu, which contains commands that affect the visibility or appearance of the image and various elements of the interface.

Note
Besides the commands described here, you may also find other entries in the menu. They are not part of GIMP itself, but have been added by extensions (plug-ins). You can find information about the functionality of a Plugin by referring to its documentation.

16.5.2   New View

The New View command creates a new image window for the current image, which you can set up differently from the existing display. You can create multiple views of any image, which are numbered .1, .2, etc., but only the zoom factor and other viewing options may be different. Any changes, other than viewing changes, which you make in one window also appear in the other displays which show the same image. The new views are not separate image files; they are simply different aspects of the same image. You might use multiple views, for example, if you were working on individual pixels at a high zoom factor. You could then see the effects your changes would have on the image at a normal size.

16.5.2.1   Activating the Command

- You can access this command from the image menubar through View → New View.

16.5.3 Dot for Dot

The Dot for Dot command enables and disables "Dot for Dot" mode. If it is enabled (checked) and the zoom factor is 100%, every pixel in the image is displayed as one pixel on the screen. If it is disabled, the image is displayed at its "real" size, the size it will have when it is printed.

The example below will illustrate this. Imagine the following image properties:

- Image size: 100x100 pixels

- Image resolution: 300 ppi (pixels per inch)

- Image displayed with Zoom=100%, "Dot for Dot" *enabled*:

    100x100 pixels

- Image displayed with Zoom=100%, "Dot for Dot" *disabled*:

    100 pixels ÷ 300 ppi = 1/3 inch   0.85 cm

For Dot for Dot mode to work properly, the resolution of the image must be the same as the screen resolution in the Preferences menu.

Enabling this mode is recommended if you are working on icons and web graphics. If you are working on images intended to be printed, you should disable Dot-for-Dot mode.

16.5.3.1 Activating the Command

- You can access this command from the image menubar through View → Dot for Dot.

16.5.4 Zoom

Figure 16.42 The "Zoom" submenu of the "View" menu

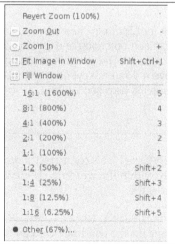

The Zoom submenu contains various commands which affect the magnification of the image in the image window (zooming). Enlarging an image (zooming in) is useful if you need to work with high precision, making pixel-level image modifications or precise selections. On the other hand, reducing an image (zooming out) is handy for getting an overall impression of the image and seeing the results of changes which affect the entire image. Please note that zooming is not undoable, since it does not affect the image data, only the way it is displayed.

> ### Tip
>
>
>
> Besides the entries in this submenu, there is also a zoom pull-down menu at the bottom edge of the image window (if the status bar is displayed), where several preset zoom levels are available.
>
> You can also make settings regarding zooming in the Navigation dialog. You can also use the Zoom tool which lets you zoom a particular area of the image.

16.5.4.1   Activate the Submenu

- You can access this submenu from the image menubar through View → Zoom. Note that the "Zoom" label on the "View" menu shows the current zoom factor, for example, Zoom (100%).

16.5.4.2   Contents of the "Zoom" submenu

The various "Zoom" submenu commands are described below, along with their default keyboard shortcuts, if any.

Revert Zoom (Shortcut: [grave accent,"backtick"]) This command will reset the zoom factor to the previous value, which is also shown by this label, for example Revert Zoom (100%). If you never changed the zoom factor of the active image, this entry is insensitive and grayed out.

Zoom Out (Shortcut: -) Each time "Zoom Out" is used, the zoom factor is decreased by about 30%. There is a minimum zoom level of 0.39%.

Zoom In (Shortcut: +) Each time "Zoom In" is used, the zoom factor is increased by about 30%. The maximum possible zoom level is 25600%.

> ### Note
>
>
>
> The keyboard shortcut for "Zoom In" has been somewhat controversial because this is a very common operation and on English keyboards, the **Shift** key must be pressed to use it. (This is not the case for European keyboards.) If you would like to have a different keyboard shortcut, you can create a dynamic shortcut for it; see the help section for User Interface Preferences for instructions.

Fit Image in Window (Shortcut: Shift-Ctrl-J). This command zooms the image to be as large as possible, while still keeping it completely within the window. There will usually be padding on two sides of the image, but not on all four sides.

Fill Window This command zooms the image as large as possible without requiring any padding to be shown. This means that the image fits the window perfectly in one dimension, but usually extends beyond the window borders in the other dimension.

A:B (X%) With these commands, you can select one of the pre-set zoom levels. Each of the menu labels gives a ratio, as well as a percentage value. Please note that each zoom pre-set has its own keyboard shortcut. The current zoom is marked with a large dot.

Other This command brings up a dialog which allows you to choose any zoom level you would like, within the range of 1:256 (0.39%) to 256:1 (25600%).

> **Tip**
>
> When you are working at the pixel level, you can use the New view command. This allows you to see what is happening to the image at its normal size at the same time.

16.5.5 Shrink Wrap

The Shrink Wrap command resizes the window so that it is exactly the same size as the image at the current zoom factor. If the image doesn't completely fit on the screen, the image window is enlarged so that the largest possible part of the image is shown. Please note that GIMP will do this automatically if you set the "Resize window on zoom" and "Resize window on image size change" options in the Image Window page of the Preferences dialog.

> **Note**
>
> Please note also that the behavior described here is not performed by GIMP itself, but by the "window manager", a part of the operating system of your computer. For that reason, the functionality described may be different on your computer, or in the worst case, might not be available at all.

16.5.5.1 Activating the Command

- You can access this command from the image menubar through View → Shrink Wrap,

- or by using the keyboard shortcut Ctrl-J.

16.5.6 Full Screen

The Fullscreen command enables and disables displaying the image window on the entire screen. When it is enabled, the image window takes up the whole screen, but the image stays the same size. When you enable full-screen mode, the menubar may not be displayed, but if this happens, you can right-click on the image to access the image menu. You can set the default appearance for full-screen mode in the Preferences menu.

Pressing the **Tab** key toggles the visibility of all present docks.

> **Note**
>
> If you use GIMP on an Apple computer, full-screen mode may not work, since Apple doesn't provide the necessary functionality. Instead, you can maximize the image window by clicking on the *Green Button*, so the image occupies most of the screen.

16.5.6.1 Activating the Command

- You can access this command from the image menubar through View → Full Screen,

- or by using the keyboard shortcut **F11**.

- In multi-window mode, you can also get it by double-clicking on the title bar of the image window.

16.5.7   Navigation Window

The Navigation Window command opens the navigation window. This allows you to easily navigate through the image, to set zoom levels and to move the visible parts of the image. You can find more information about using it in the Navigation dialog chapter.

16.5.7.1   Activating the Command

- You can access this command from the image menubar through View → Navigation Window,

- You can also access it more rapidly by clicking on the ✥ icon in the lower right corner of the image window.

16.5.8   Display Filters

This command shows a dialog window when executed. This window can be used to manage the display filters and their options. Display filters are not to be confused with the filters in the filters-menu. Display filters do not alter the image data, but only one display of it. You can imagine display filters like big panes before your screen. They change your perception of the image. This can be useful for things like soft proofing prints, controlling the color management but also simulation of color deficient vision.

16.5.8.1   Activating the Command

You can access this command from the image menubar through View → Display Filters….

16.5.8.2   Description of the "Display Filters" Dialog

Figure 16.43 The "Configure Color Display Filters" dialog

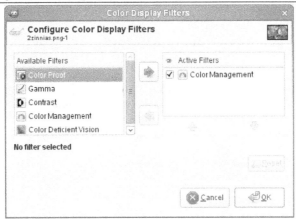

This dialog has two small selectboxes. The left selectbox displays the Available Filters. You can move a filter to the right selectbox by selecting it and clicking on the right arrow button. The Active Filters window on the right displays filters you have chosen and which will be applied if the adjacent box is checked. You can move filters from the right selectbox to the left selectbox by using the left arrow button. If you select a filter by clicking on its name, its options are displayed below the two selectboxes, in the Configure Selected Filter area.

- Simulation of deficient vision (Section 16.5.8.3; Section 16.5.8.5)

- Color Management (Section 16.5.8.6; Section 16.5.8.7)

- Others (Section 16.5.8.4)

16.5.8.3   Color Deficient Vision

The images you create, we hope, will be seen by many people on many different systems. The image which looks so wonderful on your screen may look somewhat different to people with sight deficiencies or on a screen with different settings from yours. Some information might not even be visible.

Figure 16.44 Description of the "Color Deficient Vision" dialog

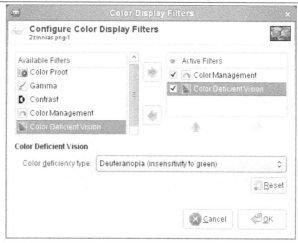

16.5.8.3.1   Options

Color Deficiency Type In this drop-down menu you can select from among:

> **Protanopia² (insensitivity to red)** Protanopia is a visual deficiency of the color red. It's the well-known daltonism (red-green color blindness). Daltonism occurs fairly frequently in the population.
>
> Protanopia is actually more complex than this; a person with this problem cannot see either red or green, although he is still sensitive to yellow and blue. In addition, he has a loss of luminance perception and the hues shift toward the short wavelengths.

> **Deuteranopia (insensivity to green)** With deuteranopia, the person has a deficiency in green vision. Deuteranopia is actually like protanopia, because the person has a loss of red and green perception, but he has no luminance loss or hue shift.

> **Tritanopia (insensitivity to blue)** With tritanopia, the person is deficient in blue and yellow perception, although he is still sensitive to red and green. He lacks some perception of luminance, and the hues shift toward the long wavelengths.

Figure 16.45 Example of protanopia

(a) *Original image*   (b) *A red-blind person cannot see the red (255,0,0) text on a black (0,0,0) background.*

---

² Greek: *proto*: first (color in the RGB Color System): *an*: negation; *op*: eye, vision.

Figure 16.46 Examples of the three types of vision deficiencies in one image

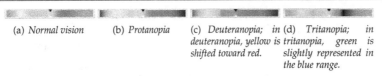

(a) *Normal vision*   (b) *Protanopia*   (c) *Deuteranopia; in deuteranopia, yellow is shifted toward red.*   (d) *Tritanopia; in tritanopia, green is slightly represented in the blue range.*

16.5.8.3.2   Examples

16.5.8.4   Gamma

Figure 16.47 The "Gamma" dialog

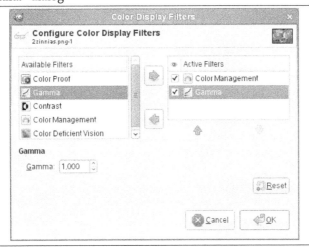

The correspondence between electrical intensity and color brightness is not exact and it depends upon the device (the camera, the scanner, the monitor, etc.). "Gamma" is a coefficient used to correct this correspondence. Your image must be visible in both dark and bright areas, even if it is displayed on a monitor with too much luminence or not enough. The "Gamma" Display Filter allows you to get an idea of the appearance of your image under these conditions.

Tip

In case you want not only to change the gamma of the current display, but the change the gamma within the image itself, you can find a description in Section 14.5.7.

16.5.8.5   Contrast

Figure 16.48 The "Contrast" dialog

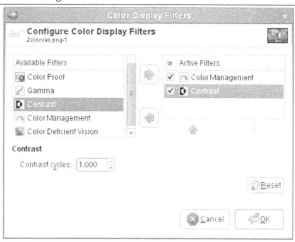

Here, we are back in the medical domain. "Contrast Sensitivity" is the capacity of the visual system to distinguish slight differences in contrast. Some people with cataracts (which means that the lens has opaque crystals that scatter light over the retina) or retinal disease (for instance, due to diabetes, which destroys the rods and cones) have a deficiency in sensitivity to contrast: for example, they would have difficulties distinguishing spots on a dress.

If you are interested in this subject, you can browse the Web for "contrast sensitivity".

16.5.8.5.1   Options

Contrast Cycles With the "Contrast" Filter, you can see the image as if you were suffering from cataracts. You may have to increase the contrast of the image so that your grandmother can see it well. In most cases, only very low values of the Contrast Cycles parameter are of interest. Higher values create a side-effect which doesn't interest us here: if you increase the luminosity value above 255, the complementary color appears.

16.5.8.6   Color Management

Figure 16.49 The "Color Management" dialog

This filter allows to enable the GIMP color management for each image window. To learn more about the color management in GIMP, please read Section 11.1.

16.5.8.6.1   Options   All the customizing for the color management in GIMP has to be done in the GIMP preferences. You can find detailed information about this in Section 12.1.14.

16.5.8.7   Color Proof

The various systems for reproducing colors cannot represent the infinity of colors available. Even if there are many colors in common between the various systems and nature, some of the colors will not be the same. The "gamut" is the color range of a system. *Color Profiles* allow you to compensate for these differences.

Before you print an image, it may be useful for you to see if you will get the result you want by applying a profile. The "Color Proof" filter shows you how your image will look after a color profile has been applied.

Figure 16.50 The "Color Proof" dialog

16.5.8.7.1 The "Color Proof" options

Profile This option allows to select a color profile that is used to simulate the color abilities of the printer. If the desired profile is not shown in the list you might want to add it by selecting a file. This can be done by selecting the last entry of the list.

Intent With this option you can select the rendering intent, which is the method used to determine how colors that can't be reproduced by a device ("are out of gamut") should be handled. The different rendering intents are described in detail in the glossary *Rendering Intent* .

Black Point Compensation Black point compensation allows a better representaion of dark colors of your image when printing.

16.5.9 Show Selection

The Show Selection command enables and disables displaying the dotted line surrounding the selection in the image window. Please note that the selection still exists, even if displaying this line is disabled.
    You can set the default for displaying the selection in the Image Window Appearance dialog.

16.5.9.1 Activating the Command

- You can access this command from the image menubar through View → Show Selection,

- or by using the keyboard shortcut Ctrl-T.

16.5.10 Show Layer Boundary

The Show Layer Boundary command enables and disables displaying the yellow dotted line that surrounds a layer in the image window. The dotted line is actually only visible when the layer is smaller than the image window. When the layer is the same size as the image window, the layer boundary is obscured by the image border.
    You can set the default for the layer boundary in the Image Window Appearance dialog.

16.5.10.1 Activating the Command

- You can access this command from the image menubar through View → Show Layer Boundary.

16.5.11 Show Guides

The Show Guides command enables and disables displaying of Guides in the image window.
You can set the default for the guides in the Image Window Appearance dialog.

16.5.11.1 Activating the Command

- You can access this command from the image menubar through View → Show Guides,

- or by using the keyboard shortcut Shift-Ctrl-T.

16.5.12 Show Grid

By using the Show Grid command, you can enable and disable displaying the grid. When you enable it, the grid overlays the image and makes it easier for you to line up selected image elements.
You can set the default for the grid in the Image Window Appearance dialog.

Tip

 See also the Configure Grid command and the Snap to Grid command.

16.5.12.1 Activating the Command

- You can access this command from the image menubar through View → Show Grid.

16.5.13 Show Sample Points

This command enables and disables showing the sample points in the image window. Sample points are used to display color informations of up to four pixels in the sample points dialog.

16.5.13.1 Activating the Command

- You can access this command from the image menubar through View → Show Sample Points.

16.5.14 Snap to Guides

The Snap to Guides command enables and disables snap to guides. When snap to guides is enabled, the guides you set (see Show Guides) almost seems magnetic; when you move a layer or selection, the guides appear to pull on it when it approaches. This is enormously useful for accurate placement of image elements.

16.5.14.1 Activating the Command

- You can access this command from the image menubar through View → Snap to Guides.

16.5.15 Snap to Grid

The Snap to Grid command enables and disables snap to grid. When snap to grid is enabled, the grid you set (see Show Grid) almost seems magnetic; when you move a layer or selection, the grid points appear to pull on it when it approaches. This is enormously useful for accurate placement of image elements.

16.5.15.1 Activating the Command

- You can access this command from the image menubar through View → Snap to Grid.

16.5.16   Snap to Canvas

If this option is enabled, when you move a selection or a layer, they appear to pull on the canvas edges when it approaches. This is useful for accurate placement of image elements.

> **Note**
>
> Canvas edges are usually mingled with image edges: the canvas has, then, the same size as the image. But you can change canvas size in Image → Canvas Size.

16.5.16.1   Activating the Command

- You can access this command from the image menubar through View → Snap to Canvas.

16.5.17   Snap to Active Path

If this option is enabled, when you move a selection or a layer, they appear to pull on the next anchor point of the active path when it approaches. This is useful for accurate placement of image elements.

16.5.17.1   Activating the Command

- You can access this command from the image menubar through View → Snap to Path.

16.5.18   Padding Color

Figure 16.51 Contents of the "Padding Color" submenu

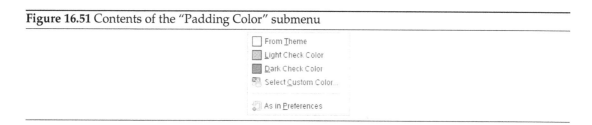

You can change the color of the canvas which surrounds the image by using the Padding Color command. The canvas is the surface the image lies on. It looks like a frame around the image in the image window. This is just a matter of personal preference, since the padding color does not have any effect on the image itself. Please note that this color is not the same as the color used by the Fill tool.

16.5.18.1   Activating the submenu

- You can access this submenu from the image menubar through View → Padding Color.

16.5.18.2   "Padding Color" Options

From Theme The color of the theme defined in Preferences Theme is used.

Light/Dark Check Color The check representing transparency, which is defined in Preferences Display is used.

Select Custom Color... Opens the Color Selector window to let you choose a color to use.

As in Preferences The color selected in the Image Window Appearance is used.

16.5.19 Show Menubar

The Show Menubar command enables and disables displaying the menubar. It may be useful to disable it if you are working in full-screen mode. If the menubar is not displayed, you can right-click on the image to access the menubar entries.

You can set the default for the menubar in the Image Window Appearance dialog.

16.5.19.1 Activating the Command

- You can access this command from the image menubar through View → Show Menubar.

16.5.20 Show Rulers

The Show Rulers command enables and disables displaying the rulers. It may be useful to disable them if you are working in full-screen mode.

You can set the default for the rulers in the Image Window Appearance dialog.

16.5.20.1 Activating the Command

- You can access this command from the image menubar through View → Show Rulers,

- or by using the keyboard shortcut Shift-Ctrl-R.

16.5.21 Show Scrollbars

The Show Scrollbars command enables and disables displaying the scrollbars. It may be useful to disable them if you are working in full-screen mode.

You can set the default for the scrollbars in the Image Window Appearance dialog.

16.5.21.1 Activating the Command

- You can access this command from the image menubar through View → Show Scrollbars.

16.5.22 Show Statusbar

The Show Statusbar command enables and disables displaying the status bar. It may be useful to disable it when you are working in full-screen mode.

You can set the default for the status bar in the Image Window Appearance dialog.

16.5.22.1 Activating the Command

- You can access this command from the image menubar through View → Show Statusbar.

16.6 The "Image" Menu

16.6.1 Overview

Figure 16.52 The Contents of the "Image" Menu

The Image menu contains commands which use or affect the entire image in some way, not just the active layer or some other specific part of the image.

> **Note**
>
> Besides the commands described here, you may also find other entries in the menu. They are not part of GIMP itself, but have been added by extensions (plug-ins). You can find information about the functionality of a Plugin by referring to its documentation.

16.6.2 Duplicate

The Duplicate command creates a new image which is an exact copy of the current one, with all of its layers, channels and paths. The GIMP Clipboard and the History are not affected.

> **Note**
>
> Don't mistake a duplicated image for a new view of this image. In a View → New View, all changes are passed on the original image.

16.6.2.1 Activating the Command

- You can access this command from the image menubar through Image → Duplicate,

- or by using the keyboard shortcut Ctrl-D.

16.6.3   Mode

Figure 16.53 The "Mode" submenu of the "Image" menu

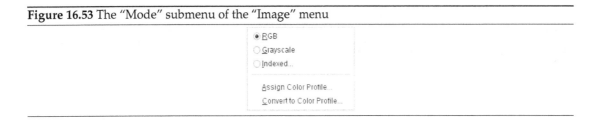

The Mode submenu contains commands which let you change the color mode of the image. There are three modes.

16.6.3.1   Activating the Submenu

- You can access this submenu from the image menubar through Image → Mode.

16.6.3.2   The Contents of the "Mode" Submenu

- RGB

- Grayscale

- Indexed

- Assign Color Profile (see Color management)

- Convert to Color Profile (see Color management)

16.6.4   RGB mode

The RGB command converts your image to RGB mode. See the RGB description in the Glossary for more information. Normally, you work in this mode, which is well-adapted to the screen. It is possible to convert an RGB image to Grayscale or Indexed mode, but be careful: once you have saved the image, you can no longer retrieve the RGB colors, so you should work on a copy of your image.

16.6.4.1   Activating the command

- You can access this command from the image menu bar through Image → Mode → RGB.

16.6.5   Grayscale mode

You can use the Grayscale command to convert your image to grayscale with 256 levels of gray, from 0 (black) to 255 (white).

16.6.5.1   Activating the Command

- You can access this command from the image menubar through Image → Mode → Grayscale.

16.6.6   Indexed mode

The Indexed command converts your image to indexed mode. See indexed colors in the Glossary for more information about Indexed Color Mode.

16.6.6.1   Activating the Command

- You can access this command from the image menubar through Image → Mode → Indexed.

16.6.6.2 The "Convert Image to Indexed Colors" dialog

The Indexed command opens the Convert Image to Indexed Colors dialog.

Figure 16.54 The "Convert Image to Indexed Colors" dialog

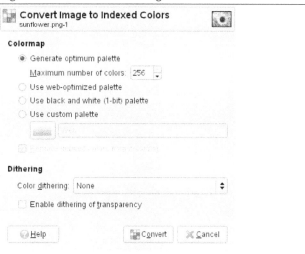

Colormap Options

- Generate optimum palette: This option generates the best possible palette with a default maximum number of 256 colors (classic GIF format). You can reduce this *Maximum Number of Colors*, although this may create unwanted effects (color banding) on smooth transitions. You may be able to lessen the unwanted effects by using dithering, however.

- Use web-optimized palette: use a palette that is optimized for the web.

- Use black and white (1-bit) palette: This option generates an image which uses only two colors, black and white.

- Use custom palette: This button lets you select a custom palette from a list. The number of colors is indicated for each palette. The "Web" palette, with 216 colors, is the "web-safe" palette. It was originally created by Netscape to provide colors that would look the same on both Macs and PCs, and Internet Explorer 3 could manage it. Since version 4, MSIE handles a 212 color palette. The problem of color similarity between all platforms has not been solved yet and it probably never will be. When designing a web page, you should keep two principles in mind: use light text on a dark background or dark text on a light background, and never rely on color to convey information.

  Some colors in the palette may not be used if your image does not have many colors. They will be removed from the palette if the Remove unused colors from final palette option is checked.

Dithering Options Since an indexed image contains 256 colors or less, some colors in the original image may not be available in the palette. This may result in some blotchy or solid patches in areas which should have subtle color changes. The dithering options let you correct the unwanted effects created by the Palette Options.

A dithering filter tries to approximate a color which is missing from the palette by instead using clusters of pixels of similar colors which are in the palette. When seen from a distance, these pixels give the impression of a new color. See the Glossary for more information on dithering.

Three filters (plus "None") are available. It is not possible to predict what the result of a particular filter will be on your image, so you will have to try all of them and see which works best. The "Positioned Color Dithering" filter is well adapted to animations.

Figure 16.55 Example: full color, with no dithering

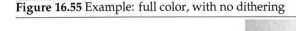

This is an example image with a smooth transition in RGB Mode.

Figure 16.56 Example: four colors, with no dithering

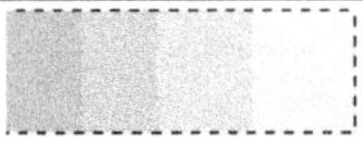

The same image, after being transformed to four indexed colors, without dithering.

Figure 16.57 Example: Floyd-Steinberg (normal)

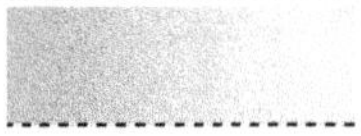

The same image, with four indexed colors and "Floyd-Steinberg (normal)" dithering.

Figure 16.58 Example: Floyd-Steinberg (reduced color bleeding)

The same image, with four indexed colors and "Floyd-Steinberg (reduced color bleeding)" dithering.

In a GIF image, transparency is encoded in 1 bit: transparent or not transparent. To give the illusion of partial transparency, you can use the Enable dithering of transparency option. However, the Semi-flatten plug-in may give you better results.

Note

 You can edit the color palette of an indexed image by using the Colormap Dialog.

16.6.7 Transform

Figure 16.59 The "Transform" submenu of the "Image" menu

The items on the Transform submenu transform the image by flipping it, rotating it or cropping it.

16.6.7.1 Activating the Submenu

- You can access this submenu from the image menubar through Image → Transform.

16.6.7.2   The Contents of the "Transform" Submenu

The Transform submenu has the following commands:

- Flip Horizontally; Flip Vertically

- Rotate 90° clockwise / counter-clockwise; Rotate 180°

- Guillotine

16.6.8   Flip Horizontally; Flip Vertically

You can flip the image, or turn it over like a card, by using the Flip Horizontally or Flip Vertically commands. These commands work on the whole image. To flip a selection, use the Flip Tool. To flip a layer, use the functions of the Layer → Transform menu or the Flip Tool.

16.6.8.1   Activate the Commands

- You can access the horizontal flip command from the image menubar through Image → Transform → Flip Horizontally.

- You can access the vertical flip command from the image menubar through Image → Transform → Flip Vertically.

16.6.9   Rotation

You can rotate the image 90° clockwise or counter-clockwise, or rotate it 180°, by using the rotation commands on the Transform submenu of the Image menu. These commands can be used to change between Portrait and Landscape orientation. They work on the whole image. If you want to rotate the image at a different angle, rotate a selection or rotate a layer, use the Rotate Tool. You can also rotate a layer by using the Layer Transform menu.

16.6.9.1   Activate the Commands

You can access these three commands from the image menubar through

- Image → Transform → Rotate 90 degrees CW,

- Image → Transform → Rotate 90 degrees CCW and

- Image → Transform → Rotate 180°.

16.6.10   Guillotine

The Guillotine command slices up the current image, based on the image's guides. It cuts the image along each guide, similar to slicing documents in an office with a guillotine (paper cutter) and creates new images out of the pieces. For further information on guides, see Section 12.2.2.

16.6.10.1   Activate the Command

- You can access this command from the image menubar through Image → Transform → Guillotine.

16.6.11   Canvas Size

The "canvas" is the visible area of the image. By default the size of the canvas coincides with the size of the layers. The Canvas Size… command opens the "Set Image Canvas Size" dialog that lets you enlarge or reduce the canvas size. You can, if you want, modify the size of the layers. When you enlarge the canvas, you create free space around the contents of the image. When you reduce it, the visible area is cropped, however the layers still extend beyond the canvas border.

When you reduce the canvas size, the new canvas appears surrounded with a thin negative border in the preview. The mouse pointer is a moving cross: click and drag to move the image against this frame.

16.6.11.1   Activating the Command

- You can access this command from the image menubar through Image → Canvas Size....

16.6.11.2   Description of the "Set Image Canvas Size" dialog

---

Figure 16.60 The "Set Image Canvas Size" dialog

Canvas Size

Width; Height You can set the Width and the Height of the canvas. The default units are pixels but
you can choose different units, e.g. percent, if you want to set the new dimensions relative to the
current dimensions. If the Chain to the right of the Width and Height is not broken, both Width
and Height keep the same relative size to each other. That is, if you change one of the values, the
other one also changes a corresponding amount. If you break the Chain by clicking on it, you can
set Width and Height separately.

Whatever units you use, information about the size in pixels and the current resolution are always
displayed below the *Width* and *Height* fields. You cannot change the resolution in the Canvas Size
dialog; if you want to do that, use the Print Size dialog.

Offset

The Offset values are used to place the image (the image, not the active layer) on the canvas. You
can see the size and the content of the canvas in the preview of the dialog window. When the canvas is
smaller than the image, the preview window shows it in a frame with a thin negative border.

X ; Y The X and Y specify the coordinates of the upper left corner of the image relative to the upper left
corner of the canvas. They are negative when the canvas is smaller than the image. You can place
the image in different ways (of course, the coordinates can't exceed the canvas borders):

- by click-and-dragging the image,

- by entering values in the X and Y text boxes,

- by clicking on the small arrow-heads. This increments the value by one pixel (unit).

- And when the focus is on a text box, you can use the keyboard arrow keys, **Up** and **Down** to
  change by one pixel (unit), or **PageUp** and **PageDown** to change the value by 10 pixels (units).

Layers Before the GIMP-2.4 version, "Canvas Size" had no influence on layer size. To change it, you had to use the Layer Boundary Size command. The "Layers" option now allows you to specify how, possibly, layers will be resized. The drop-down list offers you several possibilities:

Figure 16.61 The Resize layers list

- None: default option. No layer is resized, only the canvas is.

- All Layers: all layers are resized to canvas size.

- Image-sized layers: only layers with the same size as the image are sized to canvas size.

- All visible layers: only visible layers, marked with a ⬭ icon, in the Layer Dialog, are sized to canvas size.

- All linked layers: only linked layers, marked with a 🔗 in the Layer Dialog, are sized to canvas size.

Center The Center button allows you to center the image on the canvas. When you click on the Center button, the offset values are automatically calculated and displayed in the text boxes.

Note

When you click on the Resize button, the canvas is resized, but the pixel information and the drawing scale of the image are unchanged.

If the layers of the image did not extend beyond the borders of the canvas before you changed its size, there are no layers on the part of the canvas that was added by resizing it. Therefore, this part of the canvas is transparent and displayed with a checkered pattern, and it is not immediately available for painting. You can either flatten the image, in which case you will get an image with a single layer that fits the canvas exactly, or you can use the Layer to Image Size command to resize only the active layer, without changing any other layers. You can also create a new layer and fill it with the background you want. By doing this, you create a digital "passe-partout" (a kind of glass mount with a removable back for slipping in a photograph).

16.6.11.3 Example

Figure 16.62 Original image

We started with a green background layer 100x100 pixels, which defines a default canvas with the same size. Then we added a new red layer 80x80 pixels. The active layer limits are marked with a black and yellow dotted line. The red layer does not fill the canvas completely: the unoccupied part is transparent. The background color in the Toolbox is yellow.

Figure 16.63 Canvas enlarged (layers unchanged)

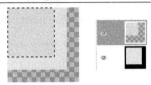

The canvas has been enlarged to 120x120 pixels. The layers size remained unchanged. The unoccupied part of the canvas is transparent.

Figure 16.64 Canvas enlarged (all layers changed)

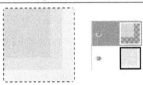

The canvas has been enlarged to 120x120 pixels. All layers have been enlarged to the canvas size. The undrawn part is transparent in the red layer and yellow (background color in Toolbox) in the green background layer.

16.6.11.4   What's Canvas Size useful for?

You may want to add some stuff around your image: enlarge canvas size, add a new layer that will have the same size as the new canvas and then paint this new layer. That's the converse of cropping.

You can also use this command to crop an image:

Figure 16.65 Resizing canvas

Click on the chain next to Width and Height entries to unlink dimensions. By modifying these dimensions and moving image against canvas, by trial and error, you can crop the part of the image you want. Click on the Center button and then on the Resize button.

Figure 16.66 Cropped image

Note

 The Crop tool is easier to use.

16.6.12   Fit Canvas to Layers

The Fit Canvas to Layers command adapts the canvas size to the size of the largest layer in the image, in both width and height.

When you create or open an image, the canvas size is defined as the image size and remains unchanged if you add new layers. If you add a layer larger than the canvas, only the area limited by the canvas will be visible. To show the whole layer, use this command.

16.6.12.1   Activate the command

- You can access this command from the image menubar through Image → Fit Canvas to Layers.

16.6.13   Fit Canvas to Selection

The Fit Canvas to Selection command adapts the canvas size to the size of the selection, in both width and height.

16.6.13.1   Activate the command

- You can access this command from the image menubar through Image → Fit Canvas to Selection.

16.6.14   Print Size

This command opens the "Set Image Print Resolution" dialog that allows you to change the *dimensions of a printed image* and its *resolution*. This command does not change the number of pixels in the image and it does not resample the image. (If you want to change the size of an image by resampling it, use the Scale Image command.)

16.6.14.1   Activating the Dialog

- You can access this dialog from the image menubar through Image → Print Size....

16.6.14.2   Options in the "Print Size" Dialog

Figure 16.67 The "Set Image Print Resolution" dialog

The output resolution determines the number of pixels used per unit length for the printed image. Do not confuse the output resolution with the printer's resolution, which is a printer feature and expressed in dpi (dots per inch); several dots are used to print a pixel.

When the dialog is displayed, the resolution shown in the boxes is the resolution of the original image. If you increase the output resolution, the printed page will be smaller, since more pixels are used per unit of length. Conversely, and for the same reason, resizing the image modifies the resolution.

Increasing the resolution results in increasing the sharpness of the printed page. This is quite different from simply reducing the image size by scaling it, since no pixels (and no image information) are removed.

Width; Height You can set the printing Width and Height by using the text boxes. You can also choose the units for these values from the dropdown list.

As soon as you change the Width or the Height, the X and/or Y resolution values automatically change accordingly. If the two resolution values remain linked, the relationship of the width to the height of the image is also automatically maintained. If you would like to set these values independently of each other, simply click on the chain symbol to break the link.

X resolution; Y resolution You can set the resolution used to calculate the printed width and height from the physical size of the image, that is, the number of pixels in it.

Use the text boxes to change these resolution values. They can be linked to keep their relationship constant. The closed chain symbol between the two boxes indicates that the values are linked together. If you break the link by clicking on the chain symbol, you will be able to set the values independently of each other.

16.6.15 Scale Image

The Scale Image command enlarges or reduces the physical size of the image by changing the number of pixels it contains. It changes the size of the contents of the image and resizes the canvas accordingly.

It operates on the entire image. If your image has layers of different sizes, making the image smaller could shrink some of them down to nothing, since a layer cannot be less than one pixel wide or high. If this happens, you will be warned before the operation is performed.

If you only want to scale a particular layer, use the Scale Layer command.

Note

If scaling would produce an image larger than the "Maximum new image size" set in the Environment page of the Preferences dialog (which has a default of 128 Mb), you are warned and asked to confirm the operation before it is performed. You may not experience any problems if you confirm the operation, but you should be aware that very large images consume a lot of resources and extremely large images may take more resources than you have, causing GIMP to crash or not perform well.

16.6.15.1 Activate the Command

- You can access this command from the image menubar through Image → Scale Image….

16.6.15.2 The "Scale Image" Dialog

Figure 16.68 The "Scale Image" dialog

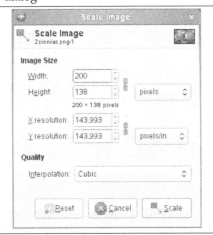

Image Size You should keep in mind that an image can be located in one of four places: in the image file, in RAM after it has been loaded, on your screen when it is displayed, or on paper after it has been printed. Scaling the image changes the number of pixels (the amount of information) the image contains, so it directly affects the amount of memory the image needs (in RAM or in a file).

However printing size also depends upon the resolution of the image, which essentially determines how many pixels there will be on each inch of paper. If you want to change the printing size without scaling the image and changing the number of pixels in it, you should use the Print Size dialog. The screen size depends not only on the number of pixels, but also on the screen resolution, the zoom factor and the setting of the Dot for Dot option.

If you enlarge an image beyond its original size, GIMP calculates the missing pixels by interpolation, but it does not add any new detail. The more you enlarge an image, the more blurred it becomes. The appearance of an enlarged image depends upon the interpolation method you choose. You may improve the appearance by using the Sharpen filter after you have scaled an image, but it is best to use high resolution when you scan, take digital photographs or produce digital images by other means. Raster images inherently do not scale up well.

You may need to reduce your image if you intend to use it on a web page. You have to consider that most internet users have relatively small screens which cannot completely display a large image. Many screens have a resolution of 1024x768 or even less.

Adding or removing pixels is called "Resampling".

Width; Height When you click on the Scale command, the dialog displays the dimensions of the original image in pixels. You can set the Width and the Height you want to give to your image by adding or removing pixels. If the chain icon next to the Width and Height boxes is unbroken, the Width and Height will stay in the same proportion to each other. If you break the chain by clicking on it, you can set them independently, but this will distort the image.

However, you do not have to set the dimensions in pixels. You can choose different units from the drop-down menu. If you choose percent as the units, you can set the image size relative to its original size. You can also use physical units, such as inches or millimeters. If you do that, you should set the X resolution and Y resolution fields to appropriate values, because they are used to convert between physical units and image dimensions in pixels.

X resolution; Y resolution You can set the printing resolution for the image in the X resolution and Y resolution fields. You can also change the units of measurement by using the drop-down menu.

Quality To change the image size, either some pixels have to be removed or new pixels must be added. The process you use determines the quality of the result. The Interpolation drop down list provides a selection of available methods of interpolating the color of pixels in a scaled image:

Interpolation

- None: No interpolation is used. Pixels are simply enlarged or removed, as they are when zooming. This method is low quality, but very fast.
- Linear: This method is relatively fast, but still provides fairly good results.
- Cubic: The method that produces the best results, but also the slowest method.
- Sinc (Lanczos 3): New with GIMP-2.4, this method gives less blur in important resizings.

Note

 See also the Scale tool, which lets you scale a layer, a selection or a path.

16.6.16 Crop to Selection

The Crop to Selection command crops the image to the boundary of the selection by removing any strips at the edges whose contents are all completely unselected. Areas which are partially selected (for example, by feathering) are not cropped. If the selection has been feathered, cropping is performed on the external limit of the feathered area. If there is no selection for the image, the menu entry is disabled and grayed out.

Note

This command crops all of the image layers. To crop just the active layer, use the Crop Layer **command.**

16.6.16.1 Activate the command

- You can access this command on the image menu bar through Image → Crop to Selection.

16.6.17 Autocrop Image

The Autocrop Image command removes the borders from an image. It searches the active layer for the largest possible border area that is all the same color, and then crops this area from the image, as if you had used the Crop tool.

Caution

Note carefully that this command only uses the *active layer* of the image to find borders. Other layers are cropped according to the same limits as limits in the active layer.

16.6.17.1 Activate the Command

- You can access this command from the image menubar through Image → Autocrop Image.

16.6.17.2 Example

Figure 16.69 "Autocrop" example

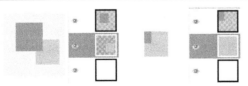

(a) *This image is made of three layers. One with a red square, another with a green square; both on a yellow semi-transparent background. Only a green layer is active.* (b) *"Autocrop" has cropped the green square and made a layer from it. The other layers have been cropped to the same size as the green one. Only a small part of the red square has been kept.*

16.6.18 Zealous Crop

The Zealous Crop command crops an image using a single solid color as a guide. It crops the edges, as with the Autocrop command, but it also crops the areas in the middle of the image which have the same color (at least, in principle).

> **Caution**
>
> Please note that Zealous Crop crops all of the layers, although it only analyzes the active layer. This may lead to a loss of information from the other layers.

16.6.18.1 Example

Figure 16.70 "Zealous Crop" Example

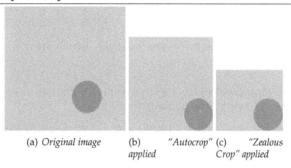

(a) *Original image*   (b)   *"Autocrop"* (c)   *"Zealous*
                                applied   *Crop" applied*

16.6.18.2 Activate the Command

- You can access this command from the image menu bar through Image → Zealous Crop.

16.6.19 Merge Visible Layers

The Merge Visible Layers command merges the layers which are visible into a single layer. Visible layers are those which are indicated on the Layers dialog with an "eye" icon.

> **Note**
>
> With this command, the original visible layers disappear. With the New From Visible command, a new layer is created at top of the stack and original visible layers persist.

16.6.19.1 Activate the Command

- You can access this command from the image menubar through Image → Merge Visible Layers…,

- or by using the keyboard shortcut Ctrl-M.

16.6.19.2   Description of the "Layers Merge Options" Dialog

Figure 16.71 The "Layers Merge Options" Dialog

Final, Merged Layer should be: Visible layers are the layers which are marked with an "eye" icon in the Layers dialog.

- *Expanded as necessary*: The final layer is large enough to contain all of the merged layers. Please note that a layer in GIMP can be larger than the image.

- *Clipped to image*: The final layer is the same size as the image. Remember that layers in GIMP can be larger than the image itself. Any layers in the image that are larger than the image are clipped by this option.

- *Clipped to bottom layer*: The final layer is the same size as the bottom layer. If the bottom layer is smaller than some of the visible layers, the final layer is clipped and trimmed to the size and position of the bottom layer.

Merge within active group only This self-explanatory option is enabled when a layer group exists.

Discard invisible layers When this option is checked, non visible layers are removed from the layer stack.

Figure 16.72 "Merge visible layers" example

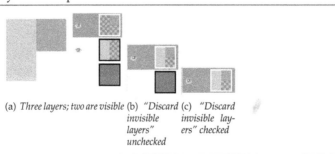

(a) *Three layers; two are visible* (b) *"Discard invisible layers" unchecked* (c) *"Discard invisible layers" checked*

16.6.20   Flatten Image

The Flatten Image command merges all of the layers of the image into a single layer with no alpha channel. After the image is flattened, it has the same appearance it had before. The difference is that all of the image contents are in a single layer without transparency. If there are any areas which are transparent through all of the layers of the original image, the background color is visible.

This operation makes significant changes to the structure of the image. It is normally only necessary when you would like to save an image in a format which does not support levels or transparency (an alpha channel).

16.6.20.1 Activate the Command

- You can access this command from the image menubar through Image → Flatten Image.

16.6.21 Align Visible Layers...

With the Align Visible Layers command, you can very precisely position the visible layers (those marked with the "eye" icon). This degree of precision is especially useful when you are working on animations, which typically have many small layers. Clicking on Align Visible Layers displays a dialog which allows you to choose how the layers should be aligned.

> ### Note
>
> In GIMP 1.2, the default base for the alignment was the top visible layer in the stack. In GIMP 2, the default alignment base is the edge of the canvas. You can still align the image on the bottom layer of the stack, even if it is invisible, by checking Use the (invisible) bottom layer as the base in the dialog.

Figure 16.73 Example image for layer alignment

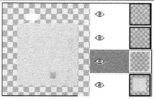

The example image contains four layers on a large (150x150 pixel) canvas. The red square is 10x10 pixels, the green rectangle is 10x20 pixels and the yellow rectangle is 20x10 pixels. The background layer (blue, 100x100 pixels) will not be affected by the command, since the Ignore lower layer option has been checked on the dialog. Note that the layers in the image seem to have a different order than their actual order in the stack because of their positions on the canvas. The yellow layer is the top layer in the image and the second one in the stack.

16.6.21.1 Activate the Command

- You can access this command from the image menubar through Image → Align Visible layers.... There is no default keyboard shortcut. If the image holds a single layer only, you get a message from GIMP telling that there must be more than one layer in the image to execute the command.

Figure 16.74 The "Not enough layers" message

16.6.21.2   Description of the "Align Visible Layers" dialog

Figure 16.75 The "Align Visible Layers" dialog

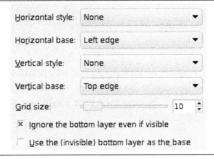

Horizontal Style; Vertical Style These options control how the layers should be moved in relationship to each other. You can choose:

- None: There will be no change in the horizontal or the vertical position, respectively.
- Collect: The visible layers will be aligned on the canvas, in the way that is determined by the Horizontal base and Vertical base options. If you select a Horizontal base of Right edge, layers may disappear from the canvas. You can recover them by enlarging the canvas. If you check the Use the (invisible) bottom layer as the base option, the layers will be aligned on the top left corner of the bottom layer.

Figure 16.76 Horizontal "Collect" alignment (on the edge of the canvas)

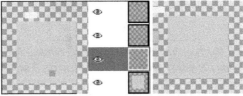

(a) *Original image with the layer stack* (b) *The layers have been moved horizontally so that their left edges are aligned with the left edge of the canvas.*

Figure 16.77 Horizontal "Collect" alignment (on the bottom layer)

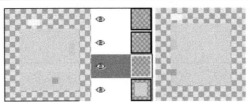

(a) *Original image with the layer stack* (b) *The layers have been moved horizontally so that their left edges align with the left edge of the bottom layer.*

- Fill (left to right); Fill (top to bottom): The visible layers will be aligned with the canvas according to the edge you selected with Horizontal base or Vertical base, respectively. The layers are arranged regularly, so that they do not overlap each other. The top layer in the stack is placed on the leftmost (or uppermost) position in the image. The bottom layer in the stack is placed on the rightmost (or bottommost) position of the image. The other layers are placed regularly between these two positions. If the Use the (invisible) bottom layer as the base option is checked, the layers are aligned with the corresponding edge of the bottom layer.

Figure 16.78 Horizontal "Fill" alignment (canvas)

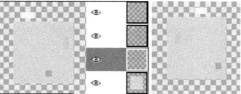

(a) *Original image with the layer stack* (b) *Horizontal filling alignment, Left to Right, with Use the (invisible) bottom layer as the base option not checked. The top layer in the stack, the green one, is placed all the way on the left. The bottom layer in the stack, the red one, is placed is on the right and the yellow layer is between the other two.*

Figure 16.79 Horizontal "Fill" alignment (bottom layer)

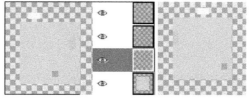

(a) *Original image with the layer stack* (b) *The same parameters as in the previous example, but with the lowest (blue) level as the base.*

- Fill (right to left); Fill (bottom to top): These settings work similarly to the ones described above, but the filling occurs in the opposite direction.

Figure 16.80 Vertical "Fill" alignment (bottom layer)

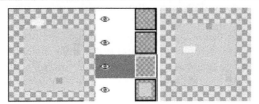

(a) *Original image with the layer stack* (b) *Vertical "Fill" alignment, bottom to top, bottom layer as base*

There must be at least three visible layers in the image to use the "Fill" options.

16.6.22   Guides

Figure 16.81 The "Guides" options of the "Image" submenu

New Guide (by Percent)...
New Guide...
New Guides from Selection
Remove all Guides

The Guides submenu contains various commands for the creation and removal of guides.

16.6.22.1   Activating the Submenu

- You can access this submenu from the image menubar through Image → Guides.

16.6.22.2   The Contents of the "Guides" Submenu

The Guides submenu contains the following commands:

- Section 16.6.23

- Section 16.6.24

- Section 16.6.25

- Section 16.6.26

16.6.23   New Guide

The New Guide command adds a guide to the image.

Tip

 You can add guides to the image more quickly, but less accurately, by simply clicking and dragging guides from the image rulers and positioning them where you would like.

16.6.23.1   Activate the Command

You can access this command from the image menubar through Image → Guides → New Guide

16.6.23.2 "New Guide" Options

When you select New Guide, a dialog opens, which allows you to set the Direction and Position, in pixels, of the new guide more precisely than by using click-and-drag.

Figure 16.82 The "New Guide" Dialog

Direction You can choose the Direction of the guide, either Horizontal or Vertical, by using the drop-down list.

Position The coordinate origin for the Position is the upper left corner of the canvas.

16.6.24 New Guide (by Percent)

The New Guide (by Percent) command adds a guide to the image. The position of the guide is specified as a percentage of the canvas Height and Width.

Tip

You can add guides to the image more quickly by simply clicking and dragging guides from the image rulers and positioning them where you would like. Guides you draw with click-and-drag are not as precisely positioned as those you draw with this command, however.

16.6.24.1 Activate the Command

You can access this command from the image menubar through Image → Guides → New Guide (by Percent).

16.6.24.2 "New Guide (by Percent)" Options

When you select this menu item, a dialog opens, which allows you to set the Direction and Position, by percent, of the new guide.

Figure 16.83 The "New Guide (by Percent)" Dialog

Direction You can choose the Direction of the guide, either Horizontal or Vertical, by using the drop-down list.

Position You can also choose the Position of the new guide. The coordinate origin is in the upper left corner of the canvas.

16.6.25   New Guides from Selection

The New Guides from Selection command adds four guide lines, one for each of the upper, lower, left and right edges of the current selection. If there is no selection in the current image, no guides are drawn.

16.6.25.1   Activating the Command

You can access this command from the image menubar through Image → Guides → New Guides from Selection.

16.6.26   Remove all guides

The Remove all Guides command removes all guides from the image. Clicking-and-dragging one or two guides onto a ruler is a quicker way to remove them. This command is useful if you have positioned several guides.

16.6.26.1   Activate the Command

You can access this command from the image menubar through Image → Guides → Remove all guides.

16.6.27   Configure Grid...

The Configure Grid command lets you set the properties of the grid which you can display over your image while you are working on it. The GIMP provides only Cartesian grids. You can choose the color of the grid lines, and the spacing and offsets from the origin of the image, independently for the horizontal and vertical grid lines. You can choose one of five different grid styles.

16.6.27.1   Activating the Command

- You can access this command from the image menubar through Image → Configure Grid....

16.6.27.2   Description of the "Configure Image Grid" dialog

Figure 16.84 The "Configure Grid" dialog

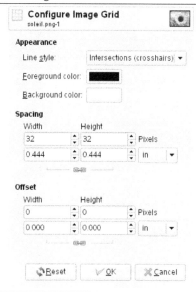

Appearance

In the Configure Grid dialog, you can set the properties of the grid which is shown when you turn on the image grid.

Line style

Intersections (dots) This style, the least conspicuous, shows a simple dot at each intersection of the grid lines.

Intersections (crosshairs) This style, the default, shows a plus-shaped crosshair at each intersection of the grid lines.

Dashed This style shows dashed lines in the foreground color of the grid. If the lines are too close together, the grid won't look good.

Double dashed This style shows dashed lines, where the foreground and background colors of the grid alternate.

Solid This style shows solid grid lines in the foreground color of the grid.

Foreground and Background colors Click on the color dwell to select a new color for the grid.

Spacing

Width and Height You can select the cell size of the grid and the unit of measurement.

Offset

Width and Height You can set the offset of the first cell. The coordinate origin is the upper left corner of the image. By default, the grid begins at the coordinate origin, (0,0).

16.6.28   Image Properties

The "Image Properties" command opens a window that shows lots of different information for the image.

16.6.28.1   Activate the Command

- You can access this command from the image menubar through Image → Image Properties,

- or by using the keyboard shortcut Alt-Return.

16.6.28.2   Options

The properties window is divided into three tabs.

Figure 16.85 "Properties" tab

16.6.28.2.1   "Properties" tab

Pixel dimensions Shows the image height and width in pixels, that is, the *physical* size of the image.

Print size Shows the size the image will have when it is printed, in the current units. This is the *logical* size of the image. It depends upon the physical size of the image and the screen resolution.

Resolution Shows the print resolution of the image in pixel per inch.

Color space Shows the images color space.

File name Path and name of the file that contains the image.

File size Size of the file that contains the image.

File type Format of the file that contains the image.

Size in memory RAM consumption of the loaded image including the images journal. This information is also displayed in the image window. The size is quite different from the size of the file on disk. That is because the displayed image is decompressed and because GIMP keeps a copy of the image in memory for Redo operations.

Undo steps Number of actions you have performed on the image, that you can undo. You can see them in the Undo History dialog.

Redo steps Number of actions you have undone, that you can redo.

Number of pixels; Number of layers; Number of channels; Number of paths Well counted!

Figure 16.86 "Color profile" tab

16.6.28.2.2 "Color profile" tab This tab contains the name of the color profile the image is loaded into GIMP with. Default is the built-in "sRGB" profile.

Figure 16.87 "Comments" tab

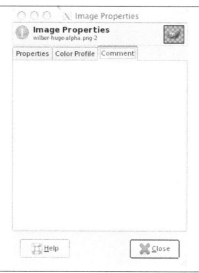

16.6.28.2.3 "Comments" tab This tab allows you to view and edit a comment for the image.

16.7 The "Layer" Menu

16.7.1 Introduction to the "Layer" Menu

Figure 16.88 The Contents of the "Layer" Menu

The items on the Layer menu allow you to work on layers.

In addition to accessing the Layer menu from the Image menubar and by right-clicking on the image window, you can get to it by right-clicking on the thumbnail of a layer in the Layers dialog. You can also perform several of the operations on this menu by clicking on buttons in the Layers dialog, for example, resizing a layer, managing layer transparency and merging layers.

Figure 16.89 The Contents of the "Layer" local pop-menu

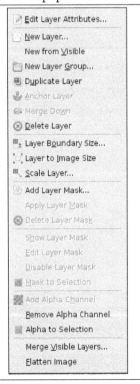

> **Note**
>
> Besides the commands described here, you may also find other entries in the menu. They are not part of GIMP itself, but have been added by extensions (plug-ins). You can find information about the functionality of a Plugin by referring to its documentation.

16.7.2 New Layer

The New Layer... command opens the "Create a New Layer" dialog that allows you to add a new, empty layer to the layer stack of the image, just above the active layer. The command displays a dialog in which you can specify the size of the new layer.

16.7.2.1 Activating the Command

- You can access this command from the image menubar through Layer → New Layer....

16.7.2.2 Description of the "New Layer" Dialog

Figure 16.90 The "New Layer" dialog

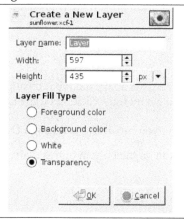

Under the title "Create a new layer" you can see the name of the image for that you create this new layer and next to the title a thumbnail of it. That is interesting to see if you have selected the good image when there is more than one image open.

Layer Name The name of the new layer. It does not have any functional significance; it is simply a convenient way for you to remember the purpose of the layer. The default name is "New Layer". If a layer with the name you choose already exists, a number is automatically appended to it to make it unique (e.g., "New Layer#1") when you click on the OK button.

Width; Height The dimensions of the new layer. When the dialog appears, the values are initialized to the dimensions of the image. You can change them by using the two text boxes. You can also change the units in the pull-down menu to the right.

Layer Fill Type There are four options for the solid color that fills the layer: the current Foreground color, the current Background color, White and Transparency.

16.7.3 New Layer Group

This command creates a new layer group directly. Please refer to Section 8.4.

16.7.3.1 Activating the Command

- You can access this command from an image menu through Layer → New Layer Group…, or from the layer context menu you get by right clicking on the layer dialog.

16.7.4 New From Visible

This command merges the visible layers into a new layer at the top of the layer stack.

The aim is to further manipulate the result, but keep the steps that created this situation. Example: You want to selectively blur some areas of your multilayer image. You create a new layer from what you see, blur it and then apply a layer mask to erase the parts you want your original work to show.

16.7.4.1 Activating the Command

- You can access this command from the image menubar through Layer → New From Visible.

16.7.5 Duplicate layer

The Duplicate Layer command adds a new layer to the image which is a nearly identical copy of the active layer. The name of the new layer is the same as the name of the original layer, but with " copy" appended to it.

If you duplicate a background layer which does not have an alpha channel, the new layer is provided with one. In addition, if there are any "parasites" attached to the active layer, they are not duplicated. (If your understanding of the word "parasites" is limited to small, unpleasant creatures, please ignore the last sentence.)

16.7.5.1 Activate the Command

- You can access this command from the image menubar through Layer → Duplicate Layer, or from the local pop-up menu that you get by right-clicking on the Layer Dialog.

- In addition, at the Layer Dialog, you can access it through Duplicate of its context pop-up menu, or clicking on the icon button on the bottom of this dialog.

16.7.6 Anchor layer

If you have created a floating selection, a temporary layer, called a "floating layer" or "floating selection", is added to the layer stack. As long as the floating layer persists, you can work only on it. To work on the rest of the image, you must "anchor" the floating layer to the former active layer with the Anchor layer command. If the image does not contain a floating selection, this menu entry is insensitive and grayed out.

Note

If there is an active selection tool, the mouse pointer is displayed with an anchor icon when it is outside of the selection.

16.7.6.1 Activate the Command

- You can access this command from the image menubar through Layer → Anchor layer,

- or by using the keyboard shortcut Ctrl-H.

16.7.6.2 Alternative Ways of Anchoring a Floating Selection

There are more ways to anchor a floating selection:

- You can anchor the floating selection to the current layer that the selection is originating from by clicking anywhere on the image except on the floating selection.

- You can also anchor the floating selection to the current layer by clicking on the anchor button of the Layers dialog.

- If you create a New Layer while there is a floating selection, the floating selection is anchored to this newly created layer.

16.7.7 Merge Down

The Merge Down command merges the active layer with the layer just below it in the stack, taking into account the various properties of the active layer, such as its opacity and layer mode. The resulting merged layer will be in Normal mode, and will inherit the opacity of the layer below. If the layer below is not opaque, or if it is in some mode other than Normal, then this command will generally change the appearance of the image.

The most common use of Merge Down is to construct a layer, by starting with a "base layer" (usually opaque and in Normal mode, so that you can see what you are doing), and adding a "modification layer" on top of it, with whatever shape, opacity, and layer mode you need. In this case, merging down the modification layer will combine the two layers into one, without changing the way the image looks.

16.7.7.1 Activating the Command

- You can access this command from the image menubar through Layer → Merge Down.

16.7.8 Delete Layer

The Delete Layer command deletes the current layer from the image.

16.7.8.1 Activate the Command

- You can access this command from the image menubar through Layer → Delete Layer.

- In addition, at the Layer Dialog, you can access it through Delete Layer of its context pop-up menu, or clicking on the 🗑 icon button on the bottom of this dialog.

16.7.9 The Text Commands of the Layer Menu

These commands are displayed only if a text layer is present.

Figure 16.91 Text commands in the Layer menu

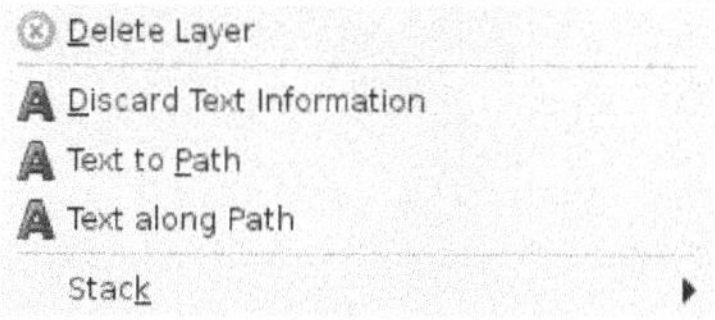

⊗ Delete Layer
A Discard Text Information
A Text to Path
A Text along Path
Stack ▶

16.7.9.1 The Text Commands

- Section 16.7.10

- Text to Path

- Text along Path

- In the Text to Selection drop-down list, the commands are identical to those of the Transparency sub-menu (in fact, the text is formed of areas of different transparency):

  - **Text to Selection:** Section 16.7.38
  - **Add to Selection:** Section 16.7.39
  - **Subtract from Selection:** Section 16.7.40
  - **Intersect with Selection:** Section 16.7.41

16.7.10   Discard Text Information

This command belongs to a group of Text commands displayed only if a text layer is present.

Figure 16.92 The Discard Text command among text commands in the Layer menu

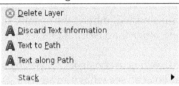

When you add text to an image, GIMP adds specific informations. This command lets you discard these informations, transforming the current text layer into a normal bitmap layer. The reason to do that is not evident.

Note that this transformation of text into bitmap is automatically performed when you apply a graphic operation to the text layer. You can get text information back by undoing the operation which modified the text.

16.7.10.1   Activating the Command

- You can access this command from the image menubar through Layer → Discard Text Information.

16.7.11   "Stack" Submenu

Figure 16.93 The "Stack" submenu

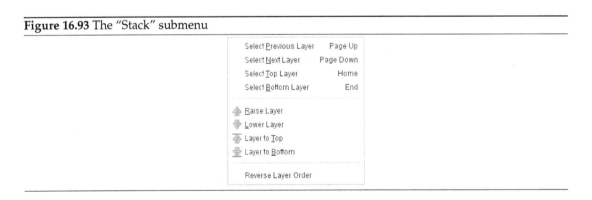

The layer stack is simply the list of layers in the Layers dialog. The Stack submenu contains operations which either select a new layer as the active layer, or change the position of the active layer in the layer stack. If your image has only one layer, these commands are grayed out.

16.7.11.1   Activating the Submenu

- You can access this submenu from the image menubar through Layer → Stack.

16.7.11.2   The Contents of the "Stack" Submenu

The Stack submenu contains the following commands:

- Section 16.7.12

- Section 16.7.13

- Section 16.7.14

- Section 16.7.15

- Section 16.7.16

- Section 16.7.17

- Section 16.7.18

- Section 16.7.19

- Section 16.7.20

16.7.12   Select Previous Layer

The Select Previous Layer command selects the layer just above the active layer in the layer stack. The command highlights the layer in the Layers Dialog and makes it the new active layer. If the active layer is already at the top of the stack, this menu entry is insensitive and grayed out.

Note

  Note that on a standard Windows-style English keyboard, the default shortcut **Page Up** does not refer to the key on the numeric keypad, but to the other **Page Up** key in the group of six keys to the left of the numeric keypad.

Tip

  The keyboard shortcuts for Select Previous Layer and Select Next Layer may be very useful if you frequently pick colors from one layer to use for painting on another layer, especially when you use them with the color-picker tool, which you get by holding down the **Ctrl** key with most of the painting tools.

16.7.12.1   Activating the Command

- You can access this command from the image menubar through Layer → Stack → Select Previous Layer,

- or by using the keyboard shortcut **Up**.

Or you simply click on the layer name in the Layers Dialog.

16.7.13   Select Next Layer

The Select Next Layer command selects the layer just underneath the active layer in the layer stack. The command highlights the layer in the Layers Dialog and makes it the new active layer. If the active layer is already at the bottom of the stack, this menu entry is insensitive and grayed out.

> **Note**
>
> Note that on a standard Windows-style English keyboard, the default shortcut **Page Down** does not refer to the key on the numeric keypad, but to the other **Page Down** key in the group of six keys to the left of the numeric keypad.

16.7.13.1 Activating the Command

- You can access this command from the image menubar through Layer → Stack → Select Next Layer,

- or by using the keyboard shortcut **Down**.

Or you simply click on the layer name in the Layers Dialog.

16.7.14 Select Top Layer

The Select Top Layer command makes the top layer in the stack the active layer for the image and highlights it in the Layers dialog. If the active layer is already the top layer in the stack, this menu entry is insensitive and grayed out.

> **Note**
>
> Note that on a standard Windows-style English keyboard, the default keyboard shortcut **Home** does not refer to the key on the numeric keypad, but to the other **Home** key in the group of six keys to the left of the numeric keypad.

16.7.14.1 Activating the Command

- You can access this command from the image menubar through Layer → Stack → Select Top Layer,

- or by using the keyboard shortcut **Home**.

Or you simply click on the layer name in the Layers Dialog.

16.7.15 Select Bottom Layer

With the Select Bottom Layer command, you can make the bottom layer in the stack become the active layer for the image. It is then highlighted in the Layers dialog. If the bottom layer of the stack is already the active layer, this menu entry is insensitive and grayed out.

16.7.15.1 Activate the Command

- You can access this command from the image menubar through Layer → Stack → Select Bottom Layer,

- by using the keyboard shortcut **End**.

Or you simply click on the layer name in the Layers Dialog.

16.7.16   Raise Layer

The Raise Layer command raises the active layer one position in the layer stack. If the active layer is already at the top or if there is only one layer, this menu entry is insensitive and grayed out. If the active layer is at the bottom of the stack and it does not have an alpha channel, it cannot be raised until you add an alpha channel to it.

16.7.16.1   Activating the Command

- You can access this command from the image menubar through Layer → Stack → Raise Layer,

- or by clicking on the up-arrow icon at the bottom of the Layers dialog.

16.7.17   Lower Layer

The Lower layer command lowers the active layer one position in the layer stack. If the active layer is already at the bottom of the stack or if there is only one layer, this menu entry is insensitive and grayed out.

16.7.17.1   Activating the Command

- You can access this command from the image menubar through Layer → Stack → Lower Layer,

- or by clicking on the down-arrow icon at the bottom of the Layers dialog.

16.7.18   Layer to Top

The Layer to Top command raises the active layer to the top of the layer stack. If the active layer is already at the top or if there is only one layer, this menu entry is insensitive and grayed out. If the active layer is at the bottom of the stack and it does not have an alpha channel, you cannot raise it until you add an alpha channel to it.

16.7.18.1   Activating the Command

- You can access this command from the image menubar through Layer → Stack → Layer to Top,

- or by pressing the **Shift** key and clicking on the up-arrow icon at the bottom of the Layers dialog.

16.7.19   Layer to Bottom

The Layer to bottom command lowers the active layer to the bottom of the layer stack. If the active layer is already at the bottom of the stack or if there is only one layer, this menu entry is insensitive and grayed out.

16.7.19.1   Activating the Command

- You can access this command from the image menubar through Layer → Stack → Layer to Bottom,

- or by pressing the **Shift** key and clicking on the down-arrow icon at the bottom of the Layers dialog.

16.7.20   The "Reverse Layer Order" command

This command is self-explanatory.

16.7.20.1   Activating the command

- From the image Menu through: Layers → Stack → Reverse Layer Order.

16.7.21   The "Mask" Submenu

Figure 16.94 The "Mask" submenu of the "Layer" menu

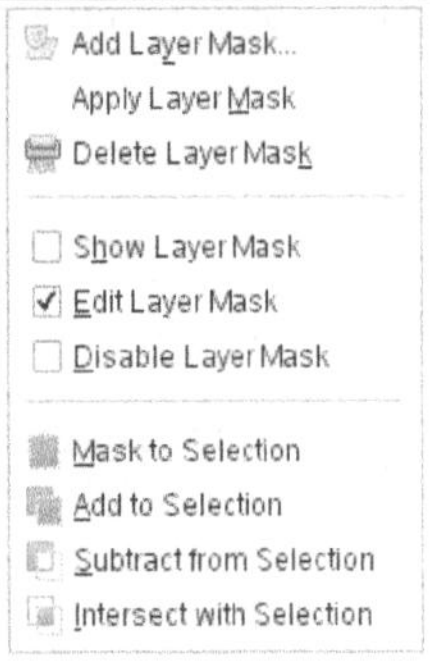

The Mask submenu of the Layer menu contains commands which work with masks: creating a mask, applying a mask, deleting a mask or converting a mask into a selection. See the Layer Masks section for more information on layer masks and how to use them.

16.7.21.1   Activating the Submenu

- You can access this submenu from the image menubar through Layer → Mask

16.7.21.2   The Contents of the "Mask" Submenu

The Mask submenu contains the following commands:

- Section 16.7.22
- Section 16.7.23
- Section 16.7.24
- Section 16.7.25
- Section 16.7.26
- Section 16.7.27
- Section 16.7.28
- Section 16.7.29
- Section 16.7.30
- Section 16.7.31

16.7.22   Add Layer Mask

The Add Layer Mask command adds a layer mask to the active layer. It displays a dialog in which you can set the initial properties of the mask. If the layer already has a layer mask, the menu entry is insensitive and grayed out.

A layer mask lets you define which parts of the layer are opaque, semi-transparent or transparent. See the Layer Mask section for more information.

16.7.22.1   Activating the Command

- You can access this command from the image menubar through Layer → Mask → Add Layer Mask

- or from the pop-up menu you get by right-clicking on the active layer in the Layers Dialog.

16.7.22.2   Description of the "Add Layer Mask" Dialog

Figure 16.95 The "Add Layer Mask" dialog

Initialize Layer Mask to This dialog allows you several choices for the initial contents of the layer mask:

White (full opacity) With this option, the layer mask will make all of the layer fully opaque. That means that you will not notice any difference in the appearance of the layer until you paint on the layer mask.

Black (full transparency) With this option, the layer mask will make all of the layer fully transparent. This is represented in the image by a checkered pattern on which you will need to paint to make any part of the layer visible.

Layer's alpha channel With this option, the contents of the alpha channel are used to fill the layer mask. The alpha channel itself is not altered, so the transparency of partially visible areas is increased, leading to a more transparent layer.

Transfer layer's alpha channel This option sets the layer mask as the previous option, but resets the layer's alpha channel to full opacity afterwards. The effect is to transfer the transparency information from the alpha channel to the layer mask, leaving the layer with the same appearance as before. The visibility of the layer is now determined by the layer mask alone and not by the alpha channel. If in doubt, select this option instead of "Layer's alpha channel", because it will leave the appearance unaltered.

Selection This option converts the current selection into a layer mask, so that selected areas are opaque, and unselected areas are transparent. If any areas are partially selected, you can click on the QuickMask button to help you predict what the effects will be.

Grayscale copy of layer This option converts the layer itself into a layer mask. It is particularly useful when you plan to add new contents to the layer afterwards.

Channel With this option the layer mask is initialized with a selection mask you have created before, stored in the Channel dialog.

Invert Mask If you check the Invert Mask box at the bottom of the dialog, the resulting mask is inverted, so that transparent areas become opaque and vice versa.

When you click on the OK button, a thumbnail of the layer mask appears to the right of the thumbnail of the layer in the Layers Dialog.

16.7.23   Apply Layer Mask

The Apply Layer Mask command merges the layer mask with the current layer. The transparency information in the layer mask is transferred to the alpha channel, that is created if it doesn't exist, and the layer mask is removed. If the active layer does not have a layer mask, the menu entry is insensitive and grayed out. See the Layer Masks section for more information.

16.7.23.1 Activating the Command

- You can access this command from the image menubar through Layer → Mask → Apply Layer Mask,

- or from the pop-up menu you get by right-clicking on the active layer in the Layers Dialog.

16.7.24 Delete Layer Mask

The Delete Layer Mask command deletes the active layer's layer mask, without modifying the active layer itself. If the active layer does not have a layer mask, the menu entry is insensitive and grayed out.

16.7.24.1 Activating the Command

- You can access this command from the image menubar through Layer → Mask → Delete Layer Mask,

- or from the pop-up menu you get by right-clicking on the active layer in the Layers Dialog.

16.7.25 Show Layer Mask

The Show Layer Mask command lets you see the layer mask better by turning the image invisible. When you click on the menu entry, a check is displayed next to it and the layer mask's thumbnail in the Layers Dialog is shown with a green border. The layer itself is not modified; you can turn it visible again later.

16.7.25.1 Activating the Command

- You can access this command from the image menubar through Layer → Mask → Show Layer Mask,

- or by holding down the **Alt** key (Ctrl-Alt on some systems) and single-clicking on the layer mask's thumbnail in the Layers Dialog.

- You can undo this action by unchecking the menu entry in the Layer → Mask submenu or by **Alt**-clicking (or Ctrl-Alt-clicking) again on the layer mask's thumbnail.

16.7.26 Edit Layer Mask

When you click on the Edit Layer Mask item on the Layer Mask submenu, a check is displayed next to it, the layer mask becomes the active component of the current layer and the layer mask is displayed in the Layers Dialog with a white border. When you uncheck it, the layer itself becomes the active component and it is displayed with a white border. You can also activate the component you want more simply by clicking on it in the Layers Dialog.

16.7.26.1 Activating the Command

- You can access this command from the image menubar through Layer → Mask → Edit Layer Mask.

- You can undo this action by unchecking the menu entry in the Layer → Mask menu or by clicking on the layer component in the Layers Dialog.

16.7.27 Disable Layer Mask

As soon as you create a layer mask, it acts on the image. The Disable Layer Mask command allows you to suspend this action. When you click on the menu entry, a check is displayed next to it and the border of the layer mask's thumbnail in the Layers Dialog turns red.

16.7.27.1   Activating the Command

- You can access this command from the image menubar through Layer → Mask → Disable Layer Mask,

- or by holding down the **Ctrl** key (Ctrl-Alt on some systems) and single-clicking on the layer mask's thumbnail in the Layers Dialog.

- You can undo this action by unchecking the menu entry in the Layer → Mask menu or by **Ctrl**-clicking (or Ctrl-Alt -clicking) again on the layer mask's thumbnail.

16.7.28   Mask to Selection

The Mask to Selection command converts the layer mask of the active layer into a selection, which replaces the selection that is already active in the image. White areas of the layer mask are selected, black areas are not selected, and gray areas are converted into feathered selections. The layer mask itself is not modified by this command.

16.7.28.1   Activating the Command

- You can access this command from the image menubar through Layer → Mask → Mask to Selection,

- or from the pop-up menu you get by right-clicking on the active layer in the Layers Dialog.

16.7.28.2   Illustration of "Layer Mask to Selection"

Figure 16.96 Illustration of "Layer Mask to Selection"

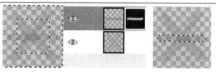

On the left, the original image with a selection. In the middle, the Layers Dialog with a layer mask created with the "Layer's alpha channel" option. On the right, the result after applying "Mask to Selection": the selection of the non-transparent pixels of the active layer replaces the initial selection.

16.7.29   Add Layer Mask to Selection

The Add to Selection command converts the layer mask of the active layer into a selection, which is added to the selection that is already active in the image. White areas of the layer mask are selected, black areas are not selected, and gray areas are converted into feathered selections. The layer mask itself is not modified by this command.

16.7.29.1   Activating the Command

- You can access this command from the image menubar through Layer → Mask → Add to Selection,

16.7.29.2   Illustration of Add Layer Mask to Selection

Figure 16.97 Illustration of Add Layer Mask to Selection

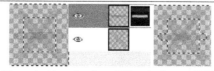

On the left, the original image with a selection. In the middle, the Layers Dialog with a layer mask created with the "Layer's alpha channel" option. On the right, the result after applying "Mask to Selection": the selection of the non-transparent pixels of the active layer is added to the initial selection.

16.7.30 Subtract Layer Mask from Selection

The Subtract from Selection command converts the layer mask of the active layer into a selection, which is subtracted from the selection that is already active in the image. White areas of the layer mask are selected, black areas are not selected, and gray areas are converted into feathered selections. The layer mask itself is not modified by this command.

16.7.30.1 Activating the Command

- You can access this command from the image menubar through Layer → Mask → Subtract from Selection,

16.7.30.2 Illustration of Subtract Layer Mask from Selection

Figure 16.98 Illustration of Subtract Layer Mask from Selection

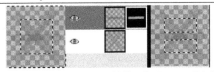

On the left, the original image with a selection. In the middle, the Layers Dialog with a layer mask created with the "Layer's alpha channel" option. On the right, the result after applying "Mask to Selection": the selection of the non-transparent pixels of the active layer is subtracted from the initial selection.

16.7.31 Intersect Layer Mask with Selection

The Intersect with Selection command converts the layer mask of the active layer into a selection. The intersection of this selection and the selection that is already active form the new selection for the image. White areas of the layer mask are selected, black areas are not selected, and gray areas are converted into feathered selections. The layer mask itself is not modified by this command.

16.7.31.1 Activating the Command

- You can access this command from the image menubar through Layer → Mask → Intersect with Selection,

16.7.31.2 Illustration of Intersecting the Layer Mask with the Selection

Figure 16.99 Illustration of Intersecting the Layer Mask with the Selection

On the left, the original image with a selection. In the middle, the Layers Dialog with a layer mask created with the "Layer's alpha channel" option. On the right, the result after applying "Intersect Mask with Selection": the selection of the non-transparent pixels of the active layer is the common part between the initial selection and the mask.

16.7.32 The "Transparency" Submenu of the "Layer" menu

Figure 16.100 The "Transparency" submenu of the "Layer" menu

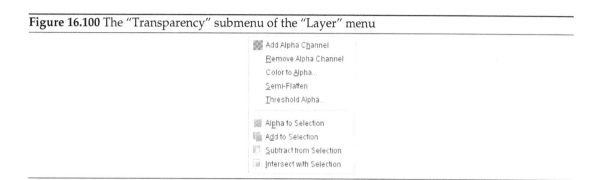

The Transparency submenu contains commands which use or affect the alpha channel of the active layer.

16.7.32.1 Activating the Submenu

- You can access this submenu from the image menu bar through Layer → Transparency.

16.7.32.2 The Contents of the "Transparency" Submenu

The Transparency submenu contains the following commands:

- Section 16.7.33

- Section 16.7.34

- Section 16.7.35

- Section 16.7.36

- Section 16.7.37

- Section 16.7.38

- Section 16.7.39

- Section 16.7.40

- Section 16.7.41

16.7.33 Add Alpha Channel

Add Alpha Channel: An alpha channel is automatically added into the Channel Dialog as soon as you add a second layer to your image. It represents the transparency of the image. If your image has only one layer, this background layer has no Alpha channel. In this case, you can Add an Alpha channel with this command.

16.7.33.1 Activate the Command

- You can access this command from the image menubar through Layer → Transparency → Add alpha Channel.

- In addition, at the Layer Dialog, you can access it through Add Alpha Channel of its context pop-up menu.

16.7.34   Remove Alpha Channel

This command removes the Alpha channel of the active layer, keeping the Apha channels of the other layers.

If the active layer is the background layer and if you have not added an Alpha channel before (then the layer name is in bold letters in the Layer Dialog), the command is grayed out, inactive.

If the active layer is not the background layer, transparency is replaced with the background color of the Toolbox.

16.7.34.1   Activate the Command

- You can access this command from the image menubar through Layer → Transparency → Remove Alpha Channel.

- In addition, at the Layer Dialog, you can access it through Remove Alpha Channel of its context pop-up menu.

16.7.35   Color to Alpha

This command is the same as Layer → Transparency: Section 16.8.34.

16.7.36   Semi-flatten

The Semi-Flatten command is described in the Semi-flatten filter chapter. The command is useful when you need an anti-aliased image with indexed colors and transparency.

16.7.36.1   Activate the Command

- You can access this command from the image menubar through Layer → Transparency → Semi-flatten.

16.7.37   Threshold Alpha

The Threshold Alpha command converts semi-transparent areas of the active layer into completely transparent or completely opaque areas, based on a threshold you set, between 0 and 255. It only works on layers of RGB images which have an alpha channel. If the image is Grayscale or Indexed, or if the layer does not have an alpha channel, the menu entry is insensitive and grayed out. If the Keep transparency option is checked in the Layers dialog, the command displays an error message.

16.7.37.1   Activating the Command

- You can access this command from the image menubar through Layer → Transparency → Threshold Alpha.

16.7.37.2 Description of the Dialog Window

Figure 16.101 The only one option of the "Threshold Alpha" dialog

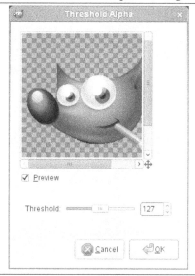

Threshold You can set the transparency value to be used as a threshold by using the slider or by entering a value between 0 and 255 in the input box. All transparency values above this threshold will become opaque and all transparency values below or equal to this threshold will become completely transparent. The transition is abrupt.

> **Note**
>
> This command will never make completely transparent pixels (alpha value = 0) opaque.

Figure 16.102 Threshold Alpha example

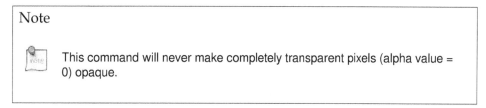

(a) *A transparency gradient 0-255.*   (b) *Threshold set to 50, 127, 210.*

16.7.38 Alpha to Selection

The Alpha to Selection command creates a selection in the current layer from the alpha channel, which encodes transparency. Opaque areas are fully selected, transparent areas are unselected, and translucent areas are partially selected. This selection *replaces* the existing selection. The alpha channel itself is not changed.

The other commands in this group of operations are similar, except that instead of completely replacing the existing selection with the selection produced from the alpha channel, they either add the two selections, subtract the alpha selection from the existing selection, or create a selection that is the intersection of the two.

16.7.38.1   Activate the Command

- You can access this command from the image menubar through Layer → Transparency → Alpha to Selection

- or from the pop-up menu which appears when you right-click on the active layer in the Layer Dialog.

16.7.38.2   Example

Figure 16.103 Applying "Alpha to Selection"

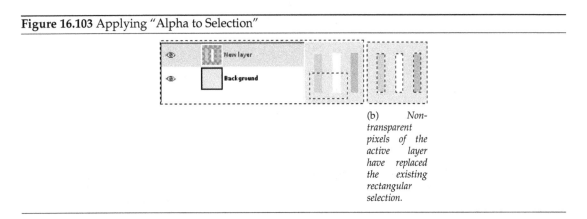

(b)   Non-transparent pixels of the active layer have replaced the existing rectangular selection.

16.7.39   Add Alpha channel to Selection

The Add to Selection command creates a selection in the current layer from the Alpha Channel. Opaque pixels are fully selected, transparent pixels are unselected, and translucent pixels are partially selected. This selection is *added* to the existing selection. The alpha channel itself is not changed.

   The other commands in this group of operations are similar, except that instead of adding to the existing selection with the selection produced from the active layer, they either completely replace the selection with a selection produced from the alpha selection, subtract the alpha selection from the existing selection, or create a selection that is the intersection of the two.

16.7.39.1   Activate the Command

- You can access this command from the image menubar through Layer → Transparency → Add to Selection.

16.7.39.2   Example

Figure 16.104 Applying "Add to Selection"

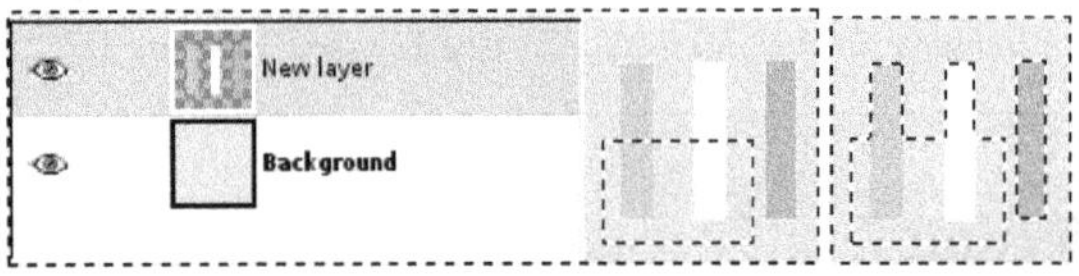

(b)   Non-transparent pixels of the active layer have been added to the existing selection.

16.7.40 Subtract from Selection

The Subtract from Selection command creates a selection in the current layer from the Alpha Channel. Opaque pixels are fully selected, transparent pixels are unselected, and translucent pixels are partially selected.This selection is *subtracted* from the existing selection. The Alpha channel itself is not changed.

16.7.40.1 Activate the Command

- You can access this command from the image menubar through Layer → Transparency → Subtract from Selection.

16.7.40.2 Example

Figure 16.105 Applying "Subtract from Selection"

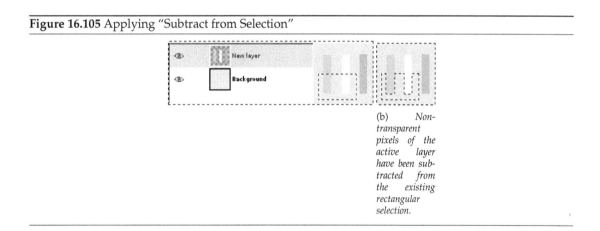

(b) Non-transparent pixels of the active layer have been subtracted from the existing rectangular selection.

16.7.41 Intersect Alpha channel with Selection

The Intersect with Selection command creates a selection in the current layer from the Alpha Channel. Opaque pixels are fully selected, transparent pixels are unselected, and translucent pixels are partially selected. This selection is *intersected* with the existing selection: only common parts of both selections are kept. The alpha channel itself is not changed.

16.7.41.1 Activate the Command

- You can access this command from the image menubar through Layer → Transparency → Intersect with Selection,

- or from the pop-up menu which appears when you right-click on the active layer in the Layers Dialog.

16.7.41.2 Example

Figure 16.106 Applying "Intersect with Selection"

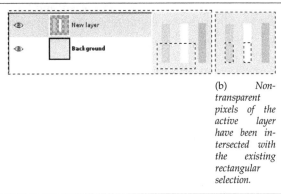

(b) Non-transparent pixels of the active layer have been intersected with the existing rectangular selection.

16.7.42 The "Transform" Submenu

Figure 16.107 The "Transform" Submenu of the "Layer" menu

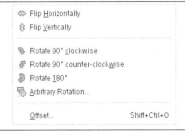

The Transform submenu of the Layer menu contains commands which flip or rotate the active layer of the image.

16.7.42.1 Activating the Submenu

- You can access this submenu from the image menubar through Layer → Transform.

16.7.42.2 The Contents of the "Transform" Submenu

The Transform submenu contains the following commands:

- Section 16.7.43
- Section 16.7.44
- Section 16.7.45
- Section 16.7.46
- Section 16.7.47
- Section 16.7.48
- Section 16.7.49

16.7.43 Flip Horizontally

The Flip Horizontally command reverses the active layer horizontally, that is, from left to right. It leaves the dimensions of the layer and the pixel information unchanged.

16.7.43.1 Activating the Command

- You can access this command from the image menubar through Layer → Transform → Flip Horizontally.

16.7.43.2 Example

Figure 16.108 Applying "Flip Layer Horizontally"

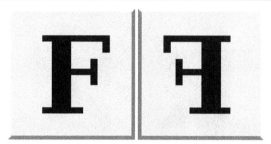

(a) *Before applying the command* (b) *The layer after it has been flipped. It looks as if the image has been reflected along the central vertical axis of the layer.*

16.7.44 Flip Vertically

The Flip Vertically command reverses the active layer vertically, that is, from top to bottom. It leaves the dimensions of the layer and the pixel information unchanged.

16.7.44.1 Activating the Command

- You can access this command from the image menubar through Layer → Transform → Flip Vertically.

16.7.44.2 Example

Figure 16.109 Applying "Flip Layer Vertically"

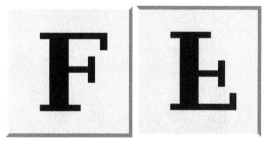

(a) *Before applying the command* (b) *The layer after it has been flipped. It looks as if the image has been reflected along the central horizontal axis of the layer.*

16.7.45 Rotate 90° clockwise

The Rotate 90° clockwise command rotates the active layer by 90° around the center of the layer, with no loss of pixel data. The shape of the layer is not altered, but the rotation may cause the layer to extend beyond the bounds of the image. This is allowed in GIMP and it does not mean that the layer is cropped. However, you will not be able to see the parts which extend beyond the boundary of the image unless you resize the image canvas or move the layer.

16.7.45.1 Activating the Command

- You can access this command from the image menubar through Layer → Transform → Rotate 90° clockwise.

16.7.45.2 Example

Figure 16.110 Applying "Rotate 90° clockwise"

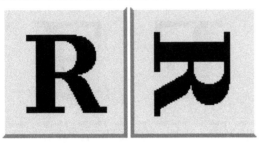

(a) *Before applying the command* (b) *The layer after it has been rotated*

16.7.46 Rotate 90° counter-clockwise

The Rotate 90° counter-clockwise command rotates the active layer by 90° counter-clockwise around the center of the layer, with no loss of pixel data. The shape of the layer is not altered, but the rotation may cause the layer to extend beyond the bounds of the image. This is allowed in GIMP and it does not mean that the layer is cropped. However, you will not be able to see the parts which extend beyond the boundary of the image unless you resize the image canvas or move the layer.

16.7.46.1 Activating the Command

- You can access this command from the image menubar through Layer → Transform → Rotate 90° counter-clockwise.

16.7.46.2 Example

Figure 16.111 Applying "Rotate 90° counter-clockwise"

(a) *Before applying the command* (b) *The layer after it has been rotated*

16.7.47 Rotate 180°

The Rotate 180° command rotates the active layer by 180° around the center of the layer, with no loss of pixel data. The shape of the layer is not altered. Since the layers have a rectangular shape, a 180° rotation only invert them and they can't extend beyond the image limits.

16.7.47.1 Activating the Command

- You can access this command from the image menubar through Layer → Transform → Rotate 180°.

16.7.47.2 Example

Figure 16.112 Applying "Rotate 180°"

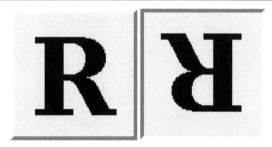

(a) *Before applying the command* (b) *The layer after it has been rotated. It is turned upside down.*

16.7.48 Arbitrary Rotation

The Arbitrary Rotation command rotates a layer by a specified angle. It is an alternate way of accessing the Rotate tool. See the section about that tool for more information.

16.7.48.1 Activating the Command

- You can access this command from the image menubar through Layer → Transform → Arbitrary Rotation,

- or by using the keyboard shortcut Shift-R.

16.7.48.2 Example

Figure 16.113 Applying "Rotate Arbitrary"

(a) *Before applying the command* (b) *The layer after it has been rotated 30° clockwise*

16.7.49 Offset

The Offset command shifts the *content* of the active layer. Anything shifted outside the layer boundary is cropped. This command displays a dialog which allows you to specify how much to shift the layer and how to fill the space that is left empty by shifting it.

16.7.49.1 Activating the Command

- You can access this command from the image menubar through Layer → Transform → Offset,

- or by using the keyboard shortcut Shift-Ctrl-O.

16.7.49.2 Using the "Offset" Command

Figure 16.114 The "Offset" dialog

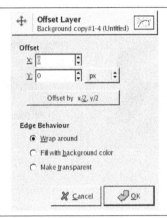

Offset

X; Y With these two values, you specify how far the contents of the layer should be shifted in the horizontal (X) and vertical (Y) directions. You can enter the offsets in the text boxes. Positive values move the layer to the right and downward. The default unit is pixels, but you can choose a different unit of measurement with the drop-down menu. A unit of "%" is sometimes useful.

Offset by x/2, y/2 With this button, you can automatically set the X and Y offsets so that the contents are shifted by exactly half the width and half the height of the image.

Edge Behavior You can specify one of three ways to treat the areas left empty when the contents of the layer are shifted:

- *Wrap around*: The empty space on one side of the layer is filled with the part of the layer which is shifted out of the other side, so none of the content is lost.

- *Fill with background color*: The empty space is filled with the background color, which is shown in the Color Area of the Toolbox.

- *Make transparent*: The empty space is made transparent. If the layer does not have an alpha channel, this choice is not available (grayed out).

16.7.49.3 Example

Figure 16.115 Using "Offset" together with "Edge Behaviors"

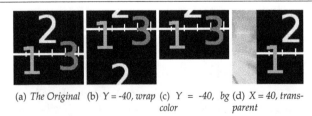

(a) *The Original* (b) *Y = -40, wrap* (c) *Y = -40, bg color* (d) *X = 40, transparent*

16.7.50 Layer Boundary Size

In GIMP, a layer is not always the same size as the others. This command changes the dimensions of a layer, but it does not scale its contents.

16.7.50.1 Activating the Command

You can access this command from the image menubar through Layer → Layer Boundary Size.

16.7.50.2 Description of the "Layer Boundary Size" dialog

Figure 16.116 The "Layer Boundary Size" Dialog

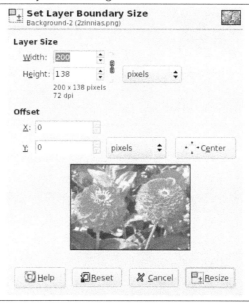

Layer Size

> **Width; Height** When the dialog is displayed, the original dimensions of the active layer are shown. You can change them by using the two text boxes. If these boxes are linked together with a chain, the width-to-height ratio is automatically maintained. If you break the chain by clicking on it, you can set the dimensions independently of each other.
>
> The default unit of measurement is pixels. You can change this by using the drop-down menu. For instance, you might use a "%" of the current size.

X Offset; Y Offset These coordinates are relative to the layer, not to the image. They are used to move a frame that determines which part of the layer content will be selected for the resized layer. In our example, the layer and the content have the same dimensions, and, of course, you have no frame to move. If you reduce Width and Height , the frame of the resized layer appears in the preview.

> Below the coordinates, a preview represents the layer with the frame of the resized layer. You can move this frame using the X and Y offsets and also dragging the cross-shaped moving pointer that appears when the mouse pointer overflies the layer area.

The Center button This button allows you to place the frame at the center of the layer.

16.7.50.3 Resizing Layer

Resizing a layer larger You can't resize a layer to bigger dimensions than that of the image.

> If the layer is smaller than the image, you can enlarge Width and/or Height . There is no good reason to do that, except if you want to enlarge the layer to the size of the image; but, in that case, it's better to use Layer to Image Size.

Resizing a layer smaller You can resize the layer to a smaller dimension to eliminate unwanted parts.

Figure 16.117 Example

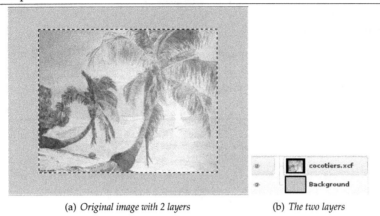

(a) *Original image with 2 layers*   (b) *The two layers*

Figure 16.118 Example

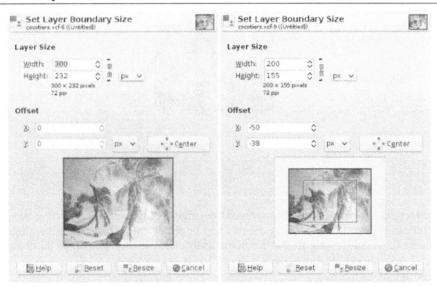

(a) *The selected layer for resizing*   (b) *The frame representing the new layer size. It has been placed at the center of the layer using the Center button.*

Figure 16.119 Result

If the image has only one layer, it's better to use the Crop tool.

16.7.51   Layer to Image Size

The Layer to Image Size command resizes the layer boundaries to match the image boundaries, without moving the contents of the layer with respect to the image.

16.7.51.1   Activating the Command

- You can access this command from the image menubar through Layer → Layer to Image Size.

16.7.52   Scale Layer

The Scale Layer command opens the "Scale Layer" dialog that allows you to resize the layer and its contents. The image loses some of its quality by being scaled. The command displays a dialog where you can set parameters concerning the size of the layer and the image quality.

16.7.52.1   Activating the Command

You can access this command from the image menubar through Layer → Scale Layer....

16.7.52.2   Description of the "Scale Layer" Dialog

Figure 16.120 The "Scale Layer" dialog

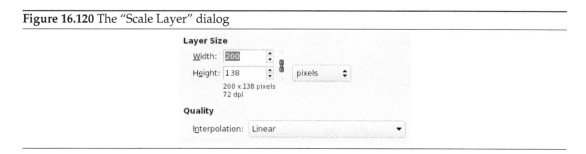

Layer Size   When you enlarge a layer, GIMP has to calculate new pixels from the existing ones. This procedure is called "interpolation". Please note that no matter which interpolation algorithm is used, no new information is added to the image by interpolation. If there are places in the layer which have no details, you will not get any new ones by scaling it. It is much more likely that the layer will look somewhat blurred after scaling. Similarly, when you reduce a layer, the image loses some of its quality when pixels are removed.

> **Width; Height**   The command displays a dialog which shows the dimensions of the original layer in pixels. You can set the new Width and Height for the layer in the two text boxes. If the adjacent chain icon is unbroken, the width and height are automatically adjusted to hold their ratio constant. If you break the chain by clicking on it, you can set them separately, but this will result in distorting the layer.
>
> However, you do not have to set the dimensions in pixels. You can choose different units from the drop-down menu. If you choose percent as units, you can set the layer size relative to its original size. You can also use physical units, like inches or millimeters. However if you do that, you should pay attention to the X/Y resolution of the image.
>
> If you enlarge a layer, the missing pixels are calculated by interpolation, but no new details are added. The more the layer is enlarged, and the more times it is enlarged, the more blurred it becomes. The exact result of the enlargement depends upon the interpolation method you choose. After scaling, you can improve the result by using the Sharpen filter, but it is much better for you to use a high resolution when scanning, taking digital photographs or producing digital images by other means. It is an inherent characteristic of raster images that they do not scale up well.

Quality   To change the size of the layer, GIMP either has to add or remove pixels. The method it uses to do this has a considerable impact on the quality of the result. You can choose the method of interpolating the colors of the pixels from the Interpolation drop-down menu.

Interpolation

None No interpolation is used. Pixels are simply enlarged or removed, as they are when zooming. This method is low in quality, but very fast.

Linear This method is a good compromise between speed and quality.

Cubic This method takes a lot of time, but it produces the best results.

Sinc (Lanczos3) The Lanczos (pronounce "lanzosh") method uses the Sinc[3] mathematical function to perform a high quality interpolation.

16.7.53   Crop to Selection

The Crop to Selection command crops only the active layer to the boundary of the selection by removing any strips at the edge whose contents are all completely unselected. Areas which are partially selected (for example, by feathering) are not cropped. If there is no selection for the image, the menu entry is insensitive and grayed out.

16.7.53.1   Activating the Command

- You can access this command from the image menubar through Layer → Crop to Selection.

16.7.53.2   Example

Figure 16.121 Applying "Crop to Selection"

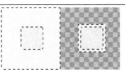

On the left: before applying the command, the layer has a selection that has feathered edges.
On the right: after applying the command, the non-transparent pixels are not cropped, even if they are only semi-transparent.

16.7.54   Autocrop Layer

The Autocrop Layer command automatically crops the active layer, unlike the Crop Tool, or the Crop Layer command which let you manually define the area to be cropped.

This command removes the largest possible area around the outside edge which all has the same color. It does this by scanning the layer along a horizontal line and a vertical line and cropping the layer as soon as it encounters a different color, whatever its transparency.

You can use this command to crop the layer to the dimensions of a subject that is lost in a solid background which is too large.

16.7.54.1   Activating the Command

- You can access this command from the image menubar through Layer → Autocrop Layer.

---

[3] Sinus cardinalis

16.7.54.2 Example

Figure 16.122 Example

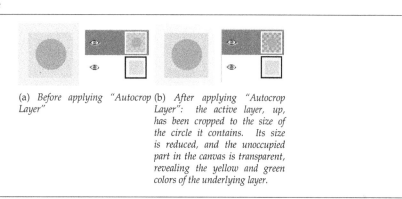

(a) *Before applying "Autocrop Layer"*

(b) *After applying "Autocrop Layer": the active layer, up, has been cropped to the size of the circle it contains. Its size is reduced, and the unoccupied part in the canvas is transparent, revealing the yellow and green colors of the underlying layer.*

16.8 The "Colors" Menu

16.8.1 Introduction to the "Colors" Menu

Figure 16.123 Contents of the "Colors" Menu

This section describes the Colors menu, which contains commands that affect the color of the image.

> **Note**
>
> Besides the commands described here, you may also find other entries in the menu. They are not part of GIMP itself, but have been added by extensions (plug-ins). You can find information about the functionality of a Plugin by referring to its documentation.

16.8.2 Colors Tools

All of the Colors tools are extensively described in the toolbox chapter, Section 14.5:

- Section 14.5.2
- Section 14.5.3
- Section 14.5.4
- Section 14.5.5
- Section 14.5.6
- Section 14.5.7
- Section 14.5.8
- Section 14.5.9
- Section 14.5.10

16.8.3 Invert

The Invert command inverts all the pixel colors and brightness values in the current layer, as if the image were converted into a negative. Dark areas become bright and bright areas become dark. Hues are replaced by their complementary colors. For more information about colors, see the Glossary entry about Color Model.

Note

 This command only works on layers of RGB and Grayscale images. If the current image is Indexed, the menu entry is insensitive and grayed out.

Warning

 Do not confuse this command with the Invert Selection command.

16.8.3.1 Activate the Command

You can access this command from the image menubar through Colors → Invert.

16.8.3.2 Example

Figure 16.124 Applying "Invert colors"

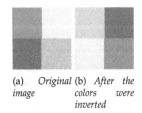

(a) Original (b) After the
image   colors were
                inverted

16.8.4 Value Invert

16.8.4.1 Overview

Figure 16.125 Example for the "Value invert" filter

(a) *Original image*   (b) *"Value Invert" applied*

This filter inverts Value (luminosity) of the active layer or selection. Hue and Saturation will not be affected, although the color will sometimes be slightly different because of round-off error. If you want to invert Hue and Saturation also, use Colors → Invert.

Note that hue and saturation can be distorted quite a bit when applying twice this filter for colors with a high luminosity (for instance, HSV 102°,100%, 98%, a bright green, gives HSV 96°, 100%, 2% after a first application of the filter , and 96°, 100%, 98% after a second application). Thus, you should not expect to be able to apply this filter twice in a row and get back the image you started with.

Figure 16.126 Example of using this filter twice

(a) *Original image*   (b) *First application of* (c) *Second application:*
                       the filter   *the image is not exactly*
                                                the same as the original
                                                one.

16.8.4.2 Activate the filter

You can access this command from the image menu bar through Colors → Value Invert.

16.8.5 Use GEGL

GEGL (Generic Graphics Library) is a graph based image processing framework that will be used in all GIMP-3.0. With GEGL, the internal processing is being done in 32bit floating point linear light RGBA. By default the legacy 8bit code paths are still used, but a curious user can turn on the use of GEGL for the color operations with this option.

In addition to porting color operations to GEGL, an experimental GEGL Operation tool has been added, found in the Tools menu. It enables applying GEGL operations to an image and it gives on-canvas previews of the results.

Warning

 Please note that GIMP remains 8-bits until GEGL covers the whole application.

16.8.5.1 Activating the option

You can access this option from the image menubar through Colors → Use GEGL. Clicking on this item toggles the use of GEGL.

16.8.6 The "Auto" Submenu

 **Figure 16.127** The "Colors/Auto" submenu

The Auto submenu contains operations which automatically adjust the distribution of colors in the active layer, without requiring any input from the user. Several of these operations are actually implemented as plugins.

16.8.6.1 Activate submenu

- You can access this submenu from the image window through Colors → Auto.

16.8.6.2 Automatic Color-Stretching

GIMP has several automatic commands for stretching the columns of the histogram for the color channels of the active layer. By pushing bright pixels to the right and dark pixels to the left, they make bright pixels brighter and dark pixels darker, which enhances the contrast in the layer.

Some of the commands stretch the three color channels equally, so that the hues are not changed. Other commands stretch each of the color channels separately, which changes the hues.

The way the stretching is done varies with the different commands and the results look different. It is not easy to predict exactly what each command will do. If you know exactly what you are doing, you can get the same results, and even more, with the Levels tool.

Here are examples of the results of these commands, all together on one page, so you can compare them more easily. The most appropriate command depends upon your image, so you should try each of them to see which command works best on it.

Figure 16.128 The original layer and its histograms

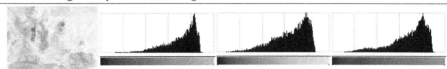

This layer doesn't have any very bright or very dark pixels, so it works well with these commands.

Figure 16.129 The Equalize command

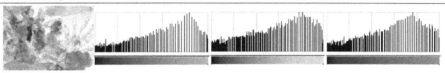

"Equalize" example

Figure 16.130 The White Balance command

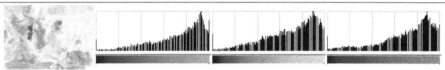

"White Balance" example

Figure 16.131 The Color Enhance command

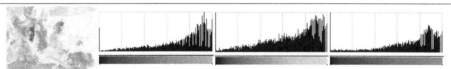

"Color Enhance" example

Figure 16.132 The Normalize command

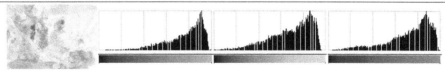

"Normalize" example

Figure 16.133 The Stretch Contrast command

"Stretch Contrast" example

Figure 16.134 The Stretch HSV command

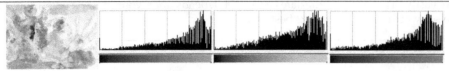

"Stretch HSV" example

16.8.7 Equalize

The Equalize command automatically adjusts the brightness of colors across the active layer so that the histogram for the Value channel is as nearly flat as possible, that is, so that each possible brightness value appears at about the same number of pixels as every other value. You can see this in the histograms in the example below, in that pixel colors which occur frequently in the image are stretched further apart than pixel colors which occur only rarely. The results of this command can vary quite a bit. Sometimes "Equalize" works very well to enhance the contrast in an image, bringing out details which were hard to see before. Other times, the results look very bad. It is a very powerful operation and it is worth trying to see if it will improve your image. It works on layers from RGB and Grayscale images. If the image is Indexed, the menu entry is insensitive and grayed out.

16.8.7.1 Activate the Command

- You can access this command from the image menubar through Colors → Auto → Equalize

- or by using the keyboard shortcut Shift-Page Down.

16.8.7.2 "Equalize" example

Figure 16.135 Original image

The active layer and its Red, Green, Blue histograms before "Equalize".

Figure 16.136 Image after the command

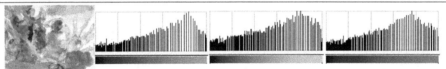

The active layer and its Red, Green, Blue histograms after treatment.
Histogram stretching creates gaps between pixel columns giving it a striped look.

16.8.8 White Balance

The White Balance command automatically adjusts the colors of the active layer by stretching the Red, Green and Blue channels separately. To do this, it discards pixel colors at each end of the Red, Green and Blue histograms which are used by only 0.05% of the pixels in the image and stretches the remaining range as much as possible. The result is that pixel colors which occur very infrequently at the outer edges of the histograms (perhaps bits of dust, etc.) do not negatively influence the minimum and maximum values used for stretching the histograms, in comparison with Stretch Contrast. Like "Stretch Contrast", however, there may be hue shifts in the resulting image.

This command suits images with poor white or black. Since it tends to create pure white (and black), it may be useful e.g. to enhance photographs.

White Balance operates on layers from RGB images. If the image is Indexed or Grayscale, the menu item is insensitive and grayed out.

16.8.8.1 Activate the Command

- You can access this command from the image menubar through Colors → Auto → White Balance.

16.8.8.2 "White Balance" example

Figure 16.137 Original image

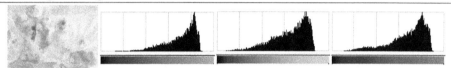

The active layer and its Red, Green and Blue histograms before "White Balance".

Figure 16.138 Image after the command

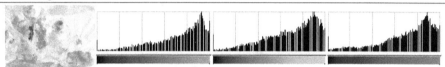

The active layer and its Red, Green and Blue histograms after "White Balance". Poor white areas in the image became pure white.
Histogram stretching creates gaps between the pixel columns, giving it a striped look.

16.8.9 Color Enhance

The Color Enhance command increases the saturation range of the colors in the layer, without altering brightness or hue. It does this by converting the colors to HSV space, measuring the range of saturation values across the image, then stretching this range to be as large as possible, and finally converting the colors back to RGB. It is similar to Stretch Contrast, except that it works in the HSV color space, so it preserves the hue. It works on layers from RGB and Indexed images. If the image is Grayscale, the menu entry is insensitive and grayed out.

16.8.9.1 Activate the command

- You can access this command from the image menubar through Colors → Auto → Color Enhance.

16.8.9.2 "Color Enhance" example

Figure 16.139 "Color Enhance" example (Original image)

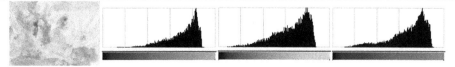

The active layer and its Red, Green and Blue histograms before "Color Enhance".

Figure 16.140 "Color Enhance" example (Image after the command)

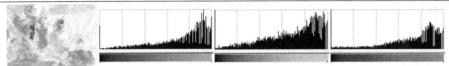

The active layer and its Red, Green and Blue histograms after "Color Enhance". The result may not always be what you expect.

16.8.10 Normalize

The Normalize command scales the brightness values of the active layer so that the darkest point becomes black and the brightest point becomes as bright as possible, without altering its hue. This is often a "magic fix" for images that are dim or washed out. "Normalize" works on layers from RGB, Grayscale, and Indexed images.

16.8.10.1 Activate the Command

- You can access this command from the image menu bar through Colors → Auto → Normalize.

16.8.10.2 "Normalize" Example

Figure 16.141 Original image

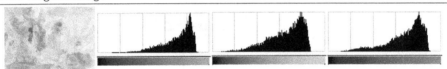

The active layer and its Red, Green and Blue histograms before "Normalize".

Figure 16.142 Image after the command

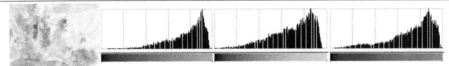

The active layer and its Red, Green and Blue histograms after "Normalize". The contrast is enhanced. Histogram stretching creates gaps between the pixel columns, giving it a striped look.

16.8.11 Stretch Contrast

The Stretch Contrast command automatically stretches the histogram values in the active layer. For each channel of the active layer, it finds the minimum and maximum values and uses them to stretch the Red, Green and Blue histograms to the full contrast range. The bright colors become brighter and the dark colors become darker, which increases the contrast. This command produces a somewhat similar effect to the Normalize command, except that it works on each color channel of the layer individually. This usually leads to color shifts in the image, so it may not produce the desired result. "Stretch Contrast" works on layers of RGB, Grayscale and Indexed images. Use "Stretch Contrast" only if you want to remove an undesirable color tint from an image which should contain pure white and pure black.

This command is also similar to the Color Balance command, but it does not reject any of the very dark or very bright pixels, so the white might be impure.

16.8.11.1 Activate the Command

- This command can be accessed from an image menubar as Colors → Auto → Stretch Contrast.

16.8.11.2 "Stretch Contrast" Example

Figure 16.143 Original image

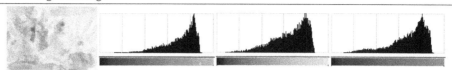

The layer and its Red, Green and Blue histograms before "Stretch Contrast".

Figure 16.144 Image after the command

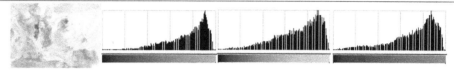

The layer and its Red and Green and Blue histograms after "Stretch Contrast". The pixel columns do not reach the right end of the histogram (255) because of a few very bright pixels, unlike "White Balance". Histogram stretching creates gaps between the pixel columns, giving it a stripped look.

16.8.12 Stretch HSV

The Stretch HSV command does the same thing as the Stretch Contrast command, except that it works in HSV color space, rather than RGB color space, and it preserves the Hue. Thus, it independently stretches the ranges of the Hue, Saturation and Value components of the colors. Occasionally the results are good, often they are a bit odd. "Stretch HSV" operates on layers from RGB and Indexed images. If the image is Grayscale, the menu entry is insensitive and grayed out.

16.8.12.1 Activate the Command

- You can access this command from the image menubar through Colors → Auto → Stretch HSV.

16.8.12.2 "Stretch HSV" example

Figure 16.145 Original image

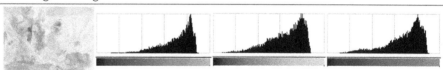

The active layer and its Red, Green and Blue histograms before "Stretch HSV".

Figure 16.146 Image after the command

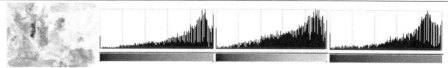

The active layer and its Red, Green and Blue histograms after "Stretch HSV". Contrast, luminosity and hues are enhanced.

16.8.13 The "Components" Submenu

This command leads to the following submenu

Figure 16.147 The "Components" submenu

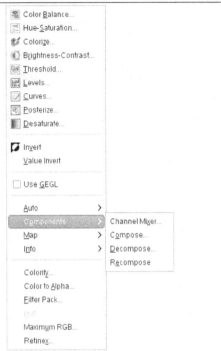

- Section 16.8.14

- Section 16.8.15

- Section 16.8.16

- Section 16.8.17

16.8.13.1 Activating the command

This command is found in the image window menu under Colors → Components.

16.8.14 Channel Mixer

16.8.14.1 Overview

Figure 16.148 Example for the "Channel Mixer" filter

(a) *Original image*   (b) *"Channel Mixer" applied*

This command combines values of the RGB channels. It works with images with or without an alpha channel. It has monochrome mode and a preview.

16.8.14.2 Activate the command

You can find this command through Colors → Components → Channel Mixer.

16.8.14.3 Options

Figure 16.149 "Channel Mixer" command options

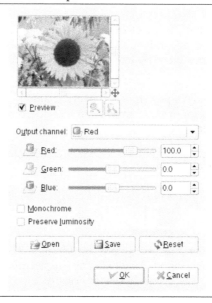

Output Channel From this menu you select the channel to mix to. Choices are Red, Green, or Blue. It is insensitive when Monochrome option is checked.

Red, Green, Blue These three sliders set the contribution of red, green or blue channel to output. Can be negative. These sliders are graduated from -200 to 200. They represent the percentage which will be attributed to the output channel. 100% corresponds to the value of the channel of the studied pixel in the image.

Monochrome This option converts the RGB image into a gray-scale RGB image. The Channel Mixer command is often used with this aim in view, because it often provides a better result than the other ways (see Grayscale in Glossary). Makes the Output Channel menu insensitive.

Note

   The 21%, 72%, 7% settings give you the same gray luminosity (Value) as the Grayscale command in Image/Mode. (They were 30%, 59%, 11% in v2.2).

Preserve Luminosity Calculations may result in too high values and an image too much clear. This option lessens luminosities of the color channels while keeping a good visual ratio between them. So, you can change the relative weight of the colors without changing the overall luminosity.

16.8.14.4   Buttons

Open Load settings from a file.

Save Save settings to a file.

Reset Set default settings.

16.8.14.5   How does Channel Mixer work?   .

In RGB mode In this mode, you have to select an Output Channel . This channel is the one which will be modified. In the dialog window, its default value is 100%, corresponding to the value of the channel in the original image. It can be increased or decreased. That's why slider ends are -200 and 200.

Three RGB sliders let you give a percentage to every channel. For every pixel in the image, the sum of the calculated values for every channel from these percentages will be given to the Output Channel. Here is an example:

Figure 16.150 The original image and its channels

RGB values of the pixels in red, green, blue, gray squares are displayed. The black rectangle is special, because black (0;0;0) is not concerned by the command (0 multiplied by any percentage always gives 0). The result can't exceed 255 nor be negative.

Figure 16.151 Output channel is red. Green Channel +50

In the red square, the pixel values are 230;10;10. Relative values are 1;0.5;0. The calculation result is 230*1 + 10*0,5 + 10*0 =235. The same reasoning is valid for the green and the blue squares.
In the gray square, which contains red color, the calculation result is above 255. It is reduced to 255. A negative value would be reduced to 0.

Figure 16.152 Output channel is red. Green Channel +50%. The Preserve Luminosity option is checked.

The values attributed to the Red Output channel are lower, preventing a too much clear image.

In Monochrome mode When this option is checked, the image preview turns to grayscale, but the image is still a RGB image with three channels, until the command action is validated.

Figure 16.153 Monochrome option checked. Red: 100% Green: 50% Blue: 0%. Preserve Luminosity unchecked.

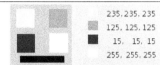

In every square, pixels have been converted into a gray level equal to the value of the Red channel in the original image (The background has been painted with pink afterwards to make all squares visible).

Here is how the Preserve Luminosity works in the monochrome mode: " For example, suppose the sliders were Red:75%, Green:75%, Blue:0%. With Monochrome on and the Preserve Luminosity option off, the resulting picture would be at 75%+75%+0% =150%, very bright indeed. A pixel with a value of, say, R,G,B=127,100,80 would map to 127*0.75+100*0.75+80*0=170 for each channel. With the Preserve Luminosity option on, the sliders will be scaled so they always add up to 100%. In this example, that scale value is 1/(75%+75%+0%) or 0.667. So the pixel values would be about 113. The Preserve Luminosity option just assures that the scale values from the sliders always adds up to 100%. Of course, strange things happen when any of the sliders have large negative values " (from the plug-in author himself).

Note

Which channel will you modify? This depends on what you want to do. In principle, the Red channel suits contrast modifications well. The Green channel is well adapted to details changes and the Blue channel to noise, grain changes. You can use the Decompose command.

16.8.15 Compose

16.8.15.1 Overview

Figure 16.154 Example for the "Compose" command

(a) *Decomposed image (RGB decomposition)*   (b) *"Compose" applied*

This command constructs an image from several grayscale images or layers, for instance from extracted RGB, HSV... components. You can also build an image from grayscale images or layers created independently.

16.8.15.2   Activate the command

- You can find this command in the image window menu under Colors → Components → Compose....
  It is enabled if your image is grayscale.

16.8.15.3   Options

Figure 16.155 "Compose" command options

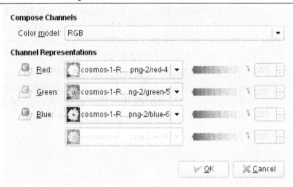

Compose Channels You can select there the color space to be used: RGB, HSV... The options are described in the following Decompose command.

Channel Representation Allows you to select which channel will be affected to each image channel. You may use this option, for example, to exchange color channels:

Figure 16.156 Channel Representation example: exchange two channels

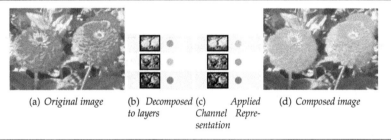

(a) *Original image*   (b) *Decomposed* (c)   *Applied*   (d) *Composed image*
                       to layers   *Channel Repre-*
                                           sentation

Mask Value: Instead of selecting a layer or an image to build the channel, you can give the channel a value from 0 to 255. But note that at least one channel must be formed from a layer or image.

Tip

If Compose options are different from Decompose ones, for instance an image decomposed to RGB then re-composed to LAB, you will get interesting color effects. Test it!

16.8.16   Decompose

16.8.16.1   Overview

Figure 16.157 Decomposition to images (RGB)

(a) *Original image*   (b) *Command "Decompose" applied (RGB decomposition) with Decompose to layers unchecked.*

Figure 16.158 Decomposition to layers (RGB)

(a) *Original image*   (b) *Command "Decompose" applied (RGB decomposition) with Decompose to layers checked.*

This command separates the channels (RGB, HSV, CMYK...) of an image into separated images or layers.

16.8.16.2   Activate the command

- You can find this command in the image window menu under Colors → Components → Decompose....

16.8.16.3   Options

Figure 16.159 "Decompose" command options

Extract Channels

Following options are described with Decompose to layers checked.

Color model

> **RGB** If the RGB radio button is clicked, a grey level image is created with three layers (Red, Green and Blue), and two channels (Grey and Alpha).
>
> This function is interesting when using Threshold tool. You can also perform operations like cutting, pasting or moving selections in a single RBG channel. You can use an extracted grayscale as a selection or mask by saving it in a channel (right-click>Select>Save to a channel).

RGBA If the RGBA radio button is clicked, a image is created similar at the RGB Decomposing with a additional Alpha layer filled with the transparencies values of the source image. Full transparent pixels are black and the full opaque pixels are white.

HSV This option decomposes image into three greyscaled layers, one for Hue, one for Saturation and another for Value.

Although Hue is greyscaled, it does represent hues. In color circle, white and black are starting and arrival points and are superimposed. They represent Red color at top of circle. Grey intermediate levels are corresponding to intermediate hues on circle: dark grey to orange, mid grey to green and light grey to magenta.

Saturation and Value: White is maximum Saturation (pure color) and maximum Value (very bright). Black is minimum Saturation (white) and minimum Value (black).

HSL This option is similar to HSV. Instead of the *Value*, the third layer contains the image's *L* component.

CMY This option decomposes image into three greyscaled layers, one for Yellow, one for Magenta and another for Cyan.

This option might be useful to transfer image into printing softwares with CMY capabilities.

CMYK This option is similar at the CMY Decomposing with an additional layer for Black.

This option might be useful to transfer image into printing softwares with CMYK capabilities.

Alpha This option extracts the image transparency stored in the Alpha channel in Channel dialog in a separate image. The full transparent pixels are Black the full opaque pixels are white. The graytones are smooth transitions of the transparency in the source image.

LAB This option decomposes image into three greyscaled layers, layer "L" for Luminance, layer "A" for colors between green and red, layer "B" for colors between blue and yellow.

The LAB Decomposing is a color model of the Luminance-Color family. A channel is used for the Luminosity while two other channels are used for the Colors. The LAB color model is used by Photoshop.

YCbCr In GIMP there is four YCbCr decompositions with different values. Each option decomposes image in three greyscaled layers, a layer for Luminance and two other for blueness and redness.

The YCbCr color model also called YUV is now used for digital video (initially for PAL analog video). It's based on the idea that the human eye is most sensitive to luminosity, next to colors. The YCbCr Decomposing use a transformation matrix and the different options are different values recommended by ITU (International Telecommunication Union) applied to the matrix

.

Decompose to Layers If this option is checked, a new grey-scaled image is created, with each layer representing one of the channels of the selected mode. If this option is not checked, every channel is represented with a specific image automatically and clearly named in the name bar.

Example 16.1 Crop marks

Foreground as registration color
Source image

Cyan component

Black component
(Magenta and Yellow components omitted.)

This option is for specialists. It is related to CMYK printing. When checked, every pixel of the current foreground color will be black in each component of the decomposed images/layers. This allows you to make crop marks visible on all channels, providing a useful reference for alignment. A thin cross printed in registration black can also be used to check whether the printing plates are lined up.

16.8.17 Recompose

16.8.17.1 Overview

Figure 16.160 Example for the "Recompose" command

(a) *Original image (decomposed to RGB)*   (b) *Command "Recompose" applied*

This command reconstructs an image from its RGB, HSV... components directly, unlike the Compose command which uses a dialog.

16.8.17.2 Activate the command

- This command is found in the image window menu under Colors → Components → Recompose: This command is active after using Decompose.

16.8.18 The "Map" Submenu

This command leads to the following submenu

Figure 16.161 The "Map" submenu

- Section 16.8.19

- Section 16.8.20

- Section 16.8.21

- Section 16.8.22

- Section 16.8.23

- Section 16.8.24

- Section 16.8.25

- Section 16.8.26

16.8.19   Rearrange Colormap

Figure 16.162 The "Rearrange Colormap" window

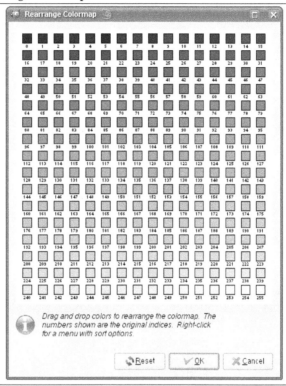

This command allows you to re-organize colors in the palette of *indexed* images. It doesn't modify the image. You can't add or remove colors; for that, see The Indexed Palette Dialog.

16.8.19.1   Activate Dialog

You can access this command from the image menu-bar through Colors → Map → Rearrange Colormap. If your image is not indexed, this command is grayed out and disabled.

16.8.19.2   Using the "Rearrange Colormap" dialog

Explanations supplied in the dialog window are enough: drag and drop colors to rearrange the colormap. You can sort colors in various ways by using the local pop-menu that you get by right-clicking:

Figure 16.163 The "Rearrange Colormap" pop-menu

Sort on Hue
Sort on Saturation
Sort on Value

Reverse Order
Reset Order

16.8.20 Set Colormap

Figure 16.164 The "Set Colormap" window

This command opens a dialog which allows you to select another palette to replace the color map of your indexed image. First click in the button with the name of the current palette (which is not the color map of your image yet) to open the Palette Selector:

Figure 16.165 The "Palette Selection" dialog

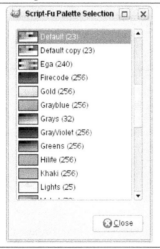

Once you have chosen the wanted palette, click the OK button in the "Set Palette" dialog to replace the image colormap.

16.8.20.1 Activate the command

This command is found in the image window menu under Colors → Map → Set Colormap.

16.8.21 Alien Map

16.8.21.1 Overview

Figure 16.166 Alien Map filter example

(a) *Original image*   (b) *Filter applied*

This filter renders very modified colors by applying trigonometric functions. Alien Map can work on images having RGB and HSV color models.

16.8.21.2 Activate the filter

You can find this filter in the image window menu under Colors → Map → Alien Map.

16.8.21.3 Options

Figure 16.167 Options for the "Alien Map" filter

Preview This preview displays results of filter application interactively.

Mode Radio buttons RGB Color Channel and HSV Color Channel let you select the color space you want to use.

Check boxes Modify ... Channel let you select RGB/HSV Channel you want to work with.

Sliders For each channel, you can set Frequency (0-5) and Phaseshift (0-360) of sine-cosine functions, using either sliders or input boxes and their arrowheads.

Frequency around 0.3 to 0.7 provides a curve that is similar to the linear function (original image), only darker or with more contrast. As you raise the frequency level, you'll get an increasing variation in pixel transformation, meaning that the image will get more and more "alien".

Phase alters the value transformation. 0 and 360 degrees are the same as a sine function and 90 is the same as a cosine function. 180 inverts sine and 270 inverts cosine.

16.8.22   Color Exchange

16.8.22.1   Overview

Figure 16.168 "Color Exchange" filter example

(a) *Original image*   (b) *Filter applied*

This filter replaces a color with another one.

16.8.22.2   Activate the filter

This filter is found in the image window menu under Colors → Map → Color Exchange.

16.8.22.3   Options

Figure 16.169 Option of the "Two color exchange" filter

Preview   In this preview, a part of the Image is displayed. A selection smaller than preview will be complete in preview. A bigger one will be cut out to be adapted to the preview.

If you middle-click inside preview , the clicked pixel color will be selected and will appear as From Color.

From color   In this section, you can choose the color to be used to select pixels that will be concerned by color exchange.

Three sliders for RVB colors: If you have clicked on preview, they are automatically positioned. But you can change them. Each slider acts on color intensity. Input boxes and arrowheads work the same. Result is interactively displayed in the From swatch box.

Three sliders for thresholds, for each color. The higher the threshold, the more pixels will be concerned. Result is interactively displayed in Preview.

Lock Thresholds: This option locks threshold sliders which will act all the same.

To color   Three cursors allow to select the color that pixels will have. Result is displayed in swatch box and in preview. You can also click on the color dwell to get a color selector.

16.8.23   Gradient Map

16.8.23.1   Overview

Figure 16.170 Example of gradient map

Example of Gradient Mapping. Top: Original image. Middle: a gradient. Bottom: result of applying the gradient to the original image with the Gradient Map filter.

This filter uses the current gradient, as shown in the Brush/Pattern/Gradient area of the Toolbox, to recolor the active layer or selection of the image to which the filter is applied. To use it, first choose a gradient from the Gradients Dialog. Then select the part of the image you want to alter, and activate the filter. The filter runs automatically, without showing any dialog or requiring any further input. It uses image color intensities (0 - 255), mapping the darkest pixels to the left end color from the gradient, and the lightest pixels to the right end color from the gradient. Intermediate values are set to the corresponding intermediate colors.

16.8.23.2   Activate the filter

You can find this filter in the image window menu under Colors → Map → Gradient Map.

16.8.24   Palette Map

16.8.24.1   Overview

This plug-in recolors the image using colors from the active palette that you choose in Dialogs → Palettes.

It maps the contents of the specified drawable (layer, selection...) with the active palette. It calculates luminosity of each pixel and replaces the pixel by the palette sample at the corresponding index. A complete black pixel becomes the lowest palette entry, and complete white becomes the highest. Works on both Grayscale and RGB image with/without alpha channel.

16.8.24.2   Activate the filter

You can access this filter in the image window menu under Colors → Map → Palette Map.

16.8.24.3   Example

Figure 16.171 The active palette is applied to a gradient image

(a) *The current palette, with 18 colors* (b) *The colors of the active palette are applied to a black to white gradient. The color with the lowest index in the palette (orange) replaces the black color in the gradient. The color with the highest index in the palette (red) replaces the white color in the gradient. The other colors spread out in the order of the palette.*

16.8.25   Rotate Colors

16.8.25.1   Overview

Figure 16.172 Example for the "Rotate Colors" filter

(a) *Original image*   (b) *Filter "Rotate Colors" applied*

Colormap Rotation lets you exchange one color range to another range.

16.8.25.2   Activating the filter

This filter is found in the image window menu under Colors → Map → Rotate Colors.

16.8.25.3   Main Options

Figure 16.173 Main Options of the "Color Map Rotation" filter

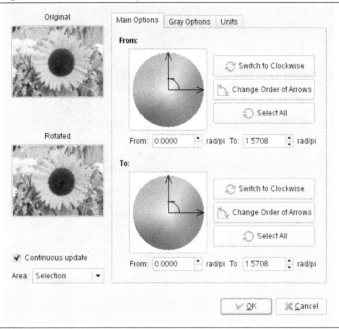

You have there two color circles, one for the "From" color range and the other for the "To" color range:

From The Color Circle: Two axis to define "From" range. The curved arrow in angle lets to recognise "From" axis and "To" axis of range. Click-drag these axis to change range.

> Switch to Clockwise/Counterclockwise: Sets the direction the range is going.

> Change Order of Arrows: Inverts From and To axis. This results in an important color change as colors in selection angle are different.

> Select All selects the whole color circle.

> From and To boxes display start axis and end axis positions (in rad/PI) which are limiting the selected color range. You can enter these positions manually or with help of arrow-heads.

To This section options are the same as "From" section ones.

16.8.25.4   Gray Options

Figure 16.174 Base image for Gray Options

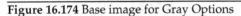
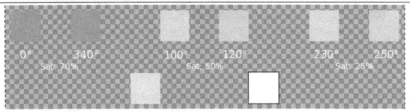

Three sectors are defined for Red, Green and Blue with different saturations. Gray and White colors are represented (0% Sat).

In this tab, you can specify how to treat gray. By default, gray is not considered as a color and is not taken in account by the rotation. Here, you can convert slightly saturated colors into gray and you can also convert gray into color.

Gray Color Circle At center of this color circle is a small "define circle". At center, it represents gray. If you increase gray threshold progressively, colors with saturation less than this threshold turn to gray.

Then, if you pan the define circle in the color circle, or if you use input boxes, you define *Hue* and *Saturation*. This color will replace all colors you have defined as gray. But result depends on Gray Mode too.

Gray Mode The radio buttons *Treat As This* and *Change As This* determine how your previous choices will be treated:

- With *Change to this*, gray will take the color defined by the define circle directly, without any rotation, whatever its position in the color circle.

- With *Treat as this*, gray will take the color defined by the define circle after rotation, according to "From" and "To" choices you made in the Main tab. With this option, you can select color only in the "From" sector, even if it is not visible in Gray tab.

Figure 16.175 Gray Mode

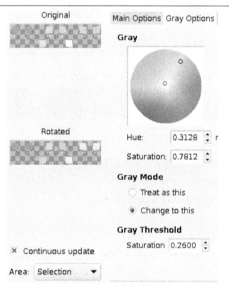

The small circle is on yellow and mode is "Change to this". Blue has changed to yellow. Note that Gray and White did so too.

Gray Threshold

Figure 16.176 Gray Threshold

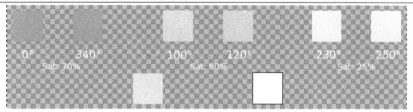

Gray-threshold is 0.25: the blue sector (sat 0.25) has turned to Gray (Note that Gray and White, that are 0% Sat., are not concerned).

You specify there how much saturation will be considered gray. By increasing progressively saturation, you will see an enlarging circle in color circle and enlarging selected areas in Preview if "Continuous update" is checked. In a black to white gradient, you can see enlarging color replacement as you increase threshold very slowly.

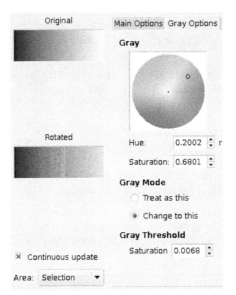

Black to White gradient, progressively filled with color, as threshold increases.

16.8.25.5 Previews

Original, Rotated The Original preview displays a thumbnail of the original image and the Rotated preview displays color changes interactively, before they are applied to the Image.

Continuous Update Continuous Update displays color changes continuously in the Rotated preview.

Area In this drop down list, you can select between

- Entire Layer: works on the whole layer (The image if there is no selection).
- Selection: displays selection only.
- Context: displays selection in image context.

16.8.25.6 Units

You can select here the angle unit used to locate colors in the Hue/Saturation circle. This choice is valid only for the current filter session: don't click on OK just after selecting unit, return to the wanted tab!

16.8.26 Sample Colorize

16.8.26.1 Overview

Figure 16.177 Example for the "Sample Colorize" filter

(a) *Original image*   (b) *Filter "Sample Colorize" applied*

This filter allows you to colorize old black-and-white images by mapping a color source image or a gradient against it.

Caution

Your gray-tone image must be changed to RGB before using this filter (Image/Image>Mode>RGB).

16.8.26.2 Activate the filter

This filter is found in the image window menu under Colors → Map → Sample Colorize.

16.8.26.3 Options

Figure 16.178 Options of the "Sample Colorize" filter

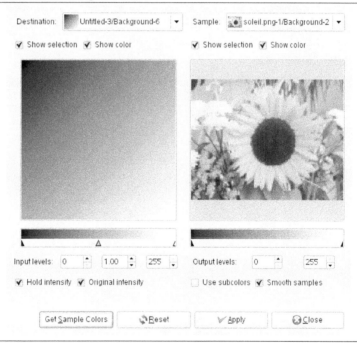

The filter window is divided into two parts: Destination on the left, Sampling on the right.

Destination, Sample By default, displayed image previews reproduce the image you invoked the filter from.

The sample can be the whole preview, or a selection of this preview. With the drop list, you can select another sample-image among the names of images present on your screen when you called the filter. If you choose From Gradient (or From Inverse Gradient), the selected gradient in Gradient Dialog (or its inverse) will be the sample. It will be displayed into the gradient bar below the sample preview. The sampling preview is greyed out and two cursors allow you to select the gradient range that will be applied to the image or selection.

Destination is, by default, the source image. The drop list displays the list of images present on your screen when you evoked the filter and allow you to select another destination image. If there is a selection in this image, it will be gray-scaled, else the whole preview will be gray-scaled.

Show Selection This option toggles between the whole image and the selection, if it exists.

Show Colors This option toggles between colors and gray-scale.

Get Sample Colors When you click on this button, the gradient bar below the sample preview displays colors of the sample. If your sample holds few colors, transitions may be abrupt. Check Smooth Sample Colors option to improve them.

Use Subcolors is more difficult to understand. Let's say first that in a greyscale image there is information only for Value (luminosity, more or less light). In a RGB image, each pixel has information for the three colors and Value. So, pixels with different color may have the same Value. If this option is checked, colors will be mixed and applied to Destination pixels having that Value. If it is unchecked, then the dominating color will be applied.

Out Levels Two input boxes and two sliders act the same: they limit the color range which will be applied to destination image. You can choose this range accurately. Result appears interactively in destination preview.

In Levels Three input boxes and three sliders allow to fix importance of dark tones, mid tones and light tones. Result appears interactively in destination preview.

Hold Intensity If this option is checked, the average light intensity of destination image will be the same as that of source image.

Original Intensity If this option is checked, the In levels intensity settings will not be taken in account: original intensity will be preserved.

16.8.27   The "Info" Submenu

This command leads to the following submenu

Figure 16.179 The "Info" submenu

- Section 16.8.28

- Section 16.8.29

- Section 16.8.30

- Section 16.8.31

16.8.28 Histogram

The Histogram dialog is documented in Section 15.2.5.

16.8.29 Border Average

16.8.29.1 Overview

Figure 16.180 Example for the "Border Average" filter

(a) *Original image*

(b)
*Filter
"Border
Aver-
age"
applied*

This plug-in calculates the most often used color in a specified border of the active layer or selection. It can gather similar colors together so that they become predominant. The calculated color becomes the foreground color in the Toolbox. This filter is interesting when you have to find a Web page color background that differs as little as possible from your image border. The action of this filter is not registered in Undo History and can't be deleted with Ctrl-Z : it doesn't modify the image.

16.8.29.2 Activating the filter

This filter is found in the image window menu under Colors+Info → Border Average.

16.8.29.3 Options

Figure 16.181 Options of the "Border Average Filter"

Border Size You can set there the border Thickness in pixels.

Number of Colors The Bucket Size lets you control the number of colors considered as similar and counted with the same "bucket". A low bucket size value (i.e. a high bucket number) gives you better precision in the calculation of the average color. Note that better precision does not necessarily mean better results (see example below).

16.8.29.4 Examples illustrating the "Border Average" filter

Figure 16.182 Original image

Original image: colors are pure Red (255;0;0), pure Blue (0;0;255), and different but similar kinds of Green (0;255;0 , 63;240;63 , 48;224;47 , 0;192;38).

Figure 16.183 "Number of Colors" is set to 8:

The resulting color is a Red (254,2,2).

The bucket size is low. So the bucket number is high. All color shades can be stored in different buckets. Here, the bucket containing red is the most filled. The resulting color is a nearly pure Red (254,2,2) and becomes the foreground color of the Toolbox.

Figure 16.184 "Number of Colors" is set to 64:

The resulting color is Green (32,224,32).

Here the bucket size is high, the number of buckets low. Similar colors (here green) are stored in a same bucket. This "green" bucket is now the most filled. All colors in this bucket have the same values for the two most significant bits: (00******;11******;00******). The remaining 6 bits may have any values from 0 to 63 for the respective channel. So in this bucket, color red channels range from 0 to 63, green channels from 192 to 255, blue channels from 0 to 63. The resulting color is Green (32,224,32), which, for every channel, is the average between the limits of the channel range $(63 + 0)/2$, $(255+192)/2$, $(63+0)/2$.

16.8.30 Colorcube Analysis

16.8.30.1 Overview

Figure 16.185 Example for the "Colorcube" filter

 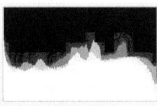

Image dimensions: 300 × 300
Number of unique colors: 44201

      (a) *Original image*   (b) *Filter "Colorcube Analysis" applied*

Information is reduced since GIMP 2.4: size and color number of the active layer.

16.8.30.2 Activating the filter

You can find this filter in the image window menu under Colors → Info → Colorcube Analysis.

16.8.31 Smooth Palette

16.8.31.1 Overview

Figure 16.186 Example for the "Smooth Palette" filter

(a) *Original image*   (b) *Filter "Smooth Palette" applied*

It creates a striped palette from colors in active layer or selection. The main purpose of this filter is to create color-maps to be used with the Flame filter.

16.8.31.2 Activating the filter

This filter is found in the image window menu under Colors → Info → Smooth Palette.

16.8.31.3 Options

Figure 16.187 "Smooth Palette" options

Parameter Settings You can set palette dimensions for Width and Height. Dimensions are linked when chain is not broken. You can also select unit.

Search Depth Increasing Search Depth (1 - 1024) will result in more shades in palette.

16.8.32 The Color Filters

The following color filters group contains miscellaneous filters to modify colors in an image, a layer or a selection. You can find some nice effects here.

- Section 16.8.33

- Section 16.8.34

- Section 16.8.35

- Section 16.8.36

- Section 16.8.37

- Section 16.8.38

16.8.33 Colorify...

16.8.33.1 Overview

Figure 16.188 Example for the "Colorify" filter

(a) *Original image*   (b) *Filter "Colorify" applied*

This filter renders a greyscaled image like it is seen through a colored glass.

For every pixel, the filter computes a weighted average value of the RGB channels (this is equivalent to desaturating the image based on Luminosity). The resulted color is the product of this average value and the "colorify color".

Hence, this filter works only on images in RGB mode.

16.8.33.2 Activate the filter

This filter is found in the image window menu under Colors → Colorify....

16.8.33.3 Options

Figure 16.189 "Colorify" filter options

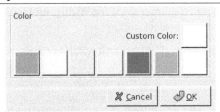

A color palette is available containing especially the RGB colors Red, Green, Blue and the CMY colors Cyan, Magenta, Yellow.

You can select your own color by clicking on the Custom Color swatch.

16.8.34 Color to Alpha...

16.8.34.1 Overview

Figure 16.190 Example for "Color to Alpha"

(a) *Original image*   (b) *"Color to Alpha" applied on blue areas*

The Color to Alpha command makes transparent all pixels of the active layer that have a selected color. An Alpha channel is created. It will attempt to preserve anti-aliasing information by using a partially intelligent routine that replaces weak color information with weak alpha information. In this way, areas that contain an element of the selected color will maintain a blended appearance with their surrounding pixels.

16.8.34.2 Activate the filter

This filter is found in the image window menu under Colors → Color to Alpha....

16.8.34.3 Options

Figure 16.191 "Color to Alfa" command options

Color Clicking on the From color swatch provides a color selection dialog where you can select a color. If selection of a precise color is required, use the Color Picker then drag and drop the selected color from the color picker to the From color swatch. Right clicking on the color will display a menu where you can select Foreground or Background colors, White or Black.

16.8.35 Filter Pack...

16.8.35.1 Overview

Figure 16.192 Example for the "Filter Pack" filter

(a) *Original image*   (b) *Filter "FilterPack" applied (more Blue, more Saturation)*

This tool offers you a collection of unified filters to treat the image. Of course, same functions can be performed by particular filters, but you have here an interesting, intuitive, overview.

16.8.35.2 Activate the filter

You can find this filter in the image window menu under Colors → Filter Pack....

16.8.35.3 Options

Figure 16.193 All the options for filter "Filter Pack"

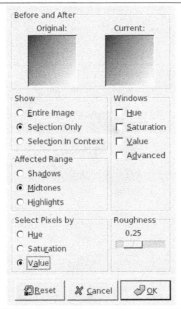

Original and Current previews Two previews display respectively before treatment and after treatment images.

Show Sets what you want to preview:

- Entire image
- Selection only: if a selection exists (default is the whole image).
- Selection in context: the selection within the image.

Windows You can choose between:

- Hue makes one preview for each of the three primary colors and the three complementary colors of the RGB color model. By clicking successively on a color, you add to this color into the affected range, according to Roughness. To subtract color, click on the opposite color, the complementary color.

Figure 16.194 Hue option of the "Filterpack" filter

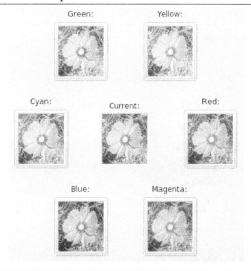

- Saturation: Three previews for more or less saturation.

Figure 16.195 The saturation option of the "Filterpack" filter

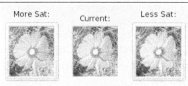

- Value: Three previews for more or less luminosity.

Figure 16.196 Value option of the "Filterpack" filter

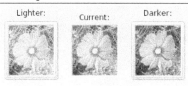

- Advanced: developed later.

Affected range Allows you to set which brightness you want to work with.

- Shadows: dark tones.
- Midtones
- Highlights: bright tones

Select pixels by Determines what HSV channel the selected range will affect. You can choose between:

- Hue
- Saturation
- Value

Roughness This slider sets how image will change when you click on a window: taking a short step or a large one (0 - 1).

Advanced Options

Figure 16.197 Advanced options of the "Filterpack" filter

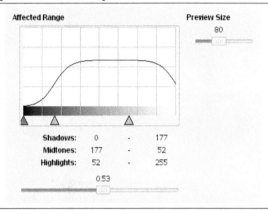

These advanced options let you work more precisely on the changes applied to the image and on the preview size.

Preview Size Something like a zoom on previews. Normal size is 80.

Tip

 In spite of Preview Size option, this size is often too small. You can compensate this by working on an enlarged selection, for instance a face on a photo. Then, you invert selection to work on the other part of the image.

Affected range Here, you can set the tone range that the filter will affect.

The curve in this window represents the importance of the changes applied to the image. The aspect of this curve depends on the Affected range you have selected: Shadows, Midtons or Highlights. You can set the curve amplitude by using the Roughness slider in the main window of the filter.

By using the available controls (slider and triangles), you can precisely set the form of this action curve.

16.8.36 Hot...

16.8.36.1 Overview

This command identifies and modifies pixels which might cause problem when displayed onto PAL or NTSC TV screen.

16.8.36.2   Activate the command

You can access the command from the image menu bar through Colors → Hot....

   This command only works on images in RGB mode, and only if the active layer does not have an alpha channel. Otherwise the menu entry is insensitive and grayed out.

16.8.36.3   Options

Figure 16.198 "Hot" options

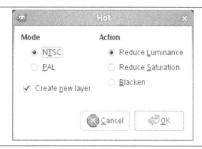

Mode   You have to select the TV mode: PAL or NTSC.

Action   You can select:

- Reduce Luminency
- Reduce Saturation
- Blacken: this will turn hot pixels to black.

Create a new layer   With this option, work will be performed on a new layer instead of the image. This will give you peace of mind!

16.8.37   Maximum RGB...

16.8.37.1   Overview

Figure 16.199 Example for the filter "Max RGB"

(a) *Original image*   (b) *Filter "Max RGB" applied*

For every pixel of the image, this filter holds the channel with the maximal/minimal intensity. The result is an image with only three colors, red, green and blue, and possibly pure gray.

16.8.37.2   Activate the filter

This filter is found in the image window menu under Colors → Maximum RGB....

16.8.37.3 Options

Figure 16.200 "Max RGB" options

Preview This preview displays, in real time, the resulting image after treatment by filter.

Parameter Settings Hold the maximal channels: For every pixel, the filter keeps intensity of the RGB color channel which has the maximal intensity and reduces other both to zero. For example: 220, 158, 175 max--> 220, 0, 0. If two channels have same intensity, both are held: 210, 54, 210 max--> 210, 0, 210.

Hold the minimal channels: For every pixel, the filter keeps intensity of the RGB color channel which has the minimal intensity and reduce both others to zero. For example: 220, 158, 175 min--> 0, 158, 0. If two minimal channels have same intensity, both are held: 210, 54, 54 min--> 0, 54, 54.

Grey levels are not changed since light intensity is the same in all three channels.

16.8.38   Retinex

16.8.38.1   Overview

Figure 16.201 "Retinex" example

(a) *Original image*   (b) *"Retinex" filter applied. Note new details in the upper right corner.*

Retinex improves visual rendering of an image when lighting conditions are not good. While our eye can see colors correctly when light is low, cameras and video cams can't manage this well. The MSRCR (MultiScale Retinex with Color Restoration) algorithm, which is at the root of the Retinex filter, is inspired by the eye biological mechanisms to adapt itself to these conditions. Retinex stands for Retina + cortex.

Besides digital photography, Retinex algorithm is used to make the information in astronomical photos visible and detect, in medicine, poorly visible structures in X-rays or scanners.

16.8.38.2 Activate the filter

This filter is found in the image window menu under Colors → Retinex....

16.8.38.3 Options

Figure 16.202 "Retinex" filter options

These options call for notions that only mathematicians and imagery engineers can understand. In actual practice, the user has to grope about for the best setting. However, the following explanations should help out the experimented GIMP user.

Level Here is what the plug-in author writes on his site [PLUGIN-RETINEX]: "To characterize color variations and the lightor, we make a difference between (gaussian) filters responses at different scales. These parameters allow to specify how to allocate scale values between min scale (sigma 2.0) and max (sigma equal to the image size)"...

Uniform Uniform tends to treat both low and high intensity areas fairly.

Low As a rule of thumb, low does "flare up" the lower intensity areas on the image.

High High tends to "bury" the lower intensity areas in favor of a better rendering of the clearer areas of the image.

Scale Determines the depth of the Retinex scale. Minimum value is 16, a value providing gross, unrefined filtering. Maximum value is 250. Optimal and default value is 240.

Scale division Determines the number of iterations in the multiscale Retinex filter. The minimum required, and the recommended value is three. Only one or two scale divisions removes the multiscale aspect and falls back to a single scale Retinex filtering. A value that is too high tends to introduce noise in the picture.

Dynamic As the MSR algorithm tends to make the image lighter, this slider allows you to adjust color saturation contamination around the new average color. A higher value means less color saturation. This is definitely the parameter you want to tweak for optimal results, because its effect is extremely image-dependent.

16.9   The "Tools" Menu

16.9.1   Introduction to the "Tools" Menu

Figure 16.203 Contents of the "Tools" menu

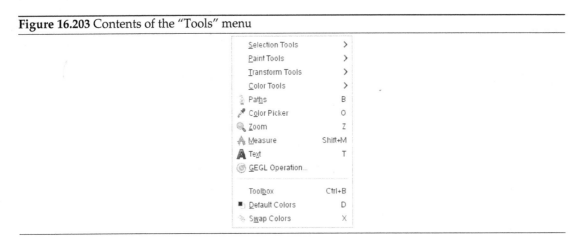

The menu entries on the Tools menu access the GIMP tools. All of the tools available in GIMP are extensively described in the Tools section.

16.10   The "Filters" Menu

16.10.1   Introduction to the "Filters" Menu

Figure 16.204 The "Filters" menu

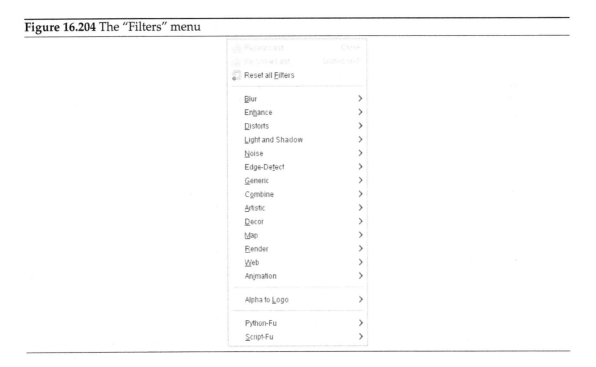

In GIMP terminology, a *filter* is a plug-in that modifies the appearance of an image, in most cases just the active layer of the image. Not all of the entries in this menu meet that definition, however; the word "filter" is often mis-used to mean any plug-in, regardless of what it does. Indeed, some of the entries in this menu do not modify images at all.

With the exception of the top three items of the Filters menu, all of the entries are provided by plug-ins. Each plug-in decides for itself where it would like its menu entry to be placed. Therefore, the appearance of this menu can be completely different for each user. In practice, though, the appearance does not vary very much, because most plug-ins come with GIMP when it is installed, and of course they are always in the same places in the menu.

Plug-ins are not restricted to just the Filters menu: a plug-in can place entries in any menu. Indeed, a number of GIMP's basic functions (for example, Semi-flatten in the Layer menu) are implemented by plug-ins. But the Filters menu is the default place for a plug-in to place its menu entries.

For general information on plug-ins and how to use them, see the section on Plug-ins. You can find information on the filters that are provided with GIMP in the Filters chapter. For filters you install yourself, please refer to the information which came with them.

16.10.2   Repeat Last

The Repeat Last command performs the action of the most recently executed plug-in again, using the same settings as the last time it was run. It does not show a dialog or request confirmation.

Note

 Please note that this command repeats the most recently executed *plug-in*, regardless of whether it is in the Filters menu or not.

16.10.2.1   Activating the Command

- You can access this command from the image menubar through Filters → Repeat `filter`,

- or by using the keyboard shortcut Ctrl-F.

16.10.3   Re-show Last

The Re-show Last command shows the dialog of the most recently executed plug-in. Unlike the "Repeat Last" command, which does not display a dialog, the "Re-show Last" command displays a dialog window, if the plug-in has one. It is displayed with the settings you used the last time you ran the plug-in (assuming that the plug-in follows the GIMP programming conventions).

Note

 Please note that this command repeats the most recently executed *plug-in*, regardless of whether it is in the Filters menu or not.

Tip

 When you are using a plug-in, especially one that does not have a preview window, you may very well have to adjust the parameters several times before you are satisfied with the results. To do this most efficiently, you should memorize the shortcuts for Undo and Re-show Last: Ctrl-Z followed by Ctrl-Shift-F.

16.10.3.1   Activating the Command

- You can access this command from the image menubar through Filters → Re-show `filter`,

- or by using the keyboard shortcut Ctrl-Shift-F.

16.10.4 Reset All Filters

Normally, each time you run an interactive plug-in, its dialog is displayed with all of the settings initialized to the ones you used the last time you ran it. This may be a problem if you made a mistake setting the values and you can't remember what they were originally. One way to recover is to exit GIMP and start again, but the Reset all Filters command is a slightly less drastic solution: it resets the values for *all* plug-ins to their defaults. Because it is a dramatic step, it asks you to confirm that you really want to do it. Be careful: you cannot undo this command.

16.10.4.1 Activating the Command

- You can access this command from the image menubar through Filters → Reset all Filters.

16.10.5 The "Python-Fu" Submenu

Figure 16.205 The "Python-Fu" submenu

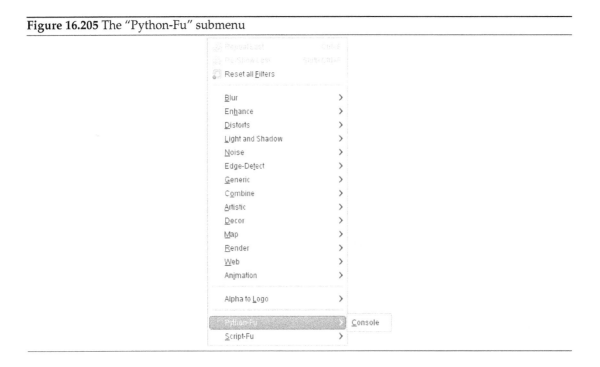

By default this submenu just contains the Python-Fu console.

Python-Fu is a set of Python modules that act as a wrapper to *libgimp* allowing the writing of plug-ins for GIMP.

16.10.5.1 Activating the submenu

- You can access this command from the image menu through Filters → Python-Fu

16.10.5.2 The Python-Fu Console

The Python-Fu console is a dialog window running a "Python shell" (a Python interpreter in interactive mode). This console is set up to make use of the internal GIMP library routines of *libgimp*.

You can use the Python-Fu console to interactively test Python commands.

The console consists of a large scrollable main window for input and output, where you can type Python commands. When you type in a Python command and then press the **Enter** key, the command is executed by the Python interpreter. The command's output as well as its return value (and its error message, if any) will be displayed in the main window.

Figure 16.206 The Python-Fu Console

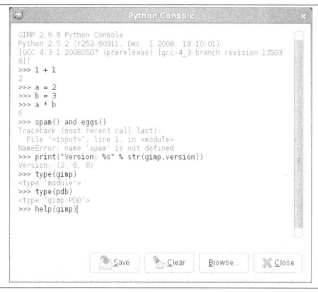

The Python-Fu Console Buttons

Save This command lets you save the content of the main window, that is the Python-Fu console input and output (including the ">>>" prompt).

Clear Wenn you click on this button, the content of the main window will be removed. Note that you can't get back the removed content using the Save command.

Browse When clicked, the procedure browser pops up, with an additional button Apply at the bottom of the window.

When you press this Apply button in the procedure browser, a call to the selected procedure will be pasted into the console window as a Python command:

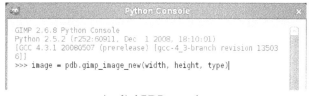

Applied PDB procedure

Now you just have to replace the parameter names (here: "width", "height", and "type") with actual values, e.g.

```
image = pdb.gimp_image_new(400, 300, RGB)
```

Then press **Enter** to execute the command.

You can (and should!) use the constants you find in the decription of the procedure's parameters, for example "RGB-IMAGE" or "OVERLAY-MODE". But note that you have to replace hyphens ("-") with underscores ("_"): RGB_IMAGE, OVERLAY_MODE.

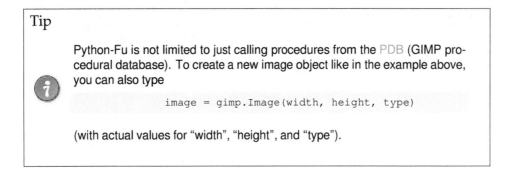

Tip

> Python-Fu is not limited to just calling procedures from the PDB (GIMP procedural database). To create a new image object like in the example above, you can also type
>
> ```
> image = gimp.Image(width, height, type)
> ```
>
> (with actual values for "width", "height", and "type").

Close Pressing this button closes the console.

16.10.6   The "Script-Fu" Submenu

Figure 16.207 The "Script-Fu" submenu

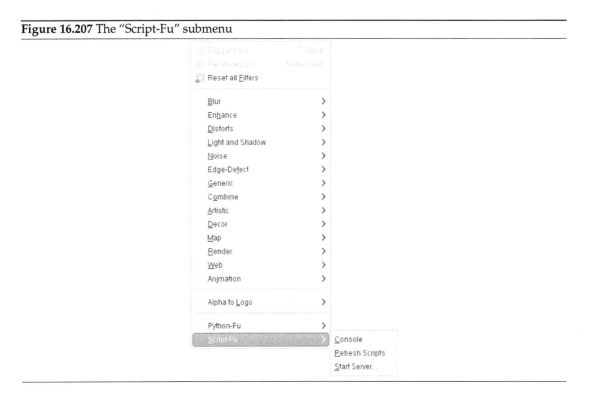

This submenu contains some Script-Fu commands, especially the Script-Fu console. Script-Fu is a language for writing scripts, which allow you to run a series of GIMP commands automatically.

16.10.6.1   Activating the submenu

- You can access this command from the image menu through Filters → Script-Fu

16.10.6.2   Refresh Scripts

You will need this command every time you add, remove, or change a Script-Fu script. The command causes the Script-Fus to be reloaded and the menus containing Script-Fus to be rebuilt from scratch. If you don't use this command, GIMP won't notice your changes until you start it again.

Note that you won't get any feedback, unless saving, if one of your scripts fails.

16.10.6.3   Script-Fu Console

The Script-Fu console is a dialog window where you can interactively test Scheme commands.

The console consists of a large scrollable main window for output and a textbox used to type Scheme commands. When you type a Scheme statement and then press the **Enter** key, the command and its return value will be displayed in the main window.

Figure 16.208 The Script-Fu Console

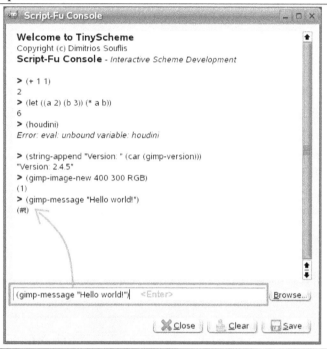

You will find more information about Scheme and examples how to use the Script-Fu console in Section 13.3.

The Script-Fu Console Buttons

Browse This button is next to the Scheme commands textbox. When clicked, the procedure browser pops up, with an additional button at the bottom of the window:

The additional button of the Procedure Browser

When you press this Apply button in the procedure browser, the selected procedure will be pasted into the text box:

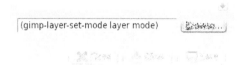

Applied PDB procedure

Now you just have to replace the parameter names (here: "layer" and "mode") with actual values, and then you can call the procedure by pressing **Enter**.

Close Pressing this button closes the Script-Fu console.

Clear Wenn you click on this button, the content of the main window will be removed. Note that you can't get back the removed content using the Save command.

Save This command lets you save the content of the main window, that is the Script-Fu console output (including the ">"-characters).

16.10.6.4   Start Server

This command will start a server, which reads and executes Script-Fu (Scheme) statements you send him via a specified port.

Figure 16.209 The Script-Fu Server Options

Server Port The port number where the Script-Fu server will listen. It is possible to start more than one server, specifying different port numbers, of course.

Server Logfile Optionally you can specify the name of a file the server will use to log informal and error messages. If no file is specified, messages will be written to stdout.

The Script-Fu Server Protocol
The protocol used to communicate with the Script-Fu server is very simple:

- Every message (Script-Fu statement) of length L sent to the server has to be preceded with the following 3 bytes:

Table 16.1 Header format for commands

Byte #	Content	Description
0	0x47	Magic byte ('G')
1	L div 256	High byte of L
2	L mod 256	Low byte of L

- Every response from the server (return value or error message) of length L will be preceded with the following 4 bytes:

Table 16.2 Header format for responses

Byte #	Content	Description
0	0x47	Magic byte ('G')
1	error code	0 on success, 1 on error
2	L div 256	High byte of L
3	L mod 256	Low byte of L

Tip

If you don't want to get your hands dirty: there is a Python script named servertest.py shipped with the GIMP source code, which you can use as a simple command line shell for the Script-Fu server.

16.11   "Windows" Menu

This menu allows you to manage GIMP windows dialogs:

The "Windows" menu name is not well adapted to the new single-window mode. Nevertheless, its functions concern multi and single modes. Its display may vary according presence or absence of images and docks:

Figure 16.210 Contents of the "Windows" Menu

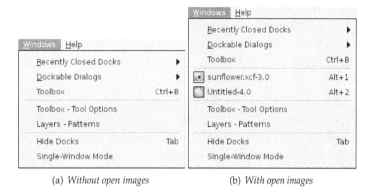

(a) *Without open images*   (b) *With open images*

1. **Recently Closed Docks**: this command opens the list of the docks you have closed recently. You can reopen them by clicking on their name. Please note that isolated windows are not concerned.

   For more information about docks, please see Dialogs and Docking.

2. **Dockable Dialogs**: this command opens the list of dockable dialogs. Please refer to Section 3.2.3.

3. **Toolbox**: clicking on this command or using the Ctrl-B shortcut, raises the toolbox usually together with the tool options dock.

4. The list of open image windows: clicking on an image name, or using the Alt-Number of the image shortcut, makes the image active.

5. The list of open docks: in this list, docks are named with the name of the active dialog in this dock. Clicking on a dock name raises this dock.

6. **Hide Docks** (**Tab**): this command hides all docks (usually to the left and right of the image), leaving the image window alone. The command status is kept on quitting GIMP; then, GIMP starts with no dock in multi-window mode, but not in single-window mode, although the option is checked!

7. **Single Window Mode**: when enabled, GIMP is in a single window mode. Please see Single Window Mode.

16.12   The "Help" Menu

16.12.1   Introduction to the "Help" Menu

Figure 16.211 Contents of the "Help" menu

The Help menu contains commands that assist you while you are working with GIMP.

> **Note**
>
> Besides the commands described here, you may also find other entries in the menu. They are not part of GIMP itself, but have been added by extensions (plug-ins). You can find information about the functionality of a Plugin by referring to its documentation.

16.12.2 Help

The Help command displays the GIMP Users Manual in a browser. You can set the browser you would like to use in the Help System section of the Preferences dialog, as described in Section 12.1.5. The browser may be the built-in GIMP help browser, or it may be a web browser.

> **Tip**
>
> If the help does not seem to work, please verify that the "GIMP Users Manual" is installed on your system. You can find the most recent help online [GIMP-DOCS].

16.12.2.1 Activating the Command

- You can access this command from the image menubar through Help → Help (**F1**).

16.12.3 Context Help

The Context Help command makes the mouse pointer context-sensitive and changes its shape to a "?". You can then click on a window, dialog or menu entry and GIMP displays help about it, if it is available. You can also access context help at any time by pressing the **F1** key while the mouse pointer is over the object you would like help about.

16.12.3.1 Activating the Command

- You can access this command from the image menu through Help → Context Help

- or by using the keyboard shortcut Shift-F1.

16.12.4 Tip of the Day

The Tip of the Day command displays the Tip of the Day dialog. This dialog contains useful tips to help you gain a better understanding of some of the subtle points of using GIMP. New users will find it very valuable to pay attention to these, because they often suggest ways of doing something that are much easier or more efficient than more obvious approaches.

16.12.4.1 Activating the Command

- You can access this command in the image menu through Help → Tip of the Day.

16.12.4.2 Description of the dialog window

Figure 16.212 "Tip of the Day"Dialog window

Some tips contain a Learn more link to the corresponding GIMP manual page.

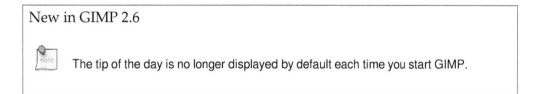

New in GIMP 2.6

The tip of the day is no longer displayed by default each time you start GIMP.

16.12.5 About

The About command shows the About window, which displays information about the version of The GIMP you are running and the many authors who wrote it.

16.12.5.1 Activating the "About" Command

- You can access this command in the image menu through Help → About

16.12.5.2 Description of the dialog window

Figure 16.213 The "About" dialog window

The Credits leads to the list of contributors to GIMP program, concerning programming, graphics and translation of the interface.

The Licence explains how to get the licence.

16.12.6   Plug-In Browser

The Plug-In Browser command displays a dialog window which shows all of the extensions (plug-ins) which are currently loaded in GIMP, both as a list and as a hierarchical tree structure. Since many of the filters are actually plug-ins, you will certainly see many familiar names here. Please note that you do not run the extensions from this dialog window. Use the appropriate menu entry to do that instead. For example, you can run filter plug-ins by using the Filter command on the image menubar.

16.12.6.1   Activating the Command

- You can access this command from the image menubar through Help → Plug-in Browser

16.12.6.2   Description of the "Plug-In Browser" dialog window

Figure 16.214 The list view of the "Plug-In Browser" dialog window

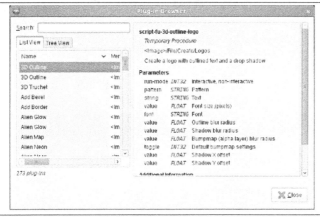

The figure above shows the list view of the Plug-In Browser. You can click on the name of a plug-in in the scrolled window to display more information about it. Select the List View by clicking on the tab at the top of the dialog.

You can search for a plug-in by name by entering part or all of the name in the Search: text box. The left part of the dialog then displays the matches found.

Figure 16.215 The tree view of the "Plug-In Browser" dialog window

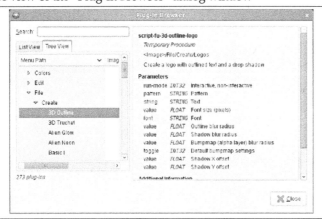

The figure above shows the tree view of the Plug-In Browser. You can click on the name of a plug-in in the scrolled window to display more information about it. You can click on the arrowheads to expand or contract parts of the tree. Select the Tree View by clicking on the tab at the top of the dialog.

You can search for a plug-in by name by entering part or all of the name in the Search: text box. The left part of the dialog then displays the matches found.

> **Note**
>
> Not everything in these huge dialog windows is visible at the same time. Use the scroll bars to view their content.

16.12.7 The Procedure Browser

The Procedure Browser command displays the procedures in the PDB, the Procedure Database. These procedures are functions which are called by the scripts or plug-ins.

16.12.7.1 Activating the Command

- You can access this command from the image menubar through Help → Procedure Browser

16.12.7.2 Description of the "Procedure Browser" dialog window

---

Figure 16.216 The "Procedure Browser" dialog window

The figure above shows the Procedure Browser dialog window. If you click on an item in the scrolled list on the left, information about it is displayed on the right. You can also search for a specific procedure by querying the procedural database with a regular expression on Search: text box:

by name Shows a list of procedures which have code names that contain the part of name you entered.

by description Shows a list of procedures which have blurbs that contain the word you entered.

by help Shows a list of procedures which have additional information text that contain the word you entered.

by author Shows a list of procedures which created by the author which has the part of name you entered.

by copyright Shows a list of procedures which copyright are hold by someone that have the part of name you entered.

by date Shows a list of procedures which have date of year that match the year you entered.

Note

This query is processed with text but not date value, so you cannot find some procedure entries even if their date contains the year you entered. For example, a procedure dated 2000-2005 does not match if you search procedures with 2001, but it matches with 2000 or 2005.

by type Shows a list of procedures which have a one of four types: "Internal GIMP procedure", "GIMP Plug-In", "GIMP Extension", or "Temporary Procedure".

16.12.8   GIMP online

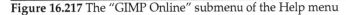

Figure 16.217 The "GIMP Online" submenu of the Help menu

The GIMP online command displays a submenu which lists several helpful web sites that have to do with various aspects of GIMP. You can click on one of the menu items and your web browser will try to connect to the URL.

Chapter 17

Filters

17.1 Introduction

A filter is a special kind of tool designed to take an input layer or image, apply a mathematical algorithm to it, and return the input layer or image in a modified format. GIMP uses filters to achieve a variety of effects and those effects are discussed here.

The filters are divided into several categories:

- Section 17.2

- Section 17.3

- Section 17.4

- Section 17.5

- Section 17.6

- Section 17.7

- Section 17.8

- Section 17.9

- Section 17.10

- Section 17.11

- Section 17.12

- Section 17.13

- Section 17.14

- Section 17.15

- Section 17.16

17.1.1 Preview

Most filters have a Preview where changes in the image are displayed, in real time (if the "Preview" option is checked), before being applied to the image.

Figure 17.1 Preview submenu

Right clicking on the Preview window opens a submenu which lets you set the Style and the Size of checks representing transparency.

17.2   Blur Filters

17.2.1   Introduction

Figure 17.2 Original for demo

This is a set of filters that blur images, or parts of them, in various ways. If there is a selection, only the selected parts of an image will be blurred. There may, however, be some leakage of colors from the unblurred area into the blurred area. To help you pick the one you want, we will illustrate what each does when applied to the image shown at right. These are, of course, only examples: most of the filters have parameter settings that allow you to vary the magnitude or type of blurring.

Figure 17.3 Gaussian blur (radius 10)

The most broadly useful of these is the Gaussian blur. (Don't let the word "Gaussian" throw you: this filter makes an image blurry in the most basic way.) It has an efficient implementation that allows it to create a very blurry blur in a relatively short time.

Figure 17.4 Simple blur

If you only want to blur the image a little bit — to soften it, as it were — you might use the simple "Blur" filter. This filter runs automatically, without creating a dialog. The effect is subtle enough that you might not even notice it, but you can get a stronger effect by repeating it. In GIMP 2.0 the filter shows a dialog that allows you to set a "repeat count". If you want a strong blurring effect, this filter is too slow to be a good choice: use a Gaussian blur instead.

Figure 17.5 Selective blur

The Selective Blur filter allows you to set a threshold so that only pixels that are similar to each other are blurred together. It is often useful as a tool for reducing graininess in photos without blurring sharp edges. (In the example, note that the graininess of the background has been reduced.) The implementation is much slower than a Gaussian blur, though, so you should not use it unless you really need the selectivity.

Figure 17.6 Pixelize

The Pixelize filter produces the well-known "Abraham Lincoln" effect by turning the image into a set of large square pixels. (The Oilify filter, in the Artistic Filters group, has a similar effect, but with irregular blobs instead of perfectly square pixels.)

Note

You can find a nice explanation of the Abraham Lincoln effect at [BACH04]. You will see the Salvador Dali's painting "Gala Contemplating the Mediterranean Sea" turning to an Abraham Lincoln's portrait when looking at it from a distance.

Figure 17.7 Motion blur

The Motion Blur filter blurs in a specific direction at each point, which allows you to create a sense of motion: either linear, radial, or rotational.

Finally, the Tileable Blur filter is really the same thing as a Gaussian blur, except that it wraps around the edges of an image to help you reduce edge effects when you create a pattern by tiling multiple copies of the image side by side.

Note

Tileable Blur is actually implemented by a Script-Fu script that invokes the Gaussian blur plug-in.

17.2.2 Blur

17.2.2.1 Overview

Figure 17.8 The Blur filter applied to a photograph

(a) *Original*   (b) *Blur applied*

The simple Blur filter produces an effect similar to that of an out of focus camera shot. To produce this blur effect, the filter takes the average of the present pixel value and the value of adjacent pixels and sets the present pixel to that average value.

Filter advantage is its calculation speed. It suits big images.

Filter disadvantage is that its action is hardly perceptible on big images, but very strong on small images.

17.2.2.2 Activate the filter

You can find this filter through: Filters → Blur → Blur

17.2.3 Gaussian Blur

17.2.3.1 Overview

Figure 17.9 Example for the "Gaussian Blur" filter

(a) *Original*   (b) *Blur applied*

The IIR Gaussian Blur plug-in acts on each pixel of the active layer or selection, setting its Value to the average of all pixel Values present in a radius defined in the dialog. A higher Value will produce a higher amount of blur. The blur can be set to act in one direction more than the other by clicking the Chain Button so that it is broken, and altering the radius. GIMP supports two implementations of

Gaussian Blur: IIR G.B. and RLE G.B. They both produce the same results, but each one can be faster in some cases.

17.2.3.2   Activate the filter

You can find this filter in the image menu under Filters → Blur → Gaussian Blur...

17.2.3.3   Options

Figure 17.10 "Gaussian" filter parameters settings

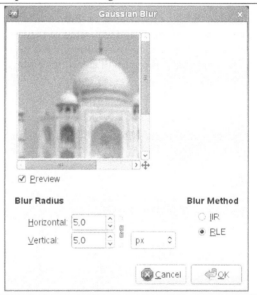

Blur Radius Here you can set the blur intensity. By altering the ratio of horizontal to vertical blur, you can give the effect of a motion blur. You can choose the unit with the drop list.

Blur Method

    IIR IIR stands for "infinite impulse response". This blur works best for large radius values and for images which are not computer generated.

    RLE RLE stands for "run-length encoding". RLE Gaussian Blur is best used on computer-generated images or those with large areas of constant intensity.

17.2.4 Selective Gaussian Blur

17.2.4.1 Overview

Figure 17.11 The Selective Gaussian Blur filter

(a) *Original*   (b) *Blur applied*

Contrary to the other blur plug-ins, the Selective Gaussian Blur plug-in doesn't act on all pixels: blur is applied only if the difference between its value and the value of the surrounding pixels is less than a defined Delta value. So, contrasts are preserved because difference is high on contrast limits. It is used to blur a background so that the foreground subject will stand out better. This add a sense of depth to the image with only a single operation.

17.2.4.2 Activate the filter

You can find this filter in the image menu under Filters → Blur → Selective Gaussian Blur...

17.2.4.3 Options

Figure 17.12 "Selective Gaussian" filter parameters settings

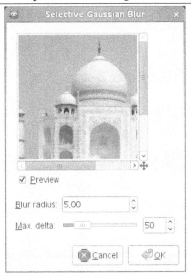

Blur radius Here you can set the blur intensity, in pixels.

Max. delta Here you can set the maximum difference (0-255) between the pixel value and the surrounding pixel values. Above this Delta, blur will not be applied to that pixel.

17.2.5 Motion Blur

17.2.5.1 Overview

Figure 17.13 Starting example for Motion Blur filter

(a) *Original image*   (b) *Linear blur*

Figure 17.14 Using example for Motion Blur filter

(a) *Radial blur*   (b) *Zoom blur*

The Motion Blur filter creates a movement blur. The filter is capable of Linear, Radial, and Zoom movements. Each of these movements can be further adjusted, with Length, or Angle settings available.

17.2.5.2 Activate the filter

You can find this filter in the image menu under Filters → Blur → Motion Blur...

17.2.5.3   Options

Figure 17.15 "Motion Blur" filter options

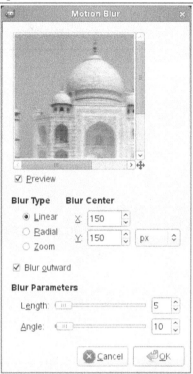

Blur Type

Linear Is a blur that travels in a single direction, horizontally, for example. In this case, Length means as Radius in other filters:it represents the blur intensity. More Length will result in more blurring. Angle describes the actual angle of the movement. Thus, a setting of 90 will produce a vertical blur, and a setting of 0 will produce a horizontal blur.

Radial motion blur that creates a circular blur. The Length slider is not important with this type of blur. Angle on the other hand, is the primary setting that will affect the blur. More Angle will result in more blurring in a circular direction. The Radial motion blur is similar to the effect of a spinning object. The center of the spin in this case, is the center of the image.

Zoom Produces a blur that radiates out from the center of the image. The center of the image remains relatively calm, whilst the outer areas become blurred toward the center. This filter option produces a perceived forward movement, into the image. Length is the main setting here, and affects the amount of speed, as it were, toward the center of the image.

Blur Parameters

Length This slider controls the distance pixels are moved (1 - 256)

Angle As seen above, Angle slider effect depends on Blur type (0 - 360).

Blur Center With this option, you can set the starting point of movement. Effect is different according to the Blur Type you have selected. With Radial Type for instance, you set rotation center. With Zoom Type, vanishing point. This option is greyed out with Linear type.

Tip

You have to set the blur center coordinates. Unfortunately, you can't do that
by clicking on the image. But, by moving mouse pointer on the image, you
can see its coordinates in the lower left corner of the image window. Only
copy them out into the input boxes.

17.2.6 Pixelise

17.2.6.1 Overview

Figure 17.16 Example for the "Pixelize" filter

(a) *Original*   (b) *"Pixelize" applied*

The Pixelize filter renders the image using large color blocks. It is very similar to the effect seen on television when obscuring a criminal during trial. It is used for the "Abraham Lincoln effect": see [BACH04].

17.2.6.2 Activate the filter

You can find this filter in the image menu through Filters → Blur → Pixelise…

17.2.6.3 Options

Figure 17.17 "Pixelize" filter options

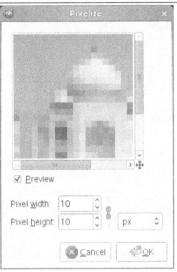

Pixel width, Pixel height Here you can set the desired width and height of the blocks.

By default, width and height are linked, indicated by the chain symbol next to the input boxes. If you want to set width and height separately, click on that chain symbol to unlink them.

Using the unit selection box you can select the unit of measure for height and width.

17.2.7 Tileable Blur

17.2.7.1 Overview

Figure 17.18 Example for the "Tileable" filter

(a) *Original*   (b) *Filter "Tileable Blur" applied*

This tool is used to soften tile seams in images used in tiled backgrounds. It does this by blending and blurring the boundary between images that will be next to each other after tiling.

> Tip
>
> If you want to treat only images borders, you can't apply filter to the whole image. The solution to get the wanted effect is as follows:
>
> 1. Duplicate layer (Layer → Duplicate Layer) and select it to work on it.
>
> 2. Apply "Tileable Blur" filter with a 20 pixels radius to this layer.
>
> 3. Select all (Ctrl-A) and reduce selection (Selection → Shrink) to create a border with the wanted width.
>
> 4. Give a feathered border to the selection by using Selection → Feather.
>
> 5. Delete selection with Ctrl-K.
>
> 6. Merge layers with Layer → Merge down.

17.2.7.2 Activate the filter

You can find this filter in the image menu under Filters → Blur → Tileable Blur....

17.2.7.3 Options

Figure 17.19 "Tileable Blur" filter options

Radius The bigger the radius, the more marked is the blur. By selecting Horizontal and Vertical, you can make the horizontal and vertical borders tileable.

Blur vertically, Blur horizontally These options are self-explanatory.

Blur type Choose the algorithm to be applied:

  IIR for photographic or scanned images.

  RLE for computer-generated images.

17.3 Enhance Filters

Figure 17.20 The Enhance filters menu

17.3.1 Introduction

Enhance filters are used to compensate for image imperfections. Such imperfections include dust particles, noise, interlaced frames (coming usually from a TV frame-grabber) and insufficient sharpness.

17.3.2 Antialias

17.3.2.1 Overview

This filter reduces alias effects (see Antialiasing) using the Scale3X edge-extrapolation algorithm.

Scale3X is derived from Scale2X, which is a graphics effect to increase the size of small bitmaps guessing the missing pixels without interpolating pixels and blurring the images.[1] Scale2X was originally developed to improve the quality of old Arcade and PC games with a low video resolution played with video hardware like TVs, Arcade monitors, PC monitors and LCD screens.[2]

The Antialias filter works as follows:

For every pixel,

1. the filter expands the original pixel in 9 (3x3) new pixels according to the Scale3X algorithm, using the colors of the pixel and its 8 adjacent pixels (extrapolation);

2. then the filter subsamples the new pixels to a weighted average pixel.

17.3.2.2 Activating the filter

You can find this filter through Filters → Enhance → Antialias.

17.3.2.3 Examples

The following examples illustrate the effect on some patterns. The small squares are one pixel in size (zoom 16:1).

---

[1] [SCALE2X].

[2] [AdvanceMAME].

Original image (zoom 16:1)

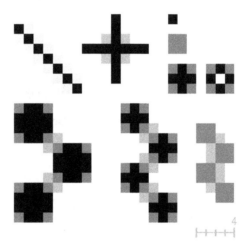

"Antialias" applied (zoom 16:1)

17.3.3 Deinterlace

17.3.3.1 Overview

Images captured by videocards, especially when fast movement is recorded, may look blurred and stripped, with split objects. This is due to how cameras work. They don't record 25 images per second, but 50, with half vertical resolution. There are two interlaced images in one frame. First line of first image is followed by first line of second image followed by second line of first image... etc. So, if there have been an important move between the two images, objects will appear split, shifted, stripped.

The Deinterlace filter keeps only one of both images and replaces missing lines by a gradient between previous and following lines. The resulting image, or selection, will be somewhat blurred, but can be improved by enhance filters

You can find interlaced images at [WKPD-DEINTERLACE].

17.3.3.2 Activating the filter

You can find this filter through Filters → Enhance → Deinterlace....

17.3.3.3 Options

Figure 17.21 Deinterlace filter options

Preview If checked, parameter setting results are interactively displayed in preview.

Keep odd fields, Keep even fields One of them may render a better result. You must try both.

17.3.3.4 Example

Figure 17.22 Simple applying example for the Deinterlace filter

(a) *Top: even lines pixels* (b) *"Keep even fields"* (c) *"Keep odd fields"*
are shifted by one pixel to the *checked.   Top: odd lines* *checked.   Top: even lines*
right. Bottom: one line is *have been shifted to the* *have been shifted to the left,*
missing. These images are *right, to align themselves to* *align themselves with*
zoomed to show pixels. *with the even lines. Bottom: the odd lines. Bottom: the*
the empty line has been *empty line persists, but*
filled with red. *joins up and down through*
a gradient.

17.3.4 Despeckle

17.3.4.1 Overview

This filter is used to remove small defects due to dust, or scratches, on a scanned image, and also moiré effects on image scanned from a magazine. You should select isolated defects before applying this filter, in order to avoid unwanted changes in other areas of your image. The filter replaces each pixel with the median value of the pixels within the specified radius.

17.3.4.2 Activating the filter

You can find this filter through Filters → Enhance → Despeckle....

17.3.4.3   Options

Figure 17.23 "Despeckle" filter options

Preview If checked, parameter setting results are interactively displayed in preview.

Median

> **Adaptive** Adapts the radius to image or selection content by analyzing the histogram of the region around the target pixel. The adapted radius will always be equal to or smaller than the specified radius.

> **Recursive** Repeats filter action which gets stronger.

Radius Sets size of action window from 1 (3x3 pixels) to 20 (41x41). This window moves over the image, and the color in it is smoothed, so imperfections are removed.

Black level Only include pixels brighter than the set value in the histogram (-1-255).

White level Only include pixels darker than the set value in the histogram (0-256).

17.3.5   Destripe

17.3.5.1   Overview

It is used to remove vertical stripes caused by poor quality scanners. It works by adding a pattern that will interfere with the image, removing stripes if setting is good. This "negative" pattern is calculated from vertical elements of the image, so don't be surprised if you see stripes on the preview of an image that has none. And if pattern "strength"; is too high, your image will be striped.

If, after a first pass, a stripe persists, rectangular-select it and apply filter again (all other selection type may worsen the result).

17.3.5.2   Activating the filter

You can find this filter through Filters → Enhance → Destripe....

17.3.5.3 Options

Figure 17.24 "Destripe" filter options

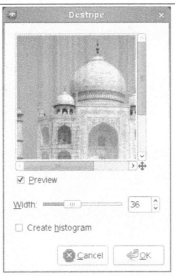

Preview If checked, parameter setting results are interactively displayed in preview. Scroll bars allow you to move around the image.

Create histogram This "histogram " is a black and white image showing the interference pattern more legibly.

Width Slider and input box allow to set "strength" of filter (2-100): more than 60 is rarely necessary and may create artifacts.

17.3.6 NL Filter

17.3.6.1 Overview

Figure 17.25 Example for the NL-Filter

(a) *Original image*   (b) *"NL Filter" applied*

NL means "Non Linear". Derived from the Unix **pnmnlfilt** program, it joins smoothing, despeckle and sharpen enhancement functions. It works on the whole layer, not on the selection.

This is something of a swiss army knife filter. It has 3 distinct operating modes. In all of the modes each pixel in the image is examined and processed according to it and its surrounding pixels values.

Rather than using 9 pixels in a 3x3 block, it uses an hexagonal block whose size can be set with the Radius option.

17.3.6.2 Activating the filter

You can find this filter through Filters → Enhance → NL Filter....

   The filter does not work if the active layer has an alpha channel. Then the menu entry is insensitive and grayed out.

17.3.6.3 Options

Figure 17.26 "NL Filter" options

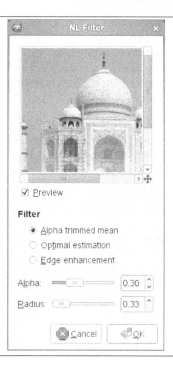

Preview When checked, parameter setting results are interactively displayed in preview.

Filter The Operating Mode is described below.

Alpha Controls the amount of the filter to apply. Valid range is 0.00-1.00. The exact meaning of this value depends on the selected operating mode. Note that this parameter is related to but not the same as the `alpha` parameter used in the **pnmnlfilt** program.

Radius Controls the size of the effective sampling region around each pixel. The range of this value is 0.33-1.00, where 0.33 means just the pixel itself (and thus the filter will have no effect), and 1.00 means all pixels in the 3x3 grid are sampled.

17.3.6.4 Operating Modes

This filter can perform several distinct functions:

Alpha trimmed mean The value of the center pixel will be replaced by the mean of the 7 hexagon values, but the 7 values are sorted by size and the top and bottom `Alpha` portion of the 7 are excluded from the mean. This implies that an `Alpha` value of 0.0 gives the same sort of output as a normal convolution (i.e. averaging or smoothing filter), where `Radius` will determine the "strength" of the filter. A good value to start from for subtle filtering is `Alpha` = 0.0, `Radius` = 0.55. For a more blatant effect, try `Alpha` = 0.0 and `Radius` = 1.0.

An `Alpha` value of 1.0 will cause the median value of the 7 hexagons to be used to replace the center pixel value. This sort of filter is good for eliminating "pop" or single pixel noise from an image without spreading the noise out or smudging features on the image. Judicious use of the `Radius` parameter will fine tune the filtering.

Intermediate values of `Alpha` give effects somewhere between smoothing and "pop" noise reduction. For subtle filtering try starting with values of `Alpha` = 0.8, `Radius` = 0.6. For a more blatant effect try `Alpha` = 1.0, `Radius` = 1.0 .

Optimal estimation This type of filter applies a smoothing filter adaptively over the image. For each pixel the variance of the surrounding hexagon values is calculated, and the amount of smoothing is made inversely proportional to it. The idea is that if the variance is small then it is due to noise in the image, while if the variance is large, it is because of "wanted" image features. As usual the `Radius` parameter controls the effective radius, but it probably advisable to leave the radius between 0.8 and 1.0 for the variance calculation to be meaningful. The `Alpha` parameter sets the noise threshold, over which less smoothing will be done. This means that small values of `Alpha` will give the most subtle filtering effect, while large values will tend to smooth all parts of the image. You could start with values like `Alpha` = 0.2, `Radius` = 1.0, and try increasing or decreasing the `Alpha` parameter to get the desired effect. This type of filter is best for filtering out dithering noise in both bitmap and color images.

Edge enhancement This is the opposite type of filter to the smoothing filter. It enhances edges. The `Alpha` parameter controls the amount of edge enhancement, from subtle (0.1) to blatant (0.9). The `Radius` parameter controls the effective radius as usual, but useful values are between 0.5 and 0.9. Try starting with values of `Alpha` = 0.3, `Radius` = 0.8.

17.3.6.4.1 Combination use The various operating modes can be used one after the other to get the desired result. For instance to turn a monochrome dithered image into grayscale image you could try one or two passes of the smoothing filter, followed by a pass of the optimal estimation filter, then some subtle edge enhancement. Note that using edge enhancement is only likely to be useful after one of the non-linear filters (alpha trimmed mean or optimal estimation filter), as edge enhancement is the direct opposite of smoothing.

For reducing color quantization noise in images (i.e. turning .gif files back into 24 bit files) you could try a pass of the optimal estimation filter (`Alpha` = 0.2, `Radius` = 1.0), a pass of the median filter (`Alpha` = 1.0, `Radius` = 0.55), and possibly a pass of the edge enhancement filter. Several passes of the optimal estimation filter with declining `Alpha` values are more effective than a single pass with a large `Alpha` value. As usual, there is a trade-off between filtering effectiveness and losing detail. Experimentation is encouraged.

17.3.7 Red Eye Removal

17.3.7.1 Overview

Figure 17.27 Example for the "Red Eye Removal" filter

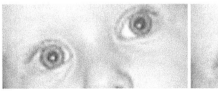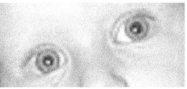

(a) *Original image*   (b) *"Red Eye Removal" applied*

The aim of this filter is - guess what - to remove red eyes from an image. Before applying the "Red Eye Removal" you must do a selection (lasso or elliptical) of the boundary of the iris of the eye(s) having a red pupil. After only you can apply the filter on this selection. If you don't make this selection, the filter inform you that : "Manually selecting the eyes may improve the results".

17.3.7.2 Activating the filter

This filter is found in the image window menu under Filters → Enhance → Red Eye Removal....

17.3.7.3 Options

Figure 17.28 "Red Eye Removal" options

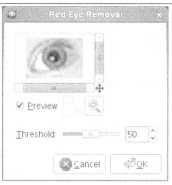

Preview If you check "Preview" you can see the modifications in real-time in the preview window. And you can choose the good value of threshold compared with what you see, and then validate it.

Threshold If you move the cursor of threshold the amount of red color to eliminate will vary.

17.3.8 Sharpen

17.3.8.1 Overview

Most of digitized images need correction of sharpness. This is due to digitizing process that must chop a color continuum up in points with slightly different colors: elements thinner than sampling frequency will be averaged into an uniform color. So sharp borders are rendered a little blurred. The same phenomenon appears when printing color dots on paper.

The Sharpen filter accentuates edges but also any noise or blemish and it may create noise in graduated color areas like the sky or a water surface. It competes with the Unsharp Mask filter, which is more sophisticated and renders more natural results.

Figure 17.29 Applying example for the Sharpen filter

(a) *Original image*   (b) *Filter "Sharpen" applied*

17.3.8.2 Activating the filter

You can find this filter through Filters → Enhance → Sharpen....

17.3.8.3   Options

Figure 17.30 "Sharpen" filter options

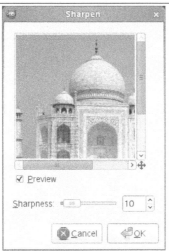

Preview If checked, parameter setting results are interactively displayed in preview. Scroll bars allow you to move around the image.

Sharpness The slider and input boxes allow you to set sharpness (1-99) and you can judge result in preview. By increasing sharpness, you may increase image blemishes and also create noise in graduated color areas.

17.3.9   Unsharp Mask

17.3.9.1   Overview

Figure 17.31 Applying example for the Unsharp Mask filter

(a) *Original image*   (b) *Filter "Unsharp mask" applied*

Out-of-focus photographs and most digitized images often need a sharpness correction. This is due to the digitizing process that must chop a color continuum up in points with slightly different colors: elements thinner than sampling frequency will be averaged into an uniform color. So sharp borders are rendered a little blurred. The same phenomenon appears when printing color dots on paper.

The Unsharp Mask filter (what an odd name!) sharpens edges of the elements without increasing noise or blemish. It is the king of the sharpen filters.

> **Tip**
>
>
>
> Some imaging devices like digital cameras or scanners offer to sharpen the created images for you. We strongly recommend you disable the sharpening in this devices and use the GIMP filters instead. This way you regain the full control over the sharpening of your images.

To prevent color distortion while sharpening, Decompose your image to HSV and work only on Value. Then Compose the image to HSV. Go to Colors → Components → Decompose.... Make sure the Decompose to Layers box is checked. Choose HSV and click OK. You will get a new grey-level image with three layers, one for Hue, one for Saturation, and one for Value. (Close the original image so you won't get confused). Select the Value layer and apply your sharpening to it. When you are done, with that same layer selected, reverse the process. Go to Colors → Components → Compose.... Again choose HSV and click OK. You will get back your original image except that it will have been sharpened in the Value component.

17.3.9.2 Activating the filter

You can find this filter through Filters → Enhance → Unsharp Mask....

17.3.9.3 Options

Figure 17.32 "Unsharp Mask" filter options

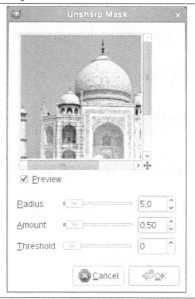

Preview If checked, parameter setting results are interactively displayed in preview. Scroll bars allow you to move around the image.

Radius The slider and input boxes (0.1-120) allow you to set how many pixels on either side of an edge will be affected by sharpening. High resolution images allow higher radius. It is better to always sharpen an image at its final resolution.

Amount This slider and input boxes (0.00-5.00) allow you to set strength of sharpening.

Threshold This slider and input boxes (0-255) allow you to set the minimum difference in pixel values that indicates an edge where sharpen must be applied. So you can protect areas of smooth tonal transition from sharpening, and avoid creation of blemishes in face, sky or water surface.

17.3.9.4   How does an unsharp mask work?

Using an unsharp mask to sharpen an image can seem rather weird. Here is the explanation:

Think of an image with a contrast in some place. The intensity curve of the pixels on a line going through this contrast will show an abrupt increase of intensity: like a stair if contrast is perfectly sharp (blue), like an S if there is some blur (yellow).

Now, we have an image with some blur we want to sharpen (black curve). We apply some more blur: the intensity variation will be more gradual (green curve).

Let us subtract the blurredness intensity from the intensity of the image. We get the red curve, which is more abrupt: contrast and sharpness are increased. QED.

Unsharp mask has first been used in silver photography. The photograph first creates a copy of the original negative by contact, on a film, placing a thin glass plate between both; that will produce a blurred copy because of light diffusion. Then he places both films, exactly corresponding, in a photo enlarger, to reproduce them on paper. The dark areas of the positive blurred film, opposed to the clear areas of the original negative will prevent light to go through and so will be subtracted from the light going through the original film.

In digital photography, with GIMP, you will go through the following steps:

1. Open your image and duplicate it Image → Duplicate

2. In the copy, duplicate the layer Layer → Duplicate layer, then drop the Filters menu down and apply Blur → Gaussian Blur to the duplicated layer with the default IIR option and radius 5.

3. In the layer dialog of the duplicated image, change Mode to "Subtract", and in the right-click menu, select "Merge down".

4. Click and drag the only layer you got into the original image, where it appears as a new layer.

5. Change the Mode in this layer dialog to "Addition".

Voilà. The "Unsharp Mask" plug-in does the same for you.

At the beginning of the curve, you can see a dip. If blurring is important, this dip is very deep; the result of the subtraction can be negative, and a complementary color stripe will appear along the contrast, or a black halo around a star on the light background of a nebula (black eye effect).

Figure 17.33 Black eye effect

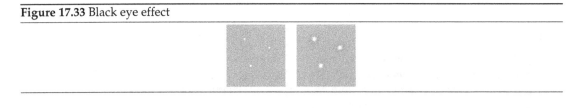

17.4   Distort Filters

Figure 17.34 The Distort filters menu

17.4.1   Introduction

The distort filters transform your image in many different ways.

17.4.2   Blinds

17.4.2.1   Overview

Figure 17.35 Applying example for the Blinds filter

(a) *Original image*   (b) *Filter "Blinds" applied*

It generates a blind effect with horizontal or vertical battens. You can lift or close these battens, but not lift the whole blind up.

17.4.2.2   Activating the filter

You can find this filter through Filters → Distorts → Blinds....

17.4.2.3 Options

Figure 17.36 "Blinds" filter options

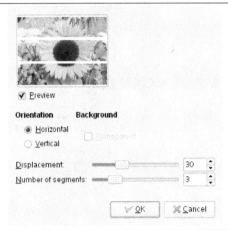

Preview All your setting changes will appear in the Preview without affecting the image until you click on OK.

Orientation Allows you to decide whether battens will be horizontal or vertical.

Background The batten color is that of the Toolbox Background. To be able to use the *Transparent* option, your image must have an Alpha channel.

Displacement Slider and input box allow to wide battens giving the impression they are closing, or to narrow them, giving the impression they are opening.

Number of segments It's the number of battens.

17.4.3 Curve Bend

17.4.3.1 Overview

Figure 17.37 Applying example for the Curve Bend filter

      (a) *Original image*   (b) *Filter "Curve Bend" applied*

This filter allows you to create a curve that will be used to distort the active layer or selection. The distortion is applied gradually from an image or selection border to the other.

17.4.3.2 Activating the filter

You can find this filter through Filters → Distorts → Curve Bend....

17.4.3.3 Options

Figure 17.38 "Curve bend" filter options

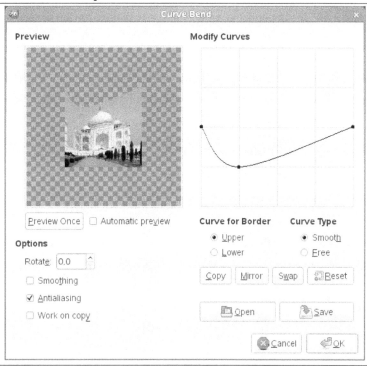

Preview The preview displays changes to image or selection without modifying the image until you press *OK*.

> **Preview once** This button allows you to update the preview each time you need it.
>
> **Automatic Preview** With this option, preview is changed in real time. This needs much calculation and may lengthen work. It is particularly evident when using "Rotation".

Options

> **Rotate** There, you can set the application angle of filter (0-360 counter-clockwise). 0 is default setting: The curve will be applied from the upper border and/or from the lower. Set to 90, it will be applied from left border and/or from the right one.
>
> **Smoothing, Antialiasing** The distort process may create hard and stepped borders. These two options improve this aspect.
>
> **Work on copy** This option creates a new layer called "Curve_bend_dummy_layer_b" which becomes the active layer, allowing you to see changes to your image in normal size without modifying the original image until you press the OK button.

Modify Curves In this grid, you have a marked horizontal line, with a node at both ends, which represents by default the upper border of image. If you click on this curve, a new node appears, that you can drag to modify the curve as you want. You can create several nodes on the curve.

You can have only two curves on the grid, one for the so named "upper" border and the other for the so named "lower" border. You can activate one of them by checking the Upper or Lower radio button.

If you use the Free *Curve Type* option, the curve you draw will replace the active curve.

Curve for Border There you can select whether the active curve must be applied to the Upper or the Lower border, according to the rotation.

 Caution

Remember that the curve border depends on the rotation. For example, with Rotate = 90° the upper curve will actually be applied to the left border.

Curve Type With the Smooth, you get automatically a well rounded curve when you drag a node.

The Free option allows you to draw a curve freely. It will replace the active curve.

Buttons

Copy Copy the active curve to the other border.

Mirror Mirror the active curve to the other border.

Swap Swap the Upper and Lower curves.

Reset Reset the active curve.

Open Load the curve from a file.

Save Save the curve to a file.

17.4.4 Emboss

17.4.4.1 Overview

Figure 17.39 Applying example for the Emboss filter

(a) *Original image*   (b) *Filter "Emboss" applied*

This filter stamps and carves the active layer or selection, giving it relief with bumps and hollows. Bright areas are raised and dark ones are carved. You can vary the lighting.

You can use the filter only with RGB images. If your image is grayscale, it will be grayed out in the menu.

17.4.4.2 Starting filter

You can find this filter through Filters → Distorts → Emboss....

17.4.4.3 Options

Figure 17.40 "Emboss" filter options

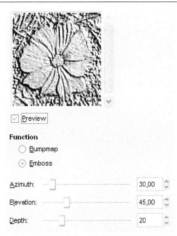

Preview All your setting changes will appear in the Preview without affecting the image until you click on OK. Don't keep Preview checked if your computer is too slow.

Function

    Bumpmap Relief is smooth and colors are preserved.

    Emboss It turns your image to grayscale and relief is more marked, looking like metal.

Azimuth This is about lighting according to the points of the compass (0 - 360). If you suppose South is at the top of your image, then East (0°) is on the left. Increasing value goes counter-clockwise.

Elevation That's height from horizon (0°), in principle up to zenith (90°), but here up to the opposite horizon (180°).

Depth Seems to be the distance of the light source. Light decreases when value increases.

17.4.5 Engrave

17.4.5.1 Overview

Figure 17.41 Example for the "Engrave" filter

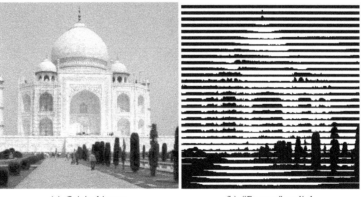

(a) Original image   (b) "Engrave" applied

This filter produces an engraving effect: the image is turned black and white and some horizontal lines of varying height are drawn depending on the value of underlying pixels. The resulting effect reminds of engravings found in coins and old book illustrations.

Note

The "Engrave" filter operates only on floating selections and layers with an alpha channel. If the active layer does not have an alpha channel please add it first.

17.4.5.2 Activating the filter

This filter is found in the image window menu under Filters → Distorts → Engrave....

17.4.5.3 Options

Figure 17.42 "Engrave" options

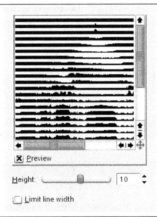

Preview The result of your settings will appear in the Preview without affecting the image until you click on OK.

Height This option specifies the height of the engraving lines. The value goes from 2 to 16.

Limit line width If this option is enabled thin lines are not drawn on contiguous color areas. See the figure below for an example of this option result.

Figure 17.43 Example result of Limit line width option

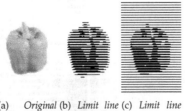

(a) Original (b) Limit line (c) Limit line
image   width   option width   option
             enabled   disabled

17.4.6   Erase Every Other Row

17.4.6.1   Overview

Figure 17.44 Example for the "Erase Every Other row" filter

(a) *Original image*   (b) *"Erase Every Other row" applied*

This filter not only can erase each other row or column of the active layer but also can change them to the background color.

17.4.6.2   Activating the filter

This filter is found in the image window menu under Filters → Distorts → Erase Every Other Row....

17.4.6.3   Options

Figure 17.45 "Erase Every Other row" options

These options are self-explanatory. Only one remark: if the active layer has an Alpha channel, erased rows or columns will be transparent. If it doesn't have an Alpha channel (then its name is in bold letters in the Layer Dialog), the Background color of the toolbox will be used.

17.4.7   IWarp

17.4.7.1   Overview

Figure 17.46 Applying example for the IWarp filter

(a) *Original image*   (b) *Filter "IWarp" applied*

This filter allows you to deform interactively some parts of the image and, thanks to its Animate option, to create the elements of a fade in/fade out animation between the original image and the deformed one, that you can play and use in a Web page.

To use it, first select a deform type then click on the Preview and drag the mouse pointer.

17.4.7.2   Activating the filter

You can find this filter through Filters → Distorts → Iwarp….

17.4.7.3   Options

The options of this filter are so numerous that they come in two tabs. The first tab contains general options. The second tab holds animation options.

Figure 17.47 "IWarp" filter options (Settings tab)

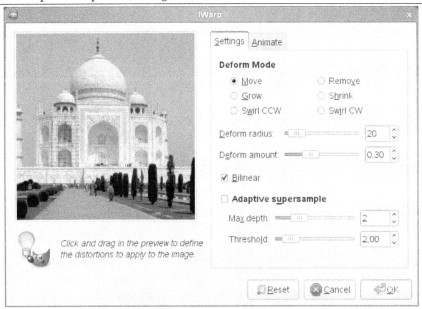

17.4.7.3.1   Settings   The Settings tab allows you to set parameters which will affect the preview you are working on. So, you can apply different deform modes to different parts of the preview.

Preview   Here, the Preview is your work space: You click on the Preview and drag mouse pointer. The underlying part of image will be deformed according to the settings you have chosen. If your work is not convenient, press the *Reset* button.

Deform Mode

> **Move**   Allows you to *stretch* parts of the image.
>
> **Remove**   This remove the distortion where you drag the mouse pointer, partially or completely. This allows you to avoid pressing Reset button, working on the whole image. Be careful when working on an animation: this option will affect one frame only.
>
> **Grow**   This option inflates the pointed pattern.
>
> **Shrink**   Self explanatory.
>
> **Swirl CCW**   Create a vortex counter clockwise.
>
> **Swirl CW**   Create a vortex clockwise.

Deform radius   Defines the radius, in pixels (5-100), of the filter action circle around the pixel pointed by the mouse.

Deform amount   Sets how much out of shape your image will be put (0.0-1.0).

Bilinear   This option smooths the IWarp effect.

Adaptive supersample   This option renders a better image at the cost of increased calculation.

> **Max Depth**   This value limits the maximum sampling iterations performed on each pixel.
>
> **Threshold**   When the value difference between a pixel and the adjacent ones exceeds this threshold a new sampling iteration is performed on the pixel.

Figure 17.48 "IWarp" filter options (Animation tab)

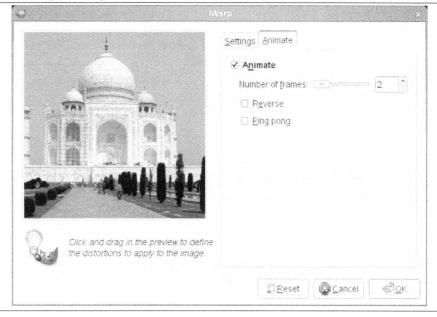

17.4.7.3.2   Animate   This tab allows to generate several intermediate images between the original image and the final deformation of this image. You can play this animation thanks to the Playback plug-in.

Number of frames   That's the number of images in your animation (2-100). These frames are stored as layers attached to your image. Use the XCF format when saving it.

Reverse This option plays the animation backwards.

Ping pong When the animation ends one way, it goes backwards.

17.4.8 Lens Distortion

17.4.8.1 Overview

Figure 17.49 Example for the "Lens Distortion" filter

(a) *Original image*   (b) *"Lens Distortion" applied*

This filter lets you simulate but also correct the typical distortion effect introduced in photo images by the glasses contained in the camera lenses.

17.4.8.2 Activating the filter

This filter is found in the image window menu under Filters → Distorts → Lens Distortion....

17.4.8.3 Options

Figure 17.50 "Lens Distortion" options

The allowed range of all options is from -100.0 to 100.0.

Preview The result of your settings will appear in the Preview without affecting the image until you click on OK.

Main The amount of spherical correction to introduce. Positive values make the image convex while negative ones make it concave. The whole effect is similar to wrapping the image inside or outside a sphere.

Figure 17.51 Example result of Main option

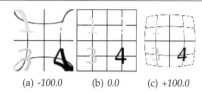

(a) -100.0   (b) 0.0   (c) +100.0

Edge Specifies the amount of additional spherical correction at image edges.

Figure 17.52 Example result of Edge option (Main set to 50.0)

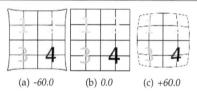

(a) -60.0   (b) 0.0   (c) +60.0

Zoom Specifies the amount of the image enlargement or reduction caused by the hypothetical lens.

Figure 17.53 Example result of Zoom option

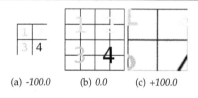

(a) -100.0   (b) 0.0   (c) +100.0

Brighten The amount of the "vignetting" effect: the brightness decrease/increase due to the lens curvature that produces a different light absorption.

The Main or Edge options must be non zero for this option to produce noticeable results.

Figure 17.54 Example result of Brigthen option (Main set to 75.0)

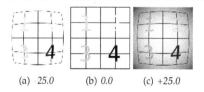

(a) -25.0   (b) 0.0   (c) +25.0

X shift, Y shift These two options specify the shift of the image produced by not perfectly centered pairs of lenses.

As above this option produces visible results only if the Main or Edge options are non zero.

Figure 17.55 Example result of X shift option (Main set to 70.0)

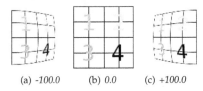

(a) -100.0   (b) 0.0   (c) +100.0

17.4.9   Mosaic

17.4.9.1   Overview

Figure 17.56 Applying example for the "Mosaic" filter

(a) *Original image*   (b) *Filter "Mosaic" applied*

It cuts the active layer or selection into many squares or polygons which are slightly raised and separated by joins, giving so an aspect of mosaic.

17.4.9.2   Activating the filter

You can find this filter through Filters → Distorts → Mosaic....

17.4.9.3   Options

Figure 17.57 "Mosaic" filter options

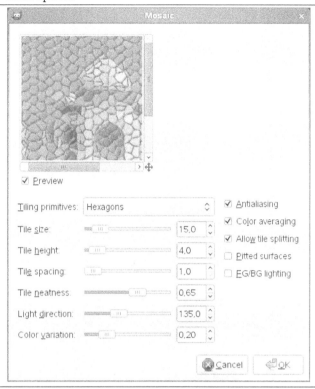

Preview All your setting changes will appear in the Preview without affecting the image until you click on OK. Note that the preview displays only a part of the whole image if the filter is applied to an selection. Don't keep Preview checked if your computer is too slow.

Tiling primitives This option is self-understanding:

    Squares 4 edges

    Hexagons 6 edges (hexa = 6)

    Octagons & squares 8 or 4 edges (octa = 8)

    Triangles 3 edges (tri = 3)

Tile size Slider and input box allow you to set the size of tile surface.

Tile height That's ledge, relief of tiles. Value is width of the lit border in pixels.

Tile spacing That's width of the join between tiles.

Tile neatness When set to 1, most of tiles have the same size. With 0 value, size is determined at random and this may lead to shape variation.

Light direction By default light comes from the upper left corner (135°). You can change this direction from 0 to 360 (counter clockwise).

Color variation Each tile has only one color. So the number of colors is reduced, compared to the original image. Here you can increase the number of colors a little.

Antialiasing This option reduces the stepped aspect that may have borders.

Color averaging When this option is unchecked, the image drawing can be recognized inside tiles. When checked, the colors inside tiles are averaged into a single color.

Allow tile splitting This option splits tiles in areas with many colors, and so allows a better color gradation and more details in these areas.

Pitted surfaces With this option tile surface looks pitted.

FG/BG lighting When this option is checked, tiles are lit by the foreground color of the toolbox, and shadow is colored by the background color. Joins have the background color.

17.4.10 Newsprint

17.4.10.1 Overview

Figure 17.58 Applying example for the Newsprint filter

(a) *Original image*   (b) *Filter "Newsprint" applied*

This filter halftones the image using a clustered-dot dither. Halftoning is the process of rendering an image with multiple levels of grey or color (i.e. a continuous tone image) on a device with fewer tones; often a bi-level device such as a printer or typesetter.

The basic premise is to trade off resolution for greater apparent tone depth (this is known as spatial dithering).

There are many approaches to this, the simplest of which is to throw away the low-order bits of tone information; this is what the posterize filter does. Unfortunately, the results don't look too good. However, no spatial resolution is lost.

This filter uses a clustered-dot ordered dither, which reduces the resolution of the image by converting cells into spots which grow or shrink according to the intensity that cell needs to represent.

Imagine a grid super-imposed on the original image. The image is divided into cells by the grid - each cell will ultimately hold a single spot made up of multiple output pixels in order to approximate the darkness of the original image in that cell.

Obviously, a large cell size results in a heavy loss in resolution! The spots in the cells typically start off as circles, and grow to be diamond shaped. This change in shape is controlled by a Spot function. By using different spot functions, the evolution in the shape of the spots as the cell goes from fully black to fully white may be controlled.

17.4.10.2 Starting filter

You can find this filter through Filters → Distorts → Newsprint....

17.4.10.3   Options

Figure 17.59 "Newsprint" filter options

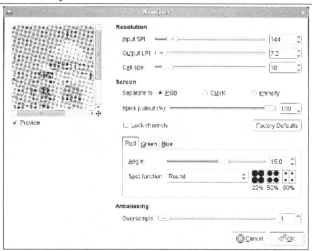

Preview All your setting changes will appear in the Preview without affecting the image until you click on OK. Note that the preview displays only a part of the whole image if the filter is applied to an selection. Don't keep Preview checked if your computer is too slow.

Resolution This group controls the cell size, either by setting the input and output resolutions, or directly.

> **Input SPI** Resolution of the original input image, in Samples Per Inch (SPI). This is automatically initialised to the input image's resolution.

> **Output LPI** Desired output resolution, in Lines Per Inch (LPI).

> **Cell size** Resulting cell size, in pixels. Most often you will want to set this directly.

Screen

> **Separate To RGB, CMYK, Intensity** Select which colorspace you wish to operate in. In *RGB* mode, no colorspace conversion is performed. In *CMYK*, the image is first internally converted to CMYK, then each color channel is separately halftoned, before finally being recombined back to an RGB image. In *Intensity* mode, the image is internally converted to grayscale, halftoned, then the result used as the alpha channel for the input image. This is good for special effects, but requires a little experimentation to achieve best results. Hint: try CMYK if you don't know which to go for initially.

> **Black pullout (%)** When doing RGB->CMYK conversion, how much K (black) should be used?

> **Lock channels** Make channel modifications apply to all channels.

> **Factory Defaults** Restore the default settings which should give pleasing results.

> **Angle** Cell grid angle for this channel.

> **Spot function** Spot function to be used for this channel (see preview in blue cell-boxes).

Antialiasing Proper halftoning does not need antialiasing: the aim is to reduce the color depth after all! However, since this plugin is mainly for special effects, the results are displayed on screen rather than by a black/white printer. So it is often useful to apply a little anti-aliasing to simulate ink smearing on paper. If you do want to print the resulting image then set the antialising to 1 (ie, off).

> **Oversample** Number of subpixels to sample to produce each output pixel. Set to 1 to disable this feature. Warning: large numbers here will lead to very long filter runtimes!

17.4.10.4   Example

Figure 17.60 Example for Newsprint

An example from plug-in author

17.4.11   Page Curl

17.4.11.1   Overview

Figure 17.61 Example for the Page Curl filter

(a) *Original image*   (b) *Filter "Page Curl" applied*

This filter curls a corner of the current layer or selection into a kind of cornet showing the underlying layer in the cleared area. A new "Curl Layer" and a new Alpha channel are created. The part of the initial layer corresponding to this cleared area is also transparent.

17.4.11.2   Activating the filter

This filter is found in the image window menu under Filters → Distorts → Page Curl....

17.4.11.3 Options

Figure 17.62 Options

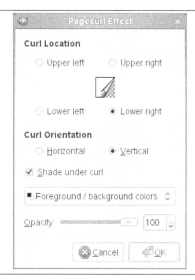

Curl Location You have there four radio buttons to select the corner you want raise. The Preview is redundant and doesn't respond to other options.

Curl Orientation *Horizontal* and *Vertical* refer to the border you want raise.

Shade under curl This is the shadow inside the cornet.

Foreground / background colors, Current gradient, Current gradient (reversed) This option refers to the outer face of the cornet.

Opacity Refers to the visibility of the layer part underlying the cornet. It may be set also in the Layer Dialog.

17.4.12 Polar Coords

17.4.12.1 Overview

Figure 17.63 Example for Polar Coords filter

(a) *Original image*   (b) *"Polar Coords" filter applied*

It gives a circular or a rectangular representation of your image with all the possible intermediates between both.

17.4.12.2   Activating the filter

You can find this filter through Filters → Distorts → Polar Coords....

17.4.12.3   Options

Figure 17.64 "Polar Coords" filter options

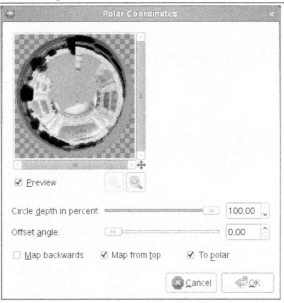

Preview The result of your settings will appear in the Preview without affecting the image until you click on OK.

Circle depth in percent Slider and input box allow you to set the "circularity" of the transformation, from rectangle (0%) to circle (100%).

Offset angle This option controls the angle the drawing will start from (0 - 359°), and so turns it around the circle center.

Map backwards When this option is checked, the drawing will start from the right instead of the left.

Map from top If unchecked, the mapping will put the bottom row in the middle and the top row on the outside. If checked, it will be the opposite.

To polar If unchecked, the image will be circularly mapped into a rectangle (odd effect). If checked, the image will be mapped into a circle.

17.4.12.4   Examples

Figure 17.65 With text

If you have just written the text, you must Flatten the image before using the filter.

Figure 17.66 With two horizontal bars

17.4.13   Ripple

17.4.13.1   Overview

Figure 17.67 "Ripple" filter example

(a) *Original image*   (b) *Filter "Ripple" applied*

It displaces the pixels of the active layer or selection to waves or ripples reminding a reflection on disturbed water.

17.4.13.2   Activating the filter

You can find this filter through Filters → Distorts → Ripple....

17.4.13.3 Options

Figure 17.68 "Ripple" filter options

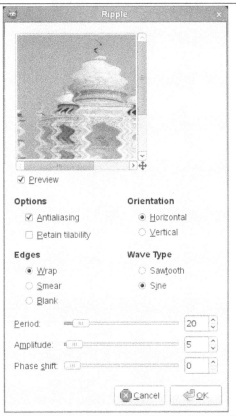

Preview The result of your settings will appear in the Preview without affecting the image until you click on OK.

Options

    Antialiasing This improves the scaled look the image borders may have.

    Retain tileability This preserves the seamless properties if your image is a tile pattern.

Orientation That's the Horizontal or Vertical direction of waves.

Edges Because ripples cause pixel displacement, some pixels may be missing on the image sides:

- With Wrap, pixels going out one side will come back on the other side, replacing so the missing pixels.
- With Smear, the adjacent pixels will spread out to replace the mixing pixels.
- With Blank, the missing pixels will be replaced by black pixels, if the layer does not have an Alpha channel. If an Alpha channel exists in the layer, transparent pixels replace the missing pixels after applying this option.

Wave Type Choose how the wave should look like:

- Sawtooth
- Sine

Period It is related to wavelength (0-200 pixels)

Amplitude It is related to wave height (0-200 pixels).

Phase shift It is angle to delay the wave (0-360 degree). Appling this filter again with the same setting but Phase shift differs by 180 brings the once processed image back to become almost similar to the first original image.

17.4.14 Shift

17.4.14.1 Overview

Figure 17.69 Example for the Shift filter

(a) *Original image*   (b) *Filter "Shift" applied*

It shifts all pixel rows, horizontally or vertically, in the current layer or selection, on a random distance and within determined limits.

17.4.14.2 Activating the filter

You can find this filter through Filters → Distorts → Shift....

17.4.14.3 Options

Figure 17.70 "Shift" filter options

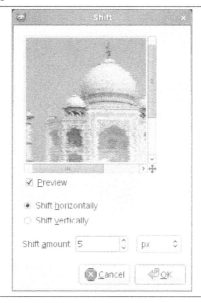

Preview The result of your settings will appear in the Preview without affecting the image until you click on OK.

Shift horizontally, Shift vertically This option sets the dimension where pixels are moved.

Pixels going out one side will come back on the other side.

Shift amount With this option, you can set the maximum shift, between 1 and 200 pixels, or in another unit of measurement.

17.4.15 Value Propagate

17.4.15.1 Overview

Figure 17.71 Example for the Value Propagate filter

(a) *Original image*   (b) *Filter "Value Propagate" applied*

This filter works on color borders. It spreads pixels that differ in a specified way from their neighbouring pixels.

17.4.15.2 Activating the filter

This filter is found in the image window menu under Filters → Distorts → Value Propagate....

17.4.15.3   Options

Figure 17.72 "Value propagate" filter options

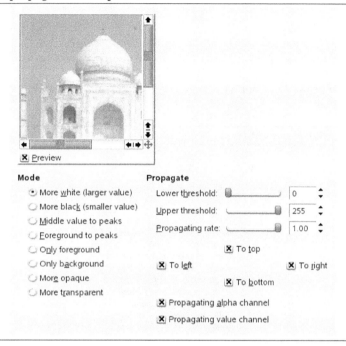

Preview The result of your settings will appear in the Preview without affecting the image until you click on OK.

Mode The examples will be about the following image:

> **More white (larger value)** Pixels will be propagated from upper value pixels towards lower value pixels. So bright areas will enlarge.

Figure 17.73 More white

Bright pixels have been propagated to dark pixels in the four directions : top, bottom, right and left. Filter applied several times to increase effect.

> **More black (smaller value)** Pixels will be propagated from lower value pixels towards upper value pixels. So dark areas will enlarge.

Figure 17.74 More black

Figure 17.75 To bottom only

The same as above with To bottom direction only checked.

Middle value to peaks On a border between the selected thresholds, the average of both values is propagated.

Figure 17.76 Middle value to peaks

(a) A thin border with a transitional color has been added to objects. It is not visible around objects with smoothed borders.

(b) Green area zoomed x800. A thin border (one pixel wide) has been added. Its value is the average between grey (90%) and green (78%) : (90 + 78) / 2 = 84.

Foreground to peaks The propagated areas will be filled with the foreground color of the toolbox.

Figure 17.77 Foreground to peaks

In this example, the foreground color in Toolbox is Red. A thin border, one pixel wide, red, is added around objects. With smoothed objects, this border is located at the furthest limit of smoothing. Here, another border appears inside. This is an artifact due to the small size of the object which makes the smoothing area of opposite sides to overlap.

Only foreground Only areas with the Toolbox Foreground color will propagate.

Figure 17.78 Only foreground

In this example, the foreground color in Toolbox is that of the green object. After applying filter several times, the green area is clearly enlarged.

Only background Only areas with the Background color will propagate.

More opaque, More transparent These commands work like "More white" and "More black". Opaque (transparent) areas will be propagated over less opaque (transparent) areas. These commands need an image with an alpha channel.

Figure 17.79 More opaque

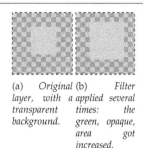

(a) *Original layer, with a transparent background.* (b) *Filter applied several times: the green, opaque, area got increased.*

Propagate

Lower threshold, Upper threshold A pixel will be propagated (spread) if the difference in value between the pixel and its neighbour is no smaller than the lower threshold and no larger than the upper threshold.

Propagating rate That's the propagating amount. The higher it will be the more colored the propagation will be.

To left, To top, To right, To bottom You can select one or more directions.

Propagating alpha channel If checked, the pixel alpha value will be propagated, otherwise the pixel will get the alpha of the neighbouring pixels. This checkbox is only visible when the active layer has an alpha channel.

Propagating value channel If checked, the pixel's color channels (gray channel on grayscaled images) will be propagated. The option is checked by default, of course. This checkbox too is only visible when the active layer has an alpha channel.

17.4.16 Video

17.4.16.1 Overview

Figure 17.80 Applying example for the "Video" filter

(a) *Original image*   (b) *Filter "Video" applied*

Apply low dot-pitch RGB simulation to the specified drawable.

17.4.16.2 Activating the filter

You can find this filter through Filters → Distorts → Video....

17.4.16.3 Options

Figure 17.81 "Video" filter options

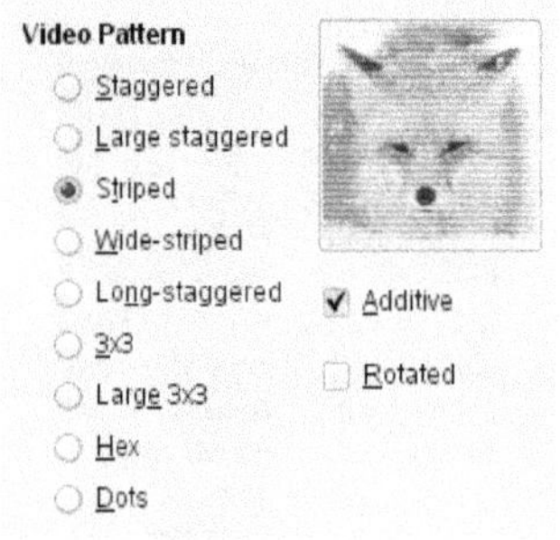

Video Pattern
- ○ Staggered
- ○ Large staggered
- ● Striped
- ○ Wide-striped
- ○ Long-staggered   ☑ Additive
- ○ 3x3
- ○ Large 3x3   ☐ Rotated
- ○ Hex
- ○ Dots

Preview This preview is unusual: Changes appear always on the same image which is not yours.

Video Pattern It would be rather difficult to describe what each pattern will render. It's best to see what they render in the Preview.

Additive Set whether the function adds the result to the original image.

Rotated Rotate the result by 90°.

17.4.17 Waves

17.4.17.1 Overview

Figure 17.82 Example for the Waves filter

(a) *Original image*   (b) *Filter "Waves" applied*

With this filter you get the same effect as a stone thrown in a quiet pond, giving concentric waves.

17.4.17.2 Activating the filter

You can find this filter through Filters → Distorts → Waves....

17.4.17.3 Options

Figure 17.83 "Waves" filter options

Preview All your setting changes will appear in the Preview without affecting the image until you click on OK. Don't keep Preview checked if your computer is too slow.

Mode

> **Smear** Because of the waves, areas are rendered empty on sides. The adjacent pixels will spread to fill them.
>
> **Blacken** The empty areas will be filled by black color.

Reflective Waves bounce on sides and interfere with the arriving ones.

Amplitude Varies the height of waves.

Phase This command shifts the top of waves.

Wavelength Varies the distance between the top of waves.

17.4.18   Whirl and Pinch

17.4.18.1   Overview

Figure 17.84 Example for the Whirl and Pinch filter

(a) *Original image*   (b) *Filter applied*

"Whirl and Pinch" distorts your image in a concentric way.

"Whirl" (applying a non-zero Whirl angle) distorts the image much like the little whirlpool that appears when you empty your bath.

"Pinch", with a nil rotation, can be compared to applying your image to a soft rubber surface and squeezing the edges or corners. If the Pinch amount slider is set to a negative value, it will look as if someone tried to push a round object up toward you from behind the rubber skin. If the Pinch amount is set to a positive value, it looks like someone is dragging or sucking on the surface from behind, and away from you.

> **Tip**
>
> The "pinch" effect can sometimes be used to compensate for image distortion produced by telephoto or fish-eye lenses ("barrel distortion").

Figure 17.85 Illustration

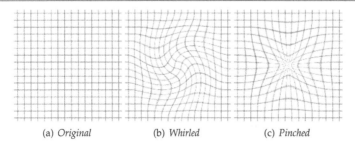

(a) *Original*   (b) *Whirled*   (c) *Pinched*

17.4.18.2   Activating the filter

You can find this filter through Filters → Distorts → Whirl and Pinch...

17.4.18.3 Parameter Settings

Figure 17.86 "Whirl and Pinch" filter options

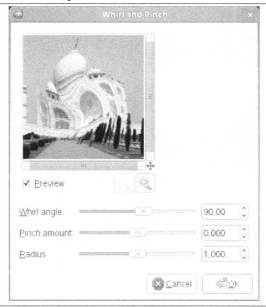

Preview Changes to parameters are immediately displayed into the *Preview*. The whirlpool is focused around the center of the current layer or selection.

Whirl angle Clockwise or counter clockwise (-360 to +360). Controls how many degrees the affected part of the image is rotated.

Pinch amount Whirlpool depth(-1 to +1). Determines how strongly the affected part of the image is pinched.

Radius Whirlpool width (0.0-2.0). Determines how much of the image is affected by the distortion. If you set *Radius* to **2**, the entire image will be affected. If you set *Radius* to **1**, half the image will be affected. If *Radius* is set to **0**, nothing will be affected (think of it as the radius in a circle with 0 in the center and 1 halfway out).

17.4.19 Wind

17.4.19.1 Overview

Figure 17.87 "Wind" filter example

(a) *Original image*   (b) *Filter "Wind" applied*

The Wind filter can be used to create motion blur, but it can also be used as a general distort filter. What is characteristic about this filter is that it will render thin black or white lines. Wind will detect the edges in the image, and stretch out thin white or black lines from that edge. This is why you can create the illusion of motion, because the edges are what will be blurred in a photograph of a moving object.

17.4.19.2 Activating the filter

You can find this filter through Filters → Distorts → Wind….

17.4.19.3 Options

Figure 17.88 "Wind" filter options

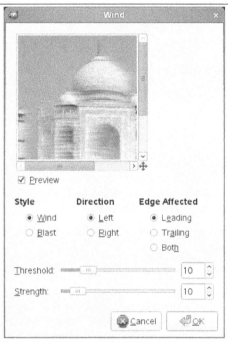

The interface is quite simple. You can set the *Strength* of the wind and a *Threshold* value. *Threshold* will restrict the effect to fewer areas of the image. *Strength* controls the amount of wind, so a high value will render a storm. You can also increase the effect by setting the *Style* to Blast, which will produce thicker lines than Wind.

You can only set the wind in two directions, either Left or Right. However, you can control which edge the wind will come from using the values Leading, Trailing or Both. Because Trailing will produce a black wind, it creates a less convincing motion blur than Leading, which will produce white wind.

The following illustrations are based on this image:

Preview All your setting changes will appear in the Preview without affecting the image until you click on OK. It reproduces a part of the image only, centred on the first modified area it encounters.

Style

   Wind This option is the most suggestive of a moving effect. Trails are thin.

Blast This option tries to suggest a blast due to an explosion. Trails are thick.

Direction You can select the direction, Left or Right, from which the wind comes.

Edge Affected

Leading Trails will start from the front border, falling on the object itself. It suggests that a violent wind is pulling color out.

Trailing Trails start from the back border of the object.

Both Combines both effects.

Threshold The threshold to detect borders. The higher it is, the fewer borders will be detected.

Strength Higher values increase the strength of the effect.

17.4.20 Apply Lens

17.4.20.1 Overview

Figure 17.89 The same image, before and after applying lens effect.

(a) *Original image*   (b) *Filter "Apply lens" applied*

After applying this filter, a part of the active layer is rendered as through a spherical lens.

17.4.20.2 Activate the filter

You can find this filter in the image window menu through Filters → Distorts → Apply Lens...

17.4.20.3 Options

Figure 17.90 "Apply Lens" filter options

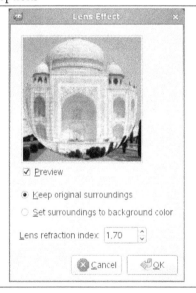

Preview If checked, parameter setting results are interactively displayed in preview. Scroll bars allow you to move around the image.

Keep original surroundings The lens seems to be put on the active layer.

Set surroundings to background color The part of the active layer outside the lens will have the background color selected in the toolbox.

Make surroundings transparent The part of the active layer outside the lens will be transparent. This option exists only if the active layer has an alpha channel.

Lens refraction index Lens will be more or less convergent (1-100).

17.5 Light and Shadow Filters

Figure 17.91 The Light and Shadow filters menu

17.5.1 Introduction

Here you will find three groups of filters:

- The original *Light Effects* filters, which render several illumination effects of the image.

- Some *Script-Fu* and *Python-Fu* scripts, which create various kinds of shadows.

- *Glass Effects* filters result in an image as if it were seen through a lens or glass tiles.

17.5.2 Gradient Flare

17.5.2.1 Overview

Figure 17.92 Example for the Gradient Flare filter

(a) *Original image*   (b) *Filter "Gradient Flare" applied*

Gradient Flare effect reminds the effect you get when you take a photograph of a blinding light source, with a halo and radiations around the source. The Gradient Flare image has three components: *Glow* which is the big central fireball, *Rays* and *Second Flares*

17.5.2.2 Activating the filter

This filter is found in the image window menu under Filters → Light and Shadow → Gradient Flare...

17.5.2.3 Options

The *Settings* tab allows you to set manually the parameters while the *Selector* tab let you choose presets in a list.

Preview When Auto update preview is checked, parameter setting results are interactively displayed in preview without modifying the image until you click on OK button.

Figure 17.93 "Gradient Flare" filter options (Settings)

17.5.2.3.1 Settings

Center You can set X and Y (pixels) coordinates of glint using the input box or by clicking into the preview. The coordinate origin is at the upper left corner.

Parameters

> **Radius** The radius of the effect. The slider limits the range of possible values, but using the input box you can enter greater values.

> **Rotation** Turn the effect.

> **Hue rotation** Change the tint (color) of the effect.

> **Vector angle** Turn the Second flares.

> **Vector length** Vary the distance applied for the Second flares.

Adaptive supersampling Settings of the anti-aliasing following parameters like Depth and Threshold. (See also *Supersampling* .)

Figure 17.94 "Gradient Flare" filter options (Selector)

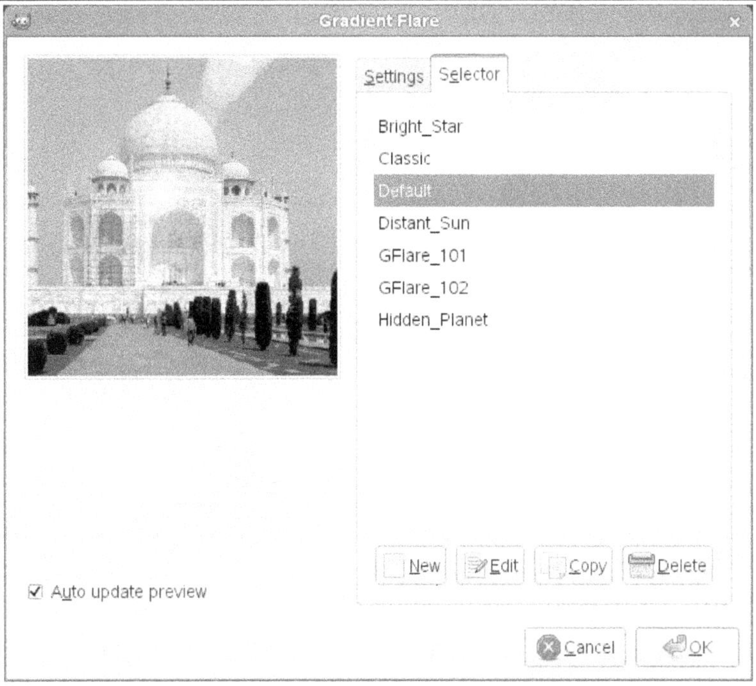

17.5.2.3.2 Selector   The Selector tab allows you to select a Gradient Flare pattern, to change it and save it.

New When you click on this button, you create a new Gradient Flare pattern. Give it a name of your choice.

Edit This button brings up the Gradient Flare Editor (see below).

Copy This button allows you to duplicate selected Gradient Flare pattern. You can edit the copy without altering the original.

Delete This button deletes the selected Gradient Flare pattern.

17.5.2.4 Gradient Flare Editor

The Gradient Flare Editor is also organized in tabs:

Figure 17.95 "Gradient Flare Editor" options (General)

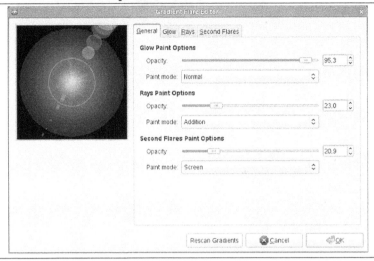

17.5.2.4.1 General

Glow Paint Options

> **Opacity** Slider and input box allows you to reduce glow opacity (0-100).
>
> **Paint mode** You can choose between four modes:
>
> > **Normal** In this mode, the glow covers the image without taking into account what is beneath.
> >
> > **Addition** Pixel RGB values of glow are added to RGB values of the corresponding pixels in the image. Colors get lighter and white areas may appear.
> >
> > **Overlay** Light/Dark areas of glow enhance corresponding light/dark areas of image.
> >
> > **Screen** Dark areas of image are enlightened by corresponding light areas of glow. Imagine two slides projected onto the same screen.

Rays Paint Options Options are the same as for Glow Paint Options.

Second Flare Paint Options Options are the same as for Glow Paint Options.

Figure 17.96 "Gradient Flare Editor" options (Glow)

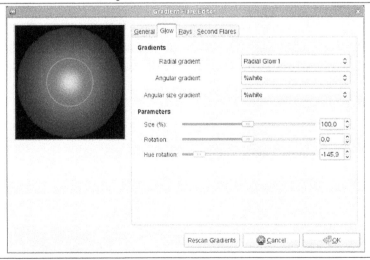

17.5.2.4.2 Glow

Gradients By clicking on the rectangular buttons, you can develop a long list of gradients. "%" gradients belong to the Editor.

Radial gradient The selected gradient is drawn radially, from center to edge.

Angular gradient The selected gradient develops around center, counter-clockwise, starting from three o'clock if the Rotation parameter is set to 0. Radial and angular gradients are combined according to the Multiply mode: light areas are enhanced and colors are mixed according to CMYK color system (that of your printer).

Angular size gradient This is a gradient of radius size which develops angularly. Radius is controlled according to gradient Luminosity: if luminosity is zero (black), the radius is 0%. If luminosity is 100% (white), the radius is also 100%.

Parameters

Size (%) Sets size of glow in percent (0-200).

Rotation Sets the origin of the angular gradient (-180 +180).

Hue rotation Sets glow color, according to the HSV color circle (-180 +180). (Cf. The triangle color selector.)

Figure 17.97 "Gradient Flare Editor" options (Rays)

17.5.2.4.3 Rays

Gradients The options are the same as for Glow.

Parameters The first three options are the same as in Glow. Two are new:

# of Spikes This option determines the number of spikes (1-300) but also their texture.

Spike thickness When spikes get wider (1-100), they look like flower petals.

Figure 17.98 "Gradient Flare Editor" options (Second Flares)

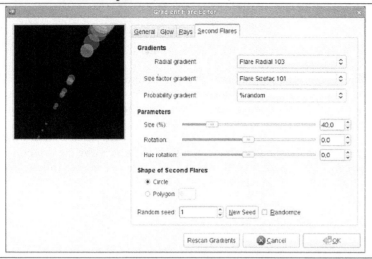

17.5.2.4.4 Second Flares

Gradients The options are the same as for Glow.

Parameters Options are the same as in Glow.

Shape of Second Flares Second flares, these satellites of the main flare, may have two shapes: Circle and Polygon. You can set the *Number* polygon sides. The option accepts 1 side (!), not 2.

Random seed The random generator will use this value as a seed to generate random numbers. You can use the same value to repeat the same "random" sequence several times.

Randomize When you click on this button, you produce a random seed that will be used by the random generator. It is each time different.

17.5.3 Lens Flare

17.5.3.1 Overview

Figure 17.99 Example for the Lens Flare filter

(a) *Original image*   (b) *Filter "Lens Flare" applied*

This filter gives the impression that sun hit the objective when taking a shot. You can locate the reflection with a reticule you can move, but you have not the possibilities that the Gradient Flare filter offers.

17.5.3.2 Activate the filter

You can find this filter in the image menu menu through Filters → Light and Shadow → Lens Flare.

17.5.3.3 Options

Figure 17.100 "Lens Flare" filter options

Preview If checked, parameter setting results are interactively displayed in preview. Scroll bars allow you to move around the image.

Center of Flare Effect You can set X and Y (pixels) coordinates of glint using the input box or by clicking into the preview. The coordinate origin is at the upper left corner.

Show position When this option is checked, a reticule appears in preview and you can move it with the mouse pointer to locate the center of Lens Flare effect.

Tip

  The mouse cursor, which looks like a cross when it moves over the preview, lets you locate the filter effect even without the reticule.

17.5.4 Lighting Effects

17.5.4.1 Overview

Figure 17.101 The same image, before and after applying Lighting filter

(a) *Original image*   (b) *Filter "Lighting Effects" applied*

This filter simulates the effect you get when you light up a wall with a spot. It doesn't produce any drop shadows and, of course, doesn't reveal any new details in dark zones.

17.5.4.2 Activate the filter

This filter is found in the image window menu under Filters → Light and Shadow → Lighting Effects....

17.5.4.3 Options

Figure 17.102 "Lighting" filter options

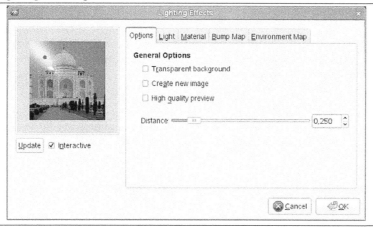

Preview When Interactive is checked, parameter setting results are interactively displayed in preview without modifying the image until you click on OK button.

If Interactive is not checked, changes are displayed in preview only when you click on the Update button. This option is useful with a slow computer.

Any other options are organized in tabs:

Figure 17.103 "Lighting" filter options (General Options)

17.5.4.3.1   General Options

Transparent background Makes destination image transparent when bumpmap height is zero (height is zero in black areas of the bumpmapped image).

Create new image Creates a new image when applying filter.

High quality preview For quick CPU...

Distance You can specify the distance of the light source from the center of the image with this slider. The range of values is from 0.0 to 2.0.

Figure 17.104 "Lighting" filter options (Light Settings)

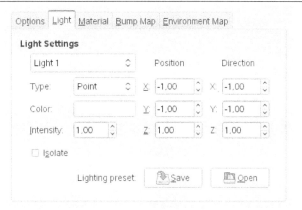

17.5.4.3.2   Light Settings
In this tab, you can set light parameters. With Light 1 ... Light 6 you can create six light sources and work on each of them separately.

Type The filter provides several *light types* in a drop-down list:

    Point Displays a blue point at center of preview. You can click and drag it to move light all over the preview.

    Directional The blue point is linked to preview center by a line which indicates the direction of light.

    None This deletes the light source (light may persist...).

Color When you click on the color swatch, you bring a dialog up where you can select the light source color.

Intensity With this option, you can set light intensity.

Position Determines the light point position according to three coordinates: X coordinate for horizontal position, Y for vertical position, Z for source distance (the light darkens when distance increases). Values are from -1 to +1.

Direction This option should allow you to fix the light direction in its three X, Y and Z coordinates.

Isolate With this option, you can decide whether all light sources must appear in the Preview, or only the source you are working on.

Lighting preset You can save your settings with the Save and get them back later with the Open.

Figure 17.105 "Lighting" filter options (Material Properties)

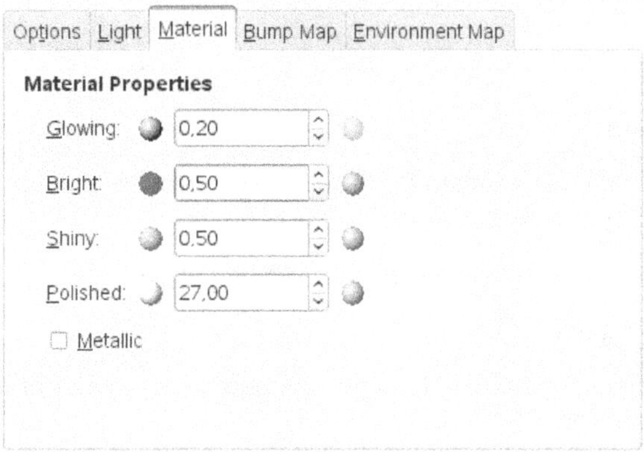

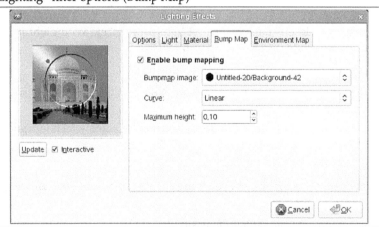

17.5.4.3.3 Material Properties These options don't concern light itself, but light reflected by objects. Small spheres, on both ends of the input boxes, represent the action of every option, from its minimum (on the left) to its maximum (on the right). Help pop ups are more useful.

Glowing With these option, you can set the amount of original color to show where no direct light falls.

Bright With this option, you can set the intensity of original color when hit directly by a light source.

Shiny This option controls how intense the highlight will be.

Polished With this option, higher values make the highlight more focused.

Metallic When this option is checked, surfaces look metallic.

Figure 17.106 "Lighting" filter options (Bump Map)

17.5.4.3.4   Bump Map   In this tab, you can set filter options that give relief to the image. See *Bump mapping* .

Enable bump mapping With this option, bright parts of the image will appear raised and dark parts will appear depressed. The aspect depends on the light source position.

Bumpmap image You have to select there the grey-scale image that will act as a bump map. See *Bump Map* plug-in for additional explanations.

Curve This option defines the method that will be used when applying the bump map; that is, the bump height is a function of the specified curve. Four curve types are available: *Linear*, *Logarithmic*, *Sinusoidal* and *Spherical*.

Maximum height This is the maximum height of bumps.

Figure 17.107 "Lighting" filter options (Environment Map)

17.5.4.3.5   Environment Map

Enable environment mapping When you check this box, the following option is enabled:

Environment image You have to select there a RGB image, present on your screen. Please note that for this option to work you should load another image with GIMP *before* using it.

An example can be found at [BUDIG01].

17.5.5   Sparkle

17.5.5.1   Overview

Figure 17.108 Applying example for the Sparkle filter

(a) *Original image*   (b) *Filter "Sparkle" applied*

This filter adds sparkles to your image. It uses the lightest points according to a threshold you have determined. It is difficult to foresee where sparkles will appear. But you can put white points on your image where you want sparkles to be.

17.5.5.2   Activate the filter

This filter is found in the image window menu under Filters → Light and Shadow → Sparkle....

17.5.5.3   Parameter Settings

Figure 17.109 "Sparkle" filter options

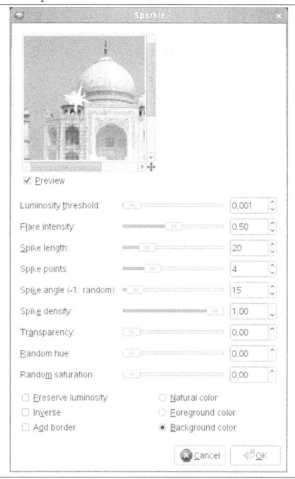

Sliders and input boxes allow you to set values.

Preview If checked, parameter setting results are interactively displayed in preview. Scroll bars allow you to move around the image.

Luminosity threshold The higher the threshold, the more areas are concerned by sparkling (0.0-0.1).

Flare intensity When this value increases, the central spot and rays widen (0.0-1.0).

Spike length This is ray length (1-100). When you reduce it, small spikes decrease first.

Spike points Number of starting points for spikes (0-16). It's the number of big spikes. There is the same number of small spikes. When number is odd, small spikes are opposite the big ones. When number is even, big spikes are opposite another big spike.

Spike angle This is angle of first big spike with horizontal (-1 +360). -1 determines this value at random. If a spot has several pixels within required threshold, each of them will generate a sparkle. If angle is positive, they will all be superimposed. With -1, each sparkle will have a random rotation resulting in numerous thin spikes.

Spike density This option determines the number of sparkles on your image. It indicates the percentage (0.0-1.0) of all possible sparkles that will be preserved.

Transparency When you increase transparency (0.0-1.0), sparkles become more transparent and the layer beneath becomes visible. If there is no other layer, sparkle saturation decreases.

Random hue This option should change sparkle hue at random... (0.0-1.0).

Random saturation This option should change sparkle saturation at random... (0.0-1.0).

Preserve luminosity Gives to all central pixels the luminosity of the brightest pixel, resulting in increasing the whole sparkle luminosity.

Inverse Instead of selecting brightest pixels in image, Sparkle will select the darkest ones, resulting in dark sparkles.

Add border Instead of creating sparkles on brightest pixels, this option creates an image border made up of numerous sparkles.

Natural color, Foreground color, Background color You can change there the color of central pixels. This color will be added in Screen mode (Multiply if Inverse is checked). "Natural color" is the color of the pixel in the image.

17.5.6 Supernova

17.5.6.1 Overview

Figure 17.110 Applying example for the Supernova filter

(a) *Original image*   (b) *Filter "Supernova" applied*

This filter creates a big star reminding a super-nova. It works with RGB and GRAY images. Light effect decreases according to $1/r$ where r is the distance from star center.

17.5.6.2 Activate the filter

This filter is found in the image window menu under Filters → Light and Shadow → Supernova....

17.5.6.3 Parameter Settings

Figure 17.111 "Supernova" filter options

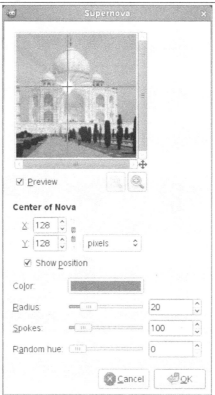

Preview If checked, parameter setting results are interactively displayed in preview. Scroll bars allow you to move around the image.

Center of Nova

> **X, Y** You can use input boxes to set horizontal (X) and vertical (Y) coordinates of SuperNova center. You can also click the SuperNova center in the *preview* box.

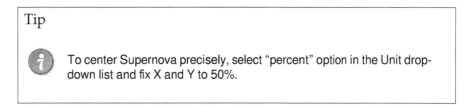

> Tip
>
> To center Supernova precisely, select "percent" option in the Unit drop-down list and fix X and Y to 50%.

Show position This option brings up a reticle in preview, centered on the SuperNova.

Color When you click on the color swatch, you bring up the usual color selector.

Radius This is radius of the SuperNova center (1-100). When you increase the value, you increase the number of central white pixels according to r*r (1, 4, 9...).

Spikes This is number of rays (1-1024). Each pixel in the nova center emit one pixel wide rays. All these rays are more or less superimposed resulting in this glittering effect you get when you move this slider.

Random hue Color rays at random. (0-360) value seems to be a range in HSV color circle.

17.5.7 Drop Shadow

17.5.7.1 Overview

Figure 17.112 Example for the "Drop Shadow" filter

(a) *Original image*   (b) *"Drop Shadow" applied (white background layer added manually)*

This filter adds a drop-shadow to the current selection or to the image if there's no active selection. Optional the filter resizes the image if that's necessary for displaying the shadow.

You may choose the color, position, and size of the shadow.

Please note that the filter does not add a background layer to make the shadow visible. The shadow's background is transparent. The white background in the above example has not been created by the filter, instead it has been added later to let you see the shadow.

17.5.7.2 Activate the filter

You can find this filter in the image menu menu through Filters → Light and Shadow → Drop Shadow....

17.5.7.3 Options

Figure 17.113 "Drop Shadow" filter options

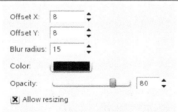

Offset X, Offset Y The layer containing the drop shadow will be moved horizontally by X pixels, vertically by Y pixels. So, X and Y offset determine where the shadow will be placed in relation to the image. High values make the imaginary source of light look like it's far away in horizontal or vertical direction, and low values will make it look closer to the image.

The offsets may be negative, leading to a shadow on the left of the selection if offset X < 0, or above the selection if offset Y < 0.

If there's no active selection, you must have Allow resizing enabled to see any effect.

Blur radius After creating the shadow, a Gaussian blur with the specified radius is applied to the shadow layer, resulting in the realistic appearance of the drop shadow. It may be necessary to enable Allow resizing, since blurring extends the shadow.

Color The shadow may have any color. Just click on the button, and select a color when the color selector pops up.

Figure 17.114 "Drop Shadow" color example

Opacity The shadow's opacity is just the opacity of the new layer containing the shadow (see Section 8.1.1). It defaults to 80%, but you may select any other value from 0 (full transparency) to 100 (full opacity) here. After applying the filter to an image you can change the opacity in the layers dialog.

Allow resizing If enabled, the filter will resize the image if that is needed to make place for the shadow. The new size depends on the size of the selection, the blur radius, and the shadow offsets.

17.5.8 Perspective

17.5.8.1 Overview

Figure 17.115 Example for the "Perspective" filter

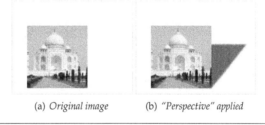

(a) *Original image*   (b) *"Perspective" applied*

This filter adds a perspective shadow to the selected region or alpha-channel as a layer below the active layer. You may select color, length and direction of the shadow as well as the distance of the horizon.

If necessary, the filter may resize the image. But it will not add a background to make the shadow visible.

17.5.8.2 Activate the filter

You can access this filter in the image window menu through Filters → Light and Shadow → Perspective....

17.5.8.3 Options

Figure 17.116 "Perspective" options

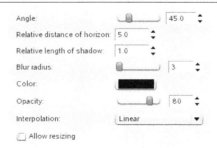

Angle The angle determines the direction of the shadow or the imaginary source of light, respectively. Values range from 0° to 180°, where 90° represents a light source just in front of the selection or layer. For angles less than 90°, the shadow is at the right side, so the light source is on the left. For angles greater than 90°, it's the other way round. Tip: think of the slider's handle as source of light.

Figure 17.117 "Angle" example

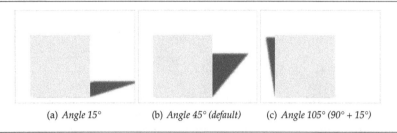

(a) *Angle 15°*　　(b) *Angle 45° (default)*　　(c) *Angle 105° (90° + 15°)*

Relative distance of horizon This option determines how far away the imaginary horizon is. The relative distance is the distance from the ground-line of the selection or layer, the "unit" of measurement is the height of the selection or layer.

Value range is from 0.1 to 24.1, where 24.1 means (nearly) "infinite". Note that the relative length of shadow must not exceed the distance of horizon.

Figure 17.118 "Distance of horizon" example

Angle = 45°. Distance = 2.4. Length = 1.8.

In the example above, the yellow area is the selection the filter is applied to. The blue line at the top represents the imaginary horizon. The angle between the selection's ground-line and the red line is 45°. The length of the red line is 1.8 times the height of the yellow selection. Extended to the horizon, the length is 2.4 times the selection's height.

Relative length of shadow With this option you can set the length of shadow with respect to the height of the selection or layer. In the above example, the red line represents the length of shadow, its length is 1.8 relative to the height of the yellow selection.

Value range is from 0.1 to 24.1, although the length of shadow must not exceed the relative distance of horizon - you can't go beyond the horizon.

Figure 17.119 "Length of Shadow" example

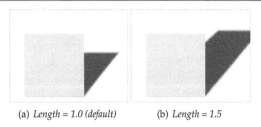

(a) *Length = 1.0 (default)*　　(b) *Length = 1.5*

Blur radius After creating the shadow, a Gaussian blur with the specified radius is applied to the shadow layer, resulting in the realistic appearance of the shadow.

Figure 17.120 Blur example

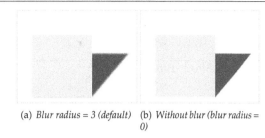

(a) *Blur radius = 3 (default)*   (b) *Without blur (blur radius = 0)*

Color Of course, the default color of the shadow is black. But a click on the button opens the color selector, where you may select any other color.

Opacity The shadow's opacity is the opacity of the new layer containing the shadow (see Section 8.1.1). It defaults to 80%, but you may select any other value from 0 (full transparency) to 100 (full opacity) here. After applying the filter to an image you can change the opacity in the layers dialog.

Interpolation This drop-down list lets you choose the method of interpolation used when the shadow layer is transformed, for example rotated by the specified angle. Using None will usually result in aliasing, using any interpolation method may change the color of the shadow in some areas. Linear is a good choice.

Allow resizing If enabled, the filter will resize the image if that is needed to make place for the shadow.

In the example below, the yellow area is the active selection, background is light blue. The white area has been added after resizing to make the shadow visible.

Figure 17.121 "Allow resizing" example

(a) *Allow resizing*   (b) *Don't allow resizing*

17.5.9 Xach-Effect

17.5.9.1 Overview

Figure 17.122 Example for the "Xach-Effect" filter

(a) *Original image* (b) *"Xach-Effect" applied*

This filter adds a subtle translucent 3D effect to the selected region or alpha channel. This 3D effect is achieved by

1. Highlighting the selection: a new layer ("Highlight") will be created above the active layer, filled with the highlight color. Then a layer mask will be added to that layer making the unmasked pixel partially transparent.

Highlight layer with layer mask

2. Painting the selection's left and top edges with the highlight color: for that the "Highlight" layer will be extended by one pixel left and up. These small areas will be opaque.

3. Creating a drop shadow at the bottom right side of the selection.

You may vary these default settings, for example select different colors for highlight or shadow and change amount and directions of offsets.

17.5.9.2 Activate the filter

The filter is found in the image window menu under Filters → Light and Shadow → Xach-Effect....

17.5.9.3 Options

There are two groups of options, each controlling the highlight or the shadow, and a checkbox for the selection behaviour.

Figure 17.123 "Xach-Effect" options

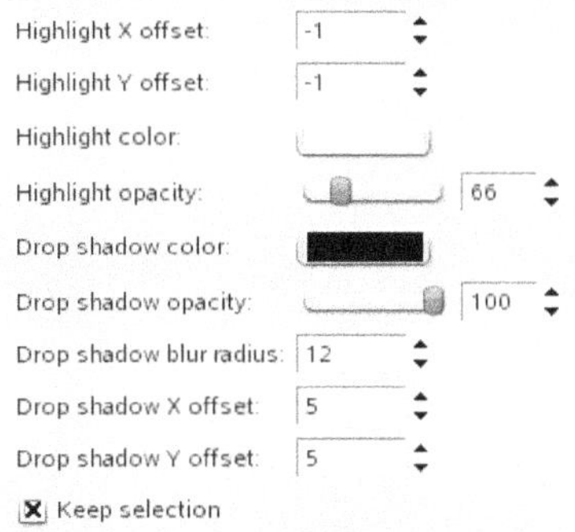

Highlight X offset: -1

Highlight Y offset: -1

Highlight color:

Highlight opacity: 66

Drop shadow color:

Drop shadow opacity: 100

Drop shadow blur radius: 12

Drop shadow X offset: 5

Drop shadow Y offset: 5

☒ Keep selection

Highlight X offset, Highlight Y offset The selection's left and top edge are painted with the highlight color. The highlight offset is the size (width or height) of the respective area. If offset is less than 0 (this is the default), the left (X offset < 0) or top (Y offset < 0) area will be colored. If offset is greater than 0, the right (X offset > 0) or bottom (Y offset > 0) area will be painted.

Highlight color This is the color used to highlight the selected area. It defaults to white, but clicking on the swatch button brings up a color selector and you may select any other color.

Highlight opacity The selection will be covered by a partially transparent area filled with the highlight color. This option lets you set the level of transparency. Since a layer mask will be used, the value ranges from 0 (full transparency) to 255 (full opacity).

The highlight opacity defaults to 66, which is equivalent to 26%.

Drop shadow options These options work like the respective Drop Shadow options (without resizing). Briefly:

Drop shadow color Click on the button to open a color selector.

Drop shadow opacity The opacity (0% - 100%) of the layer containing the shadow.

Drop shadow blur radius The radius used by the Gaussian blur filter, which will be applied to the shadow.

Drop shadow X offset, Drop shadow Y offset Direction and amount, by which the shadow will be moved from the selection.

Keep selection If checked, the active selection will remain active when the filter has been applied.

17.5.10   Glass Tile

17.5.10.1   Overview

Figure 17.124 The same image, before and after applying glass tile effect.

(a) *Original image*   (b) *Filter "Glass Tile" applied*

After applying this filter, the active layer or selection is rendered as through a glass brick wall.

17.5.10.2 Activate the filter

You can find this filter through Filters → Light and Shadow → Glass Tile

17.5.10.3 Options

Figure 17.125 "Glass Tile" filter options

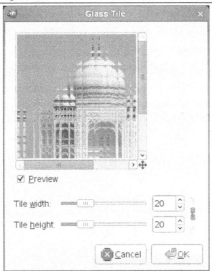

Preview If checked, parameter setting results are interactively displayed in preview. Scroll bars allow
you to move around the image.

Tile width, Tile length Sets tile width and length (10-50 pixels).

By default, width and height are linked, indicated by the chain symbol next to the input boxes. If
you want to set width and height separately, click on that chain symbol to unlink them.

17.6 Noise Filters

17.6.1 Introduction

Noise filters *add* noise to the active layer or to the selection. To *remove* small defects from an image, see
the Despeckle and Selective Gaussian Blur filters.

17.6.2   HSV Noise

17.6.2.1   Overview

Figure 17.126 Example of applying the "HSV Noise" filter

(a) *Original image*   (b) *Filter "HSV Noise" applied*

The HSV Noise filter creates noise in the active layer or selection by using the Hue, Saturation, Value (luminosity) color model.

17.6.2.2   Activate the filter

You can find this filter through Filters → Noise → HSV Noise....

17.6.2.3   Options

Figure 17.127 "HSV Noise" filter options

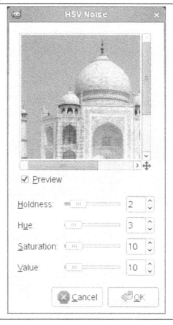

Preview This preview displays interactively changes before they are applied to the image.

Holdness This slider (1 -8) controls how much the new pixel color value is allowed to be applied compared to the existing color. A low holdness will give an important hue variation. A high holdness will give a weak variation.

Hue This slider changes the color of the pixels in a random pattern. It selects an increasing available color range in the HSV color circle starting from the original pixel color.

Saturation This slider increases saturation of scattered pixels.

Value This slider increases brightness of scattered pixels.

17.6.3 Hurl

17.6.3.1 Overview

Figure 17.128 Example for the "Hurl" filter

        (a) *Original image*   (b) *Filter "Hurl" applied*

You can find this filter through Filters → Noise → Hurl....

The Hurl filter changes each affected pixel to a random color, so it produces real *random noise*. All color channels, including an alpha channel (if it is present) are randomized. All possible values are assigned with the same probability. The original values are not taken into account. All or only some pixels in an active layer or selection are affected, the percentage of affected pixels is determined by the Randomization (%) option.

17.6.3.2   Options

Figure 17.129 "Hurl" options

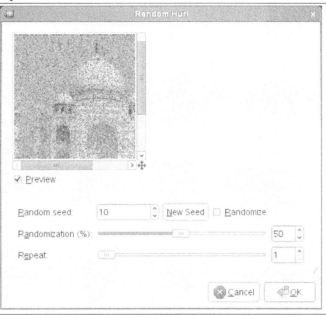

Random seed Controls randomness of hurl. If the same random seed in the same situation is used, the filter produces exactly the same results. A different random seed produces different results. Random seed can be entered manually or generated randomly by pressing New Seed button.

When the Randomize option is checked, random seed cannot be entered manually, but is randomly generated each time the filter is run. If it is not checked, the filter remembers the last random seed used.

Randomization (%) This slider represents the percentage of pixels of the active layer or selection which will be hurled. The higher value, the more pixels are hurled.

Repeat It represents the number of times the filter will be applied. In the case of the Hurl filter it is not very useful, because the same results can be obtained faster just by using a higher Randomization (%) value.

17.6.4   Pick

17.6.4.1   Overview

Figure 17.130 Example of applying the "Pick" filter

(a) *Original image*   (b) *Filter "Pick" applied*

The Pick filter replaces each affected pixel by a pixel value randomly chosen from its eight neighbours and itself (from a 3×3 square the pixel is center of). All or only some pixels in an active layer or selection are affected, the percentage of affected pixels is determined by the Randomization (%) option.

17.6.4.2   Activate the filter

You can find this filter through Filters → Noise → Pick....

17.6.4.3   Options

Figure 17.131 "Pick" filter options

Random seed Controls randomness of picking. If the same random seed in the same situation is used, the filter produces exactly the same results. A different random seed produces different results. Random seed can be entered manually or generated randomly by pressing New Seed button.

When the Randomize option is checked, random seed cannot be entered manually, but is randomly generated each time the filter is run. If it is not checked, the filter remembers the last random seed used.

Randomization (%) This slider represents the percentage of pixels of the active layer or selection which will be picked. The higher value, the more pixels are picked.

Repeat This slider represents the number of times the filter will be applied. Higher values result in more picking, pixel values being transferred farther away.

17.6.5   RGB Noise

17.6.5.1   Overview

Figure 17.132 Example of applying the "RGB Noise" filter

(a) *Original image*   (b) *Filter "RGB Noise" applied*

The RGB Noise filter adds a normally distributed noise to a layer or a selection. It uses the RGB color model to produce the noise (noise is added to red, green and blue values of each pixel). A normal distribution means, that only slight noise is added to the most pixels in the affected area, while less pixels are affected by more extreme values. (If you apply this filter to an image filled with a solid grey color and then look at its histogram, you will see a classic bell-shaped Gaussian curve.)

The result is very naturally looking noise.

This filter does not work with indexed images.

17.6.5.2   Activate the filter

You can find this filter through Filters → Noise → RGB Noise....

17.6.5.3   Options

Figure 17.133 "RGB Noise" filter options

Preview This preview displays interactively changes before they are applied to the image.

Correlated noise Noise may be additive (uncorrelated) or multiplicative (correlated - also known as speckle noise). When checked, every channel value is multiplied by an normally distributed value. So the noise depends on the channel values: a greater channel value leads to more noise, while dark colors (small values) tend to remain dark.

Independent RGB When this radio button is checked, you can move each RGB slider separately. Otherwise, sliders R, G and B will be moved all together. The same relative noise will then be added to all channels in each pixel, so the hue of pixels does not change much.

Red, Green, Blue, Alpha These slidebars and adjacent input boxes allow to set noise level (0.00 - 1.00) in each channel. Alpha channel is only present if your layer holds such a channel. In case of a grayscale image, a Grey is shown instead of color sliders.

The value set by these sliders actually determine the standard deviation of the normal distribution of applied noise. The used standard deviation is a half of the set value (where 1 is the distance between the lowest and highest possible value in a channel).

17.6.6   Slur

17.6.6.1   Overview

Figure 17.134 Example of applying the Slur filter

(a) *Original image*   (b) *Filter "Slur" applied*

Slurring produces an effect resembling melting the image downwards; if a pixel is to be slurred, there is an 80% chance that it is replaced by the value of a pixel directly above it; otherwise, one of the two pixels to the left or right of the one above is used. All or only some pixels in an active layer or selection are affected, the percentage of affected pixels is determined by the Randomization (%) option.

17.6.6.2   Activate the filter

You can find this filter through Filters → Noise → Slur....

17.6.6.3   Options

Figure 17.135 Slur filter options

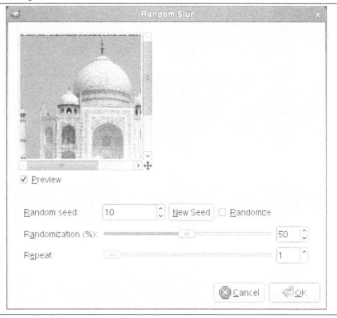

Random seed It controls randomness of slurring. If the same random seed in the same situation is used, the filter produces exactly the same results. A different random seed produces different results. Random seed can be entered manually or generated randomly by pressing New Seed button.

When the Randomize option is checked, random seed cannot be entered manually, but is randomly generated each time the filter is run. If it is not checked, the filter remembers the last random seed used.

Randomization (%) This slider represents the percentage of pixels of the active layer or selection which will be slurred. The higher value, the more pixels are slurred, but because of the way the filter works, its effect is most noticeable if this slider is set to a medium value, somewhere around 50. Experiment with it and try for yourself!

Repeat This slider represents the number of times the filter will be applied. Higher values result in more slurring, moving the color over a longer distance.

17.6.7   Spread

17.6.7.1   Overview

Figure 17.136 Example of applying the Spread filter

(a) *Original image*   (b) *Filter "Spread" applied*

The Spread filter swaps each pixel in the active layer or selection with another randomly chosen pixel by a user specified amount. It works on color transitions, not on plain color areas. No new color is introduced.

17.6.7.2   Activate the filter

You can find this filter through Filters → Noise → Spread....

17.6.7.3   Options

Figure 17.137 "Spread" filter options

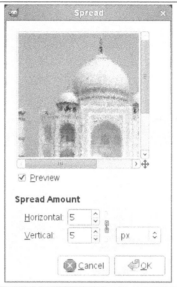

Preview   This preview displays interactively changes before they are applied to the image.

Spread Amount   You can set the distance that pixels will be moved along Horizontal and Vertical axis. The axis can be locked by clicking the Chain icon. You can also define the Unit to be used.

17.7   Edge-Detect Filters

17.7.1   Introduction

Edge detect filters search for borders between different colors and so can detect contours of objects. They are used to make selections and for many artistic purposes.

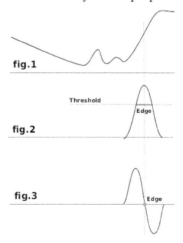

Most of them are based on gradient calculation methods and give thick border lines. Look at fig.1 which represents color intensity variations. On the left is a slow color gradient which is not a border. On the right is a quick variation which is an edge. Now, let us calculate the gradient, the variation speed, of this edge, i.e. the first derivative (fig.2). We have to decide that a border is detected when gradient is more than a threshold value (the exact border is at top of the curve, but this top varies according to borders). In most cases, threshold is under top and border is thick.

The Laplacian edge detection uses the second derivative (fig.3). The top of the curve is now at zero and clearly identified. That's why Laplace filter renders a thin border, only a pixel wide. But this derivative gives several zeros corresponding to small ripples, resulting in false edges.

Some blurring before applying edge filters is often necessary: it flattens small ripples in signal and so prevents false edges.

17.7.2 Difference of Gaussians

17.7.2.1 Overview

Figure 17.138 Applying example for the "Difference of Gaussians" filter

(a) *Original image*   (b) *Filter "Difference of Gaussians" applied*

This filter does edge detection using the so-called "Difference of Gaussians" algorithm, which works by performing two different Gaussian blurs on the image, with a different blurring radius for each, and subtracting them to yield the result. This algorithm is very widely used in artificial vision (maybe in biological vision as well!), and is pretty fast because there are very efficient methods for doing Gaussian blurs. The most important parameters are the blurring radii for the two Gaussian blurs. It is probably easiest to set them using the preview, but it may help to know that increasing the smaller radius tends to give thicker-appearing edges, and decreasing the larger radius tends to increase the "threshold" for recognizing something as an edge. In most cases you will get nicer results if Radius 2 is smaller than Radius 1, but nothing prevents you from reversing them, and in situations where you have a light figure on the dark background, reversing them may actually improve the result.

17.7.2.2 Activating the filter

You can find this filter through Filters → Edge-Detect → Difference of Gaussians....

17.7.2.3 Options

Figure 17.139 Gaussian Difference filter options

Smoothing Parameters Radius 1 and Radius 2 are the blurring radii for the two Gaussian blurs. The only constraints on them is that they cannot be equal, or else the result will be a blank image. If you want to produce something that looks like a sketch, in most cases setting "Radius 2" smaller than "Radius 1" will give better results.

Normalize Checking this box causes the brightness range in the result to be stretched as much as possible, increasing contrast. Note that in the preview, only the part of the image that is shown is taken into account, so with Normalize checked the preview is not completely accurate. (It is accurate except in terms of global contrast, though.)

Invert Checking this box inverts the result, so that you see dark edges on a white background, giving something that looks more like a drawing.

17.7.3 Edge

17.7.3.1 Overview

Figure 17.140 Applying example for the Edge filter

(a) *Original image*   (b) *After applying the filter (Sobel option)*

Figure 17.141 Applying examples for the Edge filter

(a) *After applying the filter (Prewitt compass* (b) *After applying the filter (Gradient option)*
option)

Figure 17.142 Applying example for the Edge filter

(a) *After applying the filter (Roberts option)* (b) *After applying the filter (Differential op-*
tion)

Figure 17.143 Applying example for the Edge filter

After applying the filter (Laplace option)

17.7.3.2 Activating the filter

You can find this filter through Filters → Edge-Detect → Edge....

17.7.3.3 Options

Figure 17.144 Edge filter options

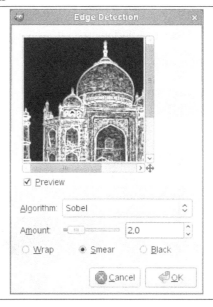

Algorithm Edge detector offers several detection methods:

> **Sobel** Here, this method has no options and so is less interesting than the specific Sobel.
>
> **Prewitt compass** Result doesn't look different from Sobel.
>
> **Gradient** Edges are thinner, less contrasted and more blurred than Sobel.
>
> **Roberts** No evident difference from Sobel.
>
> **Differential** Edges less bright.
>
> **Laplace** Less interesting than the specific one.

Amount A low value results in black, high-contrasted image with thin edges. A high value results in thick edges with low contrast and many colors in dark areas.

Wrap, Smear, Black Where the edge detector will get adjoining pixels for its calculations when it is working on the image boundaries. This option will only have an effect on the boundaries of the result (if any). Smear is the default and the best choice.

17.7.4 Laplace

17.7.4.1 Overview

Figure 17.145 Applying example for the Laplace filter

(a) *Original image*   (b) *Filter "Laplace" applied*

This filter detects edges in the image using Laplacian method, which produces thin, pixel wide borders.

17.7.4.2 Activating the filter

You can find this filter through Filtres → Edge-Detect → Laplace.

17.7.5 Neon

17.7.5.1 Overview

Figure 17.146 Applying example for the Neon filter

(a) *Original image*   (b) *Filter "Neon" applied*

This filter detects edges in the active layer or selection and gives them a bright neon effect.

You will find in GIMP a Script-Fu also named Neon, which works in a different manner. The Script-Fu is an easy shortcut to construct logo-like letters outlined with a configurable neon-effect. See Section 17.16.17 for details.

17.7.5.2 Activating the filter

You can find this filter through Filters → Edge-Detect → Neon....

17.7.5.3 Options

Figure 17.147 Neon filter options

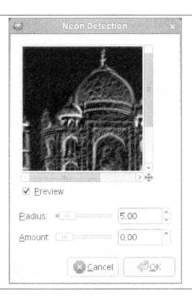

Radius This option lets you determine how wide the detected edge will be.

Amount This option lets you determine how strong the filter effect will be.

17.7.6 Sobel

17.7.6.1 Overview

Figure 17.148 Applying example of the Sobel filter

(a) *Original image*   (b) *Filter "Sobel" applied*

Sobel's filter detects horizontal and vertical edges separately on a scaled image. Color images are turned into RGB scaled images. As with the Laplace filter, the result is a transparent image with black lines and some rest of colors.

17.7.6.2   Activating the filter

You can find this filter through Filters → Edge-Detect → Sobel....

17.7.6.3   Options

Figure 17.149 Sobel filter options

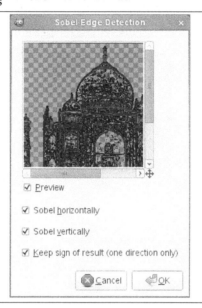

Preview If checked, changes in the image are displayed in the Preview in real time before being applied to the image.

Sobel horizontally Renders near horizontal edges.

Sobel vertically Renders near vertical edges.

Keep sign of result This option allows you to set how the filter will work if you have selected one direction for use only: a flat relief with bumps and hollows will be created.

17.8   Generic Filters

17.8.1   Introduction

Generic filters are a catch-all for filters which can't be placed elsewhere. You can find:

- The Convolution Matrix filter which lets you build custom filters.
- The Dilate filter.
- The Erode filter.

17.8.2   Convolution Matrix

17.8.2.1   Overview

Here is a mathematician's domain. Most of filters are using convolution matrix. With the Convolution Matrix filter, if the fancy takes you, you can build a custom filter.

What is a convolution matrix? It's possible to get a rough idea of it without using mathematical tools that only a few ones know. Convolution is the treatment of a matrix by another one which is called "kernel".

The Convolution Matrix filter uses a first matrix which is the Image to be treated. The image is a bi-dimensional collection of pixels in rectangular coordinates. The used kernel depends on the effect you want.

GIMP uses 5x5 or 3x3 matrices. We will consider only 3x3 matrices, they are the most used and they are enough for all effects you want. If all border values of a kernel are set to zero, then system will consider it as a 3x3 matrix.

The filter studies successively every pixel of the image. For each of them, which we will call the "initial pixel", it multiplies the value of this pixel and values of the 8 surrounding pixels by the kernel corresponding value. Then it adds the results, and the initial pixel is set to this final result value.

A simple example:

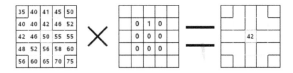

On the left is the image matrix: each pixel is marked with its value. The initial pixel has a red border. The kernel action area has a green border. In the middle is the kernel and, on the right is the convolution result.

Here is what happened: the filter read successively, from left to right and from top to bottom, all the pixels of the kernel action area. It multiplied the value of each of them by the kernel corresponding value and added results. The initial pixel has become 42: (40*0)+(42*1)+(46*0) + (46*0)+(50*0)+(55*0) + (52*0)+(56*0)+(58*0) = 42. (the filter doesn't work on the image but on a copy). As a graphical result, the initial pixel moved a pixel downwards.

17.8.2.2   Activating the filter

This filter is found in the image window menu under Filters → Generic → Convolution Matrix....

17.8.2.3 Options

Figure 17.150 "Convolution matrix" options

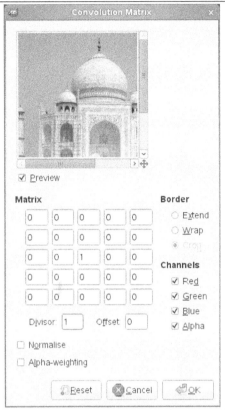

Matrix This is the 5x5 kernel matrix: you enter wanted values directly into boxes.

> **Divisor** The result of previous calculation will be divided by this divisor. You will hardly use 1, which lets result unchanged, and 9 or 25 according to matrix size, which gives the average of pixel values.

> **Offset** This value is added to the division result. This is useful if result may be negative. This offset may be negative.

Border When the initial pixel is on a border, a part of kernel is out of image. You have to decide what filter must do:

From left: source image, Extend border, Wrap border, Crop border

> **Extend** This part of kernel is not taken into account.

> **Wrap** This part of kernel will study pixels of the opposite border, so pixels disappearing from one side reappear on the other side.

> **Crop** Pixels on borders are not modified, but they are cropped.

Channels You can select there one or several channels the filter will work with.

Normalise If this option is checked, The Divisor takes the result value of convolution. If this result is equal to zero (it's not possible to divide by zero), then a 128 offset is applied. If it is negative (a negative color is not possible), a 255 offset is applied (inverts result).

Alpha-weighting If this option is not checked, the filter doesn't take in account transparency and this may be cause of some artefacts when blurring.

17.8.2.4   Examples

Design of kernels is based on high levels mathematics. You can find ready-made kernels on the Web. Here are a few examples:

Figure 17.151 Sharpen

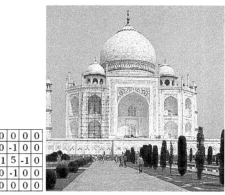

Figure 17.152 Blur

Figure 17.153 Edge enhance

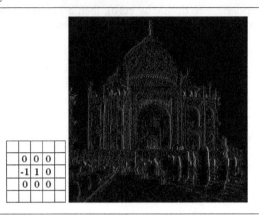

Figure 17.154 Edge detect

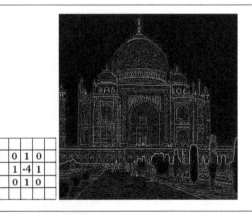

Figure 17.155 Emboss

17.8.3 Dilate

17.8.3.1 Overview

Figure 17.156 Applying example for the Dilate filter

(a) *Original image*　　　　　　　(b) *Filter "Dilate" applied*

This filter widens and enhances dark areas of the active layer or selection.

For every image pixel, it brings the pixel Value (luminosity) into line with the lowest Value (the darkest) of the 8 neighbouring pixels (3x3 matrix). So, a dark pixel is added around dark areas. An isolated pixel on a brighter background will be changed to a big "pixel", composed of 9 pixels, and that will create some noise in the image.

In this image, the studied pixel has a red border and the studied matrix has a green border. I hope you have understood how to go on with the process and get a 3x3 pixel block: when the "I" pixel is inside the green border, the studied pixel turns to black.

A larger dark area will dilate by one pixel in all directions:

The filter was applied 3 times.

On more complex images, dark areas are widened and enhanced the same, and somewhat pixellated. Here, the filter was applied 3 times:

Of course, if background is darker than foreground, it will cover the whole image.

17.8.3.2 Activating the filter

This filter is found in the image window menu under Filters → Generic → Dilate.

17.8.3.3 Examples

Figure 17.157 Dilate text

E **E**

Figure 17.158 Dilate neon effect

17.8.4 Erode

17.8.4.1 Overview

Figure 17.159 Erode noise

(a) *Original image*   (b) *Filter "Erode noise" applied*

This filter widens and enhances bright areas of the active layer or selection.

For every image pixel, it brings the pixel Value (luminosity) into line with the upper value (the brightest) of the 8 neighbouring pixels (3x3 matrix). So, a bright pixel is added around bright areas. An isolated pixel on a brighter background will be deleted. A larger bright area will dilate by one pixel in all directions.

On complex images, bright areas are widened and enhanced the same, and somewhat pixellated.

On a solid background, this filter can delete noise:

Figure 17.160 "Erode noise" example

17.8.4.2 Activating the filter

This filter is found in the image window menu under Filters → Generic → Erode.

17.9 Combine Filters

17.9.1 Introduction

The combine filters associate two or more images into a single image.

17.9.2 Depth Merge

Depth Merge is a Combine Filter which is useful to combine two different pictures or layers. You can decide which part of every image or layer will stay visible.

17.9.2.1   Overview

Figure 17.161 Filter example

(a) *Original*   (b) *Filter applied*

Every image is associated with a map which works as a mask. Simply create this map as a grayscale gradient: when applied onto the image, dark areas of the mask will show the underlying image and bright areas will mask the image.

Note

To work with this filter, images and maps must have the same size. All images to be selected must be present on screen.

You can also use this filter on an image with several layers. All layers will appear in the drop-down lists used to select images. These layers must have the same size.

17.9.2.2   Accessing this Filter

You can find this filter through Filters → Combine → Depth Merge...

17.9.2.3 Options

Figure 17.162 "Depth Merge" filter options

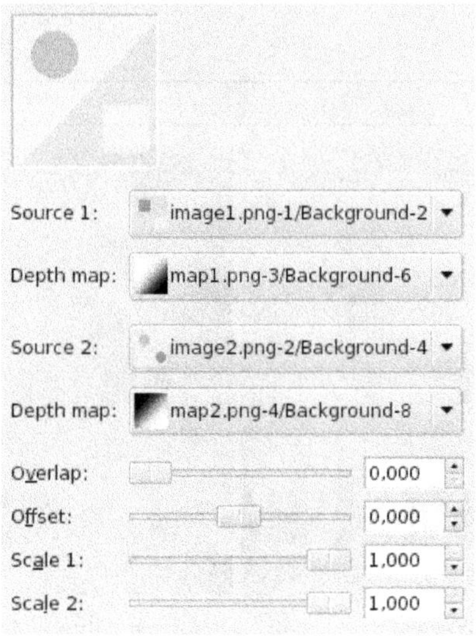

Source 1:   image1.png-1/Background-2 ▼

Depth map: map1.png-3/Background-6 ▼

Source 2:   image2.png-2/Background-4 ▼

Depth map: map2.png-4/Background-8 ▼

Overlap: 0,000

Offset: 0,000

Scale 1:   1,000

Scale 2:   1,000

Source 1, Source 2 Defines the source images to use for the blending.

Depth map Define the picture to use as transformation maps for the sources.

Overlap Creates soft transitions between images.

Offset This option shifts the merging limit, giving more or less importance to an image against the other.

Scale 1, Scale 2 Same as above for Offset, but more sensitive and applied to each map separately. When you scale to a lower value, it will affect the map image's value, making it darker. So, black is more dominant in the merge and you will see more of the image.

17.9.2.4 Using example

Maps are grayscale gradients created with the Blend tool and modified with the Curve tool.

Figure 17.163 Source images and their maps

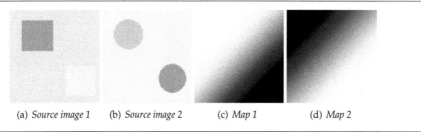

(a) *Source image 1*   (b) *Source image 2*   (c) *Map 1*   (d) *Map 2*

You can understand what's going on. Image-1 is treated by map-1: the red square is masked and the yellow square remains visible. Image-2 is treated by map-2: the red circle is masked and the green circle remains visible. In total, the green circle and the yellow square stay visible.

Figure 17.164 Results

(a) *No offset and no overlap. The limit between both images is sharp and is situated in the middle of the mask gradient.*

(b) *Offset = 0.980 : the limit be- limit, sharp, is shifted so is blurred.*

(c) *Overlap: the limit is that the image-2 area is increased.*

(d) *Scale 1 reduced to 0.056 : as with Offset, the limit is shifted. Image-1 area is increased.*

17.9.3   Filmstrip

17.9.3.1   Overview

Figure 17.165 Applying example for the Filmstrip filter

(a) *Original image*   (b) *Filter "Filmstrip" applied*

Filmstrip filter lets you merge several pictures into a photographic film drawing.

Note

This filter does not invert colors, so it does not imitate negative film like the ones used to produce prints. Instead you should think of the result as an imitation of slide film or cinema film.

17.9.3.2   Accessing this Filter

You can find this filter through Filters → Combine → Filmstrip....

17.9.3.3 Options

Figure 17.166 "Filmstrip" filter options (Selection)

17.9.3.3.1 Selection   Filmstrip

Fit height to images Applies the height of original pictures to the resulting one.

Height This option lets you define the height of the resulting picture. If originals have different sizes, they will be scaled to this size.

Color By clicking on the color dwell you can define the color of the film (around and between pictures).

    Numbering

Start index Defines the beginning number which will be used for the images.

Font Defines the font of digits.

Color By clicking on the color dwell, you can define the font color of digits.

At top, At bottom Defines the position of the number.

    Image Selection

Available images Shows the pictures which can be used for merging. The pictures are the ones already opened in GIMP.

On film Shows the pictures chosen to be merged.

Add This button allows the user to put an available image in the "On film" section.

Remove This button allows to bring a picture from "On film " to "Available images". After that, the picture will not be used anymore in the resulting document.

Figure 17.167 "Filmstrip" filter options (Advanced)

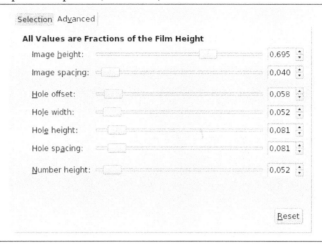

17.9.3.3.2 Advanced

Image height Defines the height of each pictures in the resulting image.

Image spacing Defines the space between the pictures as they will be inserted in the future image.

Hole offset Defines the hole position from image border.

Hole width Defines the width of the holes in the resulting image.

Hole height Defines the height of the holes in the resulting image.

Hole spacing Defines the space between holes

Number height Defines the height of the index number, proportionally to the height of the picture.

17.10 Artistic Filters

17.10.1 Introduction

Artistic filters create artistic effects like cubism, oil painting, canvas...

17.10.2 Apply Canvas

17.10.2.1 Overview

Figure 17.168 Example for the "Apply Canvas" filter

(a) *Original image*   (b) *Filter "Apply Canvas" applied*

This filter applies a canvas-like effect to the current layer or selection. It textures the image as if it were an artist's canvas.

17.10.2.2 Activate the filter

You can find this filter through Filters → Artistic → Apply Canvas....

17.10.2.3 Options

Figure 17.169 "Apply Canvas" options

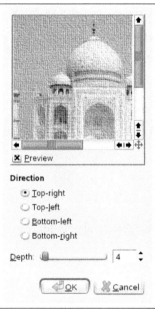

Preview Your changes are displayed in this preview before being applied to your image.

Direction Direction sets the starting direction of the canvas render. You can also consider that this option gives you the position of the light source which lightens the canvas.

Depth The Depth slider controls the apparent depth of the rendered canvas effect from 1 (very flat) to 50 (very deep).

17.10.3 Cartoon

17.10.3.1 Overview

Figure 17.170 Example for the "Cartoon" filter

(a) *Original image*   (b) *Filter "Cartoon" applied*

The Cartoon filter modifies the active layer or selection so that it looks like a cartoon drawing. Its result is similar to a black felt pen drawing subsequently shaded with color. This is achieved by darkening areas that are already distinctly darker than their neighborhood.

17.10.3.2 Activate the filter

You can find this filter in Filters → Artistic → Cartoon….

17.10.3.3 Options

Figure 17.171 "Cartoon" filter options

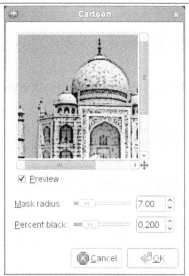

Mask radius This parameter controls the size of areas the filter works with. Large values result in very thick black areas and much less detail in the resulting image. Small values result in more subtle pen strokes and more details preserved.

Percent black This parameter controls the amount of black color added to the image. Small values make the blend from color regions to blackened areas smoother and dark lines themselves thinner and less noticeable. Larger values make the lines thicker, darker and sharper. The maximum value makes the lines aliased. The best, most natural results are usually achieved with an intermediate value.

17.10.4 Clothify

17.10.4.1 Overview

Figure 17.172 Example of Clothify

Filter "Clothify" applied (in selection)

Clothify command is a script which adds a cloth-like texture to the selected region or alpha.

If the image is in indexed colors, this menu entry is grayed out and unavailable.

This effect is achieved through the following steps:

1. Create an image in the same size as the original image, or selection or region in alpha if it is given, then add a layer to this image filled with white and noisified strongly.

2. Reproduce a layer from the recently added layer and set the mode of the upper layer to Multiply.

3. Apply Gaussian blur in different directions, horizontally on the lower layer by the given parameter Blur X as the radius, and vertically on the upper layer with Blur Y.

4. Merge these two layers into an image and make its contrast expanded as possibly, then slightly noisify again on this working image.

5. Finally do bump map on the original image by the working image with parameters Azimuth, Elevation, and Depth.

17.10.4.2 Activate the filter

This filter is found in the image window menu under Filters → Artistic → Clothify….

17.10.4.3   Options

Figure 17.173 "Clothify" filter options

Azimuth, Elevation, and Depth come from Bump Map filter.

Blur X, Blur Y   These parameters lengthen fibers of the texture, horizontally by Blur X, and vertically by Blur Y. The range of value is between 3 to 100.

Azimuth   Azimuth slider controls the bearings where light comes from according to the point of the compass. Both the minimum value (0.00) and the maximum value (360.00) are the direction of three o'clock on the dial panel of an analogue clock. Increasing value goes counter-clockwise.

Elevation   Elevation slider controls the height where light comes from. For the minimal value (0.50) the light comes from horizon, and for the maximum value (90.0) the light comes from zenith.

Depth   Depth slider controls distance between bump height and hollow depth. Increasing value causes more rugged features. Values vary from 1 to 65.

17.10.5   Cubism

17.10.5.1   Overview

Figure 17.174 Example for the "Cubism"

(a) *Original image*   (b) *Filter "Cubism" applied*

The Cubism plug-in modifies the image so that it appears to be constructed of small squares of semi-transparent tissue paper.

> **Tip**
>
> If setting possibilities of this filter are not enough for you, see GIMPressionist filter which offers more options.

17.10.5.2 Activate the filter

You can find this filter through Filters → Artistic → Cubism...

17.10.5.3 Options

Figure 17.175 "Cubism" filter options

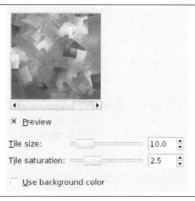

Preview Your changes are displayed in this preview before being applied to your image.

Tile size This variable determines the size, in pixels, of the squares to be used. This is, in effect, the size of the little squares of tissue paper used in generating the new image. The slider can be used, the exact pixel size can be entered into the text box, or the arrow buttons can be used.

Tile saturation This variable specifies how intense the color of the squares should be. This affects the opacity of the squares. A high value will render the squares very intensely and does not allow lower squares to show through. A lower value allows the lower squares to be more visible through the higher ones and causes more blending in the colors. If this is set to 0 and Use Background Color is not checked, the entire layer will be rendered black. If it is checked and the value here is zero, the background color will fill the entire layer.

Use background color This filter creates its tiles from all the colors of the image and paint them with a color scale which depends on the Tile Saturation. With a low Tile Saturation, this color scale lets the background color appear: default is black as you can see by setting Tile Saturation to 0. When this option is checked, the background color of the Toolbox is used. If your image has an Alpha channel, this color scale will also be transparent.

Figure 17.176 Example illustrating the action of the "Use BackGround color" option

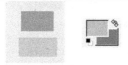

The original image and the color area of Toolbox. BG color is blue.

Figure 17.177 The option is not checked

The option is not checked. On the left is no Alpha: background is black. On the right is Alpha: background is transparent black.

Figure 17.178 The option is checked

The option is checked. On the left, no Alpha: background is blue. On the right, with an Alpha channel, background is transparent blue.

Tip

If you are using this to generate background images for web pages and the like, work with a small range of colors painted randomly on a small square. Then apply the Cubism filter with the desired settings. As a last step, try Make Seamless to adjust the image so it will tile seamlessly in your background.

17.10.6 GIMPressionist

17.10.6.1 Overview

Figure 17.179 Example for the "GIMPressionist" filter

(a) *Original image*   (b) *Filter "GIMPressionist" applied*

The GIMPressionist filter is the king of Artistic filters. It can do what Cubism and Apply Canvas do and much more. It gives your image the look of a painting. All is going as if your image was painted again on a paper and with a brush you'd have chosen. It works on the active layer or selection.

17.10.6.2 Activating the filter

You can find this filter via the image menu through Filters → Artistic → GIMPressionist....

17.10.6.3   Options

Figure 17.180 GIMPressionist options

The dialog window consists of a small Preview area on the left, which is always visible, and a huge amount of GIMPressionist options organized in tabs.

17.10.6.3.1   Preview   All your setting changes will appear in the Preview without affecting the image until you click on OK. The Update button refreshes the preview window (it is not automatic, GIMPressionist has so much work to do!), and the Reset button reverts to the original image.

Figure 17.181 "Presets" tab options

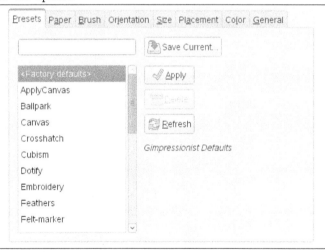

17.10.6.3.2   Presets tab   GIMPressionist has a lot of parameters. When combined, they give an astronomical number of possibilities. So, it is important, when an interesting preset has been found, to save it and also to send it to the plugin author if exceptional. Per contra, the intricacy of all these parameters makes difficult understanding and foreseeing how each one works.

Presets options

Save Current Save current parameters. You can give a name in the input box on the left and a short description in the dialog that appear.

Apply Load the parameters of the selected preset in the list.

Delete Delete the selected preset. You can delete only the presets you have created.

Refresh Update the preset list.

Figure 17.182 "Paper" tab options

17.10.6.3.3   Paper tab   This tab concerns the texture of the canvas your image will be painted on. You have a list of textures and a Preview for the selected texture. A description is displayed on the right for every texture when selected.

Paper options

Invert Inverts the paper texture: what was a hollow turns to a bump and vice-versa.

Overlay Apply the paper as it, without embossing it. It looks like if a transparent paper has been overlayed on the image.

Scale Specifies the scale of the texture (in % of the original file): controls the graininess of the texture.

Relief Specifies the amount of embossing to apply (3-150).

Figure 17.183 "Brush" tab options

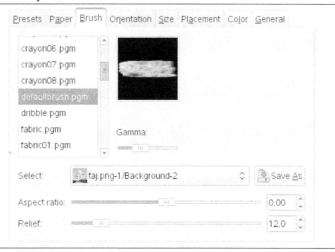

17.10.6.3.4   Brush tab   "Brush" is a general term for any material used to paint. A list of brushes is available with a Preview for the selected one.

Brush options

Gamma Changes the gamma (luminosity) of the selected brush. The gamma correction brightens or darkens midtones.

Select You can also use a brush pattern you have created by selecting its image (arrow button on the Select line). This image must be on your screen before you launch the filter to be taken in account. Of course, don't use big images.

If your image has several layers, they also will be displayed in the Select list and can be used as a brush. When selected, the layer appears in the brush preview and the normal brush is deselected.

The Save as button allows you to save the selected brush.

Aspect ratio Specifies the brush proportions, height (0 -1) and width (0 +1).

Relief Specifies the amount of paint used for each stroke. This may evoke painting with a palette knife.

Figure 17.184 "Orientation" tab options

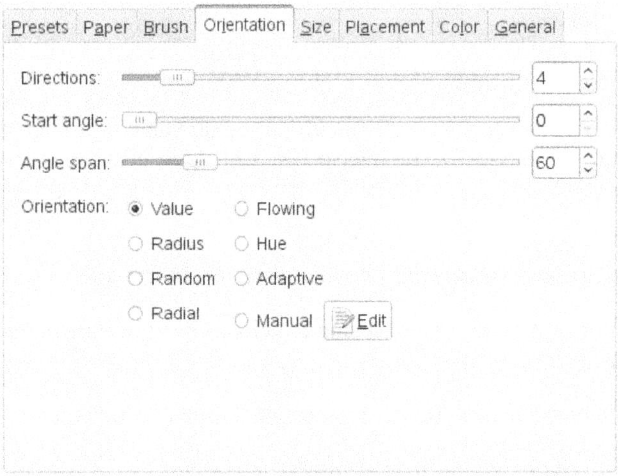

17.10.6.3.5 Orientation tab This tab allows to set the orientation of the brush strokes. A painter is not obliged to go over with the same paintbrush angle. To perform some effects, he can vary their orientation. Orientation options

Directions With this option, you can set how many times the brush will pass through a same place, with each time a different direction, resulting in a more and more thick paint.

Start angle Specifies the general direction of the strokes, the angle that the angle range will start from. Directions are often chosen to give some movement to the image.

Angle span Specifies the angle, the sector, of the stroke "fan".

Orientation Specifies the direction of the brush strokes.

>   **Value** Let the value (luminosity) of the region determine the direction of the stroke.
>
>   **Radius** The distance from the center of the image determines the direction of the stroke.
>
>   **Random** Select a random direction for each stroke.
>
>   **Radial** Let the direction from the center determine the direction of the stroke.
>
>   **Flowing** Not a direction question here: the strokes follow a "flowing" pattern.
>
>   **Hue** Let the hue of the region determine the direction of the stroke.
>
>   **Adaptive** The brush direction that matches the original image the closest is selected.
>
>   **Manual** The Edit button opens the Edit orientation Map dialog that allows you to set the directions manually.

Figure 17.185 "Size" tab options

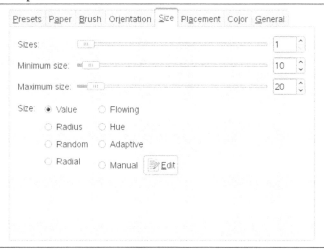

17.10.6.3.6   Size tab   This tab allows you to set the number of brush sizes that will be used to paint, the limits of variation of these sizes and the criterion used to determine them.

Size options

You can specify how many brush sizes are to be used and their sizes.

Sizes The number of brush sizes to use.

Minimum size, Maximum size The brush sizes are between these two values. The greater the size, the greater the length and width of strokes.

Size You have there options to specify how the size of strokes will be determined.

> **Value** Let the value (luminosity) of the region determine the size of the stroke.
>
> **Radius** The distance from the center of the image determines the size of the stroke.
>
> **Random** Select a random size for each stroke.
>
> **Radial** Let the direction from the center determine the size of the stroke.
>
> **Flowing** Not a length question here: the strokes follow a "flowing" pattern.
>
> **Hue** Let the hue of the region determine the size of the stroke.
>
> **Adaptive** The brush size that matches the original image the closest is selected.
>
> **Manual** The Edit button opens the Size Map Editor. That allows you to specify the size of strokes by yourself.

Figure 17.186 "Placement" tab options

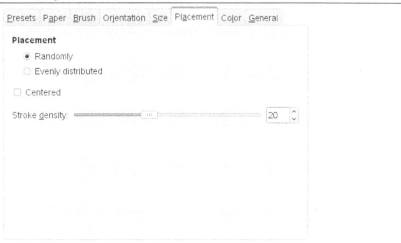

17.10.6.3.7   Placement tab   In this tab you can set how strokes will be distributed.

Placement options

Placement In the preview of the Orientation Map Editor, all small arrows look like a flow around objects. Inside this flow, strokes may be placed in two different ways:

Randomly Places strokes randomly. This produces a more realistic paint.

Evenly distributed Strokes are evenly distributed across the image.

Stroke density The greater the density the closer the strokes. With a low density, the paper or background may be visible in unstroke areas.

Centered Focus brush strokes around center.

Figure 17.187 "Color" tab options

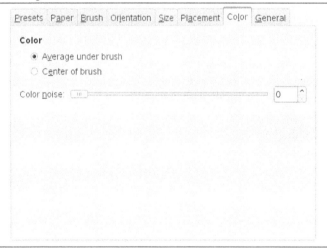

17.10.6.3.8   Color tab   In this tab, you can set what the stroke color will be.

Color options

Color You can set the stroke color in two ways:

Average under brush Stroke color is computed from the average of all pixels under the brush.

Center of brush Samples the color from the pixel in the center of the brush.

Color noise This slider, and its input box, allow you to introduce noise in the stroke color, that will look less homogeneous.

Figure 17.188 "General" tab options

17.10.6.3.9   General tab   In this tab you can set what will be the background and the relief of brush strokes.

General options

Background

    Keep original   The original image will be used as a background.

    From paper   Copy the texture of the selected paper as a background.

    Solid   By clicking on the color dwell you can select a solid colored background.

    Transparent   Use a transparent background. Only the painted strokes will be visible. This option is available only if your image has an alpha channel.

Paint edges   If it is disabled, a thin border will not be painted around the outside border of the image.

Tileable   If checked, the resulting image will be seamlessly tileable. The right side will match the left side and the top will match the bottom. This is interesting if your image will be repeatedly used in a Web background.

Drop shadow   Add a shadow effect to each brush stroke.

Edge darken   How much to darken the edges of each brush stroke. This increases paint relief or thickness.

Shadow darken   How much to darken the brush shadow.

Shadow depth   How far apart from the object the drop shadow should be.

Shadow blur   How much to blur the drop shadow.

Deviation threshold   A bail-out value for adaptive selections of brush size.

17.10.6.4   Orientation Map Editor

17.10.6.4.1   Overview   The Orientation-map editor is an annexe of the GIMPressionist filter. You can get to it by clicking on the Edit button in the Orientation tab. With this editor, you can set the direction that brush strokes given by filter will have.

Figure 17.189 Options of the "Orientation-map Editor" dialog

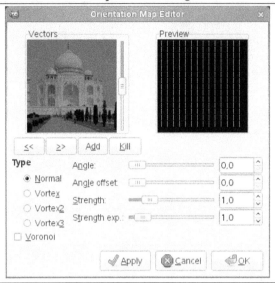

17.10.6.4.2   Options   You can place one or several vectors. You can set their direction and their strength. They will act on the corresponding area of the image.

Vectors In the left windows (Vectors) you can manage your vectors. By default, a vector is at center. Vectors are red when they are active, and grey when they are not with a white point at tip.

- By clicking on the Add button, you add a vector at center of the window, whereas clicking with the mouse Middle Button puts it where you click.

- Clicking with the mouse Left Button displaces the selected vector to the clicked point.

- When clicking with the mouse Right Button, the selected vector points to where you have clicked.

- Clicking on << and >> buttons displaces focus from a vector to another.

- The Delete button allows you to delete the selected vector.

Tip

 With the scroll bar on the right of the Vectors panel, you can set the image brightness. This can be very useful if the image is very dark/bright and you can't see vectors well.

Preview This Preview gives you an idea of the action of the various vectors. The slider on the right border lets you change the luminosity of this preview.

Type You have there some types to arrange the brush strokes within the selected vector domain. Describing them is difficult, but you can see the result in the Preview.

Voronoi A Voronoi's diagram consists in partitioning a plane with n master points into n polygons where each polygon has only one of these n master points and where any given other point of the polygon is closer to the master point than to any other. So each polygon limit is midway between two master point. Here is an example of a Voronoi's diagram:

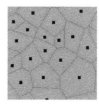

Here, when this option is checked, only the vector closest to a given point of the image influences this point.

Angle Direction of the selected vector. This slider has the same action as right-clicking (see above).

Angle offset This slider allows you to change the angle of *all* vectors.

Strength This slider acts on the influence domain of the selected vector. This influence lowers with distance. Strength is showed with the vector length.

Strength exp. This slider acts on the length of *all* vectors, and so changes the strength of all brush strokes.

17.10.6.5 Size Map Editor

17.10.6.5.1 Overview The Size-map editor is an annexe of the GIMPressionist filter. You can get to it by clicking on the Edit button in the Size tab. With this editor, you can set the size that brush strokes given by filter will have.

Figure 17.190 Size-map editor options

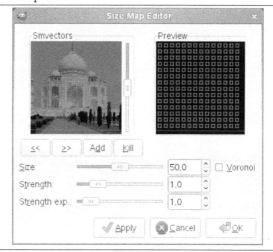

17.10.6.5.2 Options You can place one or several vectors. You can set their strength. They will act on the corresponding area of the image.

Smvectors In this window you can place your vectors. By clicking on the Add button, you add a vector at the center of the window, whereas clicking with the mouse Middle Button puts it where you click. Vectors are red when selected, and gray when they are not, with a white point at tip.

Clicking with the mouse Left Button displaces the selected vector to the clicked point.

Clicking on the mouse Right Button, has no evident action.

Clicking on << and >> buttons displaces focus from a vector to another.

The Kill button allows you to delete the selected vector.

> **Tip**
>
> With the scroll bar on the right of the Vectors panel, you can set the image brightness. This can be very useful if the image is very dark/bright and you can't see vectors well.

Preview This Preview gives you an idea of the action of the different vectors. The size of squares represent the size of the brushes and their strength.

Size Change the size of the brush strokes in the selected vector domain.

Strength This slider acts on the influence domain of the selected vector. This influence lowers with distance.

Strength exp. Change the exponent of the stroke.

Voronoi See Orientation Map Editor for an explanation.

17.10.7 Oilify

17.10.7.1 Overview

Figure 17.191 Example for the "Oilify" filter

(a) *Original image*   (b) *Filter "Oilify" applied*

This filter makes the image look like an oil painting. The Mask size controls the outcome: a high value gives the image less detail, as if you had used a larger brush.

> **Tip**
>
> The GIMPressionist filter can produce similar effects, but allows a much wider variety of options.

17.10.7.2 Activate the filter

This filter is found in the image menu through Filters → Artistic → Oilify....

17.10.7.3   Options

Figure 17.192 "Oilify" filter options

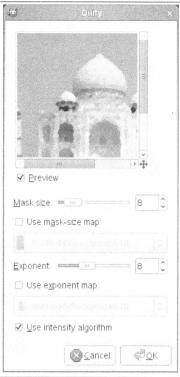

Mask size Mask size selects the size of the brush mask used to paint the oily render. Larger values here produce an oilier render.

Use mask-size map You may use a mask-size map to control Mask size partially. Mask size is reduced accordings to darkness in each pixel of the map image. You can select a map image among the current opened images of the same size as the source image.

Exponent Exponent selects density of the brush mask used to paint the oily render.

Use exponent map You may use an exponent map to control density of brush touch partially. Density is reduced accordings to darkness in each pixel of the map image. You can select a map image among the current opened images of the same size as the source image.

Use intensity algorithm "Use intensity algorithm" changes the mode of operation to help preserve detail and coloring.

17.10.8 Photocopy

17.10.8.1 Overview

Figure 17.193 Example for the "Photocopy" filter

(a) *Original image*   (b) *Filter "Photocopy" applied*

The Photocopy filter modifies the active layer or selection so that it looks like a black and white photocopy, as if toner transferred was based on the relative darkness of a particular region. This is achieved by darkening areas of the image which are measured to be darker than a neighborhood average, and setting other pixels to white.

> **Tip**
>
> You may use this filter to sharpen your image. Create a copy of the active layer and use the filter on the copy. Set the Layer Mode to Multiply and adjust the opacity slider to get the best result.

17.10.8.2 Starting filter

You can find this filter from the image menu through Filters → Artistic → Photocopy....

17.10.8.3 Options

Figure 17.194 "Photocopy" filter options

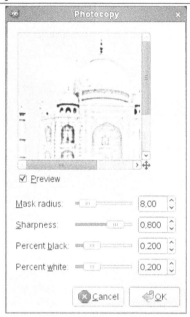

Preview Your changes are displayed in this preview before being applied to your image.

Mask radius This parameter controls the size of the pixel neighbourhood over which the average intensity is computed and then compared to each pixel in the neighborhood to decide whether or not to darken it. Large values result in very thick black areas bordering the regions of white and much less detail for black areas. Small values result in less toner overall and more details everywhere.

Sharpness With this option, you can set photocopy sharpness, from 0.0 to 1.0.

Percent black This parameter controls the amount of black color added to the image. Small values make the blend from color regions to blackened areas smoother and dark lines themselves thinner and less noticeable. Larger values make the lines thicker, darker and sharper. The maximum value makes the lines aliased. The best, most natural results are usually achieved with an intermediate value. Values vary from 0.0 to 1.0.

Percent white This parameter increases white pixels percentage.

17.10.9 Predator

17.10.9.1 Overview

Figure 17.195 Example for the "Predator" filter

(a) *Original image*   (b) *"Predator" applied*

This filter adds a "Predator" effect to the image. The predator effect makes the image/selection look something like the view the predator has in movies (kind of a thermogram and that type of thing). This will reduce the image to edges in a few basic colors on a dark background.

   If there is an active selection, the filter effect will be applied to the selected region, otherwise to the alpha channel (the filter will add an alpha channel, if necessary). The filter works best on colorful RGB images.

17.10.9.2 Activate the filter

This filter is found in the image window menu under Filters → Artistic → Predator….

17.10.9.3 Options

Figure 17.196 "Predator" options

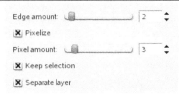

Edge amount The "predator" filter will detect edges using the Sobel edge detector. The specified "Edge amount" will be passed to the Sobel filter. A high value will result in detecting more edges.

Figure 17.197 "Edge amount" examples

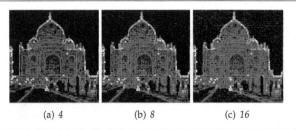

(a) *4*   (b) *8*   (c) *16*

Pixelize If checked, the filter will simplify the image into solid-colored squares using the Pixelise filter before the real predator effect will be applied. You can select the size of these squares with the option Pixel amount, which will heavily affect the result (see examples below).

Pixel amount "Pixel amount" is the size of the color blocks the image will be simplified to if Pixelize is checked. Actually you are decreasing the resolution with this option. In the examples below, you can see directly how increasing the pixel block size leads to something like "macro pixels":

Figure 17.198 "Pixelize" examples

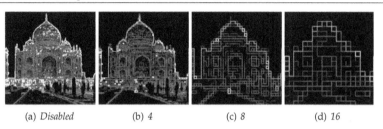

(a) *Disabled*   (b) *4*   (c) *8*   (d) *16*

Keep selection If checked, the filter will be applied to the active selection. Else, it will be applied to the active layer.

Separate layer When this option is checked, a copy of the active layer will be created above the active layer and the filter will be applied to this copy, leaving the original layer untouched. If not checked, the filter will be applied to the active layer.

17.10.9.4 Filter algorithm

Since this filter delegates the essential parts to two or three other filters the algorithm is very simple:

Figure 17.199 Making the "predator" effect

(a) *Original*   (b) *Pixelize*   (c) *Min RGB*   (d) *Edge detection*

1. The original image.

2. Optionally, the filter pixelizes the image: it renders the image by using color blocks instead of pixels, thus reducing the image resolution.

3. The colors will be reduced to pure red, green, blue (and possibly gray colors), using the minimal RGB channel for every pixel.

4. Applying the Sobel edge detecting filter, the image will be reduced further on to edges, usually on a black background, with very few colors.

17.10.10 Softglow

17.10.10.1 Overview

Figure 17.200 Example for the "SoftGlow" filter

(a) _Original image_   (b) _Filter "Softglow" applied_

This filter lights the image with a soft glow, like the old trick smearing vaseline on the lens. Softglow produces this effect by making bright areas of the image brighter.

17.10.10.2 Starting filter

You can find this file in the Image menu through: Filters → Artistic → Softglow....

17.10.10.3 Options

Figure 17.201 "Softglow" filter options

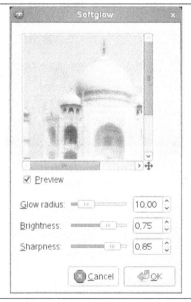

Preview Your changes are displayed in this preview before being applied to your image.

Glow radius The glow radius parameter controls the sharpness of the effect, giving a "vaseline-on-the-lens" effect.

Brightness The brightness parameter controls the degree of intensification applied to image highlights.

Sharpness The sharpness parameter controls how defined or alternatively diffuse the glow effect should be.

17.10.11   Van Gogh (LIC)

17.10.11.1   Overview

Figure 17.202 From left to right: original image, map, resulting image

Map has three stripes: a solid black area, a vertical gradient area, a solid white area. One can see, on the resulting image, that image zones corresponding to solid areas of the map, are not blurred. Only the image zone corresponding to the gradient area of the map is blurred.

"LIC" stands for Line Integral Convolution, a mathematical method. The plug-in author uses mathematical terms to name his options... This filter is used to apply a directional blur to an image, or to create textures. It could be called "Astigmatism" as it blurs certain directions in the image.

It uses a blur map. Unlike other maps, this filter doesn't use grey levels of this blur map. *Filter takes in account only gradient direction(s).* Image pixels corresponding to solid areas of the map are ignored.

17.10.11.2   Activate the filter

You can find this filter through Filters → Artistic → Van Gogh (LIC)....

17.10.11.3   Options

Figure 17.203 "Van Gogh (LIC)" filter options

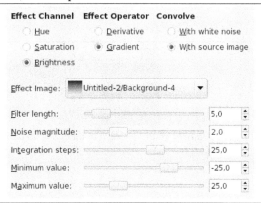

> Tip
>
>
>
> - To create a blur, check With Source Image. Only Filter Length slider and perhaps Integration Steps slider, are useful.
>
> - To create a texture, check With White Noise. All sliders can be useful.

Effect Channel By selecting Hue, Saturation or Brightness (=Value), filter will use this channel to treat image.

Effect Operator The "Derivative" option reverses "Gradient " direction:

Figure 17.204 Derivative option example

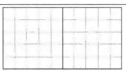

Using a square gradient map, Effect operator is on "Gradient" on the left, on "Derivative" on the right: what was sharp is blurred and conversely.

Convolve You can use two types of convolution. That's the first parameter you have to set:

With white noise White noise is an acoustics name. It's a noise where all frequencies have the same amplitude. Here, this option is used to create patterns.

With source image The source image will be blurred.

Effect image That's the map for blur or pattern direction. This map must have the same dimensions as the original image. It must be preferably a grayscale image. It must be present on your screen when you call filter so that you can choose it in the drop-list.

Figure 17.205 Blurring with vertical gradient map

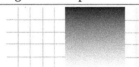

With a vertical gradient map, vertical lines are blurred.

Figure 17.206 Blurring with a square gradient map

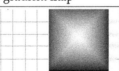

The gradient map is divided into four gradient triangles: each of them has its own gradient direction. In every area of the image corresponding to gradient triangles, only lines with the same direction as gradient are blurred.

Figure 17.207 Texture example

The "With white noise" option is checked. Others are default. With a vertical gradient map, texture "fibres" are going horizontally.

Filter length When applying blur, this option controls how important blur is. When creating a texture, it controls how rough texture is: low values result in smooth surface; high values in rough surface.

Figure 17.208 Action example of Filter Length on blur

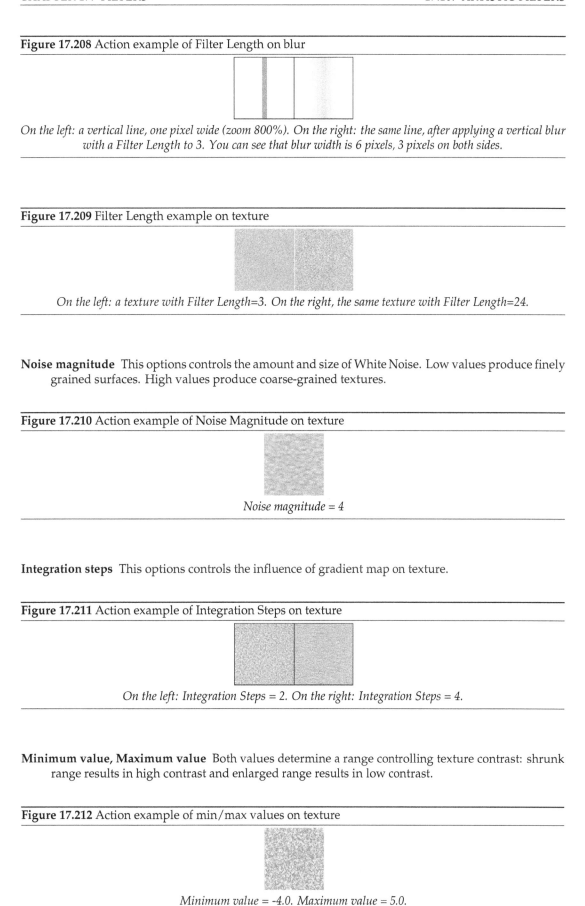

On the left: a vertical line, one pixel wide (zoom 800%). On the right: the same line, after applying a vertical blur with a Filter Length to 3. You can see that blur width is 6 pixels, 3 pixels on both sides.

Figure 17.209 Filter Length example on texture

On the left: a texture with Filter Length=3. On the right, the same texture with Filter Length=24.

Noise magnitude This options controls the amount and size of White Noise. Low values produce finely grained surfaces. High values produce coarse-grained textures.

Figure 17.210 Action example of Noise Magnitude on texture

Noise magnitude = 4

Integration steps This options controls the influence of gradient map on texture.

Figure 17.211 Action example of Integration Steps on texture

On the left: Integration Steps = 2. On the right: Integration Steps = 4.

Minimum value, Maximum value Both values determine a range controlling texture contrast: shrunk range results in high contrast and enlarged range results in low contrast.

Figure 17.212 Action example of min/max values on texture

Minimum value = -4.0. Maximum value = 5.0.

17.10.12   Weave

17.10.12.1   Overview

Figure 17.213 Example of Weave

Filter "Weave" applied

The Weave command is a Script-Fu script which creates a new layer filled with a weave effect and adds it to the image as an overlay or bump map. The result of the image looks as if it were printed over woven ribbons of paper, thin wooden sheet, or stripped bamboo.

If the image is in indexed colors, this menu entry is grayed out and unavailable.

This filter adds a "Multiply" mode layer upon the layer where you activate this command. The weave texture is rendered in gray levels.

17.10.12.2   Activate the filter

This filter is found in the image window menu under Filters → Artistic → Weave....

17.10.12.3   Options

Figure 17.214 "Weave" filter options

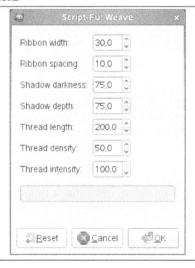

For to make coarse mesh texture, increase the ribbon spacing and/or decrease the ribbon width.

For to strain ribbons hard, decrease the shadow depth.

Ribbon width With this option you can set the tape width in pixel between 0.0 and 256.0. In default, 30.0 pixels is set.

Ribbon spacing With this option you can set the distance to the neighboring ribbon or the size of black square hole in pixel between 0.0 and 256.0. In default, 10.0 pixels is set.

Shadow darkness With this option you can set the darkness at crossings of lower ribbon in percentage. Lower value shows ribbons thinner. 75.0 percent is the default value.

Shadow depth With this option you can set the bent strength of ribbons in percentage. Higher value shows ribbons more wavy, lower value for flat surface. The actual effect is limited by the Shadow darkness. 75.0 percent is the default value.

Thread length With this option you can set the regularity of stripe texture. If this value is shorter than the summary of the ribbon width and twice of the ribbon spacing, the surface of ribbon becomes speckled. Set this value in pixel on range between 0.0 to 256.0. The default value is 200.0.

Thread density With this option you can set the density of fiber-like parallel short stripes on the surface of ribbons. To populate stripes increase this value. 50.0 percent is the default value.

Thread intensity With this option you can set the opacity of stripe texture. Lower value shows threads vague. To clear off threads set the value to 0.0 percent. The default value is 100.0 percent.

17.10.12.4   Another usage

Figure 17.215 Adding a lattice using "Weave" texture

Narrower the ribbon width, wider the ribbon spacing, and filled with the "Wood #1" pattern.

This texture can be a lattice that you can see the original image through its mesh holes. Add a new, transparent layer over the active layer for the lattice, and apply this filter. Select a black regular square in the texture layer using the Select By Color tool, then delete black squares in selection on the texture layer to be chink holes. Reverse the selection, and activate the transparent layer so that you can fill the lattice surface with a pattern, then drag and drop your favorite pattern over the image window.

17.11   Decor Filters

17.11.1   Introduction

These filters are image-dependent Script-Fu scripts. They create decorative borders, and some of them add some nice special effects to the image.

17.11.2   Add Bevel

17.11.2.1   Overview

Figure 17.216 Example for the "Add Bevel" filter

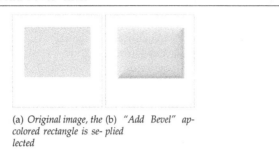

(a) *Original image, the* (b) *"Add Bevel" ap-*
colored rectangle is se- *plied*
lected

This filter adds a slight bevel to an image using a bump map (see below). If there is a selection, it is bevelled, otherwise the filter has no effect.

Figure 17.217 Another "Add Bevel" example, with bumpmap

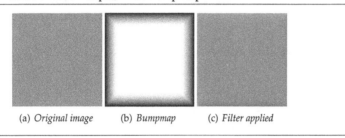

(a) *Original image*   (b) *Bumpmap*   (c) *Filter applied*

17.11.2.2   Activate the filter

You can find this filter in the image window menu under Filters → Decor → Add Bevel....

17.11.2.3   Options

Figure 17.218 "Add Bevel" options

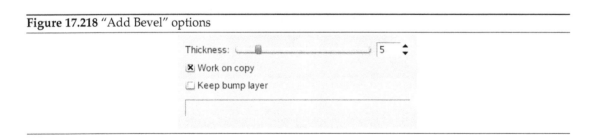

Thickness You can specify the thickness of the bevel, in pixels. Maximal thickness is 30 pixels.

Work on copy If checked, the filter creates a new window containing a copy of the image with the filter applied. The original image remains unchanged.

Keep bump layer When checked, you will keep the generated bumpmap as a new, not visible layer (below the layer dialog):

17.11.3   Add Border

17.11.3.1   Overview

Figure 17.219 Example for the "Add Border" filter

(a) *Original image*   (b) *Border added*

This filter just does what its name says: it adds a border to the image. You can specify the thickness of the border as well as the color. The four sides of the border are colored in different shades, so the image area will appear raised.

The image will be enlarged by the border size, it won't be painted over.

17.11.3.2   Activate the filter

This filter is found in the image window menu under Filters → Decor → Add Border....

17.11.3.3   Options

Figure 17.220 "Add Border" options

Border X size, Border Y size   Here you can select the thickness of the added border, in pixels. X size (left an right) and Y size (top and bottom) may be different. Maximum is 250 pixels.

Border color   Clicking on this button brings up the color selector dialog that allows you to choose an "average" border color (see below, Delta value on color).

Delta value on color   This option makes the border sides to be colored in different shades and thus makes the image to appear raised. The actual color of the respective border side is computed for every color component red, green, and blue[3] from the "average" Border color as follows (resulting values less than 0 are set to 0, values greater than 255 are set to 255):

- Top shade = Border color + Delta
- Right shade = Border color - ½ Delta

---

[3] See image types or *RGB* .

- Bottom shade = Border color - Delta

- Left shade = Border color + ½ Delta

Figure 17.221 Delta examples

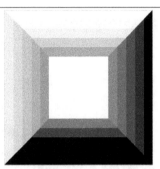

"Add Border" filter applied with Delta value 25, then with 75, 125, 175, and 225.

Example: the default color is blue (38,31,207), default delta is 25. So the shades of the borders are: top: (38,31,207) + (25,25,25) = (63,56,232), right: (38,31,207) + (-13,-13,-13) = (25,18,194), etc.

17.11.4   Coffee Stain

17.11.4.1   Overview

Figure 17.222 Example for the "Coffee Stain" filter

(a) *Original image*   (b) *"Coffee Stain" applied*

This filter adds realistic looking coffee stains to the image.

Every stain is created in a layer of its own. The stain layers are randomly moved to let the stains spread out (at the end you may see the boundary of the moved top layer). So after applying the filter you can easily edit (e.g., move, scale, remove) the coffee stains, or create additional stains using the filter again.

17.11.4.2   Activate the filter

The filter is found in the image window menu under Filters → Decor → Coffee Stain....

17.11.4.3 Options

Figure 17.223 "Coffee Stain" options

Stains The number of the coffee stains (1-10).

Darken only Since every stain is created in a layer of its own, all layers have to be merged to make the appearance of the image. If this option is checked, the relevant layer mode is set to "Darken only", otherwise it is set to "Normal".

The layer mode determines how the pixels of the layers are combined. In "Normal" mode, every coffee stain covers the pixels of the layers below. As a rule of thumb, if layer mode "Darken only" is set, coffee stains covers the corresponding pixels of the layers below them only if these pixels are lighter.

17.11.5 Fuzzy Border

17.11.5.1 Overview

Figure 17.224 Example for the "Fuzzy Border" filter

(a) *Original image*   (b) *"Fuzzy Border" applied*

This filter adds a cool fading border to an image. The border will look jagged and fuzzy, and you can specify color and thickness of the fading border. Optionally you may add a shadow to the image.

17.11.5.2 Activate the filter

You can find this filter in the image window menu through Filters → Decor → Fuzzy Border....

17.11.5.3   Options

Figure 17.225 "Fuzzy Border" options

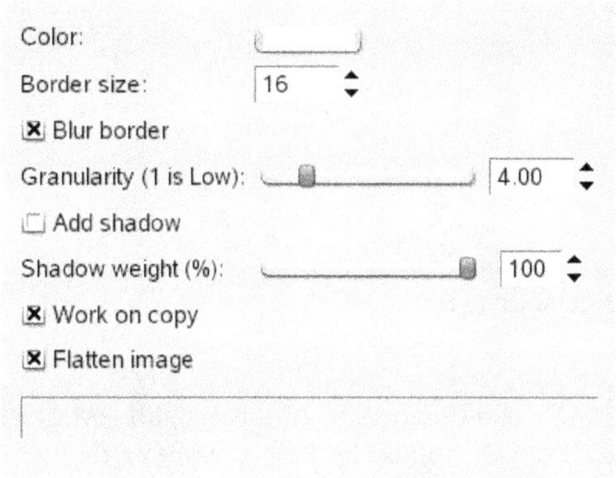

Color:
Border size: 16
☒ Blur border
Granularity (1 is Low):   4.00
☐ Add shadow
Shadow weight (%):   100
☒ Work on copy
☒ Flatten image

Color   Clicking on this button brings up the color selector dialog that allows you to choose the border color.

Border size   Here you can set the thickness of the fuzzy border, in pixels. Maximum is 300 pixels, regardless of the image width or height.

Blur border   If checked, the border will be blurred. The example below shows the effect of blurring:

Figure 17.226 "Blur border" example

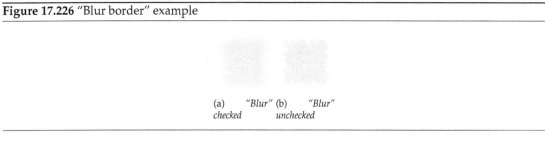

(a)   "Blur"   (b)   "Blur"
checked   unchecked

Figure 17.227 "Blur border" zoomed (1600%)

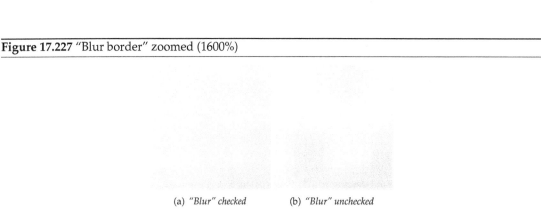

(a) "Blur" checked   (b) "Blur" unchecked

Granularity   The border's granularity is almost the size of pixel blocks spread to create the effect of a jagged and fuzzy border.

Figure 17.228 Granularity example (without blurring)

(a) Granularity 1 (b) Granularity 4 (de- (c) Granularity 16
(min)   fault)   (max)

Add shadow If checked, the filter will also create a shadow at the border.

Figure 17.229 "Add shadow" example

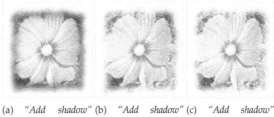

(a) "Add shadow" (b) "Add shadow" (c) "Add shadow"
checked,   shadow with   shadow weight unchecked (default)
weight 100% (default 10%.
shadow weight).

Shadow weight If Add shadow is checked, you may set the shadow opacity here. Defaults to 100% (full opacity).

Work on copy If checked, the filter creates a new window containing a copy of the image with the filter applied. The original image remains unchanged.

Flatten image If unchecked, the filter keeps the additional layers it used to create the border and the shadow (if demanded). Default is to merge down all layers.

17.11.6 Old Photo

17.11.6.1 Overview

Figure 17.230 Example for the "Old Photo" filter

(a) Original image   (b) "Old Photo" applied

This filter makes an image look like an old photo: blurred, with a jagged border, toned with a brown shade, and marked with spots.

17.11.6.2 Activate the filter

The filter is found in the image window menu under Filters → Decor → Old Photo….

17.11.6.3 Options

Figure 17.231 "Old Photo" options

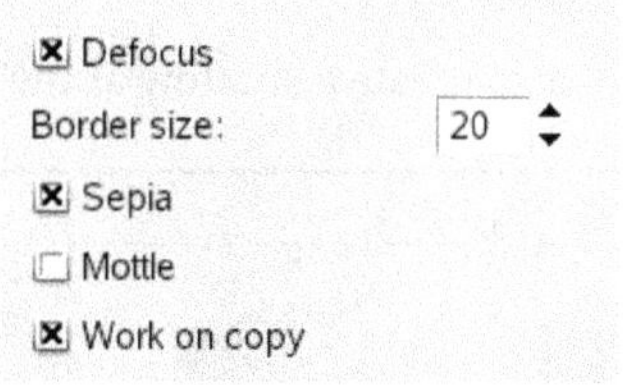

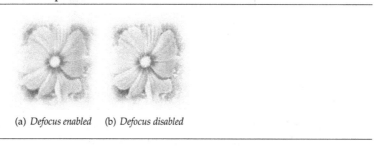

Defocus If checked, a Gaussian blur will be applied to the image, making it less clear.

Figure 17.232 Example for the "Defocus" option

(a) *Defocus enabled*   (b) *Defocus disabled*

Border size When you choose a border size > 0, the Fuzzy Border filter will be applied to the image, adding a white, jagged border.

Sepia If checked, the filter reproduces the effect of aging in old, traditional black-and-white photographs, toned with sepia (shades of brown).[4] To achieve this effect, the filter desaturates the image, reduces brightness and contrast, and modifies the color balance.[5]

Mottle When you check this option, the image will be marked with spots.

Figure 17.233 Example for the "Mottle" option

A plain white image mottled (without Defocus or Sepia)

---

[4] See Wikipedia [WKPD-SEPIA].

[5] Compare Section 14.5.2.

Work on copy If checked, the filter creates a new window containing a copy of the image with the filter applied. The original image remains unchanged.

17.11.7 Round Corners

17.11.7.1 Overview

Figure 17.234 Example for the "Round Corners" filter

(a) *Original image*   (b) *"Round Corners" applied*

This filter rounds the corners of an image, optionally adding a drop-shadow and a background layer.

The filter works on RGB and grayscale images that contain only one layer. It creates a copy of the image or can optionally work on the original. It uses the current background color to create a background layer.

17.11.7.2 Activate the filter

This filter is found in the image window menu under Filters → Decor → Round Corners....

17.11.7.3 Options

Figure 17.235 "Round Corners" options

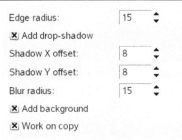

Edge radius Rounding corners is done by selecting a quarter of a circle at every corner and removing the area not covered by this selection. The "edge radius" is the radius of the constructing circle.

In the examples below, the filter was applied to a 100x100 pixels image, with varying edge radius. For radius = 50, the four quadrants just form a circle with diameter = 100, which exactly fits into the original image outline. A radius greater than 50 is possible, but look what happens...

Figure 17.236 Edge radius examples

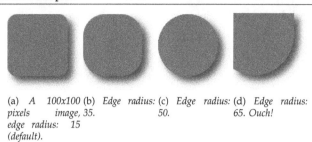

(a) A 100x100 (b) Edge radius: (c) Edge radius: (d) Edge radius:
pixels image, 35. 50. 65. Ouch!
edge radius: 15
(default).

Add drop-shadow When this option is checked, the filter will cast a shadow behind your image after rounding the image corners.

Shadow X/Y offset X and Y offset determine where the shadow will be placed in relation to the image. Offset is measured in pixels. High values make the shadow look like it's far away, and low values will make it look closer to the image.

Figure 17.237 Shadow offset examples

(a) Shadow X off- (b) Shadow X offset: 8, Y offset: 8 set: 16, Y offset: 4.
(default).

Note that the shadow offsets as well as the blur radius are limited to background area.

Blur radius When Add drop-shadow is checked, you may select a blur radius, which will be used by the Drop Shadow filter. The image will be enlarged in both dimensions depending on the blur radius and the shadow offsets.

Add background When you check this option (it is checked by default), the filter will add a background layer below the existing layer, filled with the current background color. The size of this new layer depends on the blur radius and the shadow offsets.

Work on copy If checked, the filter creates a new window containing a copy of the image with the filter applied. The original image remains unchanged.

17.11.8 Slide

17.11.8.1 Overview

Figure 17.238 Example for the "Slide" filter

(a) *Original image*   (b) *"Slide" applied*

This filter makes your image look like a slide, by adding a slide-film like black frame, sprocket holes, and labels.

If necessary, the image will be cropped to fit into an aspect ratio of width : height = 3:2. If image width is greater than image height, black frames will be added at the top and the bottom of the image, else the frames will be added on the left and right sides. You may select the color as well as the font of the text appearing on the frames. The current background color will be used for drawing the holes.

The script only works on RGB and grayscale images that contain one layer. Otherwise the menu entry is insensitive and grayed out.

17.11.8.2 Activate the filter

The filter is found in the image window menu under Filters → Decor → Slide....

17.11.8.3 Options

Figure 17.239 "Slide" options

Text A short label that will be displayed in the top and bottom (or the left and right) of the frame. The text must be really short.

Number Here you may enter a text for simulating consecutive numbers. Two numbers will be displayed: this number and this number with the character "A" appended.

Font Clicking on this button opens the Font dialog, where you can choose a font for the text on the frame.

Fontcolor Clicking on this button brings up a color selection dialog that allows you to choose the color of the text.

Work on copy If checked, the filter creates a new window containing a copy of the image with the filter applied. The original image remains unchanged.

17.11.9   Stencil Carve

17.11.9.1   Overview

Figure 17.240 Example for the "Stencil Carve" filter

(a) *Original image*   (b) *"Stencil Carve" applied*

This filter works with two images, source and target. The source image must be a grayscale image containing a single layer and no Alpha channel. This layer is used as selection mask and will work as stencil for the carving effect. The image to be carved (the target image) can be an RGB color or grayscale image, also with a single layer. This target image must have the same size as the source image.

17.11.9.2   Activating the filter

This filter is found in the image window menu under Filters → Decor → Stencil Carve....

Tip

   If this command remains grayed out although the image is grayscale, check for an
Alpha channel and delete it.

17.11.9.3 Options

Figure 17.241 "Stencil Carve" options

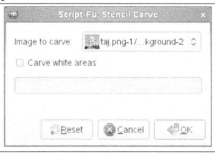

Image to carve Here you may select the target image, i.e. the image the carving effect is applied to. The
drop-down list will show you a list of opened images which may be carved.

Carve white areas If checked (default), the source image is used as stencil as described above. If unchecked,
the *inverted* source image is used as stencil, e.g.:

Figure 17.242 Engraving Masks

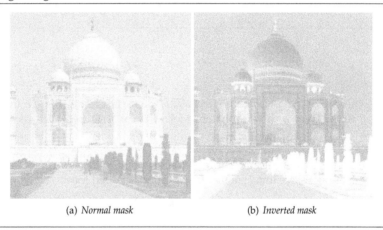

(a) *Normal mask*   (b) *Inverted mask*

In the example below, the source is a grayscale image. The target is an image with a wood pattern.

On the left, Carve white areas is enabled. The pixels of the target image corresponding to white
pixels in the stencil (around the text) have been carved. The result is an embossed text.

On the right, Carve white areas is disabled. The pixels of the target image corresponding to the
black pixels in the stencil (the text) have been carved. The result is a hollow text.

Figure 17.243 Example for "Carve white areas"

(a) *White areas carved*   (b) *Stencil*   (c) *Black areas carved*

Information about the many layers created by this filter can be found in [GROKKING].

17.11.10   Stencil Chrome

17.11.10.1   Overview

Figure 17.244 Example for the "Stencil Chrome" filter

(a) *Original image*   (b) *"Stencil Chrome" applied*

This filter provides a state of the art chrome effect. The source image must be an image in grayscale mode, containing a single layer without alpha channel. This layer is used as mask ("stencil") for the chrome effect.

The filter creates a new image with the chrome effect applied to the source image or, if a selection exists, to the selection of the source image (a nice background is added too).

17.11.10.2   Activating the filter

This filter is found in the image window menu under Filters → Decor → Stencil Chrome....

> **Tip**
>
> If this command remains grayed out although the image is in grayscale mode, check for an Alpha channel and delete it.

17.11.10.3 Options

Figure 17.245 "Stencil Chrome" options

Chrome saturation, Chrome lightness Use this option to control how saturation and lightness of the "Chrome" layer are adjusted. Negative values decrease saturation and lightness respectively.

Chrome factor This factor lets you adjust offsets, feather radius, and brush size used to construct the "Chrome" and "Highlight" layer (and the "Drop Shadow" as well).

Change with caution, decreasing this value may make the chrome effect worse. The default factor 0.75 seems to be a good choice.

Environment map The environment map is an image that is added as some kind of "noise" to the source. The effect is best to see if you use a simple map with some obvious shapes:

Using a simple environment map

The environment map must be an image in grayscale mode too. Size doesn't matter, the environment map is scaled to the size of the source image.

Highlight balance This color is used to modify the color balance of the "Highlight" layer: the amount of red, green, and blue colors is increased according to the corresponding values of the specified option.

Avoid colors with red, green or blue value > 230.

Chrome balance Same as above, but modifies the color balance of the "Chrome" layer.

Chrome white areas If checked (this is the default), the source image is used as mask. If unchecked, the *inverted* source image is used.

17.11.10.4 How to create the chrome effect

The following section provides a brief and simplified description of how the script (actually this filter is a Script-Fu) creates the chrome effect.

If you apply the filter to your source images and then look at the layer dialog of the resulting image, you will see that there are two main layers which make up the chrome effect: the "Chrome" layer and the "Highlight" layer. These layers are created as follows:

1. The script constructs a somewhat simplified and blurred layer from the source image (from the inverted source image if Chrome white areas is unchecked).

The Chrome factor controls the appearance of this layer.

2. The (scaled) environment map is blurred and merged into the above layer with 50% opacity. (Do you spot the cat in the introducing example?)

Merging the environment map

3. The brightness (value) of the layer is modified according to a spline-based intensity curve.

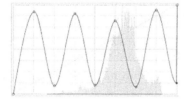 

Modifying the intensity curve

4. A layer mask is added, initialized with the source image (the "Chrome Stencil"). This is the "Chrome" layer before the final step.

   The "Highlight" layer is a copy of the "Chrome" layer where the layer mask is stroked with a white brush.

Chrome and Highlight base

5. For both layers the color balance is modified (according to Highlight balance and Chrome balance), increasing the amount of red, green, and blue, with emphasis on highlights.

   Additionally, saturation and lightness of the "Chrome" layer are modified (controlled by Chrome saturation and Chrome lightness).

Chrome and Highlight layer

Now add a drop shadow and a background layer and you get the Example image for the "Stencil Chrome" filter.

17.12   Map Filters

17.12.1   Introduction

Map filters use an object named *map* to modify an image: you map the image to the object. So, you can create 3D effects by mapping your image to another previously embossed image ("Bumpmap" Filter) or to a sphere ("Map Object" filter). You can also map a part of the image elsewhere into the same image ("Illusion" and "Make Seamless" filters), bend a text along a curve ("Displace" filter)...

17.12.2   Bump Map

17.12.2.1   Overview

Figure 17.246 "bump-map" example

On the left, the original image that we want to emboss: a solid blue. In the middle, the bump map : a grayscale image, where black pixels will emboss backwards and white pixels will emboss forwards. On the right, the bump-mapped image. The filter adds a shadow effect.

This filter creates a 3D effect by embossing an image (the card) and then mapping it to another image. Bump height depends on pixel luminosity and you can set light direction. See Emboss for more information about embossing. You can bump map any type of image, unlike the Emboss filter.

17.12.2.2   Activate the filter

This filter is found in the image window menu under Filters → Map → Bump Map....

17.12.2.3   Options

Figure 17.247 "Bump Map" filter options

Preview If checked, parameter setting results are interactively displayed in preview. Scroll bars allow you to move around the image.

Bump map This drop-down list allows you to select the image that will be used as a map for bump-mapping. This list contains images that are present on your screen when you launch the filter. Images opened after starting filter are not present in this list.

Map type This option allows you to define the method that will be used when creating the map image:

    Linear Bump height is a direct function of luminosity.

    Sinusoidal Bump height is a sinusoidal function of luminosity.

    Spheric Bump height is a spheric function of luminosity.

Compensate for darkening Bump-mapping tends to darken image. You can compensate this darkening by checking this option.

Invert bumpmap Bright pixels default to bumps and dark pixels to hollows. You can invert this effect by checking this option.

Tile bumpmap If you check this option, there will be no relief break if you use your image as a pattern for a web page: patterns will be placed side by side without any visible joins.

Azimut This is about lighting according to the points of the compass (0 - 360). East (0°) is on the left. Increasing value goes counter-clockwise.

Elevation That's height from horizon (0.50°), up to zenith (90°).

Depth With this slider, you can vary bump height and hollow depth. The higher the value, the higher the difference between both. Values vary from 1 to 65.

X offset, Y offset With this slider, you can adjust the map image position compared with the image, horizontally (X) and/or vertically (Y).

Waterlevel If your image has transparent areas, they will be treated like dark areas and will appear as hollows after bump-mapping. With this slider, you can reduce hollows as if sea level was raising. This hollows will disappear when sea level value reaches 255. If the Invert bump-map option is checked, transparent areas will be treated as bright areas, and then Waterlevel slider will plane bumps down.

Ambient This slider controls the intensity of ambient light. With high values, shadows will fade and relief lessen.

17.12.3 Displace

17.12.3.1 Overview

Figure 17.248 Displacement examples

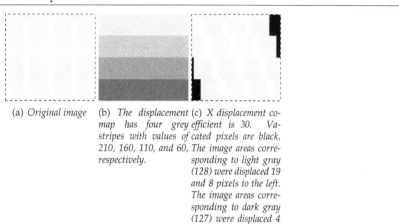

(a) *Original image* (b) *The displacement* (c) *X displacement co-map has four grey efficient is 30. Va-stripes with values of cated pixels are black. 210, 160, 110, and 60, The image areas corre-respectively. sponding to light gray (128) were displaced 19 and 8 pixels to the left. The image areas corre-sponding to dark gray (127) were displaced 4 and 15 pixels to the right.*

This filter uses a "displace-map" to displace corresponding pixels of the image. This filter displaces the content of the specified drawable (active layer or selection) by the amounts specified in X and Y Displacement multiplied by the intensity of the corresponding pixel in the 'displace map' drawables. *Both X and Y displace maps should be gray-scale images and have the same size as the drawable .* This filter allows interesting distortion effects.

17.12.3.2 Activating the filter

You can find this filter through Filters → Map → Displace...

17.12.3.3 Options

Figure 17.249 Displace filter options

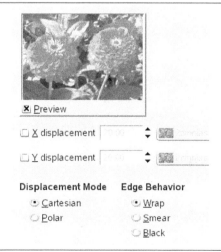

☒ Preview

☐ X displacement

☐ Y displacement

Displacement Mode **Edge Behavior**

⦿ Cartesian ⦿ Wrap

○ Polar ○ Smear

○ Black

Preview Uncheck this option if your processor is slow.

Displacement Mode You can choose working in Cartesian coordinates, where pixels are displaced in X or Y direction, or working in Polar coordinates, where the image is pinched and whirled by displacing pixels in radial or tangent direction.

Please see the next sections for details about these options.

Edge Behavior These options allows you to set displacement behaviour on active layer or selection edges:

Wrap With this option, what disappears on one edge reappears on the opposite edge.

Smear With this option, pixels vacated by displacement are replaced with pixels stretched from the adjacent part of the image.

Black With this option, pixels vacated by displacement are replaced with black.

Figure 17.250 Displace filter options (Cartesian)

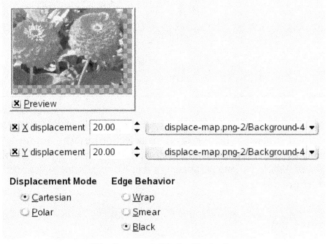

Displacement Mode: Cartesian

17.12.3.3.1 Cartesian Displacement Mode In both modes, direction and amount of displacement depend on the intensity of the corresponding pixel in the displacement map.

The map, that should be a grayscale image, has 256 gray levels (0-255), the (theoretical) average value is 127.5. The filter displaces image pixels corresponding to pixels with values less than 127.5 (0 to 127) in map to one direction, corresponding to pixels with values from 128 to 255 to the opposite direction.

X displacement, Y displacement If the respective option is activated, image pixels corresponding to pixels from 0 to 127 will be displaced to the right for X, downwards for Y, image pixels corresponding to pixels from 128 to 255 will be displaced to the left for X, upwards for Y.

What you enter in input boxes, directly or by using arrow-head buttons, is not the actual displacement. It's a coefficient used in a $displacement = (intensity x coefficient)$ formula, which gives the pixel actual displacement according to the scaled intensity [6] of the corresponding pixel in map, modulated by the coefficient you enter. Introducing intensity into formula is important: this allows progressive displacement by using a gradient map.

This value may be positive or negative. A negative displacement is reverse of a positive one. The value varies in limits equal to the double of image dimensions.

When you click on the drop-down list button, a list appears where you can select a displacement map. To be present in this list, an image must respect two conditions. First, this image must be present on your screen when you call filter. Then, this image must have the same dimensions as the original image. Most often, it will be a duplicate original image, which is transformed to grey scale and modified appropriately, with a gradient. It may be possible to use RGB images, but

---

[6] Scaled intensity = (intensity - 127.5) / 127.5; see Section 17.12.3.5.

color luminosity is used making result prevision difficult. Map may be different in horizontal and vertical directions.

Figure 17.251 Displace filter options (Polar)

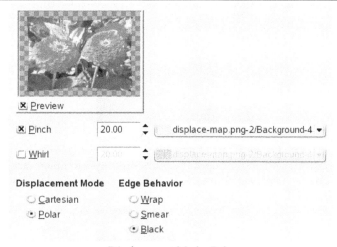

Displacement Mode: Polar

17.12.3.3.2   Polar Displacement Mode

Pinch If this option is activated, the radial coordinates (i.e. the distance to the image's midpoint, the "pole") of the pixels will be changed. Image pixels corresponding to map pixels from 0 to 127 will be displaced outwards, image pixels corresponding to pixels from 128 to 255 will be displaced towards center.

For the values and the displacement map see above ("X/Y displacement").

The displacement is independent from the polar distance, all pixels are displaced by the same amount. So the image will not only be stretched or compressed, but also distorted:

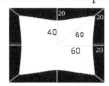

Image distortion by Pinch option

A 160x120 pixel image, plain white displacement map, and displacement coefficient 20.0: this results in a 20 pixels displacement towards center. This is a horizontal reduction in size by 25%, vertical by 33%, and diagonal by 20%, so the image will be distorted.

Whirl If this option is activated, the angular coordinates of the image pixels will be "displaced" by a map pixel dependent amount. For a plain displacement map, the image will be rotated, otherwise it will be whirled.

Image pixels corresponding to pixels from 0 to 127 in the map will be displaced counterclockwise, image pixels corresponding to pixels from 128 to 255 will be displaced clockwise.

For the values and the displacement map see above.

Note

 For a plain, non neutral map, if displace mode "Polar" is enabled, this filter works like Whirl and Pinch.

17.12.3.4   Using gradient to bend a text

Follow following steps:

1. Start with opening your image.

2. Duplicate this image. Activate this duplicate and make it gray-scaled (Image → Mode → GrayScale). Fill it with the wanted gradient. This image will be your *Displacement map*, with the dimensions of original image.

3. Activate original image. Create a *Text Layer* with your text. Set layer to image size: right-click on the layer in layer dialog and, in the pop-menu, click on "Layer to image size". Note that letters in text layer lie on a transparent background; now this filter doesn't displace transparent pixels. Only letters will be displaced.

4. Activate the text layer. Open the Displace filter window. Set parameters, particularly the displacement coefficient, according to the result in Preview. Click OK.

This method also applies to standard layers:

Tip

 To get the wanted gradient, first draw a black to white gradient. Then use the Curves tool to modify the gradient curve.

17.12.3.5   Displacement Calculation

The following section will show you how to calculate the amount of displacement, if you are interested in these details. If you don't want to know it, you can safely omit this section.

The overview example showed the X displacement using a coefficient of 30.0: 19, 8, 4, or 15 pixels, depending on the grey level of the displacement map's color.

Why just these amounts? That's easy:

$$30.0 * \frac{I - 127.5}{127.5} = D$$
$$30.0 * \frac{210 - 127.5}{127.5} = 19$$
$$30.0 * \frac{(160 - 127.5)}{127.5} = 8$$

$$30.0 * \frac{(110-127.5)}{127.5} = -4$$
$$30.0 * \frac{(60-127.5)}{127.5} = -15$$

If you check these equations, you will notice that the values they give are not exactly the results we retained in the example (using non-integers, that's not surprising). So, were the results rounded to the nearest integer and then the pixels were displaced by a whole-numbered amount? No. Every pixel is displaced exactly by the calculated amount; a "displacement by a fractional amount" is realized by interpolation. A closer look at the example image will show it:

Figure 17.252 A closer look at the displacement example

A small area zoomed in by 800 percent.

The displacement causes small (one pixel wide) areas of intermediate colors at the edges of plain color areas. E.g., the black area (zoomed in image) is caused by a displacement of -4.12, so the intermediate color is 12% black and 88% gold.

So if you select a displacement coefficient of 30.01 instead of 30.00, you will indeed get a different image, although you won't see the difference, of course.

17.12.4   Fractal Trace

17.12.4.1   Overview

Figure 17.253 Fractal Trace

(a) *Original image*   (b) *Filter "Fractal Trace" applied*

This filter transforms the image with the Mandelbrot fractal: it maps the image to the fractal.

17.12.4.2   Activate the filter

This filter is found in the image window menu under Filters → Map → Fractal trace....

17.12.4.3   Options

Figure 17.254 "Fractal trace" filter options

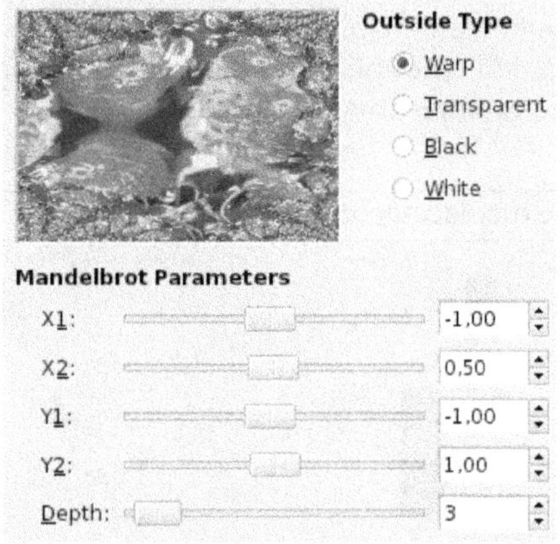

Outside Type
- ● Warp
- ○ Transparent
- ○ Black
- ○ White

Mandelbrot Parameters

X1:   -1,00
X2:   0,50
Y1:   -1,00
Y2:   1,00
Depth: 3

Mandelbrot parameters

X1, X2, Y1, Y2, Depth These parameters are similar to X/YMIN, X/YMAX and ITER parameters of the Fractal Explorer filter. They allow you to vary fractal spreading and detail depth.

Outside Type Mapping image to fractal may reveal empty areas. You can select to fill them with Black, White, Transparency or make what disappears on one side reappear on the opposite side with Wrap option.

17.12.5   Illusion

17.12.5.1   Overview

Figure 17.255 Illusion

(a) *Original image*   (b) *Filter "Fractal Trace" applied*

With this filter, your image (active layer or selection) looks like a kaleidoscope. This filter duplicates your image in many copies, more or less dimmed and split, and puts them around the center of the image.

17.12.5.2   Activate the filter

This filter is found in the image window menu under Filters → Map → Illusion....

17.12.5.3 Options

Figure 17.256 "Illusion" filter options

Preview If checked, parameter setting results are interactively displayed in preview. Scroll bars allow you to move around the image.

Divisions That's the number of copies you want to apply to image. This value varies from -32 to 64. Negative values invert kaleidoscope rotation.

Mode 1, Mode 2 You have two arrangement modes for copies in image:

Figure 17.257 From left to right: original image, mode 1, mode 2, with Divisions=4

17.12.6 Make Seamless

17.12.6.1 Overview

Figure 17.258 An example of Make Seamless.

(a) *Original*　　　　　(b) *Make Seamless applied*

This filter modifies the image for tiling by creating seamless edges. Such an image can be used as a pattern for a web-page. This filter has no option, and result may need correction.

17.12.6.2 Activation

You can find this filter through Filters → Map → Make Seamless

17.12.7 Map Object

17.12.7.1 Overview

Figure 17.259 The "Map Object" filter applied to a photograph

(a) *Original*　　　　　(b) *"Map Object" applied*

This filter maps a picture to an object (plane, sphere, box or cylinder).

17.12.7.2 Activate the filter

This filter is found in the image window menu under Filters → Map → Map Object....

17.12.7.3 Options

17.12.7.3.1 Preview This preview has several possibilities:

Preview! Preview is automatic for some options but you will have to press this button to update Preview after modifying many other parameters.

When mouse pointer is on Preview and the Light tab is selected, it takes the form of a small hand to grab the *blue point* which marks light source origin and to displace it. This blue point may not be visible if light source has negative X and Y settings in the Light tab.

Zoom out, Zoom in Zoom buttons allow you to enlarge or to reduce image in Preview. Their action is limited, but may be useful in case of a large image.

Show preview wireframe Puts a grid over the preview to make displacements and rotations more easy. Works well on a plan.

Figure 17.260 "Map Object" options (General)

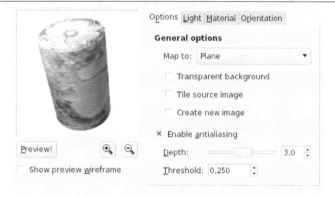

17.12.7.3.2 General Options

Map to This drop-down list allows you to select the object the image will be mapped on. It can be a *Plane*, a *Sphere*, a *Box* or a *Cylinder*.

Transparent background This option makes image transparent around the object. If not set, the background is filled with the current background color.

Tile source image When moving Plane object and displacing it with Orientation tab options, a part of the image turns empty. By checking the Tile source image, source image copies will fill this empty space in. This option seems not to work with the other objects.

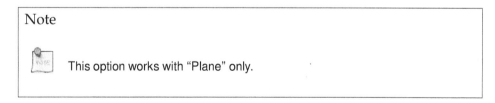

> **Note**
>
> This option works with "Plane" only.

Create new image When this option is checked, a new image is created with the result of filter application, so preserving the original image.

Enable antialiasing Check this option to conceal this unpleasant aliasing effect on borders. When checked, this option lets appear two settings:

Depth Defines antialiasing quality, to the detriment of execution speed.

Threshold Defines antialiasing limits. Antialiasing stops when value difference between pixels becomes lower than this set value.

Figure 17.261 "Map Object" options (Light)

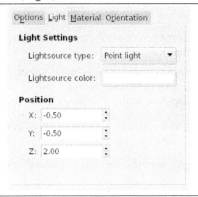

17.12.7.3.3   Light

Light Settings

> **Lightsource type** In this dropdown list, you can select among *Point light*, *Directionnal light* and *No light*.

> **Lightsource color** Press this button to open the Color Selector dialog.

Position If "Point light" is selected, you can control there light source *Position* (the blue point), according to X, Y and Z coordinates.

> If "Directional light" is selected, these X, Y and Z parameters control the "Direction vector" (effect is not evident).

Figure 17.262 "Map Object" options (Material)

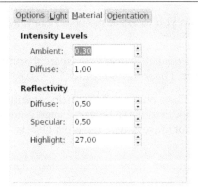

17.12.7.3.4   Material

Intensity Levels

> **Ambient** Amount of color to show where no light falls directly.

> **Diffuse** Intensity of original color when lit by a light source.

Reflectivity

> **Diffuse** Higher values make object reflect more light (looks brighter).

> **Specular** Controls how intense the highlights will be.

> **Highlight** Higher values make the highlights more focused.

Figure 17.263 "Map Object" options (Orientation)

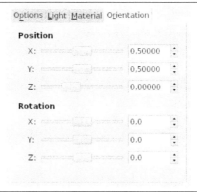

17.12.7.3.5 Orientation

Position These three sliders and their input boxes allows you to vary object position in image, according to the X, Y, Z coordinates of the object upper left corner.

Rotation These three sliders make the object rotate around X, Y, Z axes respectively.

17.12.7.3.6 Box This tab appears only when you select the Box object.

Figure 17.264 "Map Object" options (Box)

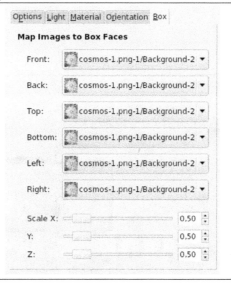

Match Images to Box Faces This function name is self explanatory: you can select an image for every face of the box. These images must be present on your screen when you call the Map Object filter.

Scale These X, Y, Z sliders allow you to change the size of every X, Y, Z dimension of the box.

17.12.7.3.7 Cylinder This tab appears only when you select the Cylinder object.

Figure 17.265 "Map Object" options (Cylinder)

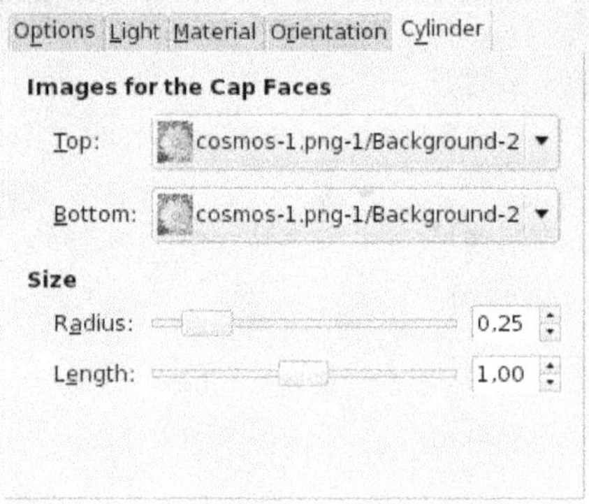

> Options | Light | Material | Orientation | Cylinder
>
> **Images for the Cap Faces**
>
> Top: [img] cosmos-1.png-1/Background-2 ▼
>
> Bottom: [img] cosmos-1.png-1/Background-2 ▼
>
> **Size**
>
> Radius: ⊟───────────────── 0.25 ⬍
>
> Length: ──────────⊟────── 1.00 ⬍

Images for the Cap Faces The name of this option is self-explanatory. Images must be present on your screen when you call the Map Object filter.

Size

> **Radius** This slider and its input boxes let you control the Cylinder diameter. Unfortunately, this setting works on the image mapped onto the cylinder and resamples this image to adapt it to the new cylinder size. It would be better to have the possibility of setting size cylinder before mapping so that we could map a whole image.
>
> **Length** Controls cylinder length.

17.12.8   Paper Tile

17.12.8.1   Overview

Figure 17.266 "Papertile" filter example.

(a) *Original image*   (b) *Filter "Papertile" applied*

This filter cuts the image (active layer or selection) into several pieces, with square form, and then slides them so that they, more or less, overlap or move apart. They can go out image borders a little.

17.12.8.2   Activate the filter

You can find this filter through Filters → Map → Paper Tile....

17.12.8.3 Options

Figure 17.267 "Paper Tile" filter options

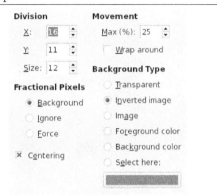

Division X, Y and Size parameters are linked, because filter starts cutting image before it displaces pieces; so, piece size and number of pieces in horizontal (X) and vertical (Y) directions must be convenient to image size.

Movement

Max (%) This is the maximum displacement percentage against the side size of squares.

Wrap around As tiles move, some can go out image borders. If this option is checked, what goes out on one side goes in on the opposite side.

Fractional Pixels Because of image cutting, original pixels can persist. There are three ways treating them:

Background Remaining pixels will be replaced with the background type defined in the following section.

Ignore Background Type option is not taken into account and remaining pixels are kept.

Force Remaining pixels will be cut also.

Background Type You can select the background type which will be used, if the Background radio-button is checked, among six options:

Transparent Background will be transparent.

Inverted image Background colors will be inverted (255-value in every color channel).

Image Background colors will be unchanged. The original image is the background.

Foreground color Remaining pixels will be replaced by the Foreground color of Toolbox.

Background color Remaining pixels will be replaced by the Background color of Toolbox.

Select here When this radio-button is checked, clicking in the color dwell will open a Color Selector where you can select the color you want for background.

Centering If this option is checked, tiles will rather be gathered together in the center of the image.

17.12.9 Small Tiles

17.12.9.1 Overview

Figure 17.268 Example for the "Small Tiles" filter

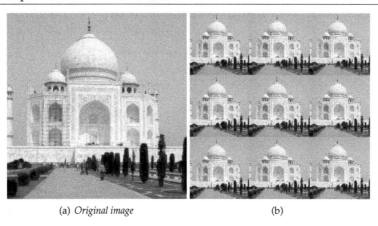

(a) *Original image*   (b)

This filter reduces the image (active layer or selection) and displays it in many copies inside the original image.

17.12.9.2 Activate the filter

You can find this filter through Filters → Map → Small Tiles....

17.12.9.3 Options

Figure 17.269 "Small Tiles" filter options

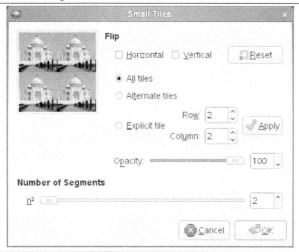

Flip You can flip tiles according to the Horizontal or/and Vertical axis by checking the corresponding option(s).

You can also decide which tiles will be flipped:

All tiles No comment.

Alternate tiles Only odd tiles will be flipped.

Explicit tile You can define a particular tile using both Row and Column input boxes. This tile will be marked with a box in Preview. Press Apply to mark this explicit tile. Repeat this procedure to mark more than one tile.

Opacity With this slider and its input box, you can set the opacity of the resulting image. This option is valid only if your image has an Alpha channel.

Number of Segments n^2 means "the image into n to the power of two tiles", where "n" is the number you set with the slider or its input box. n = 3 will make nine tiles in the image.

17.12.10 Tile

17.12.10.1 Overview

Figure 17.270 The same image, before and after applying Tile filter

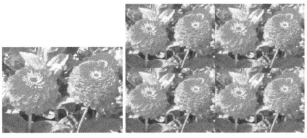

(a) *Original image*   (b) *(We have reduced image size intentionally)*

This filter makes several copies of the original image, in a same or reduced size, into a bigger (new) image.

17.12.10.2 Activate the filter

You can find this filter through Filters → Map → Tile....

17.12.10.3 Options

Figure 17.271 "Tile" filter options

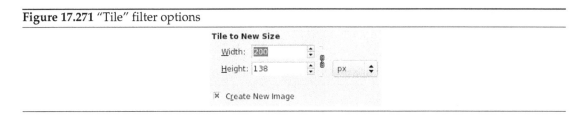

Tile to New Size

Width, Height Input boxes and their arrow-heads allow you to enter the dimensions for the new image.

Both directions are linked by default with a chain ⬚ . You can make them independent by breaking this chain. You can choose a unit else than pixel by clicking on the drop-down list button.

The new image must be bigger than the original one. Else, you will get an image sample only. Choose sizes which are multiple of original sizes if you don't want to have truncated tiles.

Create new image It's in your interest to keep this option checked to avoid modifying your original image.

17.12.11 Warp

17.12.11.1 Overview

This filter displaces pixels of active layer or selection according to the grey levels of a *Displacement map*. Pixels are displaced according to the gradient slope in the displacement map. Pixels corresponding to solid areas are not displaced; the higher the slope, the higher the displacement.

Figure 17.272 From left to right: original image, displace map, displaced image

Solid areas of displacement map lead to no displacement. Abrupt transitions give an important displacement. A linear gradient gives a regular displacement. Displacement direction is perpendicular to gradient direction (angle = 90°).

Figure 17.273 With a non-linear gradient

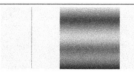

A non-linear gradient leads to curls.

Figure 17.274 With a complex gradient:

And a complex gradient, such as the Solid Noise filter can create, gives a swirl effect.

This filter offers the possibility of masking a part of the image to protect it against filter action.

17.12.11.2 Activating the filter

This filter is found in the image window menu under Filters → Map → Warp.... This filter has no Preview.

17.12.11.3   Options

Figure 17.275 Warp filter options

Basic Options

Step size "Step" is displacement distance for every filter iteration. A 10 value is necessary to get a one pixel displacement. This value can be negative to invert displacement direction.

Iterations The number of repetitions of effect when applying filter.

On edges Because of displacement, a part of pixels are driven over the borders of layer or selection, and, on the opposite side, pixels places are emptying. Four following options allow you to fix this issue:

  Wrap What goes out on one side is going into the opposite side (this is the default).

  Smear Emptying places are filled with a spreading of the neighbouring image line.

  Black Emptying places are filled with black color.

  Foreground color Emptying places are filled with the Foreground color of the color area in Toolbox.

Displacement map To be listed in this drop-down list, the displacement map, which should be a grayscaled image, must be *present on your screen when you call filter and must have the same size as the original image*.

Advanced Options

Dither size Once all pixels displaced, this option scatters them randomly, giving grain to the image. The higher this value (0.00-100.00), the thinner the grain.

Figure 17.276 With a 3.00 dither size:

Rotation angle This option sets displacement angle of pixels according to the slope direction of gradient. Previous examples have been created with a vertical gradient and a 90° angle: so, pixels were displaced horizontally and nothing went out of the image borders. Here is an example with a 10° angle and 6 iterations:

Figure 17.277 With a 10° angle and 6 iterations:

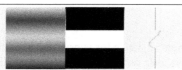

Displacement is made according to a 10° angle against vertical. Pixels going out the lower border on every iteration are going into through the upper border (Wrap option checked), giving a dotted line.

Substeps If you specify a value > 1, the displacement vector is computed in several substeps, giving you a finer control to the displace process.

Magnitude map In addition to displacement map, you can add a Magnitude map. This map should also be a grayscaled image, with the same size as the source image and which must be present on your screen when you call filter. This map gives more or less strength to filter on some parts of the image, according to the grey levels of this magnitude map. Image areas corresponding to white parts of this map will undergo all the strength of filter. Image areas corresponding to black parts of the map will be spared by filter. Intermediate grey levels will lessen filter action on corresponding areas of the image. Use magnitude map must be checked for that.

Figure 17.278 Magnitude Map example:

From left to right: original image, displacement map, magnitude map, after applying "Warp" filter. You can see that the black areas of magnitude map prevent filter to take action.

More Advanced Options
These extra options let you add two new maps, a gradient map and/or a vector map.

Note

To test these options alone, you must use a map with a solid color for all the other maps.

Gradient scale Using a gradient map, (this map should also be a grayscaled image), the displacement of pixels depends on the direction of grayscale transitions. The Gradient scale option lets you set how much the grayscale variations will influence the displacement of pixels. On every iteration, the filter works of the whole image, not only on the red object: this explains blurredness.

Figure 17.279 Gradient scale example

From left to right: original image, Gradient map, filter applied.

In the example above, "Warp" filter is applied with a gradient map (Gradient scale = 10.0). Gradient is oblique, from top left to right bottom. The part of the image corresponding to the gradient is moved obliquely, 90° rotated (Rotation angle 90° in Advanced Options).

Vector mag With this map, the displacement depends on the angle you set in the Angle text box. 0° is upwards. Angles go counter-clockwise. The *vector control map* determines by how many pixels the image will move on every iteration.

Figure 17.280 Vector mag example

From left to right: original image, displacement map, filter applied.

In the above example, "Warp" filter is applied with a Vector mag. Gradient is vertical, from top to bottom. Vector angle is 45°. The image is moved obliquely, 45° to the top left corner. The image is blurred because every iteration works on the whole image, and not only on the red bar.

Angle Angle for fixed vector map (see above).

17.13 Rendering Filters

17.13.1 Introduction

Most GIMP filters work on a layer by transforming its content, but the filters in the "Render" group are a bit different. They create patterns from scratch, in most cases obliterating anything that was previously in the layer. Some create random or noisy patterns, others regular of fractal patterns, and one (Gfig) is a general-purpose (but rather limited) vector graphics tool.

17.13.2 Difference Clouds

17.13.2.1 Overview

Figure 17.281 Example of Difference Clouds

Filter "Difference Clouds" applied

Difference Clouds command changes colors partially in cloud-like areas: The filter renders Solid Noise cloud in an automatically created new layer, and sets the layer mode to Difference, then merges this layer over the specified image.

Before merging the layer, this script opens the dialog of the Solid Noise plug-in which allows to control its effect.

If the image is in indexed colors, this menu entry is grayed out and unavailable.

17.13.2.2 Activate the filter

This filter is found in the image window menu under Filters → Render → Clouds → Difference Clouds....

17.13.2.3   Options

This script does not have its own dialog window but invokes the Solid Noise filter's dialog.

17.13.3   Fog

17.13.3.1   Overview

Figure 17.282 Example for the "Fog" filter

(a) *Original image*   (b) *"Fog" applied*

This filter adds a new layer with some clouds to the image that look like fog or smoke. The clouds are created with the Plasma texture.

17.13.3.2   Activating the filter

This filter is found in the image window menu under Filters → Render → Clouds → Fog….

17.13.3.3   Options

Figure 17.283 "Fog" options

Among the few filter options, only "Turbulence" is somewhat important, because you can't change it later and have to undo and repeat the filter if the result doesn't fit your desire.

Layer name The name of the layer. You can change it later in the Layers Dialog.

Fog color Defaults to some kind of sandy brown (240, 180, 70). Click on the color button to change this if you think that is not the natural color of fog.

Turbulence This is actually the Turbulence option of the Plasma filter: it controls the complexity of the clouds, from soft (low values) to hard (high values).

Opacity The opacity of the layer. You can change it later in the Layers Dialog.

17.13.4 Plasma

17.13.4.1 Overview

Figure 17.284 Example of a rendered plasma

Filter "Plasma" applied

All of the colors produced by Plasma are completely saturated. Sometimes the strong colors may be distracting, and a more interesting surface will appear when you desaturate the image using Colors → Desaturate.

17.13.4.2 Activating the filter

This filter is found in the image window menu under Filters → Render → Clouds → Plasma....

17.13.4.3 Options

Figure 17.285 "Plasma" filter options

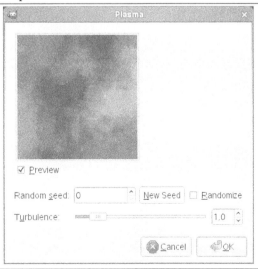

Preview If checked, parameter setting results are interactively displayed in preview.

Random seed This option controls the randomization element. The Randomize check-button will set the seed using the hardware clock of the computer. There is no reason to use anything else unless you want to be able to repeat the exact same pattern of randomization on a later occasion.

Turbulence This parameter controls the complexity of the plasma. High values give a hard feeling to the cloud (like an abstract oil painting or mineral grains), low values produce a softer cloud (like steam, mist or smoke). The range is 0.1 to 7.0.

17.13.5 Solid Noise

17.13.5.1 Overview

Figure 17.286 Example of turbulent solid noise

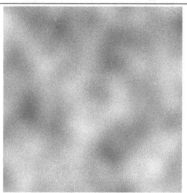

Filter "Solid noise" applied

Solid Noise is a great texture maker. Note that this noise is always gray, even if you applied it to a very colorful image (it doesn't matter what the original image looks like -- this filter completely overwrites any existing background in the layer it is applied to). This is also a good tool to create displacement maps for the Warp plug-in or for the Bump Map plug-in. With the "turbulence" setting active, the results look quite a bit like real clouds.

17.13.5.2 Activating the filter

This filter is found in the image window menu under Filters → Render → Clouds → Solid noise....

17.13.5.3 Options

Figure 17.287 "Solid Noise" filter options

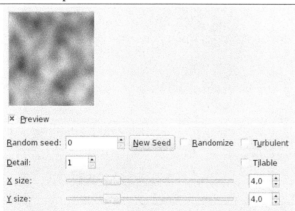

Preview If checked, parameter setting results are interactively displayed in preview.

Random seed This option controls random behaviour of the filter. If the same random seed in the same situation is used, the filter produces exactly the same results. A different random seed produces different results. Random seed can be entered manually or generated randomly by pressing New Seed button.

When the Randomize option is checked, random seed cannot be entered manually, but is randomly generated each time the filter is run. If it is not checked, the filter remembers the last random seed used.

Turbulent If you check this, you'll get very interesting effects, often something that looks much like oil on water, or clouds of smoke, or living tissue, or a Rorschach blot.

Detail This controls the amount of detail in the noise texture. Higher values give a higher level of detail, and the noise seems to be made of spray or small particles, which makes it feel hard. A low value makes it more soft and cloudy.

Tileable If you check Tileable, you'll get a noise which can be used as tiles. For example, you can use it as a background in an HTML page, and the tile edges will be joined seamlessly.

X size, Y size These control the size and proportion of the noise shapes in X (horizontal) and Y (vertical) directions (range 0.1 to 16.0).

17.13.6   Flame

17.13.6.1   Overview

Figure 17.288 Example of a rendered Flame

(b) Filter "Flame" applied

With the Flame filter, you can create stunning, randomly generated fractal patterns. You can't control the fractals as you can with the IFS Fractal filter, but you can steer the random generator in a certain direction, and choose from variations of a theme you like.

Warning

Unfortunately it turned out, that this filter is not working properly for large images. Even more unfortunate is, that its developer is currently not undertaking any actions with that plug-in at all, so there seems no quick fix in sight. Although we can't give you the exact numbers, the plug-in worked in a quick test for a 1024x768 pixel image, but didn't do it for a 2500x2500 pixel image.

Note

This plug-in was given to GIMP by Scott Draves in 1997. He also holds the copyright for the plug-in. An descriptive page for the plug-in, provided by the author can be found in the internet [PLUGIN-FLAMES].

17.13.6.2   Activating the filter

You can find this filter through Filters → Render → Nature → Flame….

17.13.6.3   Options

Figure 17.289 "Flame" filter options

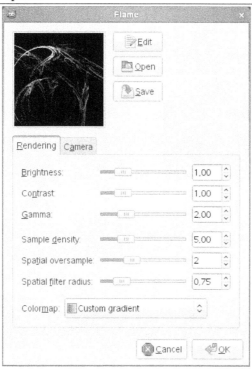

In the main window, you can set Rendering and Camera parameters. The first three parameters in the Render display are Brightness, Contrast and Gamma. The result of these options is visible in the Preview window, but it's generally better to stick to the default values, and correct the rendered image later with Image/Colors.

The other three parameters affect the rendering process and don't show in the preview window. Sample Density, which controls the resolution of the rendered pattern, is the most important of these.

The Camera parameters allow you to zoom and offset the flame pattern, until you're happy with what you see in the preview window. Flame also offers the possibility to store and load your favorite patterns.

Edit Pressing this button brings up the Edit dialog:

Figure 17.290 The Edit Flame dialog

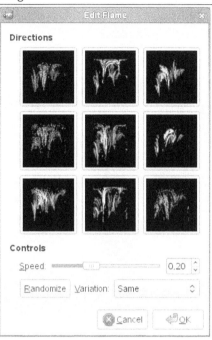

The dialog shows nine different windows. The pattern displayed in the center is the current pattern, and the eight windows surrounding it are random variations of that pattern. Clicking on the central image creates eight new variations, which can be adjusted with the Speed control. You select a variation by clicking on it, and it instantly replaces the image in the middle. To pick a certain character or theme for the variations, you can choose from nine different themes in the Variations menu. You can also use Randomize, which replaces the current pattern with a new random pattern.

Open This button brings up a file selector that allows you to open a previously saved Flame settings file.

Save This button brings up a file save dialog that allows you to save the current settings for the plug-in, so that you can recreate them later.

Rendering

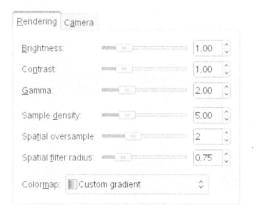

Brightness Controls the brightness of the flame object.

Contrast Controls the contrast between brighter and dimmer parts of the flame.

Gamma Sets a gamma correction for parts with intermediate brightness.

Sample density Controls the resolution of the rendered pattern. (Does not have any effect on the pre-view.) A high sample density results in soft and smooth rendering (like a spider's web), whereas low density rendering resembles spray or particle clouds.

Spatial oversample What does this do?

Spatial filter radius What does this do?

Colormap This menu gives you several options to set the color blend in the flame pattern:

- The current gradient as shown in the Toolbox.
- A number of preset colormaps.
- The colors from images that are presently open in GIMP.

Camera

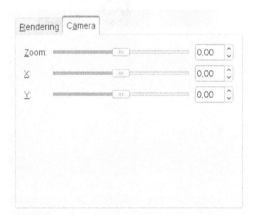

Zoom Allows you to zoom the flame in or out.

X, Y Allows you to move the flame around in the image area.

17.13.7   IFS Fractal

17.13.7.1   Overview

Figure 17.291 Applying example for the IFS Fractal filter

Filter "IFS Fractal" applied

This fractal-based plug-in is truly wonderful! With this versatile instrument, you can create amazingly naturalistic organic shapes, like leaves, flowers, branches, or even whole trees. ("IFS" stands for "Iterated Function System".)

The key to use this plug-in lies in making very small and precise movements in fractal space. The outcome is always hard to predict, and you have to be extremely gentle when you change the pattern. If you make a component triangle too big, or if you move it too far (even ever so slightly), the preview screen will black out, or more commonly, you'll get stuck with a big shapeless particle cloud.

A word of advice: When you have found a pattern you want to work with, make only small changes, and stick to variations of that pattern. It's all too easy to lose a good thing. Contrary to what you might believe, it's really much easier to create a leaf or a tree with IFS Fractal than to make a defined geometrical pattern (where you actually know what you're doing, and end up with the pattern you had in mind).

For a brief introduction to IFS's see Foley and van Dam, et al,. *Computer Graphics, Principles and Practice*[FOLEY01].

17.13.7.2 Activating the filter

This filter is found in the image window menu under Filters → Render → Nature → IFS Fractal....

17.13.7.3 Options

Figure 17.292 "IFS Fractal" filter options

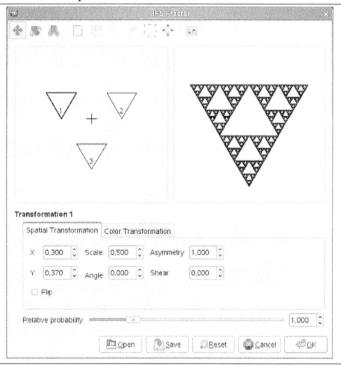

The plug-in interface consists of the compose area to the left, a preview screen to the right, and some tabs and option buttons at the bottom of the dialog. The Default setting (in the preview window) is three equilateral triangles. (This gives rise to a fractal pattern called the *Sierpinski Triangle*).

Toolbar

Click on the toolbar buttons to use the following tools, or open the context menu of the compose area.

Move, Rotate/Scale, Stretch Select the action to perform using the (mouse) pointer.

New, Delete Add or remove fractals.

Undo, Redo Standard.

Select all Link fractals and let apply actions to all fractals.

Recenter Recompute the center of the fractals. This does not have any visible effect to the resulting fractal.

Render Options

   Max. memory Enables you to speed up rendering time. This is especially useful when working with a large spot radius; just remember to use even multiples of the default value: 4096, 8192, 16384, ...

   Iterations Determines how many times the fractal will repeat itself. (A high value for Subdivide and Iterations is for obvious reasons a waste of process time unless your image is very large.)

   Subdivide Controls the level of detail.

   Spot radius Determines the density of the "brushstrokes" in the rendered image. A low spot radius is good for thin particle clouds or spray, while a high spot radius produces thick, solid color strokes much like watercolor painting. Be careful not to use too much spot radius — it takes a lot of time to render.

Spatial Transformation

Gives you information on the active fractal, and allows you to type a value instead of changing it manually. Changing parameters with the mouse isn't very accurate, so this is a useful option when you need to be exact.

X, Y, Scale, Angle, Shear Move, scale, or shear the active fractal.

Asymmetry Stretch the active fractal.

Flip Flip the active fractal.

Color Transformation

Simple Changes the color of the currently selected fractal component (default is the foreground color in the toolbox) to a color of your choice.

Full Like the Simple color transformation but this time you can manage the color transformation for each color channel and for the alpha channel (shown as a black channel).

Scale hue by, Scale value by When you have many fractals with different colors, the colors blend into each other. So even if you set "pure red" for a fractal, it might actually be quite blue in some places, while another "red " fractal might have a lot of yellow in it. Scale Hue/Value changes the color strength of the active fractal, or how influential that fractal color should be.

   Other

Relative probability Determines influence or total impact of a certain fractal.

17.13.7.4   A Brief Tutorial

This is a rather complex plug-in, so to help you understand it, we'll guide you through an example where you'll create a leaf or branch.

Many forms of life, and especially plants, are built like mathematical fractals, i.e., a shape that reproduces or repeats itself indefinitely into the smallest detail. You can easily reproduce the shape of a leaf or a branch by using four (or more) fractals. Three fractals make up the tip and sides of the leaf, and the fourth represents the stem.

1. Before invoking the filter: Select File → New Image. Add a transparent layer with Layers → Layers and Channels → New Layer. Set the foreground color in the toolbox to black, and set the background to white.

2. Open IFS Fractal. Start by rotating the right and bottom triangles, so that they point upward. You'll now be able to see the outline of what's going to be the tip and sides of the leaf. (If you have problems, it may help to know that the three vertices of a triangle are not equivalent.)

Figure 17.293 Tutorial Step 2

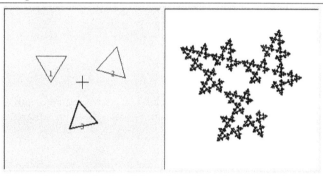

Start by rotating triangles 2 and 3, trying to keep them nearly the same size.

3. To make the leaf symmetrical, adjust the bottom triangle to point slightly to the left, and the right triangle to point slightly to the right.

4. Press New to add a component to the composition. This is going to be the stem of the leaf, so we need to make it long and thin. Press Stretch, and drag to stretch the new triangle. Don't be alarmed if this messes up the image, just use Scale to adjust the size of the overlong triangle. You'll probably also have to move and rotate the new fractal to make it look convincing.

Figure 17.294 Tutorial Step 3

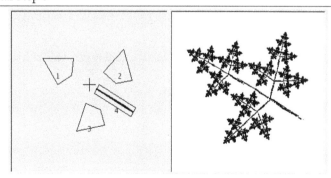

Add a fourth component, then stretch, scale, and move it as shown.

5. You still have to make it look more leaf-like. Increase the size of the top triangle, until you think it's thick and leafy enough. Adjust all fractals until you're happy with the shape. Right-click to get the pop-up menu, and choose Select all. Now all components are selected, and you can scale and rotate the entire leaf.

Figure 17.295 Tutorial Step 4

Enlarge component 1, arrange the other components appropriately, then select all, scale and rotate.

6. The final step is to adjust color. Click on the Color Transformation tab, and choose a different color for each fractal. To do this, check Simple and press the right color square. A color circle appears, where you can click or select to choose a color.

Figure 17.296 Tutorial Step 5

Assign a brownish color to component 4, and various shades of green to the other components.

7. Press OK to apply the image, and voilà, you've just made a perfect fractal leaf! Now that you've got the hang of it, you'll just have to experiment and make your own designs. All plant-imitating fractals (be they oak trees, ferns or straws) are more or less made in this fashion, which is leaves around a stem (or several stems). You just have to twist another way, stretch and turn a little or add a few more fractals to get a totally different plant.

17.13.8 Checkerboard

17.13.8.1 Overview

Figure 17.297 Example for the Checkerboard filter

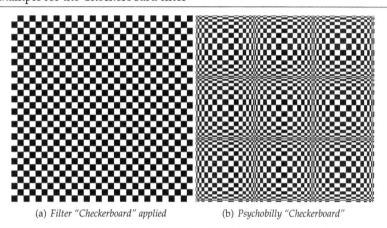

(a) *Filter "Checkerboard" applied*   (b) *Psychobilly "Checkerboard"*

This filter creates a checkerboard pattern replacing the current layer content. Colors used for pattern are current Fore- and Back ground colors of toolbox.

17.13.8.2 Starting filter

You can find this filter in the image menu through Filters → Render → Pattern → Checkerboard...

17.13.8.3 Options

Figure 17.298 "Checkerboard" filter options

Size With this option, you can set checkerboard square size, in pixels, or in your chosen unit by using the drop-down list.

Psychobilly This option gives an eiderdown look to the Checkerboard.

17.13.9   CML Explorer

17.13.9.1   Overview

Figure 17.299 Example for the "CML Explorer" filter

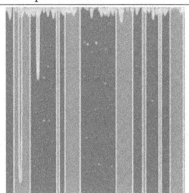

Filter "CML Explorer" applied with default options

This filter is the king of texture creating filters. It is extremely efficient but very complex. It uses a mathematical method named Cellular Automata [WKPD-CA].

17.13.9.2   Activating the filter

You can find this filter from the image menu through Filters → Render → Pattern → CML Explorer....

17.13.9.3   Options

17.13.9.3.1   General Options   Filter options are distributed among Hue,Saturation, Value, Advanced, Others and Misc Ops. tabs. Some more options are available. They will be described in following section.

Preview   This filter offers you a Preview where you can see the result of your settings before they are applied to the image.

New Seed, Fix Seed, Random Seed   Random plays a large part in creating patterns. With these options, you can influence the way random is generated. By clicking on the New Seed button, you can force random to use a new source of random. The preview will show you the result. Fix Seed lets you keep the same seed and so to reproduce the same effect with the filter. Random Seed generates a random seed at random.

Open, Save   With these both command buttons you can save pattern settings in a file, and to get them back later.

Figure 17.300 Hue tab

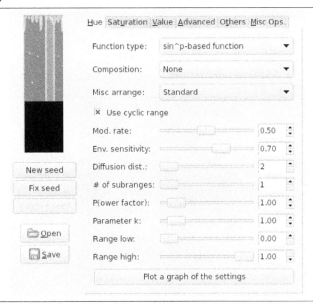

17.13.9.3.2 "CML Explorer" filter options (Hue)   This filter works in the HSV color model. In this tab, you can set options for Hue.

Function type   In this drop-down list, you can select the method that will be used to treat the current layer. These methods are:

> **Keep image's values**   With this option, image hue values will be kept.
>
> **Keep the first value**   With this option, starting color will be standard cyan.
>
> **Fill with parameter k**   Pattern look will depend on k that you will set later in options.
>
> **Miscellaneous f(k)**   See above, "Fill with k parameter".
>
> **Delta function, Delta function stepped**   // TODO
>
> **sin^p-based function, sin^p, stepped**   These options create wave-like patterns, like aurora borealis or curtain folds.

Composition   Here, these options concern Hue. You can choose among several functions, and a book could be filled with results of all these functions. Please, experiment!

Misc. arrange   This drop-down list offers you several other parameters. Also a book would be necessary to explain all possibilities of these parameters.

Use cyclic range   // TODO

Mod. rate   With this slider and the input box, you can set modification rate from 0.0 to 1.0. Low value results in a lined pattern.

Env. sensitivity   Value is from 0.0 to 1.0

Diffusion dist.   Diffusion distance: from 2 to 10.

# of subranges   Number of sub-rangers: from 1 to 10.

(P)ower factor   With this option you can influence the Function types using the p parameter. Value from 0.0 to 10.0.

Parameter k   With this option you can influence the Function types using the k parameter. Value from 0.0 to 10.0.

Range low   Set lower limit of hue that will be used for calculation. values vary from 0.0 to 1.0.

Range high   Set the upper limit of hue that will be used for calculation. Variations are from 0.0 to 1.0.

Plot a Graph of the Settings By clicking on this large button, you can open a window that displays the graph of hue present settings.

Figure 17.301 Function graph of present settings

Figure 17.302 Saturation tab

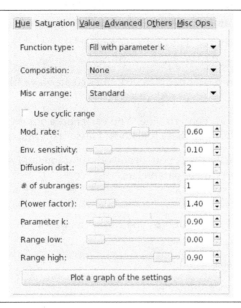

17.13.9.3.3 "CML Explorer" filter options (Saturation) In this tab, you can set how Saturation component of the HSV color model will be used in pattern calculation.

These options are similar to Hue tab options.

Figure 17.303 Value tab

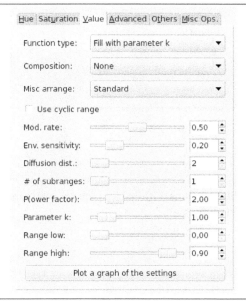

17.13.9.3.4 "CML Explorer" filter options (Value)   In this tab, you can set how the Value (Luminosity) component of the HSV color model will be used in pattern calculation.

These options are similar to Hue tab options.

Figure 17.304 Advanced tab

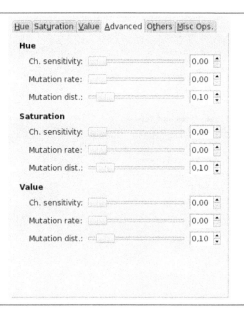

17.13.9.3.5 "CML Explorer" filter options (Advanced)   These tab settings apply to the three HSV channels.

Channel sensitivity // TODO

Mutation rate // TODO

Mutation distance // TODO

Figure 17.305 Others tab

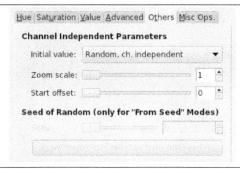

17.13.9.3.6 "CML Explorer" filter options (Others)   In this tab, you can find various parameters about image display and random intervention.

Initial value // TODO

Zoom scale // TODO

Start offset // TODO

Seed of Random // TODO

Figure 17.306 Miscellaneous options tab

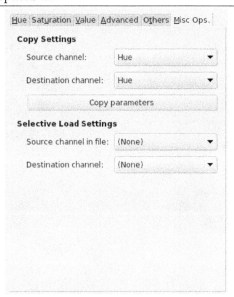

17.13.9.3.7 "CML Explorer" filter options (Misc Ops.)   In this tab you can find various options about copy and loading.

Copy Settings These options allow you to transfer information from one of the HSV channel to another one.

Selective Load Settings With the Open button of this filter, you can load previously loaded settings. If you don't want to load all of them, you can select a source and a destination channel here.

17.13.10 Diffraction Patterns

17.13.10.1 Overview

Figure 17.307 Two examples of diffraction patterns

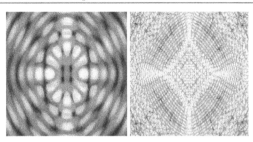

This filter lets you make diffraction or wave interference textures. You can change the Frequency, Contours and Sharp Edges for each of the RGB channels. You can also set Brightness, Scattering and Polarization of the texture. There is no automatic preview, so you must press the preview button to update. On a slow system, this may take a bit of time. Note that result doesn't depend on the initial image.

This is a very useful filter if you want to create intricate patterns. It's perfect for making psychedelic, batik-like textures, or for imitating patterns in stained glass (as in a church window).

It seems clear that the plugin works by simulating the physics of light striking a grating. Unfortunately, the original authors never got around to writing down the theory behind it, or explaining what the parameters mean. The best approach, then, is just to twiddle things and see what happens. Fortunately, almost anything you do seems to produce interesting results.

17.13.10.2 Activating the filter

This filter is found in the image window menu under Filters → Render → Pattern → Diffraction Patterns....

17.13.10.3 Options

Figure 17.308 "Diffraction Patterns" filter options

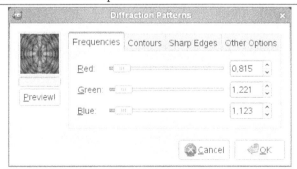

17.13.11   Grid

17.13.11.1   Overview

Figure 17.309 Applying example for the Grid filter

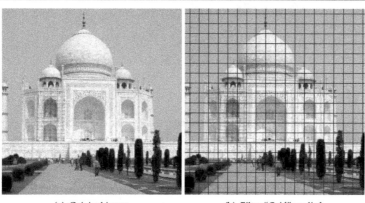

(a) *Original image*	(b) *Filter "Grid" applied*

It renders a Cartesian grid in the active layer, on top of the existing contents. The width, spacing, offsets, and colors of the grid lines can all be set by the user. By default, the lines are with the GIMP's foreground color. (Note: this plug-in was used to create demonstration images for many of the other plug-ins.)

> Tip
>
> If you set the grid line widths to 0, then only the intersections will be drawn, as plus-marks.

17.13.11.2   Activating the filter

This filter is found in the image window menu under Filters → Render → Pattern → Grid....

17.13.11.3 Options

Figure 17.310 "Grid" filter options

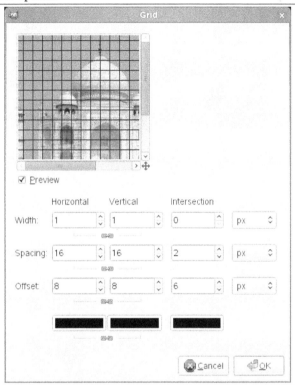

There are separate options for controlling the horizontal grid lines, vertical grid lines, and intersections. By default, the horizontal and vertical settings are locked together, so that all changes are applied symmetrically. If you want to change just one of them, click on the "chain" symbol below it to unlock them. The results of changing the Intersection parameters are rather complex.

Besides, for some options, you can select the unit of measurement thanks to a drop-down list.

Width Sets the widths of the horizontal or vertical grid lines, or of the symbols drawn at their intersections.

Spacing Sets the distance between grid lines. The Intersection parameter clears the space between the intersection point and the end of the arms of the intersection crosses.

Offset Sets the offset for grid lines with respect to the upper left corner. For intersections, sets the length of the arms of the intersection crosses.

Color Selectors These allow you to set the colors of the grid lines and intersection marks.

Figure 17.311 Intersection parameters

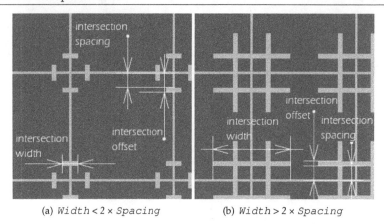

(a) *Width < 2 × Spacing*   (b) *Width > 2 × Spacing*

17.13.12 Jigsaw

17.13.12.1 Overview

Figure 17.312 Jigsaw filter example

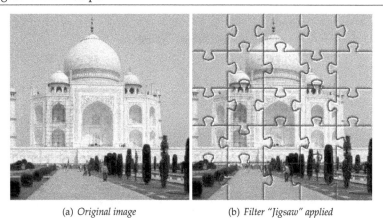

(a) *Original image*   (b) *Filter "Jigsaw" applied*

This filter will turn your image into a jigsaw puzzle. The edges are not anti-aliased, so a little bit of smoothing often makes them look better (i. e., Gaussian blur with radius 1.0).

> **Tip**
>
> If you want to be able to easily select individual puzzle-piece areas, render the jigsaw pattern on a separate layer filled with solid white, and set the layer mode to Multiply. You can then select puzzle pieces using the magic wand (fuzzy select) tool on the new jigsaw layer.

17.13.12.2 Activating the filter

This filter is found in the image window menu under Filters → Render → Pattern → Jigsaw....

17.13.12.3 Options

Figure 17.313 "Jigsaw" filter options

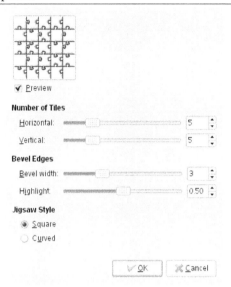

Number of Tiles How many tiles across the image is, horizontally and vertically.

Bevel Edges

Bevel width The Bevel width slider controls the slope of the edges of the puzzle pieces (a hard wooden puzzle would require a low Bevel width value, and a soft cardboard puzzle would require a higher value).

Highlight The Highlight slider controls the strength of the highlight that will appear on the edges of each piece. You may compare it to the "glossiness" of the material the puzzle is made of. Highlight width is relative to the Bevel width. As a rule of thumb, the more pieces you add to the puzzle, the lower Bevel and Highlight values you should use, and vice versa. The default values are suitable for a 500x500 pixel image.

Jigsaw Style

You can choose between two types of puzzle:

Square Then you get pieces made with straight lines.

Curved Then you get pieces made with curves.

17.13.13   Maze

17.13.13.1   Overview

Figure 17.314 An example of a rendered maze.

Filter "Maze" applied

This filter generates a random black and white maze pattern. The result completely overwrites the previous contents of the active layer. A typical example is shown below. Can you find the route from the center to the edge?

17.13.13.2   Activating the filter

This filter is found in the image window menu under Filters → Render → Pattern → Maze....

17.13.13.3   Options

Figure 17.315 "Maze" filter options

Maze Size

Width, Height These sliders control how many pathways the maze should have. The lower the values for width and height, the more paths you will get. The same happens if you increase the number of pieces in the Width and Height Pieces fields. The result won't really look like a maze unless the width and height are equal.

Algorithm

Seed You can specify a seed for the random number generator, or ask the program to generate one for you. Unless you need to later reproduce exactly the same maze, you might as well have the program do it.

Depth first, Prim's algorithm You can choose between these two algorithms for maze. Only a computer scientist can tell the difference between them.

Tileable If you want to use it in a pattern, you can make the maze tileable by checking this check-button.

17.13.14 Qbist

17.13.14.1 Overview

Figure 17.316 Applying examples for the Qbist filter

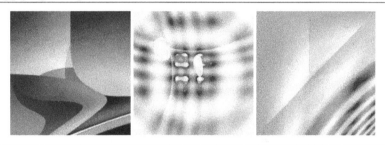

The Qbist filter generates random textures containing geometric figures and color gradients.

17.13.14.2 Activating the filter

This filter is found in the image window menu under Filters → Render → Pattern → Qbist...

17.13.14.3 Options

Figure 17.317 "Qbist" filter options

The Qbist filter generates random textures. A starting texture is displayed in the middle square, and different variations surround it. If you like one of the alternative textures, click on it. The chosen texture now turns up in the middle, and variations on that specific theme are displayed around it. When you have found the texture you want, click on it and then click OK. The texture will now appear on the currently active layer, completely replacing its previous contents.

Antialiasing If you check this, it will make edges appear smooth rather than stair-step-like.

Undo Lets you go back one step in history.

Open, Save These buttons allow you to save and reload your textures. This is quite handy because it's almost impossible to re-create a good pattern by just clicking around.

17.13.15 Sinus

17.13.15.1 Overview

Figure 17.318 Applying example for the Sinus filter

Filter "Sinus" applied

You can find this filter from the image menu through Filters → Render → Pattern → Sinus....

The Sinus filter lets you make sinusoidally based textures, which look rather like watered silk or maybe plywood. This plug-in works by using two different colors that you can define in the Colors tab. These two colors then create wave patterns based on a sine function.

You can set the X and Y scales, which determine how stretched or packed the texture will be. You can also set the Complexity of the function: a high value creates more interference or repetition in the pattern. An example is shown below.

17.13.15.2 Options

Figure 17.319 "Sinus" filter options (Settings)

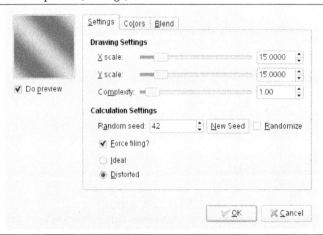

17.13.15.2.1 Settings Drawing Settings

X scale, Y scale A low X/Y value will maximize the horizontal/vertical stretch of the texture, whereas a high value will compress it.

Complexity This controls how the two colors interact with each other (the amount of interplay or repetition).

Calculation Settings

Random seed This option controls the random behaviour of the filter. If the same random seed in the same situation is used, the filter produces exactly the same results. A different random seed produces different results. Random seed can be entered manually or generated randomly by pressing the New Seed button.

When the Randomize option is checked, random seed cannot be entered manually, but is randomly generated each time the filter is run. If it is not checked, the filter remembers the last random seed used.

Force tiling? If you check this, you'll get a pattern that can be used for tiling. For example, you can use it as a background in an HTML page, and the tile edges will be joined seamlessly.

Ideal, Distorted This options give additional control of the interaction between the two colors. "Distorted" creates a more distorted interference between the two colors than "Ideal".

Figure 17.320 "Sinus" filter options (Colors)

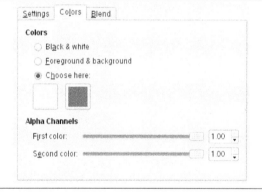

17.13.15.2.2 Colors

Colors Here, you set the two colors that make up your texture. You can use Black & white or the Foreground & background colors in the toolbox, or you can Choose a color with the color icons.

Alpha Channels This sliders allow you to assign an opacity to each of the colors. (If the layer you are working on does not have an alpha channel, they will be grayed out.)

Figure 17.321 "Sinus" filter options (Blend)

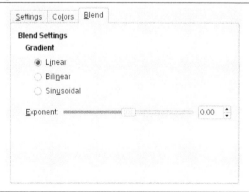

17.13.15.2.3 Blend

Gradient You can choose between three functions to set the shapes of the waves that are produced: Linear, Bilinear and Sinusoidal.

Exponent The Exponent controls which of the two colors is dominant, and how dominant it is. If you set the exponent to -7.5, the left color will dominate totally, and if you set it to +7.5 it will be the other way around. A zero value is neutral.

17.13.16 Circuit

17.13.16.1 Overview

Figure 17.322 Example of Circuit

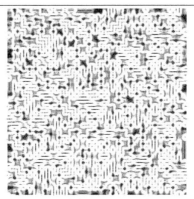

Filter "Circuit" applied.

Circuit command is a script that fills the selected region (or alpha) with traces like those on the back of an old circuit board. It looks even better when gradmapped with a suitable gradient.

Tip

 The effect seems to work best on odd shaped selections because of some limitations in the maze codes selection handling ability.

If the image is in indexed colors, this menu entry is grayed out and unavailable.

Note

 This filter creates a grey level image in RGB mode.

The resulting image doesn't depend on the original image.

17.13.16.2 Activate the filter

This filter is found in the image window menu under Filters → Render → Circuit....

17.13.16.3   Options

Figure 17.323 "Circuit" filter options

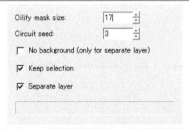

Oilify mask size With this option you can set the option value of the Oilify filter in pixels (range 3 to 50). Larger values make lines more fuzzy. 17 is the default value.

Circuit seed You can give a randomizing seed number between 1 and 3000000. The default value is 3.

No background (only for separate layer) If this option is enabled, dark pixels of the circuit are made transparent so that the underlying image is shown through these holes. This option is disabled in default settings. The Separate layer option is required.

Keep selection If an active selection exists when this script is called, you can keep the selection and its marching ants with this option. This option is enabled in default settings.

Separate layer If this option is not checked, the generated texture is drawn on the active layer. When this option is enabled (in default), this script adds a layer to draw the circuit texture is on.

17.13.16.4   Making the Circuit effect

The Circuit effect is achieved through the following steps:

1. First, draw maze with 5 pixels width pathways and walls with the "Depth First" algorithm. The pattern of maze is set by Circuit seed.

2. Oilify this maze with a brush of Oilify mask size.

3. Then apply the extract edge filter with Sobel algorithm, Smear option and Amount to 2.0, to the oilified maze image. This crowds high contrast winding curves like as a circuit map.

4. Finally, Desaturate the map with gray color in RGB mode.

17.13.17   Fractal Explorer

17.13.17.1   Overview

Figure 17.324 Example for the Fractal Explorer filter

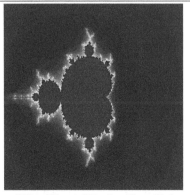

Filter "Fractal Explorer" applied

With this filter, you can create fractals and multicolored pictures verging to chaos. Unlike the IFS Fractal filter, with which you can fix the fractal structure precisely, this filter lets you perform fractals simply.

17.13.17.2   Starting filter

You can find this filter through Filters → Render → Fractal Explorer….

17.13.17.3   Options

Figure 17.325 "Fractal Explorer" filter options

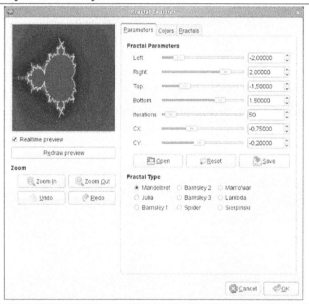

The Fractal Explorer window contains two panes: on the left there is the Preview pane with a Zoom feature, on the right you find the main options organized in tabs: Parameters, Colors, and Fractals.

17.13.17.3.1   Preview

Realtime preview Uncheck the Realtime preview only if your computer is slow. In this case, you can update preview by clicking on the Redraw preview button.

By clicking-dragging mouse pointer on preview, you can draw a rectangle delimiting an area which will be zoomed.

Zoom You have there some options to zoom in or zoom out. The Undo allows you to return to previous state, before zooming. The Redo allows you to reestablish the zoom you had undone, without having to re-create it with the Zoom In or Zoom Out buttons.

Figure 17.326 "Fractal Explorer" filter options (Parameters)

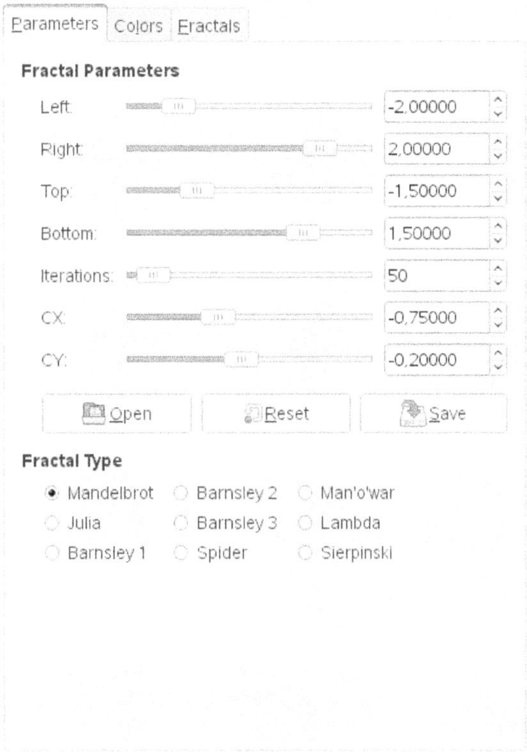

17.13.17.3.2   Parameters   This tab contains some options to set fractal calculation and select fractal type.

Fractal Parameters   Here, you have sliders and input boxes to set fractal spreading, repetition and aspect.

> **Left, Right, Top, Bottom**   You can set fractal spreading between a minimum and a maximum, in the horizontal and/or vertical directions. Values are from -3.0 to 3.0.

> **Iterations**   With this parameter, you can set fractal iteration, repetition and so detail. Values are from 0.0 to 1000.0

> **CX, CY**   With these parameters, you can change fractal aspect, in the horizontal (X) and/or vertical (Y) directions, except for Mandelbrot and Sierpinski types.

> **Open, Reset, Save**   With these three buttons, you can save your work with all its parameters, open a previously saved fractal, or return to the initial state before all modifications.

Fractal Type   You can choose what fractal type will be, for instance Mandelbrot, Julia, Barnsley or Sierpinski.

Figure 17.327 "Fractal Explorer" filter options (Colors)

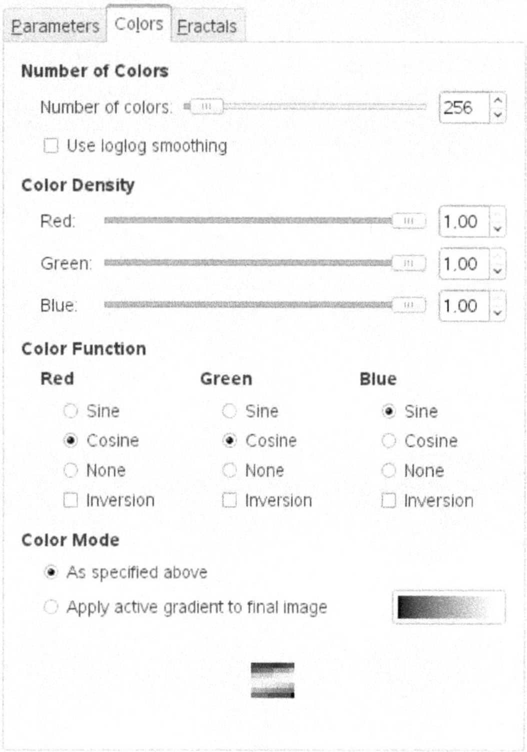

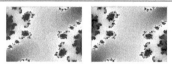

17.13.17.3.3 Colors This tab contains options for fractal color setting.
Number of Colors

Number of colors This slider and its input boxes allow you to set the number of colors for the fractal, between 2 and 8192. A palette of these colors is displayed at the bottom of the tab. Actually, that's a gradient between colors in fractal: you can change colors with "Color Density" and "Color Function" options. Fractal colors don't depend on colors of the original image (you can use a white image for fractals as well).

Use loglog smoothing If this option is checked, the band effect is smoothed.

Figure 17.328 Loglog smoothing example

Color density

Red, Green, Blue These three sliders and their text-boxes let you set the color intensity in the three color channels. Values vary from 0.0 to 1.0.

Color Function
For the Red, Green and Blue color channels, you can select how color will be treated:

Sine Color variations will be modulated according to the sine function.

Cosine Color densities will vary according to cosine function.

None Color densities will vary linearly.

Inversion If you check this option, function values will be inverted.

Color Mode

These options allow you to set where color values must be taken from.

As specified above Color values will be taken from the Color Density options.

Apply active gradient to final image Used colors will be that of active gradient. You should be able to select another gradient by clicking on the gradient source button.

Figure 17.329 "Fractal Explorer" filter options (Fractals)

17.13.17.3.4 Fractals This tab contains a big list of fractals with their parameters, that you can use as a model: only click on the wanted one.

The Refresh allows you to update the list if you have saved your work, without needing to re-start GIMP. You can delete the selected fractal from the list by clicking on the Delete.

17.13.18   Gfig

17.13.18.1   Overview

Figure 17.330 The same image, before and after using Gfig

(a) *Original image*   (b) *Filter "Gfig" applied*

This filter is a tool: You can create geometrical figures to add them to the image. It is very complex. I hope this paper will help you.

When using this filter, elements inserted in the image will be placed in a new layer. So the image will not be modified, all modifications occurring in this layer.

17.13.18.2   Starting filter

You can find this filter through Filters → Render → Gfig...

17.13.18.3   Options

Figure 17.331 "Gfig" filter options

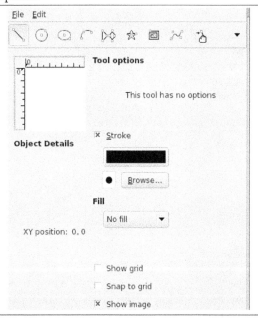

The Preview (with a horizontal and a vertical ruler) on the left of the main window actually is your working area where you are adding your figures.

You can add and modify figures using the Gfig tools (Gfig tool bar) and using the appropriate options (Gfig main window).

17.13.18.3.1   The Gfig tool bar   At the top of dialog, you can find a set of icons which represents the functions of this filter. Help pop-ups are explicit.

Functions for object drawing

On the left part of tool bar, you can find some functions for object drawing. You enable them by clicking on the corresponding icon. You can create the following objects (note that *Control points* are created at the same time as object):

Create line With this tool, you can draw lines. Click on Preview to mark start point, then drag mouse pointer to the end point.

Create rectangle With this tool, you can draw rectangles. Click on Preview to mark start point, then drag mouse pointer to create the rectangle.

Create circle With this tool, you can draw circles. Click on Preview to mark center, then drag mouse pointer to the wanted radius.

Create ellipse With this tool, you can draw ellipses. Click on Preview to mark center, then drag mouse pointer to get the wanted size and form.

Create arc With this tool, you can draw circle arcs. Click on Preview to set start point. Click again to set another arc point. Without releasing mouse button, drag pointer; when you release mouse button, the arc end point is placed and an arc encompassing these three points is drawn.

Create regular polygon With this tool, you can create a regular polygon. Start with setting side number in Tool Options at the right of Preview. Then click on Preview to place center and, without releasing mouse button, drag pointer to get the wanted size and orientation.

Create star With this tool, you can create a star. Start with setting side number (spikes) in Tool Options at the right of Preview. Then click on Preview to place center and, without releasing mouse button, drag pointer to get the wanted size and orientation.

Create spiral With this tool, you can create a spiral. Start with setting spire number (sides) and spire orientation in Tool Options at the right of Preview. Then click on Preview to place center and, without releasing mouse button, drag pointer to get the wanted size.

Create bezier curve With this tool, you can create Bézier curves. Click on Preview to set start point and the other points: the curve will be created between these points. To end point creation press **Shift** key when creating last point.

Functions for object management

In the middle of tool bar, you can find tools to manage objects:

Move an object With this tool, you can move the active object. To enable an object, click on a control point created at the same time as the object.

Move a single point With this tool, you can click-and-drag one of the control points created at the same time as object. Each of these points moves the object in a different way.

Copy an object With this tool, you can duplicate an object. Click on an object control point and drag it to the wanted place.

Delete an object Click on an object control point to delete it.

Select an object With this tool, you can select an object to active it. Simply click on one of its control points.

Functions for object organisation

At the right of tool bar, you can find tools for object superimposing (you can also get them by clicking on the drop-down list button if they are not visible). You have:

Up (Raise selected object), Down (Lower selected object) With this tool, you can push the selected object one level up or down.

Top, Bottom Self explanatory.

Functions for object display

Back, Forward These functions allow you to jump from one object to another. Only this object is displayed.

Show all objects This function shows all objects again, after using both previous functions.

> **Note**
>
> If your window is too small to show all icons, the tool bar provides a drop-down list which offers you the missing functions.

17.13.18.3.2 The Gfig main window

Object Details The XY position shows the position of your pointer.

Tool Options If the selected tool provides some options (like number of sides), you can change them here.

Stroke If this option is checked, the object will be drawn. Two buttons are available, to select color and brush type. Changes to color or brush apply to existing objects too.

Fill With help of this drop-down list, you can decide whether and how the object will be filled, with a color, a pattern or a gradient.

Show grid If this option is checked, a grid is applied on Preview to make object positioning easier.

Snap to grid If this option is checked, objects will align to the grid.

Show image When this option is checked, the current image is displayed in Preview (working area).

17.13.19 Lava

17.13.19.1 Overview

Figure 17.332 Example for the "Lava" filter

(a) *Original image*   (b) *"Lava" applied (on a selection)*

17.13.19.2 Activating the filter

This filter is found in the image window menu under Filters → Render → Lava....

17.13.19.3   Options

Figure 17.333 "Lava" options

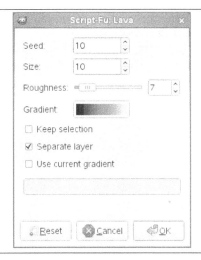

Seed TODO

Size TODO

Roughness TODO

Gradient TODO

Keep selection TODO

Separate layer TODO

Use current gradient TODO

17.13.20   Line Nova

17.13.20.1   Overview

Figure 17.334 Example for the "Line Nova" filter

(a) *Original image*   (b) *"Line Nova" applied*

The Line Nova filter fills a layer with rays emanating outward from the center of the layer using the foreground color shown in the Toolbox. The rays starts as one pixel and grew broader towards the edges of the layer.

> **Tip**
>
> This filter does not provide any option which allows you to set the center point of lines. If you need adjust the place of the radial lines where you want, create another transparent image and apply this filter on it, then add it on your image. Setting large size for the new nova image may help you not to break lines inside of your image.

17.13.20.2 Activating the filter

This filter is found in the image window menu under Filters → Render → Line Nova....

17.13.20.3 Options

Figure 17.335 "Line Nova" options

Number of lines By using this option you can set the number of lines between 40 to 1000. The default is 200.

Sharpness (degrees) This slider determines how much the rays will broaden towards the edges. The range goes from 0.0 to 10.0. If set to 0.0, nothing will be drawn. If set to 10.0, most of the area near the edges of the layer will be painted.

Figure 17.336 "Line Nova" sharpness option

From left to right: sharpness = 1; sharpness = 5; sharpness = 10

Offset radius Here you choose the distance, in pixels, from center to the starting point of the rays. If set to 0.0 the rays starts from the center. Any other value will let the starting points be on a circle at the selected distance from the center. The maximum distance is 2000 pixels. The default value is 100 pixels.

Figure 17.337 "Line Nova" offset radius option

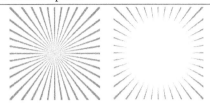

From left to right: offset radius = 0; offset radius = 50

Randomness If this slider is set to a value higher than 1, the starting point for each ray differ more or less randomly from the average starting point set as the offset radius above. With the value set to 1, all the rays will start at the circle determined by the offset radius. The maximum value is 2000. The default value is 30.

Figure 17.338 "Line Nova" randomness option

From left to right: randomness = 1; randomness = 50

17.13.21   Sphere Designer

17.13.21.1   Overview

Figure 17.339 The same image, before and after the application of "Sphere Designer" filter.

(a) *Original image*   (b) *Filter "Sphere Designer" applied*

This filter creates a three dimensional sphere with different textures. It replaces the original image.

17.13.21.2   Activating Sphere Designer

You can find this filter through Filters → Render → Sphere Designer....

17.13.21.3 Options

Figure 17.340 "Sphere Designer" filter parameters

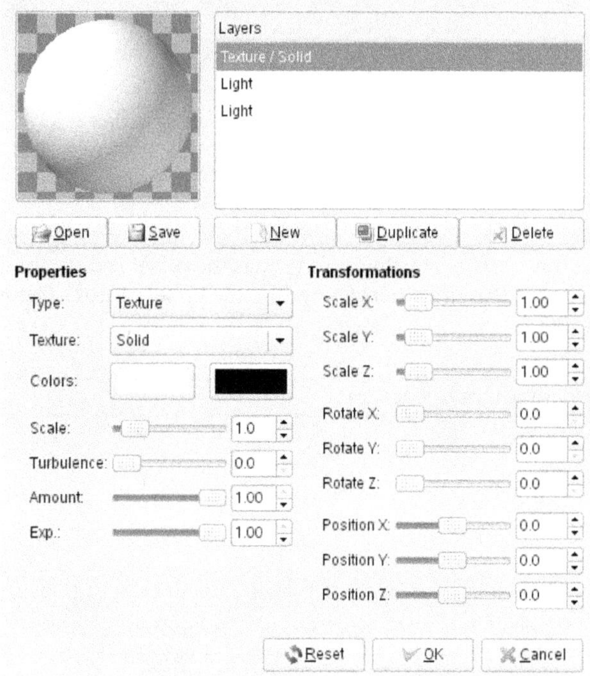

Preview All your setting changes will appear in the Preview without affecting the image until you click on OK. Note that the preview displays the whole image, even if the final result will concern a selection. Click the button *Update Preview* to see the result of the current settings.

Textures

The list of textures applied to the sphere. There textures are applied in the order listed. Each item shows the type and the name of the texture.

New Creates a new texture and adds it to the end of the list. The name and the features of this new texture are the ones which are displayed in the Texture Properties area, but you can change them by operating in this area, provided that your new texture is highlighted.

Duplicate Copies the selected texture and adds the copy to the end of the list.

Delete Deletes the selected texture from the list.

Open, Save Allows to save current settings or load previously saved settings.

Properties

Type Determines the type of action on the sphere.

> **Texture** Covers the sphere with a specific pattern.
>
> **Bumpmap** Gives some relief to the texture.
>
> **Light** Lets you set the parameters of the light shining on the sphere.

Texture Determines the pattern used by the texture type. If the texture applies to light then the light is distorted by this texture as if it was going through this texture before falling onto the sphere. If the texture applies to the texture itself, the texture is applied directly to the sphere. Several options are available.

Colors Sets the two colors to be used for a texture. By pressing the color button a color selection dialog appears.

Scale Determines the size of separate elements composing the texture. For example, for the "Checker" texture this parameter determines the size of black and white squares. Value range is from 0 to 10.

Turbulence Determines the degree of texture distortion before applying the texture to the sphere. Value range is from 0 to 10. With values of up to 1.0 you can still make out the undistorted patterns; beyond that the texture gradually turns into noise.

Amount Determines the degree of influence the texture has on the final result. Value range is from 0 to 1. With the value of 0 the texture does not affect the result.

Exponent With the Wood texture, this options gives an aspect of venetian blind, more or less open.

Transformations

Scale X, Scale Y, Scale Z Determines the degree of stretching/compression of the texture on the sphere along the three directions. The value range is from 0 to 10.

Rotate X, Rotate Y, Rotate Z Determines the amount of a turn of the texture on the sphere around the three axes. The value range is from 0 to 360.

Position X, Position Y, Position Z Determines the position of the texture relative to the sphere. When type is Light, this parameter refers to the position of the light floodlighting the sphere.

The Reset button sets all parameters to the default values.

17.13.22 Spyrogimp

17.13.22.1 Overview

Figure 17.341 Example for the "Spyrogimp" filter

(a) *Original image*   (b) *"Spyrogimp" applied*

17.13.22.2 Activating the filter

This filter is found in the image window menu under Filters → Render → Spyrogimp....

17.13.22.3 Options

Figure 17.342 "Spyrogimp" options

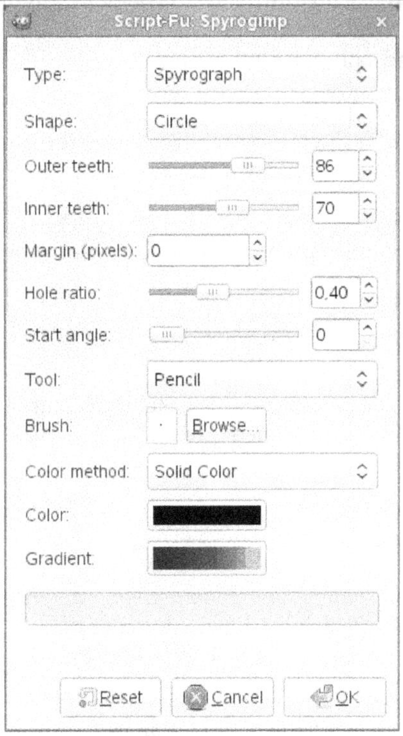

Type TODO

Shape TODO

Outer teeth TODO

Inner teeth TODO

Margin (pixels) TODO

Hole ratio TODO

Start angle TODO

Tool TODO

Brush TODO

Color method TODO

Color TODO

Gradient TODO

17.14   Web Filters

17.14.1   Introduction

Figure 17.343 The Web filters menu

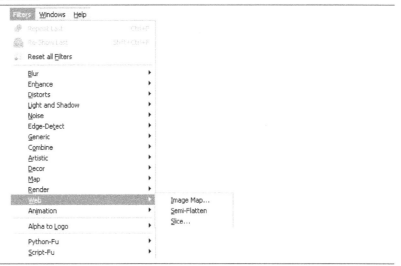

This filters are mostly used on images mentioned for web sites. The filter ImageMap is used to add clickable "hot spots" on the image. The filter Semi-Flatten is used to simulate semi-transparency in image formats without alpha channel. The Slice filter creates HTML tables of sensitive images.

17.14.2   ImageMap

In Web sensitive images are frequently used to get some effects when defined areas are enabled by the pointer. Obviously the most used effect is a dynamic link to another web page when one of the sensitive areas is clicked on. This "filter" allows you to design easily sensitive areas within an image. Web site design softwares have this as a standard function. In GIMP you can do this in a similar way.

17.14.2.1   Overview

This plug-in lets you design graphically and friendly all areas you want to delimit over your displayed image. You get the relevant part of html tags that must be merged into the right place in your page html code. You can define some actions linked to these areas too.

This is a complex tool which is not completely described here (it works about like Web page makers offering this function). However we want to describe here some of the most current handlings. If you want, you can find a more complete descriptions in Grokking the GIMP with the link [GROKKING02].

17.14.2.2   Activate the filter

From an image window, you can find this filter through Filters → Web → ImageMap...

The window is a small one, but you can magnify it. The main useful areas are:

- completely on the left are vertically displayed icons, one for pointing, three for calling tools to generate various shape areas, one to edit zone properties, and finally one to erase a selected zone; you can call these functions with the Mapping menu,

- just on the right is your working area where you can draw all the shapes areas you want with the relevant tools,

- on the right is displayed an icon vertical set; its use is obvious but a help pop-up gives you some information about each function,

- finally, even on the right is a display area, as a property list of the created areas. A click on one item of the list selects automatically the corresponding shape in the working area,

17.14.2.3   **Options**

Figure 17.344 Imagemap filter options

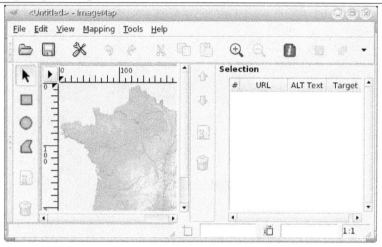

Imagemap window

17.14.2.3.1   **The Menu Bar**   The menu bar is similar to the image window menu bar, only a few menus or menu entries are different:

File

> **Save; Save As**   Contrary to other filters, this plug-in doesn't make an image but a text file. So you must save your work in a text format.

> > Tip
> >
> > 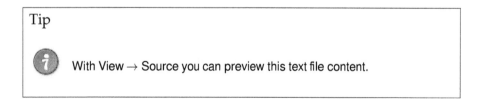 With View → Source you can preview this text file content.

> **Open; Open recent**   In the plug-in you can open the saved text file. The areas defined in your file will be loaded and overdisplayed; if the displayed image is not the original one or not with the same size, GIMP will ask you for adapting the scale.

Edit

> **Edit area info**

Figure 17.345 Editing an imagemap area

In the settings dialog you can edit the area information of a selected area. This dialog will pop up automatically whenever you create a new area.

View This menu offers you special functions:

Area list Here you can hide or show the selection area.

Source Here you see the raw data as you would save it to or read it from a file.

Color; Grayscale You can select the image mode here and work with a Grayscale display.

Mapping You will seldom use this menu, since you can more easily access selection tools by clicking on icons on the left of the working area.

Arrow The arrow here represents the Move tool. When activated tool is selected, you can select and move an area on the image.

With a polygon, you can use the arrow to move one of the red points. Right-click on a segment between two red points to open a pop-up menu that offers, with several others, the possibility to add a new point. If you right-click on a red point, you can remove it.

Rectangle; Circle; Polygon These tools let you create various shape areas: click on the image, move the pointer, and click again.

Edit Map Info

Figure 17.346 Editing the imagemap data

With this simple dialog you can enter some items, which will be written to the resulting output file; either as comments (Author, Description) or as attribute values of the HTML tags (Image name, Title, Default URL).

Tools With the "Tools" menu you can create guides and even regularly spaced rectangular areas.

> **Grid; Grid settings**

Figure 17.347 Grid options

Here you can enable and disable the image grid or configure some grid properties.

> **Use GIMP guides; Create guides** The guide lines are created at the border of the image but can be moved around by clicking on the red squares on each line something similar to the GIMP guide lines. By using the guides you are able to create active rectangles in the image.

Create guides

Figure 17.348 Guide options

The guide options

Instead of creating geometrical shapes to select the active areas you may use an array of rectangles, each representing an active area, by clicking on the "Create guides". In the menu popping up you set the width and height of the rectangles, the space between them, the number of rows and columns, and the upper and left startpoint for the array. All measures are in pixels. If you are not satisfied with the result you may adjust each rectangle by moving the red squares as usual.

17.14.2.3.2   The Tool Bar   Most entries here are just shortcuts for some functions already described. Exceptions:

Move to Front; Send to Back   Here you can move an area entry to the bottom ("Move to Front") or top ("Send to Back") of the area list.

Figure 17.349 The Working Area

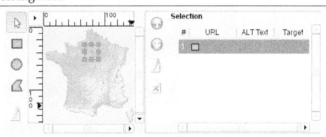

17.14.2.3.3   The Working Area   In the main area of the imagemap window, on the left side, you will find your working area where you can draw all the shapes areas you want with the relevant tools.

Beside the working area there are vertically displayed icons, one for pointing, three for calling tools to generate various shape areas, one to edit zone properties, and finally one to erase a selected zone; you can call these functions with the Mapping menu too.

Caution

   Note that the areas should not overlap.

17.14.2.3.4   The selection area   On the right is a display area, as a property list of the created areas. A click on one item of the list selects automatically the corresponding shape in the working area, then you can modify it.

Beside the display is an icon vertical set; its use is obvious but a help pop-up gives you some information about each function.

Unfortunately, the arrow symbols for moving a list entry up or down do not work here. But of course you carefully avoided to create overlapping areas, so you do not use these functions at all.

17.14.3 Semi-Flatten

17.14.3.1 Overview

The Semi-flatten filter helps those in need of a solution to anti-aliasing indexed images with transparency. The GIF indexed format supports complete transparency (0 or 255 alpha value), but not semi-transparency (1 - 254): semi-transparent pixels will be transformed to no transparency or complete transparency, ruining anti-aliasing you applied to the logo you want to put onto your Web page.

Before applying the filter, it's essential that you should know the background color of your Web page. Use the color-picker to determine the exact color which pops up as the Foreground color of the Toolbox. Invert FG/BG colors so that BG color is the same as Web background color.

Semi-flatten process will combine FG color to layer (logo) color, proportionally to corresponding alpha values, and will rebuild correct anti-aliasing. Completely transparent pixels will not take the color. Very transparent pixels will take a few color and weakly transparent will take much color.

17.14.3.2 Activate the filter

You can access this filter in the image window menu through Filters → Web → Semi-Flatten. It is available if your image holds an Alpha channel (see Section 16.7.33). Otherwise, it is greyed out.

17.14.3.3 Example

In the example below, the Toolbox Background color is pink, and the image has feathered edges on a transparent background.

Figure 17.350 Semi-Flatten example

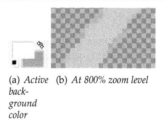

(a) *Active background color*   (b) *At 800% zoom level*

Full transparency is kept. Semi-tranparent pixels are colored with pink according to their transparency (Alpha value). This image will well merge into the pink background of the new page.

Figure 17.351 Semi-Flatten filter applied

Result, in GIF format, after applying Semi-flatten filter.

17.14.4   Slice

17.14.4.1   Overview

Figure 17.352 Example for the "Slice" filter

(a) *Original image with guides*   (b) *"Slice" applied*

This filter is a simple and easy to use helper for creating sensitive images to be used in HTML files. The filter slices up the source image (like the Guillotine command does) along its horizontal and vertical guides, and produces a set of sub-images. At the same time it creates a piece of HTML code for a table saved in a text file. Every table cell contains one part of the image. The text file should then be embedded in an HTML document.

Note that this filter is really a very simple helper. A typical HTML code produced by the filter may be not much more than this:

Example 17.1 Simple "Slice" filter example output

```
<table cellpadding="0" border="0" cellspacing="0">
  <tr>
    <td><img alt="" src="slice_0_0.png"/></td>
    <td><img alt="" src="slice_0_1.png"/></td>
  </tr>
  <tr>
    <td><img alt="" src="slice_1_0.png"/></td>
    <td><img alt="" src="slice_1_1.png"/></td>
  </tr>
</table>
```

Produced HTML code; the "style" attribute has been omitted.

When there are no guides in the image, the filter will no nothing. If, however, the guides are just hidden, the filter will work.

Tip

The ImageMap filter is a much more powerful and sophisticated tool for creating sensitive images. (But it is also much more complex...)

17.14.4.2   Activate the filter

This filter is found in the image window menu under Filters → Web → Slice....

17.14.4.3 Options

Figure 17.353 "Slice" options

Cuts an image along its guides, creates images and a HTML table snippet

Path for HTML export	tmp ▼
Filename for export	slice.html
Image name prefix	slice
Image format	● gif
	○ jpg
	○ png
Separate image folder	No
Folder for image export	images
Space between table elements	0
Javascript for onmouseover and clicked	No
Skip animation for table caps	Yes

Most options are self-explanatory, but nevertheless:

Path for HTML export Where the HTML file and the image files will be saved. By default these files will be stored in the current working directory. Clicking on the button to the right opens a pull-down menu, where you can select a different location.

Filename for export The name of the HTML file. You can change the filename using the textbox.

Image name prefix The name of an image file produced by this filter is `prefix_i_k.ext`, where `prefix` is that part of the filename which you can freely select using the textbox to the right, by default: `slice`. (i and k are the numbers of the row and the column, each starting with 0; `.ext` is the filename extension depending on the selected Image format.)

This option is particularly useful when you want to create JavaScript for onmouseover and clicked and need different sets of images.

Image format You can choose to create image files in the GIF, JPG, or PNG file format.

Separate image folder, Folder for image export When Separate image folder is enabled, a folder will be created where the image files will be placed. By default, the name of this destination folder is `images`, but you can change it in the Folder for image export textbox.

Example 17.2 With separate image folder

```
<table>
  <tr>
    <td><img src="images/slice_0_0.png"/></a></td>
```

Result of enabled "Separate image folder"

Space between table elements This value (0-15) will be passed as "cellspacing" attribute to the HTML table. The result is, that horizontal and vertical guides will be replaced with stripes of the specified width:

Example 17.3 Space between table elements

```
<table cellspacing="5">
```

Corresponding HTML code snippet

Note that the image will not be enlarged by the size of these stripes. Instead, the resulting HTML image will look like you have drawn the stripes with the Eraser tool.

JavaScript for onmouseover and clicked When this option is enabled, the filter will also add some JavaScript code. Like the HTML code, this code does not work as is, rather it's a good starting point for adding some dynamic functionality. The JavaScript code provides a function to handle events like "onmouseover":

Example 17.4 JavaScript code snippet

```
function exchange (image, images_array_name, event)
  {
    name = image.name;
    images = eval (images_array_name);

    switch (event)
      {
        case 0:
          image.src = images[name + "_plain"].src;
          break;
        case 1:
          image.src = images[name + "_hover"].src;
          break;
        case 2:
          image.src = images[name + "_clicked"].src;
          break;
        case 3:
          image.src = images[name + "_hover"].src;
          break;
      }
  }
```

Skip animation for table caps When disabled, the filter will add a `<a href="#">` ... `</a>` hyperlink stub to every table cell. When enabled (this is the default) and there are at least two horizontal or two vertical guides, the filter will not add a hyperlink stub to the first and last cell in a column or row. This may be useful when you have an image with border and you don't want to make the border sensitive.

Example 17.5 Skipped animation for table caps (simplified HTML code)

```
<table cellpadding="0" border="0" cellspacing="0">
  <tr>
    <td><img alt="" src="images/slice_0_0.png"/></td>
    <td><img alt="" src="images/slice_0_1.png"/></td>
    <td><img alt="" src="images/slice_0_2.png"/></td>
    <td><img alt="" src="images/slice_0_3.png"/></td>
  </tr>
  <tr>
    <td><img alt="" src="images/slice_1_0.png"/></td>
    <td><a href="#"><img alt="" src="images/slice_1_1.png"/></a></td>
    <td><a href="#"><img alt="" src="images/slice_1_2.png"/></a></td>
    <td><img alt="" src="images/slice_1_3.png"/></td>
  </tr>
  <tr>
    <td><img alt="" src="images/slice_2_0.png"/></td>
    <td><img alt="" src="images/slice_2_1.png"/></td>
    <td><img alt="" src="images/slice_2_2.png"/></td>
    <td><img alt="" src="images/slice_2_3.png"/></td>
  </tr>
</table>
```

Only inner cells have (empty) hyperlinks.

17.15 Animation Filters

17.15.1 Introduction

Figure 17.354 The Animation filters menu

These are animation helpers, which let you view and optimize your animations (by reducing their size). We gathered "Optimize (Difference)" and "Optimize (GIF)" filters together, because they are not much different.

17.15.2 Blend

17.15.2.1 Overview

Figure 17.355 Example for the "Blend" filter: original image

4 frames of 5 frames (white background layer omitted)

Figure 17.356 Example for the "Blend" filter: filter applied

First 8 (of 16) frames

17.15.2.2 Activating the filter

This filter is found in the image window menu under Filters → Animation → Blend....

17.15.2.3 Options

Figure 17.357 "Blend" options

Intermediate frames TODO

Max. blur radius TODO

Looped TODO

17.15.3 Burn-In

17.15.3.1 Overview

Figure 17.358 Example for the "Burn-In" filter: original image

Opaque background layer and foreground layer with transparency

Figure 17.359 Example for the "Burn-In" filter: filter applied

Resulting image with 8 frames (depending on size and speed)

17.15.3.2 Activating the filter

This filter is found in the image window menu under Filters → Animation → Burn-In....

17.15.3.3 Options

Figure 17.360 "Burn-In" options

Glow color TODO

Fadeout TODO

Fadeout width TODO

Corona width TODO

After glow TODO

Add glowing TODO

Prepare for GIF TODO

Speed (pixels/frame) TODO

17.15.4   Rippling

17.15.4.1   Overview

Figure 17.361 Example for the "Rippling" filter

(a) *Original image*   (b) *A "Rippled" frame*

17.15.4.2   Activating the filter

This filter is found in the image window menu under Filters → Animation → Rippling....

17.15.4.3   Options

Figure 17.362 "Rippling" options

Rippling strength TODO

Number of frames TODO

Edge behavior TODO

17.15.5   Spinning Globe

17.15.5.1   Overview

Figure 17.363 Example for the "Spinning Globe" filter: original image

Original image

Figure 17.364 Example for the "Spinning Globe" filter: filter applied

3 (of 10) "Spinning Globe" frames (on a white background)

17.15.5.2   Activating the filter

This filter is found in the image window menu under Filters → Animation → Spinning Globe….

17.15.5.3   Options

Figure 17.365 "Spinning Globe" options

Frames   TODO

Turn from left to right   TODO

Transparent background TODO

Index to n colors TODO

Work on copy TODO

17.15.6 Waves

17.15.6.1 Overview

Figure 17.366 Example for the "Waves" filter

(a) *Original image*   (b) *A "Wave" frame*

17.15.6.2 Activating the filter

This filter is found in the image window menu under Filters → Animation → Waves....

17.15.6.3 Options

Figure 17.367 "Waves" options

Amplitude TODO

Wavelength TODO

Number of frames TODO

Invert direction TODO

17.15.7 Optimize

17.15.7.1 Overview

An animation can contain several layers and so its size can be important. This is annoying for a Web page. The Optimize filters let you reduce this size. Many elements are shared by all layers in an animation; so they can be saved only once instead of being saved in all layers, and what has changed in each layer can be saved only.

GIMP offers two Optimize filters: Optimize (Difference) and Optimize (GIF). Their result doesn't look very different.

17.15.7.2 Activate filters

You can find these filters in the image menu:

- Filters → Animation → Optimize (Difference)

- Filters → Animation → Optimize (for GIF)

- Filters → Animation → Unoptimize

17.15.7.3 Example for the Optimize animation filters

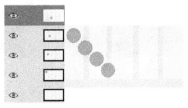

Original image

In this animation, the red ball goes downwards and past vertical bars. File size is 600 Kb.

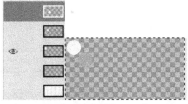

Optimize (Difference)

File size moved to 153 Kb. Layers held only the part the background which will be used to remove the trace of the red ball. The common part of layers is transparent.

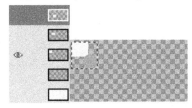

Optimize (GIF)

File size moved to 154 Kb, a bit bigger in the present example, but layer size has been reduced. Layers held only a rectangular selection which includes the part of the background which will be used to remove the trace of the red ball. The common part of layers is transparent.

17.15.7.4 Unoptimize

The "Unoptimize" filter removes any optimizations on a layer-based animation. You may need this command if you want to edit the animation and it's not possible or not useful to undo any changes and start editing from the original image.

17.15.8 Playback

17.15.8.1 Overview

This plug-in lets you play an animation from a multi-layers image (that could be saved in the GIF, MNG or even XCF format), to test it.

17.15.8.2 Activate the filter

You can find this filter through Filters → Animation → Playback...

17.15.8.3 Options

Figure 17.368 "Playback" filter options

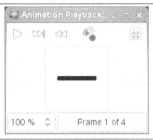

This dialog has:

Preview This preview of the animation automatically fits the frame size. The number of the displayed frame is shown below the preview.

Buttons Three buttons are available:

> **Play/Stop** Play/Stop to play or stop the animation.
>
> **Rewind** Rewind to re-launch the animation from start.
>
> **Step** Step to play the animation step by step.

17.16 Alpha to Logo Filters

17.16.1 Introduction

Figure 17.369 The Alpha to Logo filters menu

These filters correspond to the logo-generating Script-Fu scripts. They add all kinds of special effects to the alpha channel of the active layer (that is, to the pixels with a non-zero alpha value).

Note

 The menu items and the corresponding functions are enabled only if the active layer has an alpha channel. If you see that the menu items are grayed out, try to add an alpha channel.

The filter effect will always be applied according to the alpha values. The alpha of any pixel has a value ranging from 0 (transparent) to 255 (fully opaque). It is possible to apply a filter only *partially* to some (or all) pixels by using alpha values from 1 to 254.

You will notice that this is similar to selecting pixels partially. In fact, internally these filters always create a selection from the alpha channel by transferring the alpha values to the channel which represents the selection, and then work on the selection.

How to apply an "Alpha to Logo" filter to a selection?

1. If the active layer is the background layer, make sure that an alpha channel exists, otherwise add an alpha channel.

Tip

 If a layer name in the Layer Dialog is in bold, then this layer has no Alpha channel.

---

2. Invert the selection: Select → Invert.

3. Remove the (inverted) selection: Edit → Clear.

4. Apply the "Alpha to Logo" filter (the filters ignore the selection, you don't need to re-invert the selection).

17.16.2   3D Outline

17.16.2.1   Overview

Figure 17.370 Example for the "3D Outline" filter

         (a) *The "3D Outline" filter*   (b) *The "3D Outline" logo*

This filter is derived from the "3D Outline" script (File → Create → Logos → 3D Outline in the image window), which creates a logo (see above) with outlined text and a drop shadow.

The filter outlines the non-transparent areas of the active layer (determined from the Alpha channel) with a pattern and adds a drop shadow. Here, we will use the *alpha* term to refer to these areas of the active layer defined by the non-transparent pixels.

The filter uses the Sobel edge detect filter to get the alpha's outline. So with a simple alpha, for example a cleared rectangle selection, you will just get the boundary. But when you use a layer mask (don't forget to Apply the Layer Mask), as in the following example, the edge detector will find more edges and thus the filter effect will be applied to these edges too.

Figure 17.371 Example based on multicolored layer mask

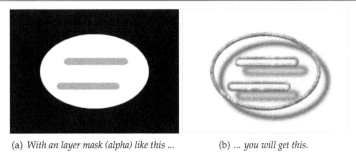

(a) *With an layer mask (alpha) like this ...*   (b) *... you will get this.*

Warning

  The image will always be resized to the active layer's size.

17.16.2.2   Activate the filter

This filter is found in the image window menu under Filters → Alpha to Logo → 3D Outline….

The filter only works if the active layer has an alpha channel. Otherwise, the menu entry is insensitive and grayed out.

17.16.2.3   Options

Figure 17.372 "3D Outline" options

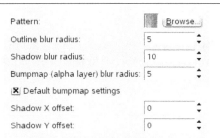

Pattern Here you can see and change the currently selected pattern. When you click on the pattern, an enlarged preview will popup. Pressing the Browse... button opens a dialog where you can select a different pattern.

Outline blur radius This radius is used to blur the alpha before the edge detector will select the area to be filled with the pattern. That's why a high value results in a wide but smeared pattern:

Figure 17.373 Outline blur radius example

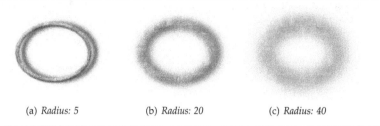

(a) *Radius: 5*   (b) *Radius: 20*   (c) *Radius: 40*

Shadow blur radius This radius is used to blur the drop shadow. A high value will smear the shadow:

Figure 17.374 Shadow blur radius example

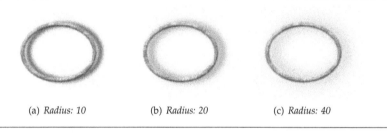

(a) *Radius: 10*   (b) *Radius: 20*   (c) *Radius: 40*

Bumpmap (alpha layer) blur radius The Bump Map used to create a 3D effect is the active layer (alpha layer) with the edge detect filter applied. Before it is used to emboss the pattern layer, another Gaussian blur will be applied with the specified radius. So a high value will reduce the 3D effect.

Default bumpmap settings If checked (this is the default) the bump map plug-in will be applied with its default options. Otherwise, the Bump Map dialog window will popup while the filter is running, and you can choose different options. Note that, when you close the window pressing the **Cancel** button, no bump map at all will be applied.

Shadow X offset; Shadow Y offset This is the amount of pixels the shadow layer will me moved to the right (X) and down (Y). Then the layer will be clipped to the image size. Note that there is no real background layer, and moving the shadow will clear its original place:

Figure 17.375 Shadow offset example

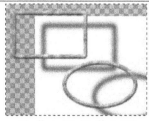

X offset: 50; Y offset: 20

17.16.3 Alien Glow

17.16.3.1 Overview

Figure 17.376 Example for the "Alien Glow" filter

(a) *The "Alien Glow" filter*   (b) *The "Alien Glow" logo*

This filter adds an eerie glow around the active layer's alpha.

The filter is derived from the "Alien Glow" script (File → Create → Logos → Alien Glow in the image window), which creates a logo with the above text effect.

> Warning
>
> The image will always be resized to the active layer's size.

17.16.3.2 Activate the filter

You can find this filter in the image window menu under Filters → Alpha to Logo → Alien Glow....

17.16.3.3 Options

Figure 17.377 "Alien Glow" options

Glow size (pixels * 4) This is actually the font size option of the "Alien Glow" Script-Fu script. However, two values will be set in relation to this size: the glow will be enlarged by "Glow size" / 30, and feather radius is "Glow size" / 4. You should probably choose the height of your objects for this option (ignore "pixels * 4").

Glow color This is the color of the "eerie" glowing. Of course it defaults to green (63,252,0), but a click on the swatch button brings up the color selector where you can choose any color.

17.16.3.4 Filter details

Reproducing an eerie alien glow is easy:

- If necessary, **create a** selection from the alpha channel of the active layer.

- Fill the selection with the following Gradient Blend: Shape = Shaped (spherical); Gradient = FG to BG (RGB), with FG = dark gray (79,79,79), BG = black.

- Create a new layer ("Alien Glow") below. Extend the selection slightly, feather it, and fill it with the Glow color.

- Create a new background layer filled with black.

17.16.4 Alien Neon

17.16.4.1 Overview

Figure 17.378 Example for the "Alien Neon" filter

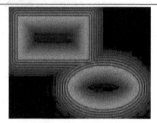

"Alien Neon" applied

Caution

   Sorry, there is no documentation for this filter as yet.

17.16.4.2 Activate the filter

This filter is found in the image window menu under Filters → Alpha to Logo → Alien Neon....

17.16.4.3 Options

Figure 17.379 "Alien Neon" options

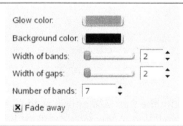

Glow color TODO

Background color TODO

Width of bands TODO

Width of gaps TODO

Number of bands TODO

Fade away TODO

17.16.5 Basic I & II

17.16.5.1 Overview

Figure 17.380 Examples for the "Basic" filters

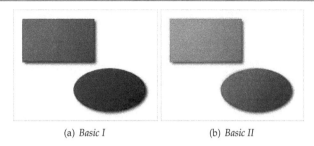

(a) *Basic I*   (b) *Basic II*

These filters add a gradient effect to the alpha channel of active layer as well as a drop shadow and a background layer.

The "Basic II" also adds a highlight layer.

> **Warning**
>
> The image will always be resized to the active layer's size.

The filters are derived from the "Basic I" and "Basic II" logo scripts (see File → Create → Logos), which draw a text with the filter effect, e.g.

The "Basic I" logo script.

17.16.5.2 Activate the filter

You can find the filter in the image window menu under Filters → Alpha to Logo → Basic I... and Filters → Alpha to Logo → Basic II....

17.16.5.3 Options

Figure 17.381 "Basic" filter options

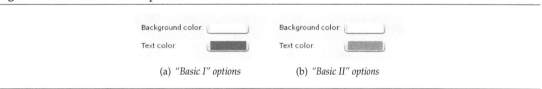

(a) *"Basic I" options*   (b) *"Basic II" options*

Background color This color is used to fill the background layer created by the filter. It defaults to white. When you click on the color swatch button, a color selector pops up where you can select any other color.

Text color The name of this option refers to the text color of the logo scripts that were mentioned above. Here this color — by default blue (6,6,206) for "Basic I" and red (206,6,50) for "Basic II" — sets the basic color of the gradient effect: this is the color the alpha channel will be filled with before the gradient effect will be applied.

17.16.5.4 Filter details

You can reproduce the gradient effect manually by using the Blend tool with the following options:

- Mode: Multiply,
- Gradient: FG to BG (RGB), where FG is white and BG is black,
- Offset: 20,
- Shape: Radial,
- Dithering: checked.

17.16.6 Blended

17.16.6.1 Overview

Figure 17.382 Example for the "Blended" filter

"Blended" applied

Caution

 Sorry, there is no documentation for this filter as yet.

17.16.6.2 Activate the filter

This filter is found in the image window menu under Filters → Alpha to Logo → Blended....

17.16.6.3 Options

Figure 17.383 "Blended" options

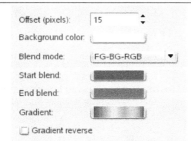

Offset (pixels) TODO

Backgroundcolor TODO

Blend mode TODO

Start blend TODO

End blend TODO

Gradient TODO

Gradient reverse TODO

17.16.7 Bovination

17.16.7.1 Overview

Figure 17.384 Example for the "Bovination" filter

"Bovination" applied

This filter adds "cow spots" to the active layer alpha channel.

> **Warning**
>
> The image will always be resized to the active layer's size.

17.16.7.2 Activate the filter

You can find this filter in the image window menu under Filters → Alpha to Logo → Bovination....

17.16.7.3 Options

Figure 17.385 "Bovination" options

Spots density X, Spots density Y The horizontal (X) and vertical (Y) spots density will be used by the Solid Noise filter as X Size and Y Size options. So these values range from 1 to 16, with high values resulting in many spots in the respective dimension, low values resulting in few spots.

Figure 17.386 "Spots density" examples

(a) *Maximum X density, min-imum Y density*   (b) *Maximum Y density, min-imum X density*

Background Color This is the color used to fill the "Background" layer; it defaults to white. When you click on the color button, you may choose any other color in the color selector dialog.

17.16.7.4 Filter details

The filter fills the alpha channel with Solid Noise:

... and maximizes the Contrast:

Besides, the filter adds a Blur layer as a light gray shadow and uses this layer as a Bump Map. Finally a (by default) white "Background" layer is added below.

So the filter will end up with these layers:[7]

17.16.8 Chalk

17.16.8.1 Overview

Figure 17.387 Example for the "Chalk" filter

(a) *Original image*   (b) *"Chalk" applied*

---

[7] If the active layer is not the top layer, it might happen that the filter messes up the layers. Then you will have to raise the active layer.

This filter creates a chalk drawing effect for the active layer.

It is derived from the "Chalk" script (File → Create → Logos → Chalk in the image window), which creates a logo from a text of your choice, for instance:

The "Chalk" logo

> **Warning**
>
> The image will always be resized to the active layer's size.

17.16.8.2 Activate the filter

You can find this filter in the image window menu under Filters → Alpha to Logo → Chalk....

17.16.8.3 Options

Figure 17.388 "Chalk" option

Background color The background color is the color of the "blackboard" you are drawing on with chalk, and of course it's black. When you click on the color button, the color selector pops up and you may select any other color.

17.16.8.4 Filter details

The "Chalk" filter

1. applies a Gaussian blur to the layer, spreads the pixels, and ripples the layer horizontally and vertically,

2. extracts edges using the Sobel edge detect filter, and

> **Note**
>
> Sometimes the sobel edge detect produces some garbage at the image sides.

3. increases the luminosity level.

Unfortunately you cannot change the tool and filter options. But you may reproduce the process step by step using the methods listed above, varying the respective options. Then you just have to add a background layer filled with any color. That's all.

17.16.9 Chip Away

17.16.9.1 Overview

Figure 17.389 Example for the "Chip Away" filter

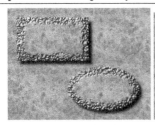

(a) *The "Chip Away" filter*   (b) *The "Chip Away" logo*

This filter adds a chipped woodcarving effect to the alpha channel of the active layer. Optionally it adds a drop shadow to the image. The content of the active layer doesn't matter, only the shape of its alpha channel does.

> **Warning**
>
> The image will always be resized to the active layer's size.

The filter is derived from the "Chip Away" Script-Fu script (File → Create → Logos → Chip Away), which creates a text logo with the effect shown above.

17.16.9.2 Activate the filter

This filter is found in the image window menu under Filters → Alpha to Logo → Chip Away....

17.16.9.3 Options

Figure 17.390 "Chip Away" options

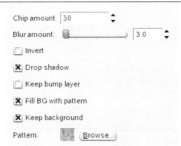

Chip amount This option lets you vary the size of chipping area. But note that "Chip amount" is not the size of this area in pixels. It is used as the maximum amount pixels are randomly spread by the Spread filter applied to the bump map. Valid range is 0-200.

Figure 17.391 "Chip amount" examples

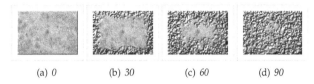

(a) *0*   (b) *30*   (c) *60*   (d) *90*

Blur amount The specified value will be passed as "Radius" option to the Gaussian blur filter, which will blur the bump layer by this amount.

Invert If checked, the bump map will be inverted and will create hollows instead of bumps, which makes the image looking carved.

Figure 17.392 "Chip Away" inverted example

Inverted, (without drop shadow)

Drop shadow If checked, a Drop shadow will be added to the image in a new layer below the active layer.

Keep bump layer By default, the bump map used to create the chipping effect will be removed after applying the filter. When this option is checked, the bump map will be kept as an invisible layer.

Fill BG with pattern If checked, the background layer (added by the filter) will be filled with the specified Pattern. Otherwise, it will be filled with white.

Keep background Whether or not to remove the background layer. This option is checked by default. You can, of course, remove this layer (or toggle its visibility) later in the Layers dialog.

Pattern This option consists of a preview area, which will produce a popup preview when you click on it and hold down the mouse button, and a Browse button. The button will popup a dialog where you can select patterns.

The default pattern is "Burlwood". Apart from that one, the plug-in author suggests the patterns "Dried mud", "3D Green", and "Slate":

Figure 17.393 Suggested "Chip Away" patterns

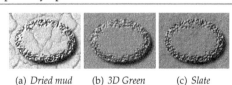

(a) *Dried mud*   (b) *3D Green*   (c) *Slate*

17.16.9.4 Filter details

To achieve a chipping effect, the filter...

1. ...creates a selection from the alpha channel in a new layer,

2. fills the selection with white,

3. spreads the pixels,

4. and applies a Gaussian blur to the layer.

5. Then it uses this layer as a Bump map, creating a 3D effect.

17.16.10   Chrome

17.16.10.1   Overview

Figure 17.394 Example for the "Chrome" filter

(a) *The "Chrome" filter applied*   (b) *The "Chrome" logo*

This filter is derived from the "Chrome" logo script (File → Create → Logos → Chrome), which — according to the script author — creates a "simplistic, but cool, chromed logo" (see above).

The filter adds this simple chrome effect to the alpha, that is the area of the active layer defined by the non-transparent pixels (think of it as a "selection by visibility"). The filter effect will always be applied according to the alpha values.

Apparently the effect only looks "cool" when the filter is applied to thin areas. For wide shapes you can try to increase the Offset value; see the examples below.

Warning

   The image will always be resized to the active layer's size.

17.16.10.2   Activate the filter

This filter is found in the image window menu under Filters → Alpha to Logo → Chrome....

17.16.10.3   Options

Figure 17.395 "Chrome" options

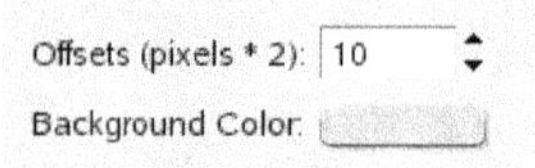

Offsets (pixels * 2): 10

Background Color:

Offset (pixels * 2)   This option is used when creating the chrome effect and for placing the drop shadow:

Figure 17.396 "Offset" examples

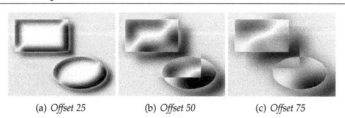

(a) *Offset 25*   (b) *Offset 50*   (c) *Offset 75*

The filter creates a drop shadow in the shape of the alpha. This shadow will be moved according to the specified offset in relation to the alpha: by 40% of the offset to the right and by 30% offset down. It will be feathered by 50% of the offset value.

The chrome effect will be achieved using some temporary layers. These layers are moved by the same amount (40% and 30% of the specified offset) and are also feathered by 50% offset. So the appearance of the alpha too is determined by the offset value.

Background Color This color is used to fill the background layer created by the filter. It defaults to light gray. When you click on the color button, a color selector pops up where you can select any other color.

17.16.11   Comic Book

17.16.11.1   Overview

Figure 17.397 Example for the "Comic Book" filter

"Comic Book" applied

Caution

 Sorry, there is no documentation for this filter as yet.

17.16.11.2   Activate the filter

This filter is found in the image window menu under Filters → Alpha to Logo → Comic Book....

17.16.11.3   Options

Figure 17.398 "Comic Book" options

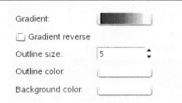

Gradient TODO

Gradient reverse TODO

Outline size TODO

Outline color TODO

Background color TODO

17.16.12 Cool Metal

17.16.12.1 Overview

Figure 17.399 Example for the "Cool Metal" filter

(a) *The "Cool Metal" filter*   (b) *The "Cool Metal" logo*

This filter creates an effect that looks like metal with a reflection in the mirrored ground, and an interesting drop shadow.

The filter is derived from the "Cool Metal" script (File → Create → Logos → Cool Metal in the image window), which creates a logo from a text as shown above.

17.16.12.2 Activate the filter

This filter is found in the image window menu under Filters → Alpha to Logo → Cool Metal....

17.16.12.3 Options

Figure 17.400 "Cool Metal" options

Effect size (pixels):	100
Background color:	
Gradient:	
☐ Gradient reverse	

Effect size (pixels) This is actually the font size option of the "Cool Metal" Script-Fu script. Some internal values will be set in relation to this size, for feathering, blurring, embossing, and creating ripple patterns.

Background color The color of the background layer added by the filter. When you click in the color swatch button, the color select dialog pops up.

Gradient The default gradient to create the cool metal is "Horizon 1". Clicking in the gradient button will open a simplified gradient dialog, where you can select any other gradient.

Gradient reverse By default, the selected gradient will be applied from top to bottom. When this option is checked, the direction will be reversed.

17.16.12.4 Filter details

At least some of the filter effects should be described briefly: how the filter creates the reflection and this nice shadow, or rather, how you can reproduce these effects manually. In fact, the only trick is to know which tool to use...

Making the reflection

Assuming that the alpha has been filled with a gradient, then:

1. Create a new layer containing the area you want to mirror, for example Copy and Paste the area in a new layer.

2. To make the reflection look more natural, scale down the layer (the filter resizes to 85% of the original height). You can do this e.g. using Scale Layer command or the Scale Tool.

3. Then flip the layer vertically and move it down.

4. Now add a layer mask, fill the layer mask with a gradient (for instance white or gray to black), and, of course, apply the layer mask.

Making the shadow

Fill the alpha with black, for instance via Duplicate Layer and Alpha to Selection, then

1. shrink and slant the layer, e.g. using the Perspective tool,

2. and apply a Gaussian Blur to the layer.

17.16.13 Frosty

17.16.13.1 Overview

Figure 17.401 Example for the "Frosty" filter

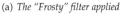

(a) The "Frosty" filter applied   (b) The "Frosty" logo

This filter is derived from the "Frosty" logo script (File → Create → Logos → Frosty in the image window), which creates a frozen logo like the example above.

The filter adds this frosty effect to the alpha, that is the area of the active layer defined by the non-transparent pixels (think of it as a "selection by visibility"). The filter effect will always be applied according to the alpha values.

> **Note**
>
> Unlike the most alpha to logo filters, the "Frosty" filter will *not* resize the image to the active layer's size.

17.16.13.2 Activate the filter

This filter is found in the image window menu under Filters → Alpha to Logo → Frosty....

17.16.13.3 Options

Figure 17.402 "Frosty" options

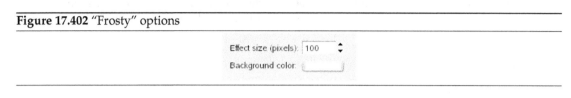

Effect size (pixels)

Figure 17.403 "Effect size" examples

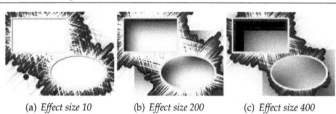

(a) *Effect size 10*   (b) *Effect size 200*   (c) *Effect size 400*

Background color This color is used to fill the background layer created by the filter. It defaults to white. When you click on the color button, a color selector pops up where you can select any other color.

17.16.14 Glossy

17.16.14.1 Overview

Figure 17.404 Example for the "Glossy" filter

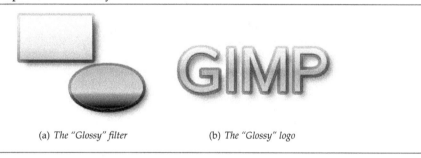

(a) *The "Glossy" filter*   (b) *The "Glossy" logo*

This filter applies gradients and patterns to the alpha. A slight 3D effect will be added using a bump map, and optionally the filter adds a drop shadow.

> **Note**
>
> Here, as a language shortcut, we use *alpha* to mean the area of the active layer defined by the non-transparent pixels. You may think of it as a selection "by visibility". Applying any effect "to the alpha" just means to apply this effect to all visible pixels of the active layer.

The filter is derived from the "Glossy" script (File → Create → Logos → Glossy in the image window), which creates a logo (see above) with a glossy outlook when used with the default options, thus the name.

This filter only works if the active layer has an alpha channel. Otherwise, the menu entry is insensitive and grayed out.

> **Warning**
>
> The image will always be resized to the active layer's size.

17.16.14.2 Activate the filter

This filter is found in the image window menu under Filters → Alpha to Logo → Glossy….

17.16.14.3 Options

Figure 17.405 "Glossy" options

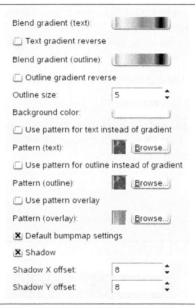

Blend gradient (text) By default, the filter will fill the alpha with a gradient blend. Clicking on the swatch button will open a simple gradient dialog, where you may select any gradient. "Text" refers to the "Glossy" logo, which creates a logo from a text, and is meaningless here.

When Text gradient reverse is checked, the alpha will be filled with a gradient blend starting at the bottom.

Pattern (text) When Use pattern for text instead of gradient is checked, the alpha will be filled with a pattern. You can open a patterns dialog to select a pattern of your choice by clicking on the Browse button. The preview area on the left will produce a popup preview of the current pattern when pressed.

Outline size This is the size of a kind of border, realised with a layer containing an enlarged copy of the alpha (details see below).

Blend gradient (outline); Pattern (outline) Just like the "text" options for the active layer, these options specify the gradient or pattern (when Use pattern for outline instead of gradient is checked) used to fill the outline area.

Use pattern overlay When checked, the original, not enlarged alpha of the outline layer will be filled with the specified pattern using the overlay mode, so that the pattern and the previous contents (pattern or gradient) will be merged.

Again, clicking on Browse button will open a patterns dialog, pressing the preview icon will produce a popup preview of the current pattern.

Default bumpmap settings This option does nothing, the filter will always apply a bump map.

Background color The color of the background layer added by the filter. When you click on the color button, a color select dialog pops up.

Shadow Optionally the filter creates a layer containing a drop shadow. The shadow layer will be moved Shadow X offset pixels to the right and Shadow Y offset pixels down. Note that this may enlarge the image, while the background layer will keep the size of the active layer.

17.16.14.4 Filter details

The numerous options may give the impression that this is a very complicate filter, but actually it is fairly simple. The interesting part is how the filter handles the active layer and the outline layer:

In the active layer, the filter creates a selection from the alpha channel and fills the selection with the specified gradient blend or pattern.

Then a new "outline" layer below the active layer will be created in a similar way: First, the active layer's alpha will be used to make a selection. But before filling the selection with a gradient or a pattern, the selection will be enlarged by Outline size pixels.

When you filled both layers with the same pattern or gradient blend, you will still see a border ("outline"), because

- a 3D effect will be applied to the outline layer using the active layer as a bump map;

- the layer mode of the active layer will be set to "Screen".

The last (optional) step is to fill the outline layer with a pattern, using the "overlay" layer mode. This will combine the pattern with the pattern or gradient used before. To learn more about the result of using the overlay mode, see the description in Section 8.2.

17.16.15 Glowing Hot

17.16.15.1 Overview

Figure 17.406 Example for the "Glowing Hot" filter

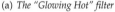

(a) *The "Glowing Hot" filter*   (b) *The "Glowing Hot" logo*

This filter adds a glowing hot metal effect to the alpha (that is to these areas of the active layer defined by the non-transparent pixels).

The filter is derived from the "Glowing Hot" script (File → Create → Logos → Glowing Hot in the image window), which creates a glowing text logo (see above).

The filter simulates a red-hot, a yellow-hot, and a white-hot area - each color representing a different metal temperature -; the alpha's outline shines through the glowing.

Warning

 The image will always be resized to the active layer's size.

17.16.15.2 Activate the filter

This filter is found in the image window menu under Filters → Alpha to Logo → Glowing Hot....

The filter only works if the active layer has an alpha channel. Otherwise, the menu entry is insensitive and grayed out.

17.16.15.3 Options

Figure 17.407 "Glowing Hot" options

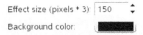

Effect size (pixels * 3) This is actually the font size option of the "Glowing Hot" logo. The value is used to calculate the size of the feathering border (cf Section 16.4.9) before the alpha is filled with red, yellow, and white. These feathered colors make the hot metal effect.

Figure 17.408 Effect size examples

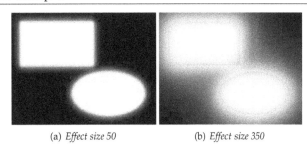

(a) *Effect size 50*   (b) *Effect size 350*

Background color This is the color used to fill the "Background" layer; it defaults to black (7,0,20). Click on the button to open a color selector, if you want to choose a different color.

17.16.15.4 Filter details

To create the glowing effect (red-hot, yellow-hot, and white-hot area), the alpha is feathered and then filled with the respective color, from red to white with decreasing feather sizes and color intensities in the feathered area.

The illustration below shows the "hot metal" colors and the width of the feathering border in percent of "Effect size" (these are the values the filter actually uses).

Figure 17.409 Effect size

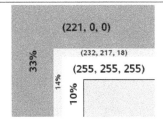

Glowing hot metal colors and their relative feather sizes

In the example images you can see how the alpha's outline shines through the glowing. This is achieved with a alpha filled with black as top layer, where the layer mode is set to overlay. Using a black overlay layer won't change pure white, but darkens light colors at the alpha's edges so that the outline appears.

17.16.16   Gradient Bevel

17.16.16.1   Overview

Figure 17.410 Example for the "Gradient Bevel" filter

"Gradient Bevel" applied

Caution

   Sorry, there is no documentation for this filter as yet.

17.16.16.2   Activate the filter

This filter is found in the image window menu under Filters → Alpha to Logo → Gradient Bevel....

17.16.16.3   Options

Figure 17.411 "Gradient Bevel" options

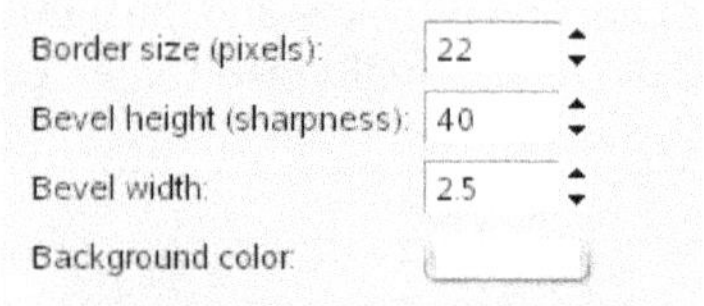

Border size (pixels):	22
Bevel height (sharpness):	40
Bevel width:	2.5
Background color:	

Border size (pixels) TODO

Bevel height (sharpness) TODO

Bevel width TODO

Background color TODO

17.16.17   Neon

17.16.17.1   Overview

Figure 17.412 Example for the "Neon" filter

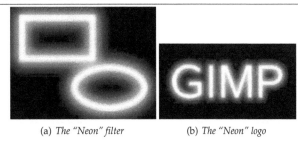

(a) *The "Neon" filter*   (b) *The "Neon" logo*

This filter converts the active layer's alpha into a neon-sign like object and optionally adds a shadow.

It is derived from the "Neon" Script-Fu script (File → Create → Logos → Neon), which creates a text effect that simulates neon lighting.

> **Warning**
>
> ⚠ The image will always be resized to the active layer's size.

17.16.17.2   Activate the filter

You can find this filter in the image window menu under Filters → Alpha to Logo → Neon....

17.16.17.3   Options

Figure 17.413 "Neon" options

Effect size (pixels * 5) This is actually the font size option of the Neon Script-Fu script. Some internal values will be set in relation to this font size, for instance tube size, shadow offset, and blur radius. So it may be a good idea to select the height of your objects as a starting point here. ("pixels * 5" is nonsense, ignore it.)

Background color This is the color used to fill the "Background" layer; it defaults to black. When you click on the color swatch button, you can choose any other color in the color selector dialog.

Glow color This is the color of the glowing neon tubes. The default is a typical neon-like light blue (38,211,255). Again, a click on the color swatch button brings up the color selector.

Create shadow Optionally, the filter can create a drop shadow, which will have the same shape as the alpha channel. The shadow color is black, and cannot be modified. Unless you don't plan to remove the background layer, you should select a different Background color.

"Neon" with shadow

17.16.17.4   Filter details

The filter uses two layers to achieve the neon effect:

Figure 17.414 The Neon effect

(a) *The "Neon Tubes" layer*   (b) *The "Neon Glow" layer*

The layer "Neon Tubes" is the active layer the filter is applied to. The content of this layer doesn't matter. Only the alpha channel does, especially its shape.

The "Neon Glow" layer below contains the glowing of the neon light.

Optional a "Shadow" layer is created below, containing a drop shadow in the same shape of the active layer's alpha channel. At the bottom a new "Background" layer is created filled with the Background color.

Overview of the Neon filter layers:

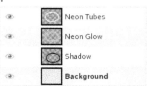

17.16.18   Particle Trace

17.16.18.1   Overview

Figure 17.415 Examples for the "Particle Trace" filter

(a) *The "Particle Trace" filter*   (b) *The "Particle Trace" logo*

To get such images, open a new image with a transparent background, create selections, fill them with any color, and apply filter.

This filter adds an effect, reminding of particle traces in a bubble chamber of nuclear physics, to the active layer alpha.

> **Warning**
>
> The image will always be resized to the active layer's size.

The filter is derived from the "Particle Trace" logo script (File → Create → Logos → Particle Trace), which creates the text effect shown in the example above.

17.16.18.2 Activate the filter

You can find this filter in the image window menu under Filters → Alpha to Logo → Particle Trace....

17.16.18.3 Options

Figure 17.416 "Particle Trace" options

Border size (pixels) Actually this option is the text layer's border of the "Particle Trace" Script-Fu Logo (hence the misleading name). Here it determines the width of the white shadow's feathering.

Hit rate This option sets the amount of light points produced by the Noise filter and thus the amount of points converted to sparkles. The value ranges from from 0.0 to 1.0, but some values may be not useful:

Figure 17.417 "Hit rate" examples

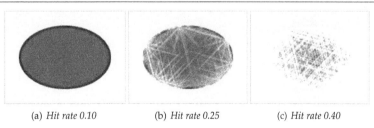

(a) *Hit rate 0.10*   (b) *Hit rate 0.25*   (c) *Hit rate 0.40*

Edge width Along the edge of the alpha, a new area will be created with radius "Edge width" (compare Section 16.4.13). This area will also be filled with the "Base color", but will be a bit darker.

Edge only If checked, the filter effect will be applied to the edge of the alpha channel only and the area of the alpha channel will be cleared.

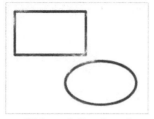

"Edge only" activated

Base color This color is used to fill the area defined by the active layer's alpha channel. It defaults to a very dark green. As usual, clicking on the color swatch button opens a color selector where you can choose any other color.

Background color This color is used to fill a new background layer. Note that above the background layer there is a white shadow layer which has opacity set to 90%, so you will see the background color only partially. If the "Edge only" option is enabled, the area of the alpha channel will be cleared and you will see the background color. Again, when you click on the color swatch button, a color selector pops up where you can select any color.

The active layer (top) and the filter layers below

17.16.18.4   Filter details

The filter adds noise to the alpha and then turns the spots into sparkles. Then it adds a feathered white shadow.

17.16.19   Textured

17.16.19.1   Overview

Figure 17.418 Example for the "Textured" filter

"Textured" applied

Caution

 Sorry, there is no documentation for this filter as yet.

17.16.19.2   Activate the filter

This filter is found in the image window menu under Filters → Alpha to Logo → Textured....

17.16.19.3   Options

Figure 17.419 "Textured" options

Border size (pixels) TODO

Pattern TODO

Mosaic tile type TODO

Background color TODO

Starting blend TODO

Ending blend TODO

Chapter 18

Keys and Mouse Reference

18.1 Help

Help — Key reference for Help menu

Help

F1 Help

Shift + F1 Context Help

18.2 Tools

Tools — Key reference for the Tools menu

Tools

Tools

R Rect Select

E Ellipse Select

F Free Select

Z Fuzzy Select

Shift + O Select By Color

I Scissors

B Paths

O Color Picker

M Move

Shift + C Crop and Resize

Shift + R Rotate

Shift + T Scale

Shift + S Shear

Shift + P Perspective

Shift + F Flip

T Text

Shift + B Bucket Fill

L Blend

N Pencil

P Paintbrush

Shift + E Eraser

A Airbrush

K Ink

C Clone

Shift + U Blur/Sharpen

S Smudge

Shift + D Dodge/Burn

Note

 Click on a tool icon to open its Tool Options dialog.

Context

X Swap Colors

D Default Colors

Note

 Click on the colors to change the colors.

18.3 File

File — Key reference for the File menu

File

Ctrl + N New image

Ctrl + O Open image

Ctrl + Alt + O Open image as new layer

Ctrl + D Duplicate

Ctrl + 1 Open recent image #1

Ctrl + 2 Open recent image #2

Ctrl + 3 Open recent image #3

Ctrl + 4 Open recent image #4

Ctrl + 5 Open recent image #5

Ctrl + 6 Open recent image #6

Ctrl + 7 Open recent image #7

Ctrl + 8 Open recent image #8

Ctrl + 9 Open recent image #9

Ctrl + 0 Open recent image #10

Ctrl + S Save image

Shift + Ctrl + S Save under a new name

Ctrl + Q Quit

18.4 Dialogs

Dialogs — Key reference for Dockable Dialogs submenu

Dockable Dialogs

Ctrl + L Layers

Shift + Ctrl + B Brushes

Shift + Ctrl + P Patterns

Ctrl + G Gradients

Note

 These open a new dialog window if it isn't open yet, otherwise the corresponding dialog gets focus.

Within a Dialog

Alt + F4, Ctrl + W Close the window

Tab Jump to next widget

Shift + Tab Jump to previous widget

Enter Set the new value

Space, Enter Activate current button or list

Ctrl + Alt + Page Up Ctrl + Alt + Page Down In a multi-tab dialog, switch tabs

> **Note**
>
> This accepts the new value you typed in a text field and returns focus to canvas.

Within a File Dialog

Shift + L Open Location

Alt + Up Up-Folder

Alt + Down Down-Folder

Alt + Home Home-Folder

Esc Close Dialog

18.5 View

View — Key reference for View menu

View

Window

F10 Main Menu

Shift + F10, right click Drop-down Menu

F11 Toggle fullscreen

Shift + Q Toggle quickmask

Ctrl + W Close document window

> **Note**
>
> Menus can also be activated by **Alt** with the letter underscored in the menu name.

Zoom

+ Zoom in

- Zoom out

1 Zoom 1:1

Ctrl + E Shrink wrap

> **Note**
>
> This fits the window to the image size.

Rulers and Guides

mouse drag Drag off a ruler to create guide

Ctrl + mouse drag Drag a sample point out of the rulers

Shift + Ctrl + R Toggle rulers

Shift + Ctrl + T Toggle guides

Note

  Drag off the horizontal or vertical ruler to create a new guideline. Drag a guideline off the image to delete it.

18.6 Edit

Edit — Key reference for Edit menu

Edit

Undo/redo

Ctrl + Z Undo

Ctrl + Y Redo

Clipboard

Ctrl + C Copy selection

Ctrl + X Cut selection

Ctrl + V Paste clipboard

Del Erase selection

Shift + Ctrl + C Named copy selection

Shift + Ctrl + X Named cut selection

Shift + Ctrl + V Named paste clipboard

Note

  This puts a copy of the selection on the GIMP clipboard.

Fill

Ctrl + , Fill with FG Color

Ctrl + . Fill with BG Color

Ctrl + ; Fill with Pattern

18.7 Layer

Layer — Key reference for Layer menu

Layers

Page Up, Ctrl + Tab Select the layer above

 Page Down, Shift + Ctrl + Tab   Select the layer below

Home Select the first layer

End Select the last layer

Ctrl + M Merge visible layers

Ctrl + H Anchor layer

18.8   Select

Select — Key reference for Select menu

Selections

Ctrl + T Toggle selections

Ctrl + A Select all

 Shift + Ctrl + A   Select none

Ctrl + I Invert selection

 Shift + Ctrl + L   Float selection

Shift + V Path to selection

18.9   Filters

Filters — Key reference for Filters menu

Filters

Ctrl + F Repeat last filter

 Shift + Ctrl + F   Reshow last filter

18.10   Zoom tool

Zoom tool — Key reference for the Zoom tool submenu

Zoom tool

click Zoom in

Ctrl + click Zoom out

mouse drag Zoom into the area

Part IV

Glossary

Alpha

An Alpha value indicates the transparency of a pixel. Besides its Red, Green and Blue values, a pixel has an alpha value. The smaller the alpha value of a pixel, the more visible the colors below it. A pixel with an alpha value of 0 is completely transparent. A pixel with an alpha value of 255 is fully opaque.

With some image file formats, you can only specify that a pixel is completely transparent or completely opaque. Other file formats allow a variable level of transparency.

Alpha Channel

An alpha channel of a layer is a grayscale image of the same size as the layer representing its transparency. For each pixel the gray level (a value between 0 and 255) represents the pixels's Alpha value. An alpha channel can make areas of the layer to appear partially transparent. That's why the background layer has no alpha channel by default.

The image alpha channel, which is displayed in the channels dialog, can be considered as the alpha channel of the final layer when all layers have been merged.

See also Example for Alpha channel.

Antialiasing

Antialiasing is the process of reversing an alias, that is, reducing the "jaggies". Antialiasing produces smoother curves by adjusting the boundary between the background and the pixel region that is being antialiased. Generally, pixel intensities or opacities are changed so that a smoother transition to the background is achieved. With selections, the opacity of the edge of the selection is appropriately reduced.

Bézier curve

A spline is a curve which is defined mathematically and has a set of control points. A Bézier spline is a cubic spline which has four control points, where the first and last control points (knots or anchors) are the endpoints of the curve and the inner two control points (handles) determine the direction of the curve at the endpoints.

In the non-mathematical sense, a spline is a flexible strip of wood or metal used for drawing curves. Using this type of spline for drawing curves dates back to shipbuilding, where weights were hung on splines to bend them. The outer control points of a Bézier spline are similar to the places where the splines are fastened down and the inner control points are where weights are attached to modify the curve.

Bézier splines are only one way of mathematically representing curves. They were developed in the 1960s by Pierre Bézier, who worked for Renault.

Bézier curves are used in GIMP as component parts of Paths.

The image above shows a Bézier curve. Points P0 and P3 are points on the Path, which are created by clicking with the mouse. Points P1 and P2 are handles, which are automatically created by GIMP when you stretch the line.

Bitmap

From *The Free Online Dictionary of Computing (13 Mar 01)* :

> bitmap — A data file or structure which corresponds bit for bit with an image displayed on a screen, probably in the same format as it would be stored in the display's video memory or maybe as a device independent bitmap. A bitmap is characterised by the width and height of the image in pixels and the number of bits per pixel which determines the number of shades of grey or colors it can represent. A bitmap representing

a colored image (a "pixmap") will usually have pixels with between one and eight bits for each of the red, green, and blue components, though other color encodings are also used. The green component sometimes has more bits than the other two to cater for the human eye's greater discrimination in this component.

BMP

BMP is an uncompressed image file format designed by Microsoft and mainly used in Windows. Colors are typically represented in 1, 4 or 8 bits, although the format also supports more. Because it is not compressed and the files are large, it is not very well suited for use in the internet.

Bump mapping

Bump mapping is a technique for displaying extremely detailed objects without increasing the geometrical complexity of the objects. It is especially used in 3-dimensional visualization programs. The trick is to put all the necessary information into a texture, with which shadowing is shown on the surface of the object.

Bump mapping is only one (very effective) way of simulating surface irregularities which are not actually contained in the geometry of the model.

Channel Mask

A channel masks is a special type of mask which determines the transparency of a selection. See Masks for a detailed description.

Channel

A channel refers to a certain component of an image. For instance, the components of an RGB image are the three primary colors red, green, blue, and sometimes transparency (alpha).

Every channel is a grayscale image of exactly the same size as the image and, consequently, consists of the same number of pixels. Every pixel of this grayscale image can be regarded as a container which can be filled with a value ranging from 0 to 255. The exact meaning of this value depends on the type of channel, e.g. in the RGB color model the value in the R-channel means the amount of red which is added to the color of the different pixels; in the selection channel, the value denotes how strongly the pixels are selected; and in the alpha channel the values denote how opaque the corresponding pixels are. See also Channels.

Clipboard

The Clipboard is a temporary area of memory which is used to transfer data between applications or documents. It is used when you Cut, Copy or Paste data in GIMP.

The clipboard is implemented slightly differently under different operating systems. Under Linux/XFree, GIMP uses the XFree clipboard for text and the GIMP internal image clipboard for transferring images between image documents. Under other operating systems, the clipboard may work somewhat differently. See the GIMP documentation for your operating system for further information.

The basic operations provided by the clipboard are "Cut", "Copy", and "Paste". Cut means that the item is removed from the document and copied to the clipboard. Copy leaves the item in the document and copies it to the clipboard. Paste copies the contents of the clipboard to the document. The GIMP makes an intelligent decision about what to paste depending upon the target. If the target is a canvas, the Paste operation uses the image clipboard. If the target is a text entry box, the paste operation uses the text clipboard.

CMY, CMYK

CMYK is a color model which has components for Cyan, Magenta, Yellow and Black. It is a subtractive color model, and that fact is important when an image is printed. It is complementary to the RGB color model.

The values of the individual colors vary between 0% and 100%, where 0% corresponds to an unprinted color, and 100% corresponds to a completely printed area of color. Colors are formed by mixing the three basic colors.

The last of these values, K (Black), doesn't contribute to the color, but merely serves to darken the other colors. The letter K is used for Black to prevent confusion, since B usually stands for Blue.

Figure 18.1 Subtractive color model

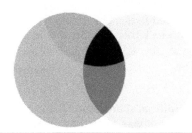

GIMP does not currently support the CMYK model. (An experimental plug-in providing rudimentary CMYK support can be found [PLUGIN-SEPARATE].)

This is the mode used in printing. These are the colors in the ink cartridges in your printer. It is the mode used in painting and in all the objects around us, where light is reflected, not emmitted. Objects absorb part of the light waves and we see only the reflected part. Note that the cones in our eyes see this reflected light in RGB mode. An object appears Red because Green and Blue have been absorbed. Since the combination of Green and Blue is Cyan, Cyan is absorbed when you add Red. Conversely, if you add Cyan, its complementary color, Red, is absorbed. This system is *subtractive*. If you add Yellow, you decrease Blue, and if you add Magenta, you decrease Green.

It would be logical to think that by mixing Cyan, Magenta and Yellow, you would subtract Red, Green and Blue, and the eye would see no light at all, that is, Black. But the question is more complex. In fact, you would see a dark brown. That is why this mode also has a Black value, and why your printer has a Black cartridge. It is less expensive that way. The printer doesn't have to mix the other three colors to create an imperfect Black, it just has to add Black.

Color depth

Color depth is simply the number of bits used to represent a color (bits per pixel : bpp). There are 3 channels for a pixel (for Red, Green and Blue). GIMP can support 8 bits per channel, referred as *eight-bit color*. So, GIMP color depth is 8 * 3 = 24, which allows 256 * 256 * 256 = 16,777,216 possible colors (8 bits allow 256 colors).

Color model

A color model is a way of describing and specifying a color. The term is often used loosely to refer to both a color space system and the color space on which it is based.

A color space is a set of colors which can be displayed or recognized by an input or output device (such as a scanner, monitor, printer, etc.). The colors of a color space are specified as values in a color space system, which is a coordinate system in which the individual colors are described by coordinate values on various axes. Because of the structure of the human eye, there are three axes in color spaces which are intended for human observers. The practical application of that is that colors are specified with three components (with a few exceptions). There are about 30 to 40 color space systems in use. Some important examples are:

- RGB
- HSV
- CMY(K)
- YUV
- YCbCr

Dithering

Dithering is a technique used in computer graphics to create the illusion of more colors when displaying an image which has a low color depth. In a dithered image, the missing colors are reproduced by a certain arrangement of pixels in the available colors. The human eye perceives this as a mixture of the individual colors.

The Gradient tool uses dithering. You may also choose to use dithering when you convert an image to Indexed format. If you are working on an image with indexed colors, some tools (such as the pattern fill tool) may also use dithering, if the correct color is not available in the colormap.

The Newsprint filter uses dithering as well. You can use the NL Filter (Non Linear filter) to remove unwanted dithering noise from your image.

Also note that although GIMP itself uses 24-bit colors, your system may not actually be able to display that many colors. If it doesn't, then the software in between GIMP and your system may also dither colors while displaying them.

See also the glossary entry on Floyd-Steinberg dithering, which is used in GIMP.

EXIF

Exchangeable image file format (official abbreviation Exif, not EXIF) is a specification for the image file format used by digital cameras. It was created by the Japan Electronic Industry Development Association (JEIDA). The specification uses the existing JPEG, TIFF Rev. 6.0, and RIFF WAVE file formats, with the addition of specific metadata tags. It is not supported in JPEG 2000 or PNG. Version 2.1 of the specification is dated June 12, 1998 and version 2.2 is dated April 2002. The Exif tag structure is taken from that of TIFF files. There is a large overlap between the tags defined in the TIFF, Exif, TIFF/EP and DCF standards [WKPD-EXIF].

Feathering

The process of Feathering makes a smooth transition between a region and the background by softly blending the edges of the region.

In GIMP, you can feather the edges of a selection. Brushes can also have feathered edges.

File Format

A file format or file type is the form in which computer data is stored. Since a file is stored by an operating system as a linear series of bytes, which cannot describe many kinds of real data in an obvious way, conventions have been developed for interpreting the information as representations of complex data. All of the conventions for a particular "kind" of file constitute a file format.

Some typical file formats for saving images are JPEG, TIFF, PNG and GIF. The best file format for saving an image depends upon how the image is intended to be used. For example, if the image is intended for the internet, file size is a very important factor, and if the image is intended to be printed, high resolution and quality have greater significance. See Format types.

Floating Selection

A floating selection (sometimes called a "floating layer") is a type of temporary layer which is similar in function to a normal layer, except that a floating selection must be anchored before you can resume working on any other layers in the image.

In early versions of GIMP, when GIMP did not use layers, floating selections were used for performing operations on a limited part of an image (you can do that more easily now with layers). Now floating selections have no practical use, but you must know what you have to do with them.

Floyd-Steinberg Dithering

Floyd-Steinberg dithering is a method of dithering which was first published in 1976 by Robert W. Floyd and Louis Steinberg. The dithering process begins in the upper left corner of the image. For each pixel, the closest available color in the palette is chosen and the difference between that color and the original color is computed in each RGB channel. Then specific fractions of these differences are dispersed among several adjacent pixels which haven't yet been visited (below and to the right of the original pixel). Because of the order of processing, the procedure can be done in a single pass over the image.

When you convert an image to Indexed mode, you can choose between two variants of Floyd-Steinberg dithering.

Gamma

Gamma or gamma correction is a non-linear operation which is used to encode and decode luminance or color values in video or still image systems. It is used in many types of imaging systems to straighten out a curved signal-to-light or intensity-to-signal response. For example, the light emitted by a CRT is not linear with regard to its input voltage, and the voltage from an electric camera is not linear with regard to the intensity (power) of the light in the scene. Gamma encoding helps to map the data into a perceptually linear domain, so that the limited signal range (the limited number of bits in each RGB signal) is better optimized perceptually.

Gamma is used as an exponent (power) in the correction equation. Gamma compression (where gamma < 1) is used to encode linear luminance or RGB values into color signals or digital file values, and gamma expansion (where gamma > 1) is the decoding process, and usually occurs where the current-to-voltage function for a CRT is non-linear.

For PC video, images are encoded with a gamma of about 0.45 and decoded with a gamma of 2.2. For Mac systems, images are typically encoded with a gamma of about 0.55 and decoded with a gamma of 1.8. The sRGB color space standard used for most cameras, PCs and printers does not use a simple exponential equation, but has a decoding gamma value near 2.2 over much of its range.

In GIMP, gamma is an option used in the brush tab of the GIMPressionist filter and in the Flame filter. The display filters also include a Gamma filter. Also see the Levels Tool, where you can use the middle slider to change the gamma value.

Gamut

In color reproduction, including computer graphics and photography, the gamut, or color gamut (pronounced / gæm t/), is a certain complete subset of colors. The most common usage refers to the subset of colors which can be accurately represented in a given circumstance, such as within a given color space or by a certain output device. Another sense, less frequently used but not less correct, refers to the complete set of colors found within an image at a given time. In this context, digitizing a photograph, converting a digitized image to a different color space, or outputting it to a given medium using a certain output device generally alters its gamut, in the sense that some of the colors in the original are lost in the process. [WKPD-GAMUT]

GIF

GIF™ stands for Graphics Interchange Format. It is a file format with good, lossless compression for images with low color depth (up to 256 different colors per image). Since GIF was developed, a new format called Portable Network Graphics (PNG) has been developed, which is better than GIF in all respects, with the exception of animations and some rarely-used features.

GIF was introduced by CompuServe in 1987. It became popular mostly because of its efficient, LZW compression. The size of the image files required clearly less disk space than other usual graphics formats of the time, such as PCX or MacPaint. Even large images could be transmitted in a reasonable time, even with slow modems. In addition, the open licensing policy of CompuServe made it possible for any programmer to implement the GIF format for his own applications free of charge, as long as the CompuServe copyright notice was attached to them.

Colors in GIF are stored in a color table which can hold up to 256 different entries, chosen from 16.7 million different color values. When the image format was introduced, this was not a much of a limitation, since only a few people had hardware which could display more colors than that. For typical drawings, cartoons, black-and-white photographs and similar uses, 256 colors are quite sufficient as a rule, even today. For more complex images, such as color photographs, however, a huge loss of quality is apparent, which is why the format is not considered to be suitable for those purposes.

One color entry in the palette can be defined to be transparent. With transparency, the GIF image can look like it is non-rectangular in shape. However, semi-transparency, as in PNG, is not possible. A pixel can only be either entirely visible or completely transparent.

The first version of GIF was 87a. In 1989, CompuServe published an expanded version, called 89a. Among other things, this made it possible to save several images in one GIF file, which is especially used for simple animation. The version number can be distinguished from the first six bytes of a GIF file. Interpreted as ASCII symbols, they are "GIF87a" or "GIF89a".

GNU

The GNU project was started in 1983 by Richard Stallman with the goal of developing a completely free operating system. It is especially well-known from the GNU General Public License (GPL) and GNU/Linux, a GNU-variant with a Linux kernel.

The name came about from the naming conventions which were in practice at MIT, where Stallman worked at the time. For programs which were similar to other programs, recursive acronyms were chosen as names. Since the new system was to be based on the widespread operating system, Unix, Stallman looked for that kind of name and came up with GNU, which stands for "GNU is not Unix". In order to avoid confusion, the name should be pronounced with the "G", not like "new". There were several reasons for making GNU Unix-compatible. For one thing, Stallman was convinced that most companies would refuse a completely new operating system, if the programs they used wouldn't run on it. In addition, the architecture of Unix made quick, easy and distributed development possible, since Unix consists of many small programs that can be developed independently of each other, for the most part. Also, many parts of a Unix system were freely available to anyone and could therefore be directly integrated into GNU, for example, the typesetting system, TeX, or the X Window System. The missing parts were newly written from the ground up.

GIMP (GNU Image Manipulation Program) is an official GNU application [WKPD-GNU].

Grayscale

Grayscale is a mode for encoding the colors of an image which contains only black, white and shades of gray.

When you create a new image, you can choose to create it in Grayscale mode (which you can colorize later, by changing it to RGB mode). You can also change an existing image to grayscale by using the Grayscale, Desaturate, Decompose, Channel Mixer, although not all formats will accept these changes. Although you can create images in Grayscale mode and convert images to it, it is not a color model, in the true sense of the word.

As explained in RGB mode, 24-bit GIMP images can have up to 256 levels of gray. If you change from Grayscale to RGB mode, your image will have an RGB structure with three color channels, but of course, it will still be gray.

Grayscale image files (8-bit) are smaller than RGB files.

Guides

Guides are lines you can temporarily display on an image while you are working on it. You can display as many guides as you would like, in either the horizontal or the vertical direction. These lines help you position a selection or a layer on the image. They do not appear when the image is printed.

For more information see Section 12.2.2.

Histogram

In digital image processing, a histogram is a graph representing the statistical frequency of the gray values or the color values in an image. The histogram of an image tells you about the occurrence of gray values or color values, as well as the contrast range and the brightness of the image. In a color image, you can create one histogram with information about all possible colors, or three histograms for the individual color channels. The latter makes the most sense, since most procedures are based on grayscale images and therefore further processing is immediately possible.

HSV

HSV is a color model which has components for Hue (the color, such as blue or red), Saturation (how strong the color is) and Value (the brightness).

The RGB mode is very well suited to computer screens, but it doesn't let us describe what we see in everyday life; a light green, a pale pink, a dazzling red, etc. The HSV model takes these characteristics into account. HSV and RGB are not completely independent of each other. You can see that with the Color Picker tool; when you change a color in one of the color models, the other one also changes. Brave souls can read *Grokking the GIMP*, which explains their interrelationship.

Brief description of the HSV components:

Hue This is the color itself, which results from the combination of primary colors. All shades (except for the gray levels) are represented in a *chromatic circle*: yellow, blue, and also purple, orange, etc. The chromatic circle (or "color wheel") values range between 0° and 360°. (The term "color" is often used instead of "Hue". The RGB colors are "primary colors".)

Saturation This value describes how pale the color is. A completely unsaturated color is a shade of gray. As the saturation increases, the color becomes a pastel shade. A completely saturated color is pure. Saturation values go from 0 to 100, from white to the purest color.

Value This value describes the luminosity, the luminous intensity. It is the amount of light emitted by a color. You can see a change of luminosity when a colored object is moved from being in the shadow to being in the sun, or when you increase the luminosity of your screen. Values go from 0 to 100. Pixel values in the three channels are also luminosities: "Value" in the HSV color model is the maximum of these elementary values in the RGB space (scaled to 0-100).

HTML notation

A hex triplet is a way of encoding a color for a computer. The "#" symbol indicates that the numbers which follow it are encoded in hexadecimal. Each color is specified in two hexadecimal digits which make up a triplet (three pairs) of hexadecimal values in the form "#rrggbb", where "rr" represents red, "gg" represents green and "bb" represents blue.

Image Hose

An image hose in GIMP is a special type of brush which consists of several images. For example, you could have a brush with footprints, which consists of two images, one for the left footprint and one for the right. While painting with this brush, a left footprint would appear first, then a right footprint, then a left one, etc. This type of brush is very powerful.

An image hose is also sometimes called an "image pipe" or "animated brush". An image hose is indicated in the Brushes dialog by a small red triangle in the lower right corner of the brush's symbol.

For information concerning creating an image hose, please see the Section 7.8 and Section 7.7.

Incremental, paint mode

Incremental mode is a paint mode where each brush stroke is drawn directly on the active layer. When it is set, each additional stroke of the brush increases the effect of the brush, up to the maximum opacity for the brush.

If incremental mode is not set, brush strokes are drawn on a canvas buffer, which is then combined with the active layer. The maximum effect of a brush is then determined by the opacity, and stroking with the brush repeatedly does not increase the effect beyond this limit.

The two images above were created using a brush with spacing set to 60 percent. The image on the left shows non-incremental painting and the image on the right shows the difference with incremental painting.

Incremental mode is a tool option that is shared by several brush tools, except those which have a "rate" control, which automatically implies an incremental effect. You can set it by checking the Incremental checkbox in the tool option dialog for the tool (Paintbrush, Pencil and Eraser).

Indexed Colors

Indexed color mode is a mode for encoding colors in an image where each pixel in the image is assigned an 8-bit color number. The color which corresponds to this number is then put in a table (the palette). Changing a color in the palette changes all the pixels which refer to this palette color. Although you can create images in *Indexed Color* mode and can transform images to it, it is, strictly speaking, not a color model.

See also the Indexed Palette section and the Convert Image to Indexed Colors command.

Interpolation

Interpolation means calculating intermediate values. When you enlarge ("digitally zoom") or otherwise transform (rotate, shear or give perspective to) a digital image, interpolation procedures are used to compute the colors of the pixels in the transformed image. GIMP offers three interpolation methods, which differ in quality and speed. In general, the better the quality, the more time the interpolation takes (see Interpolation methods).

GIMP uses interpolation when you Scale an image, Scale a layer, and when you Transform an image.

JPEG

JPEG is a file format which supports compression and works at all color depths. The image compression is adjustable, but beware: Too high a compression could severely reduce image quality, since JPEG compression is lossy.

Use JPEG to create web graphics or if you don't want your image to take up a lot of space. JPEG is a good format for photographs and for computer-generated images (CGI). It is not well suited for:

- digital line drawings (for example, screenshots or vector graphics), in which there are many neighboring pixels with the same color values, few colors and hard edges,

- Black and white images (only black and white, one bit per pixel) or

- half-toned images (newsprint).

Other formats, such as GIF, PNG or JBIG, are far better for these kinds of images.

In general, JPEG transformations are not reversible. Opening and then saving a JPEG file causes a new, lossy compression. Increasing the quality factor later will not bring back the image information which was lost.

L*a*b*

The Lab color space (also called the L*a*b* color space) is a color model developed in the beginning of the 1930s by the Commission Internationale d Eclairage (CIE). It includes all the colors that the human eye can perceive. That contains the colors of the RGB and the CMYK color spaces, among others. In Lab, a color is indicated by three values: L, a and b. Here, the L stands for the luminance component — corresponding to the gray value — and a and b represent the red-green and blue-yellow parts of the color, respectively.

In contrast to RGB or CMYK, Lab is not dependent upon the various input and output devices. For that reason, it is used as an exchange format between devices. Lab is also the internal color model of PostScript Level II.

Layer

You can think of layers as being a stack of slides which are more or less transparent. Each layer represents an aspect of the image and the image is the sum of all of these aspects. The layer at the bottom of the stack is the background layer. The layers above it are the components of the foreground.

You can view and manage the layers of the image through the Layers dialog.

Figure 18.2 Example image with layers

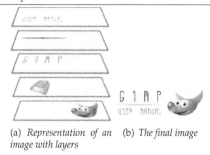

(a) *Representation of an image with layers*   (b) *The final image*

Marching Ants

Marching ants is a term which describes the dotted line which surrounds a selection. The line is animated, so it looks as if little ants are running around behind each other.

Masks

A mask is like a veil put over a layer (layer mask) or all the layers of an image (selection mask). You can remove this mask by painting with white color, and you can complete it by painting with black color. When the mask is "applied", non masked pixels will remain visible (the others will be transparent) or will be selected, according to the type of mask.

There are two types of masks:

- *Layer Mask*: Every layer can have its own mask. The layer mask represents the Alpha channel of the layer and allows you to manage its transparency. By painting on the layer mask, you can make parts of the layer opaque or transparent: painting with black makes the layer transparent, painting with white makes the layer opaque and painting with shades of gray makes the layer semi-transparent. You can use all paint tools to paint on the mask. You can also apply a filter or copy-paste. You can use the Layer mask for transition effects, volume effects, merging elements from another image, etc. See the Layer Mask section for more details.

- *Channel Mask*, also called *Selection Mask*: Channel Masks determine the transparency of a selection. By painting on a Channel Mask with white, you remove the mask and increase the selection; with black, you reduce the selection. This procedure lets you create a selection very precisely. You can also save your selections to a Channel Mask with the Save to Channel command. You can retrieve it later by using the "Channel to selection" command from the Channel menu. Channel masks are so important in GIMP that a special type has been implemented: the Quick mask. See the Selection mask section for more details.

Moiré Effect

The moiré effect (pronounce "Moa-ray") is an unintended pattern which appears when a regular pattern of grids or lines interferes with another regular pattern placed over it. This can happen, for example, when you are scanning an image with a periodic structure (such as a checkered shirt or a half-toned image), scanning a digital image, taking a digital photograph of a periodic pattern, or even when silkscreening.

If you discover the problem in time, the best solution is to move the original image a little bit in the scanner or to change the camera angle slightly.

If you cannot re-create the image file, GIMP offers some filters which may help you with the problem. For more information, see the Despeckle and NL Filter (Non-Linear) filters.

Parasite

A Parasite is additional data which may be written to an XCF file. A parasite is identified by a name, and can be thought of as an extension to the other information in an XCF file.

Parasites of an image component may be read by GIMP plug-ins. Plug-ins may also define their own parasite names, which are ignored by other plug-ins. Examples of parasites are comments, the save options for the TIFF, JPEG and PNG file formats, the gamma value the image was created with and EXIF data.

Path

A Path is a contour composed of straight lines, curves, or both. In GIMP, it is used to form the boundary of a selection, or to be *stroked* to create visible marks on an image. Unless a path is stroked, it is not visible when the image is printed and it is not saved when the image is written to a file (unless you use XCF format).

See the Paths Concepts and Using Paths sections for basic information on paths, and the Path Tool section for information on how to create and edit paths. You can manage the paths in your image with the Paths dialog.

PDB

All of the functions which GIMP and its extensions make available are registered in the Procedure Database (PDB). Developers can look up useful programming information about these functions in the PDB by using the Procedure Browser.

PDF

PDF (Portable Document Format) is a file format which was developed by Adobe to address some of the deficiencies of PostScript. Most importantly, PDF files tend to be much smaller than equivalent PostScript files. As with PostScript, GIMP's support of the PDF format is through the free Ghostscript libraries.

Pixel

A pixel is a single dot, or "picture element", of an image. A rectangular image may be composed of thousands of pixels, each representing the color of the image at a given location. The value of a pixel typically consists of several Channels, such as the Red, Green and Blue components of its color, and sometimes its Alpha (transparency).

Plugin

Optional extensions for the GIMP. Plugins are external programs that run under the control of the main GIMP application and provide specific functions on-demand. See Section 13.1 for further information.

PNG

PNG is the acronym of "Portable Network Graphic" (pronounce "ping". This recent format offers many advantages and a few drawbacks: it is not lossy and gives files more heavy than the JPEG format, but it is perfect for saving your images because you can save them several times without losing data each time (it is used for this Help). It supports True Colors (several millions of colors), indexed images (256 colors like GIF), and 256 transparency levels (while GIF supports only two levels).

PostScript

Created by Adobe, PostScript is a page description language mainly used by printers and other output devices. It's also an excellent way to distribute documents. GIMP does not support PostScript directly: it depends on a powerful free software program called Ghostscript.

The great power of PostScript is its ability to represent vector graphics—lines, curves, text, paths, etc.—in a resolution-independent way. PostScript is not very efficient, though, when it comes to representing pixel-based raster graphics. For this reason, PostScript is not a good format to use for saving images that are later going to be edited using GIMP or another graphics program.

PSD

PSD is Adobe Photoshop's native file format, and it is therefore comparable to XCF in complexity. GIMP's ability to handle PSD files is sophisticated but limited: some features of PSD files are not loaded, and only older versions of PSD are supported. Unfortunately, Adobe has now made the Photoshop Software Development Kit — which includes their file format specifications — proprietary, and only available to a limited set of developers approved by Adobe. This does not include the GIMP development team, and the lack of information makes it very difficult to maintain up-to-date support for PSD files.

Quantization

Quantization is the process of reducing the color of a pixel into one of a number of fixed values by matching the color to the nearest color in the colormap. Actual pixel values may have far more precision than the discrete levels which can be displayed by a digital display. If the display range is too small, then abrupt changes in colors (false contours, or banding) may appear where the color intensity changes from one level to another. This is especially noticeable in Indexed images, which have 256 or fewer discrete colors.

One way to reduce quantization effects is to use Dithering. The operations in GIMP which perform dithering are the Blend tool (if you have enabled the dithering option) and the Convert to Indexed command. However, they only work on RGB images and not on Indexed images.

Rendering Intent

Rendering intents are ways of dealing with colors that are out-of- Gamut colors present in the source space that the destination space is incapable of producing. There are four rendering intents defined by the ICC:

Perceptual This rendering intent is typically used for photographic content. It scales one gamut to fit into the other while maintaining the relative position of colors.

Relative colorimetric This rendering intent is typically used for spot colors. Colors that are not out of gamut are left unchanged. Colors outside the gamut are converted to colors with the same lightness, but different saturation, at the edge of the gamut.

Saturation This method is typically used for business graphics. The relative saturation of colors is mostly maintained, but lightning is usually changed.

Absolute colorimetric This rendering intent is most often used in proofing. It preserves the native device white point of the source image.

RGB

Figure 18.3 Additive color model

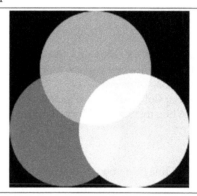

RGB is a color model which has components for Red, Green and Blue. These colors are emitted by screen elements and not reflected as they are with paint. The resulting color is a combination of the three primary RGB colors, with different degrees of lightness. If you look closely at your television screen, whose pitch is less than that of a computer screen, you can see the red, green and blue elements lit with different intensities. The RGB color model is *additive*.

GIMP uses eight bits per channel for each primary color. That means there are 256 intensities (Values) available, resulting in 256×256×256 = 16,777,216 colors.

It is not obvious why a given combination of primary colors produces a particular color. Why, for instance, does 229R+205G+229B give a shade of pink? This depends upon the human eye and brain. There is no color in nature, only a continuous spectrum of wavelengths of light. There are three kinds of cones in the retina. The same wavelength of light acting upon the three types of cones stimulates each of them differently, and the mind has learned, after several million years of evolution, how to recognize a color from these differences.

It is easy to see that no light (0R+0G+0B) produces complete darkness, black, and that full light (255R+255G+255B) produces white. Equal intensity on all color channels produces a level of gray. That is why there can only be 256 gray levels in GIMP.

Mixing two *Primary colors* in RGB mode gives a *Secondary color*, that is, a color in the CMY model. Thus combining Red and Green gives Yellow, Green and Blue give Cyan, Blue and Red give Magenta. Don't confuse secondary colors with *Complementary colors* which are directly opposite a primary color in the chromatic circle:

Figure 18.4 Colorcircle

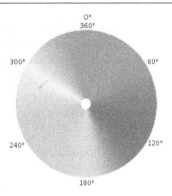

Mixing a primary color with its complementary color gives gray (a neutral color).

It is important to know what happens when you are dealing with colors in GIMP. The most important rule to remember is that decreasing the intensity of a primary color results in increasing the intensity of the complementary color (and vice versa). This is because when you decrease the value of a channel, for instance Green, you automatically increase the relative importance of the other two, here Red and Blue. The combination of these two channels gives the secondary color, Magenta, which is the complementary color of Green.

The Color Picker tool lets you find out the RGB values of a pixel and the hextriplet for the color.

Sample Merge

Sample Merged is an option you can set when you use the Bucket Fill tool, the Color Picker tool and various selection tools. It is useful when you are working on an image with several layers and the active layer is either semi-transparent or has a Layer Mode which is not set to Normal. When you check the Sample Merged option, the color which is used for the operation is the composite color of all the visible layers. When the Sample Merged option is not checked, the color used is the color of the active layer itself.

Saturation

This term refers to color purity. Imagine you add pigment to white paint. Saturation varies from 0 (white, fully toned down, fully diluted) to 100 (pure color).

Supersampling

Supersampling is a more sophisticated antialiasing technique, that is, a method of reducing jagged and stair-stepped edges along a slanted or curved line. Samples are taken at several locations *within* each pixel, not just at the center, and an average color is calculated. This is done by rendering the image at a much higher resolution than the one being displayed and then shrinking it to the desired size, using the extra pixels for calculation. The result is a smoother transition from one line of pixels to another along the edges of objects.

The quality of the result depends on the number of samples. Supersampling is often performed at a range of 2× to 16× the original size. It greatly increases the amount of time needed to draw the image and also the amount of space needed to store the image in memory.

One way to reduce the space and time requirement is to use Adaptive Supersampling. This method takes advantage of the fact that very few pixels are actually on an object boundary, so only those pixels need to be supersampled. At first, only a few samples are taken within a pixel. If the colors are very similar to each other, only those samples are used to calculate the final color. If not, more samples are used. This means that the higher number of samples is calculated only where necessary, which improves performance.

SVG

SVG stands for Scalable Vector Graphics. It is a format for two-dimensional vector graphics, both static and animated. You can export GIMP paths to SVG and you can import SVG documents into GIMP from a vector graphic software. See [WKPD-SVG] for more details.

TGA

TGA (TARGA Image File) is a file format which supports 8, 16, 24 or 32 bits per pixel and optional RLE compression. It was originally developed by the Truevision company. "TGA" stands for Truevision Graphics Adapter and "TARGA" stands for Truevision Advanced Raster Graphics Adapter.

TIFF

TIFF (Tagged Image File Format) is a file format which was developed primarily for scanned raster graphics for color separation. Six different encoding routines are supported, each with one of three different image modes: black and white, grayscale and color. Uncompressed TIFF images may be 1, 4, 8 or 24 bits per pixel. TIFF images compressed using the LZW algorithm may be 6, 8 or 24 bits per pixel. Besides Postscript format, TIFF is one of the most important formats for preliminary stages of printing. It is a high quality file format, which is perfect for images you want to import to other programs like FrameMaker or CorelDRAW.

Tile

A Tile is a part of an image which GIMP currently has open. In order to avoid having to store an entire image in memory at the same time, GIMP divides it into smaller pieces. A tile is usually a square of 64 x 64 pixels, although tiles at the edges of an image may be smaller than that.

At any time, a tile may be in main memory, in the tile cache in RAM, or on disk. Tiles which are currently being worked on are in main memory. Tiles which have been used recently are in RAM. When the tile cache in RAM is full, tiles which have been used least recently are written to disk. GIMP can retrieve the tiles from RAM or disk when they are needed.

Do not confuse these tiles with those in the Tile Filter

URI

A Uniform Resource Identifier (URI) is a string of characters that serves to identify an abstract or a physical resource. URIs are used for the identification of resources in the Internet (such as web pages, miscellaneous files, calling up web services, and for receivers of e-mail) and they are especially used in the Worldwide Web.

URL

URLs (Uniform Resource Locators) are one type of Uniform Resource Identifiers (URIs). URLs identify a resource by its primary access mechanism (commonly http or ftp) and the location of the resource in the computer network. The name of the URI scheme is therefore generally derived from the network protocol used for it. Examples of network protocols are http, ftp and mailto.

Since URLs are the first and most common kinds of URIs, the terms are often used synonymously.

Value

This term often refers to the light intensity, the luminosity of a color. It varies from 0 (black) to 100 (full light).

XCF

XCF is a file format which is special because it is GIMP's native file format: that is, it was designed specifically to store all of the data that goes to make up a GIMP image. Because of this, XCF files may be quite complicated, and there are few programs other than GIMP that can read them.

When an image is stored as an XCF file, the file encodes nearly everything there is to know about the image: the pixel data for each of the layers, the current selection, additional channels if there are any, paths if there are any, and guides. The most important thing that is *not* saved in an XCF file is the undo history.

The pixel data in an XCF file is represented in a lossless compressed form: the image byte blocks are compressed using the lossless RLE algorithm. This means that no matter how many times you load and save an image using this format, not a single pixel or other image data is lost or modified because of this format. XCF files can become very large, however GIMP allows you to compress the files themselves, using either the gzip or bzip2 compression methods, both of which are fast, efficient, and freely available. Compressing an XCF file will often shrink it by a factor of 10 or more.

The GIMP developers have made a great effort to keep the XCF file format compatible across versions. If you create a file using GIMP 2.0, it ought to be possible to open the file in GIMP 1.2.

However, some of the information in the file may not be usable: for example, GIMP 2.0 has a much more sophisticated way of handling text than GIMP 1.2, so a text layer from a GIMP 2.0 XCF file will appear as an ordinary image layer if the file is opened in GIMP 1.2.

YCbCr

YCbCr is a color model which was developed for the PAL television standard as a simple modification to the YUV color model. In the meantime, it has become the CCIR-601 standard for image and video recording. For example, it is used for JPEG pictures and MPEG videos, and therefore also on DVDs, video CDs and for most other widespread digital video standards. Note that a color model is still not a color space, since it doesn't determine which colors are actually meant by "red", "green" and "blue". For a color space, there must still be a reference to a specific absolute color value.

There are color models which do not express a color by the additive basic colors, red, green and blue (RGB), but by other properties, for example, the brightness-color model. Here, the criteria are the basic brightness of the colors (from black, through gray, to white), the colors with the largest portion (red, orange, yellow, green, blue, violet, or other pure colors that lie between them) and the saturation of the colors ("gaudy" to pale). This color model is based on the ability of the eye to recognize small differences in luminosity better than small color differences, and to recognize those better than small differences in saturation. That makes gray text written on a black background easy to read, but blue text on a red background very hard to read, even with the same basic brightness. Such color models are called brightness-color models.

The YCbCr model is a slight adaptation of such a brightness-color model. An RGB color value is divided into a basic brightness, Y, and two components, Cb and Cr, where Cb is a measurement of the deviation from gray in the blue direction, or if it is less than 0.5, in the direction of yellow. Cr is the corresponding measurement for the difference in the direction of red or turquoise. This representation uses the peculiarity of the eye of being especially sensitive to green light. That is why most of the information about the proportion of green is in the basic brightness, Y, an only the deviations for the red and blue portions need to be represented. The Y values have twice the resolution of the other two values, Cb and Cr, in most practical applications, such as on DVDs.

YUV

YUV is a color model which uses two components to represent the color information, luma (the strength of the light per area) and the chrominance, or proportion of color (chroma), where the chrominance again consists of two components. The development of the YUV color model also goes back to the development of color television (PAL), where ways were sought for transmitting the color information along with the black-and-white signal, in order to achieve backwards compatibility with old black and white televisions without having to increase the available transmission bandwidth. From the YUV color model of the analog television techiques, the YCrCb color model was developed, which is used for most kinds of digital image and video compression. Erroneously, the YUV color model is also often spoken about in those fields, although the YCbCr model is actually used. This often causes confusion.

For the calculation of the luma signals, the underlying RGB data is first adjusted with the gamma value of the output device, and an R'G'B' signal is obtained. The three individual components are added together with different weights, to form the brightness information, which also functions as the VBS signal (Video Baseband Signal, the black-and-white signal) for the old black and white televisions.

Y=R+G+B

The exact calculation is more complicated, however, since some aspects of the color perception of the human eye have to be taken into account. For example, green is perceived to be lighter than red, and this is perceived to be lighter than blue. Furthermore, in some systems gamma correction of the basic color is first performed.

The chrominance signals, and the color difference signals also, contain the color information. They are formed by the difference of blue minus luma or red minus luma.

U=B-Y

V=R-Y

From the three generated components, Y, U and V, the individual color proportions of the basic color can be calculated again later:

$Y + U = Y + (B - Y) = Y - Y + B = B$

$Y + V = Y + (R - Y) = Y - Y + R = R$

$Y - B - R = (R + G + B) - B - R = G$

Furthermore, because of the structure of the retina of the human eye, it turns out that the brightness information is perceived at a higher resolution than the color, so that many formats based on the YUV color model compress the chrominance to save bandwidth during transmission.

Part V

Bibliography

18.11   Books

[APRESS00]   Akkana Peck, *Beginning GIMP: From Novice to Professional*, Copyright © 2006 Apress Inc., Apress Inc, www.apress.com, ISBN 1-59059-587-4, http://gimpbook.com/ .

[FOLEY01]   Foley and van Dam, et al, *Computer Graphics, Principles and Practice*, Copyright © 1990 Addison Wesley, Addison Wesley, .

[GROKKING]   Carey Bunks, *Grokking the Gimp*, Copyright © 2000 New Riders Publishing, New Riders Publishing, www.newriders.com , ISBN 0-7357-0924-6, http://gimp-savvy.com/BOOK .

18.12   Online resources

[APOD]   *Astronomy Picture of the Day*, http://antwrp.gsfc.nasa.gov/apod/ .

[APOD01]   *Astronomy Picture of the Day (today)*, http://antwrp.gsfc.nasa.gov/apod/astropix.html .

[APOD02]   *Astronomy Picture of the Day - The Hubble Ultra Deep Field (2004 March 9)* , http://antwrp.gsfc.nasa.gov/apod/ap040309.html .

[APOD03]   *Astronomy Picture of the Day - M51: Cosmic Whirlpool (2002 July 10)* , http://antwrp.gsfc.nasa.gov/apod/ap020710.html .

[APOD04]   *Astronomy Picture of the Day - Saturn: Lord of the Rings (2002 February 15)* , http://antwrp.gsfc.nasa.gov/apod/ap020215.html .

[APOD05]   *Astronomy Picture of the Day - NGC 6369: The Little Ghost Nebula (2002 November 8)* , http://antwrp.gsfc.nasa.gov/apod/ap021108.html .

[APOD06]   *Astronomy Picture of the Day - Disorder in Stephan's Quintet (2000 November 13)* , http://antwrp.gsfc.nasa.gov/apod/ap001113.html .

[APOD07]   *Astronomy Picture of the Day - The Sharpest View of the Sun (2002 November 14)* , http://antwrp.gsfc.nasa.gov/apod/ap021114.html .

[ARGYLLCMS]   *Argyll Color Management System Home Page*, http://www.argyllcms.com/ .

[AdobeRGB]   *Adobe RGB (1998) ICC Profile*, http://www.adobe.com/digitalimag/adobergb.html .

[AdvanceMAME] *AdvanceMAME project*, http://advancemame.sourceforge.net/ .

[BABL]   *babl (pixel format translation library)*, http://www.gegl.org/babl .

[BACH04]   Michael Bach, *Face in blocks*, Copyright © 2004 Michael Bach, http://www.michaelbach.de/ot/fcs_mosaic/ .

[BUDIG01]   *Golden Text*, http://www.home.unix-ag.org/simon/gimp/golden.html .

[BUGZILLA]   *Bugzilla*, http://bugzilla.gnome.org .

[BUGZILLA-GIMP] *Bugzilla-GIMP*, http://bugzilla.gnome.org/browse.cgi?product=GIMP .

[CAIRO]   *Cairo*, http://www.cairographics.org .

[DARWINORTS]   *Darwin Ports Package Manager for OS X*, http://darwinports.org .

[ECI]   *ECI (European Color Initiative) Profiles*, http://www.eci.org/eci/en/060_downloads.php .

[FDL-TRANSLATION] *Unofficial translation of the GNU Free Documentation License*

[FINK]   *Fink Package Manager for OS X*, http://fink.sf.net .

[FREETYPE]   *Freetype 2 home page*, http://www.freetype.org/freetype2/index.html .

[GEGL]   *GEGL (Generic Graphics Library)*, http://gegl.org .

[GEORGIEV01] Todor Georgiev, *Image Reconstruction Invariant to Relighting*, Copyright © 2005 Todor Georgiev, http://www.tgeorgiev.net/Invariant.pdf .

[GHOSTSCRIPT] *Ghostscript project page on Sourceforge.net*, http://sourceforge.net/projects/ghostscript .

[GIMP]   *GIMP - The Gnu Image Manipulation Program*, http://gimp.org .

[GIMP-DEV]   *GIMP Development*, http://developer.gimp.org .

[GIMP-DEV-PLUGIN] *GIMP Plugin Development*, http://developer.gimp.org/plug-ins.html .

[GIMP-DOCS] *GIMP Documentation project page*, http://docs.gimp.org .

[GIMP-FONTS] *Fonts in GIMP 2.0*, http://gimp.org/unix/fonts.html .

[GIMP-NEWSYM26] *List of new symbols in GIMP 2.6*, libgimp-index-new-in-2-6.html .

[GIMP-REGISTRY] *GIMP-Plugin Registry*, http://registry.gimp.org .

[GPL]   *General Public License (GPL)*, http://www.fsf.org/licensing/licenses/gpl.html .

[GQVIEW]   *Homepage of GQview, an image browser*, http://gqview.sourceforge.net .

[GROKKING01] *Grokking the GIMP*, http://gimp-savvy.com/BOOK/index.html .

[GROKKING02] *Grokking the GIMP (9.2 Clickable Image Maps)*, http://gimp-savvy.com/BOOK/-index.html?node81.html .

[GTHUMB]   *gThumb - An Image Viewer and Browser for the GNOME Desktop*, http://gthumb.sourceforge.net .

[GUNTHER04] Gunther Dale, *Making shapes in GIMP*, Copyright © 2004 Dale (Gunther), http://gug.criticalhit.dk/tutorials/gunther1 .

[ICC]   *INTERNATIONAL COLOR CONSORTIUM*, http://www.color.org/ .

[ICCsRGB]   *ICC sRGB PROFILES*, http://www.color.org/srgbprofiles.html .

[INKSCAPE]   *Inkscape is an Open Source vector graphics editor*, http://www.inkscape.org .

[JIMMAC01]   *Alternative icon theme for GIMP 2.4*, http://jimmac.musichall.cz/zip/GIMP-Greyscale-tools-0.1.tar.bz2 .

[LPROF]   *LPROF ICC Profiler*, http://lprof.sourceforge.net/ .

[MSKB-294714] *Microsoft Knowledge Base Article 294714*, http://support.microsoft.com/kb/294714 .

[MsRGB]   *Microsoft sRVB Workspace*, http://www.microsoft.com/whdc/device/display/color/-default.mspx .

[OPENCLIPART-GRADIENT] *Open Clipart - Gradients*, http://openclipart.org/ .

[OPENICC]   *The OpenICC project*, http://freedesktop.org/wiki/OpenIcc .

[PLUGIN-EXIF] *GIMP-Plugin Exif Browser*, http://registry.gimp.org/plugin?id=4153 .

[PLUGIN-FLAMES] *GIMP-Plugin Flames*, http://draves.org/gimp/flame.html ; http://flam3.com/.

[PLUGIN-REDEYE] *A plugin to quickly remove "redeye" caused by camera flash*, http://registry.gimp.org/plugin?id=4212 .

[PLUGIN-RESYNTH] *Resynthesizer is a Gimp plug-in for texture synthesis*, http://www.logarithmic.net/-pfh/resynthesizer .

[PLUGIN-RETINEX] *A plugin providing the Retinex algorithm for GIMP*, http://www-prima.inrialpes.fr/-pelisson/MSRCR.php .

[PLUGIN-SEPARATE] *A plugin providing rudimentary CMYK support for GIMP*, http://www.blackfiveservices.co.uk/separate.shtml .

[PYTHON]   *Python Programming Language*, http://www.python.org .

[SCALE2X]   *Scale2x*, http://scale2x.sourceforge.net/ .

[SCRIBUS]   *Scribus :: Open Source Desktop Publishing*, http://www.scribus.net/ .

[SIOX]   *Simple Interactive Object Extraction*, http://www.siox.org/ .

[TUT01]   Seth Burgess, *Tutorial: How to draw straight lines*, Copyright © 2002 Seth Burgess, http://www.gimp.org/tutorials/Straight_Line .

[TUT02]   Carol Spears, *Tutorial: GIMPLite Quickies*, Copyright © 2004 Carol Spears, http://next.gimp.org/tutorials/Lite_Quickies/ .

[UNICODE]   *Unicode*, http://www.unicode.org .

[WIKIPEDIA]   Wikipedia Foundation, *Wikipedia*, Copyright © 2004 Wikipedia Foundation Inc., http://www.wikipedia.org .

[WKPD-ALPHA]   *Wikipedia - Alpha channel*, http://en.wikipedia.org/wiki/Alpha_channel .

[WKPD-BEZIER]   *Wikipedia - Bézier curve*, http://en.wikipedia.org/wiki/Bezier_curve .

[WKPD-BUMP]   *Wikipedia - Bumpmap*, http://en.wikipedia.org/wiki/Bump_Mapping .

[WKPD-BURN]   *Wikipedia - Burning*, http://en.wikipedia.org/wiki/Dodging_and_burning .

[WKPD-CA]   *Wikipedia - Cellular Automata*, http://en.wikipedia.org/wiki/Cellular_Automata .

[WKPD-CMYK]   *Wikipedia - CMYK*, http://en.wikipedia.org/wiki/CMYK .

[WKPD-COLORSPACE] *Wikipedia - Colorspace*, http://en.wikipedia.org/wiki/Colorspace .

[WKPD-DEFLATE] *Wikipedia - Deflate*, http://en.wikipedia.org/wiki/deflate .

[WKPD-DEINTERLACE] *Wikipedia - Deinterlace*, http://en.wikipedia.org/wiki/Deinterlace .

[WKPD-DITHERING] *Wikipedia - Dithering*, http://en.wikipedia.org/wiki/Dithering .

[WKPD-DODGE]   *Wikipedia - Dodging*, http://en.wikipedia.org/wiki/Dodging_and_burning .

[WKPD-EXIF]   *Wikipedia - EXIF*, http://en.wikipedia.org/wiki/EXIF .

[WKPD-FILEFORMAT] *Wikipedia - Fileformat*, http://en.wikipedia.org/wiki/Image_file_format .

[WKPD-GAMUT]   *Wikipedia - Gamut*, http://en.wikipedia.org/wiki/Gamut .

[WKPD-GIF]   *Wikipedia - GIF*, http://en.wikipedia.org/wiki/GIF .

[WKPD-GNU]   *Wikipedia - GNU*, http://en.wikipedia.org/wiki/GNU .

[WKPD-HISTOGRAM] *Wikipedia - Histogram*, http://en.wikipedia.org/wiki/Image_histogram .

[WKPD-HSV]   *Wikipedia - HSV*, http://en.wikipedia.org/wiki/HSL_and_HSV .

[WKPD-ICC]   *Wikipedia - ICC Profile*, http://en.wikipedia.org/wiki/ICC_Profile .

[WKPD-INTERPOL] *Wikipedia - Interpolation*, http://en.wikipedia.org/wiki/Interpolation .

[WKPD-JPEG]   *Wikipedia - JPEG*, http://en.wikipedia.org/wiki/JPEG .

[WKPD-LAB]   *Wikipedia - L*a*b*, http://en.wikipedia.org/wiki/Lab_color_space .

[WKPD-LZW]   *Wikipedia - LZW*, http://en.wikipedia.org/wiki/LZW .

[WKPD-MOIRE]   *Wikipedia - Moire*, http://en.wikipedia.org/wiki/Moire .

[WKPD-PACKBITS] *Wikipedia - PackBits*, http://en.wikipedia.org/wiki/PackBits .

[WKPD-PNG]   *Wikipedia - PNG,* http://en.wikipedia.org/wiki/Portable_Network_Graphics .

[WKPD-RASTER]   *Wikipedia - Raster Graphics,* http://en.wikipedia.org/wiki/Raster_graphics .

[WKPD-RETINA]   *Wikipedia - Retina,* http://en.wikipedia.org/wiki/Retina .

[WKPD-RI]   *Wikipedia - Rendering Intent,* http://en.wikipedia.org/wiki/Rendering_intent .

[WKPD-SEPIA]   *Wikipedia - Sepia,* http://en.wikipedia.org/wiki/Sepia .

[WKPD-SUBSAMPLING] *Wikipedia - Chroma subsampling,* http://en.wikipedia.org/wiki/-Chroma_Subsampling .

[WKPD-SVG]   *Wikipedia - SVG,* http://en.wikipedia.org/wiki/Scalable_Vector_Graphics .

[WKPD-URI]   *Wikipedia - URI,* http://en.wikipedia.org/wiki/Uniform_Resource_Identifier .

[WKPD-URL]   *Wikipedia - URL,* http://en.wikipedia.org/wiki/Uniform_Resource_Locator .

[WKPD-Web-colors]   *Wikipedia - Web-colors,* http://en.wikipedia.org/wiki/Web_colors .

[WKPD-YCBCR]   *Wikipedia - YCbCr,* http://en.wikipedia.org/wiki/YCbCr .

[WKPD-YUV]   *Wikipedia - YUV,* http://en.wikipedia.org/wiki/YUV .

[XDS]   *Direct Save Protocol (XDS),* http://freedesktop.org/wiki/Specifications/XDS .

[XNVIEW]   *XnView,* http://perso.orange.fr/pierre.g/xnview/enhome.html .

Part VI

GIMP History

.1 The Very Beginning

According to Peter Mattis and Spencer Kimball, the original creators of GIMP, in their announcement of GIMP 0.54:

The GIMP arose from the ashes of a hideously crafted CS164 (compilers) class project. The setting: early morning. We were both weary from lack of sleep and the terrible strain of programming a compiler in LISP. The limits of our patience had long been exceeded, and yet still the dam held.

And then it happened. Common LISP messily dumped core when it could not allocate the 17 MB it needed to generate a parser for a simple grammar using yacc. An unbelieving moment passed, there was one shared look of disgust, and then our project was vapor. We had to write something... *ANYTHING* ... useful. Something in C. Something that did not rely on nested lists to represent a bitmap. Thus, the GIMP was born.

Like the phoenix, glorious, new life sprung out of the burnt remnants of LISP and yacc. Ideas went flying, decisions were made, the GIMP began to take form.

An image manipulation program was the consensus. A program that would at the very least lessen the necessity of using commercial software under "Windoze" or on the "Macintoy". A program that would provide the features missing from the other X painting and imaging tools. A program that would help maintain the long tradition of excellent and free UNIX applications.

Six months later, we've reached an early beta stage. We want to release now to start working on compatibility issues and cross-platform stability. Also, we feel now that the program is actually usable and would like to see other interested programmers developing plug-ins and various file format support.

.2 The Early Days of GIMP

Version 0.54 Version 0.54 was released in February 1996, and had a major impact as the first truly professional free image manipulation program. This was the first free program that could compete with the big commercial image manipulation programs.

Version 0.54 was a beta release, but it was so stable that you could use it for daily work. However, one of the major drawbacks of 0.54 was that the toolkit (the slidebars, menus, dialog boxes, etc.) was built on Motif, a commercial toolkit. This was a big drawback for systems like "Linux", because you had to buy Motif if you wanted to use the faster, dynamically linked GIMP. Many developers were also students running Linux, who could not afford to buy Motif.

Version 0.60 When 0.60 was released in July 1996, it had been under S and P (Spencer and Peter) development for four months. Main programming advantages were the new toolkits, GTK (GIMP Toolkit) and gdk (GIMP Drawing Kit), which eliminated the reliance on Motif. For the graphic artist, 0.60 was full of new features like: basic layers; improved painting tools (sub-pixel sampling, brush spacing); a better airbrush; paint modes; etc.

Version 0.60 was only a developer's release, and was not intended for widespread use. It served as a workbench for 0.99 and the final 1.0 version, so functions and enhancement could be tested and dropped or changed. You can look at 0.60 as the alpha version of 0.99.

Version 0.99 In February 1997, 0.99 came on the scene. Together with other developers, S and P had made several changes to GIMP and added even more features. The main difference was the new API (Application Programming Interface) and the "PDB", which made it possible to write scripts; Script-Fus (or macros) could now automate things that you would normally do by hand. GTK/gdk had also changed and was now called GTK+. In addition, 0.99 used a new form of tile-based memory handling that made it possible to load huge images into GIMP (loading a 100 MB image into GIMP is no problem). Version 0.99 also introduced a new native GIMP file format called XCF.

The new API made it really easy to write extensions and plug-ins for GIMP. Several new plug-ins and extensions emerged to make GIMP even more useful (such as SANE, which enables scanning directly into GIMP).

In the summer of 1997, GIMP had reached version 0.99.10, and S and P had to drop most of their support since they had graduated and begun jobs. However, the other developers of GIMP continued under the orchestration of Federico Mena to make GIMP ready for prime time.

GTK+ was separated from GIMP in September 1997. GTK+ had been recognized as an excellent toolkit, and other developers began using it to build their own applications.

GIMP went into feature freeze in October 1997. This meant that no new features would be added to the GIMP core libraries and program. GUM (GIMP Users Manual) version 0.5 was also released early in October 1997. The developing work continued to make GIMP stable and ready for version 1.0.

.3 The One to Change the World

Version 1.0 GIMP version 1.0 was released on June 5, 1998. Finally, GIMP was considered stable enough to warrant a worldwide announcement and professional use.

Version 1.2 GIMP version 1.2.0 was released on December 25, 2000. Compared to the version 1.0, it included mostly fixes and improvements of the user interface.

.4 Version 2.0

First, a statistic: the GIMP code base contains about 230,000 lines of C code, and most of these lines were rewritten in the evolution from 1.2 to 2.0. From the user's point of view, however, GIMP 2 is fundamentally similar to GIMP 1; the features are similar enough that GIMP 1 users won't be lost. As part of the restructuring work, the developers cleaned up the code greatly, an investment that, while not directly visible to the user, will ease maintenance and make future additions less painful. Thus, the GIMP 2 code base is significantly better organized and more maintainable than was the case for GIMP 1.2.

Basic tools The basic tools in GIMP 2 are not very different from their predecessors in GIMP 1. The "Select Regions by Color" tool is now shown in the GIMP toolbox, but was already included in GIMP 1 as a menu option in the Select menu. The Transform tool has been divided into several specialized tools: Rotation, Scale, Shearing and Perspective. Color operations are now associated with layers in the menu Layer → Colors, but this is merely a cleanup: they were already present in the Image menu (illogically, since they are layer operations). Thus no completely new tools appear in this release, but two of the tools have been totally revamped compared to the older versions: the Text tool and the Path tool. More on this below.

The user interface for tools has also changed significantly. The "Tool Options" dialog box was modified to not resize itself when a new tool is chosen. Most users felt that the window changing size when a new tool was selected was annoying. Now, by default the "Tool Options" dialog is constantly open and docked under the toolbox, where it can easily be found.

Tool options The "Tool Options" for many tools have new possibilities that weren't available in GIMP 1. Without being exhaustive, here are the most noticeable improvements.

All selection tools now have mode buttons: Replace, Add, Subtract and Intersect. In GIMP 1 the only way to change the selection mode was to use the **Ctrl** or **Shift** buttons, which could get very confusing because those buttons also had other functions. For example, pressing and holding the **Shift** key while using the Rectangle selection tool forces the rectangle to be a square. Thus, to add a square selection you would first press **Shift**, then click the mouse, then release **Shift**, then press **Shift** again, then sweep out the selection with the mouse, then release **Shift**. It can now be done more easily.

For transformation tools, buttons now control which object (layer, selection or path) is affected by the transformation. You can for example transform a rectangular selection to various quadrilateral shapes. Path transformation in particular is now easier than it was before.

"Fade out" and "Paint Using Gradient" are now available for all drawing tools. In fact, all drawing tools now have their own individual brush, gradient and pattern settings, in contrast to GIMP 1 where there was a single global setting that applied to all drawing tools. Now you can select different brushes for the Pencil and the Paint Brush, or different patterns for the Clone and Fill tools. You can change these setting by using your mouse wheel over the relevant resource button (this is most useful for quickly and easily choosing a brush).

User Interface The most visible changes in GIMP 2 concern the user interface. GIMP now uses the GTK2+ graphical toolkit in place of GTK+. One of the nice features brought by the new libraries is dockable dialogs, and tab navigation between dialogs docked in the same window — a feature present in several popular web browsers. GIMP 1 was famous for opening dialogs anywhere on your screen; GIMP 2 can be told to use fixed boxes. Dialogs now include a little tab-customization menu, which provides maximum flexibility in organizing your workspace.

The Image window has some interesting new features. These are not necessarily activated by default, but they can be checked as options in the Preferences → Interface → Image Windows menu. "Show Brush Outline", for example, allows you to see the outline of the brush when using drawing tools. In the "Appearance" sub-section, you can toggle whether a menu bar is present at the top of image windows. You can set an option to work with the new fullscreen mode. Viewing options are also available from all image windows using right click to bring up the menu, then selecting "View". The so-called "image" menu is also available by clicking on a little triangle in the top left corner of the drawing space. The setting you choose in the "Preferences" dialog is used as the default value, and options you set from an image are used only for that image. (You can also toggle fullscreen mode by using the **F11** key; the **Esc** key also exits fullscreen mode).

GIMP 2 features keyboard accelerators to ease menu access. If you find that navigating through menus using your mouse is onerous, the solution may be to use the keyboard. For example, if the menu bar is present, to create a new image just hit Alt-F-N. Without the menu bar, hit Shift-F10 to open the top-left menu, and use direction keys or **F** then **N** to create the new image. Keyboard accelerators are different from shortcuts: accelerators are useful to navigate through menus, whereas shortcuts call a specific menu item directly. For example, Ctrl-N is a shortcut, and the quickest way to open a new image.

To ease access to your most commonly used menu items, the GIMP has provided dynamic shortcuts for many years. When a menu is open, you can hover over the desired menu item and hold down your shortcut combination. This feature is still present, but is deactivated by default in the GIMP 2.0, to avoid accidental re-assigning of existing shortcuts.

The GIMP also ships with a number of sets of key-bindings for its menus. If you would like to replace the default GIMP keybindings by Photoshop bindings, for example, you can move the file `menurc` in your user data directory to `oldmenurc`, rename `ps-menurc` to `menurc` and restart GIMP.

Handling Tabs and Docks The GIMP 2.0 introduces a system of tabbed dialogs to allow you to make your workspace look the way you want it to be. Almost all dialogs can be dragged to another dialog window and dropped to make a tabbed dialog set.

Furthermore, at the bottom of each dialog, there is a dockable area: drag and drop tabs here to attach dialogs beneath the bottom tab group.

Scripting "Python-fu" is now the standard external scripting interface for GIMP 2. This means that you can now use GIMP functions in Python scripts, or conversely use Python to write GIMP plug-ins. Python is relatively easy to understand even for a beginner, especially in comparison to the Lisp-like Scheme language used for Script-Fu in GIMP 1. The Python bindings are augmented by a set of classes for common operations, so you are not forced to search through the complete GIMP Procedural Database in order to carry out basic operations. Moreover, Python has integrated development environments and a gigantic library, and runs not only on Linux but also on Microsoft Windows and Apples Mac OS X. The biggest drawback, for GIMP 2.0, is that the standard user interface offered in Python-fu does not use the complete power of the Python language. The interface is currently designed to support simple scripts, but a more sophisticated version is a goal of future development.

GIMP-Perl is no longer distributed with the standard GIMP 2 distribution, but is available as a separate package. Currently, GIMP-Perl is supported only on Unix-like operating systems. It includes both a simple scripting language, and the ability to code more polished interfaces using the Gtk2 perl module. Direct pixel manipulation is available through the use of PDL.

Script-Fu, based on "Scheme", has the same drawbacks as before: not intuitive, hard to use and lacking a real development environment. It does, however, have one major advantage compared to Python-fu: Script-Fu scripts are directly interpreted by GIMP and do not require any additional software installation. Python-fu requires that you install a package for the Python language.

The Text Tool The big problem with the standard text tool in GIMP 1 was that text could not be modified after it was rendered. If you wanted to change anything about the text, all you could do was "undo" and try again (if you were lucky enough to have sufficient undo history available, and then of course you would also undo any other work you had done in the meantime). In GIMP 1.2 there was also a "dynamic text" plug-in that allowed you to create special text layers and keep them around indefinitely, in a modifiable form, but it was buggy and awkward to use. The second generation Text tool is an enhanced combination of the old Text tool and the Dynamic Text plugin. Now all options are available in the "Tool Options" : font, font size, text color, justify, antialiasing, indent, spacing. To create a new text item, click in the image and a little editor pops up. Text appears on the image while you are editing (and carriage returns are handled properly!). A new dedicated layer is created; this layer resizes dynamically to match the text you key in. You can import plain text from a file, and you can even do things like writing from right to left in Arabic. If you select a text layer, clicking on it opens the editor, and you can then modify your text.

The Path Tool The second generation Path tool has a completely new interface. The first major difference you notice is that paths are no longer required to be closed. A path can be made up of a number of disjoint curve segments. The next major difference is that now the path tool has three different modes, Design, Edit and Move.

In Design mode, you can create a path, add nodes to an existing path and modify the shape of a curve either by dragging edges of the curve or dragging the "handles" of a node.

In Edit mode, you can add nodes in the middle of curve edges, and remove nodes or edges, as well as change the shape of the curve. You can also connect two path components.

The third mode, Move, is, as you might expect, used to move path components. If your path has several components, you can move each path component separately. To move all components at once, use the **Shift** key.

Two other path-related features are new in the GIMP 2.0. The GIMP can not only import an SVG image as a raster image, but can also keep SVG paths intact as GIMP paths. This means that the GIMP is now more able than ever to complement your favorite vector drawing tool. The other feature which has made the path tool much better is the introduction of vector-based stroking. In previous versions, stroking paths and selections was a matter of drawing a brush-stroke along the path. This mode is still available, but it is now possible to stroke a curve accurately, using the vector library libart.

Other improvements Some other improvements in brief:

- Higher-quality antialiasing in some places — most notibly in the Text tool.
- Icons and menus are skinnable. You can create your own icon set and apply it to the toolbox using the Preference → Interface menu option. A theme called "small" is included with the standard distribution.
- An image can be saved as a template and used to create new images.
- There are four new combination modes for layers that lie one on top of another within an image: "Hard Light", "Soft Light", "Grain Extract" and "Grain Merge".
- If there is an active selection, you can crop the image directly to the selection size using image menu Image → Crop.
- As well as being able to create guides, there's now a grid functionality in GIMP. It is complementary to the guides functionality and makes it easier to position objects so that they align perfectly.
- The Layers dialog is more coherent, in that there are no more hidden functions accessed only with right click on the miniature image of the layer that appears there. You can now handle layer operations directly from the image menu: Layer Mask, Transparency, Transformation and Layer Color operations are directly in the Layer submenu.
- Color display filters are now available from the image menu View → Display Filters. Using them, you can simulate different gamma values, different contrasts, or even color deficient vision, without altering your original image. This actually has been a feature of the GIMP developer versions for a long time, but it has never been stable enough to appear in a stable version of the GIMP before.

- The color selection dialog has a new CMYK mode, associated with the printer icon.

- Data stored in EXIF tags by digital cameras are now handled in read and write mode for JPEG files.

- MNG animations are now supported. The MNG file format can be considered as animated PNG. It has all the advantages of PNG over GIF, such as more colors, 256 levels of transparency, and perhaps most importantly, lack of patent encumbrance. The format is a web standard and all recent popular web browsers support it.

- The GIMP Animation package now does onion-skinning, a bluescreen feature was added as well as audio support.

- A channel mixer filter, previously available from the web as an add-on, appears in Filters → Colors.

.5 What's New in GIMP 2.2?

Here is a brief summary of some of the most important new features introduced in GIMP 2.2. There are many other smaller changes that long-time users will notice and appreciate (or complain about!). There are also important changes at the level of plug-in programming and Script-Fu creating that are not covered here.

Interoperability and Standards Support

- You can drag-and-drop or copy-and-paste image data from the GIMP to any application which supports image/png drops (currently Abiword and Kword at least) and image/xml+svg drops (Inkscape supports this one). So you can copy-and-paste curves into the GIMP from Inkscape, and then drag a selection into Abiword to include it inline in your document.

- Patterns can now be any supported `GtkPixbuf` format, including png, jpeg, xbm and others.

- GIMP can load gradients from SVG files, and palettes from ACT and RIFF files.

- Drag-and-drop support has been extended. You can now drop files and URIs onto an image window, where they will be opened in the existing image as new layers.

> **Note**
>
> Please note, that Drag and Drop will not work for Apple Mac OS X between GIMP and the finder. This is due to a lack of functionality on Apples X11.app

Shortcut Editor You can now edit your shortcuts in a dedicated dialog, as well as continue to use the little-known dynamic shortcuts feature (which has been there since 1.2).

Plug-in Previews We have provided a standard preview widget for plug-in authors which greatly reduces the amount of code required to support previews. David Odin has integrated this widget into all the current filters, so that now many more filters in the GIMP include a preview which updates in real time, and the various previews behave much more consistently.

Real-Time Previews of Transform Operations The transform tools (shear, scale, perspective and rotate) can now show a real-time preview of the result of the operation when the tool is in "Traditional" mode. Previously, only a transforming grid was shown.

GNOME Human Interface Guide Conformance A lot of work has been done on making the GIMP's interface simpler and more usable for newcomers. Most dialogs now follows the GNOME HIG to the best of our knowledge. In addition, dialogs have separated out or removed many "Advanced" options, and replaced them with sane defaults or hidden them in an expander.

GTK+ 2.4 Migration

- Menus use the `GtkUIManager` to generate menu structure dynamically from XML data files.

- A completely revamped File Chooser is used everywhere in the GIMP for opening or saving files. The best thing about it is that it lets you create a set of "bookmarks", making it possible to navigate quickly and easily to commonly used directories.

- GIMP now supports fancy ARGB cursors when they are available on the system.

Basic Vector Support Using the GFig plug-in, the GIMP now supports the basic functionality of vector layers. The GFig plug-in supports a number of vector graphics features such as gradient fills, Bezier curves and curve stroking. It is also the easiest way to create regular or irregular polygons in the GIMP. In the GIMP 2.2, you can create GFig layers, and re-edit these layers in GFig afterwards. This level of vector support is still quite primitive, however, in comparison to dedicated vector-graphics programs such as Inkscape.

Also . . . There are many other smaller user-visible features. A rapid-fire list of some of those features is below.

- It is now possible to run the GIMP in batch mode without an X server.

- We have a GIMP binary (GIMP-console) which is not linked to GTK+ at all.

- Improved interface for extended input devices

- Editable toolbox: You can now decide which tools should be shown in the Toolbox, and their order. In particular, you can add any or all of the Color Tools to the Toolbox if you wish to.

- Histogram overlays R, G and B histograms on the Value histogram, and calculates the histogram only for the contents of the selection.

- Shortcuts are now shared across all GIMP windows.

.6 What's New in GIMP 2.4?

Refreshed Look A whole new default icon theme has been created for 2.4. The icons comply with the Tango style guidelines so GIMP doesn't feel out of place on any of the supported platforms. Regardless of whether you run GIMP under Microsoft Windows, Mac OS X or Linux (GNOME, KDE or Xfce), GIMP provides a polished, consistent look.

Figure 5 New Look of the toolbox in GIMP 2.4

Additionally the icons also have enhanced usability on dark widget themes, which is a common setting among digital artists.

For artists preferring more desaturated color theme for their icons is an alternative icon theme available for download [JIMMAC01].

Scalable Brushes The tool options now include a brush size slider that affects both the parametric and bitmap brushes. This has been an oft-requested feature from both digital painters and photo editors.

Figure 6 Scalable brushes in GIMP 2.4

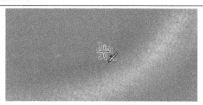

Unlike previous versions of GIMP, regardless of whether you're using a bitmap brush, parametric brush or even a picture tube (multiple bitmaps), you can easily set the brush size with either the tool options dock slider or an external device such as a MIDI slider or knob or a USB device like the Griffin Powermate.

Selection Tools The selection tools have been rewritten from scratch to allow resizing of existing selections. Additionally the rectangular selection tool includes a setting for creating rounded corners as this has been identified as a very common task among web designers.

Figure 7 Selection tools in GIMP 2.4

The learning curve for the tools has been flattened as the key functionality is available without obscure shortcuts that confused GIMP beginners. Most of the existing shortcuts still work, but the functionality is either available through the tool options or made obsolete due to the interactive move and resize on canvas.

While the tools have been redesigned to make them easier to understand for the newbies, all the former functionality is there. You can still constrain aspect ratios or specific sizes.

Foreground Select Tool Selecting individual objects on images is easier now with a new foreground select tool. It is done in two steps. First, you make select region of interest which contains the entire object. Then you paint over selected area with a brush, not crossing object's border. Release mouse button when you're done and look, if there are dark blue spots on your objects. If there are some, paint with a brush over them again and release to refine selection. When there are no more blue areas inside the object, press Enter and there you have a perfectly selected object.

Align Tool While GIMP has provided a grid and guideline functionality, the actual alignment of objects had to be done manually. A new tool comes at rescue ...

Changes in menus Most notable is the new top-level Color menu that accumulates most tools, plug-ins and scripts that adjust colors in RGB/Grayscale mode and color palettes in Indexed mode. So now you can reach functions like Levels or Curves much faster than before, unless you define your own keyboard shortcuts for them using the improved keyboard shortcuts manager.

In the new version of GIMP, some menu entries have changed their names and position. It was done mostly to simplify learning curve and improve user experience. After all, "HSV Noise" and "RGB Noise" sound more meaningful than "Scatter HSV" and "Scatter RGB", don't they? And status bar hints for all plug-ins and scripts are quite helpful too.

Support for file formats

- Support for Photoshop ABR brush format;
- Improved reading/writing EXIF in JPEG;
- Importing clipping paths in TIFF;
- Layer masks can be saved to PSD;

- 16/32 bit bitmaps and alpha-channel support in BMP;
- 24 bit and Vista icons can be opened and saved.

Fullscreen Editing The fullscreen mode has been improved to not only allow getting a full scale preview of the artwork, but also allow comfortable editing. The artist has maximum screen estate available while all functionality is quickly accessible by pressing the **Tab** key (toggles visibility of all docks) when working fullscreen.

Whether painting or touching up photos, fullscreen editing keeps all the distracting elements out of sight on a key press. It's like observing stars in a field as opposed to a light-polluted city.

Color Management and Soft-proofing GIMP now provides full support for color profiles allowing precise color modification throughout the whole "digital darkroom" process.

Figure 8 Color management in GIMP 2.4

New Crop Tool Just like the selection tools, the new crop tool has been enhanced since the last release. The resize handles actually resize the crop rectangle instead of providing both resize and move functionality. The tool behaves more naturally and consistently with other GIMP tools. For details see Section 14.4.4.

To move, simply drag the rectangle clicking within the area. Resizing is possible in one or two axes at the same time dragging the handle-bars on the sides and corners. The outside area is darkened with a nice passepartout effect to better get the idea of how the final crop will look like.

Red Eye Removal While numerous red-eye workflows exist already, GIMP now features a very convenient auto-magic filter to remove red eye from your shots.

Healing Brush The healing brush is a new tool, similar in the working of the clone tool, that permits to quickly fix small defects or imperfections due to scratching or dust. In fact the tool is smart enough to being able to *understand* where and how to modify an image to cure these defects based on image color context.

Perspective Clone Here is another clone-like new tool that is able to adapt the destination geometry, instead of color as does the healing brush, based on preselected distortion settings. As the name suggests, perfect when copying images blocks with some type of prospective changes.

Lens Distortion A very common problem exposing itself especially when using cheaper lenses is barrel distortion and vignetting. Luckily GIMP provides a brand new filter to compensate for both problems. Saving photographer's pocket is our mission!

Various Other Improvements In addition to all the above, GIMP has been improved in other areas such as:

- Better status information for tools in the window status bar.
- Various speedups in composing functions and gradient drawing.
- Zoomable preview widget for plugins.

.7 What's New in GIMP 2.6?

GIMP 2.6 is an important release from a development point of view. It features changes to the user interface addressing some often received complaints, and a tentative integration of GEGL, the graph based image processing library that will eventually bring high bit-depth and non-destructive editing to GIMP.

User Interface

Toolbox Menubar removed The toolbox menubar has been removed and merged with the image window menubar. To be able to do this a window called the empty image window has been introduced. It hosts the menubar and keeps the application instance alive when no images are opened. It also acts as a drag and drop target. When opening the first image the empty image window is transformed into a normal image window, and when closing the last image, that window becomes the empty image window.

Figure 9 New Look of the image window in GIMP 2.6

Toolbox and docks are utility windows With the empty image window acting as a natural main window, the Toolbox and Docks windows are now utility windows rather than main windows. This enables window managers to do a much better job of managing the GIMP windows, including omitting the Toolbox and Docks from the taskbar and ensuring that the Toolbox and Docks always are above image windows.

Ability to scroll beyond image border The Navigation dialog now allows panning beyond the image border; so it is no longer a problem to use a brush on the edge of an image that fills the entire display window. Also, if a utility window covers the image, you can pan the image to view or edit the portion covered by the utility window.

Figure 10 Scrolling beyond border

Minor changes

- Renamed Dialogs menu to Windows.
- Keep a list of recently closed Docks and allow reopening them.
- Make opening images in already running GIMP instances work better on Windows.
- You can now enter the image zoom ratio directly in the status bar.
- Added support for using online help instead of a locally installed GIMP Help package.
- Make it possible to lock tabs in docks to prevent accidental moving.

Tools, Filters and Plug-ins

Improved Free Select Tool The freehand select tool has been enhanced to support polygonal selections. It also allows mixing free hand segments with polygonal segments, editing of existing segments, applying angle-constraints to segments, and of course the normal selection tool operations like add and subtract. Altogether this ends up making the Free Select Tool a very versatile, powerful and easy-to-use selection tool.

Figure 11 Polygonal Selection

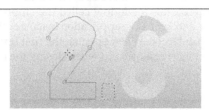

Brush Dynamics Brush dynamics uses an input dynamic such as pressure, velocity, or random, to modify brush parameters such as opacity, hardness, size, or color; every brush supports size and opacity, most support more. Velocity and random are usable with a mouse. The Ink tool, that supported velocity, has been overhauled to better handle velocity-dependent painting.

Figure 12 Brush Dynamics

Brush dynamics have enabled a new feature in stroking paths. There is now a check box under the "paint tool" option, for emulating brush dynamics if you stroke using a paint tool. What this means is that when your stroke is painted, GIMP tells the brush that the pressure and velocity are varying along the length of the stroke. Pressure starts with no pressure, ramps up to full pressure, and then ramps down again to no pressure. Velocity starts from zero and ramps up to full speed by the end of the stroke.

Minor changes

- Added a bounding box for the Text Tool that supports automatic wrapping of text within that bounding box.

Figure 13 Text tool bounding box

- Move handles for rectangle based tools like Crop and Rectangle Select to the outside of the rectangle when the rectangle is narrow.

Figure 14 Rectangle handles

- Added motion constraints to the Move Tool.
- Improved event smoothing for paint tools.
- Mark the center of rectangles while they are moved, and snap the center to grid and rulers.
- Enable brush scaling for the Smudge tool.
- Added ability to save presets in all color tools for color adjustments you use frequently.

- Allow to transfer settings from *Brightness-Contrast* to *Levels*, and from *Levels* to *Curves*.

- Allow changing opacity on transform tool previews.

- The Screenshot plug-in has been given the ability to capture the mouse cursor (using Xfixes).

- Display aspect ratio of the Crop and Rectangle Select Tool rectangles in the status bar.

- Desaturate has been given an on-canvas preview.

- The Flame plug-in has been extended with 22 new variations.

- Data file folders like brush folders are searched recursively for files.

- Replaced the PSD import plug-in with a rewritten version that does what the old version did plus some other things, for example reading of ICC color profiles.

- Several displays use Cairo library.

Figure 15 Comparing 2.6 display vs 2.4

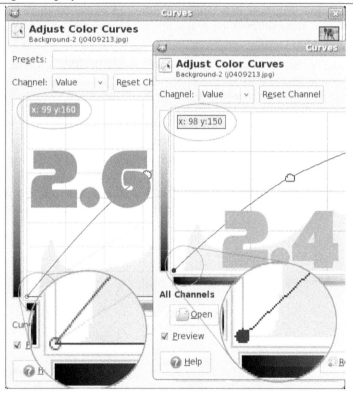

Under the Hood

GEGL Important progress towards high bit-depth and non-destructive editing in GIMP has been made. Most color operations in GIMP are now ported to the powerful graph based image processing framework GEGL [GEGL], meaning that the internal processing is done in 32bit floating point linear light RGBA. By default the legacy 8bit code paths are still used, but a curious user can turn on the use of GEGL for the color operations with Colors / Use GEGL.

In addition to porting color operations to GEGL, an experimental GEGL Operation tool has been added, found in the Tools menu. It enables applying GEGL operations to an image and it gives on-canvas previews of the results. The screenshot below shows this for a Gaussian Blur.

Figure 16 GEGL operation

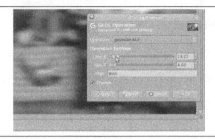

Minor changes Ported many widgets to use the 2D graphics library cairo [CAIRO] for drawing. See this comparison for an example of how much better this looks.

Miscellaneous

Plug-in Development There are new things for a plug-in developer to enjoy as well. For example, procedures can now give a detailed error description in case of an error, and the error can be propagated to the user.

GIMP 2.6 also further enhances its scripting abilities. In particular there is now a much richer API for the creation and manipulation of text layers. Here is a list of new symbols in GIMP 2.6: [GIMP-NEWSYM26].

Backwards Compatibility Some old scripts could not be used with GIMP-2.4. This has been improved and 2.6 should run 2.0 and 2.2 scripts.

Known Problems

- The Utility window hint is currently only known to work well in the Linux GNOME desktop environment and on Windows starting with GIMP 2.6.1.

- Using the Text Tool is currently not an optimal experience. Making it work better is a goal for GIMP 2.8.

- If you build GIMP yourself and don't have GVfs support on your platform you need to explicitly pass `--without-gvfs` to **configure**, otherwise opening remote files will not work properly.

Part VII

Reporting Bugs and Requesting Enhancements

Sad to say, no version of GIMP has yet been absolutely perfect. Even sadder, it is likely that no version ever will be. In spite of all efforts to make everything work, a program as complicated as GIMP is bound to screw things up occasionally, or even crash.

But the fact that bugs are unavoidable does not mean that they should be passively accepted. If you find a bug in GIMP, the developers would like to know about it so they can at least try to fix it.

Suppose, then, that you have found a bug, or at least think you have: you try to do something, and the results are not what you expect. What should you do? How should you report it?

Tip

The procedure for making an *enhancement request*—that is, for asking the developers to add a missing feature—is nearly the same as the procedure for reporting a bug. The only thing you do differently is to mark the report as an "enhancement" at the appropriate stage, as described below.

In common with many other free software projects, GIMP uses a bug-reporting mechanism called *Bugzilla*. This is a very powerful web-based system, capable of managing thousands of bug reports without losing track. In fact, GIMP shares its Bugzilla database with the entire Gnome project. At the time this is being written, Gnome Bugzilla contains 148632 bug reports–no, make that 148633.

.8 Making sure it's a Bug

The first thing you should do, before reporting a bug, is to make an effort to verify that what you are seeing really *is* a bug. It is hard to give a method for doing this that applies to all situations, but reading the documentation will often be useful, and discussing the question on IRC or a mailing list may also be quite helpful. If you are seeing a *crash*, as opposed to mere misbehavior, the odds that it is a true bug are pretty high: well written software programs are not designed to crash under *any* circumstances. In any case, if you have made an conscientious effort to decide whether it is really a bug, and at the end still aren't sure, then please go ahead and report it: the worst that can happen is that you will waste a bit of time for the development team.

Note

Actually there are a few things that are known to cause GIMP to crash but have turned out to be too inconvenient to be worth fixing. One of them is asking GIMP to do something that requires vast amounts of memory, such as creating an image one million pixels on a side.

You should also make sure that you are using an up-to-date version of GIMP: reporting bugs that have already been fixed is just a waste of everybody's time. (GIMP 1 is no longer maintained, so if you use it and find bugs, either upgrade to GIMP 2 or live with them.) Particularly if you are using the development version of GIMP, make sure that you can see the bug in the latest release before filing a report.

If after due consideration you still think you have a legitimate bug report or enhancement request, the next step is to go to GIMP's bugzilla query page (http://bugzilla.gnome.org/query.cgi), and try to see whether somebody else has already reported the same thing.

There are two forms you can use for searching bugs: a simple form to "Find a Specific Bug", and an "Advanced Search".

.8.1 Find a Specific Bug

Figure 17 Bugzilla: Find a Specific Bug

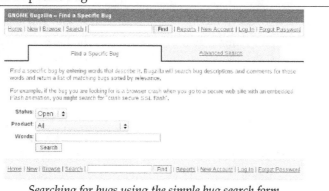

Searching for bugs using the simple bug search form

Using this form, you first should select the Product "GIMP" (classified as "Other") using the drop down list. Then you just have to enter some (space separated) search terms, e.g.

```
filter crash
```

in the text box and click on Search.

.8.2 The Advanced Bug Search Form

The alternative form, the advanced query page, allows you to search the bug database in a variety of ways:

Figure 18 Bugzilla: Advanced Search

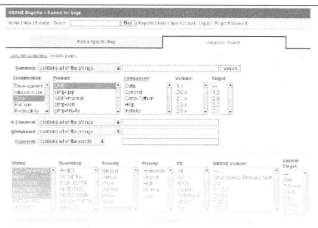

Searching for bugs using the advanced bug search form

Unfortunately this page is a bit more "complicated" to use than it really ought to be (at least, some items are hyperlinks leading to detailed help), but here is basically what you should do:

Summary Set this to "contains any of the words/strings".

In the adjoining text box, give one or more words that somebody would be likely to use in writing a one-sentence summary of a bug similar to yours. For example, if the problem is that zooming too much causes GIMP to crash, the word "zoom" would be good.

Classification Other (since GIMP is not part of the GNOME Desktop suite).

Product Set this to "GIMP" (or "GEGL", "GIMP-manual" etc., if appropriate).

Component, Version, Target Milestone Don't do anything for these.

Comment, Whiteboard, Keywords For now, leave this alone. If your search does not turn up anything, it might be worth entering your search terms in the "Comment" area here, but this often turns out to give you either great masses of stuff or nothing.

Status This field encodes the status of a bug report: whether it is still open, has been resolved, etc. You want to see all relevant bug reports, regardless of status, so you should hold down the mouse and sweep it across all entries. Leaving it alone will not work.

Resolution, Severity, Priority, OS Usually you shouldn't touch these items.

(Any other items) Don't do anything for these.

When you have set these things up, click on the "Search" button at either the top or bottom; they both do the same thing. The result is either a list of bug reports – hopefully not too long – or a message saying "Zarro boogs found". If you don't find a related bug report by doing this, it may be worth trying another search with different terms. If in spite of your best efforts, you file a bug report and it ends up being resolved as "Duplicate", don't be too upset: it has happened repeatedly to the author of this documentation, who works with GIMP Bugzilla nearly every day.

Tip

Depending on your browser configuration (i.e. whether JavaScript is enabled), you may see a link Give me some help. If you click on this link, the page will be reloaded and then moving the mouse pointer over an input widget produces a little help popup.

.9 Reporting the Bug

Okay, so you have done everything you could to make sure, and you still think it's probably a bug. You should then go ahead and file a bug report on the Bugzilla page.

Note

The first time you file a bug report, you will be asked to create a Bugzilla account. The process is easy and painless, and you probably won't even get any spam as a result.

---

1. Bugzilla: Select Classification

   Go to `http://bugzilla.gnome.org/enter_bug.cgi`, and select the classification "Other".

   If you are not logged in, you are automatically redirected to the login page. After entering your user name (login) and password, you get back to the "Select Classification" page.

2. Bugzilla: Pick Product

   Scroll down the next page until you can select the product "GIMP".

> **Tip**
>
> You can skip the above steps and go directly to http://bugzilla.
> gnome.org/enter_bug.cgi?product=GIMP (You still have to login, of
> course.)

3. Bugzilla: Enter Bug: GIMP

   Selecting "GIMP" as product takes you to the following bug report form, which you should fill out as follows. Note that most of the information you enter can be changed later by the developers if you get it wrong, so try to get it right but don't be obsessive about it.

Enter Bug: GIMP

Component Set this to the part of GIMP that the bug affects. Note that you get a short "Component Description" in the text box next to the list when you select a component.

   You have to pick something here, but if you aren't sure, make a guess and don't worry about it.

Version Set this to the version of GIMP that you are using. You always find the version in the menu of the image window: Help → About.

Severity In most cases you should either leave this as "Normal" or set it to "Enhancement", if it is an enhancement request rather than a malfunction. The maintainers will adjust the severity if they think it is warranted.

OS (Operating System) Set this to your OS unless you have a very good reason for thinking that the bug applies to all operating systems.

Summary Give a one-sentence summary that is descriptive enough so that somebody searching for similar bugs would find your bug report on the basis of the words this summary contains.

Description Describe the problem. Be as specific as you can, and include all information that you think might possibly be relevant. The classic totally useless bug report is, "GIMP crashes. This program sucks". There is no hope that the developers can solve a problem if they can't tell what it is.

There are more fields which are hidden by default. (Click "Show Advanced Fields" to show them.) You can ignore them, so we won't describe these fields here.

Sometimes it is very helpful to augment a bug report with a screenshot or some other type of data. If you need to do this, click on the button Add an attachment, and follow the directions. But please don't do this unless you think the attachment is really going to be useful—and if you need to attach a screenshot, don't make it any larger than necessary. Bug reports are likely to remain on the system for years, so there is no sense in wasting memory.

When you have filled out all of these things, press the Commit button and your bug report will be submitted. It will be assigned a number, which you may want to make note of; you will, however, be emailed any time somebody makes a comment on your bug report or otherwise alters it, so you will receive reminders in any case. You can see the current state of your bug report at any time by going to http://bugzilla.gnome.org, entering the bug number in one of the entry boxes and pressing the Find or Quick Search button.

.10 What Happens to a Bug Report after you Submit it

At any time after it is submitted, a bug report has a "Status" that describes how it is currently being handled. Here are the possible values of *Status* and what they mean:

Unconfirmed This is the initial status of a bug report, from the time it is submitted until one of the maintainers reads it and decides whether it is really a valid bug report. Sometimes the maintainers aren't sure, and in the meantime leave the status as "Unconfirmed". In the worst cases, a bug report can stay unconfirmed for a year or longer, but this is considered a bad thing and does not happen very often.

New This means that the bug report has been read by one of the maintainers, and is considered, for the moment at least, to be valid. It does not necessarily mean that anything is going to be done about it immediately: some bug reports, especially enhancement requests, may be perfectly valid and still go for a long time before anybody is able to deal with them. Many bugs, on the other hand, are fixed within hours of being reported.

Assigned This means that a specific person has agreed to work on the bug. It does not, this world being the kind of world that it is, mean that that person will actually *do* anything in particular, so for practical purposes this status means nearly the same thing as "New".

Reopened This means that the bug report was at some point considered by the maintainers to be resolved (i.e., finished), but new information came in that caused them to change their minds: most likely, a change that was intended to fix the problem did not completely work.

Needinfo This is a status you should pay particular attention to. It means that you did not supply enough information in your bug report to enable anything to be done about it. In most cases, no further action will be taken on the bug report until you supply additional information (by adding a comment). If too much time goes by without any input from you, the bug report will eventually be resolved as "Incomplete".

Resolved This means that the maintainers believe that they have finished dealing with the bug report. If you disagree, you can re-open it, but since you cannot force anybody to work on a bug against their will, you should have a good reason for doing so. Bugs can be resolved in a variety of ways. Here are the possible values of *Resolution* and what they mean:

Fixed The bug report is considered valid, and GIMP has been changed in a way that is considered to fix it.

Wontfix The maintainers agree that the bug report is valid, but it would take so much effort to fix, in relation to its importance, that it is not worth the trouble.

Duplicate This means that the same bug has already been reported by somebody else. If you see this resolution, you will also see a pointer to the earlier bug report, which will often give you a lot of useful information.

Notabug This means that the behavior described in the bug report is intentional. It may seem like a bug to you (and there may be many people who agree with you), but the program is working the way it was intended to work, and the developers don't want to change it.

NotGnome The bug report is valid, but it can't be addressed by changing GIMP. Problems in operating systems, window managers, or libraries that GIMP depends on will often be given this resolution. Sometimes the next appropriate step is to file a bug report for the software that is really at fault.

Incomplete The bug report did not contain enough information for anything to be done about it, and the reporter did not respond to requests for more information. Usually a bug report will be open for at least a month or two before it is resolved in this way.

Invalid Something is wrong with the form of the bug report: most commonly, the reporter has accidentally submitted the same bug report multiple times. (This can easily happen by mistake with some web browsers.) Bug reports that incorrectly describe how the program behaves may also be resolved as Invalid.

Note

If you disagree with the resolution of a bug report, you are always free to add your comments to it. Any comment added to any bug report, resolved or not, causes email to be sent to the GIMP Bugzilla mailing list, so it will at least be seen by the maintainers. This does not, of course, mean that they will necessarily respond to it.

Part VIII

GNU Free Documentation License

Note that any translations of the GNU Free Documentation License are not published by the Free Software Foundation, and do not legally state the distribution terms for software that uses the GNU FDL-only the original English text of the GNU FDL does that.

The GIMP Documentation Team

Copyright (C) 2000,2001,2002 Free Software Foundation, Inc. 59 Temple Place, Suite 330, Boston, MA 02111-1307 USA. Everyone is permitted to copy and distribute verbatim copies of this license document, but changing it is not allowed.

.11 PREAMBLE

The purpose of this License is to make a manual, textbook, or other functional and useful document "free" in the sense of freedom: to assure everyone the effective freedom to copy and redistribute it, with or without modifying it, either commercially or noncommercially. Secondarily, this License preserves for the author and publisher a way to get credit for their work, while not being considered responsible for modifications made by others.

This License is a kind of "copyleft", which means that derivative works of the document must themselves be free in the same sense. It complements the GNU General Public License, which is a copyleft license designed for free software.

We have designed this License in order to use it for manuals for free software, because free software needs free documentation: a free program should come with manuals providing the same freedoms that the software does. But this License is not limited to software manuals; it can be used for any textual work, regardless of subject matter or whether it is published as a printed book. We recommend this License principally for works whose purpose is instruction or reference.

.12 APPLICABILITY AND DEFINITIONS

This License applies to any manual or other work, in any medium, that contains a notice placed by the copyright holder saying it can be distributed under the terms of this License. Such a notice grants a world-wide, royalty-free license, unlimited in duration, to use that work under the conditions stated herein. The "Document", below, refers to any such manual or work. Any member of the public is a licensee, and is addressed as "you". You accept the license if you copy, modify or distribute the work in a way requiring permission under copyright law.

A "Modified Version" of the Document means any work containing the Document or a portion of it, either copied verbatim, or with modifications and/or translated into another language.

A "Secondary Section" is a named appendix or a front-matter section of the Document that deals exclusively with the relationship of the publishers or authors of the Document to the Document's overall subject (or to related matters) and contains nothing that could fall directly within that overall subject. (Thus, if the Document is in part a textbook of mathematics, a Secondary Section may not explain any mathematics.) The relationship could be a matter of historical connection with the subject or with related matters, or of legal, commercial, philosophical, ethical or political position regarding them.

The "Invariant Sections" are certain Secondary Sections whose titles are designated, as being those of Invariant Sections, in the notice that says that the Document is released under this License. If a section does not fit the above definition of Secondary then it is not allowed to be designated as Invariant. The Document may contain zero Invariant Sections. If the Document does not identify any Invariant Sections then there are none.

The "Cover Texts" are certain short passages of text that are listed, as Front-Cover Texts or Back-Cover Texts, in the notice that says that the Document is released under this License. A Front-Cover Text may be at most 5 words, and a Back-Cover Text may be at most 25 words.

A "Transparent" copy of the Document means a machine-readable copy, represented in a format whose specification is available to the general public, that is suitable for revising the document straightforwardly with generic text editors or (for images composed of pixels) generic paint programs or (for drawings) some widely available drawing editor, and that is suitable for input to text formatters or for automatic translation to a variety of formats suitable for input to text formatters. A copy made in an otherwise Transparent file format whose markup, or absence of markup, has been arranged to thwart or discourage subsequent modification by readers is not Transparent. An image format is not Transparent if used for any substantial amount of text. A copy that is not "Transparent" is called "Opaque".

Examples of suitable formats for Transparent copies include plain ASCII without markup, Texinfo input format, LaTeX input format, SGML or XML using a publicly available DTD, and standard-conforming simple HTML, PostScript or PDF designed for human modification. Examples of transparent image formats include PNG, XCF and JPG. Opaque formats include proprietary formats that can be read and edited only by proprietary word processors, SGML or XML for which the DTD and/or processing tools are not generally available, and the machine-generated HTML, PostScript or PDF produced by some word processors for output purposes only.

The "Title Page" means, for a printed book, the title page itself, plus such following pages as are needed to hold, legibly, the material this License requires to appear in the title page. For works in formats which do not have any title page as such, "Title Page" means the text near the most prominent appearance of the work's title, preceding the beginning of the body of the text.

A section "Entitled XYZ" means a named subunit of the Document whose title either is precisely XYZ or contains XYZ in parentheses following text that translates XYZ in another language. (Here XYZ stands for a specific section name mentioned below, such as "Acknowledgements", "Dedications", "Endorsements", or "History".) To "Preserve the Title" of such a section when you modify the Document means that it remains a section "Entitled XYZ" according to this definition.

The Document may include Warranty Disclaimers next to the notice which states that this License applies to the Document. These Warranty Disclaimers are considered to be included by reference in this License, but only as regards disclaiming warranties: any other implication that these Warranty Disclaimers may have is void and has no effect on the meaning of this License.

.13 VERBATIM COPYING

You may copy and distribute the Document in any medium, either commercially or noncommercially, provided that this License, the copyright notices, and the license notice saying this License applies to the Document are reproduced in all copies, and that you add no other conditions whatsoever to those of this License. You may not use technical measures to obstruct or control the reading or further copying of the copies you make or distribute. However, you may accept compensation in exchange for copies. If you distribute a large enough number of copies you must also follow the conditions in section 4.

You may also lend copies, under the same conditions stated above, and you may publicly display copies.

.14 COPYING IN QUANTITY

If you publish printed copies (or copies in media that commonly have printed covers) of the Document, numbering more than 100, and the Document's license notice requires Cover Texts, you must enclose the copies in covers that carry, clearly and legibly, all these Cover Texts: Front-Cover Texts on the front cover, and Back-Cover Texts on the back cover. Both covers must also clearly and legibly identify you as the publisher of these copies. The front cover must present the full title with all words of the title equally prominent and visible. You may add other material on the covers in addition. Copying with changes limited to the covers, as long as they preserve the title of the Document and satisfy these conditions, can be treated as verbatim copying in other respects.

If the required texts for either cover are too voluminous to fit legibly, you should put the first ones listed (as many as fit reasonably) on the actual cover, and continue the rest onto adjacent pages.

If you publish or distribute Opaque copies of the Document numbering more than 100, you must either include a machine-readable Transparent copy along with each Opaque copy, or state in or with each Opaque copy a computer-network location from which the general network-using public has access to download using public-standard network protocols a complete Transparent copy of the Document, free of added material. If you use the latter option, you must take reasonably prudent steps, when you begin distribution of Opaque copies in quantity, to ensure that this Transparent copy will remain thus accessible at the stated location until at least one year after the last time you distribute an Opaque copy (directly or through your agents or retailers) of that edition to the public.

It is requested, but not required, that you contact the authors of the Document well before redistributing any large number of copies, to give them a chance to provide you with an updated version of the Document.

.15 MODIFICATIONS

You may copy and distribute a Modified Version of the Document under the conditions of sections 3 and 4 above, provided that you release the Modified Version under precisely this License, with the Modified Version filling the role of the Document, thus licensing distribution and modification of the Modified Version to whoever possesses a copy of it. In addition, you must do these things in the Modified Version:

A. Use in the Title Page (and on the covers, if any) a title distinct from that of the Document, and from those of previous versions (which should, if there were any, be listed in the History section of the Document). You may use the same title as a previous version if the original publisher of that version gives permission.

B. List on the Title Page, as authors, one or more persons or entities responsible for authorship of the modifications in the Modified Version, together with at least five of the principal authors of the Document (all of its principal authors, if it has fewer than five), unless they release you from this requirement.

C. State on the Title page the name of the publisher of the Modified Version, as the publisher.

D. Preserve all the copyright notices of the Document.

E. Add an appropriate copyright notice for your modifications adjacent to the other copyright notices.

F. Include, immediately after the copyright notices, a license notice giving the public permission to use the Modified Version under the terms of this License, in the form shown in the Addendum below.

G. Preserve in that license notice the full lists of Invariant Sections and required Cover Texts given in the Document's license notice.

H. Include an unaltered copy of this License.

I. Preserve the section Entitled "History", Preserve its Title, and add to it an item stating at least the title, year, new authors, and publisher of the Modified Version as given on the Title Page. If there is no section Entitled "History" in the Document, create one stating the title, year, authors, and publisher of the Document as given on its Title Page, then add an item describing the Modified Version as stated in the previous sentence.

J. Preserve the network location, if any, given in the Document for public access to a Transparent copy of the Document, and likewise the network locations given in the Document for previous versions it was based on. These may be placed in the "History" section. You may omit a network location for a work that was published at least four years before the Document itself, or if the original publisher of the version it refers to gives permission.

K. For any section Entitled "Acknowledgements" or "Dedications", Preserve the Title of the section, and preserve in the section all the substance and tone of each of the contributor acknowledgements and/or dedications given therein.

L. Preserve all the Invariant Sections of the Document, unaltered in their text and in their titles. Section numbers or the equivalent are not considered part of the section titles.

M. Delete any section Entitled "Endorsements". Such a section may not be included in the Modified Version.

N. Do not retitle any existing section to be Entitled "Endorsements" or to conflict in title with any Invariant Section.

O. Preserve any Warranty Disclaimers.

If the Modified Version includes new front-matter sections or appendices that qualify as Secondary Sections and contain no material copied from the Document, you may at your option designate some or all of these sections as invariant. To do this, add their titles to the list of Invariant Sections in the Modified Version's license notice. These titles must be distinct from any other section titles.

You may add a section Entitled "Endorsements", provided it contains nothing but endorsements of your Modified Version by various parties-for example, statements of peer review or that the text has been approved by an organization as the authoritative definition of a standard.

You may add a passage of up to five words as a Front-Cover Text, and a passage of up to 25 words as a Back-Cover Text, to the end of the list of Cover Texts in the Modified Version. Only one passage of Front-Cover Text and one of Back-Cover Text may be added by (or through arrangements made by) any one entity. If the Document already includes a cover text for the same cover, previously added by you or by arrangement made by the same entity you are acting on behalf of, you may not add another; but you may replace the old one, on explicit permission from the previous publisher that added the old one.

The author(s) and publisher(s) of the Document do not by this License give permission to use their names for publicity for or to assert or imply endorsement of any Modified Version.

.16 COMBINING DOCUMENTS

You may combine the Document with other documents released under this License, under the terms defined in section 5 above for modified versions, provided that you include in the combination all of the Invariant Sections of all of the original documents, unmodified, and list them all as Invariant Sections of your combined work in its license notice, and that you preserve all their Warranty Disclaimers.

The combined work need only contain one copy of this License, and multiple identical Invariant Sections may be replaced with a single copy. If there are multiple Invariant Sections with the same name but different contents, make the title of each such section unique by adding at the end of it, in parentheses, the name of the original author or publisher of that section if known, or else a unique number. Make the same adjustment to the section titles in the list of Invariant Sections in the license notice of the combined work.

In the combination, you must combine any sections Entitled "History" in the various original documents, forming one section Entitled "History"; likewise combine any sections Entitled "Acknowledgements", and any sections Entitled "Dedications". You must delete all sections Entitled "Endorsements".

.17 COLLECTIONS OF DOCUMENTS

You may make a collection consisting of the Document and other documents released under this License, and replace the individual copies of this License in the various documents with a single copy that is included in the collection, provided that you follow the rules of this License for verbatim copying of each of the documents in all other respects.

You may extract a single document from such a collection, and distribute it individually under this License, provided you insert a copy of this License into the extracted document, and follow this License in all other respects regarding verbatim copying of that document.

.18 AGGREGATION WITH INDEPENDENT WORKS

A compilation of the Document or its derivatives with other separate and independent documents or works, in or on a volume of a storage or distribution medium, is called an "aggregate" if the copyright resulting from the compilation is not used to limit the legal rights of the compilation's users beyond what the individual works permit. When the Document is included in an aggregate, this License does not apply to the other works in the aggregate which are not themselves derivative works of the Document.

If the Cover Text requirement of section 4 is applicable to these copies of the Document, then if the Document is less than one half of the entire aggregate, the Document's Cover Texts may be placed on covers that bracket the Document within the aggregate, or the electronic equivalent of covers if the Document is in electronic form. Otherwise they must appear on printed covers that bracket the whole aggregate.

.19 TRANSLATION

Translation is considered a kind of modification, so you may distribute translations of the Document under the terms of section 5. Replacing Invariant Sections with translations requires special permission from their copyright holders, but you may include translations of some or all Invariant Sections in addition to the original versions of these Invariant Sections. You may include a translation of this License, and all the license notices in the Document, and any Warranty Disclaimers, provided that you also include the original English version of this License and the original versions of those notices and disclaimers. In case of a disagreement between the translation and the original version of this License or a notice or disclaimer, the original version will prevail.

If a section in the Document is Entitled "Acknowledgements", "Dedications", or "History", the requirement (section 5) to Preserve its Title (section 2) will typically require changing the actual title.

.20 TERMINATION

You may not copy, modify, sublicense, or distribute the Document except as expressly provided for under this License. Any other attempt to copy, modify, sublicense or distribute the Document is void, and will automatically terminate your rights under this License. However, parties who have received copies, or rights, from you under this License will not have their licenses terminated so long as such parties remain in full compliance.

.21 FUTURE REVISIONS OF THIS LICENSE

The Free Software Foundation may publish new, revised versions of the GNU Free Documentation License from time to time. Such new versions will be similar in spirit to the present version, but may differ in detail to address new problems or concerns. See http://www.gnu.org/copyleft/.

Each version of the License is given a distinguishing version number. If the Document specifies that a particular numbered version of this License "or any later version" applies to it, you have the option of following the terms and conditions either of that specified version or of any later version that has been published (not as a draft) by the Free Software Foundation. If the Document does not specify a version number of this License, you may choose any version ever published (not as a draft) by the Free Software Foundation.

.22 ADDENDUM: How to use this License for your documents

To use this License in a document you have written, include a copy of the License in the document and put the following copyrightand license notices just after the title page:

> Copyright (c) YEAR YOUR NAME. Permission is granted to copy, distribute and/or modify this document under the terms of the GNU Free Documentation License, Version 1.2 or any later version published by the Free Software Foundation; with no Invariant Sections, no Front-Cover Texts, and no Back-Cover Texts. A copy of the license is included in the section entitled "GNU Free Documentation License".

If you have Invariant Sections, Front-Cover Texts and Back-Cover Texts, replace the "with...Texts." line with this:

> with the Invariant Sections being LIST THEIR TITLES, with the Front-Cover Texts being LIST, and with the Back-Cover Texts being LIST.

If you have Invariant Sections without Cover Texts, or some other combination of the three, merge those two alternatives to suit the situation.

If your document contains nontrivial examples of program code, we recommend releasing these examples in parallel under your choice of free software license, such as the GNU General Public License, to permit their use in free software.

Part IX

Eeek! There is Missing Help

Sorry, but a help item is missing for the function you're looking for. You may be able to find it in the online version of the help at the GIMP docs website.

Feel free to join us and fill the gap by writing documentation for GIMP. For more information, subscribe to our Mailing list. Generally, it's a good idea to check the GIMP project page.

Found a **content error** or just something which doesn't look right? Report an error in Bugzilla and let us know.

Index

—
.gif, 66
.jpeg, 67
.jpg, 67
.png, 822
.psd, 822
.xcf, 821, 825
.xcf.gz, 825
3D Outline, 778

A
Acquire, 402
Add Alpha channel, 487
Add Bevel, 684
Add Border, 685
Addition, 121
Airbrush, 254
Alien Glow, 781
Alien Map, 521
Alien Neon, 782
Align, 273
Align visible layers, 465
Alpha, 488, 813
Alpha Channel, 107
Alpha channel, 813
Anchor Layer, 476
Animation
    Animated GIF options, 67
    Creating an animated brush, 90
    Optimize, 776
    Playback, 777
Antialias, 566
Antialiasing
    Explanation, 813
    Preserve anti-aliasing, 488
Apply Layer Mask (command), 483
Apply Lens, 608
Autocrop, 462

B
Background color, 206
Background layer, 107
Basic I, 783
Basic II, 783
Basic Setup, 17
Behind (paint mode), 234
Black point, 303
Blend, 246, 770
    Tool, 246
Blended, 784
Blinds, 577
Blur, 558
Blur/Sharpen, 265
BMP, 814
Border, 434
Border Average, 531
Bovination, 785

bpp, 815
Browser
    Plug-In, 552
    Procedure, 553
Brush, Pattern, Gradient area
    Preferences, 156
Brushes, 355
    Add New, 89
    Animated brushes
        Introduction, 88
    Clipboard brush, 359
    Color, 88
    Dialog, 355
    File formats, 89
    Filter brush, 261
    History brush, 261
    Introduction, 87
    Ordinary, 87
    Parametric, 88
    Toolbox Indicator Area, 207
    Varying brush size, 94
Bucket Fill, 243
Buffers
    Copy named, 379
    Cut named, 379
    Dialog, 379
    Named Buffers: Cut/Copy/Paste, 418
    Paste named, 379
Bugs, 851
Bump Map, 699
Burn, 117
Burn-In, 771
Button
    Script-Fu-generated, 183
Bézier's curve, 315

C
Cage, 290
Calibrate monitor, 161
Canvas
    effect, 657
    Fit canvas size to layers, 459
    Fit canvas size to selection, 459
    Padding color, 449
    Size, 455
    Snap to canvas, 449
Canvas effect, 657
Cartoon, 659
Chain icon, 110
Chalk, 786
Channel, 16, 515, 814
    Channel mask, 338
    Channel to Selection, 336
    Create a New Channel Mask, 336
    Delete Channel Mask, 336
    Dialog, 334
    Duplicate Channel Mask, 336

Edit Channel Attributes, 336
Move Channel Mask, 336
Channel Mixer, 510
Channels
    Menu, 337
Checkerboard, 731
Chip Away, 788
Chrome, 790
Circuit, 746
Clear, 418
Clipboard Brush, 359
Clipboard pattern, 361
Clipping
    Transform, 271
Clone, 257
Close, 411
Clothify, 660
CML Explorer, 732
CMYK, 513, 515, 517, 814
Coffee Stain, 686
Color, 124, 145
    Additive color model, 823
    Adjust level colors, 303
    Color Balance, 293
    Color display, 442
    Colorize, 297
    Deficient vision, 443
    Dithering, 815
    Grab color, 318
    HTML notation, 819
    Indexed colors, 819
    Merging layer Modes, 111
    Padding color of canvas, 449
    Palettes, 369
    Palettes (color map), 101
    Saturation, 824
    Selection by color, 222
    Subtractive color synthesis, 814
    Value, 825
Color Area, 206
Color area
    Preferences, 156
Color Balance, 293
Color depth, 815
Color Enhance, 507
Color Erase (paint mode), 235
Color Exchange, 522
Color Management, 162, 163, 823
Color management, 146, 446
Color model, 815
Color Picker, 318
Color Profile, 162
Color profile, 146
Color proof, 446
Color Selector, 352
Color to Alpha, 488
Color Tool Presets, 293
Color tools, 292
Colorcube Analysis, 532

Colorify, 534
Colorize, 297
Colormap, 344
    Rearrange, 519
    Set, 520
Colors, 540
    Alien Map, 521
    Auto, 504
    Border Average, 531
    Color enhance, 507
    Colorcube Analysis, 532
    Colorify, 534
    Components
        Channel mixer, 510
        Compose, 513
        Decompose, 515
        Recompose image from its components, 517
    Convert to gray scale, 313
    Equalize, 506
    Exchange colors, 522
    Filter Pack, 536
    Hot, 538
    Invert, 502
    Map
        Gradient Map, 524
        Palette Map, 524
    Max RGB, 539
    Normalize, 508
    Rotate, 525
    Sample Colorize, 528
    Smooth Palette, 533
    Stretch colors in HSV space, 509
    Stretch contrast, 508
    Stretching, 504
    Tools, 502
    Use GEGL, 503
    Value Invert, 503
    White balance, 506
Comic Book, 791
Command line Arguments, 12
Comment, 402
Compose, 513, 515
Composition guides, 215
Concepts, 15
Context menus, 397
Contrast, 445, 508
Convolution Matrix, 646
Cool Metal, 792
Copy Named, 379
Copy Visible, 415
Copy Visible (Layers), 415
Create Template, 410
Crop, 278
    Autocrop layer, 500
Crop Layer, 500
Crop to selection, 461
CSS Keywords, 354
Cubism, 661
Curve Bend, 578

Curves, 308
Customize
    Shortcuts, 174
    Splash-screen, 176
Cut, 415
Cut Named, 379

D
Darken only, 122
Data folders
    Preferences, 170
Decompose, 515
Decor, 683
Deinterlace, 567
Depth Merge, 652
Desaturate, 313
Despeckle, 568
Destripe, 569
Device Status, 388
Dialog
    Sample Points, 393
Dialogs
    Brushes, 355
    Buffers, 379
    Channels, 334
    Color Selector, 352
    Colormap, 344
    Device Status, 388
    Docking, 25
    Document History, 382
    Fonts, 377
    Gradient Dialog, 362
    Histogram, 346
    Images, 381
    Introduction, 329
    Layers, 329
    Palettes, 369
    Paths, 340
    Patterns, 359
    Pointer, 395
    Preferences, 149
        Color Management, 162
        Data folders, 170
        Default image, 156
        Display, 161
        Environment, 150
        Folders, 169
        Help System, 153
        Image Windows, 158, 159
        Interface, 151
        Theme, 152
        Title and Statusbar, 160
        Tool Options, 154
        Toolbox, 155
        Window management, 168
    Templates, 383
    Undo History, 350
Difference, 121
Difference Clouds, 719

Difference of Gaussians, 640
Differential, 642
Diffraction patterns (filter), 737
Dilate, 651
Disable Layer Mask, 484
Displace, 701
Display
    Dot for Dot, 439
    Full Screen, 441
    Preferences, 161
Dissolve, 113
Distort Selection, 435
Dithering, 815
Divide, 114
Docking, 25
Docks
    Add Tab, 28
    Add tab, 729
    Close tab, 28
    Context Menu, 28
    Detach tab, 28
    Lock tab, 29
    Preview size, 29
    Tab menu, 27
    Tab style, 29
    View as List/Grid, 29
Document History, 382
Dodge, 117
Dodge/Burn, 268
Dot for Dot, 439
Dot for dot, 158
Draw, 47
Drawable, 107
Drop Shadow, 624
Duplicate, 451
Duplicate Layer, 476
Dynamics, 235
Dynamics Matrix, 238
Dynamics Options, 242

E
Edge, 642
Edge feathering (Selections), 211
Edge-Detect, 639
Edit Layer Mask, 484
Edit Template, 384
Editor, 428
Ellipse Selection Tool, 215
Emboss, 580
Engrave, 581
Environment preferences, 150
Equalize, 506
Erase Every Other Row or Column, 583
Eraser, 252
Erode, 652
Error console, 389
EXIF, 68, 816
Export, 410
Export As, 410

Export File, 391
Export Image as GIF, 66
Export Image as JPEG, 67
Export Image as MNG, 72
Export Image as PNG, 69
Export Image as TIFF, 71
Export Images, 65
Eye Dropper, 318

F
Fade, 414
Feathering, 816
File
   New image, 61
File format, 816
Files, 65
   Open, 61
Fill transparent areas, 245
Fill with Background color, 419
Fill with Foreground Color, 419
Fill with Pattern, 420
Filmstrip, 655
Filter Pack, 536
Filters
   Add Bevel, 684
   Add Border, 685
   Alpha to Logo
     3D Outline, 778
     Alien Glow, 781
     Alien Neon, 782
     Basic I, 783
     Basic II, 783
     Blended, 784
     Bovination, 785
     Chalk, 786
     Chip Away, 788
     Chrome, 790
     Comic Book, 791
     Cool Metal, 792
     Frosty, 793
     Glossy, 794
     Glowing Hot, 796
     Gradient Bevel, 798
     Introduction, 777
     Neon, 799
     Particle Trace, 800
     Textured, 802
   Animation
     Blend, 770
     Burn-In, 771
     Introduction, 770
     Optimize, 776
     Playback, 777
     Rippling, 773
     Spinning Globe, 774
     Waves, 775
   Artistic
     Canvas effect, 657
     Cartoon, 659

     Clothify, 660
     Cubism, 661
     GIMPressionist, 663, 669, 671
     Introduction, 657
     Oilify, 672
     Photocopy, 674
     Predator, 676
     Softglow, 678
     Van Gogh, 679
     Weave, 682
   Blur, 556
     Blur, 558
     Gaussian Blur, 558
     Motion Blur, 561
     Pixelise, 563
     Selective Gaussian, 560
     Tileable Blur, 564
   Combine
     Depth Merge, 652
     Filmstrip, 655
     Introduction, 652
   Common functions
     Introduction to filters, 542
     Re-show last, 543
     Repeat Last, 543
     Reset all, 544
   Decor
     Coffee Stain, 686
     Fuzzy Border, 687
     Introduction, 683
     Old Photo, 689
     Round Corners, 691
     Slide, 693
     Stencil Carve, 694
     Stencil Chrome, 696
   Distorts
     Blinds, 577
     Curve Bend, 578
     Emboss, 580
     Engrave, 581
     Erase Every Other Row, 583
     Introduction, 577
     IWarp, 584
     Lens Distortion, 586
     Mosaic, 588
     Newsprint, 590
     Page Curl, 592
     Polar Coords, 593
     Ripple, 595
     Shift, 597
     Video, 601
     Whirl and Pinch, 604
     Wind, 605
   Edge Detect
     Difference of Gaussians, 640
     Edge, 642
     Introduction, 639
     Laplace, 644
     Neon, 644

Sobel, 645
Enhance
    Antialias, 566
    Deinterlace, 567
    Despeckle, 568
    Destripe, 569
    Introduction, 566
    NL filter, 570
    Red Eye Removal, 572
    Sharpen, 573
    Unsharp Mask, 574
Generic
    Convolution Matrix, 646
    Dilate, 651
    Erode, 652
    Introduction, 646
Glass Effects, 609
Introduction, 555
Light and Shadow, 609
    Apply Lens, 608
    Drop Shadow, 624
    Glass Tile, 629
    Gradient Flare, 609
    Lens Flare, 614
    Lighting effects, 616
    Perspective, 625
    Sparkle, 620
    Supernova, 622
    Xach-Effect, 628
Light Effects, 609
Map
    bump-map, 699
    Displace, 701
    Fractal Trace, 705
    Illusion, 706
    Introduction, 699
    Make Seamless, 708
    Map Object, 708
    Paper Tile, 712
    Small Tiles, 714
    Tile, 715
    Warp, 716
Menu, 542
Noise
    HSV Noise, 631
    Hurl, 632
    Introduction, 630
    Pick, 634
    RGB Noise, 635
    Slur, 637
    Spread, 638
Render
    Checkerboard, 731
    Circuit, 746
    CML Explorer, 732
    Difference Clouds, 719
    Diffraction, 737
    Flame, 723
    Fog, 720

Fractal Composition, 726
Fractal Explorer, 747
Gfig, 752
Grid, 738
Introduction, 719
Jigsaw, 740
Lava, 754
Line Nova, 755
Maze, 742
Plasma, 721
Random textures, 743
Sinusoidal textures, 744
Solid Noise, 722
Sphere Designer, 757
Spyrogimp, 759
Web
    Clickable image, 761
    Introduction, 761
    Semi-Flatten, 766
    Slice, 767
Fit canvas to layers, 459
Fit canvas to selection, 459
Flame, 723
Flatten, 464
Flip, 289, 455
Flip horizontally (layer), 492
Flip vertically (layer), 493
Floyd-Steinberg, 816
Fog, 720
Fonts
    Add, 134
    Dialog, 377
    Problems, 136
Foreground color, 206
Foreground Select, 226
Formats
    BMP, 814
    GBR, 89
    GIF, 66
    GIH, 89
    JPEG, 67
    MNG, 72
    PDF, 822
    PNG, 69
    PostScript, 822
    PSD, 822
    SVG, 824
    TGA, 825
    TIFF, 71
    VBR, 89
    XCF, 825
Fractal Explorer, 747
Fractal trace, 705
Frosty, 793
Full Screen, 441
Fuzzy Border, 687
Fuzzy Selection, 220

G

Gamma, 303, 444, 817
Gamut, 817
Gaussian Blur, 558
GBR, 89
GEGL, 503
GEGL operation, 325
Gfig, 752
GIF, 66, 817
GIH, 89
GIMP
  Bugs, 851
  Getting Unstuck, 53
  History, 837
  Introduction, 3
GIMP Online, 554
GIMPressionist, 663, 669, 671
Glass Tile, 629
Glossary, 813
Glossy, 794
Glowing Hot, 796
Gradient, 642
  Dialog, 362
  Editor, 364
  From palette, 373
  New gradient, 368
  Overview, 96
  Toolbox Indicator Area, 207
Gradient Bevel, 798
Gradient CSS code snippet, 364
Gradient Flare, 609
Gradient Map, 524
Grain extract, 119
Grain merge, 120
Grayscale
  Convert to grayscale, 452
  Overview, 818
Grid
  configure, 470
  Default setting, 157
  Grid filter, 738
  Overview, 171
  Show/Mask Grid, 448
  Snap to Grid, 448
Guide
  Add, 468
  Add by percent, 469
  Move, 278
Guides, 468
  Add from selection, 470
  Overview, 171
  Remove, 470
  Selection guides, 215
  Show/Mask Guides, 448
  Snap to Guides, 448
  Transform, 272
  Using, 818
Guillotine, 455

H

Hard light, 118
Heal, 261
Help, 153, 550
  Context help, 550
  Menu, 549
  Online, 554
  Overview, 551
  Tip of the Day, 550
Histogram, 346, 818
Hot, 538
HSV, 513, 515, 517
HSV Noise, 631
HTML notation, 819
Hue, 124
Hue-Saturation, 295
Hurl, 632

I

ICC profile, 145
IFS Fractal, 726
Illusion, 706
Image, 381
  Acquire an image, 402
  Active Image Thumbnail, 156
  Canvas size, 455
  change Mode, 40
  Close image, 411
  Color modes
    Menu, 452
  Comment, 402
  Convert
    To grayscale, 452
    To indexed mode, 452
    To RGB mode, 452
  Crop
    According to color, 462
    Autocrop, 462
    To selection, 461
    Tool, 278
  crop, 38
  Cut off image according to guides, 455
  Export As, 410
  Flip, 42
  Grid and guides, 171
  Guides, 468
  Image size
    When creating, 400
  information, 39
  New, 399
  Open, 404
    As layers, 406
    Open location, 406
    Open recent, 407
  Paste as, 417
  Paths, 83
  Print size, 459
  Reload the image, 409
  Resize after zooming or scaling, 158
  Resolution

Setting when creating, 401
Rotate, 44
save, 35
Save image
    Save, 390
    Save a copy, 409
    Save as, 407
Scale, 32
scale, 34
Text, 134
Transform, 454
Image Hose, 819
Image hoses, 88
Image Properties, 471
Image size, 158, 400
Image window
    Menus, 438, 501
Image Windows
    Basic settings, 168
    Preferences, 158, 159
Image windows
    Description, 22
ImageMap, 761
Images
    Types, 59
Incremental, 819
Indent, 324
Indexed Colors, 819
Indexed colors, 452
Indexed palette, 101
Ink, 256
Input Controllers, 166
Input Devices, 165
Interface
    Preferences, 151
Invert colors, 502
IWarp, 584

J
Jigsaw, 740
Jitter, 233
JPEG, 67, 820
Justify, 324

K
Keyboard Shortcuts, 151, 423

L
Languages, 11, 151
Laplace, 642, 644
Lasso, 218
Lava, 754
Layer, 515, 820
    Anchor the floating layer, 476
    Boundaries, 110
    Clear
        Clear layer content, 418
    Copy, 415
        Copy visible layers, 415

Creating new layers, 126
Cut (/Paste)
    Cut layer content, 415
Dialog, 329
Fill
    Fill with background color, 419
    Fill with foreground color, 419
    Fill with pattern, 420
Mask managing
    Add a mask, 482
    Add layer mask to selection, 485
    Apply, 483
    Convert layer mask to a selection, 485
    Delete layer mask, 484
    Disable, 484
    Edit, 484
    Intersect layer mask with selection, 486
    Show layer mask, 484
    Subtract layer mask from selection, 486
Modes, 111
Move, 278
Paste, 416, 417
Preview size, 29
Scale, 283
Size, 110
Size managing
    Auto-crop, 500
    Crop according to selection, 500
    Resize current layer and its content, 499
    Resize current layer but not its content, 497
    Resize current layer to image size, 499
Stack managing
    Align visible layers, 465
    Bottom layer, 480
    Create a new layer, 475
    Create a new layer from visible layers, 476
    Delete current layer, 477
    Layer duplicate, 476
    Lower current layer to the bottom of stack, 481
    Lower layer, 481
    Merge current layer with the underlying layer, 477
    Merge visible layers, 463
    Move current layer one position up, 481
    Move current layer to the top of stack, 481
    Next layer, 479
    Open image as layers, 406
    Previous layer, 479
    Reverse layer order, 481
    Select top layer, 480
Sub-menu
    Mask, 482
    Stack, 478
    Transform, 492
    Transparency, 487
Text, 478
Transform
    Flip horizontally, 492

Flip vertically, 493
Rotation, 493–495
Shift layer content, 495
Transparency managing
    Add Alpha channel to background layer, 487
    Add non-transparent areas to selection, 490
    Intersect non-transparent areas with selection, 491
    Make colors transparent, 488
    Preserve anti-aliasing, 488
    Remove Alpha Channel, 488
    Selection according to opacity, 489
    Subtract non-transparent pixels from selection, 491
    Threshold, 488
Type, 109
Layer boundary
    Show/mask layer boundary, 447
Layer Boundary Size, 497
Layer Group
    New, 475
Layer mask, 333
Layer Modes
    Addition, 121
    Burn, 117
    Color, 124
    Darken only, 122
    Difference, 121
    Dissolve, 113
    Divide, 114
    Dodge, 117
    Grain extract, 119
    Grain merge, 120
    Hard light, 118
    Hue, 124
    Lighten only, 123
    Multiply, 114
    Normal, 112
    Overlay, 116
    Saturation, 124
    Screen, 115
    Soft light, 119
    Subtract, 122
    Value, 125
Layers, 107
    Linkage, 110
    Merge all layers, 464
Lens Distortion, 586
Lens Flare, 614
Levels tool, 303
Lighten only, 123
Lighting effects, 616
Line
    Drawing a straight line, 103
Line Nova, 755
Line spacing, 324
List search field, 29
Lock alpha channel, 331
Lock pixels, 331

Logo
    Script-Fu-generated, 183

M
Magic Wand, 220
Make Seamless, 708
Map Object, 708
Marching ants speed, 158
Masks
    Channel mask, 338
    Layer mask, 333
        Add, 482
        Add to selection, 485
        Apply, 483
        Convert to a selection, 485
        Delete, 484
        Disable, 484
        Edit, 484
        Intersect with selection, 486
        Overview, 110
        Show, 484
        Subtract from selection, 486
    Overview, 821
    Quick Mask
        Using Quick Mask, 83
    Quick mask, 338
    Selection mask, 338
Max RGB, 539
Maze, 742
Measure, 321
Measure a distance, 321
Measure a surface, 321
Measure an angle, 321
Menu
    File, 399
    Help, 549
Menu-bar
    Show/Mask menu bar, 450
Menus
    Edit, 413
    File menu, 399
    Filters, 542
    Image, 451
    Introduction, 397
    Layer, 474
    Selection, 425
    Tools, 542
    Windows, 548
Merge Down, 477
Merge Visible Layers, 463
MNG, 72
Modes (color)
    Grayscale, 452
    Indexed, 452
    RGB, 452
Modes (Colors)
    Submenu, 452
Modes of layers, 111
Module Manager, 423

Modules, 423
Moiré, 821
Mosaic, 588
Motion Blur, 561
Mouse cursors, 159
Move, 276
Multiply, 114

N
Navigation
    Dialog, 349
        Navigation button, 25
        Preview size, 151
        View Navigation window, 442
Navigation preview, 22
Neon, 644, 799
New, 399
New Image, 399
New image
    Default setting, 156
New instance, 12
New Layer, 475
New View, 438
Newsprint, 590
NL filter, 570
Nonlinear filter, 570
Normalize, 508

O
Offset, 495
Oilify, 672
Old Photo, 689
Opacity
    Brush, 232
    Layers dialog, 331
Open, 404
Open as layers, 406
Open Location, 406
Open Recent, 407
Overlay, 116

P
Padding color, 449
Page Curl, 592
Paint Modes
    Behind, 234
    Color Erase, 235
Paint Tools, 230
Paintbrush, 251
Palette
    Delete, 370
    Dialog, 369
    Duplicate, 370
    Editor, 374
    Import, 371
    Introduction, 101
    Menu, 371
    New palette, 370
    Refresh, 370

Palette Color Selector, 353
Palette Map, 524
Paper Tile, 712
Parasite, 821
Particle Trace, 800
Paste, 416
Paste as new brush, 417
Paste as New Layer, 417
Paste as new pattern, 417
Paste Into, 416
Paste Named, 379
Path
    Move, 278
    Scale, 283
    Snap to active path, 449
Paths
    Dialog, 340
    Stroke, 421
    Tool, 315
    Transform, 273
    Using, 83
Patterns
    Add a pattern to layer, 719
    Clipboard pattern, 361
    Clone, 259
    Dialog, 359
    Introduction, 98
    Script-Fu-generated, 182
    Toolbox Indicator Area, 207
PDF, 822
Pencil, 249
Perspective, 287, 625
Perspective Clone, 263
Photocopy, 674
Photography, 137
Pick, 634
Pixel, 822
Pixelise, 563
Plasma, 721
Playback, 777
Plugins
    Browser, 552
    Definition, 822
    Install, 178
    Introduction, 177
    Write, 179
PNG, 69, 822
Pointer, 395
Polar Coords, 593
Polygonal Selection, 218
Portrait/Landscape mode, 401
Posterize, 312
Predator, 676
Preferences, 149
    Image grid, 157
    Input Controllers, 166
    Input Devices, 165
Preferences (command), 423
Presets

Introduction, 103
Presets Dialog, 386
Tool Preset Editor, 388
Preview
    Filter, 555
    Navigation preview, 22
    Navigation preview size, 151
    Transformation tools, 272
Previews, 151
    Tab preview size, 29
Prewitt compass, 642
Print Size, 459
Printing
    Print command, 411
    Printing your photos, 143
    Size and resolution, 459
Procedure
    Browser, 553
PSD, 822
Python-Fu
    Sub-menu, 544

Q
Qbist, 743
Quantization, 822
QuickMask, 81
Quit GIMP, 412

R
Re-show Last, 543
Rearrange Colormap, 519
Recompose, 517
Rectangle
    Drawing a rectangle, 103
Red Eye Removal, 572
Red-eyes, 142
Redo, 414
Remove Alpha channel, 488
Repeat Last, 543
Reset All, 544
Resolution, 16
    Printing, 459
    Setting when creating, 401
Retinex..., 540
Revert (command), 409
RGB, 452, 513, 515, 517, 823
RGB Noise, 635
Ripple filter, 595
Rippling, 773
Roberts, 642
Rotate, 281, 495
Rotate 180°, 494
Rotate 90° clockwise, 493
Rotate 90° counter-clockwise, 494
Rotate Colors, 525
Rotation, 455
Round Corners, 691
Rounded rectangle, 436
Rulers

Show/Mask rulers, 450
Running GIMP, 11

S
Sample Colorize, 528
Sample Points, 393, 448
Saturation, 124, 824
Save, 390
Save a copy, 409
Save as, 407
Save/Export Images, 65
Scale Image, 460
Scale layer, 499
Scale Layer, selection contour or path, 283
Scissors tool, 224
Screen, 115
Screenshot, 403
Script-Fu
    Button, 183
    Install, 180
    Introduction, 180
    Logo, 183
    Standalone, 182
    Sub-menu, 546
    Tutorial, 183
Scroll-bars
    Show/Mask scrollbars, 450
Selection
    According to opacity, 489
    Add / Subtract selections, 81
    Add alpha channel, 490
    Add layer mask to selection, 485
    Anchor the floating selection, 476
    By Color select, 428
    Change shape, 254
    Clear selection content, 418
    Copy, 415
    Create a selection border, 434
    Create a selection from Path, 428
    Cut selection content, 415
    Delete selections, 426
    Distort, 435
    Editor, 428
    Ellipse selection, 215
    Feather selection edges, 431
    Fill
        Fill with background color, 419
        Fill with foreground color, 419
        Fill with pattern, 420
    Floating selection, 816
    Floating selection (command), 427
    Foreground Select, 226
    Free Selection, 218
    Fuzzy selection, 220
    Grow, 433
    Intersect with Alpha channel, 491
    Invert selection, 426
    Modes, 211
    Move selection, 79

Paste, 416, 417
Polygonal Selection, 218
Rectangle selection, 211
Remove the feathering of border selection, 432
Rounded Rectangle, 436
Save selection to channel, 437
Scale, 283
Select All, 426
Selection boundary
  Show/Mask selection boundary, 447
Selection by color, 222
Selection mask, 338
Selection to Path
  Advanced options, 430
Shrink the size of selection, 432
Stroke selection, 420
Subtract non-transparent pixels, 491
Toggle QuickMask, 437
Transform selection to path, 437
Selections
  Common Features, 209
  Concepts, 77
  Using, 79
Selective Gaussian Blur, 560
Semi-Flatten, 766
Set Colormap, 520
Setup, 13
Sharpen, 573
Shear, 285
Shift, 597
Shortcuts, 174
Show Grid, 448
Show Guides, 448
Show Layer Boundary, 447
Show Layer Mask (command), 484
Show Menubar, 450
Show Rulers, 450
Show Scrollbars, 450
Show Selection, 447
Show Statusbar, 450
Shrink Wrap, 441
Sinus, 744
Slice, 767
Slide, 693
Sliders, 209
Slur, 637
Small Tiles, 714
Smooth Palette, 533
Smudge, 267
Snap to active path, 449
Snap to canvas, 449
Snap to Grid, 448
Snap to Guides, 448
Sobel, 642, 645
Soft light, 119
Soft proof, 446
Softglow, 678
Solid noise, 722
Space bar, 158, 277

Sparkle, 620
Sphere Designer, 757
Spinning Globe, 774
Splash-screen, 176
Spread, 638
Spyrogimp, 759
Stack, 478
Status bar
  Image window, 22
  Preferences, 160
  Show/Hide status bar, 450
Stencil Carve, 694
Stencil Chrome, 696
Stoke path, 421
Straight Line, 231
Stretch Contrast, 508
Stretch HSV, 509
Stroke Selection, 420
Subtract, 122
Supernova, 622
Supersampling, 824
SVG, 824
Swap folder, 170

T
Tab menus, 398
Tags, 376
TARGA, 825
Tear-off line, 397
Tear-off menus, 397
Temp folder, 170
Template
  Create Template, 410
  Edit, 384
  Menu, 400
Templates, 383
Text
  Context Menu, 132
  Discard information, 478
  Editing text, 129
  Editor, 324
  Embellishing text, 134
  Fonts, 134
  Load from file, 325
  Managing Text Layer, 130
  Move, 278
  Text Area, 129
  Text Toolbox, 131
  Tool, 322
Text along Path, 133
Text to Selection, 478
Textured, 802
TGA, 825
Theme, 152
Threshold, 299
TIFF, 71, 825
Tile, 715
Tile cache, 173
Tileable Blur, 564

Tip of the Day, 550
Title bar
    Preferences, 160
Toolbox, 205
    Active image area, 207
    Color Area, 206
    Configuration, 156
    Indicator Area, 207
    Introduction, 20
    Paint Tools, 230
    Preferences, 155
Tools
    Airbrush, 254
    Align, 273
    Blend, 246
    Blur/Sharpen, 265
    Brightness-Contrast, 298
    Brush, 243
    Bucket Fill, 243
    Cage Tool, 290
    Clone, 257
    Color, 292
    Color Balance, 293
    Color Picker, 318
    Colorize, 297
    Colors, 502
    Crop, 278
    Curves, 308
    Dodge/Burn, 268
    Dynamics, 235
    Dynamics Matrix, 238
    Dynamics Options, 242
    Ellipse Selection, 215
    Eraser, 252
    Flip, 289
    Foreground Select, 226
    Free Selection, 218
    Fuzzy Selection, 220
    GEGL operation, 325
    Heal, 261
    Hue-Saturation, 295
    Ink, 256
    Levels, 303
    Measure, 321
    Miscellaneous, 314
    Move, 276
    Paint, 230, 243
    Paintbrush, 251
    Path, 315
    Pencil, 249
    Perspective, 287
    Perspective Clone, 263
    Posterize, 312
    Preferences, 154
    Rectangle Selection, 211
    Rotate, 281
    Scale, 283
    Scissors, 224
    Selection by color, 222

Shear, 285
Smudge, 267
Text, 322
Threshold, 299
Transform Tools, 270
Zoom, 320
Transform, 454
    Clipping, 271
    Guides, 272
    Paths, 273
Transparency
    Alpha channel, 813
    Background layer transparency, 107
    Brush opacity, 232
    Eraser tool, 252
    Exporting images with transparency, 74
    Keep Layer Transparency, 331
    Layer opacity, 331
    Lock Alpha channel, 331
    Representation, 161
Triangle Color Selector, 353
Tutorial, 32, 34, 35, 38–40, 42, 44, 45, 47
Tutorials
    Create image, 61
    Drawing a rectangle, 103
    Drawing a straight line, 103
    New gradient, 368

U
Undo, 31, 413
Undo History, 350, 414
Unit Editor, 424
Unit of measurement, 424
Units, 424
Unsharp Mask, 574
URI, 825
URL, 825

V
Value, 125, 825
Value Invert, 503
Value Propagate, 598
Values, 303
Van Gogh (LIC), 679
VBR, 89
Video, 601
View
    Introduction, 438
    Padding color of canvas, 449
Visibility
    Icon, 109
Voronoi, 670

W
Warp, 716
Watercolor Color Selector, 353
Waves, 602, 775
Weave, 682
Web

Images for the web, 72
Whirl and Pinch, 604
White Balance, 506
White point, 303
Wind, 605

X
Xach-Effect, 628
XCF, 821, 825
XDS, 21

Y
YCbCr, 513, 515, 517, 826
YUV, 513, 515, 517, 826

Z
Zealous Crop, 462
Zoom, 158, 320, 439